PEARSON CUSTOM LIBRARY

Professor Abbas Mehdi
Department of Sociology
St. Cloud State University

PEARSON

ISBN 10: 1-269-78046-8
ISBN 13: 978-1-269-78046-9

Table of Contents

Part Three: The Problems of Inequality

Inequality

Global Inequality

Part Four: The Problems of Changing World

Population Problems

The outline of this book emerged when, a few years ago, I began developing a course on social problems. There are far more materials than can ever be covered in one semester, and a course about social problems can be approached from different perspectives. However, my intention for the design and content of this book is to increase the students' understanding of different sociological theories and sociological approaches to social problems, and how these theories and approaches may affect their understanding of, and their answers to, the social problems.

One attraction of this second edition of Social Problems: A Sociological Perspective is that it should be a relatively slim book. Therefore, the book has been restructured by dropping some chapters. In considering which changes should be made and which chapters should be dropped in the second edition, I conducted a large survey of students in social problems classes over several semesters. I would like to thank those students very much for responding so promptly with their views, which helped me in my restructuring of this book.

In selecting theses contributors, my aim has been the same since the beginning: to give a direct introductory exposition of the views of different authors whose ideas are currently the subject of interest and debate. I conceive of this book as an introductory and basic resources book giving a general overview of the field.

To achieve the purpose and the goals of the book, it is divided into five parts:
Part I is about Sociology and social problems and describes the nature, causes, process, and outcomes of social problems, and the studying of social problems in the twenty-first century.

Part II deals with troubles in social institutions. It deals with social problems of education, economic, and problems of politics and government. Part III deals with problems of inequalities in the USA, global inequality and globalization. Part IV deals with population problems. Part V deals with the following topic: "Can Social Problems be Solved?"

Acknowledgment
I would like to express my appreciation and thanks to the students at St. Cloud State University for responding so promptly with their views, which helped me in my restructuring this book. This book was constructed with them in mind and with their input. I would also like to thank Chris Robinson and Pearson publishing company for putting this book together.

About the professor
Abbas S. Mehdi received his B.A. in Economics from Al-Mustansiriyah University, Baghdad, Iraq and his M.A. in Management from Bath University, Bath, UK. He received his Ph.D. in Sociology from Ohio State University, Ohio, USA. He is currently a professor of Sociology at St. Cloud State University, Minnesota, USA.

Part One: Social Problems

Sociology and Social Problems

PhotoEdit Inc.

- What is a social problem?

- What part do social movements play in creating social problems?

- What are the sociological perspectives that are used to analyze social problems?

- How do sociologists study social problems?

- How can we evaluate the claims made about them?

From Chapter 1 of *Social Problems*, 10/e. James William Coleman. Harold R. Kerbo. Copyright © 2010 by Pearson Education. All rights reserved.

"It was the best of times, it was the worst of times, it was the age of wisdom, it was the age of foolishness, . . . it was the season of Light, it was the season of Darkness, it was the spring of hope, it was the winter of despair. . . ." These are the opening words in Charles Dickens's famous novel *A Tale of Two Cities,* and they apply as well now in the twenty-first century as they did when he wrote them in the nineteenth. On the one hand, we are healthier, longer lived, and better educated, and we enjoy more technological conveniences than in any other period in human history. On the other hand, perennial problems such as poverty, discrimination, and violence show no sign of fading away, and the specter of overpopulation and environmental catastrophe looms menacingly on the horizon.

Indeed, the list of our social problems is so depressingly long that many people just throw their hands up and decide there is nothing they can do to help. But is that really true? The sociological study of social problems is founded on the belief that something can indeed be done if we first make the effort to study our problems systematically and then act on our understanding.

Politicians and community officials spend much of their careers trying to solve social problems that include everything from double parking to the threat of nuclear war. Voters select the candidates who claim to have the best solutions, but the public's ideas about many social problems are distorted or confused. Although the serious study of social problems can clear up much of this confusion and misunderstanding, beginning students often have the uncomfortable feeling that the more they read, the less they understand. There are so many conflicting viewpoints, and even the results of objective, scientific research may appear to be contradictory.

Sociology The scientific study of societies and social behavior.

Sociology—the scientific study of society and social behavior—provides a framework for sorting out all these facts, ideas, and beliefs. It provides the perspective and the tools we need to make sense of our social problems. Using this perspective, we can develop programs to deal with our problems and evaluate their results once they have been put into effect. This is not to say that all sociologists agree on the exact causes of our social problems or how we should solve them; fortunately, such disagreements can result in a richer understanding for the student who is willing to examine all sides of the issues involved.

What Is a Social Problem?

Social problem A condition that a significant number of people believe to be a problem. A condition in which there is a sizable difference between the ideals of a society and its actual achievements.

Most people think of a **social problem** as any condition that is harmful to society; but the matter is not so simple, for the meanings of such everyday terms as *harm* and *society* are far from clear. Conditions that some people see as social problems harm some segments of society but are beneficial to others. Consider air pollution. On the one hand, an automobile manufacturer might argue that government regulation of free enterprise is a social problem because laws requiring antipollution devices on cars raise costs, decrease gasoline mileage, and stimulate inflation. On the other hand, residents of a polluted city might argue that the government's failure to completely outlaw noxious automobile emissions is a social problem because the smog created by such emissions harms their health and well-being. One person's social problem is another person's solution. Clearly, most people define a social problem as something that harms (or seems to harm) their own interests.

A more precise sociological definition holds that *a social problem exists when there is a sizable difference between the ideals of a society and its actual achievements.*[1] From this perspective, social problems are created by the failure to close the gap between the way people want things to be and the way things really are. Thus, racial discrimination is a social problem because, although we believe that everyone should receive fair and equal treatment, some groups are still denied equal access to education, employment, and housing. Before this definition can be applied, someone must first examine the ideals and values of society and then decide whether these goals are being achieved. Sociologists and other experts thus decide what is or is not a problem because they are the ones with the skills necessary for measuring the desires and achievements of society.

Critics of this approach point out that no contemporary society has a single, unified set of values and ideals. When using this definition, sociologists must therefore decide which standards they will use for judging whether or not a certain condition is a social problem. Critics charge that those ideals and values used as standards are selected on the basis of the researcher's personal opinions and prejudices, not objective analysis.

Another widely accepted sociological definition holds that *a social problem exists when a significant number of people believe that a certain condition is, in fact, a problem.*[2] Here the public (not a sociologist) decides what is or is not a social problem. The sociologist's job is to determine which problems concern a substantial number of people. Thus, in this view, pollution did not become a social problem until environmental activists and news reports attracted the public's attention to conditions that had actually existed for some time.

The advantage of this definition is that it does not require a value judgment by sociologists who try to decide what is and is not a social problem; such decisions are made by "the public." However, a serious shortcoming of this approach is that the public is often uninformed or misguided and does not clearly understand its problems. If thousands of people were being poisoned by radiation leaking from a nuclear power plant but didn't know it, wouldn't that still be a social problem? Another shortcoming of this approach is that relatively powerless groups with little money or political organization will not be able to get their problems recognized as social problems.

All the topics discussed in the chapters that follow qualify as social problems according to both sociological definitions. Each involves conditions that conflict with strongly held ideals and values, and all are considered social problems by significant groups of people. The goal of every chapter is to discuss these problems fairly and objectively. From time to time, we will also consider the problems of the powerless that have not been widely recognized by society. It is important to understand, however, that even selecting the problems requires a value judgment, whether by social scientists or by concerned citizens, and honest disagreements about the nature and importance of the various issues competing for public attention cannot be avoided.

QUICK REVIEW

- What are the two common definitions of social problems?
- What are the advantages and disadvantages of each?

Social Problems and Social Movements

The social issues that concern the public change from time to time, and a comparison of the numerous surveys of public opinion that have been done over the years reveals some interesting trends. War and peace and various economic issues have consistently ranked high on the public's list of social concerns. Interest in other problems seems to move in cycles. Thus, concern about taxes, foreign policy, illegal drug use, and lack of religious belief and morality is high in some years and low in others. Still other social problems are like fads, attracting a great deal of interest for a few years before dropping from public attention.[3]

These changes have many different causes: shifts in ideals and values, the solution of an old problem, the creation of new ones. One of the most important forces affecting changes in public opinion is **social movements** (groups of people who have banded together to promote a particular cause). For example, none of the polls in the 1930s and 1940s showed civil rights or race relations to be significant problems, even though racial discrimination was widespread and openly practiced. It was not until the civil rights movement began in the late 1950s that polls began to reflect an interest in this problem. The problem of racial discrimination would probably have remained buried if a powerful social movement had not developed to demand that society change its ways.

Social movements ■ Groups of people who have banded together to promote a particular cause.

UPI Photo/JimRuymen/NewsCom

Social movements create public awareness about social problems and push the government to take action to resolve them. This photograph shows a demonstration against the war in Iraq.

Such movements tend to follow a typical pattern of development. They begin when a large number of people start complaining about some problem they share. Such a group may be composed of people who believe they have been victimized, such as African American victims of racial discrimination or female victims of gender discrimination; or it may be made up of concerned outsiders, such as opponents of alcohol use or those who favor the death penalty. As people with a common interest in an issue begin to talk with one another and express their feelings about the problem, individuals step forward to lead the developing movement.[4] Martin Luther King, Jr., was such a leader for the civil rights movement in the United States, just as Nelson Mandela was for the movement to liberate South Africa from its racial oppression.

The leader's first job is to mold separate groups of dissatisfied people into an organized political movement. The success of the movement depends on publicity, for it is only through publicity that the general public can be made aware of the problem and be encouraged to do something about it. In other words, it is through publicity that the problem of a particular group becomes a social problem.

In order for this to happen, however, a social movement must have the necessary resources. In other words, just feeling discriminated against, deprived, or wronged in some way is not enough. African Americans in the United States did not suddenly decide they were discriminated against and deprived in the 1950s when the civil rights movement began. This reasoning would have to suggest that African Americans in the United States were not unhappy with their extreme poverty, discrimination, and even being lynched by whites in the past! What happened to stimulate the civil rights movement in the 1950s were such things as the movement of African Americans from small farm towns in the South to big cities after World War II and the Democratic Party's drive for black votes to win national elections. In big cities, the abuse of African Americans could not be hidden as easily, and with larger numbers concentrated in cities, they were able to lend each other support. It was at this time also that the Democratic Party started to lose its dominance of politics in the southern United States and began giving greater recognition to African American issues to gain their votes.

Once a social movement takes off, three factors help it gain public support and favorable action by government: political power, its appeal to values and prejudices, and strength of the opposition. The most important is the political power of the movement and its supporters. If the movement's supporters are numerous, highly organized, wealthy, or in key positions of power, it is more likely to be successful.

The second factor is the strength of the movement's appeal to the people's values and prejudices. For example, a movement to protect children from sexual abuse is much more likely to gain widespread support than an effort to protect the civil liberties of child molesters. Likewise, the pride the United States takes in calling itself a nation of equal opportunity was helpful when African Americans were able to show that it was not true for them.

The strength of the opposition to a movement is the third element determining its success or failure. Money is always limited, and the advocates of various social programs must compete with one another for funds. For example, few people object to the proposition that our children deserve a better education; however, a variety of opponents quickly emerge when someone suggests raising taxes to pay for improving the schools. Opposition to social movements also comes from people whose special interests are threatened by the goals of the movement. Thus, a proposal to raise the minimum wage for farmworkers is bound to be opposed by agricultural businesses.

A principal goal of many social movements is to create awareness of a social problem and then mobilize government action to resolve it; but even when a movement achieves these objectives, government action may be ineffective. Governments all over the world have created huge bureaucracies to deal with poverty (departments of welfare), health care (national health services), pollution (environmental protection agencies), and crime (police, courts, and prisons), but like all bureaucracies, these agencies are clumsy and slow moving, and they are often more concerned with their own survival than with the problems they are supposed to solve. After all, if narcotics enforcement agencies stopped all drug abuse, if police departments prevented all crime, or if mental hospitals quickly cured all their patients, then most of the employees of these agencies would soon be out of work. Occasionally, it appears that the agencies set up to deal with a particular social problem are not actually expected to solve it. Politicians have been known to approve funds for a social program just to silence troublesome protesters, creating new agencies with impressive titles but no real power.

QUICK REVIEW

— push gov to take action

■ How do social movements affect our social problems?

Foundations of the Sociological Approach

Over the years, sociologists have built up a body of basic knowledge about society and how it operates that can help us get perspective on conflicting claims and counterclaims about our social problems. A great deal of this book is devoted to helping students develop this kind of sociological understanding of the world. Before we can proceed, however, we must look at some basic concepts that provide the foundation on which the sociological approach is built. (A wide variety of sociological concepts, including all the key terms defined in the margins, are included in the glossary at the end of the book, so if you run across an unfamiliar concept while you are reading, be sure to check the glossary.) As we go through our daily lives dealing with our friends, relatives, and acquaintances, most of us see a group of unique individual people, but the sociologist also sees a set of social roles. In the theater or in the movies, a role is the part a particular person plays in the show. Sociologists use the term in much the same way, except that the role is played in real-life social situations. A **role** is usually defined as the set of behaviors and expectations associated with a particular social position (often known as a *status*). All roles—daughter, son, student, automobile driver, and countless others—offer certain rights and duties to the player. A student, for example, has the right to attend classes, to use the school's

Role ■ A set of expectations and behaviors associated with a social position.

Lessons from Other Places

The American Value System

I was in Germany several years ago during national elections, and I saw a rather striking contrast between German and American voters. Chancellor Helmut Kohl was running for reelection during a particularly bad economic time. Unemployment was high (about 12 percent), and the economy had been stalled with little growth for several years. Taxes in Germany are quite high compared to taxes in the United States (then more than 50 percent for the average German compared to 25 percent to 30 percent for the average American), with welfare spending much higher in Germany. German workers, for example, are guaranteed about 80 percent of their wage for two years after becoming unemployed, and approximately 60 percent of their wage for life if they still don't find a job.

Considering the strong economy in the United States with low taxes and little welfare spending, some German politicians were calling for Germany to follow the U.S. model. So Chancellor Kohl (of the Christian Democratic Party) began running for reelection on a platform of cutting taxes and welfare in Germany, while his opponent, Gerhard Schroeder (of the Social Democratic Party), pledged to keep taxes and government welfare spending high. Gerhard Schroeder won the election primarily on this pledge of keeping high taxes and welfare. My first thought was, "This is not America."

As we begin our study of social problems in the United States, we need to recognize that there are important differences in value orientation between Americans and people of other industrial nations,* and that these differences have an enormous impact on both the causes of social problems and their potential solutions. Polls show us that Americans have less trust in government, more dislike of taxes and welfare programs, and greater tolerance for poverty. These differences are in large part a result of the stronger belief in "individualism" among Americans. In the United States, most people see each individual as an autonomous actor who is responsible for his or her own destiny, whereas in most other countries the family and community are seen to be far more important in determining our fate. Americans don't support welfare programs or high unemployment benefits because they see such problems as the result of the personal failure of the individuals involved.

Studies also show that Americans are less informed about social problems than Europeans. For example, a recent study of attitudes about income inequality in North America and Europe found that, although Americans accept more poverty in their country than Europeans, both Americans and Europeans generally agree that there should be limits on top corporate salaries. Europeans were, however, more angry about high corporate salaries in their countries than Americans, even though American CEO salaries are four to 10 times higher than corporate salaries in Europe. Americans were generally not angry about corporate salaries because few people realized how high they were.

Harold Kerbo

*For opinion poll data on contrasting American values, see Everett Ladd and Karolin Bowman, *Attitudes Toward Economic Inequality* (Washington, DC: American Enterprise Institute, 1998), and the annual Gallup Poll. Also see Harold R. Kerbo and Hermann Strasser, *Modern Germany* (New York: McGraw-Hill, 2000), and Lars Osberg and Timothy Smeeding, "'Fair' Inequality? Attitudes Toward Pay Differentials: The United States in Comparative Perspective," *American Sociological Review*, 2006, 71: 450–473.

facilities, and to be graded fairly. The student also has the duty to read the texts, complete assigned work, and behave in an orderly manner. However, the way actual people carry out their roles often differs enormously from such idealized expectations.

Roles are one of the basic building blocks of our social world, and every society has countless positions with roles attached. Roles are interwoven in complex ways, so it is often impossible to understand a particular role apart from the social network in which it is embedded. How, for example, can the role of wife be defined without reference to the roles of husband, daughter, son, mother, and father? This interdependence stems from the fact that the rights of one position (wife, for example) are interlaced with the duties of other positions (husband, daughter, son). Each of us is judged by our performance as we carry out our roles. The negligent mother, the abusive father, the incompetent professor, and the disruptive student are judged harshly because they fail to meet our role expectations.

The standards we use to make such judgments are known as *norms*. A **norm** is simply a social rule that tells us what behavior is acceptable in a certain situation—and what is not. Every human group, be it a small circle of friends or an entire society, generates norms that govern its members' conduct. An individual who violates a group's norms is often labeled a **deviant** and given some kind of formal or informal punishment.

Norm ■ A social rule that tells us what behavior is acceptable in a certain situation and what is not.

Deviant ■ An individual who violates a social norm. An individual who is labeled as a deviant by others.

A person who violates the norm against taking the lives of others may be tried and formally punished with a prison term, whereas a person who violates the trust of his or her friends is informally punished by ridicule or exclusion from the group. Just as the various roles we play may place conflicting demands on us, so the norms of various groups may conflict. Thus, we are sometimes placed in the uncomfortable position of being forced to violate the norms of one group in order to meet the norms of another.

Although some of the roles we play involve nothing more than a small group or a single individual, social roles tend to be woven together into larger units. Social institutions are relatively stable patterns of roles and behavior that focus on particular social tasks. The family, for example, is a basic institution in all known societies. It usually handles many of the duties of child rearing and provides emotional and sometimes economic support for its older members.

Social class is one of the most useful of all these basic sociological ideas. Although everyone has some idea of what it means, few of us use the concept in a clear or consistent way. Sociologists define social class as a category of people with a similar position in a society. People of the same social class have a similar chance in life: a similar opportunity to get an education, to receive health care, to acquire material possessions, and so on. Thus, the people you see sleeping on the heating grates outside an office building are from one social class and the executives who speed past them on their way to the parking lot are from another.

Many nineteenth-century thinkers, including Karl Marx and his followers, defined social class solely in economic terms.[5] Today, most sociologists use a broader definition taken from the work of the German sociologist Max Weber.[6] According to Weber, the valuables a society distributes include social status and power as well as money, so to accurately assess the class positions of individuals or groups, we must know where they stand on all three. *Status* rests on a claim to social prestige inherited from one's family or derived from occupation and lifestyle. *Power* is the ability to force others to do something whether they want to or not, and it is another key to understanding the class system and, for that matter, social life in general. Power is often associated with politics in the public mind, and high political position certainly brings a large measure of power with it; but power has many other sources as well, such as wealth or control of the means of violent force.

Sociologists use several different schemes to describe the class system in contemporary societies, but the most common divides these societies into four different classes (see Figure 1). The *upper class* is composed of individuals with great wealth who often hold key positions of corporate power. Next comes the *middle class,* which is made up of an upper segment of highly paid professionals, successful executives, and entrepreneurs, and a much larger group of middle-level managers and white-collar (nonmanual) workers. The *working class* is about the same size as the middle class, but its members are mainly blue-collar (manual) workers and lower-level service workers who would traditionally have been defined as white-collar workers but actually have the low pay and low prestige associated with working-class jobs. Although the best-paid blue-collar workers earn more money than many white-collar employees, average members of the working class earn far less than their middle-class counterparts. At the bottom of the social hierarchy is the *lower class,* whose members live in conditions of poverty or near poverty. There is a popular belief that most Americans are middle class, perhaps because the majority of the people we see on television and in the movies are from that class, but the truth of the matter is much different. Of every 100 people in the United States, only one is from the upper class, 15 to 20 are from the lower class, and the remainder are more or less evenly divided between the working class and the middle class (see Figure 1).[7]

The most all-encompassing concepts in sociology are those of society and culture. In everyday speech, *culture* refers to the refinements of civilization, such as art, music, and literature; but to sociologists, culture is the way of life of the people in a certain geographic area, and particularly the ideas, beliefs, values, patterns of thought, and symbols that make it possible. A culture provides individuals with a way of understanding the world and making it meaningful. A subculture is a culture that exists within a

Social institutions ■ Relatively stable patterns of roles and behavior centered on the performance of important social tasks.

Social class ■ A category of people with similar shares of the things that are valued in a society.

Culture ■ The way of life of the people in a certain geographic area, particularly their ideas, beliefs, values, patterns of thought, and symbols.

Subculture ■ A culture that exists within and is influenced by a larger culture but has its own unique ideas and beliefs.

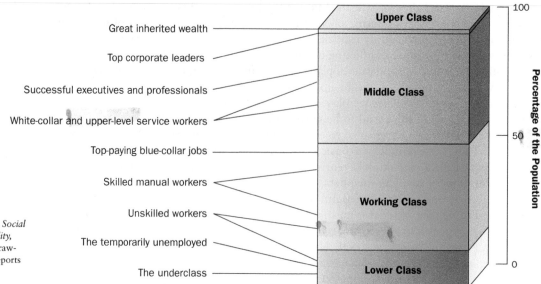

Figure 1
The Class System

Source: Harold R. Kerbo, *Social Stratification and Inequality,* 6th ed. (New York: McGraw-Hill, 2006) and current reports of the U.S. Bureau of the Census.

larger culture that influences it but has its own distinctive ideas and beliefs; for example, the gang members who cover our cities with their graffiti are part of a subculture that places its own special meaning on such symbols.

Although culture and society cannot be separated in real life, sociologists sometimes distinguish between the two so that each can be studied more easily. **Society** refers to a group of people in a particular geographic area who share common institutions and traditions, whereas *culture* refers to the physical and mental products of those people. All societies have an overall **social structure,** which is simply an organized pattern of behavior and social relationships. They also have many more focused social structures, such as a particular pattern of family life, social class, and government.

Society ■ A group of people in a geographic area who share common institutions and traditions.

Social structure ■ The organized patterns of human behavior and social relationships in a society.

QUICK REVIEW

■ Look at the list of key terms at the end of this chapter and make sure you can define each one.

Sociological Perspectives on Social Problems

All sociologists use the concepts discussed in the preceding section, but there are significant differences in their perspectives and approaches. Although the profusion of different theories and opinions can be confusing, a few broad theoretical perspectives underlie many of these differences. Aside from helping us make sense of the theories themselves, a knowledge of these basic perspectives leads to a better understanding of our social problems by drawing our attention to important social forces often neglected by the media and politicians when they discuss these issues. These general sociological perspectives (and other more narrow theories as well) tend to focus on one of two different levels. Theories of society (*macro theories*) try to make sense of the behavior of large groups of people and the workings of entire societies, whereas **social psychological theories** (*micro theories*) are concerned primarily with the behavior of individuals and small groups. Of course, society depends on its individual members, and those individuals depend on society; in the last two decades, sociologists have increasingly come to recognize that a complete understanding depends on the integration of these two different levels of analysis.

Social psychological theories ■ A large group of theories that attempts to explain the effects of individuals and social groups on each other.

Supporters of one theory often have harsh criticisms of other theories. But even though some theories are clearly more effective than others in analyzing a particular problem, none of the broad perspectives can be said to be all right or all wrong. Not only can many different theories be applied to the same problem, but also in most cases the deepest understanding comes from combining the insights gained from different theoretical perspectives. In this book, for example, some chapters draw more heavily from one theoretical perspective and some from another, depending on the nature of the problem under discussion, but all the problems are examined from many different standpoints. The objective is always to keep an open mind and draw insight wherever it can be found.

Most sociologists divide the macro-level theories of society into two broad perspectives—*functionalism* and *conflict theory*—and we will begin with those two approaches. Next we will look at *feminist theory,* which combines both macro and micro levels of analysis, and then at *interactionist theory,* which is by far the most influential of the social psychological (micro) theories in sociology. When reading the following explanations of these approaches, remember that they are only broad summaries. There are many theoretical differences among functionalists, conflict theorists, feminists, and interactionists, and many sociologists combine elements from all these theories into a more integrated approach.

The Functionalist Perspective

Many early theorists who held a **functionalist perspective** saw society as something like a living organism. Just as people have a heart and circulatory system, muscles, blood, and a brain, a society has a set of economic, political, religious, family, and educational institutions. Just as all the parts of a living organism work together to keep it alive, so all the parts of society must work together to keep it going. Each institution has a set of **functions** it must perform in order to keep society healthy; for instance, the function of the economic institution is to provide the food, shelter, and clothing that people need to survive, whereas the functions of the government include coordinating the activities of other institutions, dealing with unmet social needs, and protecting society from foreign aggressors. These various institutions make up a balanced whole, so changes in one institution are likely to require changes in another. Thus, from the functionalist perspective, we all have a common stake in helping to maintain society, and all of a society's institutions work together for the common good. However, societies, like machines and biological organisms, do not always work the way they are supposed to work. Things get out of whack. Even when things are going well, changes introduced to correct one imbalance may produce other problems. An action that interferes with the effort to carry out essential social tasks is said to be **dysfunctional.** For example, educators may train too many people for certain jobs. Those who cannot find positions in their area of expertise may become resentful, rebelling against the system that they feel has treated them unfairly. Thus, "overeducation" may be said to be a dysfunction of our educational institutions. Functionalists also realize there are sometimes unintended consequences from our efforts to change society. For example, the effort to reduce the amount of drugs available on the streets may work to push up the crime rate. As the supply of illegal drugs is reduced, the street price of drugs goes up, and addicts may have to commit more crimes to pay for their drug habit. Therefore, the functional perspective warns us that we must make a systemic analysis of functions and dysfunctions within a society before we attempt a program of social change.

Functionalists see a common set of norms and values as the glue that holds groups, institutions, and whole societies together. Small tribal societies in which everyone is in constant close contact usually have little difficulty in maintaining these common ideals, but as the great French sociologist Emile Durkheim pointed out, as societies have become ever larger and more complex, it has become increasingly difficult to maintain a social consensus about basic norms and values.[8] Thus, one of the major sources of contemporary social problems is the weakening of the social consensus. Functionalists can cite considerable evidence to show that when social rules lose their power to control our behavior, people become lost and confused and are more susceptible to suicide, mental disorders, and drug problems.

Functionalist perspective ■ A broad sociological approach that sees society as a delicate balance of parts, each with its own functions and dysfunctions, and holds that most social problems result from the disorganization of society.

Function ■ The contribution of each social institution to the maintenance of a balanced order.

Dysfunction ■ The way in which a social phenomenon interferes with the maintenance of a balanced social order.

Social disorganization ■ The condition that exists when an institution or an entire society is poorly organized and fails to carry out essential social functions satisfactorily.

Functionalists also feel that social problems arise when society, or some part of it, becomes disorganized. This **social disorganization** involves a breakdown of social structure so that its various parts no longer work together as smoothly as they should. Functionalists see many causes of social disorganization: Young people may be inadequately socialized because of problems in the institution of the family, or society may fail to provide enough social and economic opportunities to some of its members, thus encouraging them to become involved in crime or other antisocial activities. Sometimes a society's relationship to its environment may be disrupted so that it no longer has sufficient food, energy, building materials, or other resources. However, in modern industrial societies, one cause of social disorganization—rapid social change—promotes all the others.

Social disorganization is particularly severe in the modern era because more change has occurred in less time than during any other period of human history. Basic institutions have undergone drastic changes, with technology advancing so rapidly that other parts of the culture have failed to keep pace. This *cultural lag* is one of the major sources of social disorganization. For instance, when knowledge about nutrition, public health, and medical technology began spreading through the world in the nineteenth century, many lives, especially those of infants, were saved. Yet traditional attitudes toward the family have not changed fast enough to adjust to the fact that more children survive to adulthood. The result has been a worldwide population explosion.[9]

Although functionalism has been a standard theoretical approach to social problems for many years, it has numerous critics. Despite its claims of objectivity, many sociologists see functionalism as a politically conservative philosophy that too quickly assumes that society is good as it is and should be preserved without major changes. Functionalism sometimes blames social problems on individual deviance or temporary social disorganization while seeming to ignore what some see as more basic deficiencies in the structure of society. The critics of functionalism claim that it is often impossible to say whether or not a particular social phenomenon is functional for society as a whole because such phenomena usually have different impacts on different groups. For example, a law that forbids sleeping in the lobbies of public buildings would benefit wealthy people who may be disturbed by such behavior but hurt the homeless, who have nowhere else to go. The critics charge that what the functionalists often really mean when they say something is functional is that it works to the benefit of the status quo.

The Conflict Perspective

Conflict perspective ■ A broad sociological approach that sees the conflict between different groups as a basic sociological process and holds that the principal source of social problems is the exploitation and oppression of one group by another.

When theorists with a **conflict perspective** look out at contemporary society, they see a very different world. Where the functionalists see a more or less integrated whole working to maintain itself and promote the common good, the conflict theorists see a diverse collection of social groups, all struggling for wealth, power, and prestige. Whereas functionalists emphasize the importance of shared values, attitudes, and norms in holding society together, conflict theorists insist that social order is maintained more by authority backed by the use of force. For example, functionalists hold that most people obey the law because they believe that it is the right thing to do. Conflict theorists, on the other hand, say that most people obey the law because they are afraid of being arrested, jailed, or even killed if they don't. Another important difference between the functionalist and conflict perspectives is seen in their assumptions about social change. Functionalists tend to view a healthy society as being relatively stable; they assert that too much change is disruptive and that society has a natural tendency to regain its balance whenever it is disturbed. Conflict theorists see society in more dynamic terms: Because people are constantly struggling with one another to gain power, change is inevitable. One individual or group is bound to gain the upper hand, only to be defeated in later struggles.

Neither the conflict nor the functionalist perspective can be said to be a single unified theory. Rather, each consists of several related theories that share many common elements. One of the most important differences among conflict theorists concerns the type of conflicts they see as most central to modern society. Karl Marx, the famous nineteenth-century scholar and revolutionary who had so much to do with the origins of conflict theory, placed primary emphasis on **class conflict.** For Marx, the position a person holds in the system of production determines his or her class position. In a capitalist society, a person may be in one of two different positions. Some people own capital and capital-producing property (for example, factory owners, landlords, and merchants) and are, therefore, members of the *bourgeoisie.* Other people work for wages as producers of capital (for example, factory workers, miners, and laborers of all kinds). Marx called this class the *proletariat.* He asserted that these two classes have directly opposing economic interests because the wealth of the bourgeoisie is based on exploitation of the proletariat. He thought that workers would develop an increasing awareness of their exploitation by the bourgeoisie and that this awareness, combined with growing political organization, would eventually result in violent class conflict. Marx believed that the workers would overthrow their masters in this great revolution and establish a classless society. Private property and inheritance would be abolished, steeply graduated income taxes would be introduced, education and training would be free, and production would be organized for use, not profit.[10]

Modern conflict theorists continue to see class conflict as a central fact of life in contemporary society. Even though Marx's ideas have had an enormous impact on the world, many conflict theorists look at the class structure in quite different terms than Marx did, instead preferring the approach of another famous German sociologist, Max Weber, which we have already discussed. Even many contemporary Marxists have come to see the vision of a popular revolution that will establish a just society without class distinctions as something that will occur only in the distant future, if at all.

Although virtually no conflict theorist would deny the importance of class conflict in modern society, some place greater emphasis on other types of conflict. In the wake of the civil rights and ethnic power movements in the United States and the worldwide epidemic of ethnic strife, some have come to place more importance on *ethnic conflict*— the struggle for power, wealth, and status between the members of different ethnic groups. Conflict theorists influenced by feminism place greater emphasis on gender and the inequalities based on it. Whether they emphasize class, ethnicity, or gender, conflict theorists generally agree on some basic criticisms of the functionalists. Conflict theorists deny that our most serious problems arise primarily from a weakening of social values or the unintentional problems created when an important social institution becomes dis-

Class conflict ■ The struggle for wealth, power, and prestige among the social classes.

Phyllis Picardi/ImageState/International Stock Photography Ltd.

Contemporary society has huge inequalities in the distribution of wealth, power, and prestige, and conflict theorists hold that fact to be one of the most basic causes of our social problems.

organized. Rather, most social problems are the result of the intentional or unintentional exploitation of weak groups by powerful ones. For example, conflict theorists argue that the serious problems faced by Latinos and African Americans in the United States are not caused by the disorganization of the social system that makes it difficult to fully integrate these minorities into the mainstream of society, but by exploitation by whites who profit from the economic and political subordination of minority groups.

World system theory ■ A theory that sees global inequality as the product of the exploitation of poor nations by rich ones.

A conflict perspective is also well suited to move from an analysis of individual nations to a global level. Modern **world system theory,** for example, is a variety of conflict theory that helps us understand the differences between rich and poor nations. Adherents of this theory argue that there is something like an international class system in which the rich nations, having more power and wealth, are able to exploit poor nations for their own advantage. From this global conflict perspective, we can see how poor nations may sometimes be forced to remain poor because it is in the interests of richer nations to keep them that way so as to exploit their resources and their labor. At the same time, a global conflict perspective can help us understand the impact of the **globalization** of the world economy on individual nations such as the United States. For example, globalization may be of most benefit to the rich people in the advanced nations because the exploitation of poor nations can produce fat profits. On the other hand, globalization can hurt the workers of rich nations as their jobs move overseas to places with cheaper labor. Global conflict theorists argue that one reason that poverty has remained high and wages have shown little growth in the United States despite a long economic boom is that working-class Americans have faced ever-increasing competition for jobs with poor people from around the world.

Globalization ■ The process by which the nations of the world become increasingly interdependent.

Just as functionalism has been criticized for being too conservative, the conflict perspective has been criticized for being too radical. Critics say that conflict theorists overemphasize the role of conflict, arguing that if there were as much of it as these theorists claim, society would have collapsed long ago. Moreover, they charge that conflict theorists are too one-sided in their approach. The critics say that although conflict theorists see nothing but the bad side of capitalism, capitalist nations actually do a much better job of dealing with their social problems than do other kinds of societies.

The Feminist Perspective

Feminist theory ■ A group of approaches to understanding society and social behavior that focus on the importance of gender and the inequalities based on it.

Like the other approaches examined here, **feminist theory** is not really a single theory but a group of theories that share a concern with the same basic questions. In their analysis of contemporary feminist theory, Patricia Madoo Lengermann and Jill Niebrugge-Brantley hold that the two most important of those questions are "And what about the women?" and "Why is woman's situation as it is?"[11] Throughout most of its history, sociology, like the rest of the humanities and social sciences, saw human experience from a male perspective. Although there was certainly much in this approach that applied to both genders, women's experience was often ignored or given a decidedly secondary importance. So when feminist theory was first beginning to emerge as an influential force in sociology in the 1960s, the first question it posed was "What about the women?" In other words, these thinkers set out to describe the world and women's place in it from a female perspective to counterbalance the male-oriented view of the traditional sociological theories. Feminist theory emphasizes the idea that women's lives are markedly different from men's because women are given the primary responsibility for child rearing and are socialized to care for the emotional and physical needs of others. But the position of women is not just different from that of men, it is *unequal* as well. On average, women have less wealth, less power, and lower status than men. Thus, feminists often describe contemporary society as a **patriarchy**—that is, a society dominated by men and run in their interests.

Patriarchy ■ A society dominated by men and run in their interests.

In their attempts to explain why a woman's situation is the way it is, feminists tend to split into different theoretical camps. The largest group is probably the *liberal feminists*. Liberal feminists see social activity in our society divided into two separate spheres: the public sphere, which is man's central concern, and the private sphere, which is woman's realm. Liberal feminists view the private sphere as an endless round of demanding, undervalued tasks, such as housework and child care, while the real rewards of life—power, money, and prestige—are to be found in the public sphere. They generally accept the American values of freedom and individualism, but they argue that women have been confined to the private sphere and denied a fair opportunity to compete. The fundamental cause of this exclusion is **sexism**—stereotypes, prejudice, and discrimination based on gender. The solution to this injustice is, therefore, to attack the sexist traditions that have been handed down from previous generations and to allow everyone to develop their own unique abilities and pursue their interests regardless of their gender.

Sexism ■ Stereotypes, prejudice, and discrimination based on gender.

To the *socialist feminists,* the liberals take a far too rosy view of contemporary society. In their view, the roots of the exploitation of women are to be found in the capitalist economic system and the feudal system from which it evolved. Capitalism is based on the exploitation of labor, and women are the most exploited group of all. They are exploited by their husbands, providing unpaid labor for child care and housework, and they are exploited by the larger economy, providing a reserve pool of low-wage industrial labor to be used when necessary and then cast out. To the socialist feminists, a mere attack on sexist stereotypes will have little real impact on women's oppression unless the capitalist system itself is fundamentally transformed to free both women and men.

The *radical feminists* go a step beyond the others, arguing not just that the women's world is different from the men's world but that it is *better.* Men created and sustained our current social order, which is an oppressive patriarchal system that exploits and represses women, and their primary tool has been violence against women—rape, spouse abuse, incest, and murder. The radical feminists call for a "woman-centered" society that separates women from the repression of men.

The critics of feminist theory fall into three different camps. One group argues that the feminists are completely wrong when they charge that society, and especially the family, oppresses women. In this view, the family fulfills and enriches women, and the feminists are leading a misguided effort to make women become more like men. A second group of critics accepts the idea that women are indeed oppressed but argues that most men are oppressed, too. These critics assert that feminists foster the same kinds of stereotypes of men that our culture has created of women and that feminists try to blame men for injustices that are actually caused by impersonal historical forces. Finally, the third group has criticized feminist theory and the feminist movement for assuming all women have the same experience as white, middle-class women. Much attention has been given to rectifying this problem, but it is still important to ask whether or not women who are poor, women who are older, women of color, and women whose sexual identities are not heterosexual are being included in current feminist perspectives.

The Interactionist Perspective

The sociological approach to social psychology is dominated by a single broad perspective known as **interactionism.** In fact, many of the ideas of the interactionists have become so widely accepted that they are often not even seen as part of a separate theory but simply as a standard part of basic sociology. Interactionism explains our behavior in terms of the patterns of thoughts and beliefs we have and in the meaning we give to our lives. To understand individual behavior, the interactionist tries to look at the world through the eyes of the actors involved to see how they define themselves and their environment. This understanding of the conditions in which we find ourselves, known as the **definition of the situation,** is learned through interaction with other people and is the foundation on which we base all our behavior. For example, a gang member who sees the police as the storm troopers of a racist society will respond differently to an officer's calls for help than a banker who sees the police as the defenders of law and order. Our interactions with others, however, teach us far more than how to define a particular social situation or even how to define the world in general. They are also the basis for the ideas we develop about who and what we are; and such an understanding, in

Interactionism ■ A theory that explains behavior in terms of the way individuals define themselves, their social relationships, and the world as a whole.

Definition of the situation ■ People's understanding of the conditions in which they find themselves.

turn, tells us what to expect from other people and how to act in a particular social context.

To the interactionist, reality is not something out there in the world waiting to be discovered. Reality is a socially created agreement constructed by the efforts of people acting together in social groups. Meanings are created as we struggle to define ourselves and the world around us and then share those meanings with others. In interactionist theory, human culture is nothing more than a complex system of shared meanings; those meanings, in turn, determine our behavior.

The work of American philosopher George Herbert Mead was the original force behind interactionist theory.[12] Mead argued that the ability to communicate in *symbols* (principally words and combinations of words) is the key feature that distinguishes humans from other animals. Children develop the ability to think and to use symbols in the process known as **socialization.** At first, young children blindly imitate the behavior of their parents, but eventually they learn to "take the role of the other," pretending to be "mommy" or "daddy." From such role taking, children learn to understand the relationships among different roles and to see themselves as they imagine others see them. According to Mead, the key to a child's psychological development is the creation of a **self-concept** (the relatively stable mental image we all have of who and what we are). This self-concept is created out of the responses a child receives from the important people in his or her life. For example, if a girl's parents constantly tell her how smart she is, she is likely to formulate a concept of herself as an intelligent person. This concept of self is not a fixed, unchanging structure, however. If later in life her teachers and friends begin to treat her as if she isn't really very bright, her self-concept is likely to change. The concept of self is one of the most important in social psychology, for it influences almost every aspect of our behavior. Another important influence on behavior, according to Mead, is the *generalized other,* the idea we form of what kind of behavior people expect of us (in other words, our conscience).

After Mead's death in 1931, his ideas continued to gain stature among sociologists and social psychologists. Those who adhered most closely to Mead's original ideas became known as *symbolic interactionists.*[13] They have been especially active in the study of social problems and have contributed a great deal to our understanding of critical social issues. For example, differential association theory, an important explanation of delinquency and crime, is a direct offshoot of Mead's theories, as is the labeling theory that is used to explain crime and mental disorder. Over the years, however, interactionist theory has grown far beyond Mead's original vision and has absorbed insights from many other approaches.

Despite its enormous influence, interactionist theory has many critics. The most common complaint is that interactionism is vague and difficult to substantiate scientifically. A more telling criticism is that interactionism has an overly intellectual view of human nature. Classic interactionism sees human behavior entirely in terms of ideas and thoughts; it leaves out feelings and emotions. As a result of such criticism, interactionists have begun to direct more attention to the way our ideas and definitions are linked to emotions and to the role emotion plays in social life.[14]

Other Social Psychological Perspectives

Like sociologists, psychologists have long been involved in the study of social psychology, and they have developed their own perspectives to explain it. One of the most influential approaches is known as **behaviorism.** Originally, behaviorists felt science should investigate only observable behavior and that it is a waste of time to explore thoughts, feelings, or anything else that cannot be directly measured. They argued that all behavior is learned as the result of the patterns of rewards and punishments we receive from our environment.[15] Obviously, this approach is quite different from that of the interactionists and all their emphasis on thoughts and symbols. However, both perspectives see human behavior as learned, not inherited, and more recent behaviorist thinkers who are

Socialization ■ The process by which individuals learn their culture's ways of thinking and behaving.

Self-concept ■ Our image of who and what we are.

Behaviorism ■ A theory that holds behavior is learned from the rewards and punishments we receive.

more willing to look at the subjective side of behavior actually end up with conclusions that are quite compatible with those of the interactionists.[16]

Among the most popular psychological perspectives are the **personality theories**. **Personality** refers to the stable characteristics and traits that distinguish one person from another. Personality theorists believe it accounts for most differences in individual social behavior. Psychologists usually see personality differences as the result of a child's interactions with parents and other early experiences, although some hold that personality has an inherited component as well. Various ideas about personality have often been used to explain social problems. For example, criminals are sometimes said to break the law because they have "sociopathic personalities" (impulsive, unstable, and immature), and racial prejudice is attributed to an "authoritarian personality" (rigid, insecure, and with repressed feelings of guilt and hostility).

One of the most basic and long-running disputes in the social sciences is sometimes called the "nature versus nurture" controversy. Those who support the "nurture" side of the debate, including most sociologists, feel that the majority of human behavior is learned. Those on the "nature" side argue that most human behavior is determined by our inherited biological makeup. The **biosocial perspective** comprises a loose grouping of "nature" theories that emphasize the role of biology in determining human behavior. Originally, biological theorists saw virtually all human behavior as caused by inherited patterns of action they called *instincts*. Given the enormous range of human culture and behavior, few contemporary scientists still claim that all behavior is inherited. Contemporary biosocial theorists, therefore, emphasize the importance of the interaction between biological predispositions and the social environment. For example, many criminologists who argue that there is a hereditary predisposition toward crime see the problem as being as much with society as with genetics. They argue that people with low intelligence, which they hold to be a biological characteristic, are rejected by teachers and more competent students because they do poorly in school. As a result, they are more likely to become rebellious and antisocial. Many biosocial theorists focus their studies on the evolutionary process in hopes that an understanding of the forces that shaped the development of humankind will enable us to get a clearer picture of behavioral predispositions that have been passed down from our ancestors.

Personality theories ■ A group of theories that holds that social behavior is determined by differences in personality.

Personality ■ The relatively stable characteristics and traits of a person that distinguish him or her from another.

Biosocial perspective ■ A loose grouping of theories that emphasizes the importance of biology in determining human behavior.

Applying the Sociological Perspectives: An Example

At first, these abstract theoretical perspectives may not seem to have much to do with all the pressing problems facing our society. If we take a concrete example, however, it is easy to show how these perspectives work to help us build an understanding of the issues at hand. Suppose, for instance, that you often stop at a small market on your way home from class. One day you realize that the woman who is sitting in the park across the street with her three children is there every time you come in. You ask the clerk about it, and she tells you that they are living in their van, which is parked in an alley around the corner. A few weeks later, you go to the market and notice that a police car is parked on the street. You see two officers are talking with the woman, and after that you never see her or her children again.

Of course, we would need much more information before we could come to any firm conclusions about why this particular family is in such trouble, but the sociological perspectives can help us learn about the general causes of homelessness and poverty, and that is really the more important question if we are to deal with the roots of the problem. The macro-level approaches lead us to take a broad perspective and to link the family's problem with powerful sociological forces that operate throughout our society. The functionalists see the origins of this kind of problem in the social disorganization that plagues so many parts of modern society. They are particularly likely to see such problems as the product of the weakening of the institution of the family. Some functionalists argue, for example, that the growing strength of the ideals of individualism and freedom is leading us to neglect our community obligations. In the past, people were expected to stay in a marriage, even a difficult one, for the sake of the children and society as a whole. But the weakening of such norms has resulted in more and more husbands and wives splitting up, often leaving a weakened family unit in serious financial straits.

Feminists, on the other hand, see this problem in far different terms. To them, this family's problems are far more likely to be the result of sexism and discrimination. Society expects this woman to assume responsibility for her children and to sacrifice her future for their sake. Yet when a marriage breaks up, the mother is likely to face a job market that discriminates against women, offering only jobs that pay less than the cost of the child care, transportation, food, shelter, and clothing her family requires.

Although most conflict theorists are likely to agree with the feminists, they would also point out that this mother also suffers from exploitation by the classes above her in the social hierarchy. The reason there are no decent jobs available is that powerful business interests intentionally work to keep wages low so they can maximize their profits. Similarly, welfare benefits are kept at the lowest possible level: just enough to prevent the underprivileged from rising up and disrupting the system but far less than would really be needed to lift them out of poverty. When the homeless become a nuisance to affluent neighbors, the police force the homeless to move on.

Interactionists are more likely to seek the origins of this family's plight in the way family members see themselves and their social world. They point out that people from disadvantaged backgrounds often come to define the world in ways that make it difficult to escape poverty. For example, research shows that poor people are more likely to see their lives in fatalistic terms and feel that there is little or nothing they can do to change their situation. Moreover, the way poor people talk, act, and define the world is likely to be extremely different from the way people from a higher-class background do, and their attitudes and behavior may shut poor people out of many occupational and social opportunities. Interactionists are also likely to see this family as a victim of labeling. The people they interact with near the park are likely to label them as "bums" or "riffraff" and then treat them on that basis—excluding them from jobs, social contacts, and support. Eventually, the members of the family are likely to start believing those labels are really true, and they will develop an increasingly negative image of themselves and their place in the world. Such beliefs soon create a self-fulfilling prophecy as the mother gives up hope of finding a good job and increasingly avoids the company of "respectable" people. As one early interactionist, W. I. Thomas, put it: If people "define situations as real, they are real in their consequences."[17]

After reading these explanations of the woman's problem, it is tempting to ask which theory is actually the correct one. The answer quite often is that they all are. If we knew more details about this particular woman and her children, we might say one theory better explains her particular situation. But when we consider the poor and homeless in general, each theory helps us understand some aspects of their social problem that could be missed by using only one theory. If you were interested in taking the next step and actually doing something about the problem of poverty and homelessness, then each perspective could also suggest some possible courses of action. For example, some functionalists believe that we must work to strengthen our family system and to reinforce the values that place family obligations ahead of individual self-interest. Liberal feminists call for tough new laws to fight occupational discrimination and for better welfare benefits. Conflict theorists and socialist feminists call for the poor and underprivileged, women, and minorities to band together with their supporters from other groups and demand fundamental structural changes to reduce inequality and make this a more just society. Taking conflict theory to a global level suggests that something must be done about the ability of big corporations to move their operations to poor countries, thus reducing jobs and wages for American workers. Interactionists advocate education and training programs, not only to teach the disadvantaged new skills but also to help them redefine their world and the way they see themselves. Interactionists would also say that the family needs more supportive contacts with members of the larger community. Of course, these approaches are not mutually exclusive, and just as we can combine their theoretical insights to gain a more complete picture of the problem, so we can combine

Table 1

SOCIOLOGICAL PERSPECTIVES

The Functionalist Perspective

- Macro level
- Society is held together by shared norms and values.
- Society is a joint effort of many institutions working together for the common good.
- The primary cause of social problems is social disorganization, which often results from rapid social change.

The Feminist Perspective

- Macro and micro levels
- Gender is a basic organizing principle of contemporary society.
- The social position of women is not only different from that of men but also unequal.
- The primary cause of social problems is the exploitation of women by men.

The Conflict Perspective

- Macro level
- Society is held together by power, authority, and coercion.
- Society is a struggle for dominance among competing social groups.
- The primary cause of social problems is the exploitation and oppression of some groups by others.
- International conflicts between rich and poor nations help explain persistent world poverty.

The Interactionist Perspective

- Micro level
- Individual behavior is based on the symbols and shared meanings we learn.
- This learning occurs during interactions between individuals and other people and groups.
- The primary cause of social problems is the way we define ourselves and our social situation.

various proposals for change into a more comprehensive response. (See Table 1 for a comparison of the four perspectives.)

QUICK REVIEW

- Briefly describe the main points of the functionalist, conflict, feminist, and interactionist theories.
- What are the strengths and weaknesses of each theory?

Doing Sociological Research

The theoretical perspectives discussed so far serve as a guide and a point of reference for the student of social problems. Theories are of little value, however, unless they deal with facts, and in the study of social problems, people often disagree about what "the facts" really are. Because their task is so difficult, sociologists give a great deal of attention to the study of **methodology**—that is, how to do research. Volumes have been written on this subject, yet no one can say that any particular technique is better than all the others. The decision about which research techniques to use must be based on the nature of the problem being studied and the skills and resources of the researcher. Among many possible alternatives, the four most common sources of sociological data are public records and statistics, case studies, surveys, and experiments.

Methodology ■ The study of how to do research.

Public Records and Statistics

Governments and organizations such as the United Nations and the World Bank publish a wealth of statistics and information. A look through the references in this book will reveal numerous citations to data from the Bureau of the Census, the Bureau of Justice

Statistics, the United Nations Development Programme, and similar organizations because such information is vital to sociologists' efforts to understand today's social problems. One of the oldest and most reliable sources of statistics is the U.S. census, which is taken every 10 years. The goal of the census is to count all the people in the United States and determine such characteristics as their age, gender, and employment status. Such an effort to get direct information about every person in the country is obviously a massive undertaking, so most of the information we have comes from surveys that question only a sample of the total population. There are periodic government surveys of selected groups, such as the elderly or the unemployed, as well as general surveys designed to measure, for example, the number of people who have been the victims of crime. Other important sources of data are the bureaucracies that register births, marriages, divorces, and deaths and the official records of government agencies, such as the federal budget and the *Congressional Record*.

Despite their importance to the sociologist, such data still have serious shortcomings. Almost every researcher has had the experience of spending long hours looking through official publications searching for a particular figure that is nowhere to be found. You might, for example, be interested in comparing the income and educational levels of Chinese Americans and Filipino Americans, only to find that the Bureau of the Census lists only whites, blacks, Hispanics, and "others." More serious is the problem of bias and distortion. For example, it has long been known that many African American males from the underclass vanish from census reports in their early years of adulthood only to reappear in middle age. Government statistics may also be biased by political considerations. Such things as the rates of poverty, unemployment, and crime are often hot social issues, and many sociologists have charged that the standards and procedures for calculating those figures are slanted for political reasons. Government agencies may also be pressured to stop collecting and distributing data that are embarrassing to powerful political interests. The U.S. Bureau of the Census, for example, stopped publishing figures on the numbers of "working poor" after the start of the second Bush administration, which had a strong ideological opposition to both higher minimum wages and most welfare programs.

The Case Study

Case study ■ A detailed examination of specific individuals, groups, or situations.

A detailed examination of specific individuals, groups, or situations is known as a **case study**. There are many different sources of information for such investigations, including the official records just discussed, histories, biographies, and newspaper reports. *Personal interviews* and *participant observation* are two of the most direct ways of gathering information for a case study.

Suppose you were interested in studying juvenile delinquency. To do personal interviews, you might locate a gang of delinquent boys and ask each boy why he became involved in the gang, what he does with the other gang members, what his plans for the future are, and so on. You would then study the replies, put them together in some meaningful way, and draw your conclusions. To do a participant observation study, you would actually take part in gang activities. You might disguise yourself and work your way into the gang as a regular member, or you might tell the boys your purpose and ask their permission to watch their activities. One problem with the interview technique is that we can never be sure the subjects are telling the truth, even if they think they are. Although the participant observation technique avoids this problem, it is difficult and sometimes even dangerous to study people in this way because they often resent the intrusion of nosy outsiders. Then, too, people often act differently when they know a sociologist is watching them.

When compared with other research methods, the case study has the advantage of allowing researchers to come into close contact with the objects of their study. Interviews and direct observation can provide rich insights that cannot be obtained from statistics, but the case study method has its limitations, especially when the cases selected for study are not typical. For instance, a researcher might unknowingly select a group of delinquents who are strongly opposed to drug use when all the other gang members in the same area are heavy drug users. Another common criticism of the case study method is that it relies too heavily on the ability and insights of the person doing the study. Although this problem is common to all research methods, it is especially troublesome in case studies because all the "facts" that are gathered for examination are filtered by the researcher.

The Survey

Rather than concentrating on an in-depth study of a few cases, the **survey** asks more limited questions of a much larger number of people. It is seldom possible to question everyone concerned with a certain social problem; therefore, a **sample** is used. For instance, suppose you were interested in the relationship between people's age and their attitudes toward the abortion issue. You might select an appropriate city for your study and randomly select a sample of 500 names from the city directory. If the sample is properly drawn (that is, each person in the city's population had an equal chance of being selected), it will usually be representative of all the adults in the city. Each person in the sample would then be interviewed to determine his or her age and attitude toward abortion. Next, you would analyze the responses statistically and try to determine the relationship between the two variables.

The survey is an invaluable tool for measuring the attitudes and behaviors of large numbers of people. The Gallup and Harris polls, which gauge public opinion about dozens of topical issues, are good examples of the way the survey method can be used effectively. However, because most surveys gather answers to only a limited number of fixed questions, they are not as effective as the case study approach in developing new ideas and insights. Another problem is that people do not always answer the questions honestly, particularly if the survey deals with sensitive issues such as sexual behavior or crime. A third difficulty is that surveys are expensive and time consuming. When conducted properly, however, a survey ensures that the people studied are not misleading exceptions; case studies can seldom provide this assurance.

Survey ■ A research technique in which a sample of people are asked about their attitudes or activities, either in personal interviews or by means of questionnaires.

Sample ■ A cross section of subjects selected for study as representative of a larger population.

The Experiment

The **experiment,** in which the researcher performs some activity and watches the results, provides an opportunity for the most carefully controlled type of research. Although there are many types of experimental design, experimenters usually divide their subjects into an experimental group and a control group. The experimental group is then

Experiment ■ A research method in which the behavior of individuals or groups is studied under controlled conditions, usually in a laboratory setting.

AP Wide World Photos

The survey, in which a sample of people are asked a series of questions about their opinions or behavior, is one of the most common methods of sociological research.

manipulated in some way, but the other group is not. By comparing the two groups at the end of the experiment, researchers try to discover the effects of what was done to the experimental group. To illustrate, suppose you were interested in the effects of violent programs on television viewers. You might select two groups of people and show one, the experimental group, violent television programs and the other, the control group, nonviolent programs. You would then test the two groups to see whether the violent programs caused any increase in violent behavior or attitudes.

A major problem arises because most experimental studies of human behavior must be conducted in laboratory settings. Watching violent television programs in a laboratory is likely to have different effects from watching the same programs at home because the conditions in the two settings differ so greatly. True "social experiments," in which a social change is introduced into real-life settings to determine its effect on a social problem, are rare because few social scientists have the authority or the money to carry out such research. Another problem with experimental research is that the subjects may be inadvertently harmed by the experimental manipulations; many potentially valuable experiments cannot be done for ethical reasons.

QUICK REVIEW

■ Discuss the advantages and disadvantages of the use of surveys, case studies, experiments, and public records in doing sociological research.

Interpreting Claims About Social Problems

Even those of us who never do research on social problems sooner or later will have to interpret claims about them. Politicians, journalists, and sociologists, as well as an assortment of cranks and oddballs, constantly bombard the public with opinions and "facts" about these problems. Each person must decide whether or not to believe these claims. Many of them are patently false, but some are presented with impressive-sounding arguments. Reasonable skepticism is an important scientific tool; it should be practiced by anyone who is interested in knowing how social problems arise, persist, and change.

Some people find it easy to believe almost anything they see in print, and they even accept the exaggerated claims of television commercials and newspaper advertisements. In addition, the ability to speak well may be taken as a sign that the speaker is trustworthy and honest. The belief that those who lie in public are usually sued or even put in jail adds to the credibility of public speakers, but there are many ways of telling lies without risking trouble with the law. One technique is to lie about groups rather than individuals. Although someone could get in trouble saying that John Jones is a drug addict without some proof, a speaker could say that college students or musicians are addicts. Another technique is to imply guilt by association. Consider, for example, the difference between these two statements:

> Mary Jones, Islamic terrorists, and student revolutionaries agree that there are great injustices in the American economic system.

> Mary Jones, the National Council of Churches, and Supreme Court justices agree that there are great injustices in the American economic system.

Another way to convey a misleading impression is to quote out of context. This sort of misrepresentation has been brought to the level of a fine art by the merchandisers of mass market paperback books. For example, a reviewer in *The New York Times* might say something like this: "This book is somewhat interesting, but certainly not one of the greatest books of the decade." And the reviewer might end up being quoted like this:

> Interesting . . . one of the greatest books of the decade.
> —*New York Times.*

It is essential to carefully read claims about social problems and their solutions. Wild propaganda and intentional distortions are usually self-evident. However, most people who are concerned about social issues do not intentionally lie or distort the truth. They may merely be vague, using phrases such as "many people believe" and "it is widely thought" because their knowledge is incomplete. People also tend to unconsciously distort their perceptions to fit their own biases, and misleading statements are hardest to detect when the speaker is sincere. There are a number of standards that can be used to measure the validity of a statement, but none is foolproof.

The Author

One of the best places to begin evaluating an article or speech is with the author. What are his or her qualifications? Why should the speaker or writer know anything more about the problem than the audience? Titles and academic degrees in themselves do not mean much unless they have some clear relation to the problem under consideration. For instance, a professor of physics might be qualified to talk about nuclear power, but her opinion about the influence of international politics on our oil supplies could well be of little value. A professor of sociology might be qualified to comment on the causes of crime but might know little or nothing about the fine points of criminal law. An impressive title does not always guarantee authority or expertise.

It is also helpful to know an author's biases. These will often become clear through a look at the author's other work. For example, suppose that an economist who has always supported the Social Security system publishes a study concluding that the system has been a failure. These findings should be given more weight than the same conclusions published by a longtime opponent of Social Security. The same is true of articles published by people with special interests. An article concluding that criminals have been mistreated by the police is more persuasive if it is written by a police officer than by a burglar.

The Support

Scientific research projects are expensive. If the authors say their assertions are based on research, then it is important to know who paid for the research and what, if anything, its supporters stand to gain from its conclusions. Few organizations, including the federal government, will fund a study that is likely to arrive at conclusions harmful to their interests. It is not surprising to find that a study funded by an oil company asserts that oil drilling will produce little environmental damage or that a study funded by a tobacco company says smoking cigarettes is as safe as playing badminton. However, a study funded by an oil company that concludes oil drilling will cause serious damage to the environment merits attention.

The Distribution

Where an article is published or a speech is given can be another important clue to the reliability of the statements made. You can usually assume that articles published in recognized journals such as the *American Journal of Sociology* or *Social Problems* meet some minimal professional standards. But an article on race relations published in a newspaper affiliated with the Ku Klux Klan, an article on the minimum wage published in a trade union weekly, and a speech on gun control before the National Rifle Association are likely to contain few surprises.

The Content

There are no firm rules for judging which conclusions are reasonable and which are not. Some research papers are so technical that only an expert can judge their value. But most books, magazine articles, and speeches about social problems are not directed at expert audiences, so readers and listeners need no special qualifications to judge the accuracy of what is said. Asking the following questions is a good way to assess the value of an article or speech.

DOES THE ARTICLE OR SPEECH MAKE SENSE? It is important to get involved with what is being said rather than just passively accepting it. Are the author's arguments logical? If a person says that drug addiction is widespread because enemy agents are trying to weaken the country by enslaving its youth, ask yourself whether it is reasonable to claim that such things could be done in secret. It is also logical to ask why those who are being enslaved by drugs are the least powerful people in the population. Do the author's conclusions seem to follow from the evidence presented? There is good reason to reject an argument that, for example, asserts that college students who smoke marijuana do so because of poverty. Subtler gaps in logic can also be detected by the attentive listener.

WHY DOES THE WRITER OR SPEAKER USE A PARTICULAR STYLE? A book or speech need not be boring to be accurate. Nevertheless, there is a difference between a calm, thoughtful analysis and demagoguery. Skillful speakers who give emotion-packed examples of human suffering may only be trying to get an audience's attention, or they may use such examples to cloud the issue. Most articles, speeches, and books necessarily contain some vague claims or assertions. One should always ask whether the vagueness is necessary because some facts are unknown or because the author is trying to obscure the subject or conceal information. Conversely, a collection of numbers and statistics does not guarantee that conclusions are valid. An old saying holds that figures do not lie but liars figure.

DO AN AUTHOR'S CLAIMS FIT IN WITH WHAT OTHERS SAY ABOUT THE SUBJECT? The truth of a proposition is not decided by democratic vote. Majorities can be wrong and minorities right. Even an individual who strays far from what most people—including experts—accept as true is not necessarily wrong. In scientific work, a successful experiment by a lone researcher can challenge truths that have long been accepted, but if an author's claims differ greatly from those of others who know something about the subject, there is reason to be skeptical. The question to be asked is whether the author presents enough evidence to justify rejection of the old ideas and accepted beliefs.

QUICK REVIEW
■ What are the best ways of evaluating the claims people make about our social problems?

Summary

There are two major sociological definitions of the term *social problem*. One says that social problems are created by gaps between a society's ideals and actual conditions in that society. The other defines a social problem as a condition that a significant number of people consider to be a problem.

The public's perceptions of social problems change from time to time. The major forces influencing these changes are social movements that try to bring about social change. These movements usually begin when people who share a common problem communicate with each other and commit themselves to finding a solution. If the supporters of a social movement are powerful, or if they can appeal to popular values and prejudices, then the movement has a good chance of success. If the opponents of the social movement have more influence, then action is far less likely to be taken. Even if the government takes official action, the agencies that are supposed to deal with the problem may do little or nothing to change it.

Over the years, sociologists have developed a body of knowledge, theories, and methods to aid in the study of social problems. Basic concepts used by virtually all sociologists include role, norm, institution, class, culture, subculture, and society.

Sociologists approach the study of social problems from different theoretical perspectives. The two major approaches that deal with large groups and entire societies are the *functionalist perspective* and the *conflict perspective*. Functionalists see a society as something like an organism or machine in which all the parts usually work together for the common good. Every society has a set of needs that must be fulfilled if it is to survive, and all the components of a society have functions that they perform to meet these needs. But they may also have dysfunctions or harmful consequences for society. Social problems occur when a society becomes so disorganized that its basic functions cannot be performed as well as they should be. Conflict theorists see social order as a set of power relationships. Coercion, not shared values and beliefs, is the strongest cement holding a society together. Some conflict theorists emphasize class conflict, and others emphasize conflicts between people from different ethnic groups or between the genders. But they all agree that the oppression of one group by another is a basic cause of social problems. Conflict theory can also be taken to a global level to understand how rich nations are able to exploit poor nations and the impact such exploitation has both at home and abroad. *Feminist theory* attempts to counterbalance the male-oriented view of the traditional sociological perspectives by describing the world and women's place in it from a woman's viewpoint. They argue that men's and women's lives are not only distinctly different but also unequal and that contemporary society is a patriarchy that benefits men at the expense of women. The dominant social psychological perspective in sociology is known as *interactionism*. Interactionists explain our behavior in terms of the patterns of thoughts and beliefs we have. They place particular emphasis on the importance of the way we define ourselves (self-concept) and the way we define our social environment (definition of the situation), both of which are in large measure learned from our interactions with others.

Theory is an important guide, but it becomes effective only when applied to facts. Social scientists use four principal methods to gather data to test theories and uncover the facts. *Public records and statistics* provide social scientists with a rich source of data so that they do not have to collect it themselves. The *case study* is a detailed examination of specific individuals, groups, or situations. *Surveys* put questions to cross sections of the population. *Experiments* usually try to duplicate the social world in a laboratory so that the various factors being studied can be carefully controlled.

Even those who never do research on social problems should be able to interpret and judge the claims of others. There are at least four commonsense methods for evaluating speeches, books, and articles about social problems: (1) check the qualifications and biases of the author, (2) check the biases of the people who pay the bills of the speaker or author, (3) check the publishers of articles and the special interests of the audience listening to a speech, and (4) check the content of the speech or article and the logic of the arguments the author uses to support a point.

QUESTIONS FOR CRITICAL THINKING

One of the most vital sociological skills is the ability to take a general understanding about the way society operates and apply it to our own personal lives. List the two or three most serious problems facing you in your own life. How do the social forces examined by the different sociological perspectives influence those problems? Is one sociological approach better than the others in helping you understand those problems? If so, why?

KEY TERMS

behaviorism	experiment	personality
biosocial perspective	feminist theory	personality theories
case study	function	role
class conflict	functionalist perspective	sample
conflict perspective	globalization	self-concept
culture	interactionism	sexism
definition of the situation	methodology	social class
deviant	norm	social disorganization
dysfunction	patriarchy	social institutions

social movements	social structure	subculture
social problem	socialization	survey
social psychological	society	world system theory
theories	sociology	

INTERNET EXERCISE

Because of the hundreds of agencies concerned about different kinds of social problems, there are also many Websites related to all aspects of social problems. To begin your exploration of these Websites, go to the *Companion Website*™ at www.pearsonhighered.com/coleman. Enter Chapter 1 and choose the Web destination module from the navigation bar.

Among other topics in this first Chapter, we have considered how social problems are defined differently by people in different societies. One way to judge differing views on social problems is to examine opinion polls in different countries. The first Web exercise in the book for Chapter 1 directs you to the Gallup Poll Website containing opinion poll data from the *Gallup International Millennium Survey*. Go to www.gallup-international.com, under "MENU," click on "Survey archive," then "Millennium Survey." Read through topics and go to the section on the environment. Do the opinion poll data show significant differences around the world with respect to concern about the environment? Are there major differences between rich countries and poor countries in concern over pollution and the future of the environment?

NOTES

1. See Robert K. Merton, "The Sociology of Social Problems," in Robert K. Merton and Robert Nisbet, eds., *Contemporary Social Problems*, 4th ed. (New York: Harcourt Brace Jovanovich, 1976).

2. Herbert Blumer, "Social Problems as Collective Behavior," *Social Problems* 18 (1971): 298–306; Malcolm Spector and John I. Kitsuse, "Social Problems: A Reformation," *Social Problems* 21 (1973): 145–159.

3. http://www.gallup.com. Also see Robert H. Lauer, "Defining Social Problems: Public Opinion and Textbook Practice," *Social Problems* 24 (1976): 122–130.

4. See Howard S. Becker, *Outsiders* (New York: Free Press, 1963).

5. Karl Marx, *Capital: A Critique of Political Economy* (New York: Random House, 1906).

6. Max Weber, *From Max Weber: Essays in Sociology*, ed. and trans. Hans H. Gerth and C. Wright Mills (New York: Oxford University Press, 1946).

7. See Harold R. Kerbo, *Social Stratification and Inequality: Class Conflict in Historical and Comparative Perspective*, 5th ed. (New York: McGraw-Hill, 2003).

8. See Emile Durkheim, *Division of Labor in Society* (Glencoe, IL: Free Press, 1947). For some classic works on functionalism, see Emile Durkheim, *The Elementary Forms of Religious Life* (New York: Free Press, 1965); Robert K. Merton, *Social Theory and Social Structure*, rev. ed. (New York: Free Press, 1957); and Talcott Parsons, *The Social System* (New York: Free Press, 1964).

9. See Marx, *Capital*; Max Weber, *The Theory of Social and Economic Organization* (Glencoe, IL: Free Press, 1947); and Randall Collins, *Conflict Sociology* (New York: Academic Press, 1979).

10. Karl Marx and Friedrich Engels, *The Communist Manifesto*, ed. Samuel Beer (New York: Appleton Century Crofts, 1955).

11. Patricia Madoo Lengermann and Jill Niebrugge-Brantley, "Contemporary Feminist Theory," in George Ritzer, *Sociological Theory*, 4th ed. (New York: McGraw-Hill, 1996), pp. 436–488.

12. George Herbert Mead, *Mind, Self, and Society* (Chicago: University of Chicago Press, 1934).

13. See, for example, Herbert Blumer, *Symbolic Interactionism: Perspective and Method* (Englewood Cliffs, NJ: Prentice Hall, 1969), and Tamotsu Shibutani, *Society and Personality* (Upper Saddle River, NJ: Prentice Hall, 1961).

14. For a good summary of contemporary interactionist theory, see John P. Hewitt, *Self and Society: A Symbolic Interactionist Social Psychology*, 9th ed. (Boston: Allyn & Bacon, 2003).

15. See B. F. Skinner, *About Behaviorism* (New York: Knopf, 1974).

16. See, for example, Albert Bandura, *Social Learning Theory* (Upper Saddle River, NJ: Prentice Hall, 1977).

17. W. I. Thomas, *The Child in America* (New York: Knopf, 1928), p. 572.

Studying Social Problems in the Twenty-First Century

THINKING SOCIOLOGICALLY

- Why are social problems everybody's problem?

- How does sociology differ from "common sense" in explaining social problems?

- Do you agree with this statement: "Guns don't kill people; people kill people"? Is this sound sociological thinking?

From Chapter 1 of *Social Problems in a Diverse Society*, Sixth Edition. Diana Kendall. Copyright © 2013 by Pearson Education, Inc. Published by Pearson Social Science & Art. All rights reserved.

((•─[**Listen** to the **Chapter Audio** on **mysoclab.com**

So we were all freaking out, and it was ... I don't know ... it was scary. ... Oh my gosh. There could be someone else out there. But there was literally cops everywhere you turned. There were a couple of policemen standing right there and blocking off certain areas where they didn't know if it was safe to walk yet.

—"Hailey," a University of Texas sophomore, explains how she felt as she watched from her classroom during a university-wide lockdown when SWAT teams swarmed her campus university after another student opened fire with an assault rifle, shooting randomly into both the air and the ground, before killed himself (Klaus, 2010; Fleming, 2010).

None of us thought it was gunshots. [The shooter] didn't say a single word the whole time. He didn't say get down. He didn't say anything. He just came in and started shooting. ... I'm not sure how long it lasted. It felt like a really long time but was probably only a minute or so. He looked like, I guess you could say, serious. He didn't look frightened at all. He didn't look angry. Just a straight face.

—Trey Perkins, a Virginia Tech University student, describes a scene of violence in the lecture hall where his German class met. Before the lone gunman ended his shooting spree, thirty-three people were dead and more than two dozen others were wounded (msnbc.com, 2007).

For those of us who spend our days in a college setting, few things scare us more than the thought that violence might shatter our "protected" social environment in a lecture hall or other campus facility. Sadly, however, such shootings are becoming an all-too-common occurrence in educational settings, from elementary and secondary schools to colleges and universities across the United States. And schools are only one of the many settings in which seemingly random acts of violence, typically involving guns and multiple injuries or deaths, take place. Violence has also become all too common in locations such as shopping malls, workplaces, hospitals, and other public spaces. Regardless of where the violence occurs, it leaves behind shock and anguish. ***Violence* is the use of physical force to cause pain, injury, or death to another or damage to property**. On an almost daily basis, the Internet and global television news channels quickly spread word of the latest bombing, the latest massacre, or the latest murder. In the United States today, gunfire is one of the leading causes of death—only vehicular accidents take a higher toll on the lives of young people in this country. Indeed, the United States has the highest homicide rate of any high-income nation. In this chapter, we explore what we can learn from sociology about social problems such as this.

USING SOCIOLOGICAL INSIGHTS TO STUDY SOCIAL PROBLEMS

Sociologists who specialize in the study of social problems often focus on violence as a pressing social issue because it inflicts harm not only on victims and their families but also on entire communities and the nation. The study of social problems is one area of inquiry within *sociology*—**the academic discipline that engages in the systematic study of human society and social interactions**. A sociological examination of social problems focuses primarily on issues that affect an entire *society* **—a large number of individuals who share the same geographic territory and are subject to the same political authority and dominant cultural expectations**—and the groups and organizations that make up that society. *Culture* **refers to the knowledge, language, values, customs, and material objects that are passed from person to person and from one generation to the next in a human group or society**. Culture helps us define what we think is right or wrong and identify the kinds of behavior we believe should be identified as a social problem.

What Is a Social Problem?

A *social problem* is a social condition (such as poverty) or a pattern of behavior (such as substance abuse) that harms some individuals or all people in a society and that a sufficient number of people believe warrants public concern and collective action to bring about change. Social conditions or certain patterns of behavior are defined as social problems when they systematically disadvantage or harm a significant number of people or when they are seen as harmful by many of the people who wield power, wealth, and influence in a group or society. Problems that disadvantage or harm a significant number of people include violence, fear of crime, environmental pollution, and inadequate access to health care.

Problems that may be viewed as harmful to people who have power, wealth, and influence are conditions that adversely affect their economic livelihood and social well-being, such as a weakening economy, inadequate schools that do not produce the quality of workers that employers need, and high rates of crime that threaten their safety and security. To put it another way, social problems are social in their causes, consequences, and sources of possible resolution. Because social problems are social in their causes, public perceptions of what constitutes a social problem change over time (see Table 1). It is no surprise, for example, that concerns about economy, unemployment, and the federal budget deficit are important to people in the United States today given the difficult times that many people have experienced in recent years as well as extensive media coverage of economic concerns as dominant national issues.

Sociologists apply theoretical perspectives and use a variety of research methods to examine social problems. Some social problems—such as violence and crime—are commonly viewed as conditions that affect all members of a population. Other social problems—such as racial discrimination—may be viewed (correctly or incorrectly) as a condition that affects some members of a population more than others. However, all social problems may be harmful to all members in a society whether they realize it or not. As an example, sociological research has documented the extent to which racial discrimination by whites against African Americans and other people of color wastes the energies and resources of those individuals who engage in such racist actions as well as harming the targets of their actions (see Feagin and Vera, 1995).

TABLE 1 Changing Perceptions of What Constitutes a Social Problem, 1950–2011

Nationwide polls taken over the last half century reflect dramatic changes in how people view social problems. Notice how responses to the question "What do you think is the most important problem facing the country today?" have changed over the years.

1950		1965		1975	
War	40%	Civil rights	52%	High cost of living	60%
The economy	15%	Vietnam War	22%	Unemployment	20%
Unemployment	10%	Other international problems	14%	Dissatisfaction with government	7%
Communism	8%	Racial strife	13%	Energy crisis	7%
1990		**2005**		**2011**	
Budget deficit	21%	War in Iraq	19%	Economy in general	26%
Drug abuse	18%	The economy/jobs	18%	Unemployment	19%
Poverty, homelessness	7%	Terrorism (general)	6%	Federal budget deficit	17%
The economy	7%	Health care	5%	Dissatisfaction with government	13%
		Social Security	4%	Health care	9%
		Moral/family values	4%	Education	6%

Sources: *The New York Times*, 1996b; The Polling Report, 2005; J. Jones, 2011.

Social problems often involve significant discrepancies between the ideals of a society and their actual achievement. For example, the United States was founded on basic democratic principles that include the right to "Life, Liberty, and the pursuit of Happiness," as set forth in the Declaration of Independence. The rights of individuals are guaranteed by the U.S. Constitution, which also provides the legal basis for remedying injustices. Significant discrepancies exist, however, between the democratic ideal and its achievement. One such discrepancy is *discrimination*—**actions or practices of dominant group members (or their representatives) that have a harmful impact on members of subordinate groups**. Discrimination may be directed along class, racial, gender, and age lines. It also may be directed against subordinate group members whose sexual orientation, religion, nationality, or other attributes are devalued by those who discriminate against them. Sometimes, discrimination is acted out in the form of violence. This type of violent act is referred to as a *hate crime*—**a physical attack against a person because of assumptions regarding his or her racial group, ethnicity, religion, disability, sexual orientation, national origin, or ancestry**. Hate crime laws have been adopted on the federal and state level that increase the penalties for crimes committed when the perpetrator is motivated by the race, color, national origin, religion, sexual orientation, gender, or disability of the victim. For example, some states have laws criminalizing interference with religious worship. However, hate crime laws vary widely, and five states have no hate crime laws and any complaints would have to be dealt with as a civil action. Among those states that have passed hate crime laws, some of the laws do not protect sexual orientation, which remains a heavily debated issue regarding hate crime legislation. For many people, hate crimes are a personal problem because they believe that they have been the victim of violent attacks based on their race, ethnicity, religion, sexual orientation, or other devalued attributes.

When hate crimes have been reported prominently by the news media, some political leaders have taken a stronger stand against such violence, thus moving the problem from the personal to the social level. For example, when an African American man in New York City was attacked with a baseball bat, leaving him with a fractured skull, the city's mayor made public appearances around the city to show that the city would actively confront racial violence and would not tolerate it. As Mayor Michael R. Bloomberg stated, "I cannot stress it enough: We are going to live together, and nobody, nobody, should ever feel that they will be attacked because of their ethnicity, their orientation, their religion, where they live, their documented status, or anything else. Period. End of story" (quoted in Rutenberg and Kilgannon, 2005:A15). Public statements such as this and corresponding changes in social policy and law are the point at which personal problems and social issues begin to connect. Sociologists use a perspective known as the sociological imagination to explain this phenomenon.

The Sociological Imagination: Bringing Together the Personal and the Social

How do our personal problems relate to the larger social problems in our society and around the world? Although each of us has numerous personal problems, ranging from how to pay our college tuition and where to find a job to more general concerns about safety, health, and war, we are not alone in these problems, and there are larger societal and global patterns that we can identify that are related to these issues. In one of the most popular phrases in the social sciences, sociologist C. Wright Mills uniquely captured the essence of how our personal troubles are related to the larger social issues in society. According to Mills, the *sociological imagination* is **the ability to see the relationship between individual experiences and the larger society**. The sociological imagination enables us to connect the private problems of individuals to public issues. Public issues (or social problems) are matters beyond a person's control that originate at the regional or national level and can be resolved only by collective action. Mills (1959b) used unemployment as an example of how people may erroneously separate personal troubles from public issues in their thinking. The unemployed individual may view his or her unemployment as a personal trouble concerning only the individual, other family members, and friends. However, widespread unemployment resulting from economic changes, corporate decisions (downsizing or relocating a plant abroad), or technological innovations (computers and advanced telecommunications systems displacing workers) is a public issue. As another example, it is easy for the victims of violent crimes and their families to see themselves as individual victims rather than placing such attacks within the larger, collective context of a society that often tolerates violence. The sociological imagination helps us shift our focus to the larger social context and see how personal troubles may be related to public issues.

Enron employees leave the company's headquarters after being laid off December 3, 2001, in Houston, Texas. Business scandals such as the one involving Enron Corporation show the wide gap between those corporate executives who made millions of dollars from questionable business practices that eventually brought down their companies and the employees who lost their jobs and benefits when those companies folded.

Sociologists make connections between personal and public issues in society through microlevel and macrolevel analysis. *Microlevel analysis* **focuses on small-group relations and social interaction among individuals.** Using microlevel analysis, a sociologist might investigate how fear of unemployment affects workers and their immediate families. In contrast, *macrolevel analysis* **focuses on social processes occurring at the societal level, especially in large-scale organizations and major social institutions such as politics, government, and the economy.** Using macrolevel analysis, a sociologist might examine how the loss of about 7.9 millions jobs in Great Recession of 2007–2009 affected the U.S. economy. As Mills suggested, a systematic study of a social problem such as unemployment gives us a clearer picture of the relationship between macrolevel structures such as the U.S. economy and microlevel social interactions among people in their homes, workplaces, and communities.

What can we gain by using a sociological perspective to study social problems? A sociological examination of social problems enables us to move beyond myths and common-sense notions, to gain new insights into ourselves, and to develop an awareness of the connection between our own world and the worlds of other people. According to sociologist Peter Berger (1963:23), a sociological examination allows us to realize that "things are not what they seem." Indeed, most social problems are multifaceted. When we recognize this, we can approach pressing national and global concerns in new ways and make better decisions about those concerns. By taking a global perspective on social problems, we soon realize that the lives of all people are closely intertwined and that any one nation's problems are part of a larger global problem. Examining violence as a social problem, for example, makes it possible for us to look at the causes and consequences of this type of behavior on a global basis. It also makes it possible for us to look more closely at our own society to see how we respond to such problems through social policy. An example is the renewed call by many members of society for gun control in the aftermath of each new episode of gun-related violence and the contradictory assertion from organizations such as the National Rifle Association that gun-control laws are neither needed nor effective (see Box 1). As this example shows, what constitutes a social problem and what should be done about that problem is often a controversial topic.

DO WE HAVE A PROBLEM? SUBJECTIVE AWARENESS AND OBJECTIVE REALITY

A subjective awareness that a social problem exists usually emerges before the objective reality of the problem is acknowledged. Subjective awareness tends to be expressed as a feeling of uneasiness or skepticism about something, but the feeling is not founded on any concrete evidence that a problem actually exists. A subjective awareness that there is potential for violent acts in public settings such as schools, day-care centers, businesses, and churches exists even when there has been no recent violence in one of these settings. However, when new killings take place, our subjective awareness shifts to being an objective reality.

Consider, for example, the differences in subjective awareness and objective reality when it comes to violence in the media. Many people feel uncomfortable with the increasingly graphic nature of portrayals of violence on television and in films and video games.

Social Problems and Social Policy

Box 1

"Packing Heat": Should College Students Be Allowed to Carry Guns on Campus?

It's strictly a matter of self-defense. I don't ever want to see repeated on a Texas college campus what happened at Virginia Tech, where some deranged, suicidal madman goes into a building and is able to pick off totally defenseless kids like sitting ducks.

—Texas State Senator Jeff Wentworth comments on why he supported legislation in Texas to give college students and professors the right to carry guns on campus (Vertuno, 2011)

There is no scenario where allowing concealed weapons on college campuses will do anything other than create a more dangerous environment for students, faculty, staff and visitors.

—Glen Johnson, Oklahoma Chancellor of Higher Education, explains why he is opposed to concealed handguns on campus (Vertuno, 2011).

Although few states have actually enacted a law expressly allowing individuals to carry concealed weapons on public college campuses, the issue of whether students, faculty, and staff (in addition to public safety personnel) should be allowed to possess guns or other concealed weapons on campuses comes up quite often. Social policy questions regarding this issue typically are framed in terms of "concealed weapons," but the focus of these discussions is primarily on guns. As Katherine S. Newman and her associates found in a study of public school violence, gun availability is a key reason why many school shootings are so deadly: "Mass murders tend not to happen—in school or anywhere else—when knives are the only weapon available" (Newman, Fox, Harding, Mehta, and Roth, 2004:69). To curb the high number of deaths related to firearms in this nation, pro-gun-control advocates believe that we need social policies that regulate the gun industry and gun ownership. However, opponents of gun-control measures argue that regulation will not curb random violence perpetrated by a few disturbed or frustrated individuals.

What is social policy and how is it supposed to alleviate such problems as violence in society? Social scientists use the term *social policy* to refer to a written set of ideas and goals that are formally adopted by a relevant decision-making body, for example, a government bureaucracy, a state legislature, or the U.S. Congress. According to sociologist Joel Best (1999:143), we often think of social policy as a means of "declaring war" on a social problem. Social policy discussions on gun-related violence at the state and federal levels have focused on how to win the "war" on guns. However, as Best (1999:147) notes, "Warfare presumes that fighting

the enemy is a common cause for the entire society; individuals should set aside their doubts and reservations and join in the larger struggle. . . . Declaring war, then, is a call for a united, committed campaign against a social problem."

In the case of gun-related violence, however, there is a profound lack of societal consensus on the causes of the problem and what should be done about it. Some favor regulation of the gun industry and gun ownership; others believe that regulation will not curb random violence perpetrated by frustrated individuals. Underlying the arguments for and against gun control are these words from the Second Amendment to the U.S. Constitution: "A well regulated Militia, being necessary to the security of a free State, the right of the people to keep and bear Arms, shall not be infringed." Those in favor of legislation to regulate the gun industry and gun ownership argue that the Second Amendment does not guarantee an individual's right to own guns: The right to keep and bear Arms applies only to those citizens who do so as part of an official state militia. However, the U.S. Supreme Court ruled in 2008 that the Second Amendment protects an individual's right to own a gun for personal use. In other words, people have a constitutionally protected right to keep a loaded handgun at home for self-defense. This is in keeping with an argument long made by spokespersons for the National Rifle Association (NRA), a powerful group with about 4.3 million members nationwide, which has stated that gun control regulations

To curb the high number of deaths related to firearms in this nation, pro-gun-control advocates believe that we need social policies that regulate the gun industry and gun ownership. However, opponents of gun-control measures argue that regulation will not curb random violence perpetrated by a few disturbed or frustrated individuals.

Social Problems and Social Policy

Box 1 continued

violate the individual's constitutional right to own a gun and would not be an effective means of curbing random acts of violence on school campuses and elsewhere.

What solutions exist for the quandary over gun regulations? Declaring war on a social problem such as gun-related violence is difficult for several reasons. First, social problems are not simple issues: Most problems have multiple causes and a variety of possible solutions. Second, it is difficult to determine what constitutes victory in such a war. Third, it takes a long time to see the outcome of changes in social policies, and efforts to produce change may receive reduced funding or be eliminated before significant changes actually occur. Finally, it is impossible to rally everyone behind a single policy, and much time is therefore spent arguing over how to proceed, how much money to spend, and who or what is the real enemy. In the final analysis, the problem of gun violence is a chronic problem in the United States that has yet to be successfully addressed by social policy and its implementation.

In the meantime, we return to the question we initially raised about students possessing guns at college. Those persons who believe that students should be allowed to carry guns on campus for self-defense assert that no acts of violence have occurred at universities where students are legally allowed to carry concealed handguns. They also note that many states set the legal age limit at twenty-one for obtaining a concealed handgun license, which means that the students who obtain such a license typically are juniors or seniors, not beginning college students. By contrast, those individuals and organizations that strongly object to non–law enforcement personnel "packing heat" on college campuses argue that when guns are readily available, there is a greater likelihood of lethal outcomes because people have violent force right at their fingertips when they fear for their safety or become involved in an emotionally volatile situation.

What will be the future of guns on college campuses? If gun rights lobbyists have their way, more states will allow concealed guns on college campuses; if most people in the academic community and other concerned citizens are listened to when they declare their opposition to laws granting students the right to carry firearms at their college or university, we hopefully will not have the deadly mix of students, guns, and campus life in the name of "self-defense." How do you feel about this very polarizing social policy issue? Would you feel more—or less—safe if you knew that many people were carrying concealed weapons on your campus?

Initially, parents have a subjective awareness that these depictions might be harmful for their children and perhaps for the larger society. However, it is only when we have facts to support our beliefs that there is a link between media violence and actual behavior that we move beyond a subjective awareness of the issue. Indeed, numerous studies show that media violence, including excessive use of violent video games, influences how young people think and act. For example, children who frequently watch violence on television may become less sensitive to pain and suffering of others. They may become more fearful of the world around them, and ultimately, they may be more likely to behave in aggressive or harmful ways toward other people. As researchers gather additional data to support their arguments, the link between extensive media watching and the potential for violence grows stronger, moving into the realm of objective reality rather than being merely a subjective awareness of isolated individuals. Of course, most studies are not without their critics, and this is the case for studies on media and violence. Debates flourish in scholarly journals between some researchers who believe that the risks of media violence have been exaggerated (such as Ferguson and Kilbrun, 2010) and other scholars (such as Bushman, Rothstein, and Anderson, 2010) whose findings support the belief that violent media, including video games, increase aggressive thoughts, angry feelings, and aggressive behaviors and decrease empathic feelings and prosocial behaviors.

However, even the gathering of objective facts does not always result in consensus on social issues. Individuals and groups may question the validity of the facts, or they may dispute the facts by using other data that they hope demonstrate a different perspective. Examples of objective conditions that may or may not be considered by everyone to be social problems include environmental pollution and resource depletion, war, health care, and changes in moral values. Religious and political views influence how people define social problems and what they think the possible solutions might be. Often, one person's solution to a problem is viewed as a problem by another person. For example, some people see abortion as a solution to an unwanted pregnancy, whereas others believe that abortion is a serious social problem. Abortion and end-of-life decisions (such as assisted suicide and "right to die" cases) are only two of the many issues that are strongly influenced by religion and politics in the United States. To analyze the conditions that must be met before an objective reality becomes identified as a social problem, see Box 2.

Just like other people, sociologists usually have strong opinions about what is "good" and "bad" in society and what might be done to improve conditions. However, sociologists know their opinions are often subjective. Thus, they use theory and systematic research techniques and report their findings to other social scientists for consideration. In other words, sociologists strive to view social problems *objectively*. Of course, complete objectivity may not be an attainable—or desirable—goal in studying human behavior. Max Weber, an early German sociologist, acknowledged that complete objectivity might be impossible but pointed out that *verstehen* ("understanding" or "insight") was critical to any analysis of social problems. According to Weber, *verstehen* enables individuals to see the world as others see it and to empathize with them. *Verstehen*, in turn, enables us to use the sociological imagination and employ social theory rather than our own opinions to analyze social problems.

USING SOCIAL THEORY TO ANALYZE SOCIAL PROBLEMS

To determine how social life is organized, sociologists develop theories and conduct research. A *theory* is a **set of logically related statements that attempt to describe, explain, or predict social events**. Theories are useful for explaining relationships between social concepts or phenomena, such as age and unemployment. They also help us interpret social reality in a distinct way by giving us a framework for organizing our observations. Sociologists refer to this theoretical framework as a *perspective*—**an overall approach or viewpoint toward some subject**. Three major theoretical perspectives have emerged in sociology: the functionalist perspective, which views society as a basically stable and orderly entity; the conflict perspective, which views society as an arena of competition and conflict; and the interactionist perspective, which focuses on the everyday, routine interactions among individuals. The functionalist and conflict perspectives are based on macrolevel analysis because they focus on social processes occurring at the societal level. The interactionist

---

Critical Thinking and You Box 2

Determining What Constitutes a Social Problem

Which of the following is defined as a major social problem in the United States?

- Driving a motor vehicle, which results in approximately 32,708 U.S. deaths each year
- Playing contact sports in school, which results in many injuries and deaths among young people
- Hunting for wild game, which results in numerous injuries and deaths among hunters and bystanders

If you answered "None of the above," you are correct. Although driving a motor vehicle, playing contact sports, and hunting may have hazardous potential consequences, few people view these actions in and of themselves as being a social problem. In other words, not all behavior that may result in violence or even death is classified as a social problem.

What questions should we ask to determine if something is a social problem? Here are a few suggestions:

1. Is there a public outcry about this conduct or this condition? Are people actively discussing the issue and demanding that a resolution be found?

2. Does the conduct or condition reflect a gap between social ideals and social reality? What social ideals are involved? What is the social reality about the situation?

3. Are a large number of people involved in defining the problem and demanding that a solution be found? Does the matter have national attention? If not, is a special-interest group the primary source of demands that something be done about the condition?

4. Can a solution be found for the problem? If not, can we reduce the problem or alleviate the suffering of some victims of the problem?

Based on these questions, what pressing social issues are we overlooking in our nation or on a global basis that should be considered as social problems requiring immediate action? What issues receive too much attention from the media and the public? How do culture, religion, and politics influence our definition of what constitutes a social problem?

perspective is based on microlevel analysis because it focuses on small-group relations and social interaction.

The Functionalist Perspective

The functionalist perspective grew out of the works of early social thinkers such as Auguste Comte (1798–1857), the founder of sociology. Comte compared society to a living organism. Just as muscles, tissues, and organs of the human body perform specific functions that maintain the body as a whole, the various parts of society contribute to its maintenance and preservation. According to the *functionalist perspective*, **society is a stable, orderly system composed of a number of inter-related parts, each of which performs a function that contributes to the overall stability of society** (Parsons, 1951). These interrelated parts are social institutions (such as families, the economy, education, and the government) that a society develops to organize its main concerns and activities so that social needs are met. Each institution performs a unique function, contributing to the overall stability of society and the well-being of individuals (Merton, 1968). For example, the functions of the economy are producing and distributing goods (such as food, clothing, and shelter) and services (such as health care and dry cleaning), whereas the government is responsible for coordinating activities of other institutions, maintaining law and order, dealing with unmet social needs, and handling international relations and warfare.

Manifest and Latent Functions

Though the functions of the economy and the government seem fairly clear-cut, functionalists suggest that not all the functions of social institutions are intended and overtly recognized. In fact, according to the functionalist perspective, social institutions perform two different types of societal functions: manifest and latent. *Manifest functions* are intended and recognized consequences of an activity or social process. A manifest function of education, for example, is to provide students with knowledge, skills, and cultural values. In contrast, *latent functions* are the unintended consequences of an activity or social process that are hidden and remain unacknowledged by participants (Merton, 1968). The latent functions of education include the babysitter function of keeping young people off the street and out of the full-time job market and the matchmaking function whereby schools provide opportunities for students to meet and socialize with potential marriage partners. These functions are latent because schools were not created for babysitting or matchmaking, and most organizational participants do not acknowledge that these activities take place.

Dysfunctions and Social Disorganization

From the functionalist perspective, social problems arise when social institutions do not fulfill their functions or when dysfunctions occur. *Dysfunctions* are the undesirable consequences of an activity or social process that inhibit a society's ability to adapt or adjust (Merton, 1968). For example, a function of education is to prepare students for jobs, but if schools fail to do so, then students have problems finding jobs, employers have to spend millions of dollars on employee training programs, and consumers have to pay higher prices for goods and services to offset worker training costs.

Explore the Concept
Social Explorer Activity: The Dissipation of the Agricultural Industry on mysoclab.com

In other words, dysfunctions in education threaten other social institutions, especially families and the economy.

Dysfunctions can occur in society as a whole or in a part of society (a social institution). According to functionalists, dysfunctions in social institutions create social disorganization in the entire society. **Social disorganization refers to the conditions in society that undermine the ability of traditional social institutions to govern human behavior.** Early in the twentieth century, sociologists Robert E. Park (1864–1944) and Ernest W. Burgess (1886–1966) developed a social disorganization theory to explain why some areas of Chicago had higher rates of *social deviance*, which they defined as a pattern of rule violation, than other areas had. Social disorganization causes a breakdown in the traditional values and norms that serve as social control mechanisms, which, under normal circumstances, keep people from engaging in nonconforming behavior. **Values are collective ideas about what is right or wrong, good or bad, and desirable or undesirable in a specific society** (R. M. Williams, 1970). Although values provide ideas about behavior, they do not state explicitly how we should behave. Norms, on the other hand, have specific behavioral expectations. **Norms are established rules of behavior or standards of conduct**. French sociologist Emile Durkheim (1858–1917) suggested that social problems arise when people no longer agree on societal values and norms. According to Durkheim, periods of rapid social change produce *anomie*—a loss of shared values and sense of purpose in society. During these periods, social bonds grow weaker, social control is diminished, and people are more likely to engage in nonconforming patterns of behavior such as crime.

Early sociologists, examining the relationship between social problems and rapid industrialization and urbanization in Britain, western Europe, and the United States in the late nineteenth and early twentieth centuries, noted that rapid social change intensifies social disorganization. **Industrialization is the process by which societies are transformed from a dependence on agriculture and handmade products to an emphasis on manufacturing and related industries**. At the beginning of the Industrial Revolution, thousands of people migrated from rural communities to large urban centers to find employment in factories and offices. New social problems emerged as a result of industrialization and *urbanization,* **the process by which an increasing proportion of a population lives in cities rather than in rural areas**. During this period of rapid technological and social change, a sharp increase occurred in urban social problems such as poverty, crime, child labor, inadequate housing, unsanitary conditions, overcrowding, and environmental pollution.

Applying the Functionalist Perspective to Problems of Violence

Some functionalists believe that violence arises from a condition of anomie, in which many individuals have a feeling of helplessness, normlessness, or alienation. Others believe that violence increases when social institutions such as the family, schools, and religious organizations weaken and the main mechanisms of social control in people's everyday lives are external (i.e., law enforcement agencies and the criminal justice system).

One functionalist explanation of violence, known as the *subculture of violence hypothesis*, **states that violence is part of the normative expectations governing everyday behavior among young males in the lower classes**. Violence is considered a by-product of their culture, which idealizes toughness and even brutality in the name of masculinity. According to criminologists Marvin E. Wolfgang and Franco Ferracuti (1967), who originated this theory, violent subcultures (for example, violent juvenile gangs and organized crime groups) are most likely to develop when young people, particularly males, have few legitimate opportunities available in their segment of society and when subcultural values accept and encourage violent behavior. In this context, young people come to consider aggression or violence a natural response to certain situations. More recent studies have linked the subculture of violence hypothesis to neighborhood codes of violence that are disproportionately found in violent inner-city neighborhoods

with large minority populations (Matsueda, Drakulich, and Kubrin, 2006). For many years, however, this perspective has been criticized for exclusively focusing on violence among young males, often persons of color, in the lower classes because it does not provide any explanation regarding violence perpetrated by people in the middle or upper classes.

Still other functionalist explanations of violence focus on how changes in social institutions put some people at greater risk of being victims of violent crime than others. According to the *lifestyle-routine activity approach*, **the patterns and timing of people's daily movements and activities as they go about obtaining the necessities of life—such as food, shelter, companionship, and entertainment—are the keys to understanding violent personal crimes and other types of crime in our society**. Looking at violence crime, for example, social institutions and people's lifestyle may contribute to the rate of certain types of offenses. Even when rates of violent crime in the United States dropped to the lowest level in nearly 40 years in 2011, cities such as Flint, Michigan, and New York City saw the number of violent crimes increase for all four types of violent crime—murder, rape, robbery, and aggravated assault (Oppel, 2011). What factors might contribute to these increases? We can only speculate because many variables are involved. However, a few structural factors we might consider in Flint, Michigan, are the closing of automobile and parts manufacturing plants, creating high rates of structural unemployment, and the prevalence of drugs and gangs. By contrast, structural factors contributing to high rates of violent crime in New York City might include the following:

- Many people reside in close proximity to each other but remain virtual strangers who are less likely to notice if something unusual happens.
- Many people live alone (because of being single, widowed, or divorced) and do not have others who look out for them.
- Many people walk or take public transportation and thus have greater vulnerability to unscrupulous individuals.
- Many people have variable work and leisure schedules that place them on the streets at all hours of the day and night and make them more vulnerable to violent attack.

These are just a few of the many factors related to the social structure and fabric of urban life that may increase the odds of being murdered, raped, robbed, or assaulted in some cities. The lifestyle-routine activity approach suggests that people who willingly put themselves in situations that expose them to the potential for violent crime should modify their behavior or that society should provide greater protection for people whose lifestyle routine leaves them vulnerable to attackers. The lifestyle-routine activity approach is good as far as it goes, but it does not address other issues such the causes of violence in the home and other supposedly safe havens in society.

How would a functionalist approach the problem of violence? Most functionalists emphasize shared moral values and social bonds. They believe that when rapid social change or other disruptions occur, moral values may erode and problems such as school violence or hate crimes are likely to occur. Functionalists believe that to reduce violence, families, schools, religious organizations, and other social institutions should be strengthened so that they can regenerate shared values and morality. Most functionalists also believe that those who engage in violent criminal behavior should be prosecuted to the full extent of the law.

The functional approach to social problems has been criticized for its acceptance of the status quo and for its lack of appreciation of how problems in society are associated with vast economic and social inequality, racism, sexism, ageism, and other forms of discrimination that keep our society from being an equal playing field for everyone.

The Conflict Perspective

The *conflict perspective* **is based on the assumption that groups in society are engaged in a continuous power struggle for control of scarce resources**. Unlike functionalist theorists, who emphasize the degree to which society is held together by a consensus on values, conflict theorists emphasize the degree to which society is characterized by conflict and discrimination. According to some conflict theorists, certain groups of people are privileged while others are disadvantaged through the unjust use of political, economic, or social power. Not all conflict theorists hold the same views about what constitutes the most important form of conflict. We will examine two principal perspectives: the value conflict perspective and the critical-conflict perspective.

The Value Conflict Perspective

According to value conflict theorists, social problems are conditions that are incompatible with group values. From this perspective, value clashes are ordinary occurrences in families, communities, and the larger society, in which individuals commonly hold many divergent values. Although individuals may share certain core values, they do not share all values or a common culture. As previously stated, culture refers to the knowledge, language, values, customs, and material objects that are passed from person to person and from one generation to the next in a human group or society.

Discrepancies between ideal and real culture are a source of social problems in all societies. *Ideal culture* refers to the values and beliefs that people claim they hold; *real culture* refers to the values and beliefs that they actually follow. In the United States, for example, members of the National Association for the Advancement of Colored People (NAACP), La Raza, the Ku Klux Klan, and the White Aryan Resistance all claim to adhere to ideal cultural values of equality, freedom, and liberty; however, these ideal cultural values come into direct conflict with real cultural values when issues of racial-ethnic relations arise. Peaceful celebrations held by members of the NAACP to celebrate the birthday of slain African American civil rights leader Martin Luther King, Jr., and KKK rallies in states such as Kentucky and Virginia to reclaim "White Power" are concrete examples of the clash between ideal and real cultural values. Groups may claim that they advocate for peace, justice, and fairness but their real culture, the values and beliefs they actually follow, are quite different (for an example, visit this website: http://kkkknights.com).

Critical-Conflict Perspective

Unlike the value conflict approach, critical-conflict theorists suggest that social problems arise out of the major contradictions inherent in the way societies are organized. Some critical-conflict perspectives focus on class inequalities in the capitalist economic system; others focus on inequalities based on race, ethnicity, or gender.

Most class perspectives on inequality have been strongly influenced by Karl Marx (1818–1883), a German economist and activist, who recognized that the emergence of capitalism had produced dramatic and irreversible changes in social life. *Capitalism* **is an economic system characterized by private ownership of the means of production, from which personal profits can be derived through market competition and without government intervention**. In contemporary capitalist economies, businesses are privately owned and operated for the profit of owners and corporate shareholders. According to Marx, members of the *capitalist class* (*the bourgeoisie*), who own and control the means of production (e.g., the land, tools, factories, and money for investment), are at the top of a system of social stratification that affords them different lifestyles and life chances from those of the members of the *working class* (the *proletariat*), who must sell their labor power (their potential ability to work) to capitalists. In selling their labor power, members of the working class forfeit control over their work, and the capitalists derive excessive profit from the workers' labor.

Marx believed that capitalism led workers to experience increased levels of impoverishment and alienation—a feeling of powerlessness and estrangement from other people and from oneself (Marx and Engels, 1847/1971:96). He predicted that the working class would eventually overthrow the capitalist economic system. Although Marx's prediction has not come about, Erik Olin Wright (1997) and other social scientists have modified and adapted his perspective to apply to contemporary capitalist nations. In today's capitalist nations, according to Wright, ownership of the means of production is only one way in which people gain the ability to exploit others. Two other ways in which individuals gain control are through control of property and control over other people's labor. In this view, upper-level managers and others in positions of authority gain control over societal resources and other individuals' time, knowledge, and skills in such a manner that members of the upper classes are able to maintain their dominance (Wright, 1997; Wright and Rogers, 2010).

Some critical-conflict perspectives focus on racial and gender subordination instead of class-based inequalities. Critical-conflict theorists who emphasize discrimination and inequality based on race or ethnicity note that many social problems are rooted in the continuing exploitation and subordination of people of color by white people. For example, Native Americans have the highest rates of poverty in the United States because of extended periods of racial subordination and exploitation throughout this country's history.

Critical-conflict theorists who use a feminist approach focus on *patriarchy*, a system of male dominance in which males are privileged and women are oppressed. According to a feminist approach, male domination in

Unions and other workers' organizations empower workers to voice their concerns in the capitalist system. Since the economic downturn that began in 2008, members of unions such as the United Auto Workers have joined in protests against what they see as destructive banking practices, excessive profits, and corporate tax breaks that destroy communities and hurt working families.

society contributes not only to domestic violence, child abuse, and rape but also to poverty and crimes such as prostitution. Feminist scholars state that gender inequality will not be eliminated in the home, school, and workplace until patriarchy is abolished and women and men are treated equally.

Finally, some critical-conflict theorists note that race, class, and gender are interlocking systems of privilege and oppression that result in social problems. For

Critical-conflict theorists observe that African American women are disproportionately affected by flooding, property damage, and housing displacement from hurricanes and other natural disasters.

example, black feminist scholar Patricia Hill Collins (1991, 2005) has pointed out that race, class, and gender are simultaneous forces of oppression for women of color, especially African American women. Critical-conflict analysts focusing on these intersections believe that equality can come about only when women across lines of race and class receive equal treatment (Andersen and Collins, 2009; Collins, 2005). Throughout this text, we will use critical-conflict theory (rather than the value conflict approach) to highlight the power relations that result in social problems.

Applying the Conflict Perspective to Problems of Violence

Conflict theorists who focus on class-based inequalities believe that the potential for violence is inherent in capitalist societies. In fact, say these theorists, the wealthy engage in one form of violence, and the poor engage in another. They note that the wealthy often use third parties to protect themselves and their families from bodily harm as well as to secure their property and investments in this country and elsewhere in the world. For example, the wealthy who live in the United States or other high-income nations and own factories (or own stock in factories) in middle- and low-income nations use the governments and police of those nations—third parties—to control workers who threaten to strike. The wealthy also influence U.S. government policy. For instance, they are likely to support U.S. military intervention—and thus violence—in nations where they have large investments at stake. However, sometimes the wealthy want the U.S. government to look the other way and not intervene in these nations in order to protect investments in countries in which dictators have made their investments profitable.

In contrast, these theorists say, when the poor engage in violence, the violence is typically committed by the individual and is a reaction to the unjust social and economic conditions he or she experiences daily on the bottom rung of a capitalist society. The economic exploitation of the poor, these theorists note, dramatically affects all aspects of the individual's life, including how the person reacts to daily injustices, stress, and other threatening situations. In violent street crimes, the vast majority of offenders—as well as victims—are poor, unemployed, or working in low-level, low-paying jobs. In fact, most violent street crime is an intraclass phenomenon: Poor and working-class people typically victimize others who are like themselves.

The conflict perspective argues that the criminal justice system is biased in favor of the middle and upper classes. Because it is, its definition of violence depends on where a person's race, class, and gender locate him or her in the system of stratification. In this way, violent crimes are but one part of a larger system of inequality and oppression. Sexism and racism are reinforced by the overarching class structure that benefits the powerful at the expense of the powerless. Exploitation of people of color and the poor creates a sense of hopelessness, frustration, and hostility in them that may boil over into violent acts such as rape or murder. At the same time, it is important to note that violent acts, including murder, occur across all class and racial-ethnic categories in the United States.

The conflict perspective that focuses on feminist issues specifically examines violence against women, for example, rape and most spousal abuse. One feminist perspective suggests that violence against women is a means of reinforcing patriarchy. According to the feminist perspective, in a patriarchal system, the sexual marketplace is characterized by unequal bargaining power, making transactions between men and women potentially coercive in nature. Gender stratification is reinforced by powerful physical, psychological, and social mechanisms of control, including force or the threat of force. Fear of violence forces women to change their ways of living, acting, and dressing and thus deprives them of many basic freedoms (Hunnicutt, 2009). The conflict perspective that focuses on racial-ethnic inequalities points out that racism is an important factor in explaining such violent acts as hate crimes. For example, contemporary brutality against African Americans, particularly men, may be traced to earlier periods when hanging or dragging was used to punish slave insurrections and to keep African Americans subservient during the Reconstruction and the subsequent years of legal racial segregation in the South.

No matter what approach conflict theorists take, they all agree on one thing: Violence is unlikely to diminish significantly unless inequalities based on class, gender, and race are reduced at the macrolevel in society. However, social problems must also be examined at the microlevel, where individuals actually live their daily lives.

The Symbolic Interactionist Perspective

Unlike the conflict perspective, which focuses on macrolevel inequalities in society, the symbolic interactionist perspective focuses on a microlevel analysis of how people act toward one another and how they make sense of their daily lives. The *symbolic interactionist perspective*

views society as the sum of the interactions of individuals and groups. Most symbolic interactionists study social problems by analyzing how certain behavior comes to be defined as a social problem and how individuals and groups come to engage in activities that a significant number of people and/or a number of significant people view as a major social concern.

What is the relationship between individuals and the society in which they live? One early sociologist attempted to answer this question. German sociologist Georg Simmel (1858–1918), a founder of the interactionist approach, investigated the impact of industrialization and urbanization on people's values and behavior within small social units. Simmel (1902/1950) noted that rapid changes in technology and dramatic urban growth produced new social problems by breaking up the "geometry of social life," which he described as the web of patterned social interactions among the people who constitute a society. According to Simmel, alienation is brought about by a decline in personal and emotional contacts. How people interpret the subjective messages that they receive from others and the situations that they encounter in their daily life greatly influences their behavior and their perceptions of what constitutes a social problem.

Labeling Theory and the Social Construction of Reality

While Simmel focused on how people interpret their own situations, other symbolic interactionists have examined how people impose their shared meanings on others. According to sociologist Howard Becker (1963), *moral entrepreneurs* are people who use their own views of right and wrong to establish rules and label others as deviant (nonconforming). Labeling theory, as this perspective is called, suggests that behavior that deviates from established norms is deviant because it has been labeled as such by others. According to this theory, deviants (nonconformists) are people who have been successfully labeled as such by others. Labeling theory raises questions about why certain individuals and certain types of behavior are labeled as deviant but others are not.

According to some symbolic interaction theorists, many social problems can be linked to the *social construction of reality*—the process by which people's perception of reality is shaped largely by the subjective meaning that they give to an experience (Berger and Luckmann, 1967). From this perspective, little shared reality exists beyond that which people socially create. It is, however, this social construction of reality that influences people's beliefs and actions.

Other symbolic interactionists suggest that how we initially define a situation affects our future actions. According to sociologist W. I. Thomas (1863–1947), when people define situations as real, the situations become real in their consequences. Elaborating on Thomas's idea, sociologist Robert Merton (1968) has suggested that when people perceive a situation in a certain way and act according to their perceptions, the end result may be a *self-fulfilling prophecy*—**the process by which an unsubstantiated belief or prediction results in behavior that makes the original false conception come true**. For example, a teenager who is labeled a "juvenile delinquent" may accept the label and adopt the full-blown image of a juvenile delinquent as portrayed in television programs and films: wearing gang colors, dropping out of school, and participating in gang violence or other behavior that is labeled as deviant. If the teenager subsequently is arrested, the initial label becomes a self-fulfilling prophecy.

Applying Symbolic Interactionist Perspectives to Problems of Violence

Symbolic interactionist explanations of violence begin by noting that human behavior is learned through social interaction. Violence, they state, is a learned response, not an inherent characteristic, in the individual. Some of the most interesting support for this point of view comes from studies done by social psychologist Albert Bandura, who studied aggression in children (1973). Showing children a film of a person beating, kicking, and hacking an inflatable doll produced a violent response in the children, who, when they were placed in a room with a similar doll, duplicated the person's behavior and engaged

Read the Document

Is Violence Against Women About Women or About Violence? on mysoclab.com

in additional aggressive behavior. Others have noted that people tend to repeat their behavior if they feel rewarded for it. Thus, when people learn that they can get their way by inflicting violence or the threat of violence on others, their aggressive behavior is reinforced.

Symbolic interactionists also look at the types of social interactions that commonly lead to violence. According to the *situational approach*, **violence results from a specific interaction process, termed a "situational transaction."** Criminologist David Luckenbill (1977) identified six stages in the situational transaction between victim and offender. In the first stage, the future victim does something behavioral or verbal that is considered an affront by the other (e.g., a glare or an insult).

"If It Bleeds, It Leads"? News Reporting on Violence

At least 125 people killed and over 1,000 injured in deadly tornado in Joplin, Missouri.

Local man shoots his wife and two children, and then turns the gun on himself.

Animal control officers confiscate 23 neglected dogs and cats at a local residence.

Will it rain anytime soon? Stay tuned and we'll tell you all about it.

Anyone who has watched the evening news on local television has heard "teasers" such as these. On both local and national news, the lead story is often about war- or terror-related violence, followed by violence in the United States or the local community. Then a human interest story follows to grab viewers' attention and give them a feeling of revulsion about the brutal mistreatment of children or animals. Frequent viewers are aware that stations use routine formulas for putting together the nightly news;

however, many are less aware of how stories are written and presented. For this reason, sociologists with an interest in the media study how journalists, producers, and others frame news stories about events and social problems. Members of the media have the power to determine what makes the news, including which stories get covered, what news items get the most attention, how journalists organize and present their stories, and what effects a particular story might have on viewers. To study social problems effectively we must be aware of how both politics and media processes shape popular understanding and policy responses to pressing social issues such as violence.

In an analysis of media processes, we use the term *media framing* to describe the process by which information and entertainment is packaged by the media (newspapers, magazines, radio and television networks and stations, and the Internet) before being presented to an audience. How

In the second, the offended individual verifies that the action was directed at him or her personally. In the third, the offended individual decides how to respond to the affront and might issue a verbal or behavioral challenge (e.g., a threat or a raised fist). If the problem escalates at this point, injury or death might occur in this stage; if not, the participants enter into the fourth stage. In this stage, the future victim further escalates the transaction, often prodded on by onlookers siding with one party or the other. In the fifth stage, actual violence occurs when neither party is able to back down without losing face. At this point, one or both parties produce weapons, which may range from guns and knives to bottles, pool cues, or other bludgeoning devices, if they have not already appeared, and the offender kills the victim. The sixth and final stage involves the offender's actions after the crime; some flee the scene, others are detained by onlookers, and still others call the police themselves.

The situational approach is based, first, on the assumption that many victims are active participants in the violence perpetrated against them and, second, on the idea that confrontation does not inevitably lead to violence or death. In the first four stages of the transaction, either the victim or the offender can decide to pursue another course of action.

According to symbolic interactionists, reducing violence requires changing those societal values that encourage excessive competition and violence. At the

macrolevel, how the media report on violence may influence our thinking about the appropriateness of certain kinds of aggressive behavior (see Box 3). However, change must occur at the microlevel, which means that agents of socialization must transmit different attitudes and values toward violence. The next generation must learn that it is an individual's right—regardless of gender, race, class, religion, or other attributes or characteristics—to live free from violence and the devastating impact it has on individuals, groups, and the social fabric of society.

> **DID YOU KNOW**
>
> Statistics show that the following crimes are committed with a firearm:
> - 68 percent of all murders
> - 42 percent of all robberies
> - 22 percent of all aggravated assaults

USING SOCIAL RESEARCH METHODS TO STUDY SOCIAL PROBLEMS

Sociologists use a variety of research methods to study social problems such as violence. Research methods are strategies or techniques for systematically collecting

Social Problems in the Media

Box 3 continued

the media frame stories about social problems influences how we ourselves view the causes, effects, and possible solutions to the problem (Kendall 2011).

In the process of framing a news story, journalists engage in frame amplification, meaning that they highlight some issues, events, or beliefs while downplaying or neglecting other seemingly less important concerns. When news frames highlight some key details or privilege certain stories over others, we say that the highlighted factors are elevated in salience—they are made more noticeable, meaningful, or memorable to audiences. One way in which the reporting of violence is given salience, for example, is the extent to which a few stories garner most of the media coverage, and, in the most widely publicized cases, gain twenty-four-hour coverage of the "latest breaking news." Sensational murder trials are covered around the clock, even when journalists have nothing new to report.

Another way in which the reporting of violence is given salience is through episodic news framing, which focuses on the role of the individual while discounting societal factors. Episodic framing tells a news story in terms of personal experience, focusing on the part that individuals play in a situation. As one report concluded, "Generally speaking, newspaper and television journalists report a small percentage of individual violent incidents at great length and with great precision" (J. E. Stevens, 2001:7); however, this approach typically neglects the bigger picture of factors that may increase the risk of violence. These factors include "the ready availability of firearms and alcohol, racial discrimination, unemployment, violence in the media, lack of education, abuse as a child, witnessing violence in the home or neighborhood, isolation of the nuclear family, and belief in male dominance over females" (J. E. Stevens, 2001:8). Episodic framing highlights the importance of individual responsibility for acts of violence and reinforces the dominant ideology that individuals must be held accountable for their actions. This type of framing suggests to media audiences that public officials, business leaders, and other influential

people are not accountable for any part that they may have played in creating a situation that produced the violence. For example, lobbyists who pressure legislators to pass lenient gun-control legislation (or none at all) are seldom held accountable for gun-related deaths, nor are the legislators and politicians who control the political process.

Standing in sharp contrast to episodic framing is thematic framing, which provides a more impersonal view of what the nature of the social problem is. Journalists using thematic framing often tell the story through the use of statistics and discussions of trends ("Is the problem growing worse?" "Should we fear for our safety?"). Thematic framing emphasizes "facts" based on statistical data, such as the number of people killed in drive-by shootings or school violence in recent years. Thematic framing does not focus on the human tragedy of social problems such as violence or poverty, and when bombarded by continuous coverage of this sort, television viewers may conclude that little can be done about the problem. Rather than hearing from the victims of gun violence or poverty, for example, media reports typically emphasize "expert opinion" from "talking heads" who provide information that often supports the reporter's own point of view.

Questions for Consideration

1. Do you think guns should be allowed on college campuses? Why or why not?
2. Would you feel more or less safe if you knew that students and professors might be carrying a weapon?

Independent Research

What effect do blogs and comments on social networking sites such as Facebook and Twitter have on how we think about social problems? Visit your favorite sites to compare how people frame issues on social media as opposed to mainstream media outlets such as television, radio, the Internet, and newspapers.

---

data. Some methods produce *quantitative data* that can be measured numerically and lend themselves to statistical analysis. For example, the Uniform Crime Reports (UCRs), published annually by the Federal Bureau of Investigation (FBI), provide crime statistics that sociologists and others can use to learn more

👁 Watch on mysoclab.com
Qualitative vs. Quantitative Research on mysoclab.com

about the nature and extent of violent crime in the United States. Other research methods

produce *qualitative data* that are reported in the form of interpretive descriptions (words) rather than numbers. For example, *qualitative data* on violence in the United States might provide new insights on how the victims or their families and friends cope in the aftermath of a violent attack such as school shootings or terrorist bombings.

Sociologists use three major types of research methods: field research, survey research, and secondary analysis of existing data. Although our discussion focuses on each separately, many researchers use a combination of methods to enhance their understanding of social issues.

Field Research

Field research **is the study of social life in its natural setting: observing and interviewing people where they live, work, and play.** When sociologists want firsthand information about a social problem, they often use participant observation—field research in which researchers collect systematic observations while participating in the activities of the group they are studying. Field research on social problems can take place in many settings, ranging from schools and neighborhoods to universities, prisons, and large corporations.

Field research is valuable because some kinds of behavior and social problems can be studied best by being there; a more complete understanding can be developed through observations, face-to-face discussions, and participation in events than through other research methods. For example, field research over the past 40 years on the effects of violence in the media on children have indicated that some children behave more aggressively after viewing violence. Children were shown episodes of either *Batman* and *Spiderman* or *Mister Rogers' Neighborhood* (a children's show featuring "Mr. Rogers" who encouraged children to be kind and share with others) for several weeks, after which they were observed for an additional two weeks to see how they behaved. Children who saw the violent cartoons were more likely to interact aggressively with other children than those who watched *Mr. Rogers' Neighborhood* and became more willing to share their toys and cooperate with others. Other studies exposed children to shows such as *Mighty Morphin Power Rangers* and the results were similar: Children who saw episodes containing violence were more prone to aggressive behavior, such as hitting, kicking, shoving, and insulting others, than were children who did not see the episode (Kaiser Family Foundation, 2003).

Sociologists who use field research must have good interpersonal skills. They must be able to gain and keep the trust of the people they want to observe or interview. They also must be skilled interviewers who can keep systematic notes on their observations and conversations. Above all, they must treat research subjects fairly and ethically. The Code of Ethics of the American

Using field research, sociologists have studied gang violence and found that gang members are not all alike. Some do not approve of violence; others engage in violence only to assert authority; still others may engage in violence only when they feel threatened or want to maintain their territory.

Sociological Association provides professional standards for sociologists to follow when conducting social science research.

Survey Research

Survey research is probably the research method that is most frequently used by social scientists. *Survey research* **is a poll in which researchers ask respondents a series of questions about a specific topic and record their responses.** Survey research is based on the use of a sample of people who are thought to represent the attributes of the larger population from which they are selected. Survey data are collected by using self-administered questionnaires or by interviewers who ask questions of people in person or by mail, telephone, or the Internet.

The U.S. Bureau of Justice Statistics, for example, conducts survey research every year with its national crime victimization survey (NCVS), which fills in some of the gaps in the UCR data. The NCVS interviews 100,000 randomly selected households to identify crime victims, whether the crime has been reported or not. These surveys indicate that the number of crimes committed is substantially higher than the number reported in the UCR.

Survey research allows sociologists to study a large population without having to interview everyone in that population. It also yields numerical data that may be compared between groups and over periods of time. However, this type of research does have certain limitations. The use of standardized questions limits the types of information researchers can obtain from respondents. Also, because data can be reported numerically, survey research may be misused to overestimate or underestimate the extent of a specific problem such as violence.

Secondary Analysis of Existing Data

Whereas the NCVS is primary data—data that researchers collected specifically for that study—sociologists often rely on *secondary analysis of existing data*—**a research method in which investigators analyze data that originally were collected by others for some other purpose**. This method is also known as *unobtrusive research* because data can be gathered without the researcher's having to interview or observe research subjects. Data used for secondary analysis include public records such as birth and death records, official reports of organizations or governmental agencies such as the U.S. Census Bureau, and information from large databases such as the general social surveys, which are administered by the National Opinion Research Center.

Secondary analysis often involves *content analysis*, a systematic examination of cultural artifacts or written documents to extract thematic data and draw conclusions about some aspect of social life. Although it is a number of years old, the National Television Violence Study is the most definitive study of violence on television. During a nine-month period each year from October 1994 to June 1997, researchers at several universities selected a variety of programs, including drama, comedy, movies, music videos, reality programs, and children's shows on twenty-three television channels, thus creating a composite of the content in a week of television viewing. The viewing hours were from 6:00 A.M. until 11:00 P.M. for a total of seventeen hours a day across the seven days of the week (National Television Violence Study, 1998). Although the study's findings are too numerous to list all of them, here are a few (NTVS, 1998:26–31):

- Much of television violence is glamorized, sanitized, and trivialized. Characters seldom show remorse for their actions, and there is no criticism or penalty for the violence at the time that it occurs.
- Across the three years of the study, violence was found in 60 percent of the television programs taped—only a few of which carried antiviolence themes—and the networks and basic cable stations increased the proportion of programs containing violence during prime

time (the three-hour period each night that draws the most viewers).
- "High-risk" depictions (those that may encourage aggressive attitudes and behaviors) often involve (1) "a perpetrator who is an attractive role model," (2) "violence that seems justified," (3) "violence that goes unpunished," (4) "minimal consequences to the victim," and (5) "violence that seems realistic to the viewer."
- The typical preschool child who watches cartoons regularly will come into contact with more than 500 high-risk portrayals of violence each year. For preschoolers who watch television for two to three hours a day, there will be, on average, about one high-risk portrayal of violence per hour in cartoons.

Clearly, researchers can learn much from content analysis that they could not learn through other research methods because it allows them to look in more depth at a specific topic of concern and to systematically analyze what they find.

A strength of secondary analysis is its unobtrusive nature and the fact that it can be used when subjects refuse to be interviewed or the researcher does not have the opportunity to observe research subjects firsthand. However, secondary analysis also has inherent problems. Because the data originally were gathered for some other purpose, they might not fit the exact needs of the researcher, and they might be incomplete or inaccurate.

IS THERE A SOLUTION TO A PROBLEM SUCH AS GUN VIOLENCE?

Sociologists view social problems from a variety of perspectives. As shown in Table 2, each sociological perspective is rooted in different assumptions, identifies differing causes of a problem, and suggests a variety of possible solutions for reducing or eliminating a social problem such as gun violence.

Functionalists, who emphasize social cohesion and order in society, commonly view social problems as the result of institutional and societal dysfunctions, social disorganization, or cultural lag, among other things. Conflict theorists, who focus on value conflict or on structural inequalities based on class, race, gender, or other socially constructed attributes, suggest that social problems arise either from disputes over divergent values or from exploitative relations in society, such as those between capitalists and workers or between women and men. In contrast, symbolic interactionists focus on

		TABLE 2 Sociological Perspectives on Social Problems	
Perspective	**Analysis Level**	**Nature of Society and Origins of Social Problems**	**Causes and Solutions to Violence**
Functionalism	Macrolevel	Society is composed of interrelated parts that work together to maintain stability within society. Social problems result from dysfunctional acts and institutions.	The weakening of social institutions such as schools, families, and religion has produced an increase in violent behavior. Social institutions must be strengthened, and individuals should be taught to conform to society's rules, which must be reinforced by the criminal justice system.
Conflict theory	Macrolevel	Society is characterized by conflict and inequality. Value conflict theory attributes social problems to lack of agreement on values. Critical-conflict theory focuses on oppression due to class, race, gender, and other social divisions.	Factors such as sharp divisions on values, increasing social inequality, and unresolved discrimination contribute to violence in capitalist societies. To significantly reduce violence, fundamental changes are needed in political and economic institutions to bring about greater equality.
Symbolic interactionism	Microlevel	Society is the sum of the interactions of people and groups. Social problems are based on the behavior people learn from others; how people define a social problem is based on subjective factors.	Violence is learned behavior, and children must be taught attitudes and values that discourage such behavior. At the societal level, we must change those societal values that encourage excessive competition and violence.

individuals' interactions and on the social construction of reality. For symbolic interactionists, social problems occur when social interaction is disrupted and people are dehumanized, when people are labeled deviant, or when the individual's definition of a situation causes him or her to act in a way that produces a detrimental outcome.

No matter what perspectives sociologists employ, they use research to support their ideas. All research methods have certain strengths and weaknesses, but taken together, they provide us with valuable insights that go beyond commonsense knowledge about social problems and stereotypes of people. Using multiple methods and approaches, sociologists can broaden their knowledge of social problems such as violence in the United States and other nations.

In this chapter, we have looked at violence from these sociological perspectives. Like many other social problems, people do not always agree on the extent to which gun violence really is a major social problem in the United States or if the media tend to overblow each isolated incident because it can easily be sensationalized by tying it to other, previous occurrences. For example,

how was the shooting at Virginia Tech similar to, or different from, the one that occurred at Northern Illinois University? Just as people do not share a consensus on what constitutes a social problem, they often do not agree on how to reduce or solve problems such as gun violence.

Functionalist/Conservative Solutions

Those who adhere to a functionalist approach argue that violence can be reduced by strengthening major social institutions (such as the family, education, and religion) so that agents (such as parents, teachers, and spiritual leaders) can be effective in instructing children and young adults and thereby repressing negative attitudes and antisocial behaviors that might otherwise result in violent behavior, such as school and mall shootings.

Some people who embrace a functionalist theoretical perspective on violence also view themselves as being aligned with conservative political sectors that are comprised of individuals who believe that people should be free of government intervention and control when it comes to their "fundamental" rights, including the right to bear arms. From this side of the political arena, social policy solutions to reducing violence, such as passing and enforcing more stringent gun-control measures, are unacceptable means of trying to reduce the number of acts of violence that take place each year. Some political conservatives argue that gun control constitutes an aggressive disarmament strategy that violates the individual's constitutional rights while undermining the nation's overall well-being as a democratic and "free" society.

To reduce violence in the United States, the functionalist approach would suggest that it is important to maintain and preserve traditional moral and social values. Functionalists and political conservatives also believe that we should reinforce the importance of conformity to society's rules and laws through effective use of the criminal justice system, including the passage of tougher laws, more aggressive policing, and the imposition of more severe penalties in the courtroom. Conservative political viewpoints tend to reaffirm this approach by suggesting that positive social behavior, as well as violent behavior, is passed down from generation to generation through families. As a result, positive behavior must be reinforced through positive family life. Child abuse, domestic violence, and other antisocial behavioral problems within the family must not be tolerated because these contribute to larger societal problems of violence and crime.

Conflict/Liberal Solutions

Unlike functionalist sociological perspectives and conservative political approaches to solving the problem of violence, conflict theorists and liberal political analysts generally view increasing social inequality and unresolved discrimination as major factors that contribute to violence in societies. Some conflict theorists highlight the ways in which social problems are linked to the lack of agreement on values in our society. Critical-conflict theorists emphasize that oppression—based on class, race, gender, and other social divisions—is a major factor that contributes to social problems such as gun violence. In the political arena, liberal analysts similarly emphasize how a lack of economic opportunities encourages violence in a society. Based on these viewpoints, if we are to significantly reduce violence in our society, we must push for major changes in our nation's political and economic institutions.

From this approach, one factor contributing to gun violence is poverty and growing inequality. Research has shown, for example, that the risk of sustaining a firearm injury is greatest for young males who have already been involved in the criminal justice system and who have few opportunities for legitimate jobs. Although functionalist theorists might view this situation as being one in which behavioral interventions should occur that target these high-risk people and those individuals who supply them with guns and other contraband items, conflict analysts argue that the problem can be solved only if underlying problems such as poverty, racism, and chronic unemployment are systematically addressed rather than focusing on the people who commit gun-related violence or on suppressing the availability of firearms throughout the nation. From this approach, ways to eventually reduce gun-related violence might include passing legislation that requires that workers be paid a wage high enough that they can adequately support their families; improving public schools so that young people will receive a better education and be able to find decent jobs; and having community, state, and national economic development programs that create good jobs and benefit all people, not just a small percentage of the world's wealthiest people. This approach is most useful in explaining violence in low-income urban areas and other communities where few legitimate opportunities exist for individuals and most economic opportunities are of an illegal nature. It does not explain, however, why recent gun violence has been perpetrated by middle- and upper-middle-class high school students living in the suburbs and by college students with good academic records who appear to have a bright future in front of them.

Symbolic Interactionist Solutions

Finally, symbolic interactionist perspectives focus on how violence is learned behavior that comes from people's interactions in their daily lives. As a result, if we are to prevent violence, we must teach children the attitudes and values that discourage such behavior. If children are exposed to aggressive behavior or violence in their own homes, they may come to view such behavior as the norm rather than the exception to the norm. Some analysts believe that those children who spend large amounts of unsupervised time watching violence in films and on television or playing violent video games will demonstrate more violent behavior themselves. However, other analysts disagree with this assessment, claiming that violence in the media and gaming worlds provides people with an opportunity to vicariously vent their frustrations and feelings without ever actually engaging in violence themselves. Since peer groups are an important source of social learning for children and young people, some symbolic interactionists might suggest that parents, teachers, and other adult caregivers must become aware of the friends and acquaintances of the children for whom they are responsible.

Based on symbolic interactionist perspectives, one way to reduce violence is to teach people of all ages to engage in nonviolent conflict resolution where they learn how to deal with frustrating situations, such as when tensions are running high among individuals or social relationships are breaking down. The focus on competition in nations such as ours encourages people to think of everyone else as their competitors and that, in all situations, what one individual gains is another person's loss. Beliefs such as this tend to foster conflict rather than cooperation, and individuals who think that they have been marginalized (and thus taken out of the competition for friends, material possessions, or other valued goods, services, or relationships) may act out toward their perceived enemies in an aggressive or violent manner. If people learn socially acceptable ways of responding to conflict and intense competition, they may be less likely to engage in violent behavior. However, according to symbolic interactionists and other theorists who use a microlevel approach, we must first recognize as a community or nation that violence is a problem that must be solved, and then we must work collectively to reduce the problem. Although the symbolic interactionist approach is a microlevel perspective, some advocates suggest that changes must also be made at the societal level if we hope to change those societal values that encourage excessive competition and may contribute to negative behavior including gun violence.

Critique of Our Efforts to Find Solutions

How successful are our attempts to solve the problem of gun violence? The answer to this question is mixed. The United States has been somewhat successful in reducing certain types of violence, at least for several years running; however, most of our efforts have focused on particular types of violence or particular populations or categories of people, rather than on bringing about systemic change throughout the nation. Unless our nation and its political leaders face up to the fact that violence in this country is a major social problem that may lie dormant for a period of time but then rise up to leave us frightened and astonished, we are unlikely as a nation to seriously deal with the underlying causes and consequences of such violent actions, which is a necessary prerequisite for reaching the point where we might successfully reduce the problem.

When we think about the problem of gun violence or other pressing social issues, we must acknowledge that these problems have existed for many years. We have a long way to go in identifying real solutions to many of these problems, and that is why it is important that you are enrolled in this course and pursuing new ideas for the future. Please join me now as we explore a number of crucial problems we face in the second decade of the twenty-first century.

SUMMARY

✓—[Study and Review on mysoclab.com

- **How do sociologists define a social problem?**
  According to sociologists, a social problem is a social condition (such as poverty) or a pattern of behavior (such as substance abuse) that people believe warrants public concern and collective action to bring about change.

- **How do sociologists view violence?**
  Sociologists view violence as a social problem that involves both a subjective awareness and objective reality. We have a subjective awareness that violence can occur in such public settings as schools, day-care centers, businesses, and churches. Our subjective awareness becomes an objective reality when we can measure and experience the effects of violent criminal behavior.

- **How do sociologists examine social life?**
  Sociologists use both microlevel and macrolevel analyses to examine social life. Microlevel analysis focuses on small-group relations and social interaction among individuals; macrolevel analysis focuses on social processes occurring at the societal level, especially in large-scale organizations and major social institutions.

- **How does the functionalist perspective view society and social problems?**
  In the functionalist perspective, society is a stable, orderly system composed of interrelated parts, each of which performs a function that contributes to the overall stability of society. According to functionalists, social problems such

as violence arise when social institutions do not fulfill the functions that they are supposed to perform or when dysfunctions occur.

How does the conflict perspective view society and social problems?

The conflict perspective asserts that groups in society are engaged in a continuous power struggle for control of scarce resources. This perspective views violence as a response to inequalities based on race, class, gender, and other power differentials in society.

How does the value conflict perspective differ from the critical-conflict perspective?

According to value conflict theorists, social problems are conditions that are incompatible with group values. From this perspective, value clashes are ordinary occurrences in families, communities, and the larger society, in which people commonly hold many divergent values. In contrast, critical-conflict theorists suggest that social problems arise out of major contradictions inherent in the way societies are organized.

Why are there so many different approaches in the conflict perspective?

Different conflict theorists focus on different aspects of power relations and inequality in society. Perspectives based on the works of Karl Marx emphasize class-based inequalities arising from the capitalist system. Feminist perspectives focus on patriarchy—a system of male dominance in which males are privileged and women are oppressed. Other perspectives emphasize that race, class, and gender are interlocking systems of privilege and oppression that result in social problems. However, all of these perspectives are based on the assumption that inequality and exploitation, rather than social harmony and stability, characterize contemporary societies.

How does the symbolic interactionist perspective view society and social problems?

Unlike the functionalist and conflict perspectives, which focus on society at the macrolevel, the symbolic interactionist perspective views society as the sum of the interactions of individuals and groups. For symbolic interactionists, social problems occur when social interaction is disrupted and people are dehumanized, when people are labeled deviant, or when the individual's definition of a situation causes him or her to act in a way that produces a detrimental outcome.

How do sociological research methods differ?

In field research, sociologists observe and interview people where they live, work, and play. In survey research, sociologists use written questionnaires or structured interviews to ask respondents a series of questions about a specific topic. In secondary analysis of existing data, sociologists analyze data that originally were collected for some other purpose.

KEY TERMS

capitalism	microlevel analysis	sociology
conflict perspective	norms	subculture of violence hypothesis
culture	perspective	survey research
discrimination	secondary analysis of existing data	symbolic interactionist perspective
field research	self-fulfilling prophecy	theory
functionalist perspective	situational approach	urbanization
hate crime	social disorganization	values
industrialization	social problem	violence
lifestyle-routine activity approach	society	
macrolevel analysis	sociological imagination	

QUESTIONS FOR CRITICAL THINKING

1. The functionalist perspective focuses on the stability of society. How do acts of violence undermine stability? Can a society survive when high levels of violence exist within its borders? Do you believe that violence can be controlled in the United States?

2. Value conflict theorists suggest that social problems are conditions that are incompatible with group values. How would value conflict theorists view debates over gun-control laws?

3. Some critical-conflict theorists believe that social problems arise from the major contradictions inherent in capitalist economies. What part do guns play in a capitalist economy?

4. Using feminist and symbolic interactionist perspectives, what kind of argument can you make to explain why males are more frequently involved in acts of physical violence than females? What do your own observations tell you about the relationship between social norms and aggressive or violent behavior?

Glossary

capitalism an economic system characterized by private ownership of the means of production, from which personal profits can be derived through market competition and without government intervention.

conflict perspective a framework for viewing society that is based on the assumption that groups in society are engaged in a continuous power struggle for control of scarce resources.

culture the knowledge, language, values, customs, and material objects that are passed from person to person and from one generation to the next in a human group or society.

discrimination actions or practices of dominant-group members (or their representatives) that have a harmful impact on members of subordinate groups.

field research the study of social life in its natural setting: observing and interviewing people where they live, work, and play.

functionalist perspective a framework for viewing society as a stable, orderly system composed of a number of interrelated parts, each of which performs a function that contributes to the overall stability of society.

hate crime a physical attack against a person because of assumptions regarding his or her racial group, ethnicity, religion, disability, sexual orientation, national origin, or ancestry.

industrialization the process by which societies are transformed from a dependence on agriculture and handmade products to an emphasis on manufacturing and related industries.

lifestyle-routine activity approach the belief that the patterns and timing of people's daily movements and activities as they go about obtaining the necessities of life—such as food, shelter, companionship, and entertainment—are the keys to understanding violent personal crimes and other types of crime in our society.

macrolevel analysis focuses on social processes occurring at the societal level, especially in large-scale organizations and major social institutions such as politics, government, and the economy.

microlevel analysis focuses on small-group relations and social interaction among individuals.

norms established rules of behavior or standards of conduct.

perspective an overall approach or viewpoint toward some subject.

secondary analysis of existing data a research design in which investigators analyze data that originally were collected by others for some other purpose.

self-fulfilling prophecy the process by which an unsubstantiated belief or prediction results in behavior that makes the original false belief come true.

situational approach the belief that violence results from a specific interaction process, termed a "situational transaction."

social disorganization the conditions in society that undermine the ability of traditional social institutions to govern human behavior.

social problem a social condition (such as poverty) or a pattern of behavior (such as substance abuse) that people believe warrants public concern and collective action to bring about change.

society a large social grouping that shares the same geographic territory and is subject to the same political authority and dominant cultural expectations.

sociological imagination the ability to see the relationship between individual experiences and the larger society.

sociology the academic and scholarly discipline that engages in systematic study of human society and social interactions.

subculture of violence hypothesis   the hypothesis that violence is part of the normative expectations governing everyday behavior among young males in the lower classes.

survey research   a poll in which researchers ask respondents a series of questions about a specific topic and record their responses.

symbolic interactionist perspective   views society as the sum of the interactions of individuals and groups.

theory   a set of logically related statements that attempt to describe, explain, or predict social events.

urbanization   the process by which an increasing proportion of a population lives in cities rather than in rural areas.

values   collective ideas about what is right or wrong, good or bad, and desirable or undesirable in a specific society.

violence   the use of physical force to cause pain, injury, or death to another, or damage to another's property.

References

NOTE: References in blue are new to the Sixth Edition.

Andersen, Margaret L., and Patricia Hill Collins (Eds.). 2009. *Race, Class, and Gender: An Anthology* (7th ed.). Belmont, CA: Cengage/Wadsworth.

Bandura, Albert. 1973. *Aggression: A Social Learning Analysis.* Upper Saddle River, NJ: Prentice Hall.

Becker, Howard S. 1963. *Outsiders: Studies in the Sociology of Deviance.* New York: Free Press.

Berger, Peter. 1963. *Invitation to Sociology: A Humanistic Perspective.* New York: Anchor.

Berger, Peter, and Thomas Luckmann. 1967. *The Social Construction of Reality: A Treatise in the Sociology of Knowledge.* Garden City, NY: Anchor Books.

Best, Joel. 1999. *Random Violence: How We Talk about New Crimes and New Victims.* Berkeley: University of California Press.

Bushman, Brad J., Hannah R. Rothstein, and Craig A. Anderson. 2010. "Much Ado About Something: Violent Video Games Effects and a School of Red Herring: Reply to Ferguson and Kilburn." *Psychological Bulletin* 136(2):182–187.

Collins, Patricia Hill. 1991. *Black Feminist Thought: Knowledge, Consciousness, and the Politics of Empowerment.* New York: Routledge.

Collins, Patricia Hill. 2005. *Black Sexual Politics: African Americans, Gender, and the New Racism.* New York: Routledge.

Feagin, Joe R., and Hernán Vera. 1995. *White Racism: The Basics.* New York: Routledge.

Ferguson, Christopher J., and John Kilburn. 2010. "Much Ado about Nothing: The Misestimation and Overinterpretation of Violent Video Game Effects in Eastern and Western Nations: Comment on Anderson, et al." *Psychological Bulletin* 136(2):174–178.

Fleming, Justin. 2010. "College Shootings Shock Nation." *Campus Times,* University of Rochester (September 30). Retrieved May 25, 2011. Online: http://www.campustimes.org/2010/09/30/college-shootings-shock-nation/

Hunnicutt, Gwen. 2009. "Varieties of Patriarchy and Violence Against Women." *Violence Against Women* 15(5; May). Retrieved May 25, 2011. Online: http://vaw.sagepub.com/content/15/5/553.abstract

Jones, Jeffrey M. 2011. "Budget Rises as Most Important Problem to Highest Since '96." Gallup.com (April 13). Retrieved May 26, 2011. Online: http://www.gallup.com/poll/147086/Budget-Rises-Most-Important-Problem-Highest.aspx

Kaiser Family Foundation. 2003. "Key Facts: TV Violence" (Spring). Retrieved May 25, 2011. Online: http://www.kff.org/entmedia/upload/Key-Facts-TV-Violence.pdf

Kendall, Diana. 2011. *Framing Class: Media Representations of Wealth and Poverty in America* (2nd ed.). Lanham, MD: Rowman & Littlefield.

Klaus, Rikki. 2010. "University of Texas Student Talks about Shooting." whnt.com (September 28). Retrieved May 26, 2011. Online: http://www.whnt.com/news/whnt-university-of-texas-shooting-092810,0,1061492.story?track=rss

Luckenbill, David F. 1977. "Criminal Homicide as a Situated Transaction." *Social Problems,* 25:176–186.

Marx, Karl, and Friedrich Engels. 1971. "The Communist Manifesto." (orig. published in 1847). In Dirk Struik (Ed.), *The Birth of the Communist Manifesto.* New York: International.

Matsueda, Ross L., Kevin Drakulich, and Charis E. Kubrin. 2006. In Ruth D. Peterson, Lauren J. Krivo, and John Hagan (Eds.), *The Many Colors of Crime: Inequalities of Race, Ethnicity and Crime in America.* New York: New York University Press, pp. 549–584.

Merton, Robert King. 1968. *Social Theory and Social Structure* (enlarged ed.). New York: Free Press.

Mills, C. Wright. 1959b. *The Sociological Imagination.* London: Oxford University Press.

msnbc.com 2007. "Witness: Gunman 'Didn't Say a Single Word.'" msnbc.com (April 16). Retrieved March 24, 2008. Online: http://www.msnbc.msn.com/id/18139889

National Television Violence Study. 1998. "Executive Summary," *National Television Violence Study,* vol. 3. Retrieved October 31, 1999. Online: http://www.ccsp.ucsb.edu/execsum.pdf

Newman, Katherine S., Cybelle Fox, David J. Harding, Jal Mehta, and Wendy Roth. 2004. *Rampage: The Social Roots of School Shootings.* New York: Basic Books.

New York Times. 1996b. "Where the Drugs Come From" (March 2):5.

Oppel, Richard A., Jr. 2011. "Steady Decline in Major Crime Baffles Experts." *New York Times* (May 23). Retrieved May 24, 2011. Online: http://www.nytimes.com/2011/05/24/us/24crime.html?_r=1&scp=1&sq=violent%20crime%20rates%20down&st=cse

Parsons, Talcott. 1951. *The Social System.* New York: Free Press.

The Polling Report. 2005. "Problems and Priorities." Retrieved June 23, 2005. Online: http://www.pollingreport.com/prioriti.htm

Rutenberg, Jim, and Corey Kilgannon. 2005. "2 More White Men Are in Custody in Attack on Black MAN." *New York Times* (July 1):A15.

Simmel, Georg. 1950. *The Sociology of Georg Simmel.* Trans. Kurt Wolff. Glencoe, IL: Free Press (orig. written in 1902–1917).

Stevens, Jane Ellen. 2001. In "Reporting on Violence: New Ideas for Television, Print and Web" (Ed. Lori Dofman). Berkeley: Berkeley Media Studies Group. Retrieved June 30, 2005. Online: http://www.bmsg.org/content/handbook2ndEd.pdf

Vertuno, Jim. 2011. "Texas Legislature Set to Allow Guns on College Campuses." Star-Telegram.com (February 21). Retrieved May 26, 2011. Online: http://www.star-telegram.com/2011/02/20/v-print/2863470/texas-legislature-appears-set.html

Williams, Robin M., Jr. 1970. *American Society: A Sociological Interpretation* (3rd ed.). New York: Knopf.

Wolfgang, Marvin E., and Franco Ferracuti. 1967. *The Subculture of Violence: Towards an Integrated Theory in Criminology.* Beverly Hills, CA: Sage.

Wright, Erik Olin. 1997. *Class Counts: Comparative Studies in Class Analysis.* Cambridge, England: Cambridge University Press.

Wright, Erik Olin, and Joel Rogers. 2010. *American Society: How It Actually Works.* New York: Norton.

Photo Credits

Text Credits

Part Two: Trouble Institutions

Education

Problems of Education

Problems of Education

Ellen Senisi

- Why is an educated population so important to modern societies?

- Does our educational system favor rich and middle-class children?

- Do our schools do a good job of educating minority students?

- Why don't our students score better on achievement tests?

- Why are our schools so violent?

- How can we improve our educational system?

There was nothing special about it. As in thousands of other cash-strapped school districts, New York City school officials recently decided to lay off a fourth-grade teacher from Public School (PS) 41 in Greenwich Village. The parents, of course, were shocked and upset, especially when they found out that Lauren Zangara's layoff would force a big increase in the average class size—from 26 to 32 students. What was different was that the parents banded together and quickly raised the money to pay Zangara's salary. This seemingly generous offer raised a furor on the school board and left many difficult questions for us to ponder. Most of us would agree that there is nothing more important to the future of society than the education of our children, so why do so many of our schools seem to be teetering on the edge of financial disaster? Most people would also agree that all children should get an equal chance for a good education whether their parents are rich or poor, so why is it that the wealthier kids always seem to get all the advantages? Is it fair for the parents of PS 41 to pay for an extra teacher when the parents in many other city schools can't afford to do the same? The school board solved the problem at PS 41 in the most politically expedient way. They refused the parents' offer of financial support but found enough of their own money to return Zangara to her classroom. Most conflicts of this kind are not, however, resolved so easily, and the troubling question this case raises remains unresolved.[1]

One thing is clear: We place tremendous faith in education. We expect it to provide a guiding light for the young and to pass on the democratic traditions of our society. Education is seen as a path out of the slums for new immigrants and a ladder out of poverty for the sons and daughters of the disadvantaged, but it is also essential for the "good life" and the professional careers so highly valued by the middle class. As technology becomes more sophisticated, even our hopes for our economic future are coming to rest on the quality of our educational system and its graduates.

Although our goals and aspirations continue to grow, however, our educational institutions seem to be mired in one crisis after another. Several national reports have issued stinging attacks on the quality of American education, and some corporate leaders complain that our workforce is not as well trained as those of nations such as Germany and Japan. Every year, we lose tens of thousands of good teachers like Laura Zangara, and many of our students become alienated and rebellious. The poor and minority groups charge that the system has shut them out, while many in the middle class have growing doubts about how well it is serving their needs.

The picture is not all so bleak, however. Although our high school students often do not score as well on standardized achievement tests as students in other industrialized nations, it is generally agreed that U.S. universities are the best in the world, and North Americans are more likely to receive a higher education than the citizens of most other industrialized countries.[2] Moreover, the history of our educational institutions is one of continual expansion. In 1890, only 7 percent of children of high school age in the United States were in school; today, more than 10 times that percentage actually graduate.[3] This growth has transformed education into a big business. Virtually every American receives some formal education, and most people spend a good portion of their lives in school.

What are the reasons for this enormous growth? In small traditional societies, education took place in the home and in children's informal day-to-day association with adults. Training for the few specialized occupations that existed was the responsibility of those who held the jobs, usually members of the same family. Customs and traditions were passed along from one generation to the next without the assistance of schools or professional teachers. In more complex societies, specialized organizations developed for the transmission of knowledge. In the beginning, these schools were mostly for the training of priests and other religious officials, but secular education soon followed. Until the nineteenth century, however, education was reserved for aristocrats and a few of their important servants. The masses had little need to read or write, and some aristocrats saw any attempt to develop these skills in the lower classes as a threat to their power. It was only a little more than 200 years ago that the British governor of the colony of Virginia condemned all popular education: "Thank God there are no free schools or printing . . . for learning has brought disobedience and heresy into the world, and printing has divulged them . . . God keep us from both."[4]

It was not until the end of the eighteenth century, when democratic revolutions took place in America and France, that the idea of education for the common people began to catch on. Education for the lower classes became more important as technological advances created the demand for a more highly skilled workforce. In fact, historical research has shown that the increasing level of education in the United States was a major cause of its economic growth in the twentieth century.[5] An even earlier contribution to the popularity of mass education came from Protestant religious groups, which placed increasing emphasis on the need for everyone to be able to read the Bible. Yet progress toward equality has been slow, and the children of the wealthy continue to receive more and better education than the children of the poor.

QUICK REVIEW

■ Why have our educational institutions expanded so much in the last two centuries?

Equal Educational Opportunity for All?

In the past, the keys to economic success usually involved such things as the ownership of good farmland or the canny skills of the small-business owner. As formal education and professional training have gained in importance, so has the issue of educational equity. Many critics have charged that our educational system fails to provide equal opportunity for all; as a result, the poor, immigrants, women, and minorities don't get a fair shot at economic success. To understand this significant issue, we will first examine the role that social class plays in a student's academic achievement and then look at how good a job the educational system does in meeting the needs of minority and female students.

Social Class and Achievement

Grade school teachers and university professors alike can easily see that the children of affluent parents tend to do better in school than the children of the poor. In fact, numerous studies have found social class to be the most effective predictor of achievement in school.[6] As Robert James Parelius and Ann Parker Parelius put it:

> Whether we look at scores on standardized ability or achievement tests, classroom grades, participation in academic rather than vocational high school programs, involvement in extracurricular activities, number of years of schooling completed or enrollment in or completion of college and professional school, children from more socioeconomically advantaged homes outperform their less affluent peers.[7]

There are two principal explanations for this difference. One focuses on the advantages higher-status children have because they come from home environments in which books, a large vocabulary, and an emphasis on achievement are common. The other holds that the schools themselves are often organized in ways that ignore the educational needs of the poor.

FAMILY BACKGROUND Lower-class children live in a strikingly different world from that of middle-class children. The homes of the poor tend to have fewer books, newspapers, and magazines, and the parents have less education. People with low incomes are less likely to read for entertainment; thus, children in low-income homes are less likely to be encouraged to learn that vital skill. In 2003, about half of children in families with an income of $20,000 or less used a computer at home, whereas more than 90 percent of the children in families with an income over $75,000 did.[8] Lower-class families are also larger and are more often headed by only one adult. Children in such families frequently receive less parental contact, guidance, and educational encouragement. Another factor is health: Poor children are more likely to be undernourished than their middle-class counterparts, and they are sick more days in a year.[9] And unhealthy children simply do not learn as well as healthy ones. On the other hand, some of the academic success of children from affluent homes stems from the fact that their parents have higher expectations. Several surveys have shown that children from wealthy families have higher educational aspirations than children from poorer backgrounds.[10] One reason is that middle-class homes are more likely to define the world in a way that sees a college education to be essential for future success and happiness. Some of this difference also reflects a realistic adjustment by poor children to the fact that they have less chance of getting a good education.

Another major obstacle for some children is linguistic. Children whose first language is something other than English face obvious obstacles in most North American schools because they have to learn a new language along with the rest of the school curriculum. There has, moreover, been an explosive growth in the number of such students. In 1979, 8.5 percent of American children grew up speaking some other language than English in their home; by 2004, that percentage had more than doubled to 18.9.[11] Language differences among different social classes also have an important impact on educational achievement. **Standard English** is more commonly spoken by African Americans with middle-class backgrounds, whereas those from the lower class are more likely to speak the dialect known as **Ebonics,** which can be difficult for other English speakers to understand and is certainly not considered "correct" English by most teachers. Similar language differences are found among Americans from European backgrounds. People from the lower class tend to use short, simple sentences, while middle-class people use longer, more complex sentences containing more abstract concepts and a larger vocabulary. These differences give middle-class students, whatever their ethnic backgrounds, a big head start in their schoolwork and make it easier for them to understand their teachers.

THE SCHOOLS   In addition to the obstacles in the home environment of many lower-class students, the school system itself favors the education of middle- and upper-class students. This fact is obvious, first of all, in the way schools are financed. Even a brief examination of the U.S. system of school finance reveals glaring inequities both in how taxes are levied and in how they are spent. For one thing, there are great differences among the various states in the importance placed on education and in the states' ability to pay for it. For example, New Jersey spends almost three times as much money per pupil as Utah.[12] Moreover, the differences between local school districts within the same state can be even greater. Because property taxes are a major source of school funding, districts with expensive homes and other valuable real estate often receive much more revenue than poor districts. In Illinois, for example, the richest districts spend about six times as much per student as the poorest districts; in New York, they spend almost eight times as much.[13] Moreover, such inequities can occur even when rich school districts have lower tax rates than poor ones.

Defenders of the current system of financing point to studies that conclude that the amount of money spent per student has little direct effect on educational achievement.[14] There is certainly little doubt that a badly run school can spend a great deal of money and still achieve poor results, but such findings hardly justify the practice of making the disadvantaged pay higher property taxes than the rich while their children languish in understaffed and underfunded schools.

There have been some serious efforts to correct this inequitable system through the courts. Numerous lawsuits have challenged inequalities in state education finance, and courts in many states have ordered basic reforms.[15] But because the U.S. Supreme Court has refused to get involved in this issue, the process of reform is a hit-or-miss affair. Some courts have upheld the methods their states use to fund public education even when more money is allocated to educate rich children than poor children, and no challenge has yet been made in many other states. Moreover, such cases do nothing to rectify the great imbalance in school funding among different states.

Family finances also have an important effect on educational achievement. Despite the fact that public education itself is free, children from poor families simply cannot afford as much education as those from more well-to-do backgrounds. Students from poor homes are more likely to drop out of school and go to work. At the college and university level, the cost of tuition, books, and transportation puts extra pressure on poor students.

Standard English ■ The English dialect spoken by most of the middle and upper classes.

Ebonics ■ The English dialect most commonly spoken among disadvantaged African Americans.

Many highly qualified lower-class students must attend local community colleges that emphasize technical careers because they cannot afford a university education. Less-qualified upper- and middle-class students may go to expensive private universities to prepare for professional careers. Moreover, the financial pressure on college students has gotten substantially worse in recent years. The cost of college tuition and required fees tripled in the last 20 years, and other costs have shown rapid increases as well.[16]

Of course, colleges and universities are not the only educational institutions that charge their students. Compared to other industrialized nations, the United States devotes a far higher percentage of its educational spending to private schooling.[17] In 2003, about 11 percent of American children attended private schools.[18] The quality, the cost, and the philosophical orientation of these schools vary enormously, however. The most prestigious of them are the so-called **prep schools**; they offer a much higher quality of education than most public schools, but only to the children of families who can afford to pay the price (or the gifted few who receive scholarships). Thus, many of the finest primary and secondary schools are largely closed to poor, working-class, and even most middle-class children. Even less prestigious and less affluent private schools have a major advantage over the public schools: It is far easier for them to exclude troublemakers and low achievers and thereby isolate their students from disruptive influences. Public schools must try to meet the needs of *all* the young people in their communities, even those having social or academic problems.

Because children from upper-class families generally receive a better secondary education, they have easier access to the elite universities that lead students to top positions in government and corporations. Moreover, some less-qualified students from upper-class families are able to attend elite universities because of admission programs that favor the children of alumni and the children of big contributors to fund-raising campaigns.

Aside from differences in the quality of schools, achievement is also affected by the expectations that teachers have for their students. Considerable evidence indicates that teachers expect less from lower-class students, in terms of both academic achievement and behavior, and that for some students those exceptions become self-fulfilling prophecies.[19] Robert Rosenthal and Lenore Jacobson performed an interesting experiment to demonstrate this.[20] Experimenters gave a standard IQ test to pupils in 18 classrooms in a neighborhood elementary school. However, teachers were told that the instrument was the "Harvard Test of Inflected Acquisition" (which does not exist). Next, the experimenters arbitrarily selected 20 percent of the students' names and told their teachers that the test showed these students would make remarkable progress in the coming year. When the students were retested eight months later, those who had been singled out as intellectual bloomers showed a significantly greater increase in IQ than the others. As you might expect, these findings created quite a controversy when they were first published, and many similar studies have since been done. Most of them supported Rosenthal and Jacobson's findings, but some did not, and it is still not clear under exactly what conditions a teacher's expectations are most likely to become a self-fulfilling prophecy.[21] One thing we do know is that lower-class and minority students are the ones most likely to be harmed by this process because they are the ones for whom teachers hold the lowest expectations. For example, when D. G. Harvey and G. T. Slatin gave teachers photos of students and asked them to evaluate their chances for success in school, the teachers reported the highest expectations for white students who appeared to be from middle- and upper-class backgrounds.[22]

Recent research has used the concept of **cultural capital** to help us understand these influences. *Capital* refers to something people own, so cultural capital refers to knowledge and skills a person "owns," "higher culture" from the upper middle class. Research has shown that when working-class children have such cultural capital—such as "knows how to play the violin or cello" or "attends ballet classes"—the status of these children goes up in the eyes of their teachers. Thus, acquiring cultural capital can help working-class students improve their academic achievement because it increases the expectations of teachers.[23]

Prep schools ■ Private schools that focus on preparing their students for college.

Cultural capital ■ Knowledge of "higher culture," such as art and music, that facilitates acceptance into high-status groups.

Even if lower-class students are lucky enough to attend a good high school, they still often do not get the same quality of education as their middle-class schoolmates. Most high school students are placed in one of several different "tracks" or "ability groups." The "most promising" are put into college-preparatory courses, while others go into vocational or "basic" classes. There is considerable evidence that lower-class students are more likely to be placed in the vocational or basic track.[24] Tracking is supposed to be based on such criteria as academic record, performance on standardized tests, and the students' own feelings about college, but there is little doubt that the schools themselves have lower expectations for students from the lower classes. Even when there is no bias, a serious problem remains: Once students have been placed in a lower track, they will be exposed to less challenging material and teachers will have lower expectations of them. When isolated from college-bound students, even the best students in the lower tracks are less likely to want to go to college. Karl Alexander, Martha Cook, and Edward L. Dill found that students in a college-preparatory track were 30 percent more likely to plan to go on beyond high school than equally motivated and able students in non-academic tracks.[25]

Minority Education

The history of minority education has not been a bright one, and African Americans have been the victims of particularly harsh treatment. During the era of slavery, they were seldom given any education at all. Only 60 years ago, most African Americans in the South were forced to attend **segregated schools** that were clearly inferior to those attended by whites. A landmark Supreme Court decision in 1954 recognized the fact that segregated schools were inherently unequal and declared them unconstitutional. In the turmoil that followed, intentional legal segregation was ended, but unlike **de jure** (legal) **segregation, de facto** (actual) **segregation** has been resistant to change. Although African Americans and whites were assigned to the schools nearest their homes regardless of race, most schools remained segregated because most neighborhoods were segregated.

To deal with this problem, the Court ruled that school districts must aim for racial balance in their schools, even when it is necessary to bus students long distances. Intense opposition from whites made school busing an inflammatory racial issue for two decades. At first, busing and other court-ordered **desegregation** programs proved effective, and the segregation of ethnic minorities sharply declined. But because of the migration of the middle class to the suburbs, the fact that many urban whites send their children to private schools, and a heavy influx of new immigrants, in many big cities too few white children remain to create truly integrated schools. As a result, many city schools have become **resegregated.** According to a study by the Harvard Project on School Desegregation, two-thirds of African American students in the United States attend schools in which most of the students are from minority backgrounds. Moreover, Latino students are even more segregated than African Americans. Almost three-fourths of Latino students in the United States attend predominantly minority schools.[26]

The debate over school integration has generated a great deal of concern about the effects of integration on students. The famous Coleman report published in 1966 found that the quality of schools attended by African Americans and by whites was similar when measured by such factors as physical facilities, curriculum, and the qualifications of teachers.[27] The greatest influence on achievement was found to be the students' class background. Middle-class students did much better than students from the lower class. However, Coleman found that disadvantaged students did better when they were in the same classes with middle-class students. He concluded, logically enough, that the performance of lower-class African American children would improve if they were integrated in the same classes as middle-class white students. The effects of desegregation on academic performance have been the subject of dozens of studies since the Coleman report was published. These studies vary widely in methodology and overall quality and have reached contradictory conclusions. Rita E. Mahard and Robert L. Crain reviewed 93 different works on this topic; after eliminating the poorly designed studies, they analyzed

Segregated schools ■ Schools in which students are separated according to their racial, ethnic, or class background.

De jure segregation ■ A system in which the law requires the separation of different ethnic or racial groups.

De facto segregation ■ A system in which different ethnic or racial groups are, in fact, separated from each other even though the law does not require it.

Desegregation ■ The attempt to eliminate school segregation.

Resegregation ■ A return to racial or ethnic segregation that occurs after official desegregation programs have started.

the others and came to some interesting conclusions. Desegregation did indeed improve the academic performance of African American students, but mainly in the primary grades, not in junior high or high school. Moreover, there seems to be an optimum ratio of white students to African American students, which varied in the different studies from 3 to 1 to 9 to 1. Finally, the most successful approach to desegregation was the so-called metropolitan plan, which integrated inner-city and suburban schools.[28]

In addition to the academic benefits, school integration may help reduce racism and create understanding among the nation's many diverse ethnic groups. Minorities may, however, be resegregated into different classes within an integrated school. For example, academic tracking often results in predominantly white college-preparatory classes and predominantly minority vocational classes. Well-intentioned bilingual and compensatory education programs may also result in the removal of minority students from regular classrooms for a large part of the day.[29] Thus, to realize the full benefits of an integrated education, it is necessary to do more than just integrate the schools. Administrators, teachers, and concerned parents must work to create an integrated and supportive environment within individual schools as well.

How well are minority groups doing in today's educational system? The answer is a complex one. As far as standardized achievement tests go, the conclusion is not positive. A study released by the U.S. Department of Education shows that over the last 30 years there has been little overall improvement in the gap between blacks and whites on math, science, and reading scores.[30] With respect to years of school completed, and especially high school graduation rates, the picture looks better. The gap between Americans of European and African descent has narrowed considerably in the last 30 years. Approximately 85 percent of whites, 81 percent of African Americans, and 88 percent of Asians and Pacific Islanders—but only 59 percent of Latinos—had graduated from high school in 2002. (See Figure 1.) At the college level, however, a huge gap remains. About 28 percent of whites but only 18 percent of African Americans and 12 percent of Latinos have completed a four-year college degree. Asian groups, however, have done extremely well, ranking considerably above whites at about 50 percent (Pacific Islanders are also included in this statistical group although they have lower levels of educational attainment than Asians).[31]

Why do Latinos rank lower than African Americans when they share a similar socioeconomic position in American society? One important factor is language. Some Latinos come into English-speaking schools with little knowledge of that language, and many others are less proficient in English than their classmates who grew up speaking it

Figure 1

High School Graduates

African Americans and Latinos are less likely to finish high school than European Americans.

Source: U.S. Bureau of the Census, *Statistical Abstract of the United States, 2006* (Washington, DC: U.S. Government Printing Office, 2006), p. 147.

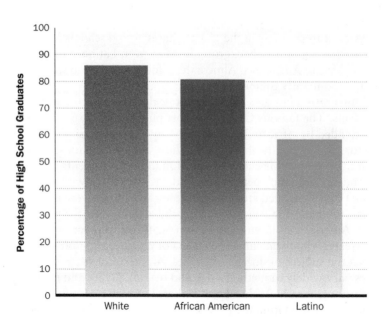

at home, and that obviously creates a host of difficult educational problems. A second factor is immigration. There has been a heavy influx of new immigrants from Latin America, and they frequently come from low-income groups that received inadequate educations in their own countries.

Gender Bias

In the past, our educational system openly discriminated against women and girls in much the same way it discriminated against minorities. The traditional attitude held that it was far more important to educate sons, who would have to go out and find jobs, than daughters, who would just stay home and take care of the house, and our educational system clearly reflected this bias. Boys were given more and better education than girls, and many of the top universities did not even admit women. Although today's students may think this kind of blatant discrimination is a thing of the distant past, such practices actually continued until quite recently. Harvard University, for example, excluded women from its law school until 1950 and from its graduate business program until 1963.

Important progress toward gender equality has unquestionably been made since then. The most blatant barriers to equal educational opportunities for female students have been removed, and there has been a remarkable increase in educational achievement among women. In fact, young women are now actually better educated than young men. A higher percentage of young women have graduated from high school and college than young men. In 2005, 58.2 percent of bachelor's degrees were earned by women.[32]

Nonetheless, many subtle forms of **sexism** remain and continue to affect the occupational chances of women today. The attitudes and behavior of teachers often reflect the same gender stereotypes that are found among other groups, and many times girls are subtly discouraged from pursuing "masculine" interests in subjects such as science and math. At least partially as a result, although more females graduate from college, they are less likely to be in the technologically oriented majors that often lead to the highest-paying jobs. In 2001, for example, only 18 percent of bachelor's degrees in engineering were awarded to females. There have, nonetheless, been important improvements in this area as well. The percentage of females earning bachelor's degrees in business and management increased from only 9 percent in 1971 to 50 percent in 2001. In that same period, biology graduates (usually a key to medical school admission) increased from 29 percent female to 60 percent. The changes among students in prelaw programs are even more striking. In 1971, only 5 percent were female compared to almost 73 percent in 2001.[33]

Sexism ■ Stereotyping, prejudice, and discrimination based on gender.

✳ QUICK REVIEW

■ How does social class affect student achievement?

■ Discuss the history of ethnic discrimination in education and how we have tried to correct it.

■ How well do females do in our educational system?

The Quality of Education

The controversy about the quality of our educational system has jumped out of specialized journals and onto the political stage. Several prestigious national commissions have been highly critical of our schools, and many people fear that American students are falling behind their counterparts in other countries. Such attention is certainly long overdue, but before we can go very far to make the schools more effective, we must first decide what they are supposed to do. Should they teach students to do well on standardized tests of academic achievement? Teach the skills of critical, independent thinking? Essay

Lessons from Other Places

Education in Germany, Thailand, and Japan

While I was living in Thailand and teaching at a Thai university, my Thai next-door neighbors had just returned from the United States, where both the mother and father had finished their PhDs. At dinner I once asked their two daughters, ages 10 and 14, what they missed most about returning to Thailand after four years in the United States. Both replied immediately, "Pizza." I then asked them what they disliked most about being back in Thailand. Again, both replied immediately, "The homework!" It is clear that one of the major reasons that American students don't score as well on standardized tests is that they don't study as much.

But that isn't the whole story. I remember being surprised a few years ago while living in Tokyo when I opened a newspaper containing a front-page article titled "Japanese Education System Should Copy the United States." Considering that Japan has a much higher rate of literacy and high school completion, that Japanese high school seniors score higher than any other country in tests of math and science, and that (at that time anyway) there was almost no violence in Japanese schools, the title of the article seemed rather odd. But the report by a government commission studying Japanese education had a point: Japanese students' heads are filled with facts, figures, and dates, but their critical reasoning skills are usually poor. The Japanese educational system is geared far more toward passing exams than building skills in critical thinking and analysis. Most of the Nobel Prizes in science went to Americans in the twentieth century, partly because independent thinking and critical reasoning are important in American schools. The Japanese Ministry of Education has instituted many changes in attempts to overcome this lack of critical thinking, but so far with little success.

There are, however, other aspects of the educational systems in Europe and Japan that we may well want to emulate. Although only half as many people in European countries graduate from four-year universities as in the United States, they have excellent systems of vocational education geared toward specific occupational skills. In Germany, for example, at the beginning of what would be the high school years for Americans, young people must go on either a college-bound track or a vocational or apprenticeship school track. Those students seeking to enter a good university go on to the famous *gymnasiums,* which are more like junior colleges, during their last two (high school) years. For those German students who choose the vocationally oriented high schools, they receive the basics in math, science, writing, and language, but as they move to their final years of school they spend more and more of their school week in practical job training than in the classroom. In Japan, there are high schools specifically oriented toward helping students pass the extremely difficult college entrance exams, and many students also spend additional hours in private schools, generally called *juku,* to help improve their chances of getting into a good university. All of this means that typical college-bound students in Japan have little time left to themselves because of all the long hours of study. Japan also has excellent "industrial high schools" that, like those in Germany, are specifically geared to train students for technical and industrial jobs, as well as the basics in math, science, and language.

Several reports have shown that American corporations have higher labor costs and lower productivity in lower-level positions because so many workers lack basic skills. Although an educational system that includes high-quality vocational training could help solve this problem, there has been strong resistance to such proposals. Most American parents do not like the idea of their children being placed in a noncollege track at such an early age, and there is no question that it does restrict their life chances. It is rare for a German or Japanese worker to change course in midlife and go back and get a university education. Again, we must understand how American values of individual freedom and equality of opportunity restrict the options we might consider for reforming our educational system. Of course, the plus side is that the values of independence and individualism help Americans acquire critical thinking skills and make innovations that have given the United States an edge in the world economy during the last few years. A combination of the German and Japanese educational systems with the most positive aspects of the American system would be the ideal. But value preferences, as is often the case, restrict our options in such matters.

Harold Kerbo

writing? Higher mathematics? Public citizenship? Or should they focus on students' social needs, such as preventing delinquency and drug abuse? In this section, we will discuss some of the main issues in the current debate about our educational system, but because the parties to this debate do not agree about the system's underlying goals, they tend to see its problems in starkly different terms.

Authority and Rebellion

Our leaders are fond of talking about the need to teach children democratic principles and the ability to think for themselves. Most schools, however, are large bureaucracies that demand obedience to a rigid set of rules over which the students, and even most teachers, have little influence. Our schools have been compared to factories in which workers (teachers) turn raw materials (students) into finished products (educated citizens) under the strict supervision of the management (school administration); they have even been likened to prisons, with principals as wardens and teachers as guards. Although such comparisons can easily be taken too far, it is hard to see most schools as places that encourage creativity or individual initiative.

In one sense, the bureaucratic structure of our schools both reflects and requires **authoritarianism.** Students are required by law to go to school, where they are compelled to spend large amounts of time in classrooms and truancy is considered a form of delinquency. All bureaucracies require strict rules and regulations if they are to coordinate the activities of large numbers of people. Without such rules, school life would quickly degenerate into chaos; however, some observers believe that schools carry the emphasis on authority and obedience to harmful extremes. They argue that many schools are experiencing a problem common to bureaucracies: **goal displacement.** In this case, there has been a shift from education to the maintenance of order and authority as the primary goal of the schools. Many conflict theorists charge that there is, thus, a **hidden curriculum** in our schools: that along with reading, writing, and arithmetic, students are taught conformism and obedience to authority. Those who do not learn this lesson are doomed to failure in the educational bureaucracy, no matter how academically talented they may be.

Although some people criticize the authoritarianism of schools, others condemn what they see as chaos in the classroom. Numerous opinion polls have shown that the public believes "lack of discipline" to be the biggest problem in schools today. To most people, this lack of discipline conjures up images of disrespectful students refusing to do their work or getting in fights on the school grounds. Of course, this is hardly a new problem, and students have been getting in fights as long as there have been schools. Unfortunately, there have been frequent reports of far more serious problems: drug dealing, students carrying weapons, and vicious assaults and rapes directed against students and even teachers.[34]

Authoritarianism ■ An extreme belief in the importance of authority and in the individual's responsibility to submit to it.

Goal displacement ■ The substitution of a new goal or goals for the officially stated objectives of an organization.

Hidden curriculum ■ Things students must learn in order to succeed in school that are not part of the formal curriculum, such as obedience to authority.

Bonnie Kamin/PhotoEdit Inc.

Violence and bullying are a problem among students from all economic and social groups.

Given the dramatic outbreaks of violence in our schools in recent years—such as the 12 students and one teacher killed at Columbine High School in Littleton, Colorado; the four students and one teacher killed at Westside Middle School in Jonesboro, Arkansas; and the three students killed at Heath High School in Kentucky—it certainly seems that our schools are becoming more dangerous all the time. But such headline-grabbing incidents can actually confuse us about the realities of life in school today. Although they are certainly not as safe as we want them to be, schools are not the most dangerous places in the United States. Students ages 12 to 18 are almost three times more likely to be the victim of a violent crime when they are away from school than when they are at school.[35] Although 2.6 percent of students reported being victims of violence in school in 2000, the rate of violent crime in U.S. schools actually came down slightly *from the previous* decade.[36]

In response to the increasing fear of violence in our schools, the federal government passed the Gun-Free Schools Act in 1994 that required schools receiving federal aid (almost all public schools) to expel for at least one year any student who takes a gun to school. But many states have gone well beyond the federal mandate and adopted "zero-tolerance" policies for all forms of weapons and drugs. Although the supporters of these policies claim they are starting to bring down the rate of school violence, their inflexibility has produced many extreme reactions. For example, an 8-year-old Louisiana girl was suspended for a month because she took her grandfather's gold pocket watch to school; on the same chain was a 1-inch knife he used to clean his fingernails. A 13-year-old in Ohio was suspended for nine days for taking a bottle of Midol to school.[37] Some schools in high-crime areas have even taken to using metal detectors to check students for weapons before entering campus. However, 64 percent of the students in the Los Angeles survey mentioned earlier said that metal detectors don't keep weapons off campus.[38]

Aside from the life-threatening violence, there has been a growing awareness of the problem of bullying in schools. Much of this new concern is the result of the numerous highly publicized school shootings in which students who were made fun of and victimized over a period of several years finally exploded in violent rage. Bullying tends to be done differently by gender. For boys, the bullying and teasing often centers on sexual orientation. Being called a "girl," "sissy," "faggot," "queen," or "queer" is a common way for boys to taunt other boys. Unfortunately, the consequences can be severe. Victims of intense bullying often drop out of school, see their academic performance drop, or succumb to depression. Gay and bisexual teenaged boys attempt suicide seven times more often than other boys their age, and the younger they are when they recognize their sexual orientation, the more likely they are to try. Bullying done by girls tends to center on appearance, especially on clothes. Although bullying is often excused as normal behavior—"Kids will be kids, after all"—it can have severe consequences on the victim. Underachieving, dropping out, life-threatening eating disorders, and depression are all common reactions.

Educational Achievement

Functionally illiterate ■ Having skills in reading and writing that are so poor that a person cannot perform many of the basic tasks necessary to daily life in an industrial society.

It is estimated that at least 3 million Americans cannot read or write at all. Moreover, more than 10 times that number are **functionally illiterate**—that is, their skills at reading and writing are so poor that they cannot perform many of the basic tasks necessary to daily life in an industrial society.[39] The demand for a more educated workforce has made the problem of illiteracy an increasingly serious one. The long-range trends have actually been toward an increase in the number of years the average person spends in school and a decline in illiteracy among native-born Americans. However, the recent influx of poorly educated immigrants has resulted in a decline in literacy in some sectors of the population.[40]

Even though people are getting more years of education, many people are concerned that educational achievement is not high enough among secondary school students. One of the statistics given the most attention is the scores on the Scholastic Aptitude Test (SAT)—the most widely used college admission examination. Overall, SAT scores declined about 7 percent from their peak in the mid-1960s until 1980. Math scores finally returned to their 1967 levels in 2000, but by 2005 verbal scores were still not back up to their previous highs.[41] Data from the U.S. Department of Education's "National Assessment of Educational Progress" are a bit more optimistic. They show little change between 1977 and 2001 in scores for reading and writing and a small improvement in math and science scores.[42] So, overall, the data are quite mixed. Educational achievement may have improved a bit in the last few years, but there is still a long way to go if it is to keep up with the ever-growing need for a well-educated population.

Another serious source of concern is that American students often do poorly in comparisons with students from other wealthy nations. For example, data from the Program for International Student Assessment for 2003 ranks the United States below average in both math and science, and only about average in reading, even though many of the 18 nations included have significantly lower per capita incomes.[43] In tests of geographic knowledge, young Americans again rank dead last among the citizens of the industrialized nations. In fact, in one study, young people (ages 18 to 24) from Sweden, Mexico, Canada, Germany, Japan, and France knew more about the U.S. population than did young Americans.[44] Sadly, American adults don't do any better in their of knowledge of international current events, scoring lower in polls than the citizens of any other industrialized nation.[45]

It is not surprising that this poor educational performance has a major impact on the U.S. economy. It is estimated that U.S. business loses between $25 billion and $30 billion a year because of poor literacy among workers, and the National Association of Manufacturers concluded that about one-fourth of U.S. firms have trouble reorganizing work activities and upgrading products because employees can't learn the necessary skills.[46]

There are three common explanations for these educational problems. The first explanation attacks the tests themselves, arguing that test scores don't accurately reflect how much students are actually learning; the second explanation holds the schools responsible; and the third explanation blames the problem on the students' social environment. Critics of the validity of these tests point out that some (but not all) of the decline in scores on college entrance examinations can be attributed to the increasing number of poor and minority students who are taking the tests. They also argue that the growing number of immigrants who do not speak English well has driven down test

Charles Gupton/Stock Boston

The Japanese students shown here are likely to go to school more hours a day, do more homework, and score higher on standardized tests of academic achievement than their American counterparts.

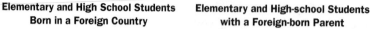

Elementary and High School Students Born in a Foreign Country

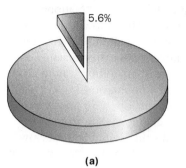

5.6%

(a)

Elementary and High-school Students with a Foreign-born Parent

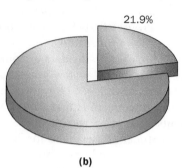

21.9%

(b)

Figure 2

Students and Parents from Other Countries

Source: U.S. Bureau of the Census, *Statistical Abstract of the United States, 2006* (Washington, DC: U.S. Government Printing Office, 2006), p. 146.

scores in our public schools. (See Figure 2.) The critics also raise a more fundamental issue: Such tests, they assert, focus on only one or two types of educational skills and should not be used to make an overall evaluation of educational achievement. The other side generally agrees that these tests do not measure all aspects of educational achievement, but they argue that the tests are a valid indicator of some critical skills. Moreover, they argue that there is no reason to believe American students do any better in the kinds of skills that are not tested than in the ones that are.

Those who blame the schools for the weak test scores attribute much of it to a decline in academic rigor. As more and more students come into school from unstable families, the schools have taken on numerous new tasks, from teaching about AIDS and family life to preventing drug abuse. One study found that in their four years of high school, American students spend less than half as many hours studying academic subjects as students in France, Germany, or Japan.[47] Moreover, many critics also charge that pressure not to flunk out disadvantaged poor and minority students has led to a watering down of academic standards and lower overall expectations. For example, surveys show that fewer than 40 percent of 12th graders do an hour or more of homework a night.[48] Such softening of standards has often been covered up by the practice of grade inflation: assigning grades of A or B to students who have barely learned the subject at hand.

Whatever the shortcomings of the schools, experts agree that home environment has an enormous influence on how well students master their studies, and there are good reasons to believe that the environment of many of today's students is less conducive to educational achievement than in the past. For example, the average high school senior now spends almost three hours a day in front of the television.[49] A survey by the Educational Testing Service found that 13-year-old Americans were more likely to report watching a great deal more television and failing to do their homework than 13-year-olds in any other country studied.[50] Obviously, children who sit in front of television sets instead of playing basketball will not become good basketball players. Just as obviously, children who watch television and play video games instead of reading books will not become good readers and, consequently, will not learn to write well either.

Teachers often complain that their students have been growing more rebellious and less interested in their studies, but it is difficult to determine whether such comments reflect a real change in students or just an idealization of the "good old days." There is, however, one good reason to believe that these complaints are accurate: the huge increase in the percentage of families in which there is only one parent or in which both parents work outside the home. These changes in family structure often reduce the amount of time and energy parents have to devote to their children, and it seems reasonable to assume that some students' behavior at school suffers as a result. These structural changes in the family may also mean that parents are not able to spend as much time assisting their children with their studies or getting involved in the educational programs of their schools.

QUICK REVIEW

■ Are our schools too authoritarian or too lenient?

■ What are the causes of low student achievement?

Solving the Problems of Education

The problems of education are also economic and political problems. Some proposals for change call for a sweeping restructuring of society that goes far beyond our educational institutions. Educational problems are also bureaucratic problems, so other proposals for change call for improved efficiency in the existing school system and its teaching methods. Proposals to upgrade the educational system fall into two broad categories: recommendations for providing more equal educational opportunities for everyone and suggestions for improving the quality of education itself.

Toward Equal Educational Opportunity

Almost everyone agrees that there should be equal educational opportunity for all, but there is widespread disagreement about what equal opportunity means and how it can be achieved. Integration of students from different ethnic backgrounds into the same schools is often proposed as a solution to educational inequality. Another approach is to set up **compensatory education programs** to provide special assistance to disadvantaged students or programs to help fight gender inequality. Finally, many people propose that we change the way education is financed so that the same amount of money is spent on both rich and poor students.

Compensatory education programs ■ Programs designed to help make up for the educational difficulties that disadvantaged students experience.

EFFECTIVE INTEGRATION For years, the U.S. government, particularly the judicial branch, has been trying to achieve racial and ethnic integration in the schools. Despite many advances, this goal has still not been met. Following court-ordered integration, unofficial desegregation often occurred as whites moved to the suburbs or enrolled their children in private schools. The metropolitan plan reduces resegregation by merging suburban school districts with inner-city school districts and then busing children within each district. One difficulty with this proposal is distance. Some suburban communities are so far from city centers that bused students spend a large part of their school day in transit. Another difficulty is prejudice. The proposal does nothing to discourage white parents from putting their children in private schools; in fact, it might encourage more prejudiced whites to do so.

As an alternative, some districts have created voluntary desegregation plans that give students the right to attend any school they wish, provided it does not have a higher percentage of students of their ethnic group than their neighborhood school. A related idea is the creation of **magnet schools** with unique educational programs that attract students from all ethnic groups. The goal of these plans is to reduce "white flight" while still allowing minority and lower-class students to attend integrated middle-class schools if they wish. Critics of such plans argue that they are not likely to significantly reduce segregation because most students choose to attend their neighborhood schools, and most neighborhoods are still segregated to one degree or another.

Magnet schools ■ Schools with special enriched programs designed to attract students from diverse ethnic groups in order to encourage integration.

Another approach encourages the integration of residential areas so that neighborhood schools are automatically integrated. In many ways, this is the most appealing solution because it provides the broadest possible opportunity for development of interracial friendships and cooperation. However, daunting obstacles stand in the way of efforts to create truly integrated communities. For one thing, a long history of prejudice and suspicion makes many Americans prefer to live in neighborhoods in which the residents have similar economic and ethnic backgrounds. Moreover, the poor and minorities simply cannot afford to live in affluent neighborhoods. One possible solution is to create more subsidized housing for low-income families in wealthy neighborhoods, along with tax incentives for affluent families who refurbish and live in older homes in lower-income neighborhoods. Such proposals, however, often run into intense opposition from wealthy homeowners, who fear that low-cost housing will decrease their property values, and from residents of low-income neighborhoods, who fear they will be displaced by more prosperous newcomers.

COMPENSATORY EDUCATION Another way to boost the educational achievement of the poor and minorities is to provide them with special programs and assistance. The most popular and widely known compensatory program of this kind is Project Head Start, which gives preschool instruction to disadvantaged children. The original research on

Mark Richards/PhotoEdit Inc.

Compensatory education programs, such as this Head Start class, are one of the best hopes for improving the educational achievement of disadvantaged students.

the Head Start program indicated that it produced significant educational gains among its students, but follow-up studies found that most of the early benefits faded away by the time the children reached the second or third grade.[51] However, research on the Perry Preschool Program, which is similar to Project Head Start but spends about twice as much per student, has shown real long-term benefits. A study that followed a group of students from ages 3 to 27 found that those who attended the Perry Preschool Program earned more money, had more stable marriages, and were less likely to use illegal drugs than those in a matched control group. The researchers estimated that because of these benefits, the Perry Preschool Program saved taxpayers $7.16 for every dollar spent.[52] A related program under Title I of the Elementary and Secondary Education Act provides federal money to give extra help to disadvantaged students who are already in school. More than 5 million elementary school students are aided under this program, and its supporters credit it with helping make real improvements in the educational performance of poor and minority students. But critics point to studies showing that the benefits of elementary school programs do not carry over into high school.[53]

Research on both Head Start and Title I programs thus reaches much the same conclusion: These programs significantly improve the performance of the underprivileged students who are enrolled, but the benefits tend to diminish after they finish the program.[54] The solution to this problem is obvious: Don't stop the programs after only a few years. Disadvantaged students should continue to receive extra help as long as they need it, which in many cases would probably be until their final years of high school. The difficulty with this proposal is, of course, money—but such an investment would pay enormous dividends in terms of a healthier, more competitive economy, lower rates of crime and welfare dependency, and, most important, a more just society.

The No Child Left Behind program begun in 2001 attempted to deal with the problem of educational inequality by focusing on improving schools. It instituted a national testing program and provided extra assistance for students in poorly performing schools and a mechanism for students to transfer from underperforming schools. There has, however, been intense criticism of the program with critics charging that it creates huge bureaucratic burdens for school districts, forces schools to teach "to the test," and is not adequately funded.

A variety of educational opportunity programs have also been established at the college level. Generally, these programs make special provisions for the admission of disadvantaged and minority students who do not meet standard admissions requirements. They also provide tutoring and assistance to help these students stay in school. Although these programs have their critics, they have become an accepted part of most colleges and universities. One common problem is that such programs often fail to provide enough academic help after the disadvantaged students are admitted, so their graduation rate remains significantly lower than it is for other students. However, the greatest conflicts have arisen over special admissions programs for graduate and professional schools. Competition for places in these schools is intense, and white students complain that they are the victims of "reverse discrimination" because some whites are rejected in favor of less-qualified minority students. Supporters of special admissions programs argue that minorities have already been subjected to a great deal of discrimination and that **affirmative action programs** merely attempt to compensate for some small part of it. The majority of the American public, however, is opposed to any kind of preference based on race or ethnic group,[55] and recent legislation and court rulings have been undermining affirmative action in college admissions. A 1996 initiative in California banned such preferences, and the result has been a sharp drop in the percentage of African Americans attending the most prestigious schools in University of California system and its many graduate schools. On the other hand, the percentage of Asian students has shown a big increase. Court rulings in other parts of the nation have also created new obstacles to ethnically based affirmative action programs. Particularly important was *Hopwood v. State of Texas,* which invalidated race-based admission criteria for the University of Texas law school. One response to this trend has been a shift to programs that seek to provide better access to higher education to students from low-income families regardless of their ethnic background. This "racially blind" approach can still help to improve educational equality without flouting strongly held public opposition to programs that are perceived to provide racial preferences.

Affirmative action program ■ A program designed to make up for past discrimination by giving special assistance to members of the groups that were discriminated against.

FIGHTING GENDER AND SEXUAL INEQUALITY Although the sharp increase in the number of women earning college and postgraduate degrees shows that our schools have made significant progress in providing more equal opportunity for both genders, much remains to be done before full equality is achieved. The funding and attention given to male and female athletics, for example, remain highly unequal. Moreover, many schools continue to tailor their curricula to reflect traditional gender stereotypes: nutrition classes for girls and auto shop for boys. More effort also needs to be made to convince girls that math and sciences aren't just "boys' classes" and that they too should get involved. The biggest challenge, however, is teachers. Like most other people in our society, teachers have many stereotypes about what kinds of behavior are appropriate for girls and for boys and about how girls' and boys' abilities and interests should differ. A comprehensive training program that sensitizes teachers to the negative effects of such stereotypes and teaches them how to keep such biases out of the classroom could help transform our schools from institutions that reinforce gender inequality to ones that actively promote equality.

There is also growing concern about the sexual harassment students often experience from other students. Of course, Title IX of the Educational Amendments of 1972 and the equal protection clause of the 14th Amendment already prohibit sexual harassment. All schools that receive federal funds are obligated to ensure that their students are protected from sexual harassment and discrimination. Unfortunately, that obligation has seldom been met. In 1999, the case of *Nabozny* v. *Podlesny* drove this point home. In his high school in Ashland, Wisconsin, Jamie was mock raped in a classroom while 20 students watched. He was urinated on in a school bathroom, and he was kicked so severely that he required surgery to stop the internal bleeding. When notified of this harassment by Jamie and his parents, a school official simply said that he had to expect that sort of treatment because he was homosexual. Fortunately, the courts disagreed; the school district eventually had to pay $900,000 in damages. Also in 1999, the Supreme Court decided in *Aurelia Davis* v. *Monroe County Board of Education* that school districts can be held liable if employees of the school are indifferent to complaints of peer-to-peer sexual harassment. One of the most critical issues is class size. When classes are large (more than 25 students), it is much more difficult for teachers to be aware of the problems that are developing in class. Another essential task is to make teachers more aware of the damage such behavior causes and their obligation to help prevent it.

REFORMING SCHOOL FINANCE As pointed out earlier, schools in rich districts often receive much more money per student than do schools in poor districts. Although this problem could be dealt with by reforming the system of school finance in individual states, such an approach does nothing to rectify the huge inequalities among states. The only solution to that dilemma is much more federal funding. For example, if the federal government paid for all primary and secondary education, it could provide equitable funding for all schools. There is, however, a strong tradition of local control of the schools in the United States, and many people fear that national financing would mean federal control that would be unresponsive to the needs of local communities.

Although such concerns are certainly well grounded, there appear to be few alternatives to increased federal aid to education, even if it stops far short of complete financial support. When economic distress causes troubled school districts and financially strapped states to cut back on education, the result may be a vicious cycle in which poorer education creates a less competent workforce that causes more economic problems. Federal money is needed to break this cycle. There is, moreover, another important reason for the federal government to get more involved: It is the only level of government that has the resources to significantly increase overall funding for education. It is worth noting that most funding for public education in the other industrial nations comes primarily and sometimes exclusively from the national or federal government rather than from local governments. In the United States, the federal government pays only about 7 cents of every dollar spent for education.[56]

Improving the Schools

The original Coleman report created a furor when it was published in 1966 because it found that none of the measures of school quality it used—funding, teacher qualifications, or physical facilities—had much effect on the educational achievement of the students. These results were widely interpreted to mean "Schools don't make any difference." Subsequent research has shown that those results were largely a product of the extremely narrow questions the researchers asked; in truth, their conclusions were highly misleading. For instance, Michael Rutter's study of London high schools found that they had a critical impact on student achievement. It is not surprising that the best schools were those that maintained high standards, required more homework, and had clear and well-enforced standards of discipline yet still created a comfortable, supportive atmosphere for students.[57] Coleman himself later acknowledged that schools do make a substantial difference. In a comparison of private and public schools, Coleman and his colleagues wrote that "the indication is that more extensive academic demands are made in the private schools, leading to more advanced courses, and thus to higher achievement."[58] In addition to the idea of requiring more work, reformers also propose reorganizing the school system and hiring better teachers.

REQUIRING MORE WORK One obvious way to improve academic performance is to raise the schools' requirements and make students work harder. In the 1960s, schools were heavily criticized for their bureaucratic rigidity, and the curriculum was loosened to allow more individual choice. Now, with the increasing concern about scholastic achievement, electives are being replaced with tougher requirements for more academic courses. A related proposal is to increase the amount of homework so that students must meet higher standards in the courses they do take. A criticism sometimes heard from minority leaders is that tougher requirements force disadvantaged students who cannot compete to leave school and go out on the streets. Efforts to make our schools more rigorous must therefore be accompanied by the kinds of compensatory educational programs discussed in the last section; otherwise, the result is likely to be lower, not higher, academic performance among some groups.

Programs to raise academic standards and require more homework win at least verbal support from teachers and school administrators, but those groups often oppose another fundamental change that needs to be made: an increase in the amount of time students spend in school. The United States has one of the shortest school years of any major industrialized nation, and things are not much better in Canada. The average student in the United States goes to school about 180 days a year, whereas in Japan schools are in session for 244 days and in Germany about 210 days. Moreover, the average school day is only six hours in North America, whereas eight-hour days are common in other nations.[59] It is unrealistic to expect American students to compete with their counterparts abroad who have as many as 30 percent more school days a year. As far back as 1983, the National Commission on Excellence in Education recommended that the average school day be increased to seven hours and the school year be increased to between 200 and 220 days, but its conclusions were largely ignored. So were the similar recommendations by the National Commission on Education and Learning made in 1994 and again in 1999.[60] But in the long run, it is hard to see how North American students can remain competitive without this kind of reform.

RESTRUCTURING THE SCHOOLS   The last two decades have been a time of ferment in our educational system, and there are literally dozens of proposals for restructuring our schools. One of the most popular among conservatives is the **voucher system.** (See the Debate in this chapter.) Under most versions of this plan, automatic support for existing public schools would be withdrawn, and parents would be given vouchers that could be "spent" at any public or private school. Advocates of the voucher system claim it would stimulate competition among the schools and force schools and teachers to provide top-quality education or go out of business. Critics of these proposals, who include many of the nation's leading educators, say that such changes would create educational chaos: Tens of thousands of independent schools would spring up with enormous differences in quality, curriculum, and objectives. California's superintendent of public instruction described the voucher proposals as "dangerous claptrap" that would produce the same disastrous results as the deregulation of the savings and loan industry, and Wisconsin's superintendent likened this approach to "nuking" the public school system.[61] Liberals are also concerned that a voucher-based school system would promote an increasing fragmentation of our society as children go to schools that only have children just like themselves. Thus, the children of Christian fundamentalists, Muslims, Catholics, and progressive liberals, for example, would have little or no contact with each other at school.

Voucher system ■ A program in which the government gives vouchers to pay for children's education at any school their parents choose.

A less radical proposal is to open the enrollment of public schools so that students can attend any school they want. The idea is that such programs cause a mass exodus from weak schools and force them to improve in order to get their students back. Left unanswered are the questions of how the good schools could physically accommodate all the students who would want to come and what would happen to the teachers and facilities at the weaker schools. One of the best-known success stories among school choice programs is in the East Harlem section of New York City. Starting in the 1970s, the district slowly developed a network of alternative elementary and junior high schools, each using its own unique educational approach. By the mid-1980s, reading scores in East Harlem had risen from the lowest in the New York City school system to about average. Improvements in other districts have caused the position of East Harlem schools to slip a bit since then, but they continue to produce impressive results for a district in which the overwhelming majority of students come from poor and minority backgrounds.[62]

Baltimore tried an even more radical approach by turning nine public schools over to a private company to run them for a profit. The company claimed that by cutting administrative overhead and staff salaries (but not teacher salaries) it could increase the amount of money actually reaching the classroom. After a year of operation, the company claimed that it had raised test scores in its schools by nearly a whole grade level. When the National Federation of Teachers commissioned its own study, however, it discovered that test scores had actually gone down, and Baltimore ultimately canceled the company's contract and reclaimed control of the schools.[63]

The most popular educational reform of the last decades is based on the call for public schools to be made more accountable by making comparative evaluations of the performance of their students on standardized tests of basic academic skills. According to this concept, schools should create a more rigorous curriculum that focuses on the basic skills of reading, writing, and mathematics, while student, teacher, and school

Debate

Educational Vouchers: A Good Idea?

YES Parents have become increasingly concerned about the education their children are receiving in the public school system. Class sizes are too large, children aren't safe on the school grounds, and academic achievement is subpar. Too many children simply fall through the cracks in our current system. Moreover, if given the choice, many parents would prefer to send their child to a school that fits their religious or philosophical views.

Educational vouchers will give parents a choice. Children in big cities who are trapped in dangerous ghetto schools will have a way out, and middle-class parents will have more control over their children's education. Using the voucher system will even the playing field. Parents can find a school that produces higher academic achievement and safer conditions. If parents are not pleased with the schools their children are attending, they can shop around for different schools that better fit the needs of their children. This will create a healthy competition among schools, and those schools that are not performing well will either improve or go out of business.

The educational voucher system will make schools more accountable for the safety and academic achievement of their students. The voucher system will also give schools an incentive to be more economically efficient. Individual choice and competition to bring better service are the American way.

NO School vouchers sound like a wonderful idea, but in fact considerable research shows that school vouchers will only serve to aggravate our educational woes. First, private schools can't provide any better education for their students than public schools unless they spend more money per student. The students in many private schools do better on standardized tests because the schools only accept good students to begin with. Private schools that are paid for by government vouchers would have neither of these advantages.

Will our educational system be more cost-effective under a voucher system? Again, the answer is no. Careful estimates show that educating our children with vouchers will actually cost billions of dollars more every year. Disseminating information, additional transportation costs, the numerous parallel administrative units, and the need for government supervision and the adjudication of problems are just a few of the reasons.

Some people argue that vouchers will give children in low-income neighborhoods an avenue to escape inadequate schools. Evidence drawn from the Milwaukee Voucher experiment, however, shows that parents who choose to use their vouchers have more education and higher socioeconomic status than those who do not. Sadly, a voucher system will therefore lead to greater socioeconomic and racial segregation of students. And that is not all. It will also lead to the segregation of students based on religion, ethnic background, and their parents' political and educational views. In 1954, our Supreme Court ruled that "separate educational facilities are inherently unequal." It would be a tragedy for this country to reverse 200 years of educational progress by turning to a voucher system.

performance should be continually evaluated by standardized tests. Teachers whose students do better on the tests would be rewarded while teachers with poorly performing students would be penalized or removed. School principals and administrators would be held accountable for the performance of the entire school in much the same fashion, and in addition the schools' ratings would be publicized so that parents can bring additional pressure on the schools or in some programs by removing their children from underperforming schools. The 2002 revision of the Elementary and Secondary Education Act, popularly known as the No Child Left Behind Act, brought the full force of the federal government behind this approach. This act requires schools that receive federal funding to give annual performance tests to students from the third to eighth grades. Schools that are found deficient are at first given special financial aid to improve, but if they continue to fall below fixed standards, they will then be subject to severe sanctions. Despite the increasing popularity of this approach, troubling questions remain. Many educators are complaining about the rigidity of the federal standards that are being applied to them and the loss of local control. Moreover, as standardized tests are given ever-increasing importance, teachers have been accused of "teaching to the test"—that is, sacrificing the broader goals of education and focusing exclusively on the skills that improve test scores.

Moreover, many educators reject the idea that successful education involves nothing more than teaching students to excel at basic skills. Is it better, they ask, to produce creative, well-adjusted children or to turn out neurotic overachievers who ace standardized tests but lack essential social skills? Obviously, the matter is not that simple, but many alternative approaches hold out a much broader ideal for education. The famous Summerhill "free" school, for example, encourages open expression and democratic principles among its students and allows them to focus their studies on whatever subjects interest them most,[64] and the Waldorf schools place as much importance on art and personal development as on basic academic skills.[65]

Finally, the most radical approach to restructuring our schools is advocated by supporters of the **home schooling** movement, who recommend that parents keep their children home and teach them themselves. Supporters of home schooling are generally critical of the quality of public education and feel that children's parents are likely to give them far more attention and concern than a professional teacher can. These parents also worry about the negative influence that close contact with other schoolchildren may have on their own child, and they object to some of the public school curriculum. Critics of home schooling point out that even though some parents can do an excellent job of educating their own children, others cannot. Moreover, even the best home schooling is likely to provide only a narrow perspective that primarily reflects the personal viewpoints of the parents. These critics say that every child should have the right to hear a much broader range of views and perspectives and that social contact with other schoolchildren is essential for normal social development in our diverse society.

Home schooling ▪ Educating students at home rather than in public or private schools.

BETTER TEACHERS In the long run, nothing is more important to the schools than the quality and dedication of teachers. Recruiting and keeping the best possible faculty is, therefore, a vital task facing our schools. Unfortunately, we have not been doing a good job of it. A report by the National Commission on Teaching and America's Future concluded that one-fourth of the nation's classroom teachers were not fully qualified, and it called the current state of teacher training a "national shame."[66] There is less prestige in being an elementary or secondary teacher than there was in the past; one way to improve the quality of our teachers is to offer a substantial increase in pay to attract and retain high-quality professionals. In 2005, the average salary for an American teacher was only $45,884, far less than most other occupations that require a similar amount of professional training. The United States ranks last among major industrialized nations in how generously it compensates its teachers.[67] One proposal already implemented in some school districts provides additional merit pay for superior teachers. A related approach is to create "master teacher" programs in which a school's best teachers are given extra pay to provide counseling and assistance to other teachers. (See the Personal Perspectives for a firsthand account of some of the problems our teachers face.)

Personal Perspectives

A Junior High School Teacher

Teaching is a rewarding profession, but as we can see from the following account by a male teacher in his 30s, it also can be extremely frustrating.

I love teaching. It's something I've always done and always will do. But the restrictions and expectations and frustrations you have to put up with to be a teacher here are horrific. The lack of support that the students get at home and the lack of support that the teachers get in the system make it so that whatever pleasure you get in a student's progression is overshadowed by the frustrations.

Kids who don't have consistent discipline at home cause problems at school. . . . The more the parents are involved in a child's education, the more everyone can learn. Then teachers don't have to spend all their time on discipline problems. Ideally, a child should come to school ready to learn. Another problem is that the school system doesn't necessarily know how to parent. Some teachers and administrators do the wrong thing. It's a tightrope between doing what's needed and not doing what will get you into trouble. For example, some children who desperately need hugs don't get them because teachers are afraid it could be construed as sexual abuse.

Too little money, however, is not the only problem. Teachers also complain about the frustrations of working within a bureaucracy that is often more concerned about the smooth functioning of its schools than about education. Other sources of discontent are excessive paperwork and the conflict between the demand that teachers be classroom police officers and their need to be educators. It is no surprise, then, that teachers suffer such a high burnout rate. Fewer than one in five new teachers is still in the profession after 10 years.[68]

Even streamlining the bureaucracy and increasing pay will not guarantee that schools can recruit enough top-quality teachers. Success will depend largely on society's attitude toward education. As Tom Hayden, the former chair of the California Assembly's Subcommittee on Higher Education, put it:

> The desire to teach is fostered in a social climate that supports the personal mission of helping others grow, of creating and sharing knowledge and pursuing a higher quality of life. Such values are not promoted in a climate of self-serving shortsightedness that lures people toward the quick fix, the fast buck, and the easy answer. Until a new emphasis on public service and social responsibility arises to balance narrow self-interest, the teaching crisis will remain difficult to resolve.[69]

VALUING LEARNING A strange paradox in American culture underlies many of the educational problems we have discussed in this chapter. Americans place tremendous faith in education in general, but at the same time they don't seem to value learning itself highly. In European countries such as France and Germany, and even more so in Asian countries such as Japan, South Korea, and Taiwan, intellectuals and scholars not only have great prestige but also comprise a powerful political force. The same is often true in less developed countries as well—two of the last four presidents of Mexico, for example, have had PhD's. In the United States, intellectuals are viewed with far more suspicion and kept on the margins of political life. But the problem goes far deeper than just politics. A student who scores at the top of the class in Japan is some kind of a celebrity in school, but the brilliant student in the United States is often seen as something of a "nerd." For the boys, it is the star athletes who win the most admiration, and for the girls it is often those with knockout good looks. International polls also show that Americans read fewer books and newspapers than people in other industrialized nations and are less informed about global events.[70]

In addition to the kinds of new programs and policies we have just discussed, the revitalization of American education will require cultural changes as well. The idea that there is some kind of contradiction between those who think and study and those who take action in the "real world" is nothing but an unfounded prejudice. Most of the world's greatest revolutionary leaders, from Thomas Jefferson to Mao Zedong, have been intellectuals as well. Earning a top score in the SAT is at least as difficult a task as winning a football game, and it is far more likely to lead to a successful career. But aside from any external benefits we may derive from an education, it is vital to recognize the intrinsic rewards of learning itself in enriching our lives and the lives of those around us.

QUICK REVIEW

■ What can we do to give everyone more equal educational opportunities?

■ How can we improve the quality of the education our children receive?

Sociological Perspectives on Problems of Education

There seems to be a virtually endless debate about the deficiencies of our educational system and what to do about them, and because the opposing sides do not even agree about the goals of a good education, the discussion often produces more confusion than consensus. A look at the problems of education from each of the major sociological perspectives can clarify the situation by linking criticisms of the educational system and proposals for change with the broader vision of society from which they arise.

The Functionalist Perspective

Functionalists see education as a basic institution that must meet a growing list of social needs. Originally, the two principal functions of education were to teach students a body of skills and knowledge and to grade them on how well they had mastered their studies. Education also became an important channel for social mobility for talented students from disadvantaged backgrounds. As industrial societies became more diverse and education became virtually universal, the schools took on an increasingly important role in transmitting values and attitudes as well as skills. They also assumed the important **latent** (hidden) **function** of reducing unemployment by keeping many young people out of the labor market. Finally, as the traditional family unit became more unstable, educational institutions were asked to take up some of the slack by launching programs to prevent delinquent behavior and to help deal with students' social and psychological needs. Many functionalists believe our schools have been given so many conflicting tasks that they are unable to do any of them well; as a result, their efforts to achieve one goal often conflict with other goals. For example, the time spent on drug education or "teen skills" can detract from the schools' academic programs, and attempts to modify the curriculum to prevent disadvantaged students from getting discouraged may lower the achievement of more gifted students. Functionalists also complain that many schools have become disorganized because of poor management and a lack of sufficient concern on the part of parents and the community.

Latent function ■ A hidden function performed by a social institution or agency.

All functionalists do not agree on how to make schools more effective, however. Many advocate the elimination of some of the new programs that have been introduced in recent years. Although such changes might well improve fundamental education, they are also likely to disrupt efforts to deal with other pressing social problems. Proposals for employing more effective teaching methods are also compatible with the functionalist perspective, but most functionalists argue that such reforms can work only if accompanied by a reorganization of the schools. For example, teachers must be rewarded for good teaching rather than for being efficient bureaucrats or for the length of time they have spent on the job. Finally, many functionalists advocate better planning and coordination with other social institutions in order to reduce the problem of unemployment and underemployment among the educated. But such a program must be combined with an effort to reduce the instability of our economic institutions because it is extremely difficult to train students to meet the needs of an economy that is in a state of rapid and unpredictable flux.

Schools do much more than teach reading, writing, and arithmetic. One of their most important functions is to provide for students' social and recreational needs.

The Conflict Perspective

Conflict theorists are not convinced that providing equal opportunity and encouraging upward mobility for the poor have ever been goals of our educational system. Rather, they argue that the schools are organized to do just the opposite: to keep members of subordinate groups in their place and prevent them from competing with members of more privileged classes. They point to the fact that free public education for all children is a relatively new idea and that even today many poor children must drop out of school to help support their families. Moreover, expensive private schools provide a superior education for children from the upper classes, whereas the public schools that serve the poor are underfunded, understaffed, and neglected. Conflict theorists

Bonnie Kamin/PhotoEdit Inc.

also argue that the old system of officially segregated education and the current system of de facto segregation serve to keep oppressed minorities at the bottom of the social heap. Their general conclusion is that the social and cultural biases in the educational system are not an accident but reflect a social system that favors the powerful.

Conflict theorists also see the schools as powerful agents of socialization that can be used as a tool for one group to exercise its cultural dominance over another. For example, they argue that by demanding that all students learn English, U.S. schools serve to perpetuate the domination of those from one linguistic background over those from all the others.

From the conflict perspective, the best and perhaps the only way to change these conditions is for the poor and minorities to organize themselves and reshape the educational system so that it provides everyone with equal opportunity but does not indoctrinate students in the cultural values and beliefs of any particular group. All children must be given the same quality of education that is now available in private schools; cash subsidies must be provided for poor students who would otherwise be forced to drop out of school; and special programs must be set up to provide extra help for children whose parents have weak educational backgrounds. Nevertheless, most conflict theorists probably agree with Christopher Jencks, who concluded that the educational system can do little to reduce inequality without changes in the broader society. Even if there were complete educational equality and everyone were given a college education, social and economic disparities would remain. Such changes would not produce more interesting, highly paid professional jobs or reduce the number of menial, low-paying ones. Thus, educational and social change must be carried out together.

The Feminist Perspective

Feminists are deeply concerned about the role of the schools in perpetuating gender stereotypes and failing to encourage the highest possible academic achievement from female students. From a feminist standpoint, an effective school system needs to do more than just eliminate obvious gender and ethnic discrimination: It needs to be an active agent for social change—encouraging full gender equality, not just in academic performance but also in our social relationships.

Another feminist priority is to ensure that our children are in schools where they feel safe no matter what their gender, sexual orientation, or ethnic heritage. They understand that learning cannot occur when a student feels marginalized and threatened. From this standpoint, it is important that prejudice, discrimination, and bullying behavior are eradicated from the schools. Feminists urge students and their parents to demand an end to this kind of behavior and take a stand, strong and firm, against the type of brush-off that they often receive from school administrators. They argue that administrators must be held accountable to enforce the laws that have been passed to prevent children from being marginalized and abused.

Many feminists also view the schools in the context of our broader social problems, and they see a vital role for the schools in helping relieve some of the enormous pressures on today's families. The standard of a six-hour school day for nine months of the year fit well with the rhythms of the farm, when children were needed as laborers during the summer harvest season and there was always somebody home after school. But in most of today's families, either both parents work or there is only a single parent in the home. So some feminists call for a new style of school that stays open 12 or 14 hours a day year-round, providing not only more academic work but also recreational and social programs. Feminists argue that such a program could improve the stability of our families, the security of our parents, and the academic achievement of our children.

The Interactionist Perspective

Interactionists are concerned with the vital role the schools play in shaping the way their students see reality. Many have commented on the possibility that the authoritarianism so common in our schools impedes learning and encourages undemocratic behavior in later life. Moreover, schools create serious difficulties for students who for one reason or another do not fit into the educational system. The schools show their students a world in which individual competition and achievement is of central importance, and this heavy emphasis on competition and the consequent fear of failure are disturbing to those students who are already anxious and insecure. Students who do not do well in school are often troubled by feelings of depression and inadequacy, and the failure to live up to the academic expectations of parents and teachers is a major contributor to teenage suicide. Many alternative schools, such as Summerhill and Waldorf, attempt to improve this socialization process by deemphasizing competition for grades and placing more importance on enhancing self-esteem. Of course, some children do poorly in such an environment and benefit from a great deal of discipline and an emphasis on obedience to authority. Authoritarian environments may, however, impede the ability of other children to learn and to function effectively; thus, it seems logical to provide the greatest possible range of educational alternatives so that the needs of each student can be met.

The finding that teachers' expectations have a huge influence on student achievement comes as no surprise to interactionists. Interactionists have long known that our behavior is shaped by the way we define the world, so if students are made to feel like high achievers, they will act like high achievers. Interactionists, therefore, call for teacher-training programs to encourage teachers to understand the critical importance of their role in influencing a student's view of the world, and they urge teachers to avoid branding students with negative labels that often become self-fulfilling prophecies.

QUICK REVIEW

- What would a functionalist, a conflict theorist, a feminist, and an interactionist say about the problems of our educational system? ✗
- Which approach do you think is most useful?

Summary

Education was originally reserved for the elite. Today, however, it has become a big business, employing millions of teachers and administrators. Children from the lower classes generally do not do as well in school as children from the middle and upper classes. Poor children usually come to school with a variety of economic and cultural handicaps, and the school system discriminates against these children in many ways. Racial and ethnic discrimination in the U.S. educational system goes back to the days of slavery. Since the Supreme Court's decision outlawing school segregation, most legal (de jure) discrimination has been abolished. However, de facto (actual) segregation arising from segregated housing patterns is still widespread. In the same way that schools have helped to perpetuate ethnic inequality, they have often served to promote gender inequality.

Schools are always struggling to deal with the twin problems of authority and rebellion. If schools lack discipline, students run wild and education suffers; but if discipline is too strict, students learn antidemocratic values and attitudes, and rebellion and delinquency may increase. There is also great concern about the quality of our educational system given the ever-growing need for an educated population. Some critics argue that the tests that show relatively poor educational achievement are not good measures of educational quality, others claim that the problem lies in the changing family environment of today's students, and still others hold the schools themselves responsible.

Many proposals for creating more equal education have been offered. These include programs to achieve more effective integration, give special assistance to poor and minority students, and promote gender equality, as well as reforms in school financing. Suggestions for improving the educational process itself include raising academic standards and requiring more homework, lengthening the school year, restructuring the schools to give teachers and local administrators more power, making education a more attractive career so that schools can hire better teachers, and increasing the cultural value we place on learning.

Functionalists argue that the educational system is not running smoothly and that solving the problems of education is mostly a matter of reorganizing schools so that they will operate more efficiently. Conflict theorists are prone to look beyond the stated goals of the educational system and argue that economic and political elites use the schools to help maintain the status quo and the privileges those groups enjoy. Feminists argue that the schools need to actively promote gender equality and institute programs to help relieve some of the pressure on today's families. Interactionists are concerned with the way the schools help shape their students' views of reality and with the harmful impact that negative labeling and an excessive emphasis on competition can have.

QUESTIONS FOR CRITICAL THINKING

Take a critical look at your own education. Were you one of the privileged students, or did you suffer from some kind of educational disadvantage? How good an education do you think you have received so far? How would you compare the quality of your education with that of a typical American student? This chapter discussed many different problems in our educational system. Which ones did you encounter in your own education?

KEY TERMS

affirmative action program	desegregation	magnet schools
authoritarianism	Ebonics	prep schools
compensatory education	functionally illiterate	resegregation
programs	goal displacement	segregated schools
cultural capital	hidden curriculum	sexism
de facto segregation	home schooling	Standard English
de jure segregation	latent function	voucher system

INTERNET EXERCISE

Because of the importance of education in modern societies and because of the many changes and problems in educational institutions today, there are many governmental and nonprofit organizations with Websites about education in the United States and other countries around the world. To begin your exploration of these Websites, go to the *Companion Website*™ at www.pearsonhighered.com/coleman. Enter Chapter 3 and choose the Web destination module from the navigation bar.

Visit the U.S. Census Bureau at www.census.gov, and find the latest report on educational attainment in the United States.

The report is compiled each year in the U.S. Census Bureau's Current Population Reports, which can be found by clicking "C" in the alphabetical index. Once you are in Current Population Reports, locate "P20 Population Characteristics," and find tables providing information about the highest degree obtained by people over 25 years of age and for people 25 years to 29 years of age in the United States. These tables also show differences among men and women in educational attainment.

What do these figures tell us about the level of education in the general U.S. population? What do these figures tell us about differences in educational attainment between men and women in the United States in recent years? What are the likely outcomes of the differences in educational attainment between men and women for the future of gender inequality in the United States?

NOTES

1. Romesh Ratnesar, "Class-Size Warfare," *Time*, October 6, 1997, p. 85.
2. U.S. Bureau of the Census, *Statistical Abstract of the United States, 2003* (Washington, DC: U.S. Government Printing Office, 2003), p. 850.
3. U.S. Bureau of the Census, *Statistical Abstract of the United States, 1996* (Washington, DC: U.S. Government Printing Office, 1996), p. 158.

4. Quoted in Mavis Hiltunen Biesanz and John Biesanz, *Introduction to Sociology*, 2nd ed. (Upper Saddle River, NJ: Prentice Hall, 1973), p. 616.

5. See Pamela Barnhouse Walters and Richard Rubinson, "Educational Expansion and Economic Output in the United States, 1890–1969," *American Sociological Review* 48 (1983): 480.

6. See Harold R. Kerbo, *Social Stratification and Inequality*, 4th ed. (New York: McGraw-Hill, 2000), pp. 362–365.

7. Robert James Parelius and Ann Parker Parelius, *The Sociology of Education*, 2nd ed. (Upper Saddle River, NJ: Prentice Hall, 1987), p. 265.

8. U.S. Bureau of the Census, *Statistical Abstract of the United States, 2006* (Washington, DC: U.S. Government Printing Office, 2006), Table 249.

9. See S. Leonard Syme and Lisa F. Berkman, "Social Class, Susceptibility and Sickness," in Howard D. Schwartz, ed., *Dominant Issues in Medical Sociology*, 2nd ed. (New York: Random House, 1987), pp. 643–649.

10. Kerbo, *Social Stratification and Inequality*, pp. 359–361.

11. U.S. Bureau of the Census, *Statistical Abstract of the United States, 2006*, Table 222.

12. U.S. Bureau of the Census, *Statistical Abstract, 1996*, p. 170.

13. William Celis III, "Michigan Votes for Revolution in Financing Its Public Schools," *The New York Times*, March 17, 1994, pp. A1, A9; Bob Secter, "Gaps Between Rich, Poor Schools Ignite Legal Fights," *Los Angeles Times*, November 26, 1990, pp. A1, A20.

14. James S. Coleman et al., *Equality of Educational Opportunity* (Washington, DC: U.S. Government Printing Office, 1966); Christopher Jencks et al., *Inequality: A Reassessment of the Effects of Family and Schooling in America* (New York: HarperCollins, 1972); Harvey A. Averch et al., *How Effective Is Schooling: A Critical Synthesis and Review of Research Findings* (Upper Saddle River, NJ: Prentice Hall, 1974); Samuel Bowles and Herbert Gintis, *Schooling in Capitalist America* (New York: Basic Books, 1976).

15. Elizabeth Ross, "A Leveling of Granite State Schools," *Christian Science Monitor*, March 14, 1994, p. 10.

16. U.S. Bureau of the Census, *Statistical Abstract of the United States, 2003*, p. 189.

17. Lawrence Mishel and Jared Bernstein, *The State of Working America, 1992–93* (Armonk, NY: M. E. Sharpe, 1993), p. 374.

18. U.S. Bureau of the Census, *Statistical Abstract, 2006*, Table 225.

19. See Parelius and Parelius, *The Sociology of Education*, pp. 293–296.

20. Robert Rosenthal and Lenore Jacobson, *Pygmalion in the Classroom* (New York: HarperCollins, 1969).

21. See Roy Nash, *Teacher Expectations and Pupil Learning* (London: Routledge & Kegan Paul, 1976); Parelius and Parelius, *The Sociology of Education*, pp. 293–296.

22. D. G. Harvey and G. T. Slatin, "The Relationship Between a Child's SES and Teacher Expectations," *Social Forces* 54 (1975): 140–159.

23. Kerbo, *Social Stratification and Inequality*, pp. 138–139, 232–233, 363.

24. See Jeannie Oakes, *Multiplying Inequalities* (Santa Monica, CA: Rand Corporation, 1990); Kerbo, *Social Stratification and Inequality*, pp. 362–363.

25. Karl Alexander, Martha Cook, and Edward L. Dill, "Curriculum Tracking and Educational Stratification," *American Sociological Review* 43 (1978): 47–66.

26. William Celis III, "Study Finds Rising Concentration of Black and Hispanic Students," *The New York Times*, December 14, 1993, pp. A1, A11; William J. Eaton, "Segregation in U.S. Schools on Rise, Study Finds," *Los Angeles Times*, December 14, 1993, pp. A1, A22.

27. Coleman et al., *Equality of Educational Opportunity*.

28. Rita E. Mahard and Robert L. Crain, "Research on Minority Achievement in Desegregated Schools," in Christine H. Rossell and Willis D. Hawley, eds., *The Consequences of School Desegregation* (Philadelphia: Temple University Press, 1983), pp. 103–125.

29. See Janet Eyler, Valerie J. Cook, and Leslie E. Ward, "Resegregation: Segregation Within Desegregated Schools," in Rossell and Hawley, *The Consequences of School Desegregation*, pp. 126–162.

30. U.S. Department of Education, *National Assessment of Educational Progress* (Washington, DC: U.S. Government Printing Office, 2000).

31. U.S. Bureau of the Census, *Statistical Abstract, 2006*, Table 214.

32. Ibid., Table 288.

33. U.S. Bureau of the Census, *Statistical Abstract, 2003*, p. 192.

34. See, Richard Lee Colvin, "14% of Students Have Carried Weapon to School, Study Says," *Los Angeles Times*, March 10, 1997, pp. B1, B3.

35. Phillip Kaufman et al., *Indicators of School Crime and Safety 1998* (Washington, DC: National Center for Educational Statistics, October 1998); U.S. Bureau of the Census, *Statistical Abstract, 1999* (Washington, DC: U.S. Government Printing Office), p. 221.

36. U.S. Bureau of the Census, *Statistical Abstract, 2003*, p. 174.

37. Tamar Lewin, "School Codes Without Mercy Snare Pupils Without Malice," *The New York Times*, March 12, 1997, pp. A1, A13.

38. See John Devine, *Maximum Security* (Chicago: University of Chicago Press, 1996).

39. Irwin S. Kirsch, Ann Jungeblut, Lynn Jenkins, and Andrew Kolstad, *Adult Literacy in America: A First Look at the Results of the National Literacy Survey* (Washington, DC: Department of Education, 1993).

40. Kirsch et al., *Adult Literacy*.

41. U.S. Bureau of the Census, *Statistical Abstract, 2006*, Table 254.

42. U.S. Bureau of the Census, *Statistical Abstract, 2003*, p. 175.

43. U.S. Bureau of the Census, *Statistical Abstract, 2006*, Table 1322.

44. William Celis III, "International Report Card Shows U.S. Schools Work," *The New York Times*, December 9, 1993, pp. A1, A8; Andrew L. Shapiro, *We're Number One: Where America Stands and Falls in the New World Order* (New York: Vintage, 1992), pp. 64–69.

45. Stanley Meisler, "Americans Get No Gold Stars for Current Events Answers," *Los Angeles Times*, March 16, 1994, p. A9.

46. Louis B. Gerstner, Jr., "Our Schools Are Failing. Do We Care?" *The New York Times*, May 27, 1994, p. A15.

47. National Commission on Education and Learning, *Prisoners of Time* (Washington, DC: U.S. Government Printing Office, April 1994).

48. Robert J. Samuelson, "Why School Reform Fails," *Newsweek*, May 27, 1991, pp. 62, 68.

49. Applebome, "U.S. Gets Average Grades in Math and Science Studies."

50. Shapiro, *We're Number One*, p. 71.

51. Parelius and Parelius, *The Sociology of Education*, pp. 334–335.

52. William Celis III, "Study Suggests Head Start Helps Beyond School," *The New York Times*, April 20, 1993, p. A9; see also John R. Berrueta-Clement et al., *Changed Lives: The Effects of the Perry Preschool Program on Youths Through Age 19* (Ypsilanti, MI: High/Scope, 1984).

53. David G. Savage, "U.S. School Aid: Looking for Results," *Los Angeles Times*, April 11, 1985, sec. 1, p. 1.

54. For an exception to this rule, see Berrueta-Clement et al., *Changed Lives*.

55. Seymour Martin Lipset, *American Exceptionalism: A Double-Edged Sword* (New York: Norton, 1996), pp. 125–131.

56. See *International Herald Tribune*, October 11, 2000.

57. Michael Rutter, *15,000 Hours: Secondary Schools and Their Effect on Children* (Cambridge, MA: Harvard University Press, 1979).

58. James S. Coleman, Thomas Hoffer, and Sally Kilgore, *High School Achievement: Public, Catholic and Private Schools* (New York: Basic Books, 1982), p. 178.

59. Shapiro, *We're Number One*, p. 60; Michael J. Barrett, "The Case for More School Days," *Atlantic*, November 1990, pp. 78–106.

60. Dennis Kelly, "Panel: Extend School Year," *USA Today*, May 5, 1994, p. 53A; U.S. Department of Education, *National Assessment of Educational Progress*.

61. Tom Morganthau, "The Future Is Now," *Newsweek*, Special Edition on Education, Fall–Winter 1990, pp. 72–76.

62. David L. Kirp, "What School Choice Really Means," *Atlantic Monthly*, November 1992, pp. 119–132.

63. Associated Press, "Baltimore Ends School Privatization Experiment," *San Luis Obispo Telegram-Tribune*, November 23, 1995, p. A6; George Judson, "Improved Schools at a Profit: Is a Private Effort Working?" *The New York Times*, November 14, 1994, pp. A1, A12; William Celis III, "Hopeful Start for Profit Making Schools," *The New York Times*, October 6, 1993, pp. A1, B3.

64. A. S. Neil, *Summerhill: A Radical Approach to Child Rearing* (New York: Hart, 1960).

65. Ronald E. Kotzsch, "Waldorf Schools: Education for Head, Hands, and Heart," *Utne Reader*, September–October 1990, pp. 84–90.

66. Elaine Woo, "Study Calls Poor Teacher Training a 'National Shame,'" *Los Angeles Times*, May 26, 1997, pp. A1, A5.

67. U.S. Bureau of the Census, *Statistical Abstract, 2006*, Table 241; Shapiro, *We're Number One*, p. 63.

68. Jonathan H. Mark and Barry Anderson, "Teacher Survival Rates: A Current Look," *American Journal of Educational Research* 15 (1978): 379–383.

69. Tom Hayden, "Running Short of Good Teachers," *Los Angeles Times*, June 24, 1983, sec. 2, p. 5.

70. See Shapiro, *We're Number One*.

Problems in Education

Thinking Sociologically

- What factors have contributed to your success in school? Have you also experienced problems that caused you to fall short of some of your objectives?

- Major sociological perspectives differ on problems related to education. What are the major causes, effects, and possible solutions for problems in today's schools according to each of these approaches?

- How do race, class, and gender affect people's educational opportunities?

((•—[**Listen** to the **Chapter Audio** on **mysoclab.com**

When we were in junior high school, my friend Rich and I made a map of the school lunch tables according to popularity. This was easy to do, because kids only ate lunch with others of about the same popularity. We graded them from A to E. "A" tables were full of football players and cheerleaders and so on. "E" tables contained the kinds with mild cases of Down's syndrome, which in the language of the time we called "retards."

We sat at a "D" table, as low as you could get without looking physically different. We were not being especially candid to grade ourselves as D. . . . Everyone in the school knew exactly how popular everyone else was, including us. . . . I know a lot of people who were nerds in school, and they all tell the same story: there is a strong correlation between being smart and being a nerd, and an even stronger inverse correlation between being a nerd and being popular. Being smart seems to make you unpopular. . . . And that, I think, is the root of the problem. Nerds serve two masters. They want to be popular, certainly, but they want even more to be smart. And popularity is not something you can do in your spare time, not in the fiercely competitive environment of an American secondary [middle and high] school. . . . Merely understanding the situation [nerds are in] should make it less painful. Nerds aren't losers. They're just playing a different game, and a game much closer to the one played in the real world.

—Paul Graham (PhD in computer science from Harvard, designer of ARC language, and creator of Yahoo Store) describes in his recent book, Hackers & Painters: Big Ideas from the Computer Age *(2004), how he and other "nerds" have become successful as adults, an accomplishment that he does not attribute to American public schools.*

Most of us have memories about our junior high and high school years that include where we thought we fit in to the student pecking order. Often this hierarchy or pecking order was symbolized by the people we ate with and where we sat at lunch because this was one brief period in the school day when we were allowed to make personal choices about our interactions with other people. Individuals like Paul Graham remember the school hierarchy as being based on athletic ability, personal appearance, and one's general popularity while others remember their cafeteria as having enclaves where students "chose" to sit with others from their own racial or ethnic category (see Tatum, 2003). At the individual level (microlevel), some people realize that their school's social environment did not mesh with their personal interests and aptitudes while others describe their school years as being among the best in their lives. At the societal level (macrolevel), sociologists who study *education*—**the social institution responsible for transmitting knowledge, skills, and cultural values in a formally organized structure**—are particularly interested in factors that contribute to the success of schools and problems that cause them to fall short of their ideals and objectives. Today, we have a wide gap between the ideals of U.S. education and the realities of daily life in many schools. As a result, many business and political leaders, parents, teachers, students, and other concerned citizens identify a number of problems with U.S. education. In this chapter, we examine contemporary problems in education and assess how these problems are intertwined with other social problems in the United States and worldwide. We'll begin with an overview of sociological perspectives on problems in education.

DID YOU KNOW

- Fourteen percent of U.S. adults (about 30 million people) do not read well enough to fill out a job application.

- A higher percentage of secondary school teachers are threatened with injury by students, but a higher percentage of elementary school teachers are actually physically attached by students.

- The average cost of center-based child care is higher than the average cost of public university tuition in a majority of U.S. states.

- Parents' level of education is a stronger predictor of students' standardized test scores than the amount of public money spent on education.

SOCIOLOGICAL PERSPECTIVES ON EDUCATION

The way in which a sociologist studies education depends on the theoretical perspective he or she takes. Functionalists, for example, believe that schools should promote good citizenship and upward mobility and that problems in education are related to social disorganization, rapid social change, and the organizational structure of schools. Conflict theorists believe that schools perpetuate inequality and that problems in education are the result of bias based on race, class, and gender. Meanwhile, interactionists focus on microlevel problems in schools, such as how communication and teachers' expectations affect students' levels of achievement and dropout rates.

Functionalist Perspectives

Functionalists believe that education is one of the most important social institutions because it contributes to the smooth functioning of society and provides individuals with opportunities for personal fulfillment and upward social mobility. According to functionalists, when problems occur, they can usually be traced to the failure of educational institutions—schools, colleges, universities—to fulfill one of their manifest functions. **Manifest functions are open, stated, and intended goals or consequences of activities within an organization or institution.** Although the most obvious manifest function of education is the teaching of academic subjects (reading, writing, mathematics, science, and history), education has at least five major manifest functions in society:

Socialization. From kindergarten through college, schools teach students the student role, specific academic subjects, and political socialization. In kindergarten, children learn the appropriate attitudes and behavior for the student role (Ballantine and Hammack, 2009). In primary and secondary schools, students are taught specific subject matter that is appropriate to their age, skill level, and previous educational experience. At the college level, students expand their knowledge and seek out new areas of study. Throughout, students learn the democratic process.

Transmission of culture. Schools transmit cultural norms and values to each new generation and play a major role in assimilation, the process whereby recent immigrants learn dominant cultural values, attitudes, and behavior so that they can be productive members of society.

Social control. Although controversy exists over whose values should be taught, schools are responsible for teaching values such as discipline, respect, obedience, punctuality, and perseverance. Schools teach conformity by encouraging young people to be good students, conscientious future workers, and law-abiding citizens.

Social placement. Schools are responsible for identifying the most qualified people to fill available positions in society. Students are often channeled into programs on the basis of their individual ability and academic achievement. Graduates receive the appropriate credentials for entering the paid labor force

Change and innovation. Schools are a source of change and innovation. To meet the needs of student populations at particular times, new programs—such as HIV/AIDS education, computer education, and multicultural studies—are created. College and university faculty members are expected to conduct research and publish new knowledge that benefits the overall society. A major goal of change and innovation in education is to reduce social problems.

In addition to these manifest functions, education fulfills a number of *latent functions*—**hidden, unstated, and sometimes unintended consequences of activities in an organization or institution.** Consider, for example, these latent functions of education: Compulsory school attendance keeps children and teenagers off the streets (and, by implication, out of trouble) and out of the full-time job market for a number of years (controlling the flow of workers). High schools and colleges serve as matchmaking institutions where people often meet future marriage partners. By bringing people of similar ages, racial and ethnic groups, and social class backgrounds together, schools establish social networks.

Functionalists acknowledge many dysfunctions in education, but one seems overriding today: Our public schools are not adequately preparing students for jobs and global competition. In comparative rankings of students across countries on standardized reading, mathematics, and science tests, U.S. students are lagging. However, the current state of the U.S. economy, including high rates of unemployment and low levels of job creation, also contribute to this problem in many regions of the country.

Functionalist and conservative efforts to improve education were introduced during the first term of the Bush administration. To reform education, President George W. Bush signed into law the No Child Left Behind (NCLB) Act of 2001. Proponents of this law hoped to improve education for the nation's children by changing the federal government's role in kindergarten through twelfth grade and by asking schools to be accountable for students' learning. Several critical steps were set forth to produce a more "accountable" education system:

- States created a set of standards—beginning with math and reading—for what all children should know at the end of each grade in school; other standards would be developed over a period of time.
- States were required to test every student's progress toward meeting those standards.
- States, individual school districts, and individual schools are all expected to make yearly progress toward meeting the standards.
- School districts must report results regarding the progress of individual schools toward meeting these standards.
- Schools and districts that do not make adequate progress are to be held accountable and could lose funding and pupils; in some cases, parents can move their children from low-performing schools to schools that are meeting the standards.

After the 2008 presidential election, NCLB was subsequently opposed by the Obama administration; however, the end products of this act remain in effect in the nation's schools. During the NCLB era, some improvements were made in fourth- and eighth-grade reading and math scores nationwide, particularly among African American and Hispanic students. However, critics believed that NCLB did not accurately address the main problems facing U.S. education—lack of money and lack of incentives for teaching and learning, not more testing of students and teachers.

In 2010, the Obama administration issued "A Blueprint for Reform" in an effort to reauthorize the Elementary and Secondary Education Act, an initiative that had been in place prior to the NCLB era. Four major priorities were included in this blueprint:

1. Improving teacher and principal effectiveness to ensure that every classroom has a great teacher and every school has a great leader
2. Providing information to families to help them evaluate and improve their children's schools, and to educators to help them improve their students' learning

3. Implementing college- and career-ready standards and developing improved assessments aligned with those standards
4. Improving student learning and achievement in America's lowest-performing schools by providing intensive support and effective interventions (U.S. Department of Education, 2010)

Overall, the plan's purpose is to produce greater equity and opportunity for all students. A "Race to the Top" in education, built on the American Recovery and Reinvestment Act of 2009, was supposed to provide additional competitive grants to expand innovations in education, support effective charter schools, promote public school choice, and provide assistance to magnet schools. However, with the United States facing financial crises at home and international problems abroad, the national political climate has not been conducive to adding more money to overburdened state and local school budgets. Consequently, even with those with a functionalist/conservative perspective highlighting the importance of education, it remains difficult to determine if progress will be made in improving schools through the Obama plan or similar proposals in the future. Critics claim such plans cannot be adequately funded in difficult economic times and that these blueprints for change are usually too ambitious.

Conflict Perspectives

Sociologists using a conflict framework for analyzing problems in education believe that schools—which are supposed to reduce social inequalities in society—actually perpetuate inequalities based on class, race, and gender (Apple, 1982). In fact, conflict theorists such as Pierre Bourdieu argue that education *reproduces* existing class relationships (see Bourdieu and Passeron, 1990). According to Bourdieu, students have differing amounts of *cultural capital* that they learn at home and bring with them to the classroom. Children from middle- and upper-income homes have considerable cultural capital because their parents have taught them about books, art, music, and other forms of culture. According to Bourdieu, children from low-income and poverty-level families have not had the same opportunities to acquire cultural capital. Some social analysts believe that it is students' cultural capital, rather than their "natural" intelligence or aptitude, that is measured on the standardized tests used for tracking. Thus, test results unfairly limit some students' academic choices and career opportunities (Oakes, 1985).

Other sociologists using the conflict framework focus on problems associated with the hidden curriculum, a term coined by sociologist John C. Holt (1964) in his study of why children fail. The **hidden curriculum refers to how certain cultural values and attitudes, such as conformity and obedience to authority, are transmitted through implied demands in the everyday rules and routines of schools** (B. R. Snyder, 1971). These conflict theorists suggest that elites use a hidden curriculum that teaches students to be obedient and patriotic—values that uphold the status quo in society and turn students into compliant workers—to manipulate the masses and maintain their power in society.

Although students from all social classes experience the hidden curriculum to some degree, studies in the past have shown that working-class and poverty-level students are the most adversely affected (Ballantine and Hammack, 2009). According to these studies, when middle-class teachers teach students from lower-class backgrounds, the classrooms are more structured, and teachers have lower expectations of students. Studies have also shown that schools that primarily serve upper-middle and upper-class families primarily focus on developing students' analytical powers and critical thinking skills, such as teaching them how to apply abstract principles to problem solving. These schools also emphasize creative activities so that students can express their own ideas and apply them to different areas of study. By contrast, schools for children from working-class and poverty-level families tend to spend much more time each day on disciplinary procedures and remedial programs to help students catch up and make higher scores on standardized tests. From the conflict approach, the hidden curriculum teaches working-class and poverty-level students that they are expected to arrive on time, follow bureaucratic rules, take orders from others, and to endure boredom without complaining (Ballantine and Hammack, 2009). The limitations on what and how these students are taught mean that many of them do not get any higher education and therefore never receive the credentials to enter high-paying professions. Our society emphasizes *credentialism*—a process of social selection that gives class advantage and social status to people who possess academic qualifications (R. Collins, 1979).

Credentialism is closely related to *meritocracy*—a social system in which status is assumed to be acquired through individual ability and effort (Young, 1994). People who acquire the appropriate credentials for a job are assumed to have gained the position through what they know, not who they are or who they know. According to conflict theorists, however, the hidden curriculum determines in advance that credentials will stay in the hands of the elites, so the United States is not a meritocracy even if it calls itself one.

Symbolic Interactionist Perspectives

Whereas functionalists examine the relationship between the functions of education and problems in schools and conflict theorists focus on how education perpetuates inequality, symbolic interactionists study classroom dynamics and how practices such as labeling affect students' self-concept and aspirations.

Symbolic interactionists believe that education is an integral part of the socialization process. Through the formal structure of schools and interpersonal relationships with peers and teachers, students develop a concept of self that lasts long beyond their schooling. Overall, social interactions in school can be either positive or negative. When students learn, develop, and function effectively, their experience is positive. For many students, however, the school environment and peer group interactions leave them discouraged and unhappy. When students who might do better with some assistance from teachers and peers are instead labeled "losers," they might come to view themselves as losers and thus set the stage for *self-fulfilling* prophecies. A self-fulfilling prophecy occurs when an unsubstantiated belief or prediction results in behavior that makes the original false belief come true. Past studies have shown that teachers who distinguish among children based on perceived levels of intelligence do create self-fulfilling prophecies in children who typically perform according to how the teacher has treated them: The allegedly "bright" children do extremely well and become successes, and the other children are labeled as underachievers or failures.

Standardized tests can also lead to labeling, self-fulfilling prophecies, and low self-esteem. In fact, say symbolic interactionists, standardized tests such as IQ (intelligence quotient) tests particularly disadvantage racial, ethnic, and language minorities in the United States. IQ testing first became an issue in the United States in the early 1900s when immigrants from countries such as Italy, Poland, and Russia typically scored lower than immigrants from northern Europe did. As a result, teachers did not expect them to do as well as children from families with northern European backgrounds and therefore did not encourage them or help them overcome educational obstacles (Feagin, Baker, and Feagin, 2006). In time, these ethnic groups became stigmatized as less intelligent.

Today, the debate over intelligence continues, but the focus has shifted to African Americans. In their highly controversial book *The Bell Curve: Intelligence and Class Structure in American Life*, Richard J. Herrnstein and Charles Murray (1994) argue that intelligence is genetically inherited and people cannot be "smarter" than they are born to be, regardless of their environment or education. According to Herrnstein and Murray, certain racial-ethnic groups differ in average IQ and are likely to differ in "intelligence genes" as well. To bolster their arguments, Herrnstein and Murray point out that on average, people living in Asia score higher on IQ tests than white Americans and that African Americans score 15 points lower on average than white Americans.

👁 **Watch** on **mysoclab.com**

Inequities in Education
on **mysoclab.com**

Many scholars have refuted Herrnstein and Murray's conclusions, but the idea of inherited mental superiority and inferiority tends to take on a life of its own when some people want to believe that such differences exist (Duster, 1995; Hauser, 1995; H. F. Taylor, 1995). In 2008, the British psychologist Richard Lynn's *The Global Bell Curve: Race, IQ, and Inequality Worldwide*, expanded the ideas of Herrnstein and Murray to include the nations of the world. According to Lynn, in multiracial nations, people of Jewish and east Asian ancestry have the highest average IQ scores and socioeconomic positions, followed by whites, south Asians, Hispanics, and people of African descent. Lynn attributes people's positions in the socioeconomic hierarchy to differences in intelligence on the basis of race-ethnicity. Today, so-called IQ fundamentalists continue to label students and others on the basis of IQ tests, claiming that these tests measure some identifiable trait that predicts the quality of people's thinking and their ability to perform. By contrast, critics of IQ tests argue that these exams measure a number of factors—including motivation, home environment, type of socialization at home, and quality of schooling—not intelligence alone (Yong, 2011). But, perhaps the most important criticism of IQ testing is how this practice can lead to the self-fulfilling prophecy for individuals. According to symbolic interactionists, labels about intelligence and other innate characteristics stigmatize students and *marginalize* them—put people at the lower or outer limits of a group—in their interactions with parents, teachers, and other students, and lead to self-fulfilling prophecies. Likewise, students who are labeled as having above-average intellectual ability, academic aptitude, creative or productive thinking, or leadership skills may achieve at a higher level because of the label.

PROBLEMS IN U.S. EDUCATION

Although we have already identified a variety of problems in education, other issues must be addressed in planning for the future of this country. These issues include the problem of illiteracy; the impact of high rates of immigration on educational systems; race, class, and gender inequalities in educational opportunities; and growing concerns about violence in schools.

Functional Illiteracy

In her memoir *Life Is Not a Fairy Tale*, Fantasia Barrino, a popular U.S. singer and former *American Idol* winner, explained that she is functionally illiterate and that she had to fake her way through portions of the televised talent show that required her to read lines. The story of her life was dictated to a freelance writer, but she committed herself to learning how to read because she wants to be able to read to her daughter. Moreover, Fantasia Barrino's situation is not an isolated case. People were shocked with a recent study by the National Institute for Literacy found that about 47 percent of adults in Detroit, Michigan, are *functionally illiterate—* **unable to read and/or write at the skill level necessary for carrying out everyday tasks**. Although similar studies have not been conducted throughout the United States in recent years, functional illiteracy remains a problem in many cities.

It is estimated that as many as 30 million people over age sixteen (which would be 14 percent of the U.S. adult population) do not read well enough to fill out a job application or understand a newspaper story with an eighth-grade reading level (ProLiteracy.org, 2010). Higher rates of functional illiteracy typically are found in areas with higher percentages of minority and immigrant populations. This may be partly due to larger, underlying social problems, such as high rates of poverty and lack of available resources to help people gain a better education. Especially telling is the fact that more than 60 percent of inmates in state and federal correctional facilities can barely read and write (ProLiteracy.org, 2010).

Illiteracy is a social problem that we may be able to reduce with adequate time and resources. Various organizations seek to reduce illiteracy by offering classes to help children and adults learn how to read and write.

Some social analysts believe that illiteracy will not be as big a problem in the future because new technologies will make reading and writing as we know it obsolete. These analysts note that the information age increasingly depends on communication by computers and other smart machines, not on basic reading and math computation skills. Still other educators and community leaders believe that illiteracy can be overcome through televised instruction in basic skills and courses on the Internet. However, not all social analysts believe that technology is the answer: Knowing how to read the printed word remains the access route to every other form of intellectual information. People need basic literacy skills before they can benefit from computers and other information technologies. Business and industry are now playing a role in solving the problem. Some critics say that the illiteracy problem is largely an immigration problem. Recent immigrants to this country continue to speak their own languages rather than learn English. However, high rates of illiteracy should not necessarily be blamed on U.S. immigration policies because many persons who have lived in this country since birth have this problem.

Immigration and Increasing Diversity in Schools

Debates over the role of schools in educating immigrants for life in the United States are not new. In fact, high rates of immigration—along with the rapid growth of industrial capitalism and the factory system during the Industrial Revolution—brought about the free public school movement in the second half of the nineteenth century. Many immigrants arriving in U.S. cities during this time spoke no English and could neither read nor write. Because of the belief that democracy requires an educated citizenry, schools were charged with the responsibility of "Americanizing" immigrants and their children. Workers needed basic reading, writing, and arithmetic skills to get jobs in factories and offices. Initially, an eighth-grade education was considered sufficient for many jobs, but soon a high school diploma became a prerequisite for most jobs above the level of the manual laborer. Schooling during this era was designed primarily to give people the means to become self-supporting. Educational systems were supposed to turn out workers who had the knowledge and skills needed to enter the labor market and produce profits for managers and owners.

In the second half of the twentieth century, this country again experienced high rates of immigration from many nations around the world, and many of the newcomers were school-age children. In the twenty-first century, some recent groups of immigrants are well educated, but most have limited formal education and few job skills. Today, about 20 percent of U.S. residents age five and older speak a language other than English at home (see Table 1). Because we use language to communicate with others, develop a sense of personal identity, and acquire knowledge and skills necessary for survival, schools must cope with language differences among students.

Although most recent immigrants rely on public schools to educate their children, some supplement school efforts with additional educational opportunities. For example, some Asian and Pacific American parents have established weekend cram schools, which are similar to the *juku* in Japan, *buxiban* in the People's Republic of China, and *hagwon* in Republic of Korea, also known as South Korea (see Box 1). Students spend a full day on subjects such as math and English and get specialized help in building study skills and learning test-taking strategies. Their parents are willing to pay for these classes so that the children will not experience language and cultural barriers that limit opportunities.

How best to educate children of recent immigrants with lower levels of education and income is a pressing problem in states that have high levels of immigration, such as California, New York, Florida, Texas, and New Jersey. Some school districts establish transitional programs for newcomers, six months to four years of classes taught in English and in the student's native language. Some schools offer bilingual education in as many as ten languages in major subjects such as math, science, and social studies.

Educational Opportunities and Race, Class, and Gender

Most research on access to educational opportunities for minority students has focused on how racially segregated schools affect student performance and self-esteem. Indeed, more than fifty years after the 1954 Supreme Court ruling in *Brown v. The Board of Education of Topeka, Kansas*, which stated that "separate but equal" schools are unconstitutional because they are inherently unequal, racial segregation or resegregation appears to be increasing in education rather than decreasing. Progress in bringing about racial *desegregation* (the abolition of legally sanctioned racial-ethnic segregation) and *integration*, which, for schools, involves taking specific action to change the racial or class composition of the student body, has been extremely slow for African Americans because segregated schools mirror race- and class-based residential segregation. Today, students of color make up the vast majority of the student body in some urban school districts, whereas middle- and upper-class white students make up the majority of the student body in private urban schools or suburban public schools. According to sociologists, schools in which racial and ethnic minorities are in the majority typically have high teacher–student ratios (more students per teacher), inexperienced teachers who are sometimes less qualified, lower expectations of students, and high dropout rates (Feagin et al., 2006).

Read the Document

Detours on the Road to Equality: Women, Work and Higher Education
on mysoclab.com

TABLE 1 Principal Languages Spoken at Home (United States)	
Language Used at Home	**Persons Five Years Old and Over Who Speak It**
English only	227,366,000
Spanish	34,560,000
Chinese	2,466,000
Tagalog	1,488,000
French	1,333,000
German	1,122,000
Korean	1,052,000
Russian	864,000
Arabic	786,000
Italian	782,000
Portuguese	661,000
French Creole	646,000
Polish	620,000
Hindi	560,000
Japanese	440,000
Persian	379,000
Urdu	353,000
Greek	337,000
Gujarathi	333,000
Serbo-Croatian	274,000
Armenian	231,000
Hebrew	213,000
Mon-Khmer (Cambodian)	183,000
Navaho	171,000
Yiddish	169,000
Other Native North American languages	193,000

Source: U.S. Census Bureau, 2010.

How segregated are U.S. schools? Here are a few facts: More than half of all African American public school students in Illinois, Michigan, and New York

Cramming for Success in Japan and South Korea

It's no secret that the Japanese have long been obsessed with education. Students flock to shrines to write prayers on wooden tablets asking for good grades. The lure of top schools is so strong that even kindergartners sometimes study for months before entrance exams, and students who fail college entrance tests are known to spend a year or two polishing their skills for another shot. For years that obsession has paid off in global leadership in innovation and design for Japan. These days, though, the country is losing its edge.

—Business journalists Ian Rowley and Hiroko Tashiro (2005) describe the emphasis placed on education in Japan as a prelude to explaining why cram schools have become a billion-dollar industry.

The students here were forsaking all the pleasures of teenage life. No cell phones allowed, no fashion magazines, no television, no Internet. No dating, no concerts, no earrings, no manicures—no acting their age. All these are mere distractions from an overriding goal . . . to clear the fearsome hurdle that can decide their future—the national college entrance examination.

—Journalist Choe Sang-Hun (2008) of the New York Times *explains the "boot camp" atmosphere of a cram school in Yongin, South Korea (also known as Republic of Korea), to show how much importance parents and students place on getting high marks on the exam that determines whether students will be admitted to a top-notch university.*

Cram schools, or *juku, buxibani,* and *hagwon,* have been around for many years in nations such as Japan, People's Republic of China, and Republic of Korea (South Korea); however, they are growing in popularity as the need to excel on standardized entrance examinations for college has become increasingly important to many families. What are cram schools? These schools are afternoon, evening, and weekend tutoring schools where students receive additional instruction in academic subjects, while specifically focusing on how to score high on standardized exams. At Jongro Yongin Campus, students are miles away from any kind of transportation and they do nothing but cram from 6:30 A.M. to past midnight, seven days a week. To attend a cram school, major family commitments are required: Money from parents and time from young people. In Japan, for example, Atsuki Yamamoto's parents pay $9,200 a year for him to attend Nichinoken four evenings a week from 5 to 9 P.M. and take exams every Sunday to prepare for entrance exams at elite junior high schools. The Yamamotos hope that if Atsuki is admitted to an elite private junior high school, he will later be accepted at a top high school and, eventually, a prestigious university (Rowley and Tashiro, 2005). In South Korea, Park Hong-ki spends $1,936 a month for his son's tuition at Jongro and admits that "It's a big financial burden for me" (Sang-Hun, 2008). The Yamamotos in Japan and the Hong-kis in South Korea are not alone in their hopes and aspirations for their children, as evidenced by the popularity of cram schools in these Southeast Asian nations.

In Japan, the People's Republic of China, and South Korea, education is everything to many people: The job you get depends on the university you attended, which depends on the high school you went to, which in turn depends on your elementary school, which, finally, depends on where you went to preschool. Thus, the sooner a child begins cramming, the better: Three- and four-year-olds prepare for preschool entrance exams by sitting at little desks in a ninety-minute class designed to improve performance on IQ tests. Even at this young age, the competition to attend the better schools is so strong that children may see each other as rivals rather than as classmates. In cities such as Hong Kong, the top cram school teachers are thought of as educational "stars," and students compete to get the best teachers in these "tutorial schools."

Cram schools have increased in popularity not only with parents but also with business investors. Many of the *juku* in Japan, for example, are owned by national corporations that advertise extensively and earn profits in the billions each year. According to business journalists, "Japan's new insecurity over its age-old obsession [education], it seems, is good for business" (Rowley and Tashiro, 2005). As long as the future of so many students hangs on scores from one major exam, the future of top tutors and cram schools is probably secure in many nations.

Questions for Consideration

1. How does the emphasis on high test scores and educational achievement in Japan and South Korea compare with the major educational concerns in U.S. education?

2. Do children in nations such as Japan, China, and South Korea pay too high a price for educational achievement? Why or why not?

3. What might students in the United States gain from intensive educational tutoring in cram school? What problems might U.S. students face in such a high-pressure environment?

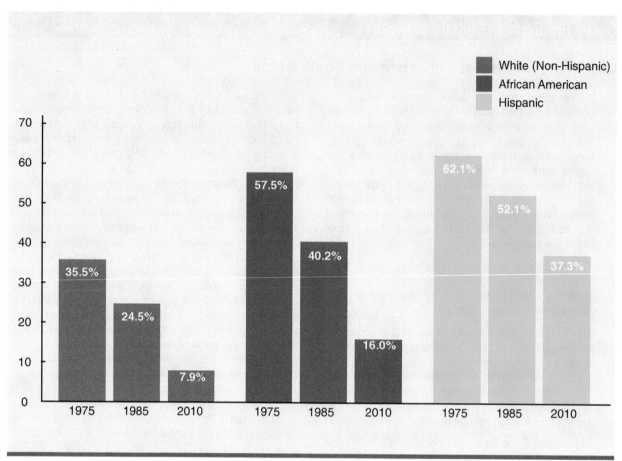

Figure 1 Percentage of persons 25 years and over not completing high school by race and Hispanic origin, 1975, 1985, and 2010
Source: U.S. Census Bureau, 2010.

Urban high schools face many challenges today. One pressing concern is how to provide the best educational opportunities for a highly diverse group of students.

state attend predominately black schools. In Maryland, Alabama, Mississippi, Tennessee, Georgia, and Texas, approximately 30 percent of African American public school students attend schools that have at least a 95 percent African American population. Children of color now constitute more than half of public school students in a number of states because White (non-Hispanic) children are more often enrolled in charter schools, suburban school districts, or private schools with a high percentage of white students (Dewan, 2010). Even more problematic is the high percentage of Latinos/as (Hispanics) who have dropped out of school or otherwise not completed high school (see Figure 1).

Why are dropout rates so high for Latino/a students? One explanation for the

Box 2

Report Card Framing: Does Education Get an A or an F?

Some *New York Times* headlines read:

- "U.S. Students Remain Poor at History, Tests Show" (Dillon, 2011b)
- "Failing Grades on Civics Exam Called a 'Crisis'" (Dillon, 2011a)
- "12th-Grade Reading and Math Scores Rise Slightly After a Historic Low in 2005" (Dillon, 2010)

The scores go up slightly; the scores go down slightly; or they remain "poor" or "failing." What's going on in U.S. schools when it comes to test scores as reported in the media? Media reports showing the latest results of national exams given to students in U.S. schools are routinely found in newspapers, on Internet websites, and on television news broadcasts. In most cases, bad test scores receive more attention than good scores in media accounts. In fact, the media often use test scores to "grade" students and schools in much the same way that educators use report cards to inform students and their parents about how students are doing in school.

Some sociologists who study the media use the terminology *report card framing* to refer to this type of coverage. Media framing refers to the manner in which reporters and other journalists organize information before they present it to an audience. For reporters on the "education beat," for example, part of that organization involves determining how to report on nationwide student testing and what slant to give the story regarding the positive or negative evaluation of those grades. As a result, *report card framing* refers to how the media give students, teachers, and schools "passing" or "failing" grades based on the results of standardized test scores. This type of framing assumes that such scores are a good measure of the academic achievements of students and the quality of teachers and schools. This framing does not take into account students' diverse family backgrounds in regard to class, race-ethnicity, nationality, region, and urban, suburban, or rural residential location. It also does not consider whether standardized exams may be biased against students who come from backgrounds that are different from those who prepare the questions on standardized exams. Similarly, report card framing assumes that tests are the best way to determine how well teachers teach and how well the educational system in our country functions.

In the past decade, major national newspapers such as the *New York Times* have expanded their coverage of students' test scores to include issues such as how student populations vary on the basis of race-ethnicity and country of origin in test scores. Other media sources, such as television and Internet news sites, use catchy "zippers" across the bottom of the TV screen or "pop-ups" on computer screens to get users' attention, and these sources typically do not have in-depth analysis of education statistics for fear of losing their audience. Catchy banners such as "Have U.S. students lost the competitive edge in the global economy?" are more likely to be the framing approach of this type of news coverage, leaving media audiences with little to go on except the "Pass–Fail" perspective on how students and schools are doing in the twenty-first century.

Questions for Consideration

1. Should journalists and other members of the media expand their reporting on education to cover a wider array of issues than just the results of standardized examinations?

2. To what extent do standardized test scores capture what is really happening in the classroom? Do they show what is most important in the learning process for students?

3. What other issues do you believe might be equally, or more, important for the media to cover in regard to schools and problems in education today?

high dropout rate comes from a comprehensive study of Latino/a high school graduates in Texas. Researchers found that high dropout rates were more closely linked to practices in schools and attitudes within the community than to individual or family problems (Romo and Falbo, 1996). Across lines of race and ethnicity, students from poor families are three to four times more likely to become school dropouts than are students from affluent families.

Another explanation for high dropout rates among all students of color, is that students may be "pushed out" of school because low-achieving students are viewed as bringing down standardized test scores, which are used to evaluate not only students but also teachers and administrators. Media reports may further contribute to the emphasis placed on standardized tests as a means of "passing" or "failing" students, teachers, and schools (see Box 2).

Even racially integrated schools often recreate segregation in the classroom when tracking or ability grouping is used. ***Tracking* is the practice of assigning students to specific courses and educational programs on the basis of their test scores, previous grades, or both.** Lower-level courses and special education classes are disproportionately filled with children of color, while gifted-and-talented programs and honors courses are more likely to be filled with white and Asian and Pacific American students.

Does gender bias in schools negatively affect female students? An extensive national survey on gender and self-esteem by the American Association of University Women (1992) found that girls were shortchanged in schools at that time. For example, reading materials, classroom activities, and treatment by teachers and peers often contributed to a feeling among many girls and young women that they were less important than male students. The accepted wisdom was that, over time, differential treatment undermines females' self-esteem and discourages them from taking certain courses, such as math and science, which have been dominated by male teachers and students. The *AAUW Report: How Schools Shortchange Girls* highlighted inequalities in women's education and started a national debate on gender equity. However, since this report was published, improvements have occurred in girls' educational achievement, as females have attended and graduated from high school and college at a higher rate than their male peers. More females have enrolled in advanced placement or honors courses and in academic areas, such as math and science, where they had previously lagged (AAUW, 2008). After many years of discussion about how schools disadvantaged female students, the emphasis has shifted to the issue of whether girls' increasing accomplishments have come at the expense of males. However, this assumption is false, according to the AAUW (2008:2): "Educational achievement is not a zero-sum game, in which a gain for one group results in a corresponding loss for the other. If girls' success comes at the expense of boys, one would expect to see boys' scores decline as girls' scores rise, but this has not been the case."

Although changes have occurred in regard to race, class, and gender and educational opportunities, differences still remain: White (non-Hispanic) American children are more likely to graduate from high school and college than are their African American and Hispanic peers. Likewise, children from higher-income families are more likely to graduate from high school than children from lower-income families who are also less likely

to attend college. Females may be gaining in certain areas, but they have a long way to go in others (AAUW, 2008). Schools increasingly have been encouraged to foster the development of all students regardless of their gender, race, or class; however, many factors—including lack of adequate funding and other resources—make it difficult for this already hard-pressed social institution to meet the needs and demands of highly diverse student populations.

School Safety and Violence

School officials are increasingly focusing on how to improve safety at schools and how to reduce or eliminate violence. In many schools, teachers and counselors are instructed in anger management and peer mediation, and they are encouraged to develop classroom instruction that teaches values such as respect and responsibility (National Center for Education Statistics [NCES], 2010a). Some schools create partnerships with local law enforcement agencies and social service organizations to link issues of school safety to larger concerns about safety in the community and the nation.

Clearly, some efforts to make schools a safe haven for students and teachers are paying off. Statistics related to school safety continue to show that U.S. schools are among the safest places for young people. According to "Indicators of School Crime and Safety," jointly released by the National Center for Education Statistics (NCES) and the U.S. Department of Justice's Bureau of Justice Statistics, young people are more likely to be victims of violent crime at or near their home, on the streets, at commercial establishments, or at parks than they are at school (NCES, 2010a). However, these statistics do not keep many people from believing that schools are becoming more dangerous with each passing year and that all schools should have high-tech surveillance equipment to help maintain a safe environment.

Even with all of these safety measures in place, violence and fear of violence continue to be pressing problems in schools throughout the United States. This concern extends from kindergarten through grade twelve because violent acts have resulted in deaths in communities such as Jonesboro, Arkansas; Springfield, Oregon; Littleton, Colorado; Santee, California; Red Lake, Minnesota; and an Amish schoolhouse in rural Pennsylvania.

About fifteen students are murdered at U.S. schools each year, but fortunately, this number is lower late in the second decade of the twenty-first century than it

Prison, airport, or school? Security guards and metal detectors have become an increasingly visible scene in many social institutions, including schools, throughout the United States. Do such measures deter school violence? Why or why not?

1,000 students in 2007 to 47 victimizations per 1,000 students in 2008 (NCES, 2010a).

Teachers, too, may be the victims of bullying or violence on school premises. During the 2007–2008 school year, 10 percent of teachers in city schools reported that they had been threatened with injury. This was a slightly higher percentage than for teachers in smaller communities (7 percent) or suburban or rural schools (6 percent each). Although a greater percentage of secondary school teachers (8 percent) reported that they had been threatened with injury by a student than elementary school teachers (7 percent), elementary school teachers were actually the victims of physical attach (6 percent) more often than teachers in secondary schools (2 percent) (NCES, 2010a). Providing safety at school for students and teachers alike is only one crisis facing school districts that are burdened with shrinking budgets, decaying buildings, and heightened demands for services.

PROBLEMS IN SCHOOL FINANCING

Because financing affects all other aspects of schooling, perhaps it is the biggest problem in education today. Most educational funds come from state legislative appropriations and local property taxes: State sources contribute less than half of public elementary–secondary school system revenue, and the rest comes from local sources and the federal government. In 2008–2009, for example, states contributed slightly less than 47 percent of total public school revenue, as compared to nearly

was in the 1990s. In collecting data on school violence, the CDC includes killings that occur at elementary, middle, or high schools, on school-sponsored trips, or while students are on their way to or from school. Even though the numbers and rates are somewhat lower than in the past, violence and the threat of violence remain a serious problem in many schools. Today, some school buildings look like fortresses or prisons with high fences, bright spotlights at night, and armed security guards. Many schools have installed metal detectors at entrances, and some search students for weapons, drugs, and other contraband as they enter. However, most educational analysts acknowledge that technology alone will not rid schools of violence and crime. Organizations such as the American Federation of Teachers have called for enhancing safety in schools by requiring higher student standards of conduct and achievement and giving teachers and administrators the authority to remove disruptive students. Some school districts require students to wear uniforms in an effort to reduce violence and crime because it was assumed that, if all students are required to dress alike, young people are less likely to be killed for their sneakers, jewelry, or designer clothes.

In 2008 (the latest year for which statistics were available), students between the ages of twelve and eighteen were victims of about 1.2 million nonfatal crimes (such as theft) at school. Although the rates of at-school crimes were lower than previously, many students still feel concern about safety at school. The total crime victimization rate of students ages twelve to eighteen at school declined from 57 victimizations per

Teacher layoffs are one of many signs of problems in today's schools where budget shortfalls are limiting students' learning opportunities.

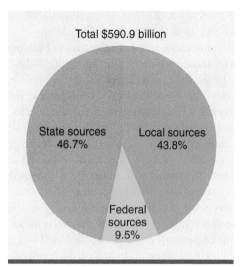

Total $590.9 billion

State sources 46.7%

Local sources 43.8%

Federal sources 9.5%

Figure 2 Percentage distribution of total public elementary–secondary school system revenue, 2008–2009

Note: Percentages may not add up to 100.

Source: Blumerman, 2011.

44 percent from local sources, and 9.5 percent from the federal government (Blumerman, 2011). The total amount of public elementary and secondary school system revenues in that same year was $590.9 billion (see Figure 2). Much of the money from federal sources is earmarked for special programs for students who are disadvantaged (e.g., the Head Start program) or who have a disability.

School funding is in crisis in many areas of the nation because of a declining property tax base. Housing foreclosures mean that families are not paying property taxes on their residences. Similarly, as small businesses and major corporations have gone out of business or relocated to other areas, local school districts have been drained of much-needed revenue for operating expenses and maintenance of facilities. The problem of erosion of local property tax revenues is further compounded by the fiscal crises of states that are unable to provide even previously promised funds to school districts. Without the funds from property taxes, schools cannot purchase the textbooks and latest computer technology for educating today's students. At the same time that educational funds are drying up, a record number of students are enrolled in the nation's schools: 76 million in 2008. In addition to meeting the daily needs of today's students and teachers, many schools are in need of major repairs or replacement because of the physical condition of these outdated structures.

Voucher Programs

Is there a way to resolve problems of unequal funding among the states, among school districts within states, and among schools within school districts? Most proposals to improve educational funding have been limited in scope and seem to benefit some groups at the expense of others. For example, some groups encourage what they refer to as "school choice," which usually means some kind of school voucher programs in which public funds (tax dollars) are provided to parents so that they can pay their child's tuition at a private school of their choice. The original idea for school choice was to provide a voucher (equal in value to the average amount spent per student by the local school district) to the family of any student who left the public schools to attend a private school. The private school could exchange the voucher for that amount of money and apply it to the student's tuition at the private school; the school district would save an equivalent amount of money as a result of the student not enrolling in the public schools. Between the origins of vouchers in 1955 and today, variations have been proposed, such as allowing vouchers to be used for transfers between public schools in the same school district, transfers from one public school district to another, transfers only to schools with no religious connections, and vouchers for use only by students from low-income families.

Many parents praise the voucher system because it provides them with options for schooling their children. Some political leaders applaud vouchers and other school choice policies for improving public school performance. However, voucher programs are controversial: Some critics believe that giving taxpayer money to parents so that they can spend it at private (often religious) schools violates some state's constitutions in regard to separation of church and state. The U.S. Supreme Court previously ruled in *Zelman v. Simmons-Harris*, a case involving a Cleveland, Ohio, school district, that voucher policies are constitutional because parents have a choice and are not required to send their children to religious-affiliated schools. Other critics claim that voucher programs are less effective in educating children than public schools. According to studies of the District of Columbia, Milwaukee, and Cleveland, public school students outperformed voucher students in both reading and math on state proficiency tests; however, neither group reached state proficiency requirements (Ott, 2011). In sum, advocates like the choice-factor in voucher programs while critics believe that vouchers undermine public education, lack accountability, and may contribute to the collapse of the public school system.

Charter Schools and For-Profit Schools

Some social analyst and political leaders believe that charter schools and for-profit schools are a more efficient way to educate children and that these schools solve some of the problems of underfunding in public education. Charter schools are primary or secondary schools that receive public money but are free from some of the day-to-day bureaucracy of a larger school district that may limit classroom performance. These schools operate under a charter contract negotiated by the school's organizers (often parents or teachers) and a sponsor (usually a local school board, a state board of education, or a university) that oversees the provisions of the contract. Some school districts "contract out" by hiring for-profit companies on a contract basis to manage charter schools, but the schools themselves are nonprofit. Among the largest educational management organizations are Imagine Schools, National Heritage Academies, The Leona Group, EdisonLearning, White Hat Management, and Mosaica Education (Molnar, Miron, and Urschel, 2010).

Charter schools provide more autonomy for individual students and teachers, and many serve an important function in education: A large number of minority students receive a higher-quality education than they would in the public schools (see J. Hardy, 2010; Winters, 2010). Charter schools attempt to maintain an organizational culture that motivates students and encourages achievement rather than having a negative school environment where minority students are ridiculed for "acting white" or making good grades. Some charter schools offer college preparatory curriculums and help students of color achieve their goal of enrolling in the college or university of their choice (J. Hardy, 2010). However, it is debatable whether charter schools save money and reduce the larger fiscal crises facing large urban school districts that are costly to operate. And, for-profit schools, as the name suggests, have as their goal making money for large corporations more than providing the highest-quality education at the lowest possible cost to students and their families.

On a final note: Some analysts believe that the economic problem of schools might be solved by significantly reducing expenditures for administration and other noninstructional activities and using that money in the classroom. More than one-third of every dollar spent on public education goes for support services rather than education. Expenses for support services include such things as the cost of administration, libraries, buses, sporting events, and repairs to buildings. However, problems in education are not limited to the elementary and secondary levels; higher education has its problems, too.

PROBLEMS IN HIGHER EDUCATION

Higher education serves several important functions in society: the transmission of specialized knowledge and skills, production of new information and technologies, and preparation of the next generation of professionals and scholars. Over the past decade, however, many public colleges and universities have come under increasing financial pressure as appropriations by state legislatures and federal funding have been cut. In response, some schools have intensified their fund-raising efforts, pursuing corporations, nonprofit foundations, and alumni. To remain solvent, many of these schools have also had to increase tuition and student fees.

Explore the Concept

Social Explorer Activity: Higher Education in America on mysoclab.com

The Soaring Cost of a College Education

One of the fastest-growing areas of U.S. higher education today is the community college, and one of the greatest challenges facing community colleges today is money. Community colleges educate about half of the nation's undergraduates. The 1,167 community colleges (including public, private and tribal colleges) in the United States enroll about 12.4 million students in credit and noncredit courses. Community college enrollment accounts for 44 percent of all U.S. undergraduate students. Women make up more than half (58 percent) of community college students. Community colleges are also important for underrepresented minority student enrollment: Fifty-five percent of all Native American college students attend a community college, as do 52 percent of all Hispanic students, 44 percent of African American students, and 45 percent of Asian American/Pacific Islanders (American Association of Community Colleges, 2011). However, across the nation, state and local governments struggling to balance their budgets have slashed funding for community colleges. In a number of regions, these cuts have been so severe that schools have been seriously limited in their ability to meet the needs of their students. In some cases, colleges have terminated programs, slashed course offerings, reduced the number of faculty, and eliminated essential student services.

At four-year colleges, increases in average yearly tuition continue to be higher than the rate of inflation. More than 12 million students attend public or private four-year colleges or universities in the United States. Although state colleges and universities typically have lower tuition rates than private colleges because they are funded primarily by tax dollars, some have grown too expensive for students from lower-income families, particularly with the decline in scholarship funds and grants. Many students must take out student loans and go into debt to attend college. Although some students find part-time jobs, their earnings make only a small dent in the cost of tuition and books.

What does a college education cost? According to the *Chronicle of Higher Education* (2010), the average tuition and fees per year at a public four-year institution are $6,319, as compared to $22,449 at a private four-year institution. Average tuition and fees per year at a public two-year institution are $2,137.

Some social analysts believe that a college education is a bargain; however, others argue that the high cost of a college education reproduces the existing class system: Students who lack money may be denied access to higher education, and those who are able to attend college receive different types of education based on their ability to pay. For example, a community college student who receives an associate's degree or completes a certificate program may be prepared for a position in the middle of the occupational status range, such as a dental assistant, computer programmer, or auto mechanic. In contrast, university graduates with four-year degrees are more likely to find initial employment with firms where they stand a chance of being promoted to high-level management and executive positions. In other words, higher educational attainment is associated with positions that offer higher earnings on average. In 2009, high school graduates had average earnings of $31,283, while those with a bachelor's degree earned about $58,613. Median earnings for a worker with a high school diploma alone were about 53 percent of the median earnings of a worker with a bachelor's degree. Average earnings for those with an advanced degree totaled $83,144 (U.S. Census Bureau, 2010).

Given the necessity of getting a college education, is any financial assistance on the way? In 2010 the Obama administration passed a student-loan bill to aid colleges and students. The legislation is designed to "cut out the middle person" by ending the bank-based system of distributing federally subsidized student loans and instead have the Department of Education give loan money directly to colleges and their students. With the savings from this approach, more money is to be put into the Pell Grant program. Unlike a loan, a federal Pell Grant does not have to be repaid. The maximum award for 2011–2012 was $5,500, but not all students were eligible for this amount. Some legislation also provides for additional assistance to historically black colleges in an effort to help more low-income students enroll and succeed in college (Basken, 2010). Many questions remain about student loans and possible long-term effects of high student debt on individuals after they complete their college education.

The Continuing Debate over Affirmative Action

For many years, affirmative action programs in higher education—programs that take race, ethnicity, and gender into consideration for admissions, financial aid, scholarships, fellowships, and faculty hiring—have been the subject of debate among academics and nonacademics alike. The legal battle over affirmative action heated up with the 1978 U.S. Supreme Court decision in *Bakke v. The University of California at Davis*. In that case, Allan Bakke, a white male, sued the University of California at Davis, claiming that its policy of allocating 16 of 100 places in the first-year class to members of underrepresented minority groups was discriminatory. Bakke claimed that he had been denied admission to the university's medical school even though his grade point average and Medical College Admissions Test score were higher than those of some minority applicants who were admitted under the university's affirmative action program. Although the Court ruled that Bakke should be admitted to the medical school, it left the door open for schools to increase diversity in their student population.

The affirmative action controversy intensified in the 1990s. In 1995, the regents of the University of California adopted a policy discontinuing any special consideration of "race, religion, sex, color, ethnicity, or national origin" in admissions criteria, and voters in California passed Proposition 209, which is a sweeping prohibition of affirmative action. Proposition 209 amended the California State Constitution to prohibit public institutions from considering race, sex, or ethnicity in admissions policies or other procedures. In 1996, the U.S. Fifth Circuit Court of Appeals ruled in *Hopwood v. State of Texas* that affirmative action programs in public education—even if they were intended to achieve a more diverse student body or to eliminate the present effects of past discrimination—unconstitutionally discriminated against whites. As a result of these and other similar events, it appeared that programs designed to increase subordinate-enrollment at institutions of higher education might become a thing of the past.

In 2003, however, the U.S. Supreme Court ruled in *Grutter v. Bollinger* (involving admissions policies of the University of Michigan's law school) and *Gratz v. Bollinger* (involving the undergraduate admissions policies of the same university) that race can be a factor for universities in shaping their admissions programs, as long as it is within carefully defined limits. Among these limits are that affirmative action plans must not involve quotas (a set number of students from a specific racial or ethnic background *must* be admitted each year, for example) or carry predetermined weight in decisions.

But this was not the end of this contentious issue. In the second decade of the twenty-first century, the University of California once again banned racial affirmative action in public university admissions. A federal lawsuit was filed challenging the constitutionality of California's ban on racial affirmative action. At the time of this writing, California Governor Jerry Brown had filed a legal opinion supporting the lawsuit and speaking out against the ban. It remains to be seen what happens next in the long battle over affirmative (or nonaffirmative) action policies in various states and throughout the nation.

In the twenty-first century, organizations such as the American Association of University Women continue to be advocates for continuing and expanding affirmative action programs in the belief that equity is still an issue. According to affirmative action advocates, greater opportunities in education and the workplace are still very important for women and people of color because discriminatory policies and covert practices often work against them. From this approach, having affirmative action programs in place also serves as a preventive measure: Making people aware that it is important to be committed to equal opportunity for all people and to diversity in education and jobs may help reduce or eliminate potential problems of bias before they occur.

Racial and Ethnic Minorities: Underrepresentation and Discrimination

One of the reasons many social analysts argue for affirmative action is that some racial and ethnic minority categories are underrepresented in higher education. How does college enrollment differ by race and ethnicity? White Americans made up slightly more than 63 percent of all college students as compared to African American enrollment at 13.5 percent and Hispanic/Latina/o enrollment at almost 12 percent (*Chronicle of Higher Education*, 2010). Native American/Alaska Native enrollment rates have remained stagnant at about 1.0 percent; however, tribal colleges on reservations have experienced growth in student enrollment. Founded to overcome racism experienced by Native American students in traditional four-year colleges and to shrink the high dropout rate among Native American college students, 37 colleges are now chartered and run by the Native American nations (American Association of Community Colleges, 2011). Unlike other community colleges, the tribal colleges receive no funding from state and local governments and, as a result, are often short of funds to fulfill their academic mission.

The proportionately low number of people of color enrolled in colleges and universities is reflected in the educational achievement of people age 25 and over, as shown in the "Census Profiles" feature. If we focus on persons who receive doctorate degrees, the underrepresentation of persons of color is even more striking. According to the *Chronicle of Higher Education* (2010), of the 84,960 doctoral degrees conferred in the 2007–2008 academic year, African Americans earned slightly less than 6 percent (4,766 degrees), Hispanics earned slightly less than 4 percent (3,199, and Native Americans/American Indians earned 0.005 percent (432). By contrast, whites (non-Hispanic) earned 47,246 PhDs, or 57 percent of the total number of degrees awarded.

Underrepresentation is not the only problem faced by students of color: Problems of prejudice and discrimination continue on some college campuses. Some problems are overt and highly visible; others are more covert and hidden from public view. Examples of overt racism include mocking Black History Month or a Latino celebration on campuses, referring to individuals by derogatory names, tying nooses on door knobs of dorm rooms or faculty offices, and having "parties" where guests dress in outfits that ridicule people from different cultures or nations.

A study by the sociologists Leslie Houts Picca and Joe R. Feagin (2007) found that many blatant racist events, ranging from private jokes and conversations to violent incidents, occurred in the presence of 600 white students at twenty-eight colleges and universities who were asked to keep diaries and record any racial events they observed. In addition to overt patterns of discrimination, other signs of racism included numerous conversations that took place "back stage" (in white-only spaces where no person of color was present) and involved derogatory comments, skits, or jokes about persons of color. According to Picca and Feagin, most of the racial events were directed at African Americans, but Latinos/as and Asian Americans were also objects of some negative comments.

ARE THERE SOLUTIONS TO EDUCATIONAL PROBLEMS?

During the twenty-first century, we must not underestimate the importance of education as a social institution. It is a powerful and influential force that imparts the values, beliefs, and knowledge that are necessary for the social reproduction of individual personalities and entire cultures (Bourdieu and Passeron, 1990). But in what direction should this tremendous social force move? As a nation, we have learned that spending more money on education does not guarantee that the many pressing problems facing this social institution will be solved (see Box 3). On the other hand, it is essential that schools be funded at a level where they can meet the

Social Problems and Statistics

Does Spending More Money Guarantee a Better Education?

When political leaders and other policy makers debate problems in education, they often use statistics to back up their arguments. Statistics show that some problems—such as large class size or inadequate school facilities—might be reduced if more money were spent on education. However, statistics also show that simply spending more money does not guarantee better outcomes for children's education. Figure 3 shows, for example, that although federal discretionary spending on education more than doubled between 1990 and 2009, this additional expenditure has not improved reading scores overall. Consider the following facts regarding education in the United States:

- Gains in reading and other subject areas occur in some testing years but do not always continue across years and at all levels (testing is done at grades 4, 8, and 12).

- The gap in reading scores across racial and ethnic categories remains. White (non-Hispanic) students continue to score higher than African American and Hispanic (Latino/a) students.

- Researchers presume the scores of Hispanic students remain lower than those of White (non-Hispanic) Americans because of language barriers.

- In subject areas other than reading, such as history, American students score poorly. Only 20 percent of fourth graders, 17 percent of eighth graders, and 12 percent of twelfth graders showing proficiency on recent history exams given by the National Assessment of Educational Progress (NAEP).

- On the civics exam, less than half of all U.S. eighth graders knew the purpose of the Bill of Rights, and 75 percent of twelfth graders could not name a power granted to Congress by the U.S. Constitution.

On the basis of these data, should we assume that less money should be spent on education? Definitely not! However, statistics do show that money alone isn't always the answer to pressing social problems in our nation. Source: Based on NCES, 2010b.

Questions for Consideration

1. If some studies show a stronger relationship between parents' income and students' academic achievement, should the United States be more concerned about addressing income inequality in this nation rather than pouring more money into schools or trying other approaches (such as "teaching to the test") to increase students' scores on standardized examinations?

2. What other factors contribute to low scores on reading, history, and civics exams? How might some of these problems be reduced or eliminated?

Independent Research

If you want to know how U.S. students score on national tests in arts, civics, economics, mathematics, reading, science, and writing, go to "The Nation's Report Card," a U.S. Government website (http://nationsreportcard.gov). These reports provide test results, sample questions, and state-by-state information about student scores. If you are writing a research paper for your social problems class (or another course), you will find useful data in these "Report Cards" that might help with your study.

needs of growing and increasingly diverse student populations. Equally important to funding issues are factors such as the quality of instruction received by students, the safety of the school environment, and the opportunity for each student to reach his or her academic and social potential. Various theoretical approaches and political perspectives provide different solutions to the educational problems that we face today.

Functionalist/Conservative Solutions

Functionalist approaches emphasize the importance of the manifest functions of education and making certain that these functions are fulfilled in contemporary schools. From this approach, greater emphasis should be placed on teaching students the basics and making certain that they have the job skills that will make it possible for them to become contributing members of the U.S. workforce. Problems such as functional illiteracy, school violence, unprepared or ineffective teachers, and school discipline issues must be dealt with so that test scores are improved and a higher percentage of students not only graduate from high school but also attend college. Functionalists typically believe that when dysfunctions exist in the nation's educational system, improvements will occur only when more stringent academic requirements are implemented for students. To make this possible, teachers must receive more rigorous training and evaluation, and high expectations must be

Box 3

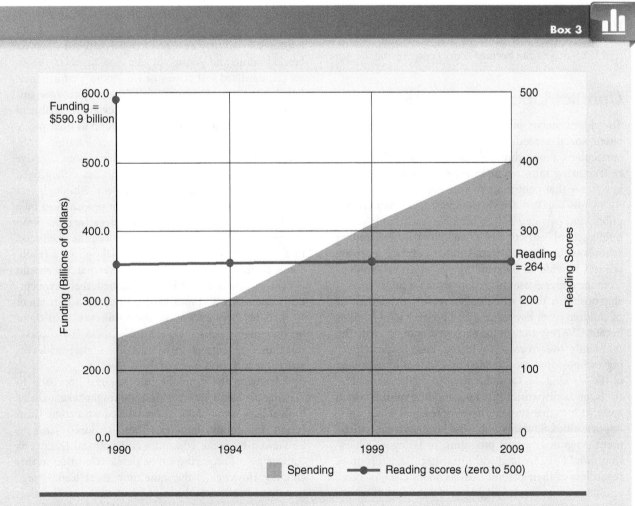

Figure 3 Education spending and reading scores, 1990–2009

Note: Reading scores are for thirteen-year-olds.

Source: Organization for Economic Cooperation and Development, 2010.

held for all students to help them reach grade-level or above achievement in all subjects they are studying.

Conservative political leaders in various states have emphasized that one possible solution to educational problems is to increase support for struggling students and underperforming schools by requiring school districts to use federal funds that have been set aside for tutoring and school choice. At the national level, there has been much discussion about rewarding the best teachers and encouraging them to take jobs in underperforming schools by providing them with additional pay and other incentives for assuming these positions. At the bottom line, the focus of functionalist/conservative approaches to solving educational problems in the United States is to make schools more competitive and to ensure that students graduate from high school prepared for jobs in the twenty-first century global marketplace. Strengthening math and science education, for example, is a key way in which political leaders believe that U.S. schools can become more competitive.

Conflict/Liberal Solutions

To address major problems in schools such as class-based social reproduction, tracking, and the hidden curriculum, many conflict theorists believe that major restructuring must occur in public education. In fact, key issues that contribute to vast educational inequality in this country are the divide that exists between public and private schools, between "rich" and "poor" public school districts, and inequalities that exist among schools within one district. Although exclusive private schools provide an outstanding education for children from the upper classes to prepare them for future leadership positions, these schools often serve to the detriment of children from low-income and poverty-level families because the resources of the affluent do not flow into the frequently overcrowded, outdated, and "underachieving" schools that are attended by children of members of the working class and the poor. In public school districts, great disparities in school funding must be done away with so that students have more equal educational opportunities. Students who would benefit from enrichment programs, special programs, or bilingual education should be provided with these necessary resources regardless of their parents' socioeconomic status, race-ethnicity, or country of origin.

Liberal political leaders typically believe that legislation must be passed or continually reaffirmed to fight race discrimination and gender and sexual inequality in schools. These are viewed as continuing problems that are not solved simply by the passage of one measure, such as Title IX of the Educational Amendments of 1972, but instead require continued vigilance across the decades. The same is true in regard to the funding of education: Increased government funding for public schools is crucial if we are to produce greater equality and more opportunity for students in the public schools of this nation. Head Start and bilingual education programs are vital to the success of students from lower-income families and those who reside in families where English is not the primary language spoken.

Symbolic Interactionist Solutions

Since symbolic interactionist approaches focus on microlevel issues, this perspective makes us aware of the importance of how we deal with individuals and small groups of people in educational settings. Problems in schools may be created or perpetuated when we label children and young adults as low achievers based on standardized test scores or classroom performance. Labeling may result in a self-fulfilling prophecy for students if they come to believe that they are incapable of learning or of achieving at the same level as their peers. As a result, one way to reduce students' learning problems in schools is to help them become more effective learners and to develop the self-confidence they need to reach greater educational attainment. Although fear of failure alone typically does not cause a child to be a less than adequate student, having a negative perception of one's own abilities certainly can reduce the likelihood that he or she will perform well in school. As a result, some symbolic interactionists believe that we should educate teachers about how important their expectations are when it comes to the student's achievement level. If teachers encourage their students, help them become higher achievers, and make them feel successful, those students often will act like higher achievers and come to expect more of themselves.

Applying the symbolic interactionist approach to viewing problems in education, we might take a closer look at how some children are labeled who come from recent immigrant families. These children tend to be viewed by some educators and political leaders as "unworthy" of acquiring a free, public education in this country. However, at the same time, these leaders suggest that education is the key to the future of this nation in the global economy. Perhaps changing our perspective on students who differ from the so-called norm of the white, middle- and upper-middle class student population that historically has been considered to be the most successful and the most popular grouping in many schools might be a starting place for reducing social divisions that become insurmountable as students progress through the educational system or decide to drop out because they perceive that school is largely unrelated to their life.

In the final analysis, schools will continue to play a key role in the future of this nation, and changes are inevitable. Other social, economic and political changes over which we have little or no control are occurring, including globalization of the marketplace and workforce, new technologies that will continually revolutionize how we work and play, and the day-to-day reality of other social problems—such as high levels of stress and bullying, peer pressure, family problems, drugs, and crime—being present in and around the schools of our nation. Unlike some social problems, analysts applying virtually all sociological and political perspectives to the problems found in schools believe that change must occur. They simply disagree on what those changes should be.

SUMMARY

✓—[Study and Review on mysoclab.com

What is education?
Education is the social institution responsible for transmitting knowledge, skills, and cultural values in a formally organized structure.

What is the functionalist perspective on education?
Functionalists believe that education contributes to the smooth functioning of society when it fulfills its manifest functions—the open, stated, and intended goals or consequences of its activities. Education has at least five major manifest functions: socialization, transmission of culture, social control, social placement, and change and innovation. Schools also fulfill a number of latent functions—hidden, unstated, and sometimes unintended consequences of its activities.

What is the conflict perspective on education?
Conflict theorists believe that schools, which are supposed to reduce inequality in society, actually perpetuate inequalities based on class, race, and gender. The sociologist Pierre Bourdieu, for example, says that children from low-income and poverty-level families come to school with less cultural capital (values, beliefs, attitudes, and competencies in language and culture) than middle- and upper-income children have. Conflict theorists also think that elites manipulate the masses and maintain their power in society through a hidden curriculum that teaches students to be obedient and patriotic and thus perpetuates the status quo in society.

What is the symbolic interactionist perspective on education?
Symbolic interactionists study classroom dynamics and how practices such as labeling affect students' self-concept and aspirations. If students are labeled "learning disabled" for example, the label might become a self-fulfilling prophecy, that is, an unsubstantiated belief or prediction that results in behavior that makes the false belief come true. A student who is erroneously labeled "learning disabled" might stop trying, and teachers might lower their expectations, with the result that the student doesn't succeed in the long run.

What is functional illiteracy and what can be done about it?
Functional illiteracy is being unable to read and/or write at the skill level necessary for carrying out everyday tasks. When the economic climate of the nation is better, leaders in business and industry are more likely to establish programs to educate functionally illiterate workers; however, their efforts are more limited in difficult economic times. Volunteer organizations that teach basic reading skills to young people and adults have been successful in helping more people learn to read, write, and engage in such important daily activities as balancing a checkbook.

Why is immigration a problem for U.S. schools?
Though some immigrants are well educated, most have limited formal education and few job skills. Also, many immigrants are children, so schools must cope with language differences among students. Some school districts offer transitional newcomer programs with bilingual instruction, but critics say that these programs are a form of segregation.

How do race, class, and gender affect educational opportunities?
The Supreme Court outlawed segregation in 1954, but segregated schools still exist because segregated schools mirror race- and class-based residential segregation. Schools in which racial and ethnic minorities are in the majority typically have high teacher–student ratios, less-qualified teachers, lower expectations of students, and high dropout rates.

How has violence affected our schools?
Many schools now look like fortresses and use metal detectors and security guards to screen entering students. To lessen the possibility of students being killed for shoes, jewelry, or designer clothes, some school districts now require students to wear uniforms.

What is the crisis in school financing?
Most educational funds come from state legislative appropriations and local property taxes, but the eroding tax base in city centers leaves schools underfunded. At the same time, record numbers of students are entering the public school system, and many schools are overcrowded and need major repairs. One proposed solution is the voucher system, whereby families are given vouchers to "buy" education at the school of their choice. Critics say that this plan would offer better opportunities to only a limited number of students and wouldn't solve the funding problem.

What are the major problems in higher education?
The soaring cost of a college education is a major problem because, say conflict theorists, it reproduces the existing class system: Those who attend college are stratified according to their ability to pay. There is also the question of affirmative action. Should race, ethnicity, and gender be taken into consideration for admissions, financial aid, scholarships, and faculty hiring?

What are the urgent educational problems of the twenty-first century?
To compete in the global economy, we must come to terms with illiteracy in our adult population and we must provide all children with a safe, high-quality education. Some experts say that the best way to achieve both goals is through holding schools and school districts accountable for the education their students receive. Others believe that we will have to tackle many other societal problems, including poverty, racism, and family discord, before we can meet our educational goals.

KEY TERMS

education
functionally illiterate
hidden curriculum
latent functions
manifest functions
tracking

QUESTIONS FOR CRITICAL THINKING

1. How do peer networks and school environment affect students' learning and their overall educational opportunities? Why are problems such as harassment and bullying so persistent in many schools? What can be done to reduce these concerns?

2. What creative solutions can you propose for the school financial crisis? That is, if the federal government doesn't increase its contribution and voters resist increased taxes, where can state legislatures find more money for education?

3. Should we think of more innovative ways to educate students who come from diverse family backgrounds and other nations of the world? Or should students be expected to quickly accept the language and cultural patterns that are prevalent in their school?

Succeed with MySocLab®   www.mysoclab.com

The new MySocLab delivers proven results in helping students succeed, provides engaging experiences that personalize learning, and comes from a trusted partner with educational expertise and a deep commitment to helping students and instructors achieve their goals.

Here are a few activities you will find for this chapter:

Watch on mysoclab.com — **Core Concepts** video clips feature sociologists in action, exploring important concepts in the study of Social Problems. Watch:
• Inequities in Education

Explore on mysoclab.com — **Social Explorer** is an interactive application that allows you to explore Census data through interactive maps. Explore:
• Social Explorer Activity: Higher Education in America

Read on mysoclab.com — **MySocLibrary** includes primary source readings from classic and contemporary sociologists. Read:
• Detours on the Road to Equality: Women, Work and Higher Education

Glossary

education the social institution responsible for transmitting knowledge, skills, and cultural values in a formally organized structure.

functionally illiterate being unable to read and/or write at the skill level necessary for carrying out everyday tasks.

hidden curriculum how certain cultural values and attitudes, such as conformity and obedience to authority, are transmitted through implied demands in the everyday rules and routines of schools.

latent functions hidden, unstated, and sometimes unintended consequences of activities in an organization or institution.

manifest functions open, stated, and intended goals or consequences of activities within an organization or institution.

tracking assigning students to specific courses and educational programs on the basis of their test scores, previous grades, or both.

Referances

NOTE: References in blue are new to the Sixth Edition.

American Association of Community Colleges. 2011. "2011 Fact Sheet." Retrieved April 18, 2011. Online: http://www.aacc.nche.edu/AboutCC/Documents/FactSheet2011.pdf

American Association of University Women. 1992. *The AAUW Report: How Schools Short-Change Girls.* Washington, DC: The AAUW Educational Foundation and National Educational Association.

Apple, Michael W. 1982. *Education and Power: Reproduction and Contradiction in Education.* London: Routledge & Kegan Paul.

Ballantine, Jeanne H., and Floyd M. Hammack. 2009. *The Sociology of Education: A Systematic Analysis* (6th ed.). Upper Saddle River, NJ: Prentice Hall.

Basken, Paul. 2010. "Pell Grant Increase Could Be Cut as Talks Intensify on Student-Aid Bill." *The Chronicle of Higher Education* (March 12). Retrieved July 17, 2011. Online: http://chroniclecareers.com/article/Pell-Grant-Increase-Could-Be/64666/

Blumerman, Lisa M. 2011. "Public Education Finances: 2009." U.S. Census Bureau (May). Retrieved July 17, 2011. Online: http://www2.census.gov/govs/school/09f33pub.pdf

Bourdieu, Pierre, and Jean-Claude Passeron. 1990. *Reproduction in Education, Society, and Culture.* Newbury Park, CA: Sage.

Collins, Randall. 1979. *The Credential Society: An Historical Sociology of Education.* New York: Academic Press.

Dewan, Shaila. 2010. "Southern Schools Mark Two Majorities." *New York Times* (January 6). Retrieved February 4, 2012. Online: http://www.nytimes.com/2010/01/07/us/07south.html

Dillon, Sam. 2010. "12th-Grade Reading and Math Scores Rise Slightly After a Historic Low in 2005." *New York Times* (November 18). Retrieved July 17, 2011. Online: http://www.nytimes.com/2010/11/19/education/19education.html?ref=nationalassessmentofeducationalprogress

Dillon, Sam. 2011a. "Failing Grades on Civics Exam Called a 'Crisis'" (May 4). Retrieved July 17, 2011. Online: http://www.nytimes.com/2011/05/05/education/05civics.html?_r=1&ref=nationalassessmentofeducationalprogress

Dillon, Sam. 2011b. U.S. Students Remain Poor at History, Tests Show." *New York Times* (June 14). Retrieved July 17, 2011. Online: http://www.nytimes.com/2011/06/15/education/15history.html

Duster, Troy. 1995. "Symposium: The Bell Curve." *Contemporary Sociology: A Journal of Reviews,* 24(2):158–161.

Feagin, Joe R., David Baker, and Clairece Booher Feagin. 2006. *Social Problems: A Critical Power-Conflict Perspective* (6th ed.). Upper Saddle River, NJ: Prentice Hall.

Graham, Paul. 2004. *Hackers & Painters: Big Ideas from the Computer Age.* Sebastopol, CA: O'Reilly.

Hardy, Jackie. 2010. "Charter Schools Closing the Achievement Gap among Minority Students." *North Dallas Gazette* (March 3). Retrieved April 29, 2011. Online: http://northdallasgazette.com/2010/03/charter-schools-closing-the-achievement-gap-among-minority-students/

Hauser, Robert M. 1995. "Symposium: The Bell Curve." *Contemporary Sociology: A Journal of Reviews,* 24(2):149–153.

Herrnstein, Richard J., and Charles Murray. 1994. *The Bell Curve: Intelligence and Class Structure in American Life.* New York: Free Press.

Holt, John C. 1964. *How Children Fail.* New York: Dell.

Lynn, Richard. 2008. *The Global Bell Curve: Race, IQ, and Inequality Worldwide.* Whitefish, MT: Washington Summit Publishers.

Molnar, Alex, Gary Miron, and Jessica L. Urschel. 2010. "Profiles of For-Profit Education Management Organizations, 2009–2010." National Education Policy Center, University of Colorado at Boulder. Retrieved April 29, 2011. Online: http://nepc.colorado.edu/files/EMO-FP-09-10.pdf

National Center for Education Statistics. 2010a. "Indicators of School Crime and Safety: 2010." Retrieved July 16, 2011. Online: http://nces.ed.gov/programs/crimeindicators/crimeindicators2010/key.asp

Oakes, Jeannie. 1985. *Keeping Track: How Schools Structure Inequality.* New Haven, CT: Yale University Press.

Ott, Thomas. 2011. "Cleveland Students Hold Their Own with Voucher Students on State Tests." Cleveland.com (February 22). Retrieved April 27, 2011. Online: http://blog.cleveland.com/metro/2011/02/cleveland_students_hold_own_wi.html

Picca, Leslie Houts and Joe R. Feagin. 2007. *Two-Faced Racism: Whites in the Backstage and Frontstage.* New York: Routledge.

ProLiteracy.org. 2010. "The Impact of Literacy." Retrieved July 16, 2011. Online: http://www.proliteracy.org/NetCommunity/Page.aspx?pid=345&srcid=191

Romo, Harriett D., and Toni Falbo. 1996. *Latino High School Graduation.* Austin: University of Texas Press.

Rowley, Ian, and Kiroko Tashiro. 2005. "Japan: Crazy for Cramming." *BusinessWeek.com* (April 18). Retrieved August 1, 2005. Online: http://www.businessweek.com/magazine/content/05_16/b3929071.htm

Sang-Hun, Choe. 2008. "A Taste of Failure Fuels an Appetite for Success at South Korea's Cram Schools." *New York Times* (August 13). Retrieved August 17, 2008. Online: http://www.nytimes.com/2008/08/13/world/asia/13cram.html

Snyder, Benson R. 1971. *The Hidden Curriculum.* New York: Knopf.

Tatum, Beverly Daniel. 2003. *Why Are All the Black Kids Sitting Together in the Cafeteria? And Other Conversations about Race.* New York: Basic Books.

Taylor, Howard F. 1995. "Symposium: The Bell Curve." *Contemporary Sociology: A Journal of Reviews,* 24(2):153–157.

U.S. Census Bureau. 2010. "The Black Population." Retrieved June 12, 2011. Online: http://www.census.gov/prod/cen2010/briefs/c2010br-06.pdf

U.S. Department of Education. 2010. "A Blueprint for Reform: The Reauthorization of the Elementary and Secondary Education Act" (March). Retrieved February 4, 2012. Online: http://www2.ed.gov/policy/elsec/leg/blueprint/blueprint.pdf

Winters, Marcus A. 2010. "For Minorities, a Charter-School Boost." *New York Post* (April 27). Online: http://www.manhattan-institute.org/cgi-bin/apMI/print.cgi

Yong, Ed. 2011. "New Evidence That IQ Is Not Set in Stone." cbsnews.com (April 26). Retrieved April 28, 2011. Online: http://www.cbsnews.com/stories/2011/04/26/scitech/main20057536.shtml

Young, Michael Dunlap. 1994. *The Rise of the Meritocracy.* New Brunswick, NJ: Transaction.

Photo Credits

Text Credits

Economy

Problems of the Economy

Richard Lord Photographer

- What is the "world economy"?

- What do we mean by globalization?

- What are the different types of capitalist economies?

- Who controls the corporations?

- Why have things gotten harder for average people?

- What can the government do to solve our economic problems?

From Chapter 4 of *Social Problems*, 10/e. James William Coleman. Harold R. Kerbo. Copyright © 2010 by Pearson Education. All rights reserved.

Don Snyder used to be an assistant professor of English at Colgate University. He had a comfortable six-bedroom house, a comfortable salary, and 18 weeks of paid vacation a year that left him plenty of time to write. Like many Americans, he thought he had it made. "I was very popular with the students, and my peers didn't hate me. I thought I was safe." Snyder soon found out he was dead wrong. His colleagues, it turned out, were not impressed with the novels he had been publishing, and he was given his pink slip. At first he denied the seriousness of his situation, and he even tried to hide the truth from his pregnant wife, Colleen. But finally, after 93 rejection letters, reality began to sink in, and he entered a two-and-a-half year path of self-destruction that included a bonfire, in which he melodramatically burned his academic books, and a near overdose of sleeping pills. Times were tough for the rest of the Snyder family, too, and sometimes they had to manage on little more than a stack of food stamps. Fortunately, Don Snyder's story has a happy ending. He eventually found employment and a surprising degree of satisfaction as a construction worker. He even wrote a book about his experiences and sold the rights to the Disney movie studios.[1]

Our economy may seem a vast and confusing system, but it is made up of countless simple stories like that of Don and Colleen Snyder. Of course, few of the millions of people who lose their jobs every year are likely to have their experiences turned into a movie, but otherwise theirs is a common story. Too often when we hear about the growing economic insecurity of the middle class, the latest figures on unemployment, or a decline in factory wages, such news seems like nothing more than dry abstractions divorced from the flesh-and-blood realities of life. So it is important to keep in mind the impact that the economic problems we discuss in this chapter have on average people. On the other hand, however, it is equally essential to realize that the economic difficulties most average people face are not just their own doing but are deeply rooted in the social and economic forces that shape our world.

The World Economy

When economic problems crop up, we tend to seek an explanation by looking at familiar events close to home. Although some problems can be understood in terms of a single nation or even a single city, today's economic problems are world problems. No one can understand the causes of inflation, unemployment, or economic inequality by looking only at a single nation in isolation from the complex international network of trade, production, and finance known as the **world economy.** As we begin the twenty-first century, that is certainly more true of the United States than at any other time in its history. So we will start our exploration of today's economic problems from a global perspective.

Globalization—the growth of a worldwide economic, political, and cultural system—has come to be the new rallying call for student protest movements of the twenty-first century. Globalization has been blamed for creating a wide range of problems: from increasing world poverty and global pollution to the loss of jobs at home in the United States. As we will see in this chapter and others to follow, many of these claims have merit, but the problem lies not so much in globalization itself but in the *way* globalization is taking place. At this beginning discussion of globalization, we must recognize a couple of facts about the process. First, it has been going on for centuries. Second, the process of globalization has gained momentum in the last 30 years and is unlikely to be reversed.[2] We can, nonetheless, learn how to promote the positive aspects of globalization and reduce the negatives. If we are to reduce these negatives, we must begin with a better understanding of the process of globalization and how nations and people are tied together through the world economy.

Although all nations are part of this world economy, all countries do not have equal roles. The principal dividing line in the modern world is between the wealthy industrialized nations and the poor nations, which are often known as the **third world** or the **less-developed countries.** Although most of the world's products are manufactured in the industrialized nations, almost 80 percent of the world's people live in the poor nations.[3]

World economy ■ The system of international economic relationships in which all countries participate.

Globalization ■ The growth of a worldwide economic, political, and social system.

Third world, less-developed countries ■ Two terms for the poor, nonindustrial nations of the world.

Most of them make their living from agriculture and the export of raw materials. Although there is a growing industrial sector in many less-developed countries, their industries pay low wages and are often owned and operated by foreigners. In contrast to the poverty of the third world, industrialized nations such as the United States have accumulated huge reserves of wealth, not just in terms of money but also in terms of the things money can buy: highways, buildings, factories, power plants, public facilities, and, of course, an educated populace and a well-trained workforce. In between these two extremes are nations such as Thailand and South Korea, which have a higher standard of living and are more industrialized than most third world countries but are still far behind such nations as the United States and Japan.

Although most third world nations have struggled to improve their position within a world economy dominated by rich capitalist countries, some have tried to follow a different road and reject the capitalist system altogether. Under **communism,** which was inspired by the ideology of Marx and Lenin, governments took direct control of all their major economic institutions. They created planned economies in which there was little competition and the important decisions were made by government officials. Originally, the communist nations sought to keep out the influence of foreign corporations and the capitalist world economy they dominate and to industrialize themselves by following their own step-by-step development plans. Although the former Soviet Union and some of the other communist nations had some success in completing the early stages of industrialization, none reached the same level of affluence enjoyed by rich capitalist countries. By the early 1990s, most communist governments in the world were gone. Today, although China and Vietnam are still ruled by their communist parties, they have made a radical shift in their economic direction, bringing in a strong dose of capitalism, and only a few isolated nations follow the old communist system.

Communism ∎ An economic system in which the government owns and controls all the major economic institutions.

To understand the problems the nations of the world face in this new global economy, we must examine the nature of **capitalism** more closely. Although difficult to define precisely, capitalist economic systems display three essential characteristics. First, there is private property. Second, a market controls the production and distribution of valuable commodities. Third, privately owned businesses compete with one another in the market, each aiming to make the greatest possible profit. The classic statement of the principles of free-market capitalism was set forth in Adam Smith's book *The Wealth of Nations,* which was first published in 1776.[4] Smith argued that individuals will work harder and produce more if allowed to work for personal profit. Private greed will be transformed into public good through the workings of a free market regulated only by supply and demand. The profit motive will drive manufacturers to supply goods that the public demands, and competition will ensure that the goods are reasonably priced. The market will regulate itself in the most efficient possible way—as though guided by an "invisible hand"—if the government does not interfere with the free play of economic forces.

Capitalism ∎ An economic system characterized by private property, profit orientation, and a competitive market for goods and labor.

Although some economists and politicians still fervently believe in the principles set forth in Smith's writings, it is clear that no real economic system operates the way Smith said it should, and no nation has completely "free" markets. Smith himself realized that businesses can reap large profits by restricting free competition and raising prices: "People of the same trade seldom meet together, even for merriment and diversion, but the conversation ends in a conspiracy against the public, or in some contrivance to raise prices."[5] Since those words were written, the major corporations have grown to a colossal size that Smith could hardly have imagined; as a result, their ability to artificially control the marketplace has become a far greater problem. Moreover, markets are now restricted in many other ways as well. Governments in the capitalist nations have all enacted numerous economic regulations and restrictions, sometimes to protect powerful special interests, sometimes to protect the public as a whole, and sometimes even to protect competition itself. Governments have also created welfare programs to help the most disadvantaged, and workers themselves have joined together into unions to demand higher wages and better treatment from their employers.

Table 1		
THREE FORMS OF CAPITALISM		
Corporate Capitalism	**Cooperative Capitalism**	**State Capitalism**
Countries	**Countries**	**Countries**
United States, Canada, United Kingdom	European Union	Japan and developing countries in East and Southeast Asia
Characteristics	**Characteristics**	**Characteristics**
Small state, little regulation, weak unions, low labor costs	Large welfare state, state regulation of economy, economic planning, strong unions	Strong state intervention, extensive regulation and planning, weak unions
Outcomes	**Outcomes**	**Outcomes**
Cheap production costs, high inequality, low benefits to workers, less job security, low unemployment, high poverty, low taxes	High production costs, low inequality, high worker benefits, high job security, high unemployment, low poverty, high taxes	Medium production costs, low inequality, medium worker benefits, medium job security, low unemployment, low poverty, low taxes

Source: Harold Kerbo, *Social Stratification and Inequality: Class and Class Conflict in Historical, Comparative and Global Perspective* (New York: McGraw-Hill, 2005), Chapter 14.

Corporate capitalism ■ A capitalist economic system that emphasizes free markets and has relatively few restrictions on corporate power.

Cooperative capitalism ■ A capitalist economic system in which corporate elites and the working class share power.

It is important to recognize that the capitalist economies in the United States, continental Europe, and Asia are significantly different, with a different balance of power among their classes.[6] The United States, and to a lesser degree Britain, have what some refer to as a *neoliberal system* or a free-market economy in which the government stays relatively uninvolved (with little economic planning and almost no government ownership of industry), resulting in more freedom for the corporations to run the economy as they wish. In this style of free-market economy, known as **corporate capitalism,** there is a relatively weak working class with less power to win government protection with labor laws, income protection, and social benefits.

A significantly different capitalist system, which is found in varying degrees in continental European countries (especially Germany and France), can be called **cooperative capitalism.** As shown in Table 1, in this system the corporate elites and working class, in alliance with government, have arrived at a sort of power-sharing agreement so that the government helps to organize the economy and protect the interests of both parties. A central component of cooperative capitalism, in contrast to the U.S. corporate-dominated system, is strong labor unions and labor laws restricting what corporate elites can do in the economy and political system.

State capitalism ■ A capitalist economic system in which the state has a high degree of independent political power and influence over the economy.

Finally, although less studied by Western social scientists, the most rapidly growing economies of the world, especially in Asia, have what can generally be called *state development capitalism* or simply **state capitalism.**[7] In this model of capitalism, the state has more independent political power, as well as more control over the economy. As in the case of the second largest economy in the world, Japan, there is little government ownership of industry, but the private sector is rigidly guided and restricted by bureaucratic government elites. Because these bureaucratic government elites are not elected officials, they are less subject to influence by either the corporate elites or the working class through the political process. The advantage of this approach is that government ministries can have the freedom to plan the economy and look to long-term national interests without having their economic policies disrupted by the short-term and narrow interests of corporate elites or the working class. The danger is that these powerful ministries may become self-serving or inflexible and lead their nation in the wrong direction.

The global economic competition of the twenty-first century will be played out among these differing forms of capitalism. Will the twenty-first century belong to a resurgent U.S. economy with its wide-open but often ruthless competition? Or will the better-trained, better-paid, and more powerful labor force of continental Europe be able to overcome the U.S. economic momentum? Or will the state capitalism of East and Southeast Asia with their government-guided and protected economies be the wave of the future? The stakes are extremely high for the citizens of rich and poor countries alike.

QUICK REVIEW

- What is the world economy?
- What are the differences among corporate capitalism, state capitalism, and cooperative capitalism?

Understanding Our Economic System

The first step in understanding our economic system is to see its role in the world economy. But we cannot get far in our efforts without also looking at its internal structures and the way they operate. In this section, we examine the four most important players in the U.S. economy: corporations, government, small businesses, and workers.

The Corporations

If all the world's largest organizations—including its governments—were listed in order of size, half would be corporations. Such giants as Wal-Mart, General Electric, Exxon, Mobil, and Ford have hundreds of thousands of employees, and their assets are worth billions of dollars. Moreover, the largest corporations keep growing, both in absolute size and in the percentage of the economy they control. The 10 largest U.S. corporations alone had revenues of just under $2 trillion in 2006, making them twice the size of the total economies of Mexico, Australia, or the Netherlands and almost three-fourths the size of the French and British economies.[8] This staggering concentration of wealth obviously gives these corporations enormous power to influence the government and shape the way average people live their lives.

When the United States was first industrializing, several of the new corporate giants that sprang up seized monopolistic control of entire industries and were able to charge exorbitant prices unrestrained by any serious competition. As a result, the federal government and many individual states passed **antitrust laws** that forbid **monopolies** (the control of industries by single firms), as well as any arrangements among competitors to work together to keep prices artificially high. Although these laws did prevent most U.S. industries from falling under the control of a single firm, they have failed in several other important ways.

Few of today's markets are controlled by outright monopolies, but the markets for many important products and services, ranging from automobiles and soft drinks to pharmaceuticals and telecommunications, are dominated by a few enormous firms—an arrangement known as an **oligopoly**. Most of the goods and services produced in the United States are made in industries dominated by such oligopolies. Even in these restricted markets, one giant is often larger and stronger than any other, thus allowing it to have a considerable degree of market control. Although antitrust laws forbid collusion among the members of these oligopolies to rig prices or restrict competition in other ways, these laws have never been effectively enforced, and there is little doubt that such activities are still common. Moreover, wave after wave of corporate mergers have gone on largely unimpeded by government action. In 2003 alone, there were more than $1.3 trillion in mergers and acquisitions in the United States.[9]

Antitrust laws ▪ Laws designed to protect free competition in the marketplace.

Monopoly ▪ The control of a market or an entire industry by a single firm.

Oligopoly ▪ The control of a market or an entire industry by a few large companies.

111

At best, antitrust laws have been only modestly successful at encouraging open competition, and in recent years they seem to be creating a new kind of economic difficulty for U.S. firms competing in the world economy. Although these laws have discouraged U.S. firms from linking themselves together into cartels and corporate interest groups, their foreign competition faces no such restrictions. Not only do these foreign corporate groups provide many of their members with financial and technical support for their ventures, but also they relieve a great deal of the pressure for short-term profits that plagues many U.S. companies. For example, most of the stock in major Japanese corporations is held by the other firms in their corporate groups, whereas private individuals hold a much larger share of U.S. firms. Although the U.S. system may sound like a better arrangement, private stockholders are primarily concerned with a corporation's quarterly profits and the dividends it allows them to pay out, whereas corporate stockholders are likely to take a much longer view of successful management.[10]

WHO RUNS THE CORPORATIONS? The modern corporation is a vast financial network. The relationships between a given corporation and its competitors, banks, subcontractors and suppliers, stockholders, directors and managers, workers, unions, and various local and national governments are extremely complex and may change without warning. Moreover, researchers who try to determine who, or what, controls this network rarely have the cooperation of corporations. Because researchers must rely on secondhand data on this politically charged issue, their conclusions are often contradictory.

Current studies show that few major corporations are now controlled by an individual family, as were Standard Oil, Morgan Bank, DuPont, and many others 100 years ago.[11] Supporters of the U.S. corporate system today claim that corporations are democratic institutions owned by many different people, and they point to the fact that tens of millions of citizens own stock in U.S. corporations. However, studies show that although some 60 percent of the American people own stock, most own such a small amount of any individual corporation's stock that their voice is insignificant. (Each share of stock usually brings one vote in the affairs of the company, mostly through helping to elect the board of directors that oversees company operations.) The biggest blocks of stock in major corporations today are owned either by a small group of wealthy individuals or institutional stockholders such as banks, insurance companies, and pension and investment funds. About 1 percent of the wealthiest and most powerful Americans control about 50 percent of family-held stock in U.S. corporations.[12] The other half of corporate stock owned by individuals is so widely dispersed that the small-time stockholders are unable to unite to offer much of a counterbalance to the power of the elite. Other powerful sources of elite influence are the banks and other financial institutions that exercise great influence over corporate decision making through their power to grant or reject loans.[13]

All of this means that U.S. corporations and, in turn, the U.S. economy are run by a small group of people that can be called a *corporate class*. As economist John Kenneth Galbraith pointed out many years ago, most national and international corporations are no longer run by a single powerful person, such as Andrew Carnegie or John D. Rockefeller. Decisions are made by executives and managers who spend their entire careers gaining the technical skills and knowledge needed to manage a modern corporation. However, the managers of U.S. corporations must still serve the primary interest of their stockholders—making profits—or they risk losing their jobs. David R. James and Michael Soref, for example, found that declining profits were the single major reason that corporate presidents lost their jobs, regardless of whether the firm was owned by a large number of stockholders or by a single individual.[14]

Corporate managers do not make their decisions simply on the basis of their knowledge and skills, however. High-level corporate managers are a distinct social class, and they act to promote their own self-interest.[15] If young managers are to get to the top, they must have more than just technical skills, ability, and drive. They must also accept the ideology and worldview of the corporate elite and support its interests. As C. Wright Mills put it back in the 1950s (when almost all corporate executives were males), "In personal manner and political view, in social ways and business style, [the new manager] must be like those who are already in, and upon whose judgments his own success rests."[16]

U.S. corporate executives have been especially aggressive in pursuing their own interests and now have by far the world's highest pay—roughly double that in other industrial countries. When the value of the stock options given many top executives is included, it is estimated the **chief executive officers (CEOs)** of the 200 largest corporations in the United States averaged more than $11 million each in total compensation in 2005.[17] Furthermore, the gap between the average worker's pay and that of top corporate executives has shown a staggering increase. In the nine years from 1990 to 1998 alone, it jumped from 40 to 1 to 419 to 1. This gap between the top executive and average worker is far greater than in any other industrial nation and still rising fast.[17a] If we look at just the largest 100 U.S. corporations, the pay gap was even bigger. In 2002, their CEOs averaged $33 million in a year in compensation, *not* including stock options. This brought them an average of $1,017 per hour compared to $16 for the average worker and $60 an hour for medical doctors.[18]

Chief executive officer (CEO) ■ The head of a corporation.

THE MULTINATIONALS In recent years, most large corporations have expanded across national boundaries, setting up a complex web of sales, manufacturing, distribution, and financial operations. Although these firms are usually based in a single country and run by people of that nationality, they are often transnational in organization and perspective. One of the most global of corporations today is certainly the Carlyle Group.[19] This international conglomerate specializes in investment funds in countries around the world. It is also the 11th largest defense contractor in the world, securing arms deals in almost all the world's trouble spots. Carlyle is also a major real-estate developer, operates health-care systems, and is heavily involved in global telecommunications. The Carlyle Group, however, is probably most unique in its collection of top corporate actors. Carlyle's board chairman is Frank Carlucci, former secretary of defense under Ronald Reagan and also former deputy director of the CIA. Other board directors for the Carlyle Group are former President George H. W. Bush, former British Prime Minister John Major, former Speaker of the U.S. House of Representatives Thomas Foley, former Secretary of State James Baker III, and former Thai prime minister Anand Panyarachum. Other board members are also executives from Boeing, BMW, and Toshiba. As one might expect, the Carlyle Group has been doing quite well financially in recent years, pulling off profitable deals all over the world. If anyone would be qualified to be members of a global corporate class at the beginning of the twenty-first century, it would be board members of the Carlyle Group.

Les Stone/The Image Works

The symbols of powerful multinational corporations can be seen all over the world, and their expansion into weak and impoverished nations often brings with it the fear of foreign domination.

Jonathan Schell argues that the contemporary corporate executive is no longer "dependent on the labor, capital or technical knowledge of any particular country. He can pick and choose from anywhere in the world. . . . [He] is not an 'American' business-man or a 'Japanese' businessman. He belongs to no country."[20] Although Schell may be overstating the case a bit, this transnational perspective is clearly growing stronger year by year. Furthermore, those who invest in corporations are developing the same transnational orientation as the managers as more and more investors buy stock in foreign nations.[21]

Multinational corporation ■ A corporation that has manufactur-ing, service, and sales operations in many countries around the world.

The growth of powerful **multinational corporations** has generated tremendous controversy. Some people see their rise as the first step toward world unity. They are convinced that by linking the economies of the world's nations, the multinationals are laying the foundation for a global government that will usher in a new era of peace and prosperity. In contrast, the critics of the multinationals see them as international bandits that exploit small countries and play large ones against one another.

The expansion of multinational corporations among the industrialized countries has created many problems of international control and regulation. Canadians, for example, are extremely concerned about the economic power of U.S. multinationals, which hold 80 percent of all foreign investment in Canada.[22] Even though the Canadian government has made repeated efforts to promote economic independence, more of Canada's economy is in foreign hands than is true of any other industrialized nation. Many Canadians have come to see foreign economic domination as a grave threat to their national inde-pendence. Even in the United States, many people are concerned about the growing influence of foreign capital. The relentless globalization of the world's economy has blurred the line between domestic and foreign products and left many formally U.S. firms under foreign control. The Chrysler Corporation, for example, only survived the 1980s by making an emotional pitch to American nationalism, arguing that the govern-ment needed to bail it out to save the U.S. auto industry. The rescue program was successful—perhaps too much so. By the late 1990s, Chrysler had become an attractive target for acquisition and was purchased by the German corporation that makes Mercedes Benz.

The worst abuses of the multinational corporations have resulted from their expan-sion into the less-developed countries of Africa, Asia, and Latin America. Although the multinationals bring advanced technology and encourage some types of economic devel-opment, the "host" nations must pay a heavy price. Foreign corporations wield tremen-dous political power in the poor countries in which they invest, and critical economic decisions are too often made by foreign corporate executives who have little concern for the welfare of the local people. Moreover, there are grounds for questioning how much economic benefit poor nations actually reap from foreign investment. Although there is considerable controversy over which poor countries have been helped and which have been hurt, several studies have concluded that foreign investment produces only short-term economic rewards. These studies indicate that once the initial investment is made, and the multinationals begin taking home their profits, the economies of nations with large foreign investments begin to fall behind those of nations that rely on their own resources for their economic development. Thus, in the long run, more self-reliant na-tions have greater economic growth.[23] It must be stressed, however, that not all poorer nations are harmed by the investments coming from powerful multinational corpora-tions, and this is especially true for some of the Asian nations that have had so much foreign investment in recent decades. Thailand, for example, has reduced poverty from 50 percent of the population in 1960 to only 15 percent by 2000, and China has seen its own economy boom with dramatic poverty reduction.[24]

Then there are the negative effects of this process of globalization has on the well-being of American workers. No one knows the exact number of American jobs that have been lost, because the U.S. government does not keep such records, but the estimates of the job losses are in the millions. Many factories have moved overseas, and more and more jobs are being "outsourced"—that is, laborers in foreign countries are taking over from domestic workers and doing such things as answering telephones and maintaining financial records. This is also a primary reason that salaries in the United States have stayed low even in a time of economic expansion. American workers have difficulty demanding higher wages; if they do, U.S. corporations may ship their jobs out to low-wage countries.

CORPORATE CRIMES The business world is sometimes described as a lawless jungle in which profits rule, and those who let ethics stand in their way are considered foolish and quaint. Although this is an exaggeration, there is ample evidence that the crime rate is high in the business world.

Everyone has had the experience of buying an article of clothing or an appliance that seemed to fall apart after hardly any use. Although the manufacture and sale of such merchandise do not violate the law, knowingly making false claims for a product is a type of **fraud**. There are countless examples of fraud in industries ranging from cosmetics to automobiles. The wave of corporate scandals that rippled across the United States in the opening years of the twenty-first century, for example, involved a host of fraudulent accounting schemes designed to make failing corporations look like winners to stockholders and potential investors. The most famous of these involved the Enron Corporation—once an obscure energy pipeline company that in less than a decade built itself into one of the world's largest energy-trading corporations. One key to Enron's meteoric rise was the money it spent cultivating powerful political connections. For example, the chairman of Enron, Kenneth Lay, gave the 2000 Bush presidential campaign $290,000 of his own money and was later appointed an advisor to the Bush transition team. Dozens of other top Enron executives also gave large political contributions, and the corporation itself gave hundreds of thousands of dollars in "soft money" to both parties. The company built itself into one of the largest corporations in the United States by the start of the twenty-first century through the use of deceptive financial statements, stock manipulations, and various other illegal practices. For example, when the state of California passed a law deregulating its electric power industry, one division of Enron secretly moved electric power out of the state and created widespread power outages. The cost of electric power to consumers went through the ceiling, and Enron reaped the profits. By the time Enron filed for bankruptcy in December 2001, shareholders had lost some $22 billion in equity, and thousands of employees lost their jobs and often their retirement nest eggs as well.[25]

Fraud is not, however, just a matter of money. Some fraudulent claims endanger the health or even the lives of consumers. The major pharmaceutical companies have, for example, frequently been caught making fraudulent claims about their products or concealing information to cover up their hazards. Two well-known examples are the painkiller Oraflex, which is thought to have killed 49 people and injured almost 1,000 more, and the Dalkon shield contraceptive device, which is believed to have caused the deaths of at least 17 women and about 200,000 injuries.[26]

Price-fixing, or the collusion by several companies to cut competition and set uniformly high prices, is another common corporate crime. A survey of the heads of the 1,000 largest manufacturing corporations asked whether "many" corporations engaged in price-fixing. Among those heading the 500 largest corporations, a surprising 47 percent agreed that price-fixing is a common practice. An overwhelming 70 percent of the heads of the remaining 500 corporations agreed.[27] It is quite possible that price-fixing costs consumers more than any other kind of crime.

Many companies also use illegal practices to drive their competitors out of business. One technique is for a big company to sell certain products at a loss in order to bankrupt a small competitor. The company recovers its loss and increases profits by selling the products at much higher prices after the competition has been eliminated. Another technique is for a giant corporation to buy out producers of key raw materials and cut off supplies to its smaller competitors. As with most corporate crimes, the damage extends far beyond the immediate victims to the general public, which ends up footing the bill in one way or another.

Fraud ■ Deceit or trickery used to gain some unfair economic advantage.

Price-fixing ■ Collusion by several companies to cut competition and set uniformly high prices.

The Government

Although everyone recognizes the power and importance of corporations in our economic life, many people in countries that practice individualistic capitalism underestimate the economic importance of the government. Although supporters of Adam Smith's laissez-faire ideology argue that governments should simply stay out of economic affairs and allow the free market to regulate itself, the governments of all industrialized nations are deeply involved in directing their economies. Actually, government plays two key economic roles in contemporary capitalist societies. First, as a major employer, government provides jobs and paychecks for millions of people who do everything from sweeping streets to flying bombers. Second, government regulates the economic activities of the private sector.

Some regulation is done directly through the legal system—for example, when the courts decide civil suits involving private businesses or when the government brings legal action for the violation of antitrust laws. U.S. government agencies such as the Federal Trade Commission and the Food and Drug Administration play a major role in regulating economic activities in a variety of different industries. The operation of these regulatory agencies has been the focus of considerable debate in recent years. Consumer groups charge that although these agencies were set up to protect the public interest, they often end up serving the interests of the industries they regulate: "The regulatory agencies have become the natural allies of the industries they are supposed to regulate. They conceive their primary task to be to protect insiders from new competition—in many cases, from any competition."[28] One problem is that the directors of these agencies often come from the industries they are supposed to regulate, and they return to those same industries when they leave the government. This "revolving door" between business and government obviously undermines the public interest. It brings in many people who are more sympathetic to the interests of the corporations than the public, and it makes many regulators fearful of risking their economic future by offending corporations that might someday offer them a high-paying position. Moreover, even when officials try to do their best, the power of the corporations is so great that these small, underfunded agencies are often too weak to get the job done.

On the other hand, business groups often make the opposite criticism, charging that government regulation damages the economy by requiring a mountain of costly and time-consuming paperwork and by placing unnecessary restrictions on their activities. As a result of these criticisms, several important industries have been **deregulated** since the 1980s. Unfortunately, the results of deregulation have often been disappointing. Deregulation of the airline industry, for example, not only produced a drop in ticket prices but also brought a sharp decline in the quality of service. Moreover, it touched off a wave of mergers, buyouts, and bankruptcies that has reduced competition in many markets, and prices are once again on the upswing. Deregulation of the savings and loan industry had even more serious consequences. Once freed from government controls, many managers pursued speculative high-risk investments or fraudulent schemes to enrich themselves at their companies' expense, and the result was the virtual collapse of the entire industry. The deregulation of the natural gas industry led to a similar pattern of abuses—and led the Enron Corporation to what turned out to be the single largest corporate collapse in U.S. history.

In addition to direct regulation, the government also has a variety of indirect means it can use to influence the economy. If the government wants to stimulate the economy to grow more rapidly, it can increase the size of its **budget deficit** (the difference between what the government earns in taxes and other revenue and how much it spends) or use its financial power to push down the interest rates charged on loans. As great as it is, however, the government's power is not unlimited. If it stimulates the economy too much, the result is likely to be a higher rate of **inflation** (price increases) and a greater danger of a severe economic downturn in the future. If the inflation rate gets too high or the economy appears to be growing too rapidly, the government can reverse those policies and push up interest rates or reduce the deficit. But then the likely result is more **unemployment**. Tax

Deregulation ■ The termination of government economic regulations and controls.

Budget deficit ■ The amount of money the government spends in excess of amount it receives in taxes and other revenues.

Inflation ■ An increase in prices.

Unemployment ■ The problem suffered by those in the workforce who want jobs but are unable to find them.

policies also have a tremendous impact on the economy, influencing the general rate of economic growth and providing special benefits or problems for specific industries. Whatever techniques the government uses, the average citizen now expects it to do everything possible to ensure economic prosperity. When the economy is in decline, the government is blamed and politicians have a difficult time getting reelected, but a prosperous economy is a boon to incumbent politicians. As we will see toward the end of this chapter, however, even the limited power of the U.S. government over the economy has been reduced by the growth of globalization. The fate of the U.S. economy is not determined just by what happens here but also by what happens in the European Union, Asia, and Latin America. And with their increasing ability to move jobs, factories, and investments anywhere in the world, multinational corporations can often defy the rules and regulations of any national government, even one as powerful as that of the United States.

Small Business

Although overshadowed by the huge corporate and government bureaucracies, small businesses nonetheless play a key role in the economy. Numerically, small businesses have always been the majority. With the current limitations in the growth of government employment and the downsizing of many big corporations, small businesses have played a key role in creating new jobs for the growing workforce. The share of the workforce that is self-employed has grown sharply—more than 11 percent over the last three decades.[29] Estimates of the total number of American workers who are self-employed vary widely, depending on the definitions and techniques used, but they range from about 8 percent to 13 percent of the workforce.[30] Of course, most people in the small-business sector are not self-employed but work for someone else.

Although there may be more job opportunities in small business, working conditions are quite different from those in the government or corporations. The main attraction of small business is the independence it offers to its many owner-operators, but most new businesses go bankrupt in their first year or two, and many of the entrepreneurs who succeed work long hours for a modest return. The employees of many small businesses share their boss's economic insecurity but without the compensation of greater independence. In comparison with corporate workers, the employees of small businesses are less unionized and receive lower pay and fewer fringe benefits.

Although small businesses and corporations are often lumped together as part of the private sector, there are fundamental differences in the economic environment they face. As we have seen, the large corporations are often able to restrict competition among themselves, thus safeguarding their profitability. Even when they face stiff competition, most major corporations have accumulated huge financial assets that can help see them through rough times. In contrast, small businesses generally struggle against a host of competitors and have extremely limited financial reserves to fall back on. Another important difference is political. Major corporations wield enormous political power—as a result, they can obtain many benefits and special favors from the government. Small businesses are much less influential and therefore pay higher taxes, receive fewer government benefits, and cannot expect a government bailout when they run into financial trouble. For these reasons, some economists refer to corporations as the *monopoly sector* of the economy and to small businesses as the *competitive sector*.

Perched between the corporate giants and the legions of "mom-and-pop" businesses are the medium-sized firms that are at the center of much economic innovation and

Although the owners of small businesses, such as the woman shown here, create many new jobs, they lack the political power and financial resources of big corporations.

Patti McConville/ImageState/International Stock Photography Ltd.

117

technological development. Unlike small companies, these firms have the size and economic resources necessary to develop new products and market them effectively. Compared with the giant corporations, medium-sized firms have less cumbersome bureaucracies and are more subject to the competitive pressures of the marketplace. Because medium-sized firms are not large enough to dominate their principal markets, they face the same choice as small businesses: Be efficient and competitive or go under.

The Workers

Not only are workers the heart of the economic system, but also their work is often a central focus of their lives. People's self-concepts—their ideas of who and what they are—are profoundly affected by their occupations and their place in the occupational hierarchy. Our jobs bring us into contact with specific social worlds and specific groups of people. If we consider, for example, the differences between the social worlds of a police officer and a ballet dancer, it becomes obvious how deeply people are influenced by their work.

THE WORKFORCE Both the types of jobs and the kinds of people who work at them have changed radically over the last century. Three major trends are apparent in the changing job market. First, the number of workers, owners, and managers of farms—once the largest job category—has steadily declined. Mechanization and technology have enabled a handful of workers to feed millions, so fewer people are needed on the farm. Farmers now make up less than 1.4 percent of the workforce, and the Department of Labor expects their numbers to keep declining.[31] Second, because of automation and increasing competition from foreign products, there has been a shift of workers away from higher-paying manufacturing and production jobs and into lower-paying **service occupations** (jobs that provide a service to someone else rather than making a product or extracting a natural resource). Just since 1989, the United States has lost millions of jobs in manufacturing, mining, and construction while creating 10 times that number of new service jobs.[32] In addition to the growing number of self-employed workers we have already discussed, there has been an even sharper increase among temporary workers, whose numbers have more than tripled in the last decade and a half.[33]

Although a service job may sound more attractive than working in a factory, the reality is often quite different. Service work can be just as dull, menial, and repetitive as most factory work, and on the average the pay is only 70 percent as high. The result has been a growing income gap between the working class and more highly trained managers and professionals, along with the deterioration of entire towns that depend on failing manufacturing concerns.

These changes have brought great hardship to people from all walks of life, but especially to the working class. In 2000, close to half of all Americans below the poverty line lived in families with a full-time worker—much more than in years past (see Figure 1). It is almost certain the percentage of the working poor is higher today, but the U.S. Bureau of the Census stopped providing these data in its annual reports at the beginning of the second George W. Bush administration. One obvious reason for this trend

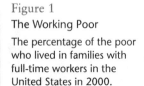

Service occupations ■ Jobs that provide a service to someone else rather than making a product or extracting a natural resource.

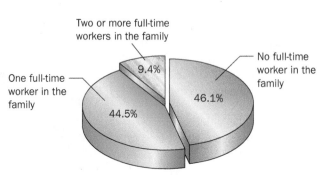

Figure 1

The Working Poor

The percentage of the poor who lived in families with full-time workers in the United States in 2000.

Source: U.S. Bureau of the Census, *Poverty in the United States, 2000* (Washington, DC: U.S. Government Printing Office, 2001), Table C.

Two or more full-time workers in the family

9.4%

One full-time worker in the family

44.5%

No full-time worker in the family

46.1%

Lessons from Other Places

Overworked Americans

When living and working in Europe, Americans are often confused at first by all the holidays and the short hours during which shops are open. Cash is getting low and you run to the bank, only to find that it is closed today for some holiday. Spain seems to have the most "bank holidays," but it may have been just my bad luck for running low on cash at all the wrong times. In Germany, almost all shops close early Saturday afternoon and do not open again until Monday morning. I am sure I have not been the only unlucky American arriving in the Frankfurt Airport on Saturday afternoon for a drive to my apartment to face an empty refrigerator. After a while, Americans began to wonder, "When do these people ever work? Are they always off on a holiday?"

These questions, of course, are exaggerated, but official statistics back up these impressions. Americans work more hours than people in any other major industrial nation. In the mid-1990s Americans passed the Japanese, who were always known as the world's premier workaholics.

During the late 1980s and early 1990s, the Japanese government began a national campaign to get Japanese people to stop working so long. Some estimates put the number of deaths from overwork—known as *karooshi*—as high as 10,000 per year. The Japanese government also figured that if the Japanese stop working such long hours,

there would be more leisure time for Japanese consumers to go out and spend money. There were posters in all the buses making the plea, and major corporations were pressured to reduce working hours. One major corporation decided to cut electrical power to its building to force managers and employees to leave. It worked, and the average hours worked by Japanese began to decline.

On the other hand, the average hours worked by Americans continued to increase. Between 1995 and 1998 alone, Americans increased their average work year by 70 hours. Now it is Americans who work more hours than people in any other major industrial nation. And with most mothers and fathers putting in these long hours, American families are experiencing increases in work-related stress and a host of related family problems.

Harold Kerbo

Harold Kerbo and John McKinstry, *Modern Japan* (New York: McGraw-Hill, 1998); Harold Kerbo and Hermann Strasser, *Modern Germany* (New York: McGraw-Hill, 2000); Juliet Schor, *The Overworked American* (New York: Basic Books, 1991); *International Herald Tribune*, September 11, 2000; Lawrence Mishel, Jared Bernstein, and Sylvia Allegretto, *The State of Working America, 2006–2007* (Ithaca, NY: Cornell University Press, 2007), Table 8-7.

is that the minimum wage hasn't kept up with the cost of living. In 2006, the federal minimum wage was slightly more than $5 an hour compared to almost $8 per hour (after adjusting for inflation) back in 1960.[34]

The third and perhaps most important of these trends involves the sweeping changes in the role of women in the workforce. For one thing, unprecedented numbers of married women have been taking jobs outside the home. In 1900, only 5 percent of married women were part of the workforce; today, more than 60 percent of all married women hold jobs.[35] As we saw in the previous chapter, another key development has been the entrance of women into occupations that used to be reserved almost entirely for men.

It is easy to overlook the unemployed, but it should be remembered that those who are out of work are still part of the workforce. The amount of unemployment goes up and down from one year to the next, depending on the state of the economy. At the beginning of the twenty-first century, the United States was well into its longest economic boom in history. In the last decade, unemployment ranged from a low of 3.8 percent of the workforce to a high of 6.6 percent. At the end of 2006, the unemployment rate stood at 4.5 percent.[36] Official unemployment statistics do not, however, count **discouraged workers,** or those who have given up looking for jobs, and those who are the victims of **underemployment**—that is, those who take part-time jobs when they want full-time work. If those two groups were added in, the unemployment figures would almost double. Although government unemployment insurance provides some help, only people officially defined as unemployed are eligible, and even among that group the number who actually receive unemployment benefits has steadily declined as eligibility standards have been raised. When people do become eligible for unemployment benefits in the

Discouraged workers ■ Workers who have given up looking for work and are not counted in unemployment figures.

Underemployment ■ The situation of workers who want permanent full-time work but can find only part-time or temporary work.

119

Personal Perspectives

An Unemployed Logger

A job is more than just a way to make a living. The loss of a job can have traumatic psychological effects. This is especially true for people like this unemployed logger, who sees little chance of getting another job as good as the one he lost.

There was a disbelief among the workers that we would ever be permanently laid off. We believed the United States needed building materials, and it had to come from somewhere. When I found out the day before Christmas that I was permanently laid off, I wasn't too worried. After 16 years, I felt I had valuable job skills in the timber industry and that I wouldn't have any problem getting another job. It didn't work out that way, though, and after a while fear of the future set in. There weren't many job prospects, and I had to lower my sights on wages.

About this time, my marriage started coming apart. I had been paying all the bills, and suddenly my wife had to start contributing to paying the bills. Her paycheck used to be just for her. This caused a problem. Arguments happened more often. About four months after I was laid off, she told me she wanted a divorce. This was a pretty low time for me. The marriage stuff was more of an emotional downer than the job stuff. All the cornerstones of my life came tumbling down.

In retrospect, it was a growth experience. You get middle aged, have a job, relationship, home . . . you coast. When it all gets taken away from you . . . well, it was a growth experience.

United States, they normally get less than 50 percent of their former wages, and even this normally ends after six months. In contrast, European nations provide far more support for the unemployed. For example, in Germany unemployed persons can receive up to 80 percent of their former wage up to two years after becoming unemployed, and thereafter up to 60 percent of their former wage for life.[37] Moreover, the severe financial difficulties created by the loss of jobs are only part of the problem, as we can see from this chapter's Personal Perspectives from an unemployed logger.

To make matters worse, the use of part-time workers has grown increasingly popular with employers. Since 1973, the percentage of workers holding part-time jobs has increased more than 11 percent and now includes 20 percent of the workforce.[38] The reason for this trend is clear: Part-time workers are cheaper. On the average, women who work part-time earn 23 percent less per hour than full-time workers, and men receive almost 40 percent less; they are both far less likely to receive medical or retirement benefits. So it is not surprising that most part-time workers really want full-time work.[39]

THE CASE OF WAL-MART   With more than $316 billion in sales in 2006, Wal-Mart is now the second biggest corporation in the world. Its sales were almost twice as much as General Electric or Microsoft. The five children of Sam Walton, the founder of Wal-Mart, have an estimated wealth of about $18 billion each, making them the seventh through the 11th richest people in the world. It comes as no surprise that, because of its size, Wal-Mart establishes trends in U.S. labor relations and shapes the production of goods all over the world—trends toward lower wages, fewer benefits, longer working hours, and the weakening of labor unions. The company admits that no one can raise a family on the $8 per hour that it gives new employees but adds that "working for Wal-Mart is maybe not right for everyone."[40] During the mid-twentieth century, the largest U.S. employer was General Motors, where unions were strong, benefits were good, and workers earned wages that put an American family far above the poverty line. Now the trend is toward low-wage employers such as Wal-Mart. In 2000, for the first time since the U.S. Census Bureau began measuring poverty in 1959, almost 50 percent of those below the poverty line lived in the household of a full-time worker.

Knowing that labor unions could help raise the wages and benefits of its employees, Wal-Mart has a strict policy forbidding union activity among its employees. If an employee even talks with a union representative, he or she may be fired or denied promotion. All new workers are required to watch a film depicting unions as corrupt and only out to take members' money. Managers of Wal-Mart branch stores are required to quickly report any union activity so the head office can rush out an "anti-union" SWAT team to make sure there is no further contact with a union.

Wal-Mart's impact on working Americans, however, is not confined to its low wages, disappearing benefits, or union busting. Wal-Mart is a leader in helping move jobs from the United States to poor countries with low-wage labor. In the early days of Wal-Mart, only 5 percent of goods bought in its stores were made in other countries. In 1985, founder Sam Walton launched his "Bring It Home to the USA" program. "Wal-Mart believes American workers can make a difference," he told his suppliers, offering to pay as much as 5 percent more for U.S.-made products. By 2002, however, around 60 percent of merchandise sold in Wal-Mart stores was made in other countries. So fierce is Wal-Mart's cost-cutting pressure that companies wishing to remain Wal-Mart suppliers are often forced to locate new factories in poor developing countries around the world. Wal-Mart now has more than 3,000 supplier factories in China alone, with many more moving to other poor countries.

Even in food retailing, Wal-Mart has established new records in price-cutting, made possible in large measure by the low wages and benefits given its employees. A cart of groceries at one of Wal-Mart's superstores, for example, costs 17 percent to 39 percent less than in better-paying grocery stores. With little union pressure or federal laws restricting Wal-Mart's antiworker policies, other U.S. retailers are being forced to follow Wal-Mart's lead if they are to stay in business.

WORKER ALIENATION Mechanization of the workplace during the Industrial Revolution led to a progressive dehumanization of workers as they were forced to change their patterns of work to meet the demands of the machines they operated. Although work hours may not be as long now as they were a century ago, many of today's factory workers still find their jobs tedious and trivial and see themselves as little more than cogs in a machine. Such feelings of **alienation** are so common that they have been given a name: the blue-collar blues. David J. Charrington's survey of worker attitudes found that "feeling pride and craftsmanship in your work" was one of the most highly desired characteristics of a job.[41] Yet technology is rapidly eliminating skilled craftspeople and replacing them with complex computer-controlled machinery. People displaced from such jobs often drift into low-skilled service industries, but even those who are retrained to repair and maintain the new equipment often lose the sense of pride that came from being directly responsible for producing a high-quality product.

Many programs have been created to help blue-collar workers gain greater satisfaction on the job. Some corporations, for example, give a group of workers responsibility for assembling a finished product rather than give each individual responsibility for only one small part of it. Other companies encourage workers to rotate from one job to another in order to vary their tasks. Some managers allow employees to set up their own work procedures and schedule their own hours. Allowing workers to participate in management decisions that affect their jobs also reduces alienation. However, conflict theorists argue that worker alienation will not be reduced significantly until workers receive a greater share of the profits of the companies that are using their labor.

Ironically, just as the corporations are discovering the problem of worker alienation among the shrinking blue-collar labor force, the computer revolution is creating similar problems among the growing numbers of clerical workers. Computers were supposed to liberate office workers from the drudgery of performing the same tasks again and again, but so far that hasn't been the result. As in the early days of factory automation, computers have been used to break down jobs into smaller and simpler tasks. The use of computers has also tended to isolate workers from other employees; at the same time, the new technology has increased employers' ability to scrutinize the actions of their workers. For example, workers who deal with the public on the phone often find that computer-generated reports show how many calls they answer and how long they spend with each customer, while supervisors randomly audit calls that exceed a given length. Moreover, repetitive movements required by some computerized equipment, such as cash registers that read bar codes, have caused huge increases in repetitive-strain injuries in the wrist and a host of eye and back problems.

Alienation ■ A feeling of estrangement from society and social groups. A feeling of the loss of control over one's activities, especially one's labor.

DEATH ON THE JOB Boredom and alienation are not the only problems workers have to face on the job. Working for the wrong company or in the wrong industry can have fatal consequences. The Centers for Disease Control and Prevention estimate that about 17 workers a day are killed on the job.[42] Overall, there were 5,575 fatal accidents in U.S. businesses during 2003. Although there has been a drop in deaths from industrial accidents in recent decades, there were still almost three deaths for every 100,000 workers in 2003.[43]

In addition to the thousands of workers who die from workplace accidents, a much larger number die more slowly from the effects of occupationally caused diseases. The U.S. government estimates there are 100,000 such deaths a year, but that figure is only an educated guess. Many workers who die from occupational diseases never know the source of their condition. Besides this huge death toll, at least 3.4 million workers a year are injured in occupational accidents, and many more are probably made ill by the work they do.[44]

It is clear that some employers simply do not care about the deaths and injuries they cause their workers. New procedures and techniques are constantly being developed by industry, but few employers take time to test them adequately before bringing them into the workplace. More than half a million chemicals are used in industry, but only a few thousand have been thoroughly tested to see if they are dangerous. Even when tests do show a chemical to be hazardous, some firms try to keep the results secret. For example, when an Italian scientist discovered that vinyl chloride (a popular plastic) causes a rare form of cancer that had been found among workers exposed to it, the Manufacturing Chemists Association joined with the European firm that sponsored the research in a coordinated effort to keep the findings secret. Confidential memos indicate that the manufacturers of asbestos followed the same policy and intentionally concealed the dangers of asbestos exposure from their workers. The ultimate death toll among these men and women is expected to be far more than 200,000.[45] Nonetheless, there are signs that things have been getting better in recent years, as we see in the box "Jobs Are Getting Safer."

LABOR UNIONS The early period of industrialization created misery among workers. Entire families labored in mines and factories. Industrialists paid subsistence wages, claiming that workers were lazy and would stop working if they were better paid. Working conditions were terrible, and deaths from occupational accidents were common. Workdays were long, often 14 hours or more, and holidays were few and far between. Conditions were so bad that Karl Marx proclaimed the workers would soon destroy capitalism in a violent revolution. The workers, however, did not respond with revolution: They responded with unionization.

Early labor unions faced bitter struggles with employers and the U.S. government, which supported employers' interests. In many places, unions were outlawed and organizers jailed; even when unionization became legal, organizers found themselves harassed at every turn. Unions gradually gained official recognition and acceptance; as they won power, the conditions of the average worker improved. Unions eventually became a major economic and political force that was often critical to the success of politicians and business enterprises alike.

Signs of Hope

Jobs Are Getting Safer

A day on the job is a difficult and dangerous affair for many workers, but there are signs that things are getting better. In 1960, about 14,000 Americans were killed on the job, or about 21 of every 100,000 workers. In 2003, in contrast, only 5,575 people died on the job, and because the workforce had grown considerably, the occupational death rate was less than one-fifth as high as in 1960. Moreover, there was a similar drop in the number of workers who suffered disabling injuries on the job.*

One reason for this improvement was the decline in the percentage of the workforce employed in heavy manufacturing jobs (which tend to be the most dangerous). Tighter government regulations, a growing concern about worker safety, and the threat of lawsuits against negligent employers also played a major role.

*Statistical Abstract of the United States, 2006 (Washington, DC: U.S. Government Printing Office), Table 641.

Mike Simons/Getty Images

Traditionally, the threat of a strike has been the unions' most effective weapon in their struggle for better pay and better working conditions. In today's anti-union climate, however, the number of successful strikes is far lower than it was in the past.

Despite the successes of the past, unions are in serious decline. By 2004, only about 8 percent of the private-sector workforce (excluding the self-employed) was unionized; that figure was close to 50 percent about 50 years ago, and it remains far higher in most European countries today. With dwindling labor union membership in the United States have come timidity and ineffectiveness. The average number of strikes a year has dropped to a fraction of what it was in earlier decades, and the wage settlements unions win are also far smaller than in the past.[46] Indeed, a growing number of strikes has resulted in the permanent replacement of the strikers with nonunion labor.

What caused this erosion of union membership and union power? Because union membership is highest in manufacturing and among **blue-collar workers,** a significant part of the decline in union membership has resulted from a decrease in the importance of those occupations. Unions are now directing more efforts toward organizing government employees and **white-collar workers,** but resistance remains strong. Today's unions face other serious problems as well: On one side are the increasingly sophisticated technologies such as industrial robots that threaten more and more union jobs; on the other side are the masses of the world's poor who will eagerly work for a fraction of union wages. Ironically, increasing their output through automation is one of the few ways workers in high-wage countries, such as the United States and Canada, can continue to compete with low-wage workers in the less-developed countries. As a result, the unions are often faced with the unpleasant choice of losing jobs to automation or to foreign labor. To make matters worse for the unions, their declining numbers have reduced their political clout, which has made it easier for business interests to win government bureaucrats and policy makers to their side.

Blue-collar workers ▪ Workers who perform manual labor.

White-collar workers ▪ Workers who perform nonmanual labor.

QUICK REVIEW

▪ Who runs the corporations?

▪ How have corporations shaped the modern economy?

▪ What role does the government play in the economy?

▪ How are conditions different for small businesses and big corporations?

▪ How did our workforce change in the twentieth century?

▪ Why has union membership declined?

The New Economic Realities

With the normal **business cycle** there are alternating periods of "boom" and "bust." During the up cycle, profits, wages, productivity of workers, and business investments tend to increase while unemployment and poverty decrease. The only downside is that those changes have tended to increase inflation as well. Eventually, the economy slows, prices and **real wages** begin to decline, and unemployment moves up again, as does poverty. Throughout the long economic expansion that began during the early 1990s in the United States, however, these things did not happen as economists predicted. Unemployment and inflation both stayed low, while the wages of average workers were stagnant, and people had to work more hours just to keep from getting behind. The rich continued to get richer, and although most of the poor did not get poorer, they showed little or no improvement in their condition. As a result, inequality continued to grow.[47] In the face of all this, too, Americans have been spending more and saving less. This long economic boom ended in 2001, but the economic recovery that started in 2002 has again been different with a far smaller increase in jobs than in similar recoveries in the past.[48] The United States has, in short, entered uncharted economic territory. We seem to be in an era of boom and bust at the same time. It is an economic boom for the wealthiest American families, while it has been more a time of bust for the less fortunate.

To deal with these new economic problems, we must understand their causes, and the first place to look is the changing world economy. Modern world system theory has made it clear that for the last 500 years the competition between powerful nations for advantage in the world economy has been an ever more important force driving economic change. The Industrial Revolution and new machine technologies brought the British dominance by the early 1800s. The further development of industrial technology, and especially assembly-line production, helped the United States win world leadership during the early twentieth century.

U.S. economic dominance was enhanced even further at the end of World War II when all the major industrialized nations—except the United States and Canada—lay in ruins. The factories of North America emerged from the war undamaged, and their products were sometimes the only ones available. As Europe and Japan began to recover from the war, they were hungry consumers of North American goods. The United States became the world's dominant economic power, and the U.S. dollar was virtually an international currency. By the early 1970s, Europe and Japan had rebuilt and developed vigorous industries of their own that could more than compete with U.S. firms in the world market. All of the new competition for American workers, however, did not come from foreign companies alone. The big U.S. corporations became truly international organizations, with little allegiance to the interests of their home country. Because the United States was the most prosperous country in the world during the postwar period, its workers received the highest wages. The availability of cheaper labor in the poor nations led large U.S. corporations to shift many of their manufacturing operations to other countries. Thus, the increasing competition faced by American workers drove wages down and unemployment up, while wealthy investors often benefited from the lower cost of labor.

Accentuating its economic problems was the fact that the United States was facing competition from the new styles of capitalism that developed in such countries as Japan and Germany after World War II. Their cooperative approach emphasizes group cooperation and national coordination to a far higher degree than in the United States, and the individualistically oriented U.S. system has had a difficult time adjusting to this new challenge. In the United States, the interests of the individual stockholders are given priority over the long-term good of the corporation, whereas in European cooperative capitalism the opposite is true. Consequently, U.S. corporations pay out a far higher percentage of their profits in stock dividends (about 80 percent) than do European or Japanese corporations (about 30 percent),[49] which obviously leaves these corporations with more money to invest in the future of their firms. Similarly, top Japanese executives are often shocked by what they see as the personal greed of their U.S. counterparts, who often raise their own salaries even when their companies are losing money. In 1990, the average CEO of a large Japanese company made 18 times more than the company's workers, whereas an average American CEO made 119 times the salary of an average worker.[50] And as Table 1 suggests, the gap is even greater today. One estimate by the Institute for Policy Studies put the ratio of factory workers' pay to CEOs' pay at 419 to 1.[51]

With the U.S. economic expansion that began in the 1990s, the list of the world's wealthiest people came to be dominated by Americans, and the average wealth of America's richest households doubled in just 10 years. Although the stock market was booming, the number of billionaires was increasing, and top executives were winning fat increases in their incomes, the wages for average workers showed little improvement, and poverty rates were going up. In simple terms, the rich were getting richer—much richer—while the poor were getting poorer.[52]

The major question is, how did the United States turn its economy around and why did the haves and have-nots fare so differently during this recovery? This first response to the United States' years of economic decline showed up during the Reagan presidency in the 1980s. Sharp drops in corporate profits and hard economic times in the 1970s led the upper strata of U.S. society to become more politically active. Through such means as lobbying, stronger political organization, and campaign contributions, the corporate class and the wealthy were able to bring about a sharp change in government economic policy. Both personal and corporate taxes were cut, whole industries were cut free of governmental regulation, welfare was reduced, and the political tide turned sharply against labor unions.[53] These changes, along with the increased competition for jobs from workers in poor countries, sent real wages, benefits, and job security down and forced American workers to work longer and longer hours. Because of the savings these changes brought to U.S. corporations, they were able to produce goods and services more cheaply and compete more effectively against firms from other industrial nations.

A second factor in the American economic turnaround was the explosive growth of high-tech industries and revolutionary innovations in computers and electronic communications. Intel, Microsoft, and many less famous firms were creating a lot of high-tech jobs and making a lot of Americans rich. The use of computer technologies also helped create dramatic improvements in the processing and distribution of information and in the manufacturing process for almost every kind of product. So U.S. corporations obtained a double benefit: Americans were working longer hours and working for less money while the technological revolution was making them increasingly efficient. Corporate profits soared and so did the stock market. Finally, a third factor that contributed to the economic boom was consumer spending. Americans have always been good at spending money for all kinds of consumer items, but confident consumers increased their spending and reduced even further what was already the lowest savings rate of any industrialized nation. Those free-spending consumers helped keep the economy racing along.

What does all this tell us about the economic future of the United States? Economic predictions and projects are so often wrong that any answer to this question has to be taken with a good deal of skepticism. Nonetheless, there are several economic clouds on the sunny horizon of today's economic prosperity. Many studies have shown that there are recurring waves of economic expansion and stagnation in the world economy. One nation usually leads the upward swing by finding more efficient ways of organizing work and creating better technologies.[54] The United States is now on top of one of those new waves. The leader's advantages, however, always decline as other nations catch on to the new ways of doing things. Currently, the Japanese and Europeans are making changes and adjustments to increase their economic competitiveness with the United States, and there are already signs they are succeeding.[55] Because the United States has already cut wages and increased working hours far more than nations such as Germany and Japan, it doesn't seem likely that U.S. business can get another boost by squeezing its workers again. A second problem is the national savings rate and unprecedented levels of consumer and government debt. Although the federal government did reduce its debt during the second half of the 1990s, the "guns and butter" policies of the second George W. Bush administration led to record levels of

During the last decade, the American lead in advanced computer and communications technology helped the U.S. economy surge ahead, but the rest of the world is rapidly catching up.

Mark Richards/PhotoEdit Inc.

federal debt at the same time that consumers were setting their own record for indebtedness. When the next big economic downturn occurs, there is a real possibility that a tidal wave of new bankruptcies will make things much worse than they would otherwise have been. Even if this doesn't happen, one of the most likely ways for U.S. corporations to stay competitive in the global economy of the future is to move even more jobs overseas to take advantage of the cheap labor in less-developed countries. This, in turn, is likely to continue to put strong downward pressure on the wages and benefits of American workers.

QUICK REVIEW

■ What are the three economic eras since the end of World War II?

■ Why did the U.S. economy stagnate in the 1970s?

■ What happened in the United States to touch off the economic boom of the 1990s?

■ What have been the results for American workers?

Solving the Problems of the Economy

In attempting to deal with the problems of our economy, politicians and economists all too often focus on short-term ups and downs and lose sight of the big picture. As we have seen, this big picture is one of growing globalization and economic competition from developing third world nations. We have seen how the prosperity of U.S. corporations since the 1990s has been to a large degree won at the expense of American workers, especially those at the bottom of the economic ladder. If we are to reform our economy so that economic competition does not mean making workers work longer for less money or shipping jobs to less-developed countries, then we must learn to adjust to the new economic realities of the global economy.

The Role of the Government: Bystander or Planner?

Some strategies to revitalize the economy cut across ideological lines. For example, proposals to improve our educational system gain supporters across the political spectrum (although liberals and conservatives often disagree about how to achieve those objectives). The overall approach of those on the political right and left, however, differs markedly.

The conservative approach is based on the free-market laissez-faire ideology that has traditionally been so strong in the United States. Conservatives generally want to cut back on the size of government in order to free more money for private investment and to sharply reduce the government's role in regulating the economy to avoid the inefficiency they believe regulation produces. They often advocate cuts in social-welfare spending, which in their view encourages people not to work, and they support a reduction in the minimum wage (or allowing it to be slowly eroded by inflation), in order to reduce the cost of labor for U.S. business. But the proposals dearest to the hearts of most conservatives are sharp cuts in taxes—especially for the well-to-do. The assumption is that tax cuts stimulate investment by putting more money into the hands of the wealthy than they are likely to spend. Conservatives argue that the economic benefits those investments produce then "trickle down" to the average citizen. Thus, conservatives advocate an individualistic approach to solving economic problems: The government should cut back on all programs and policies, whether welfare or business regulations, that restrict the free individual struggle for gain. If a big corporation is driven to the edge of bankruptcy by foreign competition, let it go under; when successful entrepreneurs make a fortune, let them enjoy their wealth without excessive taxation.

Critics argue that such policies are cruel and misguided: They rip the social safety net out from under millions of hardworking Americans, increase homelessness and malnutrition, and create an intolerable level of economic insecurity. In their view, cutting back the government's role in regulating the economy does not create more competition but less, because the wealthy and powerful are free to use their advantages to lock everyone else out of the economic game. These critics point out that in the past, tax breaks for the wealthy have often spurred spending on luxuries, such things as gold and antiques, and therefore have produced few benefits for anyone else.

In contrast to the individualistic approach of the conservatives, those on the left call for more socially oriented policies to foster greater economic cooperation. One of their principal recommendations is for more **economic planning** on the part of the government. Advocates of economic planning point out that the governments of the United States' most successful economic competitors, especially Japan and Germany, are deeply involved in planning and directing the economies of their nations. Therefore, they argue that representatives of the U.S. government, major corporations, unions, and environmental groups should work together to develop a comprehensive economic plan that identifies areas of economic strength and weakness and outlines a coherent strategy to improve the economic environment. Then all these diverse groups must be motivated to work together for the good of the entire nation. The goal of this economic planning, however, should not in the view of most of its supporters be simply to make our society more wealthy but also to make it more fair, more stable, and more environmentally sustainable.

Economic planning ■ The active involvement of government in directing the economy.

Critics of the government's role in the economy point to the damage done by some government programs in the past. They argue that, as in the communist countries, deep government involvement in the economy causes waste and inefficiency. Supporters of economic planning respond that the conditions here are now completely different and that we should seek a healthy balance that avoids both the anarchy and exploitation that come from unregulated capitalism and the oppressive centralized control of the communist system. They point out that the economies of both Japan and Germany quickly moved from the ashes of World War II to become economic powerhouses through extensive and well-managed government economic planning and that both nations have far less poverty and healthier populations than the United States.

Investing in the Future

There is a growing consensus that Americans need to take a much longer-term perspective when making key economic decisions. Although it is easy to say that we need to increase our investment in the future and lower the mountain of debt we are leaving for future generations to pay off, there seems to be little will to actually do it. The fact is

Debate

Is Freer World Trade and More Globalization the Way to Economic Prosperity at Home?

Recent years have seen some important steps toward freer world trade—including the ratification of the North American Free Trade Agreement (NAFTA), which allowed Mexico to enter the free-trade zone that already existed between the United States and Canada, and the creation of the World Trade Organization, which is charged with ensuring that no nation illegally impedes the free flow of good and services in the world economy. But are such agreements really beneficial to our own economy?

YES The record is clear. Free trade is good for the world economy, and it is good for the individual nations that participate in it. When the United States passed the Smoot-Hawley Tariff Act in 1930, the ensuing trade war established new barriers to world commerce that were a major cause of the Great Depression. After World War II, however, the industrialized nations worked together to bring down their trade barriers, and the world economy flourished.

The reasons for this are simple. Freer trade gives the businesses of each nation larger potential markets but also many more competitors. Thus, well-run businesses flourish while the incompetent go under. The result is a more efficient and more productive economy that benefits everyone.

Some people claim that freer world trade will help the Japanese, the Germans, or the third world nations more than it will the United States, but there is no reason to believe that is true. Each nation has its own unique economic strengths and weaknesses. It also makes good sense to let each nation make the products it makes best and buy from someone else the products it is not good at making. Although some nations may be hurt if they can't

produce anything that anyone else wants to buy, does anyone really think that is true of the United States or Canada? We will prosper in an open world market, and we should do everything we can to encourage its growth.

NO The world has changed, and the old answers simply don't work anymore. In the past, freer trade always benefited the most industrialized nations because their products were cheaper and better than those from other places. After World War II, for example, North American products were the best in the world—and the fewer restrictions there were on trade, the more money our businesses made.

Today things are different. There is far greater competition from such places as Germany and Japan, but the more critical problem is the third world. In the past, third world industries weren't much of a problem because they operated with inefficient management and outdated technology. But now multinational corporations bring the latest technology and management techniques to whatever country has the lowest labor costs. There are literally billions of workers in the third world who are willing to work for a few dollars a week, and their numbers and their desperation are growing every day. Free trade is a boon to the multinational corporations and their stockholders, but it will drive millions of our workers into poverty and unemployment.

Free trade can flourish only in a free world. Until we can break the third world nations' chains of poverty and despair and help them bring their runaway population growth under control, we must protect our workers with strong tariff barriers. We have no other choice!

that we cannot have our cake and eat it too: The only place to get the money is to reduce our consumer spending—in other words, to lower our current standard of living. Perhaps we should learn from the long-range perspective taken by Native Americans, who considered a major decision by asking themselves what impact it would have seven generations in the future.

Once we have committed ourselves to take a longer-term view and to invest more in the future, there are several possible ways to do it. To start with, we need to reduce the huge federal budget deficit and encourage private citizens to save more of their income. Another obvious step would be to reform the tax structure to reduce taxation on investment and increase it on spending. For example, we could increase the tax rate on corporate profits and use the money to provide tax credits and other incentives to companies that invest in more research and new plants and equipment. Another idea would be to increase the tax rate on speculative investments, such as buying and selling commodities or real estate, and reduce the rate for productive investments, such as building an environmentally sound factory that creates new jobs. More money and effort should be spent on education to improve the quality of our workforce and teach the growing population of poor and immigrant children the skills needed in a high-tech economy. The "digital divide" between Americans who can use computers and the other new technologies so essential in today's world economy and those who cannot is growing more serious all the time. If new educational programs are not directed toward less-educated Americans, a growing portion of the U.S. labor force will be unable to function effectively in the ever more demanding high-tech economy. Another pressing need is to create better systems of mass transit and rebuild our decaying highways and railroads. The rate of U.S. investment in basic infrastructure (roads, bridges, etc.) is less than half what it was in the 1960s, and we are being outspent by all our major economic competitors.[56] In addition to their long-term benefits, many of these kinds of investments are also likely to create a considerable number of the kind of well-paying working-class jobs that are currently in such short supply.

Restructuring the Workplace

Many proposals have been made to improve our productivity by restructuring workplaces and the corporations that organize and create them. One Japanese idea that is gaining popularity is known as **lean production**. Firms that use this approach cut back their overlapping layers of management, use a smaller but more flexible workforce, and strive to develop a closer working relationship with parts and equipment suppliers. Another successful Japanese idea is to give workers more responsibility in the decision-making process. This approach not only fosters a greater commitment to the organization but also takes advantage of the workers' intimate knowledge of the day-to-day problems they face on the job. In the long run, however, workers are unlikely to show more commitment to their companies unless companies also demonstrate greater commitment to them by avoiding layoffs and showing a genuine concern for their welfare.

Lean production ■ An approach to manufacturing that attempts to use the smallest possible amount of labor.

Advocates of **economic democracy** take such ideas a step further and propose programs to give workers more power over the decisions of top corporate officials as well. Past experience has shown that employees have a more cooperative attitude, accept necessary hardships, and work harder when they own a part of the company and share directly in its profits (or losses). Therefore, it seems logical that the government should assist workers to take over the ownership of financially troubled firms and help workers start new cooperative enterprises. In fact, the trend toward greater employee ownership is already under way. The number of employees participating in stock-ownership plans has grown substantially in recent years. Although most of these plans fall far short of workers owning a controlling interest in the firm, several major corporations have been acquired by their employees in recent years—one of the most successful examples being the Avis car rental company. A bolder approach would be to pass legislation as Germany has to require that worker representatives be included on the boards of directors of all major corporations. Moreover, Germany's Works Constitution Act from the 1970s requires all corporations to allow employees to elect a "works council" to represent their interests. By law, the employees elected to the works councils have the right to examine the corporate books and must be consulted by management on any hiring or firing, changes in work process, working hours, or anything related to the interests of employees. Studies have shown that worker commitment to the company and worker productivity has increased as a result of these work laws in Germany.[57] Another useful addition to corporate boards would be a public representative who could speak for the interests of the nation as a whole. However it is implemented, advocates of economic democracy argue that a fairer and more efficient system would give workers a strong voice in controlling their own occupational lives.

Economic democracy ■ A program to give workers control over the decisions that affect their lives.

Building a Sustainable Economy

If we stand back and take a hard look at the global economy, it seems shockingly irrational. Every year we are using up more and more of our limited natural resources and pouring out ever-increasing amounts of toxic pollutants in order to produce a flood of consumer goods that add little or nothing to the quality of our lives. In fact, the

Environmentalists argue that conversion to more environmentally sound technologies can create many new jobs, such as the one for the installer of this solar panel.

Sustainable society ■ A stable society that does not exceed the carrying capacity of its environment.

relentless materialism of our consumer culture is more likely an overall source of suffering than satisfaction. Spurred by the ideals of the environmental movement, many people are coming to believe that the economy should be restructured to make it more environmentally sustainable. From a theoretical standpoint, it seems clear that we must find a more harmonious way to live with our environment, yet we often fail to take even the most obvious steps toward building a more **sustainable society**. For example, it has been decades since the first "energy crisis," yet the United States is still so dependent on foreign oil that a new crisis in the Middle East could have the same or even worse consequences. Every year, increasing numbers of gas-guzzling sport utility vehicles clog the highways, the daily commute to work gets longer and longer, and new homes get ever larger, driving up both their heating and cooling costs. If we wanted to reduce this danger and cut the enormous environmental threat posed by the global warming, we could raise gasoline taxes and use the money to help communities develop local hydroelectric and solar resources. We could also conserve energy by implementing programs for such things as better insulation and more effective systems of mass transit.

A major underlying problem is that our economic system is structured to reward individuals who seek immediate short-term profits, while the costs of the long-term harm they cause are passed on to our entire society. But an even more fundamental difficulty lies in the values of our consumer culture that tell us that we can never have enough. The more riches we have, the more of the latest consumer products we own, the happier we will be. Social status comes more from what we own than the quality of our character or the contribution we make to the welfare of those around us. Later we'll explore many proposals for building a more stable, sustainable society, but we will have to take a long, hard look at our economic values before we will be willing to carry them out.

It is also important to remember that the quality of life is not measured solely by the economist's computations of average income or the standard of living. The quality of life can be improved regardless of the economic climate. Numerous suggestions for such improvements are discussed in this book, including proposals to make the workplace safer, reduce crime, improve the lives of the elderly and the poor, clean up the environment, and upgrade the educational system so that people can better understand the complexities of the world around them. Of course, all these things are expensive, but their overall cost is small compared to the benefits they bring.

QUICK REVIEW

■ What are the best ways of dealing with our economic problems?

Sociological Perspectives on Problems of the Economy

Shrinking wages, foreign competition, the hardships of unemployment, and similar difficulties seem to be matters for technically trained economists. Indeed, some economists devote their lives to the study of these problems. Sociologists, however, generally feel that a "dollars and cents" approach cannot, by itself, yield genuine understanding of our economic difficulties. To the sociologist, economic ills can be understood only in their social context. It makes no more sense to study economic problems apart from their social background than it does to try to solve social problems without understanding their economic basis. Sociologists therefore use theoretical perspectives to analyze economic problems in relationship to society as a whole.

The Functionalist Perspective

Functionalists see the economic system as a machine that produces and distributes the commodities a society needs. If the system functions efficiently to give the society what it wants, then there are few economic problems; but sometimes the machine balks or strains. One part may run faster or slower than others, throwing the whole system out of balance; for example, distribution may not keep up with production, or we may produce too many goods of one kind and not enough of another. Such maladjustments may correct themselves through the operation of the free market, or they may be corrected through government action. Economic crises occur when the whole machine becomes disorganized and coordination falters throughout the system.

Functionalists blame contemporary economic problems on the rapid changes that have thrown the traditional economic system out of balance. It took hundreds of years for Western society to develop and perfect an economic system based on open competition among private individuals in a free market, but as the system became larger and more complex, its problems multiplied. As we have seen, huge corporations sprang up and gained control of many vital markets, the government stepped in to regulate the economy, and powerful unions began to control the labor market. Thus, these new cogs destabilized the old machinery. Then, just as we were struggling to bring the system back into balance, major shifts occurring in the world economy threw North American business into intense competition with dynamic new economies around the world. Under these conditions, many of the old economic ideas no longer worked as they had in the past, and dysfunctional economic decisions followed. The breathtaking pace of economic change made it impossible to resolve old economic problems before new ones arose.

Most functionalists shy away from radical, far-reaching proposals for solving economic problems, principally because they know that change brings problems as well as solutions. Disruptive change in an unbalanced system makes a new balance even more difficult to achieve. Functionalists favor specific, limited cures for specific, limited problems, such as education and training for the unemployed and better law enforcement to deter corporate crime. The basic goal of the functionalist is to reduce the disorganization in economic institutions and improve the coordination between them and other social institutions. Only when this goal has been reached will the economic system function smoothly and efficiently.

The Conflict Perspective

Conflict theorists take a decidedly different view of the economic system. Unlike functionalists, they do not consider society a unified whole based on a consensus about norms and values. Consequently, they do not say that the economic system performs either well or badly for the entire society. Rather, they believe that it benefits certain groups at the expense of others and that who benefits, and to what degree, changes from time to time.

From the conflict perspective, society is composed of many different groups, each trying to advance its economic interests at the expense of the others. Most economic problems arise because one group—or a coalition of groups—seizes economic power and acts in ways that advance its own interests at the expense of the rest of society. Thus, conflict theorists say that recent changes in the economic system reflect competition among different groups. They each work for their own selfish interests, as Adam Smith said they should. But conflict theorists do not, like Smith, assert that this competition brings advantages to everyone. They say it benefits only the most powerful competitive groups. Conflict theorists charge that ever since businesspeople and industrialists seized power from the landed nobility, they have busily enlarged their power and their affluence at the expense of everyone else.

According to the conflict perspective, the underlying cause of most economic problems is the exploitation of workers by their employers and other members of powerful elites. If these problems are to be solved, then workers must somehow gain enough control to make the elites give up their advantages and create a more just economic order. The first step, according to Marxists, is for oppressed workers to develop **class consciousness,** a sense of unity based on the realization that they are being exploited. Then the workers must organize themselves for political action and achieve change either through peaceful struggle—elections, protests, and strikes—or, if need be, through violent conflicts. Conflict theorists, whether Marxist or not, see the widening gap between the income of the haves and have-nots as a direct result of the decline in the power of the unions and the failure of political organizations to represent the interests of working women and men. They feel that these trends must be reversed if most people are ever going to see their economic situation improve.

Class consciousness ■ A sense of unity and awareness among the members of a social class.

Conflict theorists have begun to focus more attention on globalization and the world economy to understand what is happening in the national arena and even on the local level. They argue that the rich nations are in competition among themselves for a greater share of the world's markets and wealth. The rich nations seek to dominate poorer countries (often keeping them poorer) for their own economic advantage, and the workers of the world in rich and poor countries are all in competition for jobs and wages controlled by the rich multinational corporations of the world. In this view, the expansion of this world economy, or globalization, accounts for many of the difficulties that American workers have experienced in recent decades. When corporations threaten to move jobs to the poor countries or cheap foreign products flood the marketplace, American workers are forced to accept lower wages and longer hours. Moreover, conflict theorists argue that the globalization of the world economy also hurts the poorer nations as multinational corporations take wealth and profits and leave the people of the less-developed countries without the resources necessary to improve their lives.

The Feminist Perspective

When feminists look at recent developments in our economy and the role women have played, they see two important stories. The first is the enormous flexibility women have shown in adapting to a historic change in their economic role. In earlier years, women's primary economic contribution was in the home: doing housework and taking care of the children. With the economic crisis of the 1970s, however, millions of women poured into the workforce in order to help their families make ends meet. As a result, the position of women in our society underwent a fundamental transformation, and both women and men are still struggling to adjust. Today, the average mother not only handles most of the traditional homemaking and child-care responsibilities but also puts in many long hours working outside the home.

The second story is one of continuity, not change. Unfortunately, that continuity lies in the economic exploitation of women. Although record numbers of women have entered the workforce and many have entered traditionally male jobs, the fact remains that, on the average, a woman is still paid only 77 cents for each dollar her male counterparts earn.

The solution to this problem lies in an attack on the barriers of prejudice and discrimination that still keep women second-class economic citizens. Changes in the educational system to encourage women to enter the highest-paying fields of study, tougher enforcement of antidiscrimination laws, and changes in the hostile attitudes many male workers have toward their female co-workers are just a few of the suggestions commonly made. In addition, the workplace needs to be made more "woman friendly." The fact of the matter is that women still bear the major share of the responsibility of child rearing, and employers need to create more on-site day-care centers, allow more flexible working hours, and in general take a more supportive attitude toward the needs of their employees' families.

The Interactionist Perspective

Because interactionists are concerned mainly with individuals and small groups, they rarely address large-scale economic problems directly. Instead, they are more interested in the impact of the economic system on an individual's psychological makeup, attitudes, and behavior patterns. They also examine the impact of these ways of behaving on the larger economic system. Interactionists and other social psychologists have found, for example, that unemployment has devastating psychological consequences for many workers. Feelings of boredom, uselessness, and despair are common, and some frustrated workers suffer much more serious difficulties. Studies show that the rates of such stress-related problems as high blood pressure, alcoholism, mental disorders, and suicide are significantly higher among the unemployed. Unemployed workers are also more likely to lash out at those around them. Research shows that a rise in unemployment increases the rate of child abuse and other family violence.[58]

The psychological damage caused by the economic system is not limited to the unemployed. Our competitive economy encourages a strong achievement motivation that often leads to dissatisfaction and anxiety. When a large percentage of a population is oriented toward individual competition, the culture it shares is likely to show many forms of innovation and creativity, but this system also promotes insecurity, fear, and aggression. Interactionists have observed, however, that these burdens are not equally shared by everyone in a society. On the average, the unskilled and downwardly mobile have far more social and psychological problems than other people. They are more likely to be hostile and withdrawn and to suffer from low self-esteem and bouts of intense anxiety.

Effective solutions to the psychological problems created by our economic system are not easy to find. One possibility would be to deemphasize the values of competition and achievement and instead emphasize cooperation and mutual support. Despite the fact that such values have long been stressed in family and religious institutions, their application to society at large meets strong resistance. This opposition seems to be based on the fear that reducing competitiveness will destroy initiative and creativity. Perhaps this is why more emphasis is placed on the clinical treatment of psychological disorders than on changing the economic and social conditions that produce them. Many interactionists nonetheless continue to argue that reducing economic insecurity, even in a competitive society, would improve the mental health and well-being of our entire population.

QUICK REVIEW

- What are the differences in the ways a functionalist, a conflict theorist, a feminist, and an interactionist would explain our economic problems?

Summary

Change has come so rapidly to our economic system that many people have difficulty seeing things as they really are. One common mistake is to look only at familiar events close to home and ignore the web of international relationships that makes up the world economy and the growing trend toward the globalization of our cultural and economic life. The principal dividing line in the modern world is between the wealthy industrialized nations and the poor agricultural nations. Although some poor nations have attempted to pull out of the capitalist world economy and rely on a centralized state plan to industrialize themselves, most of the nations that followed this communist system have now given it up or greatly modified it. All the rich industrialized nations practice one version or another of capitalism, although no nation adheres very closely to the ideals of the completely open free-market system advocated by Adam Smith. Today, three different styles of capitalism are practiced by the rich industrialized nations. The United States and most other English-speaking countries practice corporate capitalism with the least government regulation and the most freedom for corporations. Japan and most of Asia practice state capitalism in which the government plays a dominant role as the director and planner of the economy. Finally, France, Germany, and most other continental European countries practice cooperative capitalism in which the corporations and the working class share power.

The corporation is a major force in the modern economic system. Some corporations have grown so large that they control dozens of different companies in many countries. Although antitrust laws no longer permit most markets to be controlled by a monopoly (one corporation), many industries are dominated by an oligopoly (a few large corporations). There is considerable debate over who runs the corporations. Some people see stockholders as the owners and controllers, whereas others argue that power rests with corporate managers, who have the special technical skills needed to make effective decisions. Most sociologists hold that high-level corporate decision makers represent the interests of a small elite, but others suggest that the decision makers represent a wide variety of conflicting interests. Most large corporations are multinationals—that is, they have offices and facilities in many different nations around the world. These big multinationals are tied in to the world market, and they often have little allegiance to the interests of their home countries. Some people think the multinationals are laying the foundation for a new era of world peace and cooperation, but others see them as exploiters of the poor and the powerless. Moreover, corporations often engage in criminal activities such as fraud and price-fixing in their own countries as well.

The government, like the corporations, has come to play a key role in the economic system. The government not only is a major employer but also is deeply involved in managing the economy. With the downsizing of many corporations in recent times, small businesses have come to play an increasingly important role in the creation of jobs. However, conditions are difficult for many small businesses. Competition is generally much more intense than in the corporate sector, financial reserves are often inadequate, and, unlike the corporate giants, small businesses seldom get a government bailout when they get into trouble.

Workers are at the heart of any modern economy. Recent times have seen a sharp decline in the number of workers in farming and the old manufacturing industries, while service jobs have been on the increase. Unfortunately, most of the new jobs have been low-paying ones. Unemployment and underemployment remain significant problems. Another important trend is that women, especially married women, have been entering the workforce in ever-increasing numbers.

The United States emerged from World War II in a position of world economic dominance, and the 1950s and 1960s were an era of unprecedented economic prosperity that benefited all economic classes. The 1970s saw intense new competition from Europe and Asia that sent the whole U.S. economy into a decline. The economy turned around in the 1990s, but the benefits have gone mainly to the wealthy and the upper middle class, leading to a growing gap between the haves and have-nots.

Many proposals have been made for dealing with economic problems. Some people propose changes in the role the government plays in the economy, others say we have to invest more heavily in our economic future, while still others argue that our shortsighted exploitation of the environment is leading us to disaster, and that we have to work to build a more sustainable economy that uses it resources more wisely.

Functionalists seek to reduce economic disorganization. Conflict theorists call for the common people to ban together to demand a bigger share of the economic pie. Feminists see the need to end discrimination against women and make the workplace a friendlier place for mothers with children. Interactionists call for a greater concern with the personal problems caused by our competitive economic system.

QUESTIONS FOR CRITICAL THINKING

We can evaluate our economic system in many different ways. Economists tend to take the narrowest view and look simply at how much wealth it produces. Most sociologists think the question of how fairly wealth is distributed is often more important than how much wealth there is. Environmentalists focus their attention on the sustainability of the economic system: How much damage does it do to the environment, and does it consume resources faster than they can be replaced? Finally, from the broadest perspective, we might ask whether our economic system contributes to the overall sense of well-being and happiness of the people or whether it leaves them frustrated and unfulfilled. Do your own evaluation of our economic system in terms of each of these four viewpoints.

KEY TERMS

alienation	deregulation	price-fixing
antitrust laws	discouraged workers	real wages
blue-collar workers	economic democracy	service occupations
budget deficit	economic planning	state capitalism
business cycle	fraud	sustainable society
capitalism	globalization	third world, less-developed
chief executive officer (CEO)	inflation	countries
class consciousness	lean production	underemployment
communism	monopoly	unemployment
cooperative capitalism	multinational corporation	white-collar workers
corporate capitalism	oligopoly	world economy

INTERNET EXERCISE

Considering the impact of economic conditions on almost all aspects of American society today, it is not surprising that there are many interesting sites related to the state of the United States and world economies today. To begin your exploration of these Websites, go to the *Companion Website* at www.pearsonhighered.com/coleman. Enter Chapter 4 and choose the Web destination module from the navigation bar.

To complete the first Web exercise for Chapter 4, go to the Bureau of Census Website at www.census.gov and first click on "Subjects A to Z" tab at the top; then click on "I" to find the latest annual report titled *Income, Poverty and Health Insurance in the United States: 2006*. Read the Introduction to this report, then find the section called *Highlights*, under *Income in the United State*. From the most recent economic analysis, what has been happening to *the real median income* of households in the United States in recent years? Have American families been equally affected by economic changes in the American economy in recent years? Has income inequality among Americans been going up or down in recent years? What can we say about the relationship between economic prosperity and inequality in the United States?

NOTES

1. Curtis Rist and Mark Dagostino, "Handy Lesson," *People*, October 6, 1997, pp. 79–80.

2. See Christopher Chase-Dunn, Yukio Kawano, and Benjamin D. Brewer, "Trade Globalization Since 1795: Waves of Integration in the World-System," *American Sociological Review* (February 2000): 77–95; David Held, Anthony McGrew, David Goldblatt, and Jonathan Perraton, *Global Transformations: Politics, Economics, and Culture* (Palo Alto: Stanford University Press, 1999).

3. *World Population Data Sheet, 2006* (Washington, DC: Population Reference Bureau, 2006).

4. Adam Smith, *An Inquiry into the Nature and Causes of the Wealth of Nations* (New York: Random House, 1937 [originally pub. 1776]).

5. Ibid., p. 128.

6. See Harold R. Kerbo, *Social Stratification and Inequality*, 6th ed. (New York: McGraw-Hill, 2006), Chapter 14.

7. Chalmers Johnson, *MITI and the Japanese Miracle* (Palo Alto: Stanford University Press, 1989); Harold Kerbo and John McKinstry, *Who Rules Japan?* (Westport, Connecticut: Greenwood/Praeger, 1995); Harold Kerbo and Robert Slagter, "The Asian Economic Crisis and the Decline of Japanese Leadership in Asia," in Frank-Jurgen Richter, ed., *The Asian Economic Crisis* (New York: Quorum Press, 2000); Harold Kerbo and Robert Slagter, "Thailand, Japan, and the 'East Asian Development Model': The Asian Economic Crisis in World System

Perspective," in Frank-Jurgen Richter, ed., *The East Asian Development Model: Economic Growth, Institutional Failure and the Aftermath of the Crisis* (London: MacMillan Press, 2000); James Fallows, *Looking at the Sun: The Rise of the New East Asian Economic and Political System*, (New York: Pantheon, 1991); Ezra Vogel, *The Four Little Dragons: The Spread of Industrialization in East Asia*, Cambridge, Massachusetts, Harvard University Press, 1991).

8. Fortune, January 2007; www.money.CNN.com; Kerbo, *Social Stratification and Inequality: Class Conflict in Historical and Comparative Perspective* 6th ed. (New York: McGraw-Hill, 2006), World Bank, *World Development Report, 2000* (New York: Oxford University Press, 2000).

9. U.S. Bureau of the Census, *Statistical Abstract of the United States, 2006* (Washington, DC: U.S. Government Printing Office, 2003), Table 752.

10. See Lester Thurow, *Head to Head: The Coming Economic Battle Among Japan, Europe, and America* (New York: Morrow, 1992).

11. See Kerbo, *Social Stratification and Inequality: Class Conflict in Historical and Comparative Perspective*, 6th ed. (New York: McGraw-Hill, 2006), Chapter 7.

12. Ibid.

13. See Beth Mintz and Michael Schwartz, *The Power Structure of American Business* (Chicago: University of Chicago Press, 1985).

14. David R. James and Michael Soref, "Profit Constraints on Managerial Autonomy: Managerial Theory and the Unmaking of the Corporate President," *American Sociological Review* 46 (February 1981): 1–18.

15. See G. William Domhoff, *Who Rules America? Power and Politics in the Year 2000* (Mountain View, CA: Mayfield), 1998.

16. C. Wright Mills, *The Power Elite* (New York: Oxford University Press, 1956), p. 14.

17. www.pearlmeyer.com, January 2007; Kerbo, *Social Stratification and Inequality*.

18. *Los Angeles Times*, August 30, 1999.

19. *USA Today*, March 31, 2003.

20. Tim Shorrock, "Crony Capitalism Goes Global," *The Nation*, April 1, 2002, pp. 11–16.

21. Jonathan Schell, "Capital Is No Respecter of Ideologies," *Los Angeles Times*, June 17, 1991, p. B5.

22. Robert B. Reich, "The REAL Economy," *Atlantic*, February 1991, pp. 35–52.

23. Wayne D. Thompson, *Canada 1986* (Washington, DC: Stryker-Post, 1986), p. 106.

24. Volker Bornschier and Christopher Chase-Dunn, *Transnational Corporations and Development* (New York: Praeger, 1985); Glenn Firebaugh, "Does Foreign Capital Harm Poor Nations? New Estimates Based on Dixon and Boswell's Measures of Capital Penetration," *American Journal of Sociology* (1996) 102: 563–578.

25. Robert Slagter and Harold Kerbo, *Modern Thailand* (New York: McGraw-Hill, 2000); Harold Kerbo, *World Poverty in the 21st Century: The Modern World System and the Roots of Global Inequality* (New York: McGraw-Hill, 2005).

26. See Bethany McLean and Peter Elkind, *Smartest Guys in the Room: The Amazing Rise and Scandalous Fall of Enron* (New York: Portfolio, 2003).

27. Ibid., pp. 76–77.

28. For a review of this and other studies on price-fixing, see James William Coleman, *The Criminal Elite* (New York: St. Martin's Press, 1985), pp. 51–53.

29. Morton Mintz and Jerry S. Cohen, *America, Inc.* (New York: Dial, 1971), p. 70.

30. Lawrence Mishel, Jared Bernstein, and John Schmitt, *The State of Working America, 1996–97* (Armonk, NY: M.E. Sharpe, 1997), pp. 271–273.

31. Ibid., p. 271.

32. U.S. Bureau of the Census, *Statistical Abstract of the United States, 1996* (Washington, DC: U.S. Government Printing Office, 1996), p. 407.

33. Lawrence Mishel, Jared Bernstein, and John Schmitt, *The State of Working America, 2003* (Armonk, NY: M.E. Sharpe, 2003).

34. Ibid.

35. U.S. Bureau of the Census, *Statistical Abstract of the United States, 2003* (Washington, DC: U.S. Government Printing Office, 2003), p. 425.

36. U.S. Bureau of the Census, *Statistical Abstract of the United States, 2006*, p. 392.

37. www.bls.gov, December 2006; U.S. Bureau of the Census, *Statistical Abstract of the United States, 2003*, p. 406.

38. Kerbo and Strasser, *Modern Germany* (New York: McGraw-Hill, 2000).

39. www.bls.gov, December 2006.

40. U.S. Bureau of the Census, *Statistical Abstract of the United States, 2003*, p. 393.

41. Information in this section comes primarily from a series of investigative reports appearing in the *Los Angeles Times*, November 23, 24, and 25, 2003.

42. David J. Charrington, *The Work Ethic: Working Values and Values That Work* (New York: AMACOM, 1980).

43. Associated Press, "17 American Workers a Day Died on the Job During the 80s," *The New York Times*, April 15, 1994, p. A8; U.S. Bureau of Labor Statistics, 2001, Table A-10.

44. U.S. Bureau of the Census, *Statistical Abstract of the United States, 2006*, p. 433.

45. Ibid.

46. Ibid., pp. 10, 70–71.

47. Ibid., pp. 435–436.

48. Allen R. Myerson, "In Era of Belt-Tightening, Modest Gains for Workers," *The New York Times*, February 13, 1997, pp. C1, C4. For much more detailed analysis of the trends, see Mishel, Bernstein, and Schmitt, *The State of Working America, 1996–97*, pp. 131–239. For data on health coverage, see p. 7.

49. Louis Uchitele, "Job Growth in the U.S. Comes to Virtual Halt," *The New York Times*, January 10, 2004.

50. Thurow, *Head to Head*, p. 126.

51. Ibid., p. 138.

52. *Los Angeles Times*, August 30, 1999.

53. See data in Kerbo, *Social Stratification and Inequality*, 2006, Chapter 2.

54. Michael Useem, *The Inner Circle: Large Corporations and the Rise of Business Political Activity in the U.S. and U.K.* (New York: Oxford University Press) 1984; Kerbo, *Social Stratification and Inequality*, 2000, Chapters 6 and 7.

55. See Chase-Dunn, Kawano, and Brewer, "Trade Globalization Since 1795," 77–95; Held, McGrew, Goldblatt, and Perraton, *Global Transformations*; Volker Bornschier and Christopher Chase-Dunn, eds. *The Future of Global Conflict* (London: Sage, 1999).

56. Kerbo and Strasser, *Modern Germany*; Harold Kerbo and John McKinstry, *Modern Japan* (New York: McGraw-Hill, 1998); Kerbo, *Social Stratification and Inequality*, Chapters 13, 14, 15.

57. Thurow, *Head to Head*, p. 161.

58. Lowell Turner, *Democracy at Work: Changing World Markets and the Future of Labor Unions* (Ithaca, NY: Cornell University Press, 1991); Kathleen A. Thelen, *Unions of Parts: Labor Politics in Postwar Germany* (Ithaca, NY: Cornell University Press, 1992); Kerbo and Strasser, *Modern Germany*, 2000.

59. M. Harvey Brenner, *Estimating the Cost of National Economic Policy*, U.S. Congress, Joint Economic Committee, 1976.

ECONOMY AND WORK

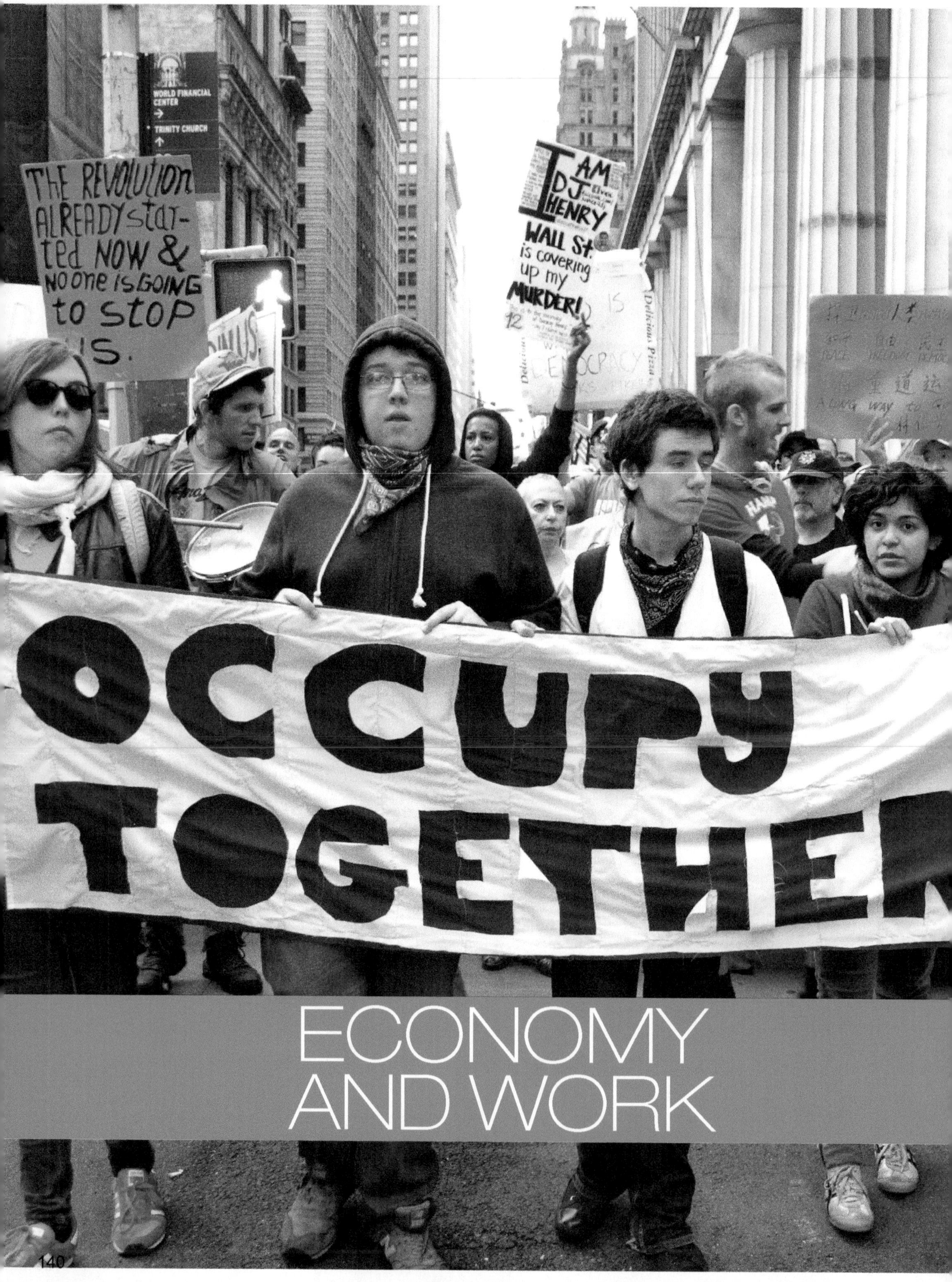
WORLD FINANCIAL CENTER
TRINITY CHURCH
THE REVOLUTION ALREADY star-ted NOW & NO ONE IS GOING to STOP
I AM DJ HENRY
WALL St. is covering up my MURDER!
OCCUPY TOGETHER

ECONOMY AND WORK

In 2011,

the U.S. economy had, technically, already dug itself out of the recent economic recession. But the news media and the American people certainly weren't acting like the country was headed for a financial upturn. Instead, the United States was undergoing another kind of debilitating kind of contraction: a confidence recession.

In strict economic terms, a recession is defined as two consecutive quarters of negative GDP growth. The first quarter of 2011 saw a modest 0.4 percent growth, and the second quarter crawled to 1 percent growth. Because this kind of growth doesn't immediately impact most Americans, they were left feeling pessimistic about their financial futures and employment prospects, reluctant to splurge on luxury purchases or invest and inclined toward stowing cash away under their mattresses.

This kind of negative thinking is spurred on by the news media, which are fond of alarmist phrases like "double-dip recession" and "crisis of confidence" and of reporting unemployment numbers daily. What's worrisome is that a confidence recession has a real impact on people's behaviors, which in turn have a real impact on the economy. With all this fear in the air, consumers, businesses, and investors get skittish about spending. The old adage about how you have to spend money to make

money is true. Without money moving around the marketplace, very little happens. New ideas don't get financed, putting a halt to technological innovations. Businesses don't expand, so new workers aren't hired. The confidence recession becomes a self-fulfilling prophecy that creates precisely the economic downturn that it feared.

The gloomy mood of the country isn't helped by the perceived political dysfunction in Washington and around the globe. Petty partisan disagreements that complicated debates over raising the nation's debt ceiling contributed to the first-ever U.S. credit downgrade. News of extreme austerity measures in Greece and the eurozone's increasing debt woes can't be ignored in a global economy. The Dow Jones industrial index declines by triple digits nearly daily. Meanwhile, swarms of protesters descended upon Wall Street in an effort to take back their financial futures from "corporate greed and corrupt politics."[1]

The government is hoping that two measures will help to renew confidence. President Obama unveiled a plan to boost job growth, and a special congressional committee convened to find a way to reduce the U.S. deficit. But Americans have little faith in the president and Congress, so it remains to be seen if they have the power to restore a battered national confidence.[2]

---Many Americans are buying gold instead of real estate, delaying vacations and retirement, and struggling to pull themselves out of unemployment. How did we get into this mess?

To understand what contributed to the recent economic recession, we need to understand a few central economic principles. How does the economy work and what factors contribute to making it prosper or decline? This chapter will discuss the different forms of economy, how they have evolved, and what roles individuals and other nations play in the economic sphere.

get the topic: HOW DO WE GET WHAT WE NEED?

Historically, governments have always been involved in their nations' economies, whether they were printing money, generating coins from precious metals, or creating a central bank to control interest on loans. The economy is the vehicle used in society to provide needed goods and services. All economic action is social. It occurs in the interactions between individuals in the pursuit of their self-interests. It, of course, also occurs in relationship to one's position in society and the power associated with it.[3] You may feel it is in your interest to drive a Porsche, but your social class and your ability to gain financing may mean you drive a Honda. The economy is, and has always been, an important part of society. But the form of the economy varies a great deal based on the form of society. As societies evolve and change, so do people's needs. People adapt their economies in ways that best allow them to attain their needs.

Stages of Society and Economic Life

In early stages of society, hunter-gatherers created simple nomadic societies. These societies primarily traded goods and services through barter. Tribal groups traded goods they wanted and/or needed within and between groups. The way in which European traders in the Americas swapped beads and skins to native peoples for blankets and other food supplies is one example of this kind of economy.

In agricultural societies, cities started to emerge and governments began to get involved in the economy. Money, taxes, and trade regulations became normal parts of life. As surplus expanded, some people accumulated wealth through trading and selling these goods. This created a new form of economy resulting from the fact that not everyone needed to be involved in basic survival efforts. The wealthiest people, or nobility, generated their fortunes through control of land. The vast majority of the population remained tied to the land, either working on it and/or trading goods.

The Industrial Revolution started in the mid-18th century in Western societies and radically changed the structure of the economy. Foremost, wealth creation became associated with manufacturing and mass production of goods. Factories emerged in cities, changing the location of work. Factory work produced goods at rates previously thought impossible. Mass production replaced the cottage-industry form of making products. Specialization of task became the norm for factory workers who

Evolution of Economies by Stages of Society

Trading and bartering

Money and taxes

Manufacturing and mass production

Globalization and knowledge economy

worked in shifts creating goods. Piecework, working on only one part of a product, replaced one worker making an entire product. Piecework, factories, and the mass urban migration also ushered in the concept of wage labor, whereby workers are paid by the hour for their time, no longer working for themselves. In addition, industry required energy to run the machinery for the factories. This too changed society, as finding and maintaining forms of energy became fundamental to the success of a society. Initially, energy came from the burning of coal and the production of steam. As time passed, newer forms of energy came into existence, but industrial societies still required energy to run their machines.

Postindustrial societies emerged in the 1960s, changing again the form of economy and work in a society. A postindustrial society is one in which service and technology jobs are the primary forms of work. The economies of such societies became even more complex, because their manufacturing base declined, but they still required manufactured goods. Globalization results as these societies look outside themselves for certain goods. Output moved from the production of goods to the production of ideas. Workers in postindustrial societies need a different skill set. They enter what is known as the "knowledge economy."[4] They no longer need mechanical skills, but require literacy, communication, and interpersonal skills. Industrialization requires people to work in one area, but in postindustrial societies, certain workers can do their jobs almost anywhere. For example, the Internet allows people to telecommute from virtual offices in their homes, hotel rooms, and trains.

FORMS OF ECONOMY

As you can see, politics and economics have similar effects on social order. This chapter will focus on politics and economics as **social institutions**—systems within a society that provide frameworks for individuals. In the United States, our government is a system with three branches; as citizens, we're allowed to vote two of those branches into office. However, if you moved to Great Britain, the system would be different and you wouldn't immediately know your place in it.

There are two basic types of **economic systems** (or **economies**): capitalism and socialism. No country has an economy that is entirely capitalist or entirely socialist; all systems will have a mixture of both, although the degrees may vary.

Capitalism is an economic system in which individuals and private corporations can own and operate the production of goods, make decisions about the price of those goods, and distribute them as they deem appropriate.[5] Capitalism is characterized by three main components: private ownership of property, profit motivation, and competition in a free market.[6]

Private ownership of property allows me to own my home, car, and television set. In general, this is a good thing. If I work hard and save money, I can acquire lots of "stuff," and that stuff is mine until I die and pass it to my children. It sounds like a pretty good idea, at least in theory.

Unfortunately, social problems arise because of this, the first, being the question of resources. Are there enough homes, cars, and TVs to go around? Does the amount of "stuff" grow as fast as the population?

SOCIAL INSTITUTIONS are organizations that provide a framework for individuals to communicate with the larger society.

ECONOMIC SYSTEM (OR ECONOMY) is a social institution that helps a society organize what it produces, distributes, and consumes, including goods and services.

CAPITALISM is an economic system in which individuals or private corporations can own and operate the production of goods, make decisions about the price of those goods, and distribute them as they deem appropriate.

MONOPOLY is the exclusive control of the production or trade of a product in the market.

FREE MARKET is an economic market that operates without government control.

ELASTICITY OF DEMAND explains the fact that demand for the product changes when the price changes.

Usually not. Allowing someone to hold onto objects creates a system that breeds inequality. If I inherit property from my uncle and rent it to someone else, I effortlessly profit from the ownership. Such a system allows for the wealth—and lack thereof—of one generation to continue to the next.

Profit motivation in capitalism can help people rise from poverty to wealth. It can also create problems in society. A seller wants the highest price he can get, and a buyer wants the cheapest price. As a seller, the best way for me to profit would be to corner the market. If I had the only sociology textbook in print, I could raise the price as high as I wanted. For this reason, the U.S. government has organizations that exist to curb the development of **monopolies**—companies with exclusive control of the production or trade of a product.

Because profit is the underlying motive of capitalism, employee-related problems can occur as well. There is always a danger of companies exploiting workers, paying them as little as possible to keep profits high. It was for this reason that the government established a minimum wage in the 1930s. Even in white-collar jobs, most employers seek to pay their workers only as much as they have to in order to keep them around (and not have to pay to train new ones).

Capitalism needs a **free market** in which it can create competition. This provides consumers with more goods while keeping prices low. In a free market, the "law of supply and demand" rules the day. If there's too much supply and too little demand, prices will drop. If there's a huge demand and too few products, prices will rise. Recently, as I walked through the mall, I was struck by the massive disparities in pricing between stores. Some "exclusive" boutiques sold men's shirts for upward of $150, while in a discount store, I could buy a similar shirt for $12. This type of variety occurs because the United States operates under a free market.

Some products have a strong **elasticity of demand**, meaning that the demand for them doesn't change much when the prices go up. If you needed a car to get to work and the price

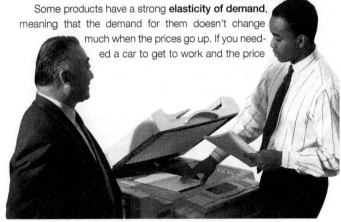

SOCIALISM is an economic system by which resources and means of production are owned collectively by the citizens.

DEMOCRATIC SOCIALISM is a type of economic system involving a blend of free market capitalism and government regulation of the economy.

of gas went up to $10 a gallon, you would still have to buy it. You might refrain from taking long trips on the weekends, but you couldn't avoid driving completely. A number of products such as electricity, health care, and prescription drugs have a strong price elasticity of demand in the U.S. economy. Generally, the price for these products doesn't matter—if you need them, you'll pay for them.

As mentioned before, no system can be purely one-sided, which is why in a capitalist economy such as the United States, there has always been some degree of government intervention. Policies such as minimum wage and Social Security are put in place by the government so that the welfare of workers is not overshadowed by corporate bottom lines. The government also controls unavoidable monopolies in order to avoid price gouging. For example, where I live, we have only one electric company. Therefore, the state regulates the price of electricity so the citizens aren't extorted.

Karl Marx, one of the first and most vocal critics of capitalism, argued that this economic system eventually leads to the exploitation of the common people. Why? A small, elite portion of the population generally gains control over the business aspects of society, leaving lower- and middle-class individuals at their mercy.[7] Under capitalism, the "haves" keep their positions and gain even more control, while the "have-nots" continue to lose ground. Of course, there's no such thing as unfettered capitalism in the United States, nor has there been since the early 1800s. That does not stop many of my students from believing we are a purely capitalist nation. Currently, as President Obama strives to expand access to health care, many of my students complain that the United States is becoming "socialist." Is it really? A clearer definition of the term will shed some light on this argument.

As an alternative to capitalism, Marx proposed **socialism**, an economic system by which resources and means of production are owned collectively by the citizens. In a pure socialist economy as imagined by Marx, the government regulates all property to avoid any possibility of exploitation. This is quite similar to a pure democracy in which the government is literally "ruled by the people," except in this case, it's the economy that's ruled by the people. Socialism is based on the idea that goods

and services are produced and distributed to meet the needs of society, not to generate a profit.

Of course, socialist economies can create social problems as well. If individual gain isn't possible, why would anyone strive to create new and innovative things? Some argue that socialism stifles individuals. Without the ability to generate personal wealth, people lack the motivation to improve their lives. The history of planned economies seems to support this notion because, historically, socialist consumers have had fewer choices of goods and services. In almost all countries that have experimented with Marxist socialism, there have generally been a small group of elites who take advantage of society and work to keep their profits from others. One problem not solved by socialism is how to keep people with power from using that power for their own benefit.

Generally speaking, pure forms of capitalism and socialism don't exist in the world today. Most countries, at least in the West, have some variation of what is known as **democratic socialism**. This type of economic system involves a blend of free-market capitalism and government regulation of the economy. The concept of democratic socialism has gained ground particularly in Europe and is often associated with the labor movement in countries such as France, Germany, Finland, and Spain.[8] Tax rates in these countries can be anywhere from 40 to 50 percent of a worker's income, with those funds being used to provide public services such as health care and unemployment coverage to the less fortunate. In such a system, the government takes an active role in redistributing the wealth of the nation to decrease inequality.

Of course, the government in the United States does this as well, but to a much lesser degree. The highest tax bracket in the nation is around 38 percent. Yet, the United States does take wealth from some and give it to others. For example, public schools are funded by everyone in society. Whether or not you have children, you still pay to educate the next generation.

People in European countries typically view the role of government and social welfare differently than people in the United States. For example, in a study of eight industrialized nations, researchers found that the people in the United States have the most negative views toward the government's redistribution of wealth, whereas people in Norway are the most likely to accept such disbursement.[9] That's not to say that Americans don't want to help the less fortunate, but they generally distrust the government's ability to do this well.

With the recent federal takeover of mortgage lenders Freddie Mac and Fannie Mae, the two largest lending institutions are now government sponsored. This serves as a real-life example of the way that capitalism

Cycle of Wealth in a Capitalist Economy

Successful company

Increased production

More jobs

More income

Increased purchasing

and socialism tend to blend together, an idea known as **convergence theory**.[10] This convergence works both ways throughout the world. Just as democratic socialism is becoming more popular in Europe, many other countries worldwide are moving away from exclusive socialism. In China, for example, the market (rather than the government) determines what goods and services are sold. Although the government still owns many of the major business, individuals are now allowed to own land. This blending of private and public ownership shows convergence as well.

Global Economy

As technology improves our ability to communicate, it becomes difficult for economic systems to remain self-contained. Business deals between companies on two separate continents can be transacted with a click of a mouse, and many corporations are establishing international satellite offices around the globe. A **corporation** is a legal entity that has an objective—typically to make a profit for its owners. Although shareholders own the company and employees run the day-to-day operations, a corporation can purchase property, acquire debt, participate in legal contracts, and enjoy most of the rights and privileges of an individual person. The people who make up international corporations are often a mixture of diverse nationalities. This is especially true for **transnational corporations** (also known as **multinational corporations**), businesses that operate in at least two countries and have the interests of their company at heart rather than the interests of their country of origin. As a dominant force in the global economy, transnational corporations generate huge profits and possess international political power.

Trends in the U.S. Economy

Layoffs, downsizings, production suspensions: No matter what it's called, job loss slowly renders an economy powerless. Unfortunately, we can all witness the real-life results of the credit crisis that began in September 2008. In that year alone, 2.6 million jobs were lost in the United States, the largest amount in more than six decades. To put it in perspective, that's as many jobs as states such as Wisconsin and Maryland have *in total*.[12]

As of June 2009, the unemployment rate was 9.7 percent.[13] If your college has around 2,000 students, imagine 194 of them being told to pack up and leave, without warning. Such could actually be the case as universities are forced to cut costs to make ends meet. A friend of mine who teaches for a public college in California told me that the school expects to eliminate 40 percent of the possible sections in sociology this year, due to economic cutbacks. All adjuncts have been fired, and full-time faculty members are required to increase their teaching loads to keep their jobs. The effects of the recession can be felt everywhere.

The economy can be fickle—what's needed one year may be insignificant in the next. (Think of fashion: Are Crocs still cool? Even if they are on your campus, they won't be by the time you finish college.) Shifts in the economy affect society. Some industries shrink, while others expand. In the economic crises of 2008, many jobs in manufacturing and construction were lost, while those in health care and social assistance grew.[14] How might this shape the future of society?

Society is also influenced by **demographics**—statistical characteristics of human populations, such as age or gender—of workers. For example, in 1980, whites had the highest participation rate in the labor force. By 2006, Hispanics overtook them, increasing their participation to 68.7 percent. By 2014, the participation rates for whites, blacks, and

CONVERGENCE THEORY describes the tendency for capitalism and socialism to converge.

CORPORATION is a legal entity that has some objective, typically to make a profit for its owners. It can purchase property, acquire debt, and participate in legal contracts.

TRANSNATIONAL CORPORATIONS operate in at least two countries and have the interests of their company at heart over the interests of their native land.

DEMOGRAPHICS are statistical characteristics of human populations, such as gender and age.

UNEMPLOYED describes people who do not have a job but have actively looked for work in the prior four weeks and are currently available for employment.

Asians are all predicted to decrease, while Hispanic participation is expected to increase even further.[15] Why? Is it due to the general increase in age of certain groups, driving many out of the workforce and into retirement? Is it due to immigration, with high rates of young Hispanics entering the United States? Perhaps it's both of these factors, or maybe it's neither.

Individuals may not be participating in the labor force for reasons other than laziness. Some are too ill to work; others suffer with a disability, have retired, or are simply unable to find a job. Although these people may not hold jobs, not all individuals who refrain from working are considered unemployed. By U.S. government standards, people are classified as **unemployed** if they do not have a job, have actively been looking for work, and are currently available to start employment. "Actively looking for a job" includes sending out résumés, searching employment registrars, or even asking friends and family members for assistance. People classified as *not* "currently available" for work include full-time students, workers on strike, and those who are absent from their

∧
∧ **Furniture store IKEA originally started in**
∧ **Sweden** but quickly became a multinational corporation. **Today, IKEA operates in 36 different countries worldwide, from Slovakia to the United Arab Emirates,** and earns over 20 billion euros in sales per year.[11]

regular jobs because of illness, vacation time, or personal reasons.[16] So, when you see U.S. unemployment numbers, remember that you're not being presented with the actual number of people without work.

Many people work for private corporations or government institutions, but some are self-employed, meaning that they operate a business as a sole proprietor or a partner. An agricultural worker (farmer) is one of the most common occupations for a self-employed individual. But as many family farms become corporately owned, the self-employed farmer is becoming a dying breed. This trend is one of the major causes for the decrease in self-employment over the last 50 years. In 2003, only 7.5 percent of the workforce was self-employed, down from 18.5 percent in 1948.[17]

Even though self-employment in farming is decreasing, individuals haven't stopped forming new businesses. The spirit of the entrepreneur is still alive in the United States. **Entrepreneurship** refers to the creation of new organizations in response to economic and social opportunities. An **entrepreneur** is a person who establishes, organizes, manages, and assumes all risks of an organization. Donald Trump is one of the most well-known entrepreneurs of our time. As a modern business mogul, Trump has built his real estate corporation from the ground up—and filed for bankruptcy no less than three separate times.[18]

One in four people in the United States will try his hand at entrepreneurship at some point in his lifetime. Certainly the decision to found a company depends on personal qualities such as motivation and individual drive. But what makes a new company successful? There's an old saying that describes the three most important aspects of business: "Location, location, location." This may be true, but research suggests that social networks and levels of competition in the marketplace play just as strong a role.[19]

Work

As discussed earlier in the chapter, the form of society influences the type of work that people engage in. You might think you are likely to choose whatever job you desire, but work is not that simple. The judgments made about work come about as a result of this position influencing what kind of work we will accept and how we will evaluate that work. Research supports the idea that our decisions about what kind of work to pursue and/or whether or not we find the work enjoyable are linked to more than our individual personalities. In fact, sociologists suggest that values, abilities, and self-concept all influence occupational choice. My undergraduate degree is in accounting. I never really liked the idea of being an accountant, but guess what both my parents did for a living? The decisions we make related to work are bounded by our backgrounds.[20]

In deciding whether we enjoy a type of work, there are two important orientations: intrinsic and extrinsic. **Intrinsic orientations** refer to how important we consider the work. Is it personally rewarding? Do we get to work in an area that supports our abilities and interests? These are the intrinsic values of work. **Extrinsic orientations** apply to the importance attached to certain parts of a job. For example, if you receive high pay and an important title, such as medical doctor, your job has high extrinsic value. A job may also have strong extrinsic value to us if it gets us where we want to go. Interestingly, intrinsic rewards for a job tend to be more important to workers who come from families with higher socioeconomic status. Perhaps this is because those who come from privilege can afford to be more focused on the value of work rather than where it is able to take you. There does not seem to be a difference in the selection between intrinsic and extrinsic rewards in the selection of careers for men and women, but family history makes a difference. The less educated a person's parents, the more important extrinsic rewards are for that person in the selection of work.[21]

Once you have selected a job, your work satisfaction depends on a number of factors. Flexibility of work environment appears to be linked to job satisfaction and to impact levels of job turnover. When workers are measured against results but given the freedom and flexibility to choose how to accomplish their tasks, they report higher rates of job satisfaction.[22]

∧
∧ In 1975, 20-year-old **Bill Gates co-founded**
∧ **a company based on the development of microcomputer software.** Eleven years later, the college dropout and Microsoft CEO became the youngest billionaire in U.S. history. It's important to note that **after working together for a number of years, Apple and Microsoft became, and remain, fierce competitors. How might this have affected both organizations?**

Factors Contributing to Job Satisfaction

EXTRINSIC VALUE

- high salary
- important title
- room for growth
- surrounded by influential people

INTRINSIC VALUE

- personally rewarding
- interesting
- makes use of one's abilities
- makes a difference in the world

TOXIC

- interpersonal conflict
- disorganization
- lack of autonomy
- unclean or dangerous facilities

Of course, not all jobs are enjoyable. Toxic work environments impact millions of workers around the world. Sociologists define these as work environments that have high levels of interpersonal conflict and disorganization while providing low rates of pay and/or lack of autonomy. Toxic work environments are problematic for workers and organizations alike. Research suggests that the majority of workers in toxic jobs believe their environments cause health problems. These jobs also result in a number of worker problems, such as high turnover, low morale, absenteeism, and tardiness. About 14 percent of workers report that they have changed jobs because of toxic working conditions.[23]

Free Trade

Governments interact with the economy all the time. They create international trade restrictions in the form of embargos or tariffs. An **embargo** is a restriction on trade that's enforced by the government. The United States imposed a trade embargo on Cuba in 1962. It's still enforced today, which is why Cuban cigars are illegal in the United States.

Tariffs, on the other hand, are taxes placed on traded items. High tariffs limit the amount of trade that occurs because the added tax makes the cost too high for consumers. Not all foreign trade involves

EMBARGO is a restriction on trade that is enforced by a government.

TARIFFS are taxes placed on traded items.

NORTH AMERICAN FREE TRADE AGREEMENT (NAFTA) is an agreement established in 1994 to allow free trade on agricultural products between the United States, Mexico, and Canada.

tariffs. The **North American Free Trade Agreement (NAFTA)** was established in 1994 to allow free trade on agricultural products between the United States, Mexico, and Canada. Removing all tariffs provided a major economic boost for these countries. Free trade policies such as NAFTA benefit both developing and developed nations; they allow developing countries the opportunity to sell their products at a fair price, as well as provide a wider variety of products with competitive pricing to wealthy countries. Of course, such policies also create controversy and lead to other social problems. For example, what might result from allowing companies to pursue cheaper labor in Mexico without having to fear import tariffs? If even more factory jobs are outsourced could this increase rates of unemployment in the United States?

The Benefits of Free Trade

No tariffs added, prices stay the same

Goods come into a country

Competitive prices for consumers

More profits for manufactures

∧
∧
∧ **Free trade allows for an increased exchange of goods among countries.** Without the addition of tariffs, consumers can afford to buy products at competitive market prices. **The more products consumers buy, the more money countries who export those products can make.**

▶▶▶ GO GL⊕BAL

Controlling the Global Economy: A Job for Everyone

Shortly after the dust settled on the disastrous economic crisis of 2008, President Obama had to address more than 20 heads of state at a global summit in London. His plan for economic recovery was much anticipated by major world leaders; however, the most contentious part of President Obama's speech revolved around what the United States could do rather than what it would do. The president announced that the United States could no longer be the sole engine of global growth. During past global economic downturns, the United States had been able to take the lead and increase spending to jump-start the international economy. This time, however, the mounting national debt had overwhelmed the nation's balance sheet. President Obama noted that the latest credit crisis wasn't caused by U.S. institutions

alone; many faulty financial regulations in Europe and Asia also contributed to the crumbling economy. Recovery, he argued, had to be a combined effort.

Although the United States will have to take a less dominate role in managing the global economy this time around, it won't be completely passive. Even though the United States can't play the part of the international financier, it shouldn't miss an opportunity to help lead the way out of the global crisis. "If there's going to be renewed growth, it cannot just be the United States as the engine," Obama said. "Everybody is going to have to pick up the pace." Many global economists agreed with this decision. "We cannot rely on the U.S. being the global locomotive," said Professor Willem H. Buiter, former member of the Bank of England Monetary Policy Committee. "Those days are gone." Now, acting as partners rather than pupils, leaders of industrialized powers, such as the United Kingdom and Japan, and

emerging powers, such as China, India, and Brazil, are working together with the United States to formulate a solution to the global economic crisis.[24]

∧
∧
∧ **President Obama had to be the one to break the news** to the international community that **the United States can no longer afford to be the world's financier.**

think social problems: HOW CAN WE THINK ABOUT THE ECONOMY?

Functionalism

Functionalists find political systems naturally balanced. According to political scientist Robert Dahl, power is distributed widely enough in democracies that groups are driven to compete *and* work with each other in order to achieve their goals. These two forces—competition and alliance—lead groups to temper their ideals, leaving society solidly in the middle, balancing between extremes.[25]

The ideas of Richard H. Thaler and Cass R. Sunstein, authors of the book *Nudge: Improving Decisions about Health, Wealth, and Happiness*, hold a similar belief. When left to our own devices, we often make wrong decisions. Do you choose Chinese takeout because it's easy or because it's healthy? Thaler and Sunstein argue that we have many competing choices in an economy such as ours, yet people don't make decisions based on what's rational, but based on what's easiest or most popular. This theory is known as **economic behaviorism**.[26] Like nudging a friend toward a salad instead of takeout, society functions best when we help people make good choices.

Contemporary sociologist Amitai Etzioni acknowledges the interrelation betweens social structures and individual choices. As one of the founders of **communitarianism**, he suggests that for society to function properly, it must have a communal set of values that guide social policies. According to communitarianism, society is made up of three components: the community, the market, and the government. Each sector has an essential role to play, but all three interact with each other constantly. Etzioni also notes that a crucial part of society is being able to see ourselves not only as individuals, but also as part of a community.[27] In this way, decisions are made with the best interests of all in mind.

ECONOMIC BEHAVIORISM states that people don't make decisions based on what is rational but what is easiest or most popular.

COMMUNITARIANISM suggests that for society to function properly, it must have communal values and set social policies according to those values.

POWER ELITE is a group comprised of top military officials, heads of major corporations, and high-ranking political leaders; this select group of people pulls the strings that control both the economy and the politics of American society.

INTERLOCKING DIRECTORATES is a practice in which the same people are placed on a variety of corporate boards, allowing separate companies to be controlled by a small, elite group.

According to Mills, the power elite comprises top military officials, heads of major corporations, and high-ranking political leaders. This select group of people pulls the strings that control both the economy and the politics of American society.[28]

A more modern theorist, William Domhoff, has suggested a similar idea: The United States is ruled by those with the most societal power. Consider corporate boards of directors. A common practice known as **interlocking directorates** involves placing the same people on a variety of corporate boards, allowing separate companies to be controlled by a small, elite group. Domhoff points out that this group often interacts with political leaders in exclusive clubs, directing (or at least strongly influencing) the course of the U.S. government.[29]

Conflict Theory

About the same time that Dahl was espousing the benefits of a balanced democratic system, sociologist C. Wright Mills was suggesting something else entirely. Mills suggested that a **power elite** runs the United States. Who are these people?

>>> **According to economic behaviorism, we make decisions based on what's easiest to do.** The most convenient way is often not the best.

Economy and Work

Economy and Work

As part of an internship program for college credit, Marco De Luca worked at the Chicago office of the U.S. Equal Employment Opportunity Commission. As a law student, he was excited to work in the Alternative Dispute Resolution (ADR) unit, so he could learn more about the process of mediation. The ADR offers mediation as an alternative to the expensive and time-consuming adjudication process.

"To be honest, I didn't know much about how mediation worked when I started my internship. It's not really a big focus in law school. As part of the internship, I was able to observe quite a few mediation conferences. Once I understood how mediation worked enough to explain the process, I was calling people who were part of cases of discrimination to find out if mediation might be an option for them. It was tricky at first, because people are kind of skeptical, like they didn't really understand who I was, why I was calling them, and if I was legit or not. I had to be careful not to pressure them so they understood that they had a legal right to take their case to court if they preferred."

Several federal laws protect workers from discrimination. They include discrimination based on sex, age, race, disability, religion, and other characteristics in terms of hiring and firing, equal pay, promotions, and other aspects of employment.

"I remember one case in particular had to do with the Equal Pay Act. A woman who worked in the office of a computer repair company claimed that she made less than a man she worked with, even though they had the same job duties and level of experience. The woman believed that this was based on her gender. It seemed like she had pretty good reason to think this; she had a lot of stories about the kidding around that would go on around the office, and a lot of it was pretty offensive to women."

The Equal Pay Act of 1963 prohibits sex-based discrimination in the payment of wages and benefits.

"The woman's boss was really glad to have the option of mediation. He probably didn't want his name attached to a legal case. Once they both had the chance to tell their sides of the story, it came out that the boss wasn't even really aware of the woman's job duties, since he didn't spend a lot of time around the office. He agreed to raise her salary and to start checking in more with his employees so that he wasn't so out of touch."

The Equal Pay Act does more than protect people from day-to-day discrimination. It also strives to ensure that women and men have the same economic opportunities. Before it was passed, it wouldn't have been uncommon for a man to control all of a household's money; he might even give his wife a weekly allowance. While the Equal Pay Act aims to give women just as much buying power as men, the wage gap still persists. In 2009, full-time working women earned just 77 percent of the salaries of their male counterparts.[32]

>>> **The Equal Pay Act** does more than protect people from day-to-day discrimination. It also **strives to ensure that women and men have the same economic opportunities.**

Symbolic Interactionism

In the mid-20th century, symbolic interactionist Erving Goffman introduced the idea of **impression management** using the metaphor of a play. In one's work life, interactions should be considered performances with the goal of delivering to the audience an impression that will help to further one's goals.[30]

A longitudinal study showed that three components of impression management positively affect an employee's performance rating: demographic similarity, supervisor-focused impression management, and self-focused impression management.[31] **Demographic similarity** refers to shared characteristics, such as race, gender, or age. **Supervisor-focused impression management** involves flattering and agreeing with your boss. **Self-focused impression management** includes acting modest about your accomplishments (even if your modesty is false), talking or bragging occasionally about successes, and showing self-assuredness through smiles and eye contact.

IMPRESSION MANAGEMENT is the process of controlling how others perceive us in order to influence them to help us achieve our goals.

DEMOGRAPHIC SIMILARITY is the extent of characteristics, such as age and race, shared among people.

SUPERVISOR-FOCUSED IMPRESSION MANAGEMENT is impression management focused on flattering and agreeing with one's superior or other person.

SELF-FOCUSED IMPRESSION MANAGEMENT is impression management focused on controlling one's own behaviors, such as acting modest, boasting only occasionally, and showing friendliness and self-assuredness.

It is normal to like people who are like us, and bosses are not immune to this feeling. Using impression management techniques, you can advance your career and look forward to your employees using impression management techniques to get on *your* good side.

discover solutions to social problems:
HOW CAN THE GOVERNMENT INFLUENCE THE ECONOMY?

Since the economic downturn of 2008, the government has made attempts to help out the economy. But the majority of American people don't feel like those efforts have been aimed at helping them. A Pew Research poll taken in July 2010 found that 70 percent or more of Americans felt that these interventions had helped large banks, financial institutions, big corporations, and wealthy people either a great deal or a fair amount. Almost 70 percent felt that small businesses and the middle class had received little or no help from

these government actions. Sixty-four percent of those polled felt that poor people had not been helped at all.

Since the government turned its focus from economic recovery to deficit reduction, the American people mostly agreed with this shift in priorities: 51 percent said deficit reduction was the higher priority, while 40 percent felt spending on economic recovery efforts was more important. In terms of what should be done to fix the economy, respondents were almost evenly split between spend-

Pro & Con

Is a free market the best kind of economy for the United States?

Pro

- A free-market economy is the most efficient way to allocate resources, because the laws of supply and demand are self-regulating.
- A free market creates more opportunities to enter the market and make a profit.
- Free markets create a drive for competition, which leads to creativity and innovation, giving consumers the best products and the most options.
- Free markets reward those who are the most efficient, productive, and innovative, while punishing those who are ineffective.

Con

- Government intervention is necessary to remedy free-market inefficiencies, such as the emergence of monopolies.
- Free markets protect the interests of the wealthy elite at the expense of the working class.
- Economies are too complex for a free market to actually exist as it is described in theory.
- Free markets lead to a very uneven distribution of wealth, so those with money exploit those without.

WRAP YOUR MIND AROUND THE THEORY

Many of our economic decisions are made based on what is easy or popular rather than what is logical. How does this type of decision making affect society as a whole?

FUNCTIONALISM

Functionalists study how systems interact to affect individuals. Dahl notes that the American form of democracy works because power is diffused enough to be shared by competing groups. Sociologist Amitai Etzioni suggests that the role of the government and the community is to balance the self-centered drive for wealth inherent in a capitalist economy. Because of these balances, our society runs smoothly.

CONFLICT THEORY

Conflict theorists assert that regardless of the form of society, the economy plays a vital role. Throughout history members of society have struggled for what is scarce. According to Marx, Mills, and Domhoff, access to wealth and power is scarce in any society. This is largely because those who have it are unwilling to let it go. Generally, they seek short-term rewards to increase their power and wealth, while ignoring the long-term societal consequences.

HOW IS POWER DISTRIBUTED IN ECONOMIC AND POLITICAL SYSTEMS?

SYMBOLIC INTERACTIONISM

Symbolic interactionists focus on how we relate to other people. By managing the impressions we give other people, we can create the outcomes we desire. This can help us achieve our career goals and advance in our professions. In doing so, we can enjoy our work in terms of both intrinsic orientations and extrinsic orientations.

According to conflict theory, those with power often use it to dominate others. **How do the economic elite dominate the lower class?**

Symbolic interactionists suggest we manage the impressions we give to other people. How can using impression management help someone achieve his or her career goals?

ing more on social programs (47 percent) and cutting taxes (42 percent).

Few Americans reported seeing the benefits of the 2009 economic stimulus. A majority said it had increased the federal deficit (66 percent).

Fewer than half of people said the stimulus improved roads and bridges in their areas. Only 35 percent thought it had prevented unemployment from worsening, and less than a third believed it had prevented state and local government layoffs and cutbacks.[33]

Economic Stimulus Package:
How it Works and Whom it Helps

Government Spending

↓

Increased government spending on infrastructure projects or goods can add to economic growth

↓

Helps employ workers on projects or at companies that make what the government buys

Cuts in Interest Rates

↓

Cuts on Federal Reserve rates make loans cheaper for businesses and consumers, broadly stimulating the economy

↓

Helps banks and big institutions that borrow large amounts of money at or near the prime rate

Tax Cuts

↓

Gives consumers bigger paychecks to boost spending

↓

Helps consumers, mostly those with high incomes

Economy and Work

MAKE CONNECTIONS

Do you take work home with you? Are you likely to be a person who would do that? If you think of the roles we play, sometimes our work life can become a "greedy role," meaning it takes away from the other possible obligations we might have. For example, I work from home on my textbooks regularly. Being an author is a greedy role. But research suggests there are factors that influence the likelihood of you blurring the lines between work and home. If you receive work-related contact outside the regular workday, you are more likely to work from home. Bringing work home is also linked to people who have greater levels of control over their schedule. They are more likely to flex their time and work while at home. Men are also more likely than women to bring work home with them. This may be related to the nature of their work and/or their higher levels of autonomy in the workplace than their female counterparts.[34]

by controlling our financial growth within a capitalist economy

HOW **CAN WE THINK ABOUT THE ECONOMY?**

in terms of competition and alliances, the distribution of power, and goals
achieved through a series of managed impressions

HOW **CAN THE GOVERNMENT INFLUENCE THE ECONOMY?**

through a complex balance of bailing out financial institutions, reducing the
federal deficit, and spending for economic stimulus

get the topic: HOW DO WE GET WHAT WE NEED?

Stages of Society and Economic Life	Work	Conflict Theory
Global Economy	Free Trade	Symbolic Interactionism
Trends in the U.S. Economy	Functionalism	

Theory

FUNCTIONALISM

- people make decisions based on what's easy, not on what's logical
- power in the United States is balanced, which helps keep society functioning smoothly

CONFLICT THEORY

- individuals struggle for what is scarce in society
- in the United States, members of the elite work to keep their power and wealth, regardless of the outcome for others

SYMBOLIC INTERACTIONISM

- in one's work life, interactions should be considered performances
- using impression management to make others view you positively can help you achieve your goals

Key Terms

social institutions are organizations that provide a framework for individuals to communicate with the larger society.

economic system (or economy) is a social institution that helps a society organize what it produces, distributes, and consumes, including goods and services.

capitalism is an economic system in which individuals or private corporations can own and operate the production of goods, make decisions about the price of those goods, and distribute them as they deem appropriate.

monopoly is the exclusive control of the production or trade of a product in the market.

free market is an economic market that operates without government control.

elasticity of demand explains the fact that demand for the product changes when the price changes.

socialism is an economic system by which resources and means of production are owned collectively by the citizens.

democratic socialism is a type of economic system involving a blend of free market capitalism and government regulation of the economy.

convergence theory describes the tendency for capitalism and socialism to converge.

corporation is a legal entity that has some objective, typically to make a profit for its owners. It can purchase property, acquire debt, and participate in legal contracts.

transnational corporations operate in at least two countries and have the interests of their company at heart over the interests of their native land.

demographics are statistical characteristics of human populations, such as gender and age.

unemployed describes people who do not have a job but have actively looked for work in the prior four weeks and are currently available for employment.

entrepreneurship is the creation of new organizations in response to economic and social opportunities.

entrepreneur is a person who establishes, organizes, manages, and assumes all risks of an organization.

intrinsic orientations are the amount of importance we place on our work, such as how rewarding or interesting it is.

extrinsic orientations are the amount of importance we attach to certain parts of our jobs, such as pay and title.

embargo is a restriction on trade that is enforced by a government.

tariffs are taxes placed on traded items.

North American Free Trade Agreement (NAFTA) is an agreement established in 1994 to allow free trade on agricultural products between the United States, Mexico, and Canada.

economic behaviorism states that people don't make decisions based on what is rational, but what is easiest or most popular.

communitarianism suggests that for society to function properly, it must have communal values and set social policies according to those values.

power elite is a group comprised of top military officials, heads of major corporations, and high-ranking political leaders; this select group of people pulls the strings that control both the economy and the politics of American society.

interlocking directorates is a practice in which the same people are placed on a variety of corporate boards, allowing separate companies to be controlled by a small, elite group.

impression management is the process of controlling how others perceive us in order to influence them to help us achieve our goals.

demographic similarity is the extent of characteristics, such as age and race, shared among people.

supervisor-focused impression management is impression management focused on flattering and agreeing with one's superior or other person.

self-focused impression management is impression management focused on controlling one's own behaviors, such as acting modest, boasting only occasionally, and showing friendliness and self-assuredness.

Sample Test Questions

These multiple-choice questions are similar to those found in the test bank that accompanies this text.

1. Which of the following is an opinion *best* associated with socialist economics?
   a. After working his way up to a high-powered corporate job, Charles becomes resentful of the amount of taxes he has to pay.
   b. Kate believes that people shouldn't have to pay high prices for essentials such as food and water.
   c. Aidan is motivated by a program on TV and joins the labor movement to promote democracy and the interests of the general public.
   d. Priya drops her philosophy class after deciding that Sartre's thoughts on Marx are too existential for her tastes.

2. What employment demographic shifts are projected for 2014?
   a. The participation rate for Hispanic workers will decrease.
   b. The participation rate for black workers will decrease.
   c. The participation rate for Hispanic workers will increase.
   d. The participation rate for black workers will increase.

3. Which of the following summarizes the main problem with interlocking directorates?
   a. The same people serve on a variety of corporate boards, effectively monopolizing a market.
   b. A group of military officials, heads of major corporations, and high-ranking political leaders pull the strings of politics and the economy.
   c. A small group in power takes advantage of society and works to keep their profits from others.
   d. An elite group of wealthy board members can influence the government by interacting with political leaders in exclusive clubs.

4. Nora recently moved to Seattle, and she needs to open a new bank account. If she bases her decision on economic behaviorism, which is she *most likely* to do?
   a. Do research online to find the best local banking options.
   b. Find the five most popular banks and visit each one.
   c. Put her money in the bank most convenient to her house.
   d. Pick the bank she saw on a bus ad while driving to work.

5. The majority of Americans think that government spending aimed at economic recovery is a higher priority than reducing the federal deficit.
   a. True
   b. False

ESSAY

1. Compare and contrast capitalist and socialist economic systems. Do you think one is likely to be more successful than the other?

2. Discuss how you felt about a job that you've had in terms of both intrinsic and extrinsic orientations.

3. Consider a goal that you have either at work or at school. Describe how you could use interaction management to help you achieve this goal.

4. Consider the idea of economic behaviorism. Do you think large groups make decisions based on what is easy and popular or what is logically correct? How does this decision-making behavior validate or invalidate the theory of group wisdom?

5. Explain which you think should be a higher priority: reducing the federal deficit or increasing spending to help the economy recover.

WHERE TO START YOUR RESEARCH PAPER

To learn more about socialism, visit the Socialist Labor Party of America's Web site at http://www.slp.org/

For more information about President Obama's 2009 economic stimulus package, see http://useconomy.about.com/od/candidatesandtheeconomy/a/Obama_Stimulus.htm

For facts about unemployment, go to the Bureau of Labor Statistics at http://www.bls.gov/bls/unemployment.htm

To read an excerpt from C. Wright Mills' *The Power Elite*, go to http://www.marxists.org/subject/humanism/mills-c-wright/power-elite.htm

To learn more about the U.S. Equal Employment Opportunity Commission, go to http://www.eeoc.gov/

ANSWERS: 1. b; 2. c; 3. d; 4. c; 5. b

Remember to check www.thethinkspot.com **for additional information, downloadable flashcards, and other helpful resources.**

1. "About," *Occupy Wall Street*, Accessed October 10, 2011, http://occupywallst.org/about.

2. Adam Shell, "A Recession in Confidence," *USA Today*, September 6, 2011, http://www.usatoday.com/MONEY/usaedition/2011-09-07-Mart-Confidence_CV_U.htm.

3. Alejandro Portes, *Economic Sociology: A Systemic Inquiry*. Princeton: Princeton Univ. Press, 2010.

4. Walter W. Powell and KaisaSnellman, "The Knowledge Economy," *Annual Review of Sociology*, 2004. 30: 199–220.

5. capitalism. (2009). In *Merriam-Webster Online Dictionary*. Accessed June 22, 2009, http://www.merriam-webster.com/dictionary/capitalism.

6. David Harvey, "The Geopolitics of Capitalism," in *Social Relations and Spatial Structures*, eds. Derek Gregory and John Urry. New York: St. Martin's Press, 1985.

7. Leslie Sklair and Peter Robbins, "Global Capitalism and Major Corporations from the Third World," *Third World Quarterly*, 2002. 23(1): 81–100.

8. Courtney D. Von Hippel, "When People Would Rather Switch Than Fight: Outgroup Favoritism Among Temporary Employees," *Group Processes and Intergroup Relations*, 2006. 9(4): 533–546.

9. Ibid.

10. Charles H. Cooley, *Human Nature and the Social Order*. New York: Schocken Books, 1964.

11. IKEA, "Facts & Figures," http://www.ikea.com/ms/en_GB/about_ikea_new/facts_figures/index.html.

12. David Goldman, "Worst Year for Jobs Since '45 Annual Loss Biggest Since End of World War II," *CNNMoney.com*, January 9, 2009, http://money.cnn.com/2009/01/09/news/economy/jobs_december/index.htm.

13. United States Bureau of Labor Statistics, "Metropolitan Area Employment and Unemployment: June 2009," http://www.bls.gov/news.release/pdf/metro.pdf.

14. U.S. Bureau of Labor Statistics, "January 2008," *Employment & Earnings*, 2008. 55(1): http://www.bls.gov/opub/ee/empearn200801.pdf.

15. U.S. Bureau of Labor Statistics, "January 2007," *Employment & Earnings*, 2007. 54(1): http://www.bls.gov/opub/ee/home.htm.

16. U.S. Bureau of Labor Statistics, "Labor Force Statistics from the Current Population Survey," Accessed June 23, 2009, http://www.bls.gov/cps/faq.htm#Ques5.

17. U.S. Department of Labor, "Self-employment Rates, 1948–2003," http://www.bls.gov/opub/ted/2004/aug/wk4/art02.htm.

18. Wayne Parry, "Donald Trump's Casino Company Files for Bankruptcy," *Huffington Post*, February 17 2009, http://www.huffingtonpost.com/2009/02/17/donald-trumps-casino-comp_n_167474.html.

19. Patricia Thornton, "The Sociology of Entrepreneurship," *Annual Review of Sociology*, 1999. 25: 19–46.

20. Monica Kirkpatrick Johnson and Jeylan T. Mortimer, "Origins and Outcomes of Judgments About Work," *Social Forces*, 2011. 89(4): 1239–1260.

21. Ibid.

22. Phyllis Moen, Erin L. Kelly, and Rachelle Hill, "Does Enhancing Work-Time Control and Flexibility Reduce Turnover? A Naturally Occurring Experiment," *Social Problems*, 2011. 58(1): 69–98.

23. Lindsey Joyce Chamberlain and Randy Hodson, "Toxic Work Environments: What Helps and What Hurts," *Sociological Perspectives*, 2010. 53(4): 455–478.

24. U.S. Census Bureau, "Voter Turnout Increases by 5 Million in 2008 Presidential Election, U.S. Census Bureau Reports Data Show Significant Increases Among Hispanic, Black and Young Voters," http://www.census.gov/Press-Release/www/releases/archives/voting/013995.html.

25. Anthony Faiola, "U.S. Signals New Era for Global Economy; Urging Nations to 'Pick Up the Pace,' Obama Says U.S. Cannot Go It Alone," *The Washington Post*, April 2, 2009.

26. Robert Dahl, *Who Governs?* New Haven, CT: Yale University Press, 1961.

27. Richard H. Thaler and Cass R. Sunstein, *Nudge: Improving Decisions About Health, Wealth, and Happiness*. New Haven, CT: Yale University Press, 2008.

28. AmitaiEtzioni, *The Spirit of Community: The Reinvention of American Society*. New York: Simon & Schuster, 1994.

29. Wright Mills, *The Power Elite: A New Edition*. New York: Oxford University Press, 2000.

30. Adam Barnhart, "Erving Goffman: The Presentation of Self in Everyday Life," *Portland State University*, Accessed October 10, 2011, http://web.pdx.edu/;tothm/theory/Presentation%20of%20Self.htm.

31. Sandy J. Wayne and Robert C. Liden, "Effects of Impression Management on Performance Ratings: A Longitudinal Study," *The Academy of Management Journal*, 1995. 38(1): 232–260.

32. U.S. Census Bureau, "Income, Poverty, and Health Insurance Coverage in the United States: 2009." Current Population Reports, P60-238. Washington DC: U.S. Government Printing Office, 2010, p. 7, http://www.census.gov/prod/2010pubs/p60-238.pdf.

33. "Government Economic Policies Seen as Boon for Banks and Big Business, Not Middle Class or Poor," *Pew Research Center for the People and the Press*, July 10, 2010, http://pewresearch.org/pubs/1670/large-majorities-say-govt-stimulus-policies-mostly-helped-banks-financial-institutins-not-middle-class-or-poor.

34. Scott Schieman and Paul Glavin, "Trouble at the Border? Gender, Flexibility at Work, and the Work-Home Interface," *Social Problems*, 2008. 55(4): 590–611.

Credits

Credits are listed in order of appearance.

PHOTO CREDITS

Tomas Abad/Alamy; **(from left):** North Wind Picture Archives/Alamy; Greg Vaughn/Alamy; C.P. Cushing/ClassicStock/Alamy; Asia Images Group Pte Ltd/Alamy; Exactostock/SuperStock; **(clockwise from top):** Shutterstock; Crocodile Images/PhotoLibrary; Getty Images/Creatas/Jupiterimages; C. Jordan Harris/PhotoEdit; Dorling Kindersley; Andre Maslennikov/Age Fotostock; Vario Images GmbH & Co./Alamy; **(from left):** Steve Gorton/Dorling Kindersley; Tomislav Forgo/Shutterstock; British Retail Photography/Alamy; Solaria/Shutterstock; Alex Slobodkin/iStockphoto; Shutterstock; Wavebreakmedia ltd/Shutterstock; **(from top):** Corbis Bridge/Alamy; Kurhan/Shutterstock; Mike Goldwater/Alamy; **(from left):** Lisa F. Young/iStockphoto; Foto Factory/Shutterstock; Keith Brofsky/Photodisc/Getty Images

Government

Problems of Government

Problems of Government

Pablo Martinez Monsivais/AP Wide World Photos

- Who runs the government?
- How do news media influence the political process?
- What are the threats to our civil liberties?
- How big a problem is government corruption?
- How can government be made more democratic?

Katherine Hicks broke into tears when she testified at the U.S. Senate hearing into the abuses of the Internal Revenue Service. The IRS, she said, had harassed her for 14 years because of an error in her master file, charged her thousands of dollars in interest for its own mistakes, and financially ruined her and her husband. "It was physically exhausting. We almost never slept. There were the visits to the attorneys and the accountants, their bills and their depressing advice: 'Pay it; it's cheaper than fighting.' My credit is completely destroyed. The IRS is judge, jury, and executioner—answerable to no one."[1]

Power is the essence of politics—the power to determine what is or is not a criminal act, the power to start or avoid wars, the power to collect vast sums of money and spend them on everything from ballpoint pens to nuclear bombs. Those who wield that power regulate thousands of aspects of our daily lives—deciding how fast we can drive, what drugs we may take, even determining whom we may or may not marry. When that power is misused, innocent people such as Katherine Hicks can suffer horrible consequences. At the same time, however, that government power is an essential part of almost any serious effort to deal with our social problems. Even such personal issues as divorce and mental disorder have their political side, and it is hard to imagine any solution to such diverse problems as crime, poverty, environmental pollution, or urban decay without effective government action.

The critical questions is, therefore: Whose interests does the government serve? Does it serve the narrow interests of its employees and officials, the interests of the wealthy and powerful, or the interests of society as a whole? Closely related questions are: How well does the government do its job? Who determines what that job is? There are almost endless examples of powerful special-interest groups that have blocked policies that are in the best interests of the nation and the vast majority of its citizens. A government that truly represents the interests of the people is the key to mounting an effective response to the numerous problems discussed in the pages of this book and the bedrock on which all our civil liberties are built.

The Growth of Government

Governments throughout the world have been growing rapidly since the beginning of the twentieth century. In 1929, the year of the great stock market crash, there were a little more than 3 million government employees in the United States; today there are almost 21 million.[2] Of course, the country's population was also increasing, but the percentage of the total workforce employed by the government still rose substantially. The often-heard accusation that there has been runaway growth in the size of the government in recent years is false, however. The number of civilians employed by the federal government declined by almost 6 percent between 1970 and 2005 while the total population almost doubled.[3] Although there is some variation from year to year, the share of our national income that funds local, state, and federal government hasn't changed much since the mid-1970s.[4] Moreover, as we can see in Table 1, only Japan has a smaller government relative to the size of its economy than the United States, and both Japan and the United States are far behind European governments.

The influence of government on the daily lives of its citizens has grown along with its size. In past centuries, most centralized governments were distant and ineffective. Important decisions were made locally and were based on long-standing customs and traditions. Today, governments are much stronger, and they are less tightly bound by traditional restraints. Most of this growth in size and influence has been a response to changes in other social institutions. For example, as the family became smaller and less stable, the government had to assume some of the functions once performed by families, such as ensuring some minimum financial support for the poor and the elderly. Similarly, as the contemporary system of industrial capitalism developed, it proved to be highly unstable, swinging from times of booming prosperity to deep depression. Even in the United States, with its deep suspicion of centralized authority, the federal government has been forced to get involved in regulating and directing the economy.

Table 1

COMPARING GOVERNMENT SIZE: GOVERNMENT SPENDING AS PERCENT OF GDP, 2004

Country	% of GDP
Sweden	57.1
France	54.4
Germany	47.7
Italy	48.6
Netherlands	48.6
Great Britain	44.1
Japan	37.3
United States	36.0

Source: Statistical Abstract of the United States, 2006 (Washington, DC: U.S. Government Printing Office), p. 878.

Bureaucracy ■ A form of social organization characterized by a division of labor, a hierarchy of authority, a set of formal rules, impersonal enforcement of rules, and job security.

When most people think about the growth of government, they think about the growth of **bureaucracy.** The huge labyrinth of federal offices and bureaus in the United States is certainly one of the largest bureaucracies that ever existed, but from a sociological standpoint, most private corporations are just as bureaucratic. In fact, one researcher concluded that more than 90 percent of all American workers are employed in some kind of bureaucratic organization.[5] What, then, is a bureaucracy? A bureaucracy is simply a formal organization in which the members perform specialized tasks and are regulated by a hierarchy of authority and a set of formal rules.[6]

Everyone seems to complain about bureaucratic waste. However, Max Weber, the great German sociologist, argued that because bureaucracies are based on rational rules that treat everyone with the same impersonal objectivity, they are actually the most stable and efficient form of organization.[7] The very strengths of a bureaucracy can also be its weaknesses, however. The formal rules that permit a government agency to function smoothly can also drown it in a sea of red tape. No system of rules is perfect. When unusual cases occur, it may be necessary to bend the rules to meet an organization's goals, but meeting those goals is not the only concern of employees. Most workers place a higher priority on holding on to their jobs, and because they can be fired for breaking rules, the tendency is to play it safe. Employees try to give at least the appearance of following all the rules, regardless of the consequences for the organization. For example, a welfare worker may know that a family is needy and deserves government assistance but is ineligible because of some technicality. An employee who is afraid to violate the rules "passes the buck" by sending the applicant to another office. At the next office, the applicant may be referred to someone else, and so on through the bureaucratic maze—while the family goes hungry. Such **goal displacement** is extremely common in bureaucracies in both government and private industry.[8] Moreover, bureaucracies often become a powerful political force in themselves, lobbying for programs and policies that may not be in the public interest. Even Max Weber was concerned about the depersonalizing effects of bureaucratization. He came to fear that the unending drive for bureaucratic efficiency would imprison people in what he called the "iron cage" of reason, with little room for human emotions.

Goal displacement ■ The tendency of bureaucracies to substitute informal goals for the official objectives of the organization.

QUICK REVIEW

■ Why has the government grown so large?

■ What is a bureaucracy, and how does it operate?

Both public and private bureaucracies have grown rapidly in the last century, and many people complain about their inefficiency and rigidity.

Rudi Von Briel/PhotoEdit Inc.

Who Runs the Government?

There is no more controversial topic in the social sciences than the question, Who really runs the government? Its enormous growth only makes that issue more important. Although most governments say they are democratic, does power really reside in the people—or is it in the hands of special-interest groups, an exclusive power elite, or the government bureaucrats and officeholders themselves? An enormous amount of research has been done on this critical issue over the years, and we will begin our discussion with a look at the major theories these researchers have developed.

Three Theoretical Approaches

Sociologists who have studied this issue generally fall into one of three theoretical camps. Perhaps the most popular theory is that of the **elite theorists** who hold that government policy is shaped by a small and relatively unified power elite. A second group sees the government as being far more democratic. These **pluralists** feel that the key government decisions are determined by competition among many different interest groups and that no single group predominates. The newest approach is that of the **structuralists,** who share the elitist view that government decisions reflect the interests of the privileged few but see the government as having far more independent power than do the elitists.

THE ELITE THEORISTS Radicals have long argued that the United States is dominated by a small group of powerful men, but it was C. Wright Mills's book, *The Power Elite,* published in the 1950s, that started much of the current debate about who runs the government. According to Mills, the power elite is a coalition of people in the highest ranks of the economy, the government, and the military, who together form a unified and self-conscious social class:

> There is no longer, on the one hand, an economy and, on the other hand, a political world, containing a military establishment unimportant to politics and to money-making. There is a political economy numerously linked with military order and decision. This triangle of power is now a structural fact, and it is the key to any

Elite theorists ■ People who believe that industrial nations are ruled by a small elite class.

Pluralists ■ People who believe that decisions in industrialized nations are made by a democratic process involving changing coalitions among many different interest groups.

Structuralists ■ Those who believe that the structure of capitalist society forces the government to support and protect the interests of a privileged few.

understanding of the higher circles in America today. For as each of these domains has coincided with the others, as decisions in each have become broader, the leading men of each—the high military, the corporation executive, the political directorate—have tended to come together to form the power elite of America.[9]

According to Mills, one of the major sources of the unity of the power elite is its members' common social background. They tend to come from upper-class and upper middle-class white families living in urban areas. They attend the same Ivy League colleges and, by and large, share the same attitudes toward the world and their position in it. In addition, the social networks that they represent are closely interconnected with many common interests. Finally, although the power elite does not represent some great conspiracy, its members meet both socially and professionally and often coordinate their activities.

Below the power elite, Mills saw two other levels of power in American society. At the bottom of the heap are the great masses of people—unorganized, ill-informed, and virtually powerless. Between these masses and the elite are the "middle levels" of power where some true competition between interest groups still exists. Mills saw the U.S. Congress as part of these middle levels of power. Although Congress decides some minor issues, the power elite ensures that no serious challenge to its control is tolerated in the political arena.

The work started by Mills has been carried on by G. William Domhoff and other contemporary elite theorists.[10] These researchers all accept Mills's conclusion that power is concentrated in the hands of the few, but they question his inclusion of the military leadership in the power elite. Although they recognize the importance of the military, they are convinced that the most critical decisions, even in the field of international relations, are made by an economic–political elite. This elite is not, however, an equal partnership between top corporate and top government officials. The lion's share of the power is held by those in key positions of corporate power. Not only do they greatly outnumber powerful government officials, but also they possess far more wealth, and their careers are not dependent on the uncertainties of the electoral process.

THE PLURALISTS Pluralists believe that democratic societies are indeed democratic. Although they recognize that there is a large apolitical mass with little power, they argue that critical political decisions are not made by a single power elite but are decided in a contest among many competing groups. David Riesman, a pluralist writing at about the same time as Mills, arrived at some starkly different conclusions than did Mills. He called interest groups "veto groups" because he thought their main objective was merely to block policies that might threaten their interests.[11] Where Mills saw common interests among powerful groups, Riesman saw divergence; where Mills saw growing concentration of power, Riesman saw growing dispersion of power.

Current pluralist thought runs along the lines taken by Riesman. However, his idea that interest groups are mainly concerned with stopping legislation they dislike is no longer widely accepted. Arnold M. Rose, a sociologist who was also a state legislator, pointed out the obvious fact that interest groups also take action on their own behalf. According to Rose:

[The pluralist] conceives of society as consisting of many elites, each relatively small numerically, and operating in different spheres of life. . . . While it is true that there are inert masses of undifferentiated individuals without access to each other (except in the most trivial respects) and therefore without influence, the bulk of the population consists not of the mass but of integrated groups and publics, stratified with varying degrees of power.[12]

The pluralists emphasize the importance of the role of government officials in transforming all those diverse interests into some kind of coherent public policy. Competing interest groups argue, negotiate, and compromise. At critical points in the decision-making process, public opinion and the common values shared by the citizenry and participants in the political process often tip the scales in favor of the public interest.

Thus, though it is far from perfect, the pluralists still see the political system as a truly democratic process.[13]

THE STRUCTURALISTS The newest theory about who runs the government comes from a group of thinkers known as the *structuralists*. Like the elite theorists, they take a conflict perspective on society, and they too believe that key government decisions are made to serve the interests of the few, not the many. However, the structuralists differ from the elitists on two important points. Although many elitists have focused their work on the ways members of the elite work to influence government policy, structuralists such as Nicos Poulantzas and Theda Skocpol argue that the upper class does not need to be involved in the political process.[14] They believe that the structure of capitalist societies forces the government to protect the interests of the upper class or risk the collapse of the whole system.

The structuralists criticize the elitists' view of the relationship between the government and the upper class in another way as well. They charge that the elitists see the government as nothing more than a passive instrument used by the power elite to advance their own interests. To the structuralists, the government and its officials are an independent power group in their own right. One way to explain the differences between structuralists and elitists such as G. William Domhoff (who has taken up research where C. Wright Mills left off) is to consider their debate over why the New Deal of President Franklin Roosevelt emerged to reform the capitalist system in United States and save it from the Great Depression of the 1930s. Domhoff provides extensive historical evidence showing that an "enlightened" faction of the American upper class realized that drastic reforms were needed or the U.S. economy might collapse. It was this faction of the upper class that pushed economic reform through Congress in the early 1930s. Skocpol, on the other hand, counters with other historical evidence and charges that it was government officials themselves who took charge of economic reforms in the 1930s and pushed these reforms on an unwilling American upper class.[15]

As is often the case in academic debates, however, the two sides of this argument are closer than it appears. Although the structuralists see the government as capable of taking autonomous action independently of the upper class, they recognize that it is only a *relative autonomy*. In the short run, the government may move against the desires of the upper class in order to stave off popular discontent or to advance its own interests; in the long run, however, it must work to promote the interests of the capitalist system and those in its key positions of economic power—or it risks being overthrown or seeing the collapse of the whole system.

The Political Process: Citizens and Special Interests

In order to evaluate these theories, we must turn our attention to the concrete operations of the political process. As most of us learned in our high school government classes, in an ideal democracy political power is shared equally by all citizens. Virtually no sociologists or political scientists feel that we actually have such a system, however. (See Figure 1.) One of the major problems of any would-be democracy is the apathy of its citizens. The number of Americans who vote has never been high, and it has declined significantly since the 1960s. Furthermore, the United States is behind all the other major industrial nations in voter turnout by its citizens.[16] Only about 61 percent of the voting-age population reported having voted in the 2004 presidential election, and the voter turnout is always substantially lower when only congressional seats are at stake.[17] A survey by the U.S. Census Bureau found that most people who did not vote said they were either "too busy" or "not interested" in voting.[18] Other forms of political participation, such as working in a political campaign or taking part in a political rally, are even less common than voting.

Of course, it is not necessary for all the citizens in a democracy to participate if those who do are representative of those who do not, but this is not the case. Studies of citizen participation reveal a strange paradox. Those who most need the government's help are

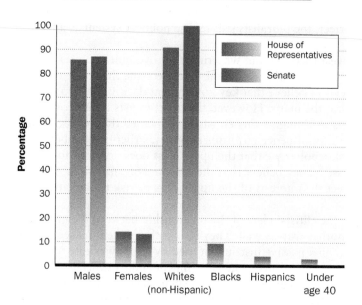

Figure 1

Who Serves in Congress?

The membership in Congress does not reflect the overall population of the United States.

Source: Statistical Abstract of the United States, 2006 (Washington, DC: U.S. Government Printing Office, 2006), p. 257.

least likely to take part in the political process. People with higher incomes and more education are much more likely to be politically active, while minorities and the poor are less likely to get involved. About 81 percent of the people in the upper-income categories report having voted in the last presidential election as compared to around 48 percent of the lower-income people. There are also considerable differences in voting by age; people in the 55-and-over age group report voting at a rate of around 73 percent, whereas young people in the 18-to-24 age group vote at a rate of around 47 percent.[19]

It seems that a primary source of voter apathy is distrust of the government and a general feeling of powerlessness. Many people do not think their votes or opinions count for much against the powerful special-interest groups and the huge number of other voters. A single vote, the argument goes, is almost never decisive even in the closest election. Furthermore, even citizens who are interested in politics often find it difficult to decide where a particular politician stands on the issues. For one thing, politicians often try to conceal their real opinions about controversial matters and try to make voters on both sides of an issue believe they support their views. In addition, the voters seldom get a chance to talk directly with candidates, relying instead on the mass media for information. Effective campaigners try to project a positive image in their advertising and television speeches, which often have little to do with the issues. Advertising agencies sell candidates in the same way they sell soap or deodorant. In a 30-second television commercial, there is little time for serious consideration of political issues. Moreover, candidates of minor political parties and those without strong financial backing have little access to the media and are thus frozen out of the arena of serious political debate.

The media have influence, however, far beyond their role in political advertising. As Thomas R. Dye, a well-known political scientist, puts it: "The media determine what the masses talk about. . . . Political issues do not just 'happen.' The media decides what are issues, problems, even crises, which must be acted upon."[20] Moreover, control of the media is concentrated in relatively few hands. Four huge media corporations account for 80 percent of the news and entertainment broadcasts on television. Most of the United States' 1,700 or so daily newspapers receive news from the Associated Press wire service, and the 15 largest newspaper conglomerates account for more than half the total newspaper circulation in the country.[21]

Despite all the obstacles, average citizens do sometimes band together into a social movement that wields significant power. One good example is the powerful voting bloc of those 65 years of age and older; another good example is the environmental movement. Although factory owners, land developers, and automobile manufacturers saw nothing wrong with their polluting activities, a growing environmental crisis was obvious to average citizens when they looked around their communities. Activists began

Bob Daemmrich/PhotoEdit Inc.

The job of the lobbyists is to get lawmakers to vote the way special-interest groups want them to vote.

forming organizations and planning protests, meetings, and demonstrations. They eventually won sympathetic media attention and came to wield significant influence on the political process.

One of the most important forces influencing legislators and other government officials is the so-called **special-interest group**—an organized group that has a stake in a particular piece of legislation. Physicians, real-estate developers, small businesses, big businesses, labor unions, and numerous others are all special-interest groups. The most common concern of such groups is financial; they actively promote legislation that will help make them money and oppose legislation that will increase their costs. People who feel strongly about a particular issue also form organizations on more idealistic grounds—for example, civil rights and peace groups. The influence of these groups depends to a large extent on their size, their degree of organization, and the money at their disposal. Big business is clearly the most powerful of all interest groups because it commands more of those resources.

Special-interest group ■ An organized group of people who have a stake in a particular area of public policy.

Personal Perspectives

A Member of the House of Representatives

Politics is like any other profession. The longer you stay in the profession, the more you learn about how to do your job. In this excerpt, a former Republican congressman lets us in on some of the conventional wisdom among elected officials that may help explain some of the problems of today's government.

The name recognition factor alone, coupled with the apathy and disinterest of most voters, should be sufficient to ensure the incumbent congressman's reelection year after year—with one exception. Here lies the rub. The exception to success in my profession occurs when an incumbent takes a position or casts a vote which a competent opponent can use to stir public apathy by creating strong feelings against the incumbent. As several elderly congressmen are wont to tell newly elected colleagues, "No man has ever been defeated on the basis of what he didn't say." The penalties in the profession of politics are applied to those who attempt to lead, take controversial positions and, most of all, allow those controversial positions to become known to their constituents.*

*Former Representative Paul N. McCloskey, Jr., *Truth and Untruth: Political Deceit in America* (New York: Simon and Schuster, 1972).

Lobbying ■ The activities of special-interest groups intended to influence government decision makers.

The effort of special-interest groups to influence lawmakers is known as **lobbying,** and it is one of their principal activities. Lobbyists aim to convince lawmakers to pass the kind of legislation the groups desire. One of their most effective tools is information: Because individual legislators are seldom well informed about all the bills they must consider, and because legislative bodies lack the funds to make independent investigations of all the issues before them, the facts and figures supplied by lobbyists can often sway lawmakers' votes. Lobbyists also try to influence legislation by cultivating the friendship of individual legislators. Many well-heeled lobbyists are notorious for their lavish parties and ingratiating manners. Moreover, a lobbyist's promise of political support from a powerful special interest often determines an elected official's decisions. Threats by a special-interest group can be effective, too. Opposition by a powerful labor union or an important corporation has resulted in the defeat of many a politician.

Money is one of the special-interest groups' main resources. Political campaigns are becoming more and more expensive, and the special interests are supplying the money. As recently as 1960, the price tag of an average congressional campaign was only about $25,000; in the 2004 presidential election, the average race for the House of Representatives cost about $1.5 million and the average Senate race cost about $5 million (see Figure 2). The total money spent by the candidates, parties, and other political groups came to almost $4 billion![22] One main source of funding are the *political action committees* (PACs) set up to represent various special-interest groups. Of course, many individual contributions come from people with a particular interest in a specific policy or program.

Politicians inevitably claim that such contributions are merely a sign of support from those who favor their policies and that money has no influence on their votes, but few outside observers find such statements to be convincing. It is too simplistic to say that most politicians overtly sell favors and influence for campaign contributions (although periodic corruption scandals show that some certainly do), but those millions of dollars often exert a dominating influence on the political process.

In theory, the ability of special interests to hire lobbyists and make campaign contributions that help elect sympathetic politicians wouldn't make much difference, as long as supporters on both sides of important issues had roughly the same amount of money to spend, but that is clearly not the case. Corporations give far more than labor unions, polluters give more than environmentalists, big businesses more than small businesses, and Republicans more than Democrats.[23] Obviously, the poor and the underprivileged will *never* be able to spend as much money to advance their political interests as the

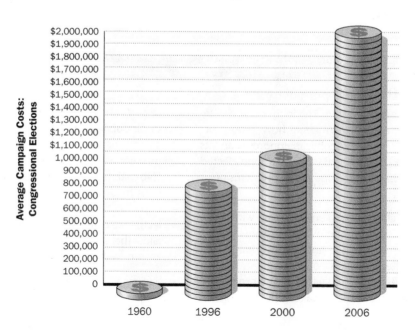

Figure 2
Running for Office
The cost of running for public office has increased enormously in recent years.

Source: U.S. Bureau of the Census, *Statistical Abstract of the United States, 2007* (Washington, DC: U.S. Government Printing Office, 2007), Table 413; Jennifer Harper, "Campaign Spending," *Washington Times,* October 22, 2004; *The New York Times,* November 25, 1997, p. A12; Theodore Caplow, *American Social Trends* (San Diego: Harcourt Brace Jovanovich, 1991), p. 114; Federal Election Commission, December 2000 (www.fec.gov).

wealthy do, just as broadly based "general-interest" groups such as environmentalists and consumer advocates are unable to match the financial power of the big corporations whose policies they oppose.

The general public is largely unaware of another important influence on government policy: the major foundations and civic associations. Large foundations, such as the Ford Foundation and the Kellogg Foundation, receive their money from donations by corporations and individuals of great wealth, and they use it, among many other things, to fund research on various social issues. The most influential policy-planning groups, such as the Council on Foreign Relations and the Business Roundtable, also generally represent the viewpoint of the established elites, and together with researchers from major universities who are funded by the foundations, they analyze public issues and make policy recommendations to the government. Because these groups provide much of the brainpower behind government policy, they exert a significant influence over its long-term direction.[24]

An Appraisal

As we have seen, the political process is a complex and multifaceted one. None of the major theoretical approaches offers all the answers, but some basic conclusions about the way the process operates do seem justified. First, numerous competing interest groups, including government officials themselves, take part in the struggle to shape government policy. These groups form shifting patterns of alliances on different issues, cooperating, competing, and compromising as called for by the political realities of their times. Second, although many diverse groups are involved in shaping political decisions, these groups are not equals. One group—made up of those who hold key positions of corporate power or great personal wealth or both—is far more powerful than any of the others. In normal times, this elite dominates the decision-making process on most of the important questions of economic and foreign policy. Third, despite all this, it would still be wrong to say that average citizens have no political power. In times of crisis, catastrophe, and mass discontent, people often band together in social movements, which on occasion have been successful in forcing fundamental changes in government policies and even in the political process itself. And, fourth, there are concrete limits to what the government can do. In times of crisis, government may be forced to carry out policies for which no sector of society has much enthusiasm, and the demands of the world economy limit the choices available to any individual nation, even a rich and powerful one.

QUICK REVIEW

- Describe the differences among the pluralist, elitist, and structuralist theories of government.
- Which theory do you think is most convincing?

The Dilemmas of Government

The most basic problem of democratic government is democracy itself: how to fairly represent the will of the people when there are so many people and so many different interests. As we have just seen, contemporary government does not always do a particularly good job with this fundamental task. In this section, we will examine some of the other major problems of government: preventing scandals and corruption, maintaining civil liberties, dealing with military issues, and deciding who is to bear the burden and receive the benefits of government policies. The fundamental need for a more democratic government underlies all these other issues, however, and will appear again and again in our discussion.

Scandals and Corruption

Most people see the problem of government corruption in personal terms: crooked politicians getting rich or getting reelected by dishonest means. There is far more to the problem than that, however, because government corruption strikes at the heart of democracy itself. The more control the influence peddlers and the corrupt interests have over government policy, the less control the people have.

Government officials can be corrupted in many ways that are completely legal. The biggest problem comes from the system of campaign financing we have already discussed. It is clearly a crime to pay a politician to vote for a certain bill or perform some other political favor, but it is perfectly legal to give large campaign contributions to that same politician and then to ask her or him to vote in the way you want—as long as no one acknowledges that the contributions were made in exchange for the vote. The fact that our politicians must carry on a continual quest for financial gifts to pay for their election campaigns creates a built-in **conflict of interest** every time a bill favored by one of their major contributors comes up for a vote.

Conflict of interest ■ The ethical dilemma that occurs when an officeholder's official duty and his or her personal interests conflict.

Another way successful politicians can reward their campaign workers and contributors is with a government job. In the nineteenth century, most government jobs were handed out in exchange for contributions and support in what came to be known as the **spoils system.** Since then, civil service reforms have sharply reduced the number of jobs that officeholders can give out as political patronage, but the practice still continues. A new president, for example, must appoint thousands of people to government positions, and it is accepted practice to give most of those jobs to friends and political supporters.

Spoils system ■ A political system in which government jobs and favors are handed out in exchange for political support.

A different kind of conflict of interest occurs when officeholders decide an issue in which they have a personal financial interest. For example, the House of Representatives reprimanded one of its members for concealing his investment in an industrial company and then voting for a bill that granted it a lucrative government contract.[25] The issues are not always that clear-cut, however. Most established politicians have considerable personal wealth, and it is almost inevitable that some of the wide-ranging decisions they are called on to make will influence their investments in one way or another. This dilemma could be avoided if officeholders would place their financial investments in a *blind trust* managed by a third party, but few politicians actually do so.

Most conflicts of interest fall into the gray area between the unethical and the illegal. There is no question, however, that outright **bribery** is still a serious problem. In earlier times, when only a small group of landholders could vote, the main problem was the bribery of the voters by politicians. In the 1757 race for the Virginia House of Burgesses, for example, George Washington was accused of giving out 50 gallons of rum, 24 gallons of wine, 46 gallons of beer, and 2 gallons of cider in a district that had only 391 voters![26] Today, of course, the bribe money normally flows in the opposite direction. Political bribery is probably most widespread at the state and local levels, often involving zoning changes or the award of government contracts. There have, of course, been numerous scandals over the years, but how much bribery goes undetected is anybody's guess. Some critics even claim that investigators sometimes inadvertently create the crimes they are supposed to prevent. For example, in the so-called Abscam case, FBI agents claimed to be working for an Arab sheik in need of some Washington favors. The agents handed out bribes to eight officeholders and subsequently arrested them. Critics of such operations (which are more commonly carried on against state and local officials) claim the agents are simply creating crime by tempting honest officeholders to break the law; others feel that the relative ease with which they find officials who will take their bribes indicates a high level of government corruption.[27] The exact level of bribery and other types of corruption is certainly difficult to determine, but see the Lessons from Other Places in this chapter for an estimate of how countries vary in their level of corruption.

Bribery ■ Giving officials money or some other reward in order to influence the way they carry out their duties.

Although conflicts of interest from campaign fund-raising are as problematic as ever, other forms of government corruption are probably less common than they were in the past. New laws requiring fuller financial disclosure by officeholders, a new interest among law-enforcement officials in investigating and prosecuting corruption cases, and,

Lessons from Other Places

Government Corruption Around the World

With all the charges of misconduct and abuse that crop up in every election, Americans often get the impression that they have the most corrupt government on Earth—or at least close to it. A look around the world, however, suggests that this is not exactly the case. In Italy, former prime ministers have been arrested on corruption charges and others have been found to have ties to Mafia leaders. In what seemed like an incorruptible government in Germany, former Chancellor Helmut Kohl, who helped unite East and West Germany, was charged with bribery. In general, however, polls by Gallup International find that Western Europeans rank their governments as less corrupt than do people in the United States. In Western Europe, 22 percent say their government is corrupt, while 29 percent of Americans believe their government is corrupt.

For the advanced industrial societies, however, recent Japanese governments have taken corruption and bribery to levels no other society can touch. From the 1970s onward, it seems that one scandal after another has brought down governments. In the middle of various bribery scandals, one top politician was still so arrogant as to be caught with $50 million worth of gold bars tucked away at home. In 1993, a new law required politicians to disclose their wealth and income for the first time. Keeping in mind that members of parliament (the Diet) in Japan were paid $160,000 per year at the time, it is interesting that the new disclosure law indicated that the average wealth of all 749 Diet members was almost $1 million each. It was also found that most of this wealth was made *after* politicians were elected to office!

A few years ago, a new international organization called Transparency International began an annual corruption ranking of governments around the world. One of its primary means of ranking these governments is to survey businesspeople who must do business in different countries to assess their direct experiences of government corruption. Among the 163 nations included in the ranking, the United States was ranked 20th. Although this means that 143 other countries were considered more corrupt, the United States was still near the bottom of the industrialized nations. The most corrupt nations tend to be newly developing countries that have yet to overcome old traditions or have fully developed legal systems in place to help guard against corruption.

Here are a few of the countries on Transparency International's 2006 list. A perfect score, meaning no corruption, is 10, with 0 given to the most corrupt nations:

Finland	9.6
New Zealand	9.6
Denmark	9.5
Singapore	9.4
Sweden	9.2
Switzerland	9.1
Norway	8.8
Netherlands	8.7
Australia	8.7
Great Britain	8.6
Austria	8.6
Germany	8.0
Japan	7.6
France	7.4
United States	7.3
Italy	4.9
Thailand	3.6
Mexico	3.3
Vietnam	2.6
Indonesia	2.4

Sources: Harold Kerbo and John McKinstry, *Who Rules Japan? The Inner Circles of Economic and Political Power* (Westport, CT: Praeger, 1995), pp. 107–108; Transparency International at www.transparency.org; data from Gallup International are also found at www.gallup-international.com.

most important, ever more stringent media scrutiny have made it harder for elected officials to get away with illegal schemes.

There has been a heavy price to pay, however, for the media's growing interest in political misbehavior. Some famous corruption cases, such as Watergate and the Iran-Contra scandal, involved important issues concerning the misuse of government power, but an insatiable appetite for scandal has led the media to focus more and more attention on politicians' sex lives and other personal matters that have little or nothing to do with their performance in office. An increasing number of elections seem to turn on the success the two sides have in digging up and publicizing "dirt" about their opponents. Political contests driven by scandal instead of real differences over the issues can hardly be expected to produce a representative government that truly reflects the will of the people. Moreover, the media's willingness to splash every detail of a politician's private life across the headlines and the increasingly negative stereotypes about government leaders in general are discouraging many talented people from pursuing careers in public service.

Public Cynicism

Closely related to the problem of government corruption is the rise in public cynicism. Opinion polls, for example, show that Americans have extremely low levels of confidence in their government. In 2005, only about 22 percent of Americans said they had "confidence" in the Congress, 41 percent in the Supreme Court, and 44 percent in the presidency.[28] Many Americans look at their government as unresponsive, bureaucratic, and inefficient, and they see those who work in it as self-serving and often corrupt. Data from Gallup International polls show that people in almost every European country have more confidence in their government and feel that elections are more fair than do people in the United States. In addition to cultural differences, there may actually be some basis in fact for these opinions. In its 2006 annual study, Transparency International found the United States to be one of the most corrupt of all major industrial nations. Only Italy received a worse rating.[29]

Of course, a reasonable skepticism about the government and its policies is a healthy thing in a democracy. As we have seen, government corruption is a serious problem, and, more important, the wealthy and powerful do often trample over the interests of the majority. When skepticism turns into the kind of corrosive cynicism that sees no possibilities for improvement, however, then the result is likely to be a growing sense of apathy and indifference that only makes those problems worse.

Why has the public's opinion of government fallen so dramatically in recent times? There is no reason to believe that the government has gotten less democratic or more corrupt; in fact, just the opposite is probably true (see, for example, the Signs of Hope box). The changes seem to be less in what the government is doing than in the way the public perceives it, and much of that can be attributed to the media. In the past, the media had a much cozier relationship to the government and were usually content to present the official version of the news. President Roosevelt was virtually never shown in his wheelchair or on his crutches for fear it might make the nation's leader look weak, and although numerous reporters knew about extramarital affairs carried on by various national leaders, such as Presidents Dwight D. Eisenhower and John F. Kennedy, they never mentioned these affairs in the press. A new era of investigative reporting has shed valuable light on numerous corrupt and undemocratic practices, but it has also fanned the flames of public cynicism. It would, however, be unfair to lay the whole problem on the media, for in many ways they merely reflect changes in our overall society, which is far more educated, more sophisticated, and more skeptical than at any time in the past.

Signs of Hope

Letting More People In

Despite the failings of our political system, which we have examined in this chapter, and the ways it favors the wealthy and the well-connected, there is no doubt that it has been growing steadily more democratic. This nation was originally ruled by a foreign king, and the elections that were allowed were restricted to white male property owners. Over the years, the vote was extended to more and more people. First, the property restrictions were dropped. Then, after the Civil War, the vote was officially extended to freed male slaves, although the southern states soon devised a variety of schemes that placed formidable barriers in the way of African Americans who wanted to exercise their new right. Next, the male establishment gave in to the demands of the "suffragettes," and women, too, obtained the right to vote. Another phase of this long process came as a result of the demands of the civil rights movement of the 1950s and 1960s, when Supreme Court rulings and new federal laws broke down the last official barriers to African American voting rights. Yet another group gained representation during the Vietnam War, when the legislature conceded that if 18-year-olds were old enough to be drafted, they were old enough to vote. The right to vote is only a first step toward true political representation, but there is no doubt that it is a critically important one.

The Military Dilemma

The military poses a dilemma in all democratic societies: It is essential but at the same time extremely dangerous. With its traditions of command, authority, and unquestioning obedience, the military often responds when disorganization and confusion paralyze an elected government. The list of struggling democracies that have been taken over by their military is a long one, particularly in the less-developed countries of Asia, Africa, and Latin America. Developed countries with long democratic traditions—such as Great Britain, Canada, the United States, and Switzerland—are in little danger of a direct military takeover, but even these nations face the danger of growing too dependent on the military, both politically and economically.

A military force is, of course, necessary for national defense. The critical question is how much of the government's budget should be spent for this purpose. Different nations answer this question in different ways. The United States spends a high percentage of its income on its military, whereas Japan and Germany, with similar economic and political systems, spend comparatively little. One point is clear, however. Although military spending can give a temporary boost to a lagging economy, serious long-range damage results. Most military products have no practical use unless there is a war: You can't eat them, wear them, or live in them. Moreover, military research and development takes scientific talent away from more productive civilian research. Many historians believe that the heavy military burden borne by Great Britain in the nineteenth century was a major cause of its economic decline and that the same thing may be happening to the United States today.

Why does the United States spend so much on its military? The prolonged struggle of World War II, closely followed by the Cold War with the Soviet Union and the Korean and Vietnam conflicts, left the United States with enormous military commitments and a vision of itself as the world's military and political leader. After each of those conflicts was resolved and draftees returned to civilian life, the military establishment ended up larger and more expensive. Military spending is once again being increased, this time to fight a sometimes vaguely defined "war on terror." Long after the collapse of the Soviet Union decimated the only military force capable of challenging U.S. global dominance, the United States continues to spend far more on its military than any other country in the world. In 2006, America's military outlays were more than $535 billion—more than the outlays of the next 20 nations combined! Almost 3 million Americans are on active duty or in the military reserves, and millions of others work in civilian industries that supply the military with the goods and services it requires.[30]

Given the enormous size and economic strength of the U.S. military, it is not surprising that many observers have expressed concern about its influence in a democratic society. One of the most unexpected warnings came from President Eisenhower, a career army officer. In his farewell address, President Eisenhower warned against the influence of the **military-industrial complex** and the growing interdependence between the military and the giant corporations. Such companies as United Technologies and Lockheed Martin are not owned by the military, but their profits come largely from military contracts. Hundreds of other companies also sell a substantial percentage of their products to the military, so corporations and the armed forces have many interests in common. The military has its own lobbyists, who wield tremendous influence in Washington. They are often assisted by lobbyists for organized labor, which sees military spending as an important source of jobs, and by lobbyists for corporations, which see military spending as good business. Even if there were no military lobbyists, senators and representatives from states with

Military-industrial complex ■ The powerful interest group formed by the military and the civilian corporations that supply it with services, materials, and equipment.

The military always poses a dilemma for a democratic society. On the one hand, it is essential for the protection of society; on the other hand, its traditions of obedience and conformity can pose a threat to democratic institutions.

David Wells/The Image Works

173

high concentrations of military bases or defense industries would still be vigorous supporters of military appropriations. Although all this does not add up to military control of the U.S. government, the military-industrial complex obviously has enormous influence and power.

Now that the Cold War is over, many new questions about the U.S. military role in the world must be faced. Supporters of the military-industrial complex argue for continuing to expand military spending, citing the wave of terrorism as proof that the world is just as dangerous a place as it was before the collapse of the Soviet Union. Skeptics, however, argue that the war in Iraq has shown that even the largest and most powerful conventional military forces are of little use against small groups of terrorists that hide from direct confrontation. They argue that it is even more doubtful that such nations as Iran or North Korea, with little technological sophistication and even less money, can pose a threat to the United States requiring anything like its current levels of military expenditures. Because the Cold War is over, common sense would seem to tell us that the U.S. military burden must be reduced to something more similar to that of its major economic competitors—but that is no easy task. Not only has the military-industrial complex gained enormous political power over the last 50 years, but a large sector of the U.S. economy has come to depend on military spending. If the U.S. military were suddenly slashed back to a size comparable to the military of Germany or Japan, there would be a devastating economic shock.

Defense conversion ■ Changing corporations and workers from military to civilian work.

Many social scientists, therefore, believe that what is necessary is a carefully thought out program of **defense conversion** to redirect corporations and workers from military to civilian work. Some military technologies are already being put to civilian purposes. For example, the global satellite system the U.S. military created to enable its soldiers to instantly find their location anywhere in the world is now forming the basis for a whole new industry that has been putting computer navigation devices in passenger cars. Advocates of defense conversion argue that the federal government must make a more concerted effort to encourage such transfers of technology, fund retraining programs for defense workers, and provide financial subsidies to help defense contractors find new civilian markets in the global economy. By itself, however, such an effort will still not be enough to head off major economic damage to local communities when a military base must be closed or the production of a expensive weapon system is stopped. Any effective program to redirect national resources from military to civilian purposes must also provide help for such beleaguered communities.

Freedom or Oppression?

Of all the dilemmas confronting modern government, none is more important than the issue of how to protect personal freedom while still maintaining social order. The fear that the government and the big corporations want to control every aspect of our lives and strip us of our basic human rights is shared by people from many walks of life. The nightmare that could come from a fusion of technology and totalitarianism—such as those depicted in books like George Orwell's *1984* and Aldous Huxley's *Brave New World*—has haunted the Western world for 50 years.

Lists of human rights usually include freedoms of speech, assembly, and movement and the right to privacy, autonomy, and political expression. The ideas embodied in these noble generalizations are, however, difficult to put into practice. The expression of one person's rights may interfere with the rights of another and the needs of the entire society, and there is always someone to claim that "the common good" or "the general welfare" requires the suppression of all individual freedom.

Blacklisting ■ The practice of denying employment and economic opportunities to people because of their political views.

The list of systematic violations of individual liberties is tragically long, even in democratic countries. One famous example is the anticommunist "witch-hunts" that took place in the United States in the 1950s. The hysterical search for communist subversives led to the **blacklisting** and professional ruin of many people whose only offense was belonging to the "wrong" political organization or holding an unpopular opinion. Another example comes from Canada, which is also a country with a long democratic tradition.

When a prominent British diplomat and a Canadian politician were kidnapped in 1970 by members of a group seeking independence for the province of Quebec, the national government invoked the War Measures Act, thereby suspending civil liberties. Membership in or support for the group responsible for the kidnapping was forbidden, and 490 "separatist sympathizers" were rounded up and jailed. Of these, 435 were eventually released without ever being charged with a crime. Polls indicated that the Canadian people clearly approved the use of the War Measures Act, just as the majority of the American people had approved of the anticommunist crusades.[31]

Watergate, one of the biggest political scandals in U.S. history, involved a different sort of violation of civil liberties. President Richard M. Nixon's White House was not riding a wave of popular fear and resentment but rather was working behind a cloak of official secrecy to harass and silence its political opponents. Among other crimes, the Watergate scandal involved burglaries of the offices of political groups, including the Democratic Party, and the use of illegal wiretaps and listening devices, tax audits, and false rumors against those on the "enemies list" put together by the White House. Once the scandal began to come to light, administration officials perjured themselves, paid bribes, and destroyed evidence in order to obstruct the investigation.[32]

Similar tactics were used by several presidential administrations to try to undercut the civil rights movement and crush opposition to the war in Vietnam. Evidence that came to light years later showed that the FBI and other government agencies used burglaries and a variety of illegal surveillance techniques to gather information. They even engaged in a direct campaign of political harassment and repression. Phony letters were sent to the friends and families of political activists, accusing them of everything from embezzlement to cheating on their spouses; false stories were planted in the media; police were urged to arrest activists on minor charges; utilities were encouraged to shut off their services; and some activists were attacked and even killed by people acting under government sponsorship. There were also many cases involving government "agents provocateurs"—that is, government agents who secretly joined a protest group to push them toward illegal activity for which they could be arrested. There are cases in which such government agents joined student movements against the Vietnam War, convinced some students they should try to destroy military buildings on campus, brought bomb-making material to these students, then tipped off police to have them arrested when the material was in their possession.[33] Such illegal activities tapered off after the end of the war and the collapse of the militant organizations the government had targeted. The bits and pieces of information that occasionally leaked out, however, show that the government's surveillance and harassment of U.S. citizens continued long after the end of the Vietnam War.[34]

The latest threat to American civil liberties comes from the September 11 terrorist attacks and the "war on terrorism" the federal government launched in response. Although a state of war was never officially declared, the government assumed a variety of wartime powers to restrict privacy and detain suspected terrorists. The most extreme abuses have occurred overseas beyond the reach of U.S. courts. More than 600 people, most of whom were captured during the war in Afghanistan, were brought to the U.S. military base in Guantanamo Bay, Cuba, because no U.S. court has jurisdiction there. They were held without charges, without trial, and without access to legal representation for months on end.[35] Despite strict secrecy, it is also becoming clear that the U.S. government used psychological torture, including prolonged sleep deprivation, threats, and nonstop interrogations to extract information from suspected terrorists. U.S. forces, however, did not stop with psychological torture. In 2004, a series of grisly photographs of the torture and sexual humiliation of prisoners held by the U.S. military in Iraq were leaked to the press and a nationwide scandal erupted. Some of these abuses were apparently for the sadistic pleasure of the guards, but it has also become clear that many of the techniques used were part of a systematic program of torture developed by the Central Intelligence Agency (CIA). This program, which appears to have been widely used by the CIA, includes three elements: (1) the use of sensory deprivation such as hooding and blindfolding subjects; (2) "self-inflicted pain" by, for example, forcing

Many believe that only totalitarian governments pose a threat to civil liberties. But democratically elected governments are also involved in many abuses as this photograph of the torture of Iraqi prisoners by American troops shows.

Washington Post/Getty Images, Inc. - Agence France Presse

someone to stand on one foot for hours at a time; and (3) what the agency calls the use of "cultural sensitivities," which, in the case of Arab prisoners, includes intimidation by dogs and sexual humiliation.

Along with the government, many private corporations now pose their own threat to civil liberties. For one thing, many companies are using a host of new techniques, including the Internet and e-mail, to peer into the private lives of their employees. A study by the American Management Association found that 63 percent of the companies surveyed had some kind of drug-testing program,[36] and other research has found that 70 percent of companies run background checks on new employees, about 50 percent examine their police records, and around 20 percent administer some kind of psychological test.[37] Supreme Court decisions have also given employers almost unlimited freedom to eavesdrop on their workers' conversations, and one study by *Macworld* magazine found that 22 percent of the firms surveyed admitted carrying on searches of employees' computer files, voice mail, or other electronic records.[38] A different sort of invasion of workers' privacy comes from employers' attempts to avoid the rising costs of health-care benefits. Not only do some companies refuse to hire smokers (who have more health problems than nonsmokers), but also current employees have been fired for off-the-job smoking.

Private firms pose a threat to more than just their employees, however, and with the proliferation of new technologies for gathering and retrieving information, privacy seems to be in danger of becoming a thing of the past. Private database firms now have cross-referenced lists of the U.S. population that include everything from the value of a family's home to children's ages. Open databases with names such as Sleuth, Asset Locator, and People Finder allow the curious to search out the private details of their friends' and neighbors' lives. Furthermore, although the convenience and portability of the cellular phone has made it a worldwide success, cellular calls are far easier for a nosy outsider to monitor. One expert estimated that 60 percent of cell phone calls in California's Silicon Valley were being taped. With the proliferation of video surveillance cameras, it has become more and more difficult to be anonymous even in public places. Denver's new international airport, for example, has no fewer than 1,500 surveillance cameras. Such equipment is now in common use in bank lobbies and parking lots and near automatic teller machines.[39] Partly in response to a long campaign of Irish Republican Army terrorist bombings, British authorities installed surveillance cameras throughout central London. Visitors to London can now expect that practically everything they do in public is being recorded by public or private surveillance cameras. One of the most advanced of the new technologies appeared in 2000 with new software called Carnivore that allows government agencies to almost instantly scan millions of e-mail and Web communications for the exact information they are seeking.

It is hardly surprising that people of all political persuasions are becoming concerned about the threat that the use of technology may pose to civil liberties. The federal government maintains hundreds of different databases that contain billions of entries about its citizens.[40] They range from files on "subversives," terrorists, and criminals, kept by investigative agencies such as the FBI, the CIA, and military intelligence agencies, to the files in the massive record-keeping systems of the Internal Revenue Service and the Social Security Administration. Clearly, government agencies need many of these files if they are to do their work efficiently, but is such efficiency dangerous? What about the growing number of private firms that are keeping their own lists and selling them to whoever is willing to buy them? The power available to those who control such information systems is obviously immense. Clearly, the totalitarian nightmares of authors such as Orwell and Huxley are now technologically possible. The problem facing all free people is to prevent them from coming true.

The legislative approach to individual privacy has tended to swing back and forth, following the mood of the nation. The Privacy Act of 1974, passed in response to the abuses of the Watergate era, was intended to protect privacy by preventing the indiscriminate sharing of files between government agencies. However, a loophole exempts routine sharing that is "compatible" with the purpose for which the information was collected, and it has been used to justify virtually any kind of exchange of information. Another concern is the fact that some of the information in government and private data files is false or misleading. People have lost their jobs or have been unable to find new ones because of false information included in a file. The Freedom of Information Act was intended to solve this problem and prevent federal agencies from covering up their mistakes by giving everyone more access to the information the government collects about itself and its citizens—but the bureaucracy has proved ingenious in developing ways to obstruct the public's access. Every year, for example, the federal government creates millions of new secrets that are exempt from the act's provisions. Even if all the information in the files were accurate, the prospect of untold numbers of hapless men and women being haunted for their entire lives by a single mistake is not a pleasant one.

After the September 11 attacks, the protection of civil liberties took a backseat to the desire to stop terrorism. The USA PATRIOT Act of 2001 sharply restricted the right to privacy by allowing the monitoring and interception of e-mail and warrantless searches in urgent cases and by giving government agencies the authority to conduct phone and Internet taps with less judicial scrutiny. The PATRIOT Act also allows law-enforcement officials to detain suspected terrorists who are not U.S. citizens for longer periods of time without a lawyer, and the Secretary of State was authorized to designate foreign groups as terrorist organizations and deport suspected terrorists. Librarians have become particularly concerned with provisions of the act that could even allow government agents access to the records of what books people check out from libraries.

Burdens and Benefits

More than any other social institution, the government is concerned with social justice. In theory, at least, it is supposed to right social wrongs through the legal codes—for example, by prohibiting discrimination against women and minorities—and by creating programs to help the disadvantaged and the deprived. In addition, the government has numerous other programs intended to help more privileged groups. But none of this comes free: Someone must bear the cost of these programs. The continuing battle over

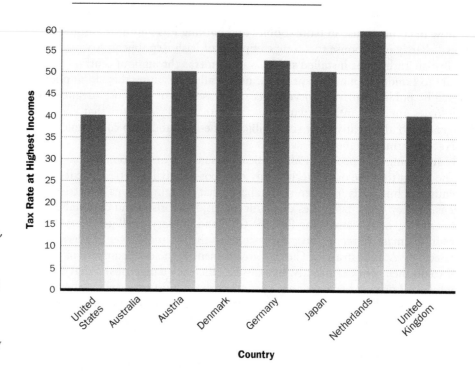

Figure 3

The Tax Burden

Despite public perception, taxes on the highest personal incomes in the United States are among the lowest of all industrial nations.

Source: World Bank, *World Development Report, 2000* (New York: Oxford University Press, 2000).

who is to receive the benefits of government action and who is to pay for them is the central feature of modern politics.

Taxation is one of the most difficult issues our political leaders must face. The voters constantly demand more and more government services, yet they do not want to pay more taxes in order to get them. Despite all the political rhetoric of recent years, the United States has the lowest overall tax rates of any industrialized nation. In Sweden, taxes total about 60 percent of the gross domestic product; in Denmark, almost half; in France, about 44 percent; in Germany, 39 percent; and in Canada, 36 percent. In the United States, the tax burden is less than 30 percent.[41] It is not surprising, then, that the tax rate for the highest-income Americans is among the *lowest* for all industrial nations. (See Figure 3.) Of course, along with lower taxes goes a much lower level of social services. For example, the United States is the only industrialized nation without some kind of national health care program for all its citizens.

In addition to the question of how much revenue must be raised is the critical issue of who is to bear the tax burden. In recent years, the overall level of taxation has remained relatively constant, but there have been some important changes in who bears it. During the 1980s, taxes on the wealthiest citizens were slashed while taxes were increased for other Americans. The tax reforms of 1993 were more favorable to middle- and low-income taxpayers, but the wealthy came out far ahead of where they started. Between 1977 and 1996, the top 1 percent of American families saw their tax burden decline by 18.5 percent while the bottom 80 percent saw their federal taxes drop only 2.5 percent.[42] This trend continued with the tax reforms of 1997, which doubled the amount of inherited wealth that is exempted from taxes and reduced the tax rate on the profits that are made on investments. Between 1996 and 1998 the wealthy saw another 6 percent decline in the share of their income paid in federal taxes.[43] The administration of George W. Bush followed the same pattern, further slashing the tax burden for the richest U.S. citizens. In 2001, the administration pushed through a long-term tax cut in which half the benefits went to the richest 1 percent of U.S. families.[44] Taxation has also been shifted away from corporations to private individuals. In 2004, corporate taxes brought in only about half as large a share of the gross domestic product as they did in 1970.[45] A second important shift in the tax burden has been from older to younger citizens as the federal government piles up more and more debt from future generations to pay off. In 1980, the federal debt was about $900 million. By 2006, it was more than

$8.5 trillion. Of course, the economy and the total population also grew over that time, but even expressed as a percentage of the total national economy, the debt almost doubled from 33 percent to 66 percent.[46]

QUICK REVIEW

- How serious a problem are conflicts of interest, bribery, and corruption in our government?
- Why has the public grown so cynical about its government?
- What dilemma does the military pose in a democratic society?
- What are the most serious threats to our civil liberties?
- Are the burdens and benefits of government fairly distributed in our society?

Solving the Problems of Government

Practically all social problems are, in part, governmental problems. The problem of the government itself, however, is the need to create a political system that is truly democratic: a government "of the people, by the people, for the people." Democracy is not just a system of government; it is a constant struggle to protect and expand the power of the people. There is little doubt that the current system is still far from the great democratic ideals we espouse, and there have been numerous proposals to solve its problems.

Campaign Finance Reform

As we have seen again and again in the pages of this chapter, the political deck is stacked in favor of wealth and against people who would challenge those already in positions of power. One of the most important reasons for this corruption of democracy is the current system of campaign financing. In the elections of 2004, for example, the average incumbent raised twice as much money as his or her opponent.[47] The obvious reason for this enormous imbalance is that those in office are in a far better position to offer political rewards to big contributors than are the challengers. PACs, for example, contribute seven times more to incumbents than to challengers.[48]

Current laws that regulate campaign financing look good on paper, but they do virtually nothing to limit the ability of the wealthy to use their money to frustrate the will of the majority. The law limits direct contributions to a candidate's election committee, but the wealthy can still spend all the money they want to help a candidate as long as they do so as individuals or give the money to PACs that support their views. Presidential candidates are eligible for federal funds if they agree to a fixed spending limit, but there are no spending limits on federal money for other candidates. Moreover, candidates have the option of refusing the federal money and the spending restraints that come with it—as the winning Democratic and Republican candidates did in the 2004 presidential primaries. Even when presidential candidates accept federal money, individuals and PACs are once again allowed to spend an unlimited amount to support a candidate so long as they do so independently of the candidate's election committee. The current system forces some politicians to sell their powers of office to the highest bidder and creates grossly unequal contests between candidates running for the same office. The best solution to this problem is to provide federal financing in all campaigns for national office, not just in presidential elections. This law would have to be written so that third-party candidates would be eligible for government financing along with candidates of the two major parties and with sufficient incentives so that all candidates would want to participate. If properly drawn, such a law could eliminate the injustices of the current system of campaign financing. A related idea, one intended to counteract the slick professional television commercials that tell so little about the real political issues, is to require the media to provide free time for all candidates to discuss their views in depth.

Should the Government Finance Our Election Campaigns?

Countless political commentators have complained about the corrupting influence of politicians' constant need to collect money for their election campaigns. The most far-reaching proposal for change would have the government, instead of private contributors, provide most or all of the money necessary for election campaigns.

YES Imagine you are a U.S. senator, and you need to raise thousands of dollars a week to pay for your next election campaign. Unless you get that money, you will probably lose your job. Now imagine that the only place you can get that kind of money is from the special-interest groups and lobbyists who want your vote when their issues come before the Senate. Don't you think you would listen more carefully to contributors who gave you tens of thousands of dollars than to an average citizen who disagreed with them but couldn't give any money?

The current system of campaign finance is based on a kind of legal bribery in which the rich and well-financed special-interest groups give millions of dollars to politicians in order to buy political influence. Of course, in some cases supporters on both sides of an important issue have equal amounts of money to spend and, therefore, balance each other out, and in other cases a courageous politician might take a risk and go against the powerful special interests. The fact remains, however, that huge campaign contributions buy political influence, and as a result we do not get a government of the people but a government of the highest bidders.

There are many proposals about how to correct this shameful state of affairs, but the only way to really do the job is to completely end politicians' dependence on gifts from contributors in order to finance their campaigns, and that means the government must provide serious candidates with the money they need to run for office. Critics claim that public financing would be a big burden on the taxpayers, but that assertion is just a smokescreen erected by politicians and special interests who have profited from the current system. Actually, the amount of money needed is a minute sum compared with the overall federal budget. If we really believe in the principles of democracy, then we must end the corrupt influence of wealthy campaign contributors once and for all.

NO Our current system of government has served us well over the years, and we shouldn't change it now. What other nation has been more prosperous, more stable, and more democratic than the United States? Why fix what isn't broken?

Although the critics are always making wild claims that our political leaders sell the powers of their office in exchange for campaign contributions, there isn't a shred of evidence that this is a common practice. Popular politicians can easily raise the money they need to run their campaigns, no matter how they vote on the issues that affect big campaign contributors, and unpopular politicians are not going to be reelected anyway. Besides, it is clearly against the law to sell votes in exchange for campaign contributions or anything else, and only very foolish politicians would take the risk of going to jail just to get a few more dollars for their campaign funds. The fact that several well-known political leaders have been convicted on bribery charges in recent years shows that the enforcement effort really works.

Placing limits on private campaign contributions may seem to be a democratic step, but it is actually just the opposite. How can a free nation tell its citizens that they cannot spend or give away their own money in order to support a cause they believe in? Moreover, government financing of election campaigns will only lead to new and serious problems. You can be sure that any legislation to create such a system would be written to favor incumbents and the candidates of the two major parties—and everyone else would be hurt. But even if that problem could be avoided, these proposals raise other troubling questions. What right do we have to take money from taxpayers to support the campaign of a politician they disagree with? Why should any taxpayers be burdened with what are really politicians' business expenses? Our current political system is working well the way it is, and these so-called reforms would only make things worse.

Restructuring Government

Many social scientists believe that the sheer growth in the size of modern nations has made governments more distant and less responsive to the will of their citizens. In a huge country with millions of citizens, most people have never even met their legislative representatives, much less the president or prime minister. Many see government policies as decisions made in distant places by officials who are not aware of or concerned with their interests—and often they are right. In response to this problem, some people suggest that government power be decentralized—in other words, they want to reduce the power of the central government and transfer it to local government. Advocates of decentralization claim that local governments are closer to the people and, therefore, more responsive to their needs. They are convinced that if local governments were given more self-determination, then many more citizens would become involved in the political process. There is, however, another side to this issue. Some political scientists argue that local governments are too close to the people to be given unrestricted power, contending that local passions and prejudices often lead to the oppression of defenseless minorities. Whether or not that actually occurs, it is clear that small local governments are too weak and divided to cope with such huge problems as pollution, warfare, and the demands of the contemporary world economy.

A different kind of reform that is already being tried in some states is to limit the number of times a person can be reelected to the same office. Advocates of such **term limits** argue that they are the only way to break the power of entrenched incumbents who enjoy built-in advantages over their challengers, and opinion polls often show public support for such proposals.[49] Critics of such ideas, however, feel that term limits make matters worse, not better. They argue that legislators, like people in any other business, need time to learn their job and that turning out everyone with any experience would cripple the government's decision-making process. Moreover, they claim that legislatures with many inexperienced members would have to rely even more heavily on lobbyists and special-interest groups.

Term limits ■ Legislation that limits the time or number of terms an elected official may serve.

Protecting Civil Liberties

The fundamental civil liberties we have grown accustomed to have been under increasing threat since the terrorist attacks of September 11, 2001. The PATRIOT Act cut back existing legal protections, the government took the unprecedented step of confining hundreds of people to an offshore military base so they would not have to be given basic legal protections, people from Middle Eastern backgrounds have been the targets of increasing suspicion and harassment because of nothing more than their ethnic heritage, and a fearful public was clearly far more concerned with catching terrorists than protecting civil liberties. Of course, civil liberties have always been curtailed in times of war and, hopefully, restored when the conflict ended. But the "war on terrorism" is different from any other we have fought. The enemy is not a nation-state, or even an organized revolutionary army, but rather a shadowy alliance of individuals, most of whose names we do not even know. For the most part, this "war on terrorism" is not being fought with conventional military forces but through surveillance, information gathering, and police work. Because the enemy is so vaguely defined, there is no clear way to know when or if it has been defeated. There is a real danger that this "war" might drag on indecisively for decades, while we grow increasingly accustomed to the restrictions on our civil liberties made in its name.

One of the most basic things we can do to protect our civil liberties is to limit government secrecy so that government actions are subject to public scrutiny. There are, of course, good reasons for some government secrets. National governments must keep military and sometimes even economic information from potential enemies; local governments must not let speculators know that a certain piece of land is about to be purchased for public use. But the "secret" stamp used for these purposes can also be used to cover up official incompetence and, worse yet, crimes and violations of civil liberties. The cold light of publicity can do a great deal to restrain overzealous government officials, and that is the reason that the Bill of Rights amended to the U.S. Constitution prohibited Congress from making any law that abridges the freedom of the press. In effect, the news media were given the duty of uncovering government secrets.

Making sure government bureaucrats inform the public about their behavior is not easy. One of the first attempts came in the Freedom of Information Act. This act requires U.S. government agencies to hand over any information they have about an individual citizen if that person requests it. Many government bureaucracies, however, respond to requests with months of stalling, and some charge fees for the information they furnish.

Other agencies protect information they do not want the public to see by classifying it as secret. In response, Congress has added amendments to the bill, establishing a deadline for responding to requests for information, limiting the fees that can be charged, and providing for judicial review of classified material. This legislation gave the public much greater access to government records, but the bureaucracies continue to put up a determined resistance. The fact of the matter is that no bureaucrats or public officials want their activities subject to close public scrutiny, and that is doubly true when it comes to the domestic surveillance and **covert operations** that are the biggest threat to civil liberties. There is clearly a compelling need for stronger laws to limit government secrecy and protect the right of free political expression. Another pressing need is for new protections for the privacy of citizens in this age of information. Tough new laws are needed to prevent the government (and private individuals and organizations) from snooping through its citizens' e-mail or keeping covert lists of which Web sites they visit or the material they choose to download onto their computers.

Covert operations ■ Secret operations carried out by government agencies such as the CIA.

Getting Politically Involved

Despite the range of complex political problems facing modern democracies, one response can help resolve them all: increased involvement of ordinary citizens in the process of government. That sounds simple enough, but there are enormous obstacles along the way to that goal. Some sociologists argue that in politics, as in sports, the media have transformed the average citizen into a passive spectator rather than an active participant. Although there is some truth to such assertions, political apathy has many other causes as well. The sheer increase in total population has meant that each elected official represents more and more people and, as a result, is less responsive to any single individual. The growing anonymity of the modern metropolis has eroded the sense of social responsibility and shared community that is so essential to the political life of traditional small-town America. As we have seen, the political deck is stacked against the average citizen, who has little influence compared with the powerful and the privileged.

There is, however, still reason for optimism. It is easy to idealize the political life of bygone small-town America, but in many important respects the United States is far more democratic today than it was in the past. In the early days of the republic, only white males who owned property could vote; but step by step, the poor, minorities, and women were let into the political process, even if they still do not enjoy equal representation. Today's society presents daunting obstacles to individual citizens who want to influence government, but history has shown us that those individuals can have an impact when they band together in political organizations to press for change.

Facing Global Competition

Before concluding our review of the problems facing the U.S. government today, we must consider the impact of the ever-growing global economy. History shows us that countries that became strong economically had a strong state that could protect their national interests and provide the things that were necessary to promote economic growth.[50] The United States emerged as a dominant economic power in large part because of its system of mass education, extensive government-sponsored transportation systems, government projects for electric power, and a small military budget that did not take resources away from government spending on education and infrastructure projects. In fact, as Paul Kennedy shows in his influential book, *The Rise and Fall of the Great Powers*, every nation that has emerged as a new economic power in the last few centuries was spending less on its military than its major economic competitors.[51]

Although the United States is now the world's dominant economic power, some people argue that it is in danger of losing that position unless education is improved, workers are better trained, transportation systems are better maintained, and military spending is cut to the same level as the other major powers. All of these changes are, of course, the responsibility of the government. Many people feel that the good economic times will not be long lasting if the philosophy of "small government" prevents it from doing the things necessary to keep its economy competitive in the ever-changing world economy and some way is not found to spread the military burden more evenly among the world's industrialized powers.

QUICK REVIEW
■ What are the best ways to respond to the problems of government?

Sociological Perspectives on Problems of Government

Practically everyone agrees that the government has serious shortcomings. Indeed, pointing out these weaknesses has become a career for some public figures. Yet there is considerable disagreement over exactly what the problems are. Conservatives are usually concerned about government inefficiency and waste, military preparedness, and what they consider excessive interference with the economy. Liberals and progressives are more worried about violations of civil liberties, protection of minority rights, erosion of the democratic process, and the government's effectiveness in dealing with society's other problems. An examination of the different sociological perspectives helps clarify the situation by pointing out the ways these diverse problems are linked to wider social forces.

The Functionalist Perspective

The government performs at least five basic functions essential to modern society. First, it enforces society's norms when other methods of social control fail. This responsibility is usually carried out by the police and the other parts of the criminal justice system, but other government agencies occasionally serve these ends as well. Second, government maintains order by acting as the final arbiter of disputes arising between individuals and groups in the thousands of lawsuits settled by the courts every year. Third, government is responsible for the overall planning and direction of society and the coordination of other social institutions. Fourth, government must deal with social needs that are left unmet by other social institutions—for example, maintaining roads and caring for homeless children. Finally, government is responsible for handling international relations and, if necessary, warfare.

According to functionalists, the rapid social changes of the past century have made it extremely difficult for many governments to perform these functions effectively. Government has accepted more and more responsibilities but has been ill prepared for its new tasks. Many governments are saddled with old-fashioned systems of organization that were adequate in the eighteenth and nineteenth centuries but are ineffectual today. Government officials often fail to understand their duties, or they pursue their own interests rather than the public's. High offices are given out to reward the supporters of victorious candidates, and bribery and corruption are everyday occurrences. Another problem is created when technological changes take place so rapidly that government officials are unable to control their application. As a result of all this, government fails to function effectively.

Functionalists suggest that steps be taken to reduce this disorganization by reshaping the government. The tasks of government bureaucracies should be spelled out in detail, and each bureau should be organized to achieve them. The decision-making mechanism should be revamped to eliminate awkward traditional structures that impede efficiency. Government waste should be cut, and more government services should be provided by private contractors who are forced to make competitive bids for the work. Tougher laws to reduce unnecessary secrecy and to protect civil liberties should also be passed. Finally, functionalists recommend that law-enforcement agencies launch a more vigorous effort to root out bribery and corruption. Perhaps the differences between functionalists and conflict theorists can best be summed up by the response of the famous functionalist Talcott Parsons to C. Wright Mills's criticism of the power of elites in his book *The Power Elite*. In Parsons's review of this book he wrote, "We must have a stronger government than we have traditionally been accustomed to, and we must come to trust it more fully."[52]

The Conflict Perspective

Conflict theorists see the government as a source of tremendous political power that is used to advance the interests of those who control it. Government works to repress conflict rather than to resolve it—that is, the groups in control of the government (the upper class) use their power to smother opposition. Vagrancy laws, for example, have been used to force the poor to work in dangerous, low-paying jobs. Tax laws with loopholes that benefit the rich are another example of the expression of class interests through legislation. When there are strong conflicts of values about the morality of a particular kind of behavior, such as homosexuality, the power of the state is often used as a tool to try to impose the standards of the dominant group.

According to the conflict perspective, control of government is a prize that is won through political conflict. Once a group gains such control, it uses the power of the government to maintain its position and, thus, the group becomes difficult to dislodge. The law and its administration become tools of the power elite and are used to exploit the masses. The solution to this problem is to give a stronger voice to the "common" man and woman. Such measures as providing government financing for political campaigns, restricting lobbying, and requiring full disclosure of all government deliberations and proceedings are steps in this direction. Conflict theorists believe that greater economic and social equality is the real key to achieving a true democracy and that the way to win a more equal distribution of both wealth and power is through greater political activism and better organization of those who are not being represented in government. The government will change only when those groups gain enough power to force it to change.

The Feminist Perspective

When feminists look at the political system, the first thing they see is the gross underrepresentation of women at all levels of government. In the United States, no woman has ever been president, vice president, or chief justice of the Supreme Court. Only one woman has ever been the prime minister of Canada, and then for only a few months. A few European countries have better records, but there isn't a single country around the world in which women have an equal share of government power. Moreover, whether we look at top officials, elected representatives, or only middle-level bureaucrats, the story is still the same.

From the feminist perspective, this situation is a real tragedy, because it not only deprives women around the world of their basic human rights but also—and perhaps just as important— deprives the decision-making process of the wisdom and common sense the world's women have to offer. Many feminists feel that this would be a more peaceful planet with more caring governments if women had their full political rights.

At least in the Western democracies, the official, legal barriers to women's political participation have been removed (although feminists point out that former slaves got the vote in the United States before women did). Today, feminists call for women and sympathetic men to ban together and force open the doors of the "old boys' club" that still dominates the political system. The majority of eligible voters in most industrialized countries are women, and feminists urge them to seize the power their numbers give them and work to create fundamental improvements in the way the old system operates.

The Interactionist Perspective

Interactionists hold that the political system, like all other social processes, is guided by the ideas, definitions, and beliefs we hold about it. If a nation values the political participation of average citizens and defines democratic rule as the only legitimate source of power, then it is likely to be democratic. If, on the other hand, average citizens come to see political participation as futile, hopeless, or just boring, then the very foundations of democracy are threatened. Thus, interactionists are concerned about the everyday cynicism that has crept into our view of the government, and they urge citizens to actively support what is good in our government and to work constructively to change what needs to be changed. In their view, the long-term health and even the survival of democratic institutions depend on such seemingly simple everyday attitudes and beliefs.

Political socialization—the way in which people learn their political values and perspectives—is another major concern of interactionists. Children learn most of their political attitudes from their parents early in life, forming their ideas about the political system and developing attachments to such symbols as the flag, patriotic slogans, and well-known public figures. As they grow older, their views are affected by their peer groups and teachers, among others. A democratic society can do little to change the home environment of its children without threatening basic civil liberties. Schools, however, can teach children to respect the rights of others, to understand how governments actually operate, and to work for the equality of all people. Another important aspect of political socialization is what we learn about political activity itself. Is it the duty of every citizen or a waste of time? Once again, the schools and the media can help encourage or discourage positive political attitudes.

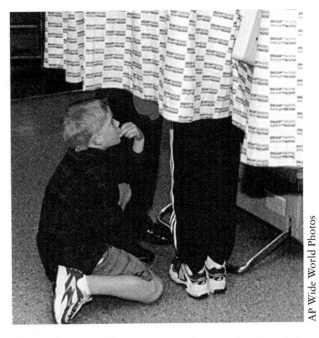

Children usually pick up their parents' political values and attitudes at an early age through a process known as *political socialization*.

QUICK REVIEW

■ What are the differences among the main sociological perspectives about the problems of government and their solutions?

Political socialization ■ The process by which people learn their political values and perspectives.

Summary

Governments and their bureaucracies have expanded rapidly in the last century as they have struggled to meet the needs of a changing society. Social scientists have exerted much effort trying to determine who really controls modern governments. There are three principal theoretical approaches. The *elitists* believe that the government is run by a small, unified power elite. The *pluralists* see many different groups competing for power and are not convinced that a single ruling class exists. Like the elitists, the *structuralists* also feel that the government works primarily in the interests of the privileged few—not because of the direct involvement of individual members of the elite, but because the structure of capitalist societies forces the government to support the interests of the upper class.

Government corruption is a serious threat to the ideals of democracy. Our current system of campaign financing creates many completely legal ways to gain corrupt influence over elected officials, and personal conflicts of interest and outright bribery are also common problems. The ever-increasing media interest in government scandals has probably made politics more honest, but it also frequently helps to shift national attention away from political issues to irrelevant details of politicians' personal lives.

The military poses a basic dilemma in a democratic society. Its traditions of unquestioning obedience and authoritarianism can be a real threat to democratic institutions, yet its power seems essential to national survival.

Protection of civil liberties is a critical task in every nation that aspires to democratic principles. There are many recent examples of governments violating individual rights and interfering with the democratic process in the name of the public good. The use of modern technology by private and public organizations to collect, store, and retrieve information about individual citizens is another growing threat to civil liberties.

Local, state, and national governments have been caught in a financial dilemma caused by the demand for lower taxes combined with a continued insistence on a high level of government services. In the last 30 years, the tax burden has been shifted away from the wealthy to the middle and lower classes and from the older generation to the younger. Overall, the U.S. tax rate is one of the lowest of all the industrialized nations, as is its level of social services.

Many responses to the problems of government have been proposed, including federal financing of election campaigns, decentralizing government, limiting government secrecy, and encouraging the political participation of average citizens.

Functionalists see the problems of government as signs of disorganization; the political institution has failed to work correctly and must be adjusted so that it runs smoothly again. *Conflict theorists* are more likely to feel that the political system creates social problems because it was intentionally designed to favor the elite and the organized special interests. They argue that if our political problems are to be resolved, this dominance must end. *Feminists* note the great underrepresentation of women in the political process and call for women to work together to win more political power. *Interactionists* place great importance on the way citizens define the government and the political process, and they emphasize the need for political socialization that recognizes the importance of democratic institutions.

QUESTIONS FOR CRITICAL THINKING

We have repeatedly described the average citizen as rather apathetic and uninvolved in government issues. How involved are you? Can you name the elected officials who represent you? What are their positions on the issues that affect you the most? Why is it that we all talk about how important democracy is but few of us ever get involved in the political process? Is it just a matter of personal choice, or is there something about the way our political system is structured that discourages the participation of average citizens?

KEY TERMS

blacklisting	elite theorists	special-interest group
bribery	goal displacement	spoils system
bureaucracy	lobbying	structuralists
conflict of interest	military-industrial complex	term limits
covert operations	pluralists	
defense conversion	political socialization	

INTERNET EXERCISE

There are many interesting Websites related to problems of governmental institutions today set up by both governments and nonprofit organizations. To begin your exploration of these Websites, go to the *Companion Website*™ for this book, www.pearsonhighered.com/coleman. Enter Chapter 5 and choose the Web destination module from the navigation bar.

Go to www.census.gov, and find the most recent *Statistical Abstracts of the United States*. Next, locate the chapter titled *Comparative International Statistics* (Section 30). Toward the end of this chapter you will find figures on military spending by different countries in the world. Among other figures provided is the amount of military spending in different countries as a percentage of the country's overall gross national product (GNP). What do these figures tell us about the level of military spending in the United States compared to other industrial nations such as Great Britain, Germany, France, and Japan? What do the figures tell us about the level of military spending among poor countries in Africa, Asia, and Latin America? From what you have learned in this Chapter, what do you think are likely outcomes for countries with high levels of military spending today?

NOTES

1. Michael Hirsh, "Behind the IRS Curtain," *Newsweek*, October 6, 1997, p. 29.

2. U.S. Bureau of the Census, *Statistical Abstract of the United States, 2006* (Washington, DC: U.S. Government Printing Office, 2003), Table 451.

3. U.S. Bureau of the Census, *Statistical Abstract of the United States, 2007* (Washington, DC: U.S. Government Printing Office, 2007), Table 480.

4. The White House, *Economic Report of the President, 2001* (Washington, DC: U.S. Government Printing Office).

5. Theodore Caplow, *American Social Trends* (San Diego: Harcourt Brace Jovanovich, 1991), p. 92.

6. Max Weber, *From Max Weber: Essays in Sociology*, trans. Hans H. Gerth and C. Wright Mills (New York: Oxford University Press, 1946), pp. 196–244.

7. Max Weber, *The Theory of Social and Economic Organization*, trans. A. M. Henderson and Talcott Parsons (New York: Free Press, 1947), p. 337.

8. See Francis Rourke, *Bureaucracy, Politics and Public Policy*, 3rd ed. (Boston: Little, Brown, 1984).

9. C. Wright Mills, "The Structure of Power in American Society," in *Power, Politics and People: The Collected Papers of C. Wright Mills* (New York: Ballantine, 1963), p. 288.

10. See, for example, G. William Domhoff, *The Power Elite and the State* (New York: Aldine de Gruyter, 1990); G. William Domhoff, *Who Rules America? Power and Politics in the Year 2000* (Mountain View, CA: Mayfield, 1998); Thomas R. Dye, *Who's Running America? The Clinton Years* (Upper Saddle River, NJ: Prentice Hall, 1995); Leonard Silk and Mark Silk, *The American Establishment* (New York: Basic Books, 1980).

11. David Riesman, *The Lonely Crowd* (New York: Doubleday, 1953).

12. Arnold M. Rose, *The Power Structure: Political Process in American Society* (New York: Oxford University Press, 1967), p. 6.

13. See Robert A. Dahl, *Dilemmas of Pluralist Democracy: Autonomy vs. Control* (New Haven, CT: Yale University Press, 1982).

14. Nicos Poulantzas, "The Problem of the Capitalist State," in Robin Blackburn, ed., *Ideology in the Social Science* (London: Fontana, 1972), pp. 238–253.

15. See Theda Skocpol, *Protecting Soldiers and Mothers: The Political Origins of Social Policy in the United States* (Cambridge, MA: Harvard University Press, 1992); Theda Skocpol and Edwin Amenta, "Did Capitalists Shape Social Security?" *American Sociological Review* 50 (1985): 572–575; Ann Shola Orloff and Theda Skocpol, "Why Not Equal Protection? Explaining the Politics of Public Social Spending in Britain, 1900–1911, and the United States, 1800s–1920," *American Sociological Review*, 49, 726–750; Domhoff, *The Power Elite and the State*; G. William Domhoff, *State Autonomy or Class Dominance? Case Studies on Policy Making in America* (New York: Aldine de Gruyter, 1996).

16. Caplow, *American Social Trends*, p. 113; Andrew L. Shapiro, *We're Number One: Where America Stands—and Falls—in the New World Order* (New York: Vintage, 1992), p. 106.

17. Kelly Holder, "Voting and Registration in the 2004 Presidential Election," U.S. Bureau of the Census, *Current Population Reports* March (Washington, DC: U.S. Government Printing Office, 2006), p. 1.

18. U.S. Bureau of the Census, "Too Busy to Vote," *Census Brief* (Washington, DC: U.S. Government Printing Office, 1998).

19. U.S. Bureau of the Census, *Statistical Abstract of the United States, 2007*, Table 405.

20. Dye, *Who's Running America?* p. 125.

21. Ibid.

22. U.S. Bureau of the Census, *Statistical Abstract of the United States, 2007*, Table 413; Jennifer Harper, "Campaign Spending," *Washington Times*, October 22, 2004.

23. Federal Election Commission, *Record*, 19:2 (February) (Washington, DC: U.S. Government Printing Office, 1993), p. 4.

24. Dye, *Who's Running America?* pp. 127–149; Domhoff, *The Power Elite and the State*.

25. James William Coleman, *The Criminal Elite: Understanding White Collar Crime* Fourth Edition, (New York: St. Martin's, 1998), pp. 31–34.

26. Ibid., pp. 102–103.

27. Ibid., p. 45.

28. U.S. Department of Justice, Bureau of Justice Statistics, *Sourcebook of Criminal Justice Statistics, 2006* (Washington, DC: U.S. Government Printing Office, 2006), Table 2.10.

29. www.transparency.org; www.gallup-international.com.

30. U.S. Bureau of the Census, *Statistical Abstract of the United States, 2007*, Table 460; Ankup Shah, "Arms Trade," www.globalissues.org.

31. Coleman, *The Criminal Elite*, pp. 55–72.

32. Ibid.

33. See Gary T. Marx, "Thoughts on a Neglected Category of Social Movement Participant: The Agent Provocateur and the Informant," *American Journal of Sociology*, 80 (1974): 402–442.

34. Brian Glick, *War at Home: Covert Action Against U.S. Activists and What We Can Do About It* (Boston: South End Press, 1989).

35. "The Argument about 'Enemy Combatants: A Few Good Men,'" *The Economist*, January 17, 2004, p. 26.

36. Marcia Staimer, "Do Workers Have Private Lives?" *USA Today*, May 13, 1991, pp. A1–A2.

37. Elys A. McLean, "Working to Avoid Violence," *USA Today*, April 27, 1994, p. B1.

38. Thomas B. Rosenstiel, "Someone May Be Watching," *Los Angeles Times*, May 18, 1994, pp. A1, A12.

39. Ibid.

40. Ibid.

41. U.S. Bureau of the Census, *Statistical Abstract of the United States, 2007*, Table 879.

42. Lawrence Mishel, Jared Bernstein, and John Schmitt, *The State of Working America, 1996–97* (Ithaca, NY: Cornell University Press, 1997), p. 103.

43. David Cay Johnston, "U.S. Richest Pay Falling Share of Tax," *International Harold Tribune*, February 27, 2001.

44. Robert Freeman, "Bush's Tax Cuts," www.counterpunch.org, April 2004.

45. U.S. Bureau of the Census, *Statistical Abstract of the United States, 2007*, p. 321.

46. Ibid., Table 459.

47. Calculated from data provided by www.fed.gov.federalelectioncomission.

48. U.S. Bureau of the Census, *Statistical Abstract of the United States, 2003* (Washington, DC: U.S. Government Printing Office), p. 322.

49. Nick Galifianakis and Marty Baumann, "How USA Feels About Terms Limits," *USA Today*, June 28, 1994, p. 1A.

50. Immanuel Wallerstein, *The Modern World System* (New York: Academic Press, 1974); Immanuel Wallerstein, *The Modern World System II* (New York: Academic Press, 1980); Immanuel Wallerstein, *The Modern World System III* (New York: Academic Press, 1989); Daniel Chirot, *Social Change in the Modern Era* (New York: Harcourt Brace College Publisher, 1986).

51. Paul Kennedy, *The Rise and Fall of the Great Powers* (New York: Random House, 1987).

52. C. Wright Mills, *The Power Elite* (New York: Oxford University Press, 1956); Talcott Parsons, "The Distribution of Power in the American Society," in G. William Domhoff and Hoyt B. Ballard eds., *C. Wright Mills and The Power Elite* (Boston: Beacon Press, 1968), pp. 60–87.

POLITICS

POLITICS

Is it just

a coincidence that politicians seem to be paying more attention than usual to Hispanic voters lately? New York Mayor Michael Bloomberg has a reputation for his repeated and amusing attempts to communicate with Hispanic voters by speaking their language, albeit not so fluently. President Barack Obama became the first president in 50 years to make an official visit to Puerto Rico, where he greeted the crowd in Spanish. While seeking the Republican presidential nomination, former Massachusetts governor Mitt Romney attended the Republican National Hispanic Assembly in Florida.

Politicians are aware of the influence Hispanic voters are expected to have in upcoming elections. In 2008, 9.5 million of the United States' 12 million registered Hispanic voters went to the polls. They made up 13 percent of voters in Colorado, 14 percent in Nevada, 15 percent in Florida, and 38 percent in New Mexico, all highly contested battlegrounds that could swing Democratic or Republican. Hispanic voters also tend to ride the fence politically. While many have conservative religious values, they also tend toward fiscal liberalism. The Hispanic vote has been decisive in the elections of both George W. Bush, who won over 40 percent of it in 2004, and President Obama, who won more than 60 percent of the Hispanic vote in 2008.

Recent legislative developments regarding undocumented immigrants bring to the forefront issues of concern for many Hispanic voters. In 2010, Arizona passed a highly criticized law requiring all immigrants in the state to register with the government and to carry registration papers with them at all times. A similar law was enacted in Arkansas. The federal DREAM Act is a bill that, under certain circumstances, would allow individuals whose parents brought them into the country illegally as children to pay in-state tuition at state colleges. Supported by President Obama, the bill has been hotly debated within many states and by Republican presidential candidates. In coming years, these and related issues are likely to draw high numbers of Hispanic voters to cast their ballots in support of the politicians they believe have their best interests in mind.

The influence of Hispanic voters is likely to continue to increase. Hispanics are the fastest-growing ethnic group in the United States. The 2010 U.S. Census reported 50.5 million Hispanics making up 16.3 percent of the U.S. population. That's up to 35.3 million or 12.5 percent of the population, since the 2000 U.S. Census.[1] This demographic shift is already having an impact on how politicians campaign. The question now is how it will affect future political outcomes.[2]

---Politics often comes to the forefront of discussions during times of upheaval. But what goes on behind the scenes when there aren't the likes of economic recessions and elections for people to pay attention to?

How are governments set up to work and what prevents them from succeeding? What types of governments exist and how do they affect society? How are other nations run? What exactly are the connections between society and political systems, and how do they affect our lives? This chapter seeks to answer these and other questions.

get the topic: HOW DO WE GOVERN TO GET WHAT WE NEED?

POLITICAL SYSTEMS are the social institutions that distribute power, set goals, and make decisions about social policies to address social problems.

POWER is the ability to get what you want done, despite the resistance of others.

GOVERNMENT is a simple or complex organization that controls and directs the power in society.

In this chapter, we investigate the social institutions that result from political systems. **Political systems** are the social institutions that distribute power, set goals, and make decisions about policies to address social problems. Political systems all revolve around power: how to get it and how to exercise it. But what is power? **Power** is the ability to get what you want done, despite the resistance of others. In a classroom, the teacher has the power; in a government, politicians have the power.

Throughout human history, we have always had some form of **government**, a simple or complex organization that controls and directs the power in society. The form of society can influence the form of government. In simple hunter–gatherer societies, alliances and power relationships are related to kinship ties and traditions. For example, a child of the tribal chief is likely to become the next chief. As societies become more complex, moving from small groups to larger cities and economies, political systems become more complex. Dictators and kings might lead in industrial, postindustrial, and even agricultural societies, but the way they maintain power is complicated. They must have the support of the elite members of society to maintain power.

Political Systems

Political sociology and political science are connected. Most colleges require students to enroll in an American government course, and anyone who has already taken that class should see that these two disciplines have important things in common. Political science uses sociology in its research methodology and theory development. Similarities between institutional and structural components of the political life, as well as the inclusion of macro and micro components of

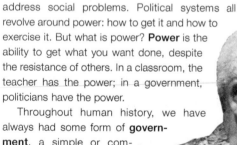

> ∧
> ∧ **Charismatic leaders have a remarkable power** to communicate with and
> ∧ inspire their followers.

the social life, make the study of political sociology a legitimate branch of sociology.[3]

In the area where sociology meets political science, both disciplines focus on cultural and global arenas. Culture takes us away from a nationalistic and simplistic understanding of what makes government work. Globalism causes us to identify the changing importance of geography. Governments and state power relationships are related to a complex series of interactions between nations that once were unrelated. This complexity shows us that the social and political worlds are highly interrelated. Sociologist Max Weber believed that political systems are based on three forms of authority: traditional, charismatic, and rational-legal.[4]

In **traditional systems**, social power is achieved through general respect for patterns of government. For example, English monarchs such as Charles I and Henry IV gained and held power because of family lineage and the tradition of monarchy. Modern examples include the government of Saudi Arabia, a traditional monarchy backed by a consultative body of officials. In 2005, King Fahd died, leaving the throne to his brother, Crown Prince Abdullah; in return, Abdullah pledged to leave the throne to another brother in the event of his death.[5] Countries that follow traditional systems are generally made up of people who share similar worldviews and, often, religious principles.

What do Nelson Mandela, Bill Clinton, and Aung San Suu Kyi have in common? All are known to be charismatic leaders. In **charismatic systems**, power is gained by a leader who has extraordinary personal attributes. Such leaders inspire their followers and often initiate influential movements. In the mid-1900s, Fidel Castro sparked revolution in Cuba when he openly protested the existing dictatorial regime. Many contribute Castro's rise in power to his powerful public speaking skills and charismatic personality.

Rational-legal authority stems from the rules and standards officially sanctified by a society. For example, American citizens have a written set of rights and regulations in the Constitution. If a U.S. president were

TRADITIONAL SYSTEMS are organizations in which social power is gained by respect for patterns of government.
CHARISMATIC SYSTEMS are political organizations in which power is gained because a leader has extraordinary personal attributes.
RATIONAL-LEGAL AUTHORITY is a system in which power stems from rules and standards that are agreed upon by society.
MONARCHY is a political system in which leadership is based on the idea that leaders are selected by divine right or heritage.

to declare himself king, it would go against agreed-upon rules and be fiercely rejected by society. However, if a woman were to walk into a voting booth on Election Day, most people would find it completely rational, in concurrence with the 19th Amendment. Likewise, a U.S. president has the constitutional authority to make executive decisions, such as deploying U.S. troops, but cannot "declare war." Authority and power are important components of any government; social problems in the political realm often occur when the authority of a government conflicts with societal rules. In the summer of 2009, Iranians took to the streets to protest manipulated election results that violated their nation's rational-legal authority.

The amount of power that a leader has is often dependent on the type of government under which a nation operates.

TYPES OF GOVERNMENT

All nations are governed in different ways. At the present, three main types of government exist: monarchy, authoritarianism, and democracy.

A **monarchy** is a political system based on the idea that leaders are selected by heritage or divine right. Monarchies are usually run by a single family that passes power down through generations. Many ancient societies were ruled by this type of government, but today only

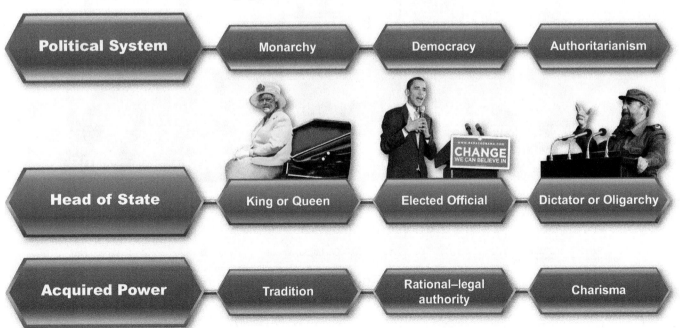

Types of Government

Political System	Monarchy	Democracy	Authoritarianism
Head of State	King or Queen	Elected Official	Dictator or Oligarchy
Acquired Power	Tradition	Rational–legal authority	Charisma

AUTHORITARIANISM is a form of government that gives citizens very little say in how the nation is run.

DICTATOR is a single person with complete control in a government system.

OLIGARCHY is a small group of influential people with complete control of the government.

a handful of nations still use this system in its pure form. In some European countries, kings and queens still sit on a recognized throne, but they have limited power and are acknowledged merely as symbols of cultural tradition. Queen Elizabeth II, for example, is still seen as a figure of authority, but it's the British Parliament and Prime Minister that truly govern the country.

Authoritarianism is a form of government that gives citizens very little say in how the nation is run and encourages absolute submission to authority. Although these governments can be lead by a king or queen, more often they are ruled by a dictator—a single person with complete control—or by an oligarchy—a small group of influential people who rule the nation together. Contrary to what you may think, not all authoritarian governments rule through use of power and fear. In 1999, General Pervez Musharraf, in reaction to the country's current political system and stressed relations with India, took control of Pakistan in a bloodless coup. During his nine-year reign as leader, Musharraf worked to decrease Islamic fundamentalism in the region and build, as he stated, a more tolerant and democratic Pakistan. His popularity among the nation's citizens rose steadily until 2006, and in 2008, President Musharraf resigned as leader and gave the government back to the people.[6]

Percentage of Minority Voters (Compared to White Voters)

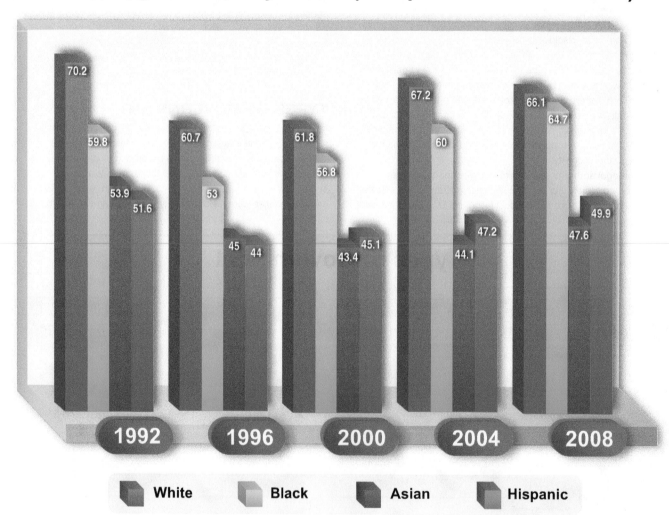

Source: U.S. Census Bureau, "Voting and Registration Data." Accessed July 29, 2008. http://www.census.gov/population/www/socdemo/voting.html

On the whole, **the percentage of minorities voting in presidential elections has been less than the percentage of whites.** What causes this discrepancy in voter turnout?

When an authoritarian government controls every aspect of citizens' lives, it becomes **totalitarianism**. In this type of system, the government can tell people how many children to have, what jobs to hold, and where they can live. Countries such as Cuba, China, and Russia have a history of totalitarian rule. Regardless of the degree of freedom, however, the average citizen's voice is not heard in authoritarian regimes.

In contrast, a **democracy** is a political system in which power is held by citizens and exercised through participation and representation (literally "rule by the people" in Greek). By definition, pure democratic societies allow citizens to make every decision, but this type of government is difficult to maintain. Can you imagine all 300 million Americans having to vote on everything the government does? Nothing would get done.

The U.S. government is an example of a representative democracy; we choose officials through state-run elections, and these officials are given the authority to make decisions for us. Of course, the problem is that not every citizen takes advantage of the right to elect leaders. In the 2008 presidential election, only 64 percent of qualified citizens voted, the highest percentage since 1968.[7]

So, why don't people vote? Explanations vary. When I ask my students, answers include "What's the point? Leaders do what they want anyway;" "No one in my family votes, so I guess I never thought about it;" "I don't really care about politics;" and the tried and true "I'm only one person, my vote doesn't matter." When citizens with the right to vote chose not to, it's known as **voter apathy**. In a democracy, such apathy poses a real problem to society, because not

everyone's voice is heard. Unfortunately, this tends to affect racial minorities the most.

Historically, the percentage of minority voters has been less than white voters. In the 2008 election, as you can see in the chart, 66.1 percent of eligible white citizens voted, while only 64.7 percent and 47.6 percent of eligible black and Asian American citizens voted, respectively.[8] One of the reasons that minorities have low election turnouts may be because they feel that, as a smaller segment of the population, their opinions will not have as large an impact on politics. However, the chart also shows that these percentages have been increasing since 1996.

No matter what the cause for voter apathy, recent elections have shown that U.S. citizens are becoming more excited about and involved in the political process. Nearly 132 million people voted in the 2008 presidential election, with previously apathetic voting groups such as young adults and ethnic minorities showing renewed interest.[9] Voter apathy may have been combated by the desire for change in the country, or the affirmation that minorities do indeed hold a prominent place in politics.

Demographics of 2008 Voters

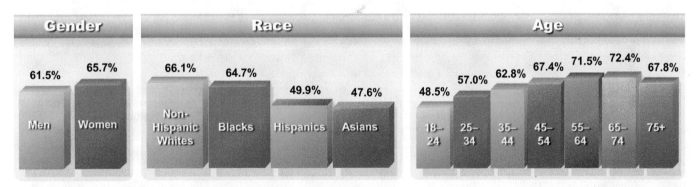

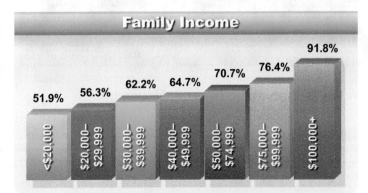

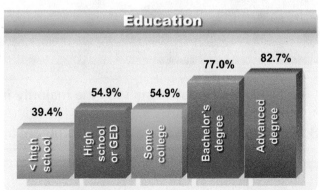

Source: U.S. Census Bureau, "Voting and Registration Data." Accessed July 29, 2008. http://www.census.gov/population/www/socdemo/voting.html

DEMOCRATIC PARTY is a political party in the United States that supports increased regulation of private institutions and a larger government.

REPUBLICAN PARTY is a political party in the United States that supports a decreased regulation of private institutions and reduced government involvement communicate with the larger society.

POLITICAL PARTIES

Politics in the United States is essentially based on a two-party system: the **Democratic Party** and the **Republican Party**. Smaller parties exist, such as the Green Party or the Constitution Party, but Democrats and Republicans dominate the political landscape. Both parties agree that social issues such as unemployment, unequal education, and problems in health care exist. However, they differ in the solutions that they propose.

Although political platforms change from year to year, Democrats tend to prefer having the government solve social problems, while Republicans prefer to have the private sector deal with them. Because of this, Democrats generally support expanded government services. Republicans, on the other hand, encourage independence from the government, suggesting that individuals can solve social issues if the government simply gets out of the way.[10] Republicans tend to focus on individual morality, such as sexual morality, whereas Democrats tend to talk about social morality, such as a lack of equality for the poor.

∧
∧
∧ In 2010, the Republicans took the majority from the Democrats in the U.S. House of Representatives, and Nancy Pelosi handed over the Speaker of the House's gavel to John Boehner. In what ways have the government's actions reflected this change?

"When a peaceful opposition overthrew the 30-year reign of Hosni Mubarak in Egypt, who would have thought that an aging academic from Harvard was responsible for its success?" When 83-year-old Boston academic Gene Sharp wrote a pamphlet 18 years ago about nonviolent opposition to repressive regimes, he didn't realize it would eventually put him on the enemy list of governments in Iran, Venezuela, and Indonesia. Foreign governments have accused him of plotting overthrows on behalf of the United States. His ideas have been popular with revolutionaries in Myanmar (Burma), Serbia, Egypt, and former Soviet republics. He has been nominated for a Nobel peace prize and has been likened to Mahatma Gandhi and Martin Luther King Jr.

Sharp's interest in promoting opposition to totalitarian regimes began when he learned about Nazi concentration camps as a high school student. He was later inspired by Gandhi's efforts to liberate India from the British Empire. His own opposition to the Korean War draft put him behind bars for several months. He taught at Harvard University and went on to write *From Dictatorship to Democracy*, which lists 198 practical methods to overthrow dictatorships. Later, he founded the Albert Einstein Institution, a nonprofit promoting nonviolent means to change. Sharp's most important point is that nonviolent protests work better than violent ones because while dictators can "do" oppression and violence, they have no idea how to handle nonviolent opposition.

Although Sharp's institution is struggling, and using the Internet is a challenge for the octogenarian, his booklet has attained the status of Karl Marx's *Das Kapital* and Mao Tse-tung's *Little Red Book*. It has been translated into 30 languages and is available for download for free. http://www.aeinstein.org/organizations/org/FDTD.pdf[11]

A Selection of Gene Sharp's 198 Methods of Nonviolent Protest and Persuasion

think social problems: HOW DO POLITICAL SYSTEMS FUNCTION?

Functionalism

Using ideas from Durkheim's notion of solidarity as well as Weber's discussion of power relationships and rational action, functionalism suggests that for a society to work, the social institutions must be connected and orderly. Thus, the process of governing involves parties, often with divergent opinions, coming together to determine the best possible outcomes for the state. The "political game" involves norms and values for governing, and it works well if all parts of the system work together.

According to political scientist Robert Dahl, power is distributed widely enough in democracies that groups are driven to compete *and* work with each other in order to achieve their goals. These two forces—competition and alliance—lead groups to temper their ideals, leaving society solidly in the middle, balancing between extremes.[12]

The U.S. federal government has three branches: executive, legislative, and judicial. Each has a specific job, and each has the responsibility to check and balance the other branches to assure citizens that no one branch of the government becomes too powerful.

Conflict Theory

Sociologist C. Wright Mills suggested that a **power elite** runs the United States. Who are these people? According to Mills, the power elite comprises top military officials, heads of major corporations, and high-ranking political leaders. This select group of people pulls the strings that control both the economy and the politics of American society.[13]

A more modern theorist, William Domhoff, has suggested a similar idea: The United States is ruled by those with the most societal power. Consider corporate boards of directors. A common practice known as **interlocking directorates** involves placing the same people on a variety of corporate boards, allowing separate companies to be controlled by a small, elite group. Domhoff points out that this group often interacts with political leaders in exclusive clubs, directing (or at least strongly influencing) the course of the U.S. government.[14]

Of interest to conflict theorists is how legislators gain benefits for their constituencies back home. Because representatives are elected locally but expected to make decisions nationally, one can see the conflict here. So-called pork-barrel projects fund the building of dams, roads, and bridges in legislators' home districts. At the same time, elected officials are under pressure to cut budgets by cutting "pork."[15]

Politically, then, we constituents may be the cause of the problem. Constituents often focus on their own short-term desires while calling elected officials to hold long-term points of view. When voters ask for benefits but complain about the costs, the very nature of the political process is called into question.[16]

POWER ELITE is a group comprised of top military officials, heads of major corporations, and high-ranking political leaders; this select group of people pulls the strings that control both the economy and the politics of American society.

INTERLOCKING DIRECTORATES is a practice in which the same people are placed on a variety of corporate boards, allowing separate companies to be controlled by a small, elite group.

Symbolic Interactionism

Symbolic interactionists focus on how people define issues, and how those definitions influence our actions. Political organizations, social movements, and special interest groups must remember this if they want their agendas to take center stage in the political arena. Organizations can gain influence through five important processes of communication. They must set an agenda, access the decision makers, suggest policies that have broad appeal, monitor the implementation of these plans, and get their issues on the government's long-term agenda.[17]

Consider the following example. Prior to the prohibition movements of the early 1900s, almost every drug was legal in the United States. The traditional viewpoint was that your body was your own property, and therefore the government should have no influence over what you put in that body. A paradigm shift occurred through the organized influence of the anti-drug and anti-alcohol movements. Now, the notion of legal and illegal drugs is so rooted in the American consciousness that few would support a reversion to the past.

∧
∧ Social movements can **gain headway if they are organized,**
∧ **have access to decision makers, and offer a plan.**

Justin Bergner remembered the first time he heard David Flores speak. He was at a neighborhood block party, listening to the man discuss politics with a small group of people. Justin had been interested in politics since he joined his high school's student council two years ago, and his awareness had expanded into local politics when he started to notice some of the growing problems in his neighborhood.

"When David began to talk about the changes he wanted to make around the city, I got interested in what he was saying. He mentioned that we needed more funding for after-school programs and more green space inside the city boundaries. He also said it was crazy how few working-class people were involved in our city's politics."

These were all issues that troubled Justin as well. "I thought it was really cool when he said he'd be running for city council in the fall. After everyone left, I went up to him and

introduced myself. I wanted to see if I could help with his campaign. He told me, 'Sure, it would be an honor to have me onboard.'"

David knew the chips were stacked against him. He only had $500 to support his campaign, and the incumbent candidate had thousands of dollars in corporate contributions. Rather than investing what little money he had in signage and advertising, David and his small group of volunteers focused on talking directly to the people. Justin remembered that summer well.

"I must've stood outside 15 different movie theaters over the course of three months. We'd each go around on the weekends when it was crowded and talk to people as they were coming and going. We'd poll them on different things, like what changes they wanted to see in the city, and David would come up and talk to them personally. He went to as many community

events as possible and always made friends with the people there, letting them know he was running for office. I think the opponent started getting scared, since a week before the election all these new signs with his name appeared on lawns, and he ran this huge full-page ad in the newspaper. David didn't have those kinds of funds, of course, but he believed that the voters would make the right decision."

David's only worry, in fact, was that enough voters wouldn't make it to the polling booths. To combat this problem, Justin suggested that the team travel door to door on Election Day and remind residents to vote.

"All five of us walked around from 7 AM to 8 PM, trying to cover as much of the city as we could. After polls closed, all we could do was wait."

In the end, it was announced that David Flores had won the election by only 55 votes.

"All of us were jumping up and down and cheering like crazy. It was great. It felt so good to see someone we believed in make it so far, and I think we proved to everyone that politics is about more than just money."

Politics

<<< **"David would come up and talk to them personally.** He went to as many community events as possible and always made friends with the people there, letting them know he was running for office."

199

WRAP YOUR MIND AROUND THE THEORY

Although the president is the nation's leader, he needs the go-ahead from Congress before he can take certain actions. What are some negative consequences of these checks and balances?

FUNCTIONALISM

Functionalists study how individuals are affected by the societal systems interacting around them. American democracy works because it diffuses power in several ways. The three branches of government, the systems of checks and balances within them, and the competing interests of at least two political parties function to balance out the competing interests of different groups.

HOW IS POWER DISTRIBUTED IN ECONOMIC AND POLITICAL SYSTEMS?

CONFLICT THEORY

Conflict theorists identify how members of society struggle for what is scarce. According to Marx, Mills, and Domhoff, access to wealth and power is scarce in any society. This is largely because those who have it are unwilling to let it go. Generally, they seek short-term rewards to increase their power and wealth, while ignoring the long-term societal consequences.

SYMBOLIC INTERACTIONISM

Symbolic interactionists are interested in the wisdom of groups. Large groups of people make better choices than individuals and can more easily influence the world around them. Interactionists also study leaders' use of personality and charisma to gain power over groups. Weber suggests that the defining mark of a leader is that he or she has the charisma to get others to follow. Charisma is a powerful tool that can be used to unite people to achieve a common goal.

In a capitalist society, people with money generally believe they have earned it and therefore don't want to share it. What are the long-term societal consequences of this kind of thinking?

Former Italian Prime Minister Silvio Berlusconi is so charismatic that his constituents reelected him despite his alleged corruption, ties to prostitution, and overall irreverent behavior on the international stage. **What are the dangers of the power of charisma in politics?**

discover solutions to social problems:
HOW DOES THE ECONOMIC SYSTEM INFLUENCE THE POLITICAL?

Political Funding

In the United States, most political campaigns are not self-funded. When a friend of mine ran for city council, he personally paid for the yard signs and flyers he passed out. However, in a major election, few people have the wealth to pay for national TV ads or print advertising. In our country, funding comes from individuals and groups that have a vested interest in the candidate or the political party that the candidate represents. For example, the National Rifle Association (NRA) might offer funds to a candidate that opposes restrictions on personal firearms, and gun owners might also support this person with smaller individual donations.

A great deal of party donations comes from **political action committees (PACs)**. PACs might allocate money to both parties, but are often

POLITICAL ACTION COMMITTEES (PACS) are interest groups that allocate money to political parties.

associated with either Democrats or Republicans. Because money can have such a profound effect on the outcome of an election, many rules and regulations are placed on how political contributions can be allocated. The McCain-Feingold-Cochran Bipartisan Campaign Reform Bill was proposed and enacted in 2002 to prevent contributions from being distributed through unethical means. Among other things, the bill involves a ban on so-called "soft money"—onetime cash contributions to national political parties from corporations, labor unions, and wealthy individuals.[18]

Pro & Con

Does the U.S. democracy actually represent "the people"?

Pro

- According to Dahl, democracy disperses power so that no one group can be in complete control.
- Shared power guarantees that everyone's voice will be heard. Those who don't vote do so of their own free will.
- Politicians seek to please voters in order to be reelected; therefore, the public's voice is always heard.
- Those who are disenfranchised need only to properly organize and they can change the system.

Con

- Plato suggested thousands of years ago that democracy was doomed to fail because not all people are intelligent enough to choose what's best for everyone. Basing a government on self-interest ultimately leads to societal collapse.
- Marx, Mills, and Domhoff all agree that power corrupts government; when left to its own devices, a government will seek short-term economic rewards.
- Corporate interests fund political campaigns, leading politicians to represent the interests of big business as opposed to the voting public.
- Democracy can work, but only if it's kept out of the hands of the power elite. So far in the United States, this has not happened.

MAKE CONNECTIONS

You Say You Want a Revolution

Gene Sharp's small book *From Dictatorship to Democracy* provides the reader with a "how-to" method to overthrow a dictatorship. Resistance, he says, requires strategy and planning to be successful. You must analyze both the strengths and weaknesses of the dictator, attacking the weaknesses and avoiding the strengths. This is why, Sharp points out, that most successful overthrows occur

through nonviolent means. Dictators by definition know how to use power and military to keep order. Attacking the military is attacking the leader at his strength, so Sharp suggests that nonviolent struggles have a better chance than violent ones. This is not to suggest that none will die in a nonviolent struggle, but that repeated efforts to repress peaceful protests often break the will of political elites and military leaders. Guns, bombs, and guerrilla attacks seem to have the opposite effect:

They often strengthen the resolve of those with power. Issues of planning, secrecy, and execution are all contained in this book, a blueprint for political overthrow.[19]

Consider the recent military overthrow of Dictator Muammar Gaddafi of Libya. Had it not been for NATO air power, do you think the protestors could have won that war? Surf the net, see what Gaddafi was willing to do to his own people to win. Do you think peaceful protest would have worked better?

HOW DO WE GOVERN TO GET WHAT WE NEED?

by creating a government that allows individuals to control their financial growth through a capitalist economy

HOW DO POLITICAL SYSTEMS FUNCTION?

through competing interests vying for power and political influence

HOW DOES THE ECONOMIC SYSTEM INFLUENCE THE POLITICAL?

through campaign funding from PACs and other special interest groups, especially through the use of soft money

get the topic: HOW DO WE GOVERN TO GET WHAT WE NEED?

Political Systems
Functionalism
Conflict Theory

Symbolic Interactionism
Political Funding

Theory

FUNCTIONALISM

- for society to work, social institutions must be connected and orderly
- governing involves divergent opinions coalescing in the best interest of the state

SYMBOLIC INTERACTIONISM

- large groups tend to make better choices than individuals
- leaders use their charismatic personalities to gain power and achieve goals

CONFLICT THEORY

- elected officials must balance showing immediate results and keeping long-term goals in mind
- constituents want to see immediate results without making any sacrifices to get them

Key Terms

political systems are the social institutions that distribute power, set goals, and make decisions about social policies to address social problems.

power is the ability to get what you want done, despite the resistance of others.

government is a simple or complex organization that controls and directs the power in society.

traditional systems are organizations in which social power is gained by respect for patterns of government.

charismatic systems are political organizations in which power is gained because a leader has extraordinary personal attributes.

rational-legal authority is a system in which power stems from rules and standards that are agreed upon by society.

monarchy is a political system in which leadership is based on the idea that leaders are selected by divine right or heritage.

authoritarianism is a form of government that gives citizens very little say in how the nation is run.

dictator is a single person with complete control in a government system.

oligarchy is a small group of influential people with complete control of the government.

totalitarianism is an authoritarian government that controls every aspect of citizens' lives.

democracy is a political system that is run by the citizens.

voter apathy is a phenomenon in which citizens with the right to vote choose not to.

Democratic Party is a political party in the United States that supports increased regulation of private institutions and a larger government.

Republican Party is a political party in the United States that supports a decreased regulation of private institutions and reduced government involvement communicate with the larger society.

power elite is a group comprised of top military officials, heads of major corporations, and high-ranking political leaders; this select group of people pulls the strings that control both the economy and the politics of American society.

interlocking directorates is a practice in which the same people are placed on a variety of corporate boards, allowing separate companies to be controlled by a small, elite group.

political action committees (PACs) are interest groups that allocate money to political parties.

Sample Test Questions

These multiple-choice questions are similar to those found in the test bank that accompanies this text.

1. Democracy can work as long as

   a. special interest groups don't sway representatives' actions.

   b. power is kept out of the hands of the elite.

   c. constituents demand short-term results.

   d. a charismatic leader is in power.

2. Which age group had the highest percentage of voters in the 2008 election?

   a. 18–24 years

   b. 35–44 years

   c. 45–54 years

   d. 65–74 years

3. In Tigrania, the government is run by a council of five, selected by the king and queen who otherwise act as figureheads. What kind of political system do the Tigranians have?

   a. monarchy

   b. totalitarianism

   c. democracy

   d. oligarchy

4. The federal DREAM Act is legislation that would

   a. offer citizenship to undocumented immigrants.

   b. offer scholarships to Hispanic students.

   c. offer in-state tuition rates to children of undocumented immigrants.

   d. offer political internships to Hispanic students.

5. Rational-legal authority would allow the president of the United States to send troops into Albania without the approval of Congress or the nation.

   a. True

   b. False

ESSAY

1. Using real-world examples, discuss how charismatic leadership could have negative outcomes.

2. What steps can the government take to combat voter apathy?

3. What political party do you associate yourself with? Explain, making reference to at least one of the three sociological theories.

4. Choose a recent issue in U.S. politics and describe how the distribution of power and system of checks and balances either helped or hindered its resolution.

5. Do you think political candidates should be able to take monetary campaign contributions from PACs or other interest groups? Why or why not? You may want to reference **From Classroom to Community** in your answer.

WHERE TO START YOUR RESEARCH PAPER

To learn more about Hispanic voters, read about the Hispanic Voter Project at http://hispanicvotedotorg.wordpress.com

To register to vote or volunteer to help combat voter apathy, go to http://www.rockthevote.org

To learn more about how money affects politics and public policy, see http://www.opensecrets.org

To download a free copy of Gene Sharp's *From Dictatorship to Democracy*, go to http://www.aeinstein.org/organizations/org/FDTD.pdf

End Notes

1. Betsy Guzmán, "The Hispanic Population," *Census 2000 Brief*, May 2001, http://www.census.gov/prod/2001pubs/c2kbr01-3.pdf.

2. Rafael Romo, "Will Hispanics Be the Swing Voting Bloc of 2010," *CNN*, September 16, 2011, http://edition.cnn.com/2011/09/15/politics/hispanic-swing-vote.

3. Alexander Hicks, "Is Political Sociology Informed by Political Science?" *Social Forces*, 1995. 73(4): 1219–1229.

4. Graham Taylor, *The New Political Sociology: Power, Ideology and Identity in the Age of Complexity*. London: Palgrave-Macmillan, 2010.

5. *BBC News*, "King Fahd of Saudi Arabia Dies," August 1, 2005, http://news.bbc.co.uk/2/hi/middle_east/4734175.stm.

6. Jane Perlez, "In Musharraf's Wake, U.S. Faces Political Disarray," *The New York Times*, August 18, 2008, http://www.nytimes.com/2008/08/19/world/asia/.

7. *BBC Online*, "Profile: Pervez Musharraf," August 18, 2008, http://news.bbc.co.uk/2/hi/south_asia/4797762.stm.

8. Tom File and Sarah Crissey, "Voting and Registration in the Election of November 2008," *U.S. Census Bureau Current Population Reports*, May 2010, http://www.census.gov/prod/2010pubs/p20-562.pdf.

9. U.S. Census Bureau, "Voting and Registration," http://www.census.gov/population/www/socdemo/voting.html.

10. U.S. Census Bureau, "Voter Turnout Increases by 5 Million in 2008 Presidential Election, U.S. Census Bureau Reports Data Show Significant Increases Among Hispanic, Black and Young Voters," http://www.census.gov/Press-Release/www/releases/archives/voting/013995.html.

11. Tony Allen-Mills, "How an 83-Year-Old American is Inspiring Middle East Revolution," *The Sunday Times*, March 6, 2011, http://www.thesundaytimes.co.uk/sto/news/focus/article570525.ece.

ANSWERS: 1. b; **2.** d; **3.** d; **4.** c; **5.** a

Remember to check www.thethinkspot.com for additional information, downloadable flashcards, and other helpful resources.

12. Robert Dahl, *Who Governs?* New Haven, CT: Yale University Press, 1961.

13. Wright Mills, *The Power Elite: A New Edition.* New York: Oxford University Press, 2000.

14. William G. Domnhoff, *Who Rules America? Power, Politics, and Social Change.* New York: McGraw-Hill, 2006.

15. Hicks.

16. Evan Thomas, "We the Problem: Washington Is Working Just Fine. It's Us That's Broken," *Newsweek*, March 8, 2010, 29.

17. Kenneth T. Andrews, "Advocacy Organizations in the U.S. Political Process," *Annual Review of Sociology*, 2004. 30: 479–506.

18. William G. Domhoff, *Who Rules America? Power, Politics, and Social Change.* New York: McGraw-Hill, 2006.

19. Gene Sharp, *From Dictatorship to Democracy.* Boston: The Albert Einstein Institution, 2003. Accessed October 9, 2011, http://www.aeinstein.org/organizations/org/FDTD.pdf.

Credits

Part Three: The Problems of Inequality

Inequality

The Poor

The Poor

John Sturrock/Alamy Images

- Who are the poor?

- Why is the gap between the rich and the poor growing wider?

- What is the underclass?

- Are the poor to blame for their poverty?

- What can we do to reduce poverty?

Ruth Acosta lives on the sixth floor of a crowded New York City apartment building with her three sons, teenage daughter, and three-year-old grandson. She is used to her small apartment; what worries her is that the refrigerator is nearly empty and there are only 10 cans of food left in her kitchen cabinet—some sweet peas, instant potatoes, peaches, and kidney beans are about all there is to eat. It's not much to feed a family when you are out of money for the month and you won't get any more food stamps for another eight days. Ms. Acosta doesn't panic—at age 37, she has been in this situation many times before. Like a lot of welfare recipients, she finds that her life follows a predictable rhythm. At the beginning of the month, when her cupboards are full, she feels pretty good about things, but as the weeks go by, her worries mount as dinner becomes less and less predictable.[1]

Our industrial economy has produced fantastic wealth for the privileged few; even middle-class Americans have luxuries never dreamed of in past centuries. The world we see in television shows, movies, and books is one of affluence and comfort, but there is an underside to our material well-being: Millions of people like Ruth Acosta and her family do not share in the abundance.

The poor in North America may not look like the starving masses in famine zones of the third world, but their misery is just as real. In fact, poverty can be more difficult in a rich country than in a poor one. There is less shame in poverty in a nation like India because so many people are poor. In North America, poor people are not only constantly confronted by the wealth they are denied but also are often blamed for their own suffering. Despite the appearance of widespread affluence, North America has some of the worst slums in the industrial world. Poor nutrition, nagging hunger, shabby clothing, and a crowded room or two in a deteriorating old building are all that many families can hope for. When compared with the people of the European countries, Americans appear to have a remarkably callous attitude toward the poor, as if people were poor simply because they didn't want to work.

Although the poor are a minority in every sense of the word, they are a sizable one. According to government estimates, there were 37 million poor people in the United States in 2005, more than 12.6 percent of the entire population.[2] Such figures should, however, be viewed with a skeptical eye because, as we will see, there is considerable debate about how to determine whether someone is poor. Although the experts may not agree about exactly how many poor people there are, there is no doubt that the problem is an enormous one. No matter how poverty is measured, there is also no doubt that the United States has a much larger percentage of its people living in poverty than any other industrial society.

The Rich and the Poor: A Widening Gap

When news commentators and politicians talk about the problem of poverty, they seldom have much to say about those at the other end of the economic ladder, but wealth and poverty are two sides of the same coin. To understand the problem of poverty, it must be seen in the context of the social and economic inequality between those at the top and those at the bottom of society.

All the data show that there is a huge gap between the haves and the have-nots and that it has been growing steadily wider for more than 25 years. There are two general ways of determining how great this gap actually is. One approach attempts to measure differences in income, and the other focuses on wealth. Although these two yardsticks are related, there are important differences between them. **Income** refers to the amount of money a person makes in a given year. **Wealth** is the total value of that person's assets: real estate and personal property, stocks, bonds, cash, and so forth.

The requirement that everyone report their income to the Internal Revenue Service makes it fairly easy to examine the distribution of income (except for the income that people hide from the tax collectors), and the U.S. Bureau of the Census conducts annual surveys that are even more accurate measures of the changes in the distribution of

Income ■ The amount of money a person earns or receives from other sources in a given year.

Wealth ■ A person's total economic assets (e.g., cash, real estate, stocks, and bonds).

The Distribution of Income

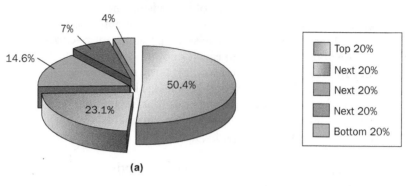

(a)

Figure 1

Distribution of Income and Wealth

Source: U.S. Bureau of the Census, *Income, Poverty and Health Insurance Coverage: 2005* (Washington, DC: U.S. Government Printing Office, 2006), p. 13; Lawrence Mishel, Jared Bernstein, and John Schmitt, *The State of Working America, 1998–1999* (Washington, DC: Economic Policy Institute, 1999), p. 262.

The Distribution of Wealth

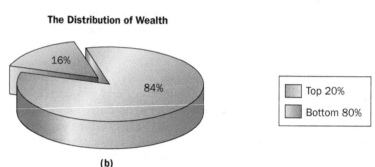

(b)

income from year to year. These data show a society deeply divided along class lines. One of the best ways to visualize the distribution of income in a society is to examine how much of the total income from an "income pie" goes to the top 20 percent of people compared to how much of that total national income goes to the poorest 20 percent of the people. When we do this, as shown in Figure 1a, we see that in 2005 the richest 20 percent of Americans received more than 50 percent of all income while the poorest 20 percent of Americans received 3.4 percent of this income.[3] In other words, in 2005 the top 20 percent of Americans received the same amount of income as everyone else combined. Thirty years ago, the top 20 percent received substantially less of the total income (43 percent) while the poorest 20 percent received more (5 percent). When we look at the very top, however, the inequality figures are even more striking. By the end of the twentieth century, the top executives of the largest corporations in the United States received an average of $10 million in income and stock options, which means their income was more than 400 times the income of their average workers.[4]

Examining the distribution of wealth is more difficult. For one thing, it is not always clear how much a particular asset, such as a painting or a mansion, is actually worth; in addition, those with great wealth often conceal many of their assets from the scrutiny of outsiders. The U.S. Bureau of the Census does not even attempt to publish yearly reports on the distribution of wealth as it does for income, but in recent times it has been trying to estimate wealth inequalities every few years. All of these studies find that wealth is far more unequally distributed than income. As can be seen from Figure 1b, while the richest 20 percent of Americans held about half of all income, the richest 20 percent held more than 84 percent of all wealth. Further, the richest 10 percent held almost 75 percent of all wealth in the United States, and the top 1 percent of people alone owned almost 40 percent of all wealth.[5]

Why is wealth distributed so much more unequally than income? There appear to be two principal reasons. First, lower-income people usually have to spend everything they make just to get by and are therefore less able to build up savings accounts, investments, or other assets. The debts of the bottom 20 percent of American families equal or exceed their assets, so they have zero net worth.[6] Second, wealth tends to be passed on from one generation to another. Poor people usually have poor parents and start out with nothing.

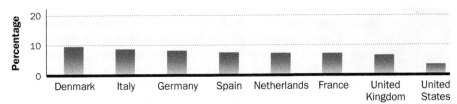

Percentage of All Income Going to the Bottom 20 Percent of the Population

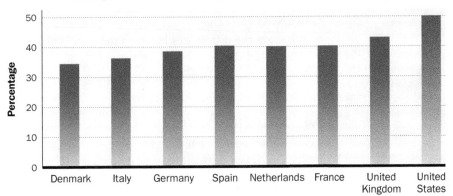

Percentage of All Income Going to the Top 20 Percent of the Population

Figure 2

Greater Inequality in the United States

Source: United Nations, *UN Development Report,* 2006, p. 335.

On the other hand, wealthy people usually have wealthy parents and are much more likely to come into a substantial estate.

Although many Americans see their country as the land of opportunity and equality, international comparisons do not bear out this view (see Figure 2). There is generally more economic inequality in the poor nations than in the industrialized countries. The research indicates, however, that the United States has by far the biggest gap between those on the top and those on the bottom of any developed nation. Canada has slightly more poverty than European countries, such as Germany and France, but less than the United States.[7] The primary reason there is so much poverty in the United States is that its government does far less than other industrial nations to fight poverty. Most European nations have welfare programs and unemployment benefits that reduce poverty by 50 percent to 80 percent of what it would be without government intervention, compared to only a 28 percent reduction because of U.S. government programs. The infant mortality rate—a common indicator of the amount of poverty in a nation—is also substantially higher in the United States than in Japan, Canada, and most Western European nations.[8]

The old saying "The rich get richer and the poor get poorer" has not always proved to be true, but since the late 1970s there has clearly been a significant widening of the gap between the haves and the have-nots. For example, between 1973 and 2000, the top 5 percent of American families saw their share of all income go up almost 30 percent while the bottom 40 percent of American families saw their share drop about 17 percent, and there was a similar trend in the concentration of wealth as well.[9] Since then, a long economic upswing helped lower- and middle-income groups in the United States make some modest gains in income, but the overall level of inequality in American society remains remarkably high and continues to grow.[10]

Many complex forces contribute to the growth of inequality of American society, but three stand out as particularly important. First, increasing globalization of the economy has placed the North American worker in direct competition with workers around the world who receive far lower wages. The managers and stockholders of multinational corporations, on the other hand, benefit from the profits made possible by lower labor costs, and the incomes of engineers, scientists, and other professionals have increased substantially because few people in the less-developed countries have the training necessary for such jobs. A second factor has been the use of technology to reduce or eliminate high-paying jobs for skilled laborers, as well as the corresponding increase in low-paying service jobs. The third cause of the growing inequality in American society is a political one. Since 1981, taxes on the rich have been substantially reduced, while government programs that benefit the poor and the working class have been cut to help make up the loss in revenue.

QUICK REVIEW

- What are the differences between the distribution of wealth and the distribution of income?
- Why has the gap between the rich and poor increased?

Measuring Poverty

Even though everyone has a general idea of what **poverty** is, it is a difficult term to define precisely. Certainly, poor people lack many of the goods and services that others enjoy. They may have insufficient food, shelter, clothing, or entertainment, but how much is "insufficient"? Are people poor if they have no shoes, no bicycle, no car, only one car?

Poverty is usually defined in one of two ways: absolute or relative. The **absolute approach** divides the poor from the nonpoor by using some fixed standard, usually the lack of money to purchase a minimum amount of food, shelter, and clothing. The **relative approach** holds that people are poor if they have significantly less income and wealth than the average person in their society.[11] Supporters of the relative approach argue that what is really important is not the fact that the poor have a low standard of living but that they are psychologically and sociologically excluded from the mainstream of society. Despite the appeal of such arguments, the absolute approach is nonetheless far more widely used both by government agencies and social scientists—perhaps because what most concerns the public is not the relative deprivation of the poor but their lack of basic necessities.

Every year the U.S. government sets a "poverty line" for families of different sizes. If a family's income falls below the line, then it is officially considered to be poor. The poverty line was originally based on studies showing that the average low-income family spent about one-third of its budget on food. The Department of Agriculture's Economy Food Budget was then multiplied by 3 to calculate the poverty line. Beginning at $3,000 in 1964, the poverty line for a family of four was just under $20,000 by 2005.[12]

Although such numbers make the poverty line sound precise and objective, it is actually a rather arbitrary figure. A different approach to these computations could easily lead to a different figure, and there is considerable debate over whether the poverty line is too high or too low. Some conservatives feel that it is too high (thus overestimating the amount of poverty) because welfare benefits that are not given in cash, such as food stamps and Medicaid, are not counted as income. Advocates for the poor counter that the original calculation that a poor family spends one-third of its income on food did not include such benefits either (although it is true that benefits are higher now than they were in 1964). They argue that if we are going to count such welfare benefits as income, we must also

Bill Bachman/PhotoEdit Inc.

Christopher Brown/Stock Boston

Wealth and poverty are two sides of the same coin. The more equally income is distributed, the less there is of both.

Poverty ■ Having insufficient resources to provide a minimum standard of living. Being significantly worse off financially than the average person in one's society.

Absolute approach ■ Defining poverty by dividing the poor from the nonpoor on the basis of some fixed standard of living.

Relative approach ■ Dividing the poor from the nonpoor on the basis of the wealth and income of the average person.

deduct the taxes the poor must pay. In recent years, however, the Census Bureau has included all of these criticisms and each year provides different poverty rates: rates that include the value of food stamps and estimates of the Medicaid value, as well as estimates that consider what the poor must pay in taxes. All of these additional poverty figures are fairly close, meaning that poverty rates do not differ much when these other items are also calculated.

Perhaps most important, however, is the criticism that the estimates of the cost of food, which are the base for calculating the poverty line, are far too low. The Department of Agriculture itself admits that its Economy Food Budget, which was originally used to calculate the poverty line, was intended only as a temporary or emergency budget, not as a way to meet long-term nutritional needs. There is also an additional problem that makes the poverty line lower than it should be to accurately reflect true costs of basic necessities. In 1969, the government stopped adjusting the poverty line on the basis of the rising cost of food and used a measure of overall inflation instead. Since then, the cost of necessities, especially housing, has gone up much faster than the consumer price index as a whole, meaning that families living at the poverty line are unable to buy as much as they could in the past. In 1995, the National Research Council examined the way the poverty level was calculated and recommended an alternative measure that adds noncash welfare benefits, subtracts out-of-pocket child-care and medical expenses, and adjusts for changing consumption patterns (for example, Americans now spend proportionately less on food and more on other expenses such as housing). The result was that about 9 million more people were counted as poor than in the official figures.[13]

Who Are the Poor?

One major reason for trying to define who is and is not poor is to discover which segments of our society experience the greatest poverty. Single-parent families, for example, have a much higher than average poverty rate, and their growing numbers have had a major impact on the problem of poverty. From 1970 to 2004, the percentage of all families with children that were headed by a single woman more than doubled, from 10 percent to 23 percent, and single mothers with children were the fastest-growing segment of the poverty population.[14] In fact, the majority of poor families with children are now headed by single women, and the poverty rate of such families is substantially greater than that of married couples.[15]

As of 2005, the official poverty rate for the United States was 12.6 percent of the population, but this rate differed substantially for various subgroups in American society. Children are among those with the highest rates of poverty in the United States. About 17 percent of those younger than 18 fall below the poverty line. Interestingly, although poverty has been rising among the young, the Social Security program has helped bring it down among the elderly (to 10.1 percent in 2005), and as the Signs of Hope box in this chapter shows, their poverty rate is now lower than the national average.[16]

Signs of Hope

Poverty Drops Among the Elderly

We have all heard the claims that government is hopelessly inefficient and that its programs to deal with our social problems are just a waste of money, but such charges are clearly false when it comes to Social Security. The use of a more generous formula for calculating Social Security benefits has had a dramatic impact in reducing poverty among the elderly. In 1970, those age 65 and older had the highest poverty rate of any group in the country: 24.6 percent. The decision to index Social Security benefits (provide an automatic adjustment for inflation) led to steadily rising benefits and a sharp decline in poverty among the aged. By 1994, the poverty rate for the elderly was only half as high as it was in 1970, and was actually lower than the national average. The rate has continued to drop since then. The 2005 poverty rate for people 65 and older was slightly more than 10 percent compared to 12.6 percent for the overall population.*

*U.S. Bureau of the Census, *Income, Poverty, and Health Insurance Coverage, 2005* (Washington, DC: U.S. Government Printing Office, 2006); U.S. Bureau of the Census, *Statistical Abstract of the United States, 1996* (Washington, DC: U.S. Government Printing Office, 1996), p. 473.

Contrary to popular stereotypes, the largest group of poor people in the United States are white, not African American or Latino. However, the percentage of the white population below the poverty line is considerably lower than it is for most minorities. For example, in 2005, 10.6 percent of all whites were poor, compared to 24.9 percent of African Americans and 21.8 percent of Latinos.[17] Family structure is also a critically important influence on poverty. Although 10.8 percent of all families were below the poverty line in 2005, families with both parents present were only about half that likely to be poor, whereas three times that percentage of female-headed families were below the poverty line.[18]

When we think about where the poor live, it is the crowded urban ghettos that come most quickly to mind, but the percentage of people below the poverty line is almost as high in rural areas.[19] The vast majority of poor people do live in cities, but that is simply because our population as a whole is so highly urbanized. The suburbs, in contrast, have the lowest poverty rate—less than half that of the central cities or rural areas—but as our original suburbs have aged, they too have developed growing pockets of poverty.[20]

The Trends in Poverty

Another important use for the statistics on poverty is to measure changes in the poverty population. Official statistics indicate that poverty declined sharply in the 1960s—from more than 22 percent of the total population at the start of the decade to around 11 percent in the early 1970s. The two main reasons for this improvement were the economic prosperity of the times and a strong government commitment to what was called the War on Poverty. As economic prosperity and the government's efforts to reduce poverty both faded, the improvements stopped and poverty again began to grow. The poverty level reached more than 15 percent in the early 1980s, then dropped a bit. It returned to that level in the early 1990s. After a long economic recovery, better economic times finally started to bring the rate down in the mid-1990s. It stood at 11.9 percent in 1999. Since then, the rate has moved back up again, hitting 12.6 percent in 2005.

Although studies indicate that there is less poverty now than 40 years ago, they also show that many problems associated with poverty have been getting worse. There has, for example, been a sharp increase in the percentage of poor people who live in **extreme poverty.** In 1975, about 30 percent of poor people had incomes that were less than half the poverty line,[21] but today that figure is 43 percent.[22] And as we shall see next, it is this group of the "poorest of the poor" who suffer most severely from their poverty.

Extreme poverty ■ The poorest of the poor. Often defined as those whose income is less than half the poverty level.

QUICK REVIEW

■ What are the two different ways of measuring poverty?

■ What type of person is most likely to be poor?

■ What are the current trends in poverty?

The Life of Poverty

Being poor in a rich country has profound psychological and sociological consequences. In our materialistic society, people are judged as much by what and how much they have as by who they are. Children of poverty lack so many of the things everyone is "supposed" to have that they often feel there is something wrong with them or their families. Poor people of all ages are constantly confronted with things they desire but have little chance to own.

The poor are deprived of more than just material possessions. In contrast to the rich and even the middle classes, those brought up in poverty often appear to speak crudely, with heavy accents and a limited vocabulary. They have less education, are less informed about the world, and are less likely to vote. Significant numbers of poor people cannot even read or write and so are cut off from much of mainstream culture. Under these conditions, poor people can hardly avoid feelings of inadequacy, frustration, and anger. Some bottle up those feelings, contributing to psychosomatic illnesses and aggravating problems such as high blood pressure and ulcers. Others express hostility and anger in violent crime. The rates of murder, assault, and rape are all much higher among poor people than among the rest of the population.

Economic uncertainty is another important part of being poor. Even poor people who are lucky enough to have a permanent job ordinarily work in low-paying, dead-end positions that are the first to be cut in bad times. Others can find only temporary work or are unemployed. Welfare sometimes helps out, but, as we shall see, the benefits are meager and the bureaucracy demeaning—and welfare programs have been sharply cut back in recent years. To make this insecurity worse, the poor have far higher rates of family instability than others. The poor marry younger and have the highest rates of divorce, separation, family violence, and out-of-marriage childbirth. This pattern of inequality even carries over into matters of life and death. Although we hear a great deal about medical miracles such as organ transplants, most of these "miracles" are reserved for people with good health insurance. As a rule, the poor receive second-rate health care, have deficient diets, and are forced to take inadequate shelter. Consequently, they catch more contagious diseases and have higher rates of infant mortality and shorter life spans.

A study of hunger released in 2000 by the Department of Agriculture estimated that more than 10 percent of Americans had faced hunger at some time in the preceding year or were worried that their food would run out. The study estimated that approximately 17 percent of America's children, about 12 million young people, did not get enough to eat. Female-headed households had the highest rate of hunger (at around 30 percent), followed by African American families (21 percent) and Hispanic families (20.8 percent). Finally, most people would find it surprising that during a period of economic boom, the people in poverty and near poverty experienced an increase in hunger between 1995 and 1999.[23]

Although these generalizations apply to all the poor to one degree or another, it is important to recognize that people who live in poverty are as diverse as those in any other class. Although some are so desperately poor they starve or freeze to death, for others poverty is a short-term condition that is soon overcome. We will devote some special attention to three overlapping groups among this diverse population: the homeless, the underclass, and the working poor.

The Homeless

We have all seen them—the bag ladies who push around everything they own in rusty shopping carts, the disheveled men sleeping on park benches or over heating grates to keep warm, an entire family living in an abandoned car. Lack of protection from the elements is the most obvious hardship they face. In the summer they swelter, and in the winter some freeze to death. Even getting enough food to eat is a constant concern for many of the homeless. Because they are almost always on the streets, they are easy targets for criminals and thugs. Aside from a few overworked charity and welfare agencies, the homeless confront a society that seems indifferent to their plight. The police, to whom most of us would turn for protection, see the homeless as a nuisance who must be moved out or arrested when their numbers become too great. (See the Personal Perspectives box.)

No one is really sure how many Americans are homeless on any given day. The Census Bureau counted 228,621 homeless people in its nationwide tally, but that figure is generally believed to be far too low, and even the bureau itself says it never set out to count every homeless person.[24] The Urban Institute estimates that there are about 600,000 homeless, the Department of Health and Human Services says 2 million, and advocates for the homeless put the figure at about 3 million or more.[25] The one thing virtually everyone agrees on is that the number of homeless men and women has grown substantially in recent years.

Personal Perspectives

A Homeless Man

What is it like not to have a home? The following account from a homeless man in his late 20s may give you some ideas.

Before I was homeless, I thought [the people] on the streets were losers—drug and alcohol abusers or mental cases. I was fairly judgmental. I remember telling one panhandler to get a job. I thought he was just lazy. Now I'm homeless and jobless. I'm willing to work, but once people see your backpack, they're scared off. People generally don't trust homeless people. They think we're flakes and don't feel safe hiring us. That makes it hard to break the cycle.

I don't eat good because I don't have much money, so my health isn't real good. I don't get medical help when I need it, also because I have no money. And I don't sleep well because I always need to have one eye open. I usually sleep behind homes or churches. They feel safer to me.

I just don't want people to prejudge me. After all, there are far more substance abusers and "flaky" people with homes than there are people who are homeless.

Who is most likely to be homeless? According to a survey of 26 major cities by the U.S. Conference of Mayors, more than half of all homeless people are African American, about one-fourth European American, and 13 percent Latino. Almost half of the homeless have some kind of alcohol or drug problem. Although one in five has a full- or part-time job, they simply can't afford a steady place to live. Perhaps the most disturbing finding of this survey was the number of homeless families.

There are several reasons why homelessness appears to have risen even in years when poverty has not. The most popular explanation is that the deinstitutionalization movement, which sharply reduced the population of state mental hospitals, has left many severely disturbed patients to wander the streets without the outpatient services that were promised. Although there is little doubt that this policy has been a major contributor to the ranks of the homeless, it is not the only factor. Articles in magazines such as *Time*, *Newsweek*, and *People* have claimed that the majority of the homeless are mentally disturbed, but several studies have put the figure much lower than 50 percent. Most research suggests that somewhere around one-third of the homeless have mental

The problem of homelessness has grown much more severe in recent years, and the sharpest increases have been among women and children.

Bruce Ayres/Getty Images Inc. - Stone Allstock

problems.[26] A study of homeless adults in Texas concluded that "the most common face on the street is not that of the psychiatrically impaired individual, but one caught in a cycle of low-paying, dead-end jobs that fail to provide the means to get off and stay off the streets."[27] The federal government has contributed to the problem by sharply reducing the amount of money spent on subsidized housing programs over the last three decades. (See the Debate below.) Equally important is the fact that large increases in the cost of rental housing have simply priced many poor people out of the market. More than 1 million "flophouse" rooms have been torn down since 1970, and the average cost of rental housing has grown twice as fast as the average income of renters.[28]

The Underclass

Originally described by sociologist Gunnar Myrdal in the early 1960s, the concept of the **underclass** was picked up in series of articles published in *New Yorker* magazine in 1981, and from there it jumped into the daily vocabulary of educated Americans. Like most such terms, it is defined differently by different people. Common to most of these definitions is the idea that the underclass comprises the bottom of the poverty class and the

Underclass ▪ Those in the lower part of the poverty class who are excluded from the economic and cultural mainstream of society.

Debate

Should the Government Provide Free Housing for the Homeless?

YES Many cities and towns provide temporary shelter for the homeless, but there are many more homeless people on the streets than the shelters can accommodate. Therefore, some people propose that federal funds be provided to guarantee every homeless person a place to sleep if he or she wants one.

A new wave of homeless men, women, and children is flooding the nation, and we must do something more than just pick up the bodies after they freeze to death. Some people say that we should rely on churches and other private charities to handle the problem. Although such an approach may have worked in a nation of small, tightly knit farming communities, it is hopelessly inadequate in a complex urban society. The charities themselves openly admit that they do not have the money or the resources to solve this problem.

The government is the one organization that can provide adequate housing for our most needy citizens. The only question is whether or not these people deserve to be helped, and the answer is a resounding "yes." More fortunate people often look down their noses at the homeless and blame them for their own misery. But no one chooses to be born into the underclass, to have a mental disorder, or to fall victim to the disease of alcoholism. And even the most zealous ideologue would have a difficult time finding a reason to blame homeless children for their plight. The real reason so many wealthy people oppose aid to the homeless is simple greed. They would rather see these unfortunates die on the streets than pay another $25 a year in taxes. Surely we are a more generous and public-spirited people than that. Our values and our traditions demand that we take forceful action to solve this tragic problem, and it is time we stopped talking and got the job done.

NO As soon as we hear about a new social problem, the first thing some people want to do is rush in and start throwing money at it. But a gigantic new government program to house the homeless would inevitably prove as wasteful and ineffective as other welfare programs have been. For one thing, the government is so inefficient and hamstrung by political pressures that most of the money is likely to be wasted before it ever gets to the homeless. Even if enough free housing were created to put roofs over their heads, that would do nothing to solve the underlying problems that made them homeless in the first place. The alcoholics and the mentally disturbed would simply be suffering from the same conditions indoors rather than on the streets.

A free housing program for the homeless would be a financial monster. It would grow bigger year by year, and eventually we would be forced to abandon it. We might begin by providing housing only to those who are now homeless, but what about the poor people who are working at low-paying jobs and still paying rent? They would soon walk away from their old apartments so that they too could become "homeless" and claim a free place to live.

The solution to the problem of the homeless is for individual citizens to give more to the private charities that have already proved they can do an efficient job dealing with the problem. Setting up another huge government bureaucracy would only make things worse.

implication that its members are excluded from the economic and cultural mainstream of society.[29] The disagreements arise over the standards that define who is in the underclass and how large a group it is. The broadest standard holds that the underclass consists of those who are trapped in long-term poverty. By that definition, the underclass would include between 40 percent and 60 percent of all poor people.[30] Another approach defines the underclass as the "poorest of the poor"—that is, those who have the lowest incomes. If we define extreme poverty as living on less than half the poverty-level income, then almost 43 percent of poor people were in the underclass in 2005.[31] Finally, the most restrictive standard would include only those who live in neighborhoods that are overwhelmingly poor. Rough estimates based on the data from census tracts (which do not follow the boundaries of actual neighborhoods) place that number at a little less than 10 percent of the poor.[32] Despite its usefulness, some sociologists have become uncomfortable with the concept of the underclass because of the sensationalistic way many journalists use the term. Herbert J. Gans, for example, writes that it is an "increasingly pejorative term that seems to be becoming the newest buzzword for the undeserving poor."[33]

However the term is defined, the underclass is, in the words of William Julius Wilson, "the heart of the problem of poverty."[34] Members of the underclass are much more likely to have been raised in poverty than the population of poor people as a whole. They are also far more likely to come from ethnic minorities, especially if we define the underclass as those living in overwhelmingly poor neighborhoods. By that definition, 65 percent of the underclass are African American and 22 percent Latino.[35] Members of the underclass tend to come from single-parent families with a poor educational background and a history of welfare dependency. A substantial proportion of the people in the underclass can't read or write and lack other job skills. In the past, such people could at least get menial work as manual laborers, but changes in the job market have left many of them now without any hope of meaningful work.

As a result of these factors, many members of the underclass are trapped in a self-perpetuating *cycle of poverty* that is extremely hard to escape. The fact is that mainstream society no longer has a use for them, and many people would rather they just disappeared. Of course, they are not going to do that, and the frustration and hopelessness of life in the underclass exact a heavy toll. Compared with other Americans and even most other poor people, members of the underclass have significantly higher rates of mental disorder, alcoholism, drug abuse, and suicide, and they are far more likely to fall victim to violent crime.

The Working Poor

We usually have the impression that people are poor because they don't work or can't work. But this is becoming less and less true. With the coming of the George W. Bush administration, the U.S. government has been releasing less information about the working poor. However, we do know that although 12.1 percent of American families were below the poverty line in 2002, the rate of poverty was still 7.9 percent among American families with at least one full-time worker. Other statistics for that year show that 26.5 percent of female-headed families were poor, but even when the mother was working, the rate of poverty for female-headed households was still 21.1 percent.[36] What these figures clearly show is that, in today's economy, even a full-time job does not guarantee people that they and their children can stay out of poverty. Furthermore, the working poor make up one of the fastest-growing groups in the poverty population. Since 1978, the number of full-time workers living in poverty has risen twice as fast as the overall poverty population.

How can so many people hold full-time or nearly full-time jobs and still be poor? The answer is simple: low wages. A study by the Bureau of the Census found that nearly one-fifth of American workers did not earn enough money to keep a family of four above the poverty line—and that was a 50 percent increase since 1979, a development the usually understated bureau termed "astounding."[37] The math, however, is simple: Working 40 hours a week for 50 weeks per year still does not bring someone with a family above the poverty line. Clearly, such low-wage jobs have been the fastest-growing segment of the labor market in recent years, and the employment prospects for young workers without high school diplomas have been growing progressively worse.

QUICK REVIEW

- How much hunger is there in the United States?
- Why has the number of homeless people increased so much?
- What is the underclass?
- Why are so many working people still below the poverty line?

Understanding the Welfare System

Before we examine the general causes of poverty, we must first take a look at the welfare system, which has become so much a part of the phenomenon of poverty. The first step in understanding the welfare system is to understand the public's attitudes toward the poor.

Attitudes Toward the Poor

Attitudes toward poverty are remarkably different in North America than in European societies. Rejection of the European class system and the availability of a vast new land to conquer helped create a tremendous faith in the value of hard work and competition among North Americans. In this way of thinking, each individual is responsible for his or her own economic destiny. Most people believe that even in a period of economic depression and high unemployment, anyone who works hard enough can be successful. It is also generally held that "there is always room at the top" for capable and hard-working people, no matter how humble their origins.

Despite its attractiveness, this belief in individual responsibility has a negative side. If the rich are personally responsible for their success, then it follows that the poor are to blame for their failure. "Poor folks have poor ways," the old saying goes. Joe R. Feagin has summarized the principal points in this **ideology of individualism** as follows:

1. Each individual should work hard and strive to succeed in competition with others.
2. Those who work hard should be rewarded with success (seen as wealth, property, prestige, and power).
3. Because of widespread and equal opportunity, those who work hard will, in fact, be rewarded with success.
4. Economic failure is an individual's own fault and reveals lack of effort and other character defects.[38]

Ideology of individualism The belief that each individual is personally responsible for his or her own economic success or failure.

Surveys show that this ideology is still a potent force in American life. When asked about the causes of poverty, most people respond with individualistic explanations that blame the poor themselves rather than with structural explanations that hold society responsible or with fatalistic explanations that blame such things as bad luck or illness. In one survey, for example, 58 percent of the respondents said that lack of thrift and proper money management is a significant cause of poverty, and 55 percent said that lack of effort by the poor is a very important cause of poverty.[39] Americans also show little support for government efforts to guarantee welfare or jobs to keep everyone above the poverty line. In contrast, 50 percent to 70 percent of the citizens of the European nations believe such efforts are a good idea.[40]

The History of the Welfare System

The ideology of individualism has had an enormous impact on the response to poverty in the United States. People receiving government assistance are often stigmatized as lazy or incompetent even when they are recognized as "truly needy." Frances Fox Piven and Richard

A. Cloward argued that the growth of the modern welfare system resulted more from an attempt to silence the political discontent of the poor than from a desire to improve their living conditions, and their findings have been supported by several more recent studies.[41]

The origins of today's welfare system are to be found in the Great Depression of the 1930s, when unemployment rose dramatically and armies of the newly impoverished demanded assistance: "Groups of men out of work congregated at local relief agencies, cornered and harassed administrators, and took over offices until their demands were met."[42] Despite such determined protests, reforms were made grudgingly. Relief for the poor was still largely a local matter, but cities and counties proved unable to shoulder the financial burden. The federal government began to give small direct payments to the unemployed, but it soon shifted to work-relief programs, which were more in tune with the ideology of individualism. With the coming of President Franklin D. Roosevelt's New Deal, a host of new government agencies was created to put unemployed Americans to work. Public opposition to these and other welfare programs nonetheless remained strong throughout the Depression. The most popular New Deal program that still survives, Social Security, is often seen more as a form of insurance than welfare.

The 1950s brought only modest increases in welfare support for the poor, but a "welfare explosion" occurred in the 1960s. From December 1960 to February 1969, the number of recipients of Aid to Families with Dependent Children (AFDC), the main welfare program providing direct financial aid to poor mothers until its elimination in 1996, increased by 107 percent.[43] Daniel Patrick Moynihan laid the blame for this increase on the deteriorating African American family and on the general increase in female-headed families.[44] Piven and Cloward disagreed, maintaining that family deterioration made only a minor contribution to the growing welfare rolls and that the real cause was increased activism among the poor, who began to demand greater social support.

The 1960s also saw the launch of President Lyndon Johnson's War on Poverty, which included such programs as the Job Corps, the Neighborhood Youth Corps, VISTA, and Head Start. These programs have often been criticized because they were inefficiently organized and because some of them were aimed primarily at young urban males and neglected females, the rural poor, and the elderly. Despite all its faults, most researchers agree that the War on Poverty did help to reduce poverty significantly in the United States.

The 1970s did not bring any new initiatives against poverty comparable to those introduced in the 1960s, but progress continued to be made. There was, however, a sharp reaction against welfare programs for the poor in the early 1980s, which was spearheaded by the incoming Reagan administration. Between 1981 and 1985, federal welfare spending dropped by 19 percent; about 400,000 families were cut from AFDC rolls, with another 300,000 receiving lower benefits; food stamp rolls were reduced by about 1 million people; and 3 million children were cut from school lunch programs.[45] The continuing growth in the number of single-parent families and the proliferation of poverty-level jobs once again forced up the number of welfare recipients. Still, welfare benefits were far less generous than they had been 20 years earlier, and many states had begun experimenting with time limits and work requirements to try to force mothers with dependent children off the welfare rolls. (See Figure 3.) As a result, the poverty rate that had stayed around 11 percent of the U.S. population during the 1970s, despite poor economic conditions, began moving up in the 1980s to roughly 15 percent. Studies show that this increase in poverty during the 1980s and early 1990s was largely related to these welfare cuts during the Reagan years.[46]

The ideology of individualism has always fostered a tendency for Americans to blame the poor for their own poverty, and during the last few decades critics have charged that welfare does everything from encouraging sexual promiscuity to undermining the economy. In one televised debate, a well-known conservative even blamed the welfare system for his lack of success in hiring a maid. Ignoring the complex sociological forces that trap so many people in poverty, these critics often presented a simplistic and unfair stereotype of welfare recipients as loafers who are living high at taxpayers' expense. This tendency to "blame the victims" for their misfortune reached new heights in a highly publicized book by Charles Murray and Richard Herrnstein. In *The Bell Curve,* they argued that poor people are biologically inferior to the affluent and that

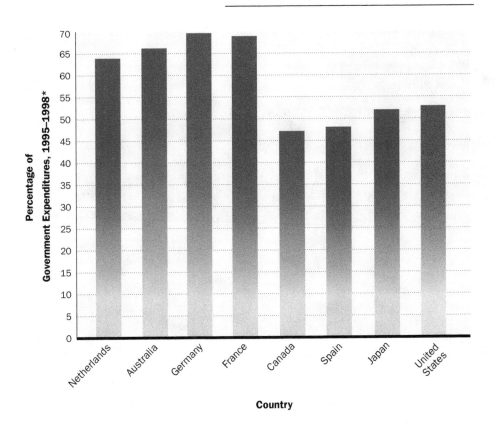

Figure 3

Welfare

The United States spends much less on welfare programs than most other industrialized nations.

*Includes Social Security.

Source: United Nations Human Development Programme, *Human Development Report, 2000* (New York: Oxford University Press, 2000), p. 300.

because their average intelligence is so low, government training or welfare programs for the poor are unlikely to do them any good.[47]

Ironically, those who attacked the welfare system ignored the largest welfare program, **Social Security,** because most of the benefits go to wealthier and more politically powerful recipients. (Social Security was supposed to be a kind of pension fund in which workers' contributions would be invested and the money returned to them when they retired, but the benefits are actually paid for directly by our taxes like any other welfare program.) Instead, the most bitter attacks were focused on AFDC—perhaps because, although it was created with the intention of assisting children whose fathers had died or been disabled, the vast majority of recipients are single women who are divorced or who have never been married. Or perhaps attacks on AFDC simply express hostility toward members of ethnic minorities, who were more likely to receive family assistance.

Social Security ■ A government-administered program providing pensions for older Americans.

The fact that there were so many unfair and unfounded attacks on the welfare system does not, however, mean that there were no reasonable criticisms. One of the biggest problems was that the welfare system was far too complex, too bureaucratic, and too wasteful. The government actually spent more in administering welfare programs (paying for welfare offices, case workers, and so on) than it paid out in benefits to the poor.[48] Another problem was that the old AFDC program tended to discourage welfare mothers from getting jobs: The money they earned was often deducted from their welfare checks, and they ran the risk of losing their Medicaid benefits if they earned too much. Another common criticism was that AFDC encouraged the breakup of families because it denied them assistance if an unemployed man was in the home. A fourth concern is that welfare programs help perpetuate the cycle of poverty because children who grow up in welfare families may fail to learn the basic work habits and attitudes necessary for success in the job market.

The Current Welfare System

The welfare system put in place in the United States with the Social Security Act of 1935 came to an abrupt end in August 1996 when President Bill Clinton signed the "welfare reform bill." The categories of welfare aid that existed in the past, such as AFDC, were

Eli Reed/Magnum Photos, Inc.

Welfare programs have never been as popular in the United States as they are in Europe. In recent years, welfare recipients have even endured an unprecedented wave of political attacks.

drastically altered. The biggest change was that each individual state was set free to design its own welfare system without the strict federal guidelines that had existed since 1935. In essence, there are now 50 different welfare systems in the United States, and the variance in who can receive aid, how much, and for how long is extensive.[49] Moreover, in many states, such as California, the welfare system is even more complex because each county has been given the task of designing some of its own welfare programs.[50]

Under this 1996 "welfare reform," the federal government did make a few important stipulations before allowing individual states to receive federal money. There had been work requirements for "able-bodied" recipients for many years, but these were made more strict—even requiring some mothers with babies just a few months old to find work or be cut off from welfare. The most important of these new requirements is the time limit on how long people can receive welfare. The basic commitment that the government should provide support for the needy has been eliminated: No longer are all "deserving people" who are hungry and poor guaranteed some aid. According to federal rules, the time limits are two years for one stay on the welfare rolls and not more than five years of welfare in a lifetime, and many states have taken up the option to make these limits even shorter. What this means is that after the time limit runs out, it doesn't matter if someone is still poor and unemployed: They will be prevented from receiving further aid from what was once the main welfare program for poor people in the United States. Some forms of limited aid, such as food stamps, may still continue, but the poor family's primary source of support is cut off.

Since 1998, when those limits began going into effect, there have been reports of increasing numbers of people asking for emergency food. However, the full impact of these sweeping changes is just starting to become clear, because many states postponed their implementation and a certain percentage of the poor are exempt from the limits. In a sense, the U.S. government "got lucky." When the time limits on receiving welfare went into effect, the country was in the longest economic boom of the twentieth century and enjoying some of its lowest unemployment rates ever. Poverty did go up a little between 2001 and 2004 when the economy slowed down slightly, but unemployment rates were still in the 4 percent to 5 percent range, and most of the poor cut from the welfare rolls have been able to find low-paying jobs. The critical question is what will happen to people with no more welfare eligibility and no job in the next major economic slowdown? Even with relatively low unemployment, most states have been reluctant to cut everyone off welfare who might have been cut, and they have temporarily extended the deadlines for hundreds of thousands of people.[51] Another consequence of the new limits on welfare assistance is just becoming apparent: The people who have been and will be removed the welfare rolls will push down wages for all low-skilled workers. Surveys have already shown that this is happening in many states,[52] and that people desperate for food and shelter are working for lower wages than those who are currently employed.

Despite all the attention paid to programs that provide cash assistance to needy families, there are also several other important welfare programs. The other major cash program is **Supplemental Security Income (SSI),** which gives financial assistance to poor people who are blind, disabled, or elderly. The federal government also has a variety of noncash programs that provide goods or services instead of money. The **food stamp program** gives recipients coupons that can be exchanged only for food, and **Medicaid** helps pay its recipients' health-care bills. (Medicaid is only for poor people; **Medicare** is for anyone over age 65.) Housing assistance is sometimes provided through rent subsidies and public housing projects that offer low rents to those poor enough to qualify. The states make a financial contribution to most of these programs, and state and local governments also supplement federal programs with short-term emergency aid and other benefits.

All things considered, we know that the real (after-inflation) value of welfare benefits in the United States has been falling for more than two decades and that the U.S. tax and welfare system already provides less help for the poor than any other industrialized nation.[53] Moreover, the United States is the only industrialized country without a comprehensive national health system or some kind of **family allowance.** If current trends continue, it may be difficult to avoid some crisis among America's poor the next time we have a sharp economic decline.

Supplemental Security Income (SSI) ■ A government program that provides financial assistance to poor people who are blind, disabled, or elderly.

Food stamp program ■ A welfare program that gives people coupons to exchange for food.

Medicaid ■ A U.S. program designed to help the poor, the blind, and the disabled pay for medical care.

Medicare ■ A U.S. program that pays a portion of the medical care costs for people 65 and older.

Family allowance ■ A welfare program that provides a small government allowance for every family with children.

QUICK REVIEW

■ What is the ideology of individualism?

■ Briefly describe the history of the American welfare system.

■ How did the 1996 reforms change the welfare system?

■ What are the main types of welfare assistance available in the United States?

Explanations of Poverty

The economic base of some societies is so fragile that hunger is a daily reality for most people. Such extreme scarcities of food, clothing, and shelter are not characteristic of modern industrial societies or even most traditional ones. The poverty problem in these societies is one of distributing wealth rather than one of producing it. There are many explanations of economic inequality, but most fall into three overlapping categories based on the analysis of: (1) economic structures, (2) political relationships among power groups, and (3) the culture of the poor.

Economic Explanations

Much poverty can be traced to simple economic causes: low wages and too few jobs for those at the bottom of the social hierarchy. We have already seen that even a full-time job at the minimum wage doesn't pay enough to keep a family out of poverty, and a growing number of people are forced to take part-time or temporary jobs because they cannot find full-time work. In technologically advanced societies such as Canada and the United States, people without education and skills are finding it increasingly difficult to secure any kind of employment, and those who find work are likely to be employed in low-paying jobs. After controlling for inflation, the average earnings of men who did not finish high school have declined by almost one-fourth in the last two decades.[54] This can only get worse with what is now called the "digital divide." With the increasing importance of computer literacy for all kinds of jobs, the less educated are likely to fall even further behind.

The average wage of all American workers declined between 1973 and 1997 while only a few slight gains have been made since then. The biggest drop has been for those who get the lowest wages.[55] Furthermore, of all the new jobs added to the U.S. economy since the 1980s, 55 percent paid wages below the poverty line.[56]

Although the unemployment rate goes up and down with the business cycle, it has seldom dropped below 4 percent in the last four decades. Moreover, the official unemployment rate is not a good measure of joblessness because it doesn't count those who have given up looking for work or those forced to take part-time jobs when they want full-time work. When those workers are added in, the picture gets far worse—in fact, the unemployment rate almost doubles.

In addition to the overall national problem, many areas have a particularly high unemployment rate because of local conditions. For example, some regions depended on industries that are no longer competitive in the world economy. The slums of the central cities are especially vulnerable to a variety of forces that combine to create an unhealthy economic climate. Low income in these areas makes it tough going for businesses that depend on local residents for their customers. A high crime rate, a lack of local services, and a significant measure of fear and racism keep the wealthy away and discourage outside investment. At the same time, inadequate transportation and long commuting distances to prosperous areas make it difficult for residents of inner-city slums to find work in other neighborhoods. For example, a study by James E. Rosenbaum and Susan J. Popkin found that poor women assigned to public housing in middle-class suburbs were much more likely to find jobs than those given housing in the central city.[57]

To add to their other problems, the poor often get less for their hard-earned dollars than do other consumers. Slum dwellers, for example, may pay more rent for a run-down apartment than people living in a small town pay for a house with a yard. More generally, because the poor are not mobile, it is difficult for them to shop around for sales and special values. They are obliged to patronize local merchants, who usually charge higher prices than those in affluent areas. Many stores in slum areas actively solicit sales on credit because the interest charges are more profitable than the sales themselves. If the customer cannot meet the installment payments, the merchandise is repossessed and sold to another poor customer.[58] When unexpected expenses occur, the poor must borrow money; but because they are not considered good credit risks, it may be impossible for them to get bank loans at standard interest rates. Instead, they must go to loan companies, which charge much higher interest rates, or to loan sharks, who charge exorbitant, illegal rates.

It is easy to look at all these difficulties as separate individual problems, but deeper roots in the basic structure of our economy link them all together. In an open capitalist society, the operation of the competitive market inevitably creates a huge gap between the rich and the poor. On the one hand, the market demands that employers pay the lowest wages and hire the fewest workers they can, or they run the risk of being driven out of business by more ruthless competitors. On the other hand, this same competitive struggle also stimulates the creation of enormous amounts of wealth, much of which goes to those who own and operate businesses. Although some workers who have skills or strong union organizations can demand better treatment, many others are inevitably left behind and sink into poverty. Of course, no capitalist economy operates in this completely unrestricted way. Governments in every capitalist nation have stepped in to help relieve some of the suffering caused by the harsh realities of the marketplace, both for humanitarian reasons and to prevent those at the bottom from rising up and threatening the whole system. But as we have seen, the U.S. government has done far less than any other industrial nation to reduce poverty and inequality.

Political Explanations

Poverty is as much a political problem as a problem of economics or culture. How much poverty a country has (at least in the relative sense) is largely determined by the policies of its government. The United States has the highest poverty rate of any industrialized country because the U.S. government redistributes less money from the wealthy and the middle class to the poor (Figure 2).[59] For example, as the Lessons from Other Places below shows, government policies in the European nations prevent high rates of unemployment from creating high rates of poverty. Inequality continues at such a high level in the United States because many Americans seem to have little concern about the poor, and those who do care are not politically organized. Politicians win votes by promising to eliminate crime and cut taxes, but few votes are won by promising to eliminate poverty. The ideology of individualism has convinced most Americans that the world is full of opportunities and that the poor deserve to be poor because they are too lazy or incompetent to seize those opportunities. As long as the poor are seen to be responsible for their own poverty, effective political action to change the conditions that cause poverty is unlikely.

Furthermore, as Herbert Gans has pointed out, poverty is valuable to the wealthy, and many powerful groups do not want it eliminated.[60] First, it ensures that society's dirty work gets done: Without poverty, few people would be willing to do low-paying, unpleasant, and dangerous jobs. Second, the low wages the poor receive for their work subsidize the wealthy by keeping the prices of goods and services low and profits high. Third, poverty creates jobs for the many people who service the poor (such as welfare workers) or try to control them (such as police officers and prison guards). Fourth, the poor provide merchants with last-ditch profits by buying goods that otherwise would be

Lessons from Other Places

Poverty Rates and Contrasting Values

Americans who live in or even just visit European countries are surprised to see so few signs of poverty. After giving relatives a tour of Germany, for example, I have even had them ask, "So where do the poor people live?" It is hard for many Americans to believe that poverty is so much less common in most of Europe than it is here.

The figures we have seen in this chapter back up these informal observations: Poverty rates in the United States are far higher than in any other industrial nation. But why is this true when we are so rich? This question is even more puzzling when we realize that the United States also has a low rate of unemployment. Germany has a poverty rate that is less than half that of the United States, even though the German unemployment rate was more than 10 percent throughout the 1990s and remained at 9.5 percent in 2005. Other major industrialized nations in Europe, such as France and Italy, are in the same situation. What is the cause of these seeming contradictions?

Although there are many economic differences between the nations on the two sides of the Atlantic, the main reason the Europeans have less poverty is that they have more effective social-welfare programs. For example, estimates suggest that Germany would have 22 percent of its population living in poverty without various types of welfare and unemployment benefits. Thus, the German welfare system has been able to reduce poverty by more than 65 percent. France, Italy, Belgium, Denmark, the Netherlands, and Sweden all have similarly low poverty levels because of their welfare programs. The same studies show that the U.S. government reduces poverty

by only 28 percent through its welfare benefits, and this was *before* the major cuts in welfare programs in 1996.

Public opinion polls show that Europeans are far more likely to demand that their government do something to pull its citizens up from poverty. Unlike Americans, Europeans still support expensive welfare and unemployment benefits even if they result in higher taxes and higher unemployment. In other words, Europeans generally recognize there is some trade-off between extensive welfare benefits and slightly higher unemployment rates, but their value preferences lead them to accept the trade-off.

Another important factor that helps keep welfare benefits low and poverty high in the United States is political. Low-income Americans are only about half as likely to vote as high-income Americans. As a result, politicians who favor more welfare and unemployment benefits are less likely to be elected. The differences in voting by economic class are much lower in Europe, so politicians are more concerned with fighting poverty.

Harold Kerbo

Sources: Harold Kerbo and Hermann Strasser, *Modern Germany* (New York: McGraw-Hill, 2000); Harold Kerbo, *Social Stratification and Inequality* (New York: McGraw-Hill, 2000), pp. 254–255, 260, Chapter 15; Lawrence Mishel, Jared Bernstein, and John Schmitt, *The State of Working America, 1998–1999* (Ithaca, NY: Cornell University Press, 1999), p. 377; Everett Carl Ladd and Karlyn H. Bowman, *Attitudes Toward Economic Inequality* (Washington, DC: AEI Press, 1998).

thrown away: stale bread, tainted meat, out-of-style clothing, used furniture, and unsafe appliances. Fifth, the poor guarantee the status of the people above them in the social hierarchy. The poor provide a group that "respectable" people can brand as deviants—examples of what happens to those who break social rules. Thus, the fact that poverty helps make the middle and upper classes more comfortable creates powerful opposition to any program that is likely to significantly reduce it.

Cultural Explanations

There are clear cultural differences among the social classes in all modern societies, and some scientists see these differences as a major cause of poverty. The foremost advocate of this position was Oscar Lewis, who argued that some poor people share a distinct **culture of poverty**.[61] Lewis did not ignore the economic basis of poverty; his thesis was simply that a separate subculture has developed among the poor as a reaction to economic deprivation and exclusion from the mainstream of society. Once a culture of poverty has taken hold, it is passed down from generation to generation. Children who grow up in poverty acquire values and attitudes that make it especially difficult for them to escape their condition.

Culture of poverty ■ A theory that holds there is a self-perpetuating subculture among some (but not all) poor people that helps trap them in poverty.

According to Lewis, the family in the culture of poverty tends to be female-centered, with the mother performing the basic tasks that keep the family going. The father, if present, makes only a slight contribution. Children have sexual relations and marry at an early age. The family unit is weak and unstable, and there is little community organization beyond it. Psychologically, those who live in the culture of poverty have weak ego structures and little self-control. Although Lewis did not use the term, most people living in the culture of poverty would clearly be part of the underclass.

Lewis studied a number of societies and concluded that the culture of poverty is international. It develops in societies with capitalist economies, persistently high unemployment rates, low wages, and an emphasis on accumulation of wealth and property. However, Lewis found several societies that have a considerable *amount* of poverty but no *culture* of poverty. India and Cuba, for example, had no culture of poverty because the poor are not degraded or isolated. Even in the United States, most poor people do not live in the culture of poverty. Lewis estimated that because of the influence of the mass media and the relatively low level of illiteracy, only 20 percent of the poor in the United States live in a culture of poverty.[62]

Most social scientists agree that poor people are more likely to have some of the characteristics described by Lewis, but there is much skepticism about claims that they have any special personality type or that they value work less than other groups. Some of Lewis's critics are not even so sure that a distinct lifestyle is passed from one generation to the next. Rather, it is argued by **situationalists** that each generation of the poor exhibits the same lifestyle because each generation experiences the same conditions: poor housing, crowding, deprivation, and isolation. Charles A. Valentine, for example, argued that the conditions Lewis described are imposed on the poor from the outside rather than being generated by a culture of poverty.[63]

Situationalists ■ Those who believe that the lifestyle of the poor is the product of their social situation rather than of a culture of poverty.

QUICK REVIEW

■ Explain the economic, political, and social causes of poverty.

Solving the Problems of Poverty

It may well be impossible to create a classless society in which all people are economically equal in an industrial nation. Certainly no such society exists today. It is, however, possible to eliminate poverty in an absolute sense, even if some people remain richer than others. We have seen that all industrial societies have made much greater progress toward this goal than the United States has, however, and some of the approaches to reducing poverty are discussed in this section.

More and Better Jobs

Reducing unemployment and creating better-paying jobs is a continuing concern of governments around the world. The easiest way to create more jobs is to stimulate the national economy by cutting taxes and interest rates or by increasing the amount of money the government spends. The problem with this kind of "quick fix" is that it often drives up inflation and the national debt, and if carried on too long it may actually cause economic harm. Long-term improvements in employment require long-term improvements in the economy, which in turn require basic structural changes. Unfortunately, reforms that aim to increase the rate of saving and investment, improve the educational system, and provide better government planning often have little political appeal because they are expensive and seldom produce results quickly enough to influence the next election. Such fundamental reforms are essential, however, if we are to make lasting progress in the struggle against poverty.

In the first years of the twenty-first century, however, the problem is not so much creating jobs as it is creating well-paying jobs. The most obvious way to do this would be a substantial increase in the minimum wage so that no one who works a full-time, year-round job would still have to live in poverty. In 1968, the minimum wage was $8 per hour in current dollars, whereas it was slightly more than $5 in 2006.[64] Critics of such proposals claim that they would create more unemployment. Although it is difficult to be sure how much of a problem that would be in today's economic environment, it would make good sense to combine an increase in the minimum wage with the kinds of basic structural reforms that can help create more jobs. Another approach is to create new education and job-training programs to give poor people the skills they need to land better jobs in today's global economy. European countries, for example, have much larger programs for **job retraining** than the countries of North America. The idea is a simple one: Teach unemployed workers skills that are in demand so that they can find new jobs. Although this approach is reasonable in this age of rapidly changing technology, it has basic limitations in times of high unemployment. If the millions of unemployed and low-wage workers were all taught the latest skills, there still wouldn't be enough good jobs to go around under current economic conditions. So, like the increases in minimum wages, such programs will be most effective if they are combined with an effort to create more jobs.

Job retraining ■ A program to teach workers new skills.

Improving Welfare

The welfare system has been attacked from all points of the political spectrum, and, if the welfare reforms the conservatives have pushed through are to have any chance for long-term success, several things will have to be done. Although few people object to the general goal of these reforms, which is getting mothers off welfare and into decent-paying jobs, progressives feel that they are being carried out in a harsh and uncaring manner and that it is unrealistic to think that these programs will meet their goals as they are currently structured. For one thing, a large number of welfare mothers are poorly educated and lack basic job skills. If they are going to have any chance of getting decent jobs, they will need much more education and training then they are now receiving. That means that in the short run an effective program will cost considerably more to set up and run than it saves. The reform legislation, however, actually cut welfare spending. The second difficulty is providing enough good, low-cost day care for the participants' children while the mothers are in training or at work. Once again, this costs more money than welfare programs are likely to be able to spend. The third problem is that the reform proposals are far too optimistic about the chances of these poor welfare mothers finding permanent jobs that keep them above the poverty line. A final drawback is that this approach is too negative. Although welfare mothers are threatened with the loss of their benefits if they do not find a job quickly enough, they are seldom given the understanding and respect they deserve for struggling to keep their families afloat. Despite these difficulties, a well-designed employment program for welfare mothers could be a positive step if it avoids a punitive approach based on stereotypes and misunderstanding. Such a program needs to provide education and comprehensive job training and placement. Even more important, it must make sure that poor children receive health care, proper nutrition, and good-quality supervision while their mothers are at work.

Another popular proposal for reform is to improve the system for keeping track of absent fathers in order to force them to contribute more to the support of their children. The advocates of such ideas claim that they can save taxpayers billions of dollars in welfare costs. Such an effort seems more likely to benefit mothers from more affluent backgrounds, however, because the fathers of children on welfare usually have few financial resources to contribute.

A different way to improve the U.S. welfare system is through administrative reforms. As currently structured, welfare programs are administered by a patchwork of federal, state, and local agencies, and a tremendous amount of time and money that might be used to help poor people is spent on determining who is eligible for assistance. Such administrative waste would be drastically reduced if more welfare services were provided to all citizens, not just to those who can demonstrate special needs. Most other industrialized nations have taken this approach, relying far more heavily on **noncategorical programs**—social programs for which everyone is eligible. Canada, for example, provides all its citizens with medical care, a small retirement pension, and a family allowance for each dependent child, and similar programs exist in all of the Western European countries. Such an approach has three major advantages. First, the poor are not discouraged from working by the threat of losing their welfare benefits when they start to earn some money. Second, welfare fraud is almost completely eliminated. Third, bureaucratic overhead is greatly reduced.

Noncategorical program ■ A welfare program with no restrictions on eligibility.

Distributing the Income More Equally

One of the most important sociological functions of the welfare system is to transfer income from the middle and upper classes to the poor people who need it most. But even a well-funded welfare program is still likely to leave a tremendous gap between the haves and have-nots. Is a day's work by the CEO of an average U.S. corporation really worth 419 times more than a day's work by an average employee? The pay gap is far less in other industrialized nations, as is the overall gap between the rich and the poor. There is no secret about how to create a more egalitarian society: The Europeans do it with a sharply progressive tax structure (one in which wealthier people must pay a higher percentage of their income in taxes) and more welfare support to the poor. Just a $1 increase in the minimum wage law could push hundreds of thousands of people above the poverty line. The United States has the lowest overall rate of taxation of any Western industrial power, and its taxes are particularly light on those with the highest income and the greatest wealth. For example, much inherited wealth is tax free. If we increased the taxes on those with the most wealth and highest incomes, we could reduce the taxes on those in the lower brackets and provide more government services, thus reducing the overall level of social inequality. The two richest Americans alone have enough wealth to eliminate all American poverty for an entire year, so a sharp reduction in poverty shouldn't be too big a task for the federal government.[65]

Organizing the Poor

Any effective program to deal with the problems of poverty is likely to have a high price tag. Although we often give lip service to the ideal of equality, the government has usually been unwilling to put that ideal into practice with the kind of financial support it requires. As we have seen, most programs to help the poor were created only when the poor organized themselves and demanded a bigger piece of the economic pie. Amid the activism of the 1960s, for example, a number of poor people's organizations sprang up to press such demands and were able to win support from more broadly based groups. As a result, the welfare system was improved and poverty decreased. If the government is once again to take new action to deal with the plight of the poor, then new organizations and new coalitions will have to be formed to push for change.

QUICK REVIEW

■ Discuss some of the best ways to deal with the poverty problem.

Sociological Perspectives on the Problems of the Poor

Poverty has not always been seen as a social problem. Although concern for poor people has a long history, until quite recently poverty was considered an inevitable part of social life or the fault of the poor themselves—a lowly status deserved by the lazy and incompetent. The Great Depression of the 1930s, tragic though it was, helped show social scientists that the conditions of poverty are institutional matters determined by large-scale economic, political, and social processes. Social scientists now agree that poverty is a social problem rather than a collection of personal problems, even though they still have different views about its causes and solutions.

The Functionalist Perspective

Functionalists consider the extremes of poverty and wealth common in most nations to be a result of malfunctions in the economy. In many parts of the world, rapid industrialization has disrupted the economic system, leaving it disorganized and unable to perform many of its essential functions. At first, people who lack job skills are forced into menial work at low wages, and later, with the coming of automation, they are not needed at all. Industrial products become outdated (horse carriages, steam engines, milk bottles), and unless rapid adjustments are made, people who manufacture those products lose their jobs. Training centers and apprenticeship programs may continue to produce graduates whose skills are no longer in demand. Discrimination, whether it is based on sex, age, race, or ethnic status, also wastes the talents of many capable people, and society is the loser.

Functionalists point out that the welfare system intended to solve the problem of poverty is just as disorganized as the economy. Administrators often show more concern for their own well-being than for their clients, and the first priority of many welfare workers has become the protection of their own jobs. Legislative bodies establish programs without enough funds to operate efficiently, and sincere welfare workers are drowned in a sea of rules, regulations, and paperwork. Inadequate communication systems fail to inform the poor about benefits to which they are entitled. Job training and educational programs are not coordinated with the needs of agriculture, commerce, and industry.

The best way to deal with poverty, according to the functionalist perspective, is to reorganize the economic system and the social service agencies so they operate more efficiently. The poor who have been cast out and neglected must be reintegrated into the mainstream of economic life. Members of the underclass must be provided with training and jobs so that they can resume their roles as productive citizens. They must also be given a new sense of hope based on the knowledge that the rest of society cares about them and is willing to help them overcome their poverty. Functionalists also recommend reforms to help stabilize the economic system so that it will not produce new poor people as others escape from poverty.

In general, however, functionalists are much more concerned about absolute poverty than about relative poverty. Many of them doubt that relative poverty (economic inequality) can or should be eliminated. Kingsley Davis and Wilbert E. Moore, for example, argued that economic inequality is actually beneficial for society.[66] Their main point is that the desire for more money motivates people to work hard to meet the standards of excellence that are required in many important jobs. Without inequality of reward, the most capable people would not be motivated to train for or perform the demanding jobs that are essential to the economic system. It should not be concluded, however, that functionalists are convinced that the social system should remain unchanged or that the amount of economic inequality should not be reduced. The functionalist conclusion is simply that some inequality is necessary for the maintenance of society as we know it. In fact, Melvin Tumin has pointed out how high inequality and poverty are actually dysfunctional for society in many important ways.[67]

The Conflict Perspective

Conflict theorists start with the assumption that because there is enormous wealth in industrialized nations, no one in such societies need be poor. Poverty exists because the middle and upper classes want it to exist. Conflict theorists argue that the working poor are exploited: They are paid low wages so that their employers can make fatter profits and lead more affluent lives. The unemployed are victims of the same system. Wealthy employers oppose programs to reduce unemployment because they do not want to pay the taxes to support them. They also oppose such programs because the fear of unemployment helps keep wages down and workers docile. Thus, conflict theorists argue that the economic system of capitalist countries operates to create and perpetuate a high degree of economic inequality. With changes in the balance of power among capitalists, labor, and other less-affluent groups, however, the extremely high level of inequality we find in the United States is not inevitable. European countries, for example, have lower levels of inequality and poverty, and workers and the less affluent have more influence on the political system.

Conflict theorists also note that wealthy and middle-class people are more likely than the poor to say that poverty stems from a lack of effort rather than from social injustice or other circumstances beyond the control of the individual. This application of the ideology of individualism enables the wealthy to be charitable to the poor by giving some assistance freely, while ignoring the economic and political foundations of poverty. Charity, including the government dole, blunts political protests and social unrest that might threaten the status quo. Moreover, some poor people come to accept the judgments passed on to them by the rest of society and adjust their aspirations and their self-esteem downward.

Conflict theorists view these adjustments to poverty as a set of chains that must be broken. They believe that the poor should become politically aware and active, organizing themselves to reduce inequality by demanding strong government action. In other words, political action is seen as the most effective response to inequality and thus to the problem of poverty. Most conflict theorists doubt that economic inequality can be significantly reduced without a concerted effort by poor people that gains at least some support from concerned members of the upper classes.

Conflict theorists argue that the wealthy want poverty to exist so they can be assured of a plentiful supply of cheap labor.

Jeff Greenberg/PhotoEdit Inc.

The Feminist Perspective

Feminists were among the first to point out what has been termed the *feminization of poverty*—that is, the long-term trend in our society for poverty to be more and more concentrated among women and children. Although there are many causes for this trend, the most important factor is the changing economic organization of our families. In the past, most of our children were raised in nuclear families with men as the primary wage earners and women as the primary caretakers of the family, but that is far less common today. The high divorce rate coupled with the growing number of unmarried women having children means that more and more women are raising children alone. Feminists point out that professions that have traditionally been open to women, such as teaching and office work, pay lower wages than occupations that are traditionally male, such as construction work. Moreover, women still earn less than men for doing the same work requiring the same education. A more egalitarian salary structure would go a long way toward lowering the poverty rate for women and children.

Feminists also question the lack of accountability men often have for their children. For example, if a woman becomes pregnant and is unmarried, she will raise the child by herself without the financial or emotional support of the father. She is also, of course, blamed for her poor judgment. The father, on the other hand, is often able to lead his life unchanged. Feminists therefore call for men to bear equal responsibility for the welfare of the children they father.

Feminists also argue that, in addition to the kinds of general approaches advocated by the functionalists and conflict theorists, special attention must be given to the other problems of single mothers if we are to create an effective program to deal with poverty. There is, for example, a crying need for a nationwide system of government-supervised and subsidized day care so that working women and men can be assured that their children are being properly cared for in their absence. A system of national health care in which basic medical services are seen as a right, not a privilege, would be another major step that would provide enormous benefits for families. Finally, more effort must be made to end occupational discrimination against women so that working mothers can earn wages high enough to keep their families out of poverty.

The Interactionist Perspective

Interactionists study the effects of attitudes and beliefs on behavior, pointing out that poor people learn to behave in the ways society expects of them. The values of those who live in the culture of poverty are passed on to their children, thus directing them into lives of poverty. For example, some people claim that the children of the poor learn to seek immediate gratification and that, unlike middle-class achievers, they are not inclined to defer small immediate rewards so that long-run goals, such as a college education, can be reached. More generally, interactionists point to cultural differences in the ways poor people and wealthy people define their worlds. They note that even when new economic opportunities arise, poor people are often unaware of them or are psychologically and socially unprepared to take advantage of them. Thus, the differences in the ways the rich and poor see the world keep the poor at the bottom of the social ladder.

Interactionists also study the psychological effects of being poor in a wealthy society. The easy availability of television and other media encourages the poor to compare themselves with more fortunate people in a fantasy world. When they do so, many come to define themselves as failures. Some blame personal shortcomings rather than social forces that are beyond their control, and the outcome is likely to be low self-esteem, which in turn precipitates a variety of personal problems, ranging from drug addiction and mental disorders to delinquency and crime. Poor people may also come to define themselves as the victims of an unjust society. On the one hand, this attitude may contribute to a healthy social activism; on the other hand, it may create a sense of hopelessness or a desire for revenge against those who have taken advantage of them.

The interactionist perspective implies that poverty traps poor people psychologically, as well as economically and socially. We could eliminate this trap by eliminating absolute poverty (the lack of adequate food, shelter, and clothing) and by opening up more opportunities for the children of the poor, thus reducing overall inequality. Interactionists also agree that the poor must be encouraged to redefine their social environment. Even if avenues for upward mobility are created, little change will occur as long as the poor are convinced that they can expect nothing better than a life of poverty. Before they will be able to take advantage of any new opportunities, many poor people will also need help to change self-images shaped by defeat and rejection.

QUICK REVIEW

- How would a functionalist and a conflict theorist disagree about the causes of poverty?
- What suggestions do feminists make for dealing with the problem of poverty?
- How can poor people's definition of themselves trap them in poverty?

Summary

Whether economic inequality is measured by income or wealth, there are large gaps among the rich, the middle class, and the poor that have grown much wider in recent years. Significant differences also exist in the cultural perspectives and lifestyles of these different groups. In cities, the poor are trapped in run-down, crime-ridden neighborhoods, while the affluent have a multitude of opportunities from which to choose. Psychologically, the poor have to cope with feelings of inadequacy and inferiority because they lack the money and goods that everyone is "expected" to have. The families of the poor are more unstable, and poor people have more health problems and shorter life spans.

There are two common ways to measure poverty. The relative approach holds that people are poor if they are significantly less well-off than the average person in their society. The absolute approach, which is used by most government agencies, defines poverty as the lack of the essentials of life, such as sufficient food, shelter, and clothing. According to the official figures, the poverty rate decreased in the late 1960s and 1970s only to increase again in the 1980s and early 1990s with cuts in poverty programs and a changing economy. It dropped during the economic boom in the late 1990s and early 2000s, and has been heading up again in the last few years. A look at the distribution of poverty shows that the young are more likely to be poor than the middle-aged or the elderly, as are children from single-parent families and members of ethnic minority groups. The poverty rate is highest in the inner city and rural areas and lowest in the suburbs.

There are many important differences among poor people. At the very bottom of the social heap are the homeless, who lack almost all the essentials of the lifestyle expected in our society. The underclass comprises the long-term poor who are shut out of the mainstream of society. The working poor are those who hold down jobs but earn too little to be above the poverty line.

The ideology of individualism, which stresses personal responsibility and self-reliance, has made Americans far more likely than citizens of other industrialized nations to blame the poor for their own condition. Nonetheless, the Great Depression of the 1930s forced the government to deal with the acute problems of poverty. Programs and benefits generally kept increasing until the 1980s, when there was a sharp conservative reaction against the welfare system. The welfare reforms enacted in 1996 are the latest in a series of efforts to cut the welfare rolls and force welfare mothers to get jobs.

There are many explanations for poverty. In some societies, the economic base is so weak that many people must go hungry, but in modern industrial societies there is more than enough to go around. The immediate causes of poverty in industrial societies are such problems as unemployment and low wages, which can in turn be traced back to the basic economic structure and the competitive demands of the capitalist marketplace. In order to relieve such economic problems, governments all over the world have programs to reduce poverty and redistribute wealth to their less fortunate citizens, but because the rich and the powerful oppose effective measures to eliminate poverty, the government's actions inevitably fall short of that goal. Another explanation for poverty is based on Oscar Lewis's idea that some nations develop a "culture of poverty" with distinctive characteristics.

There are numerous proposals for reducing poverty. First, more and better jobs could be created by improving the economy, providing job training and better education, and raising the minimum wage. Second, welfare programs could be improved by eliminating bureaucratic waste and inefficiency, providing day care and education to help welfare mothers find employment, and providing basic necessities such as health care to all citizens regardless of income. Third, the poor could organize themselves to push for government programs that really meet their needs.

Functionalists see extremes of poverty and wealth as the result of a breakdown in social organization. Conflict theorists are convinced that poverty thrives because the wealthy and powerful benefit from it. Feminists point to social changes that have forced more and more women and children into poverty. Interactionists are concerned with the problems created by being poor in an affluent society, and they note that the socialization of the poor often encourages them to develop attitudes and behavior patterns that make upward social mobility difficult.

QUESTIONS FOR CRITICAL THINKING

The problem of poverty and the welfare system needed to help deal with it has been one of the most controversial issues in U.S. politics in the last two decades. Most Americans say they believe that everyone should have an equal opportunity to succeed in life, but they also believe that people who work harder or are more capable deserve to be wealthier than others. So it comes down to questions of fairness: Do you think American society provides equal opportunities for all its citizens, whether their families are rich or poor or whether they are male or female, black, white, or brown? Are people who work at low-wage jobs paid enough for their labor? Are those at the top paid too much? What about the issue of inheritance? Is the current system fair or should the government tax inherited wealth at a higher rate?

KEY TERMS

absolute approach	job retraining	Social Security
culture of poverty	Medicaid	Supplemental Security
extreme poverty	Medicare	Income (SSI)
family allowance	noncategorical program	underclass
food stamp program	poverty	wealth
ideology of individualism	relative approach	
income	situationalists	

INTERNET EXERCISE

Many governmental agencies and nonprofit organizations are devoted to issues of poverty in the United States and the world. To begin your exploration of these Websites, go to the *Companion Website* at www.pearsonhighered.com/coleman. Enter Chapter 7 and choose the Web destination module from the navigation bar.

The most important information source about poverty in the United States is published annually by the U.S. Census Bureau. Visit the Census Bureau's Website at www.census.gov, and find the most current report on poverty, *Income, Poverty, and Health Insurance in the United States*. Then go to the section on "Poverty in the United States." From reading one of the first tables in this Census report, describe how poverty has changed in previous years. Has poverty gone up or down in the United States in the past year?

Then find the table showing changes in the rate of poverty for different sub-groups within the American society. For which group has poverty changed (up or down) most in recent years? From the explanations about poverty included in this chapter, why do you think these changes in poverty rates have occurred?

NOTES

1. Donna St. George, "For Food-Stamp Families, a More Uncertain Future," *The New York Times*, September 10, 1997, pp. C1, C8.

2. U.S. Bureau of the Census, *Income, Poverty and Health Insurance Coverage: 2005*, (Washington, DC: U.S. Government Printing Office, 2006), p. 13.

3. Ibid.; Harold R. Kerbo, *Social Stratification and Inequality*, 6th ed. (New York: McGraw-Hill, 2006), Chapter 2.

4. See *Los Angeles Times*, August 30, 1999.

5. Lawrence Mishel, Jared Bernstein, and John Schmitt, *The State of Working America, 1998–1999* (Ithaca, NY: Cornell University Press, 1999), pp. 258–262; U.S. Bureau of the Census, *Household Wealth and Assets, 1998* (Washington, DC: U.S. Government Printing Office, 1999).

6. Mishel et al., *The State of Working America, 1998–1999*, p. 278.

7. See ibid., p. 402; Kerbo, *Social Stratification and Inequality*, Chapters 2 and 9.

8. World Bank, *Economic Development Report, 2000* (New York: Oxford University Press, 2000).

9. Kerbo, *Social Stratification and Inequality*, Chapter 9.

10. Ibid., Chapter 2.

11. Ibid., pp. 250–252.

12. U.S. Bureau of the Census, *Income, Poverty, and Health Insurance Coverage, 2005*.

13. Lawrence Mishel, Jared Bernstein, and John Schmitt, *The State of Working America, 1996–97* (Ithaca, NY: Cornell University Press, 1997), p. 299.

14. U.S. Bureau of the Census, *Statistical Abstract of the United States, 2006* (Washington, DC: U.S. Government Printing Office, 2006), p. 54.

15. Mishel, Bernstein, and Schmitt, *The State of Working America, 1996–97*, p. 317.

16. U.S. Bureau of the Census, *Income, Poverty, and Health Insurance Coverage, 2005*, p. 14.

17. Ibid.

18. Ibid.

19. Ibid. Also see, Paul E. Peterson, "The Urban Underclass and the Poverty Paradox," in Christopher Jencks and Paul E. Peterson, eds., *The Urban Underclass* (Washington, DC: Brookings Institution, 1991), pp. 3–27.

20. Ibid.

21. Mishel, Bernstein, and Schmitt, *The State of Working America, 1996–97*, p. 307.

22. U.S. Bureau of the Census, *Income, Poverty, and Health Insurance Coverage, 2005*, p. 18.

23. U.S. Department of Agriculture, *Household Food Security Survey, 1999* (Washington, DC: U.S. Government Printing Office, 2000).

24. Associated Press, "Count of Homeless Useless, Official Says," *Los Angeles Times*, May 10, 1991, p. A27.

25. Anna Mulrine, "Self-Help Urged for Homeless," *Christian Science Monitor*, December 7, 1993, p. 6; Mitchel Levitas, "Homeless in America," *The New York Times Magazine*, June 10, 1990, pp. 44–45, 82–91.

26. James D. Wright, "The Mentally Ill Homeless: What Is Myth and What Is Fact?" *Social Problems* 35 (April 1988): 182–191.

27. David A. Snow, Susan G. Baker, Leon Anderson, and Michael Martin, "The Myth of Mental Illness Among the Homeless," *Social Problems* 33 (June 1986): 407–423.

28. Ibid.; Marta Elliott and Lauren J. Krivo, "Structural Determinants of Homelessness in the United States," *Social Problems* 38 (February 1991): 113–131.

29. William Julius Wilson, "Studying Inner-City Social Dislocations" and Christopher Jencks, "Is the American Underclass Growing?" in Jencks and Peterson, eds., *The Urban Underclass*.

30. U.S. Bureau of the Census, *Poverty in the United States, 1999* (Washington, DC: U.S. Government Printing Office, 2000).

31. U.S. Bureau of the Census, *Income, Poverty, and Health Insurance Coverage, 2005*, p. 18.

32. Wilson, "Studying Inner-City Social Dislocations."

33. Herbert J. Gans, "Deconstructing the Underclass: The Term's Danger as a Planning Concept," *Journal of the American Planning Association* 56 (Summer 1990): 271.

34. William Julius Wilson, *The Truly Disadvantaged: The Inner City, the Underclass, and Public Policy* (Chicago: University of Chicago Press, 1987), pp. 6–8.

35. Wilson, "Studying Inner-City Social Dislocations."

36. U.S. Bureau of the Census, *Poverty in the United States, 2002* (Washington, DC: U.S. Government Printing Office, 2003).

37. U.S. Bureau of the Census, "The Earnings Ladder: Who's at the Bottom? Who's at the Top?" *Statistical Brief* (Washington, DC: U.S. Government Printing Office, March 1994).

38. Joe R. Feagin, *Subordinating the Poor: Welfare and American Beliefs* (Upper Saddle River, NJ: Prentice Hall, 1975), pp. 91–92.

39. See Kerbo, *Social Stratification and Inequality*, Chapter 9.

40. Ibid., p. 260; Everett Carl Ladd and Karlyn H. Bowman, *Attitudes Toward Economic Inequality* (Washington, DC: AEI Press, 1998).

41. Frances Fox Piven and Richard A. Cloward, *Regulating the Poor: The Functions of Public Welfare* (New York: Vintage, 1971); Michael Betz, "Riots and Welfare: Are They Related?" *Social Problems* 21 (1974): 345–355; Larry Isaac and William Kelly, "Racial Insurgency, the State and Welfare Expansion," *American Sociological Review* 45 (1980): 1348–1386.

42. Piven and Cloward, *Regulating the Poor*, pp. 61–62.

43. Ibid., pp. 184–185.

44. Daniel Patrick Moynihan, *The Politics of a Guaranteed Income: The Nixon Administration and the Family Assistance Plan* (New York: Random House, 1973).

45. Bob Drogin, "True Victims of Poverty: The Children," *Los Angeles Times*, July 30, 1985, pp. 1, 10–11; Kevin Roderick, "Case History of a 20-Year War on Poverty," *Los Angeles Times*, July 31, 1985, pp. 1, 8–9.

46. See Kerbo, *Social Stratification and Inequality*, Chapter 9.

47. Charles Murray and Richard Herrnstein, *The Bell Curve: Intelligence and Class Structure in American Life* (New York: Basic Books, 1994).

48. Michael Harrington, *The New American Poverty* (New York: Holt, Rinehart and Winston, 1984), pp. 81–87.

49. See the *Los Angeles Times*, August 21, 1997.

50. See the *Los Angeles Times*, February 2, 1998.

51. See *International Herald Tribune*, October 2, 1998, *Los Angeles Times*, January 2, 2003.

52. See the *Los Angeles Times*, February 8 and February 9, 1998.

53. Mishel, Bernstein, and Schmitt, *The State of Working America, 1996–97*, p. 403.

54. Ibid., p. 169.

55. Ibid., p. 143.

56. Kerbo, *Social Stratification and Inequality*, p. 26.

57. James E. Rosenbaum and Susan J. Popkin, "Employment and Earnings of Low-Income Blacks Who Move to Middle Class Suburbs" in Jencks and Peterson, *The Urban Underclass*, pp. 342–358.

58. See Paul Jacobs, "Keeping the Poor Poor," in Jerome Skolnick and Elliott Currie, eds., *Crisis in American Institutions*, 5th ed. (Boston: Little, Brown, 1988), pp. 134–140.

59. Mishel, Bernstein, and Schmitt, *The State of Working America, 1996–97*, pp. 328–331.

60. Herbert J. Gans, "The Uses of Poverty: The Poor Pay All," *Social Policy* 2 (1971): 21–23.

61. Oscar Lewis, *La Vida* (New York: Random House, 1965).

62. Ibid.

63. Charles A. Valentine, *Culture and Poverty: Critique and Counter-Proposals* (Chicago: University of Chicago Press, 1968).

64. U.S. Bureau of the Census, *Statistical Abstracts of the United States*.

65. See *International Herald Tribune*, June 22 and July 14, 1999.

66. Kingsley Davis and Wilbert E. Moore, "Some Principles of Stratification," *American Sociological Review* 10 (1945): 242–249.

67. Melvin Tumin, "Some Principles of Stratification: A Critical Analysis," *American Sociological Review* 18 (1953): 387–394.

INEQUALITY: POVERTY AND WEALTH

From Chapter 2 of *Think Social Problems 2013*, Second Edition. John D. Carl. Copyright © 2013 by Pearson Education, Inc. All rights reserved.

INEQUALITY: POVERTY AND WEALTH

In the

summer of 2011, the United States was in the midst of a financial disaster felt by both its government and its people. Many clamored for congress to increase government revenue by eliminating tax breaks for the wealthiest Americans. For the time being, the tax breaks stuck, even though one of the most vocal proponents of higher taxes for the super-rich was at the time the third wealthiest person in the world. Warren Buffett is not your typical billionaire. He lives in Omaha, Nebraska, in a home he bought for $31,500, has pledged to donate 99 percent of his money to charity,[1] and doesn't appreciate being "coddled" by the government.

As Buffett explains in a *New York Times* op-ed, most "mega-rich" and "super-rich" Americans technically earn little to no actual income. Rather than earn money by working at a job, they make most of their money by investing. According to the federal tax code, money gained from these investments is classified— and taxed—differently than money earned from a job. While most middle- and lower-income Americans pay around 25 percent to 40 percent of their incomes in taxes, some of the wealthiest investors only pay around 15 percent of their capital gains and carried interest in taxes. Some of them, in fact, report no wages at all. And they aren't breaking any tax laws.

Those in favor of continuing tax breaks for the super-rich claim that if those with the most money are taxed at higher rates, they will invest less in businesses and hire fewer people in their own businesses. The purported outcome is that the net result of fewer jobs would be bad for middle- and lower-income workers. But Buffett reminds us that tax rates for the super-rich were higher in the 1980s and 1990s. Yet investors didn't stop investing because of the higher rates—after all, investing is how they make money. They could no sooner stop investing than middle-class workers could just up and quit their jobs without an alternative source of income. Higher taxes on the rich might actually cause them to hire more workers and/or pay their workers more to avoid the higher tax. This would stimulate the economy more. During the higher-tax years between 1980 and 2000, 40 million jobs were created. In 1992, the 400 Americans reporting the highest income had a combined taxable income of $16.9 billion and paid 29.2 percent of that sum in taxes. By 2008, the combined taxable income of the top 400 has reached a whopping $90.9 billion, yet they only paid taxes at a rate of 21.5 percent. The result of the tax rates lowered under George W. Bush's administration was not more jobs for the middle class; instead, fewer jobs were created and the nation fell into a deep recession.

Buffett implores the U.S. government to "get serious about shared sacrifice." To do so, he advises leaving tax rates unchanged for 99.7 percent of taxpayers. For the rest—the roughly 237,000 households making more than $1 million and roughly 8,000 bringing in $10 million or more—he would raise the rates proportionally. Buffett is not only a member of this $10-million-or-more group, but also a "legendary investor" and an "investing wizard," so he might know a thing or two about money.[2]

---More than 30 states have lotteries. Lotto slogans scream from billboards around the country: "Let Yourself Play!"

In what is widely known as the richest country in the world, the super-rich have continued to grow in their share of the income they earn. Meanwhile, the middle- and lower-income workers in this country think their best hope to become super-rich is to play their state lottery. The lottery, in effect, becomes a voluntary tax often used to support essential state functions such as education. However, lotteries do not necessarily result in increased funds for those projects.[3] Although some states earmark lottery revenues directly for programs like education, others send the money to a general fund for the legislature to use as it sees fit.[4]

Who plays state lotteries? Regular gamblers account for the majority of players. Men are more likely to play than women are, with adults between the ages of 25 and 65 years falling within the most-likely-to-play age category. A higher level of education also appears to affect how likely someone is to play the lottery.[5] As a person becomes more educated, he or she is less likely to play.

How much do people spend on lotto tickets? The average lottery expense is about the same for households earning between $10,000 and $60,000 per year. Households with income levels higher than $60,000, however, have lower levels of play. You can bet you won't see billionaire Warren Buffett playing the Mega Millions.[6]

In particular, in light of the current downturn in the U.S. economy, huge deficits, and housing woes for many, some might wonder if the government should be coaxing people to gamble away their money. Essentially, a lottery is a tax on the desperate and hopeful. Is this the best way to "share sacrifice?"As we take a look at the issues of income inequality in the United States, some fundamental questions will arise. How much inequality is there? Are we all living in a "land of opportunity?" What can we do, if anything, to ensure that everyone has the same chance?

get the topic: WHAT IS INEQUALITY AND HOW DOES IT AFFECT PEOPLE?

SOCIAL STRATIFICATION is the ranking of people and the rewards they receive based on objective criteria, often including wealth, power, and/or prestige.

INCOME is the money received for work or through investments.

WEALTH is all of an individual's material possessions, including income.

QUINTILES are the five equal segments into which sociologists and economists divide the population, each group accounting for 20 percent (one-fifth) of the population.

MEDIAN is the midpoint of a group of numbers ranked from lowest to highest.

Defining Economic Inequality

SOCIAL STRATIFICATION

Human beings have a tendency to categorize or rank things. Whether it's the "Top 10" songs for a given week or the "Five Best Cities" in which to raise your kids, people enjoy the distinction of knowing that the city, song, or book that they have chosen is well ranked by their peers. Sociologists apply the same process to people and use **social stratification** to rank individuals based on objective criteria, often wealth, power, and/or prestige. Social stratification naturally creates inequality, as some people are "haves" and some are "have-nots." This inequality causes many social conflicts, which lead to greater social problems.

Each society has its own way to rank, or stratify, the population, but the level of stratification can vary greatly.[7] In certain societies, political power may be used to separate people. For example, in Cuba, members of the Communist party often have preferential housing and access to better schools, while people with different political affiliations often live in poverty.[8] Wealth and income are other means by which societies stratify people into social classes; generally in the United States, the wealthier you are, the more important others consider you. Other societies use birth status and family origins as a way to divide people. In these societies, privileged positions may be available only to families regarded as "nobility." For example, if you're a member of the Dubai royal family, you're probably living well. That is, you have excellent health care, the trendiest cars, the finest wardrobe, and the choicest foods, among other things.

In the United States, people are often divided by their access to wealth, income, or both. **Income** refers to the money received for work or through investments. It may be the paycheck you receive every month or the dividends you receive from the stock market. **Wealth**, on the other hand, refers to all of your material possessions including income. You could probably raise a considerable sum that would be more than your monthly paychecks if you were to take everything you owned—your car, your electronics, your clothes—and place these items on eBay to sell at a fair market value. Let's look further at the distribution of wealth and income in the United States.

Share of Income by Quintile, 1968 and 2009

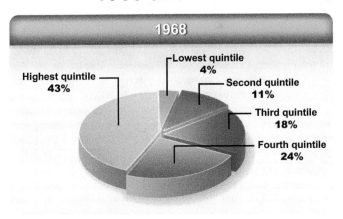

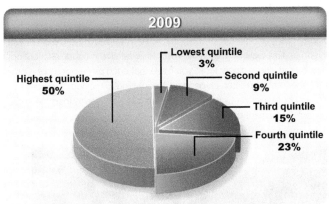

Source: U.S. Census Bureau, "Share of Aggregate Income Received by Each Fifth and Top 5 Percent of Households, All Races: 1967 to 2009," www.census.gov/compendia/statab/2011/tables/11s0693.xls.

that each account for 20 percent (one-fifth) of the population. Ranking households based on income alone shows that most Americans exist somewhere between extreme wealth and extreme poverty and gives a clearer understanding of how vague terms like "middle class" and "lower class" can be quantified. In 2009, the richest 20 percent of Americans controlled just over 50 percent of total income. The poorest quintile had only 3.4 percent of total income.[9] Between these two extremes, the second-lowest quintile accounted for 8.6 percent, the middle quintile 14.6 percent, and the second-highest for 23.2 percent of all income. The richest of the top quintile—the top 5 percent of all earners—made $180,000 or more per year and accounted for 21.7 percent of the nation's combined income.[10]

Although the **median** (or midpoint) of all household incomes that same year was $49,777, one in five households made do on less than $20,453, making up the bottom quintile. The second quintile's incomes ranged from $20,454 to $38,550; the third's, from $38,551 to $61,801; the fourth, from $61,802 to $100,000. One-fifth of U.S. households earned more than $100,000.[11]

In the United States, income inequality has increased over time. The chart at the bottom of the page provides income data across more than 50 years. As you review the chart, you'll notice that the poorest fifth of the population is actually earning less of the total U.S. income each year. At their peak in 1975, this group earned 5.6 percent of the nation's

---

<<< **In 2009, the highest-earning quintile earned a greater share of the nation's total income than it did in 1968; all other income groups saw their shares decline.** The top 5 percent earned 16.3 percent of the nation's total income in 1968 and 21.7 percent in 2009.

INCOME DISTRIBUTION

As you've probably noticed, the U.S. workplace is home to a wide range of salaries. Many families today have experienced a painful transformation in their economic situations. After an unexpected layoff, a middle-class family may go from owning a large and comfortable home in suburbia to renting a one-bedroom apartment in the bad part of town. Income earners in the United States can range from struggling workers making minimum wage to high-powered executives with six- or seven-figure salaries.

One way that sociologists and economists look at income distribution in the United States is by dividing the population into **quintiles**, five equal segments

Income Change Over Time

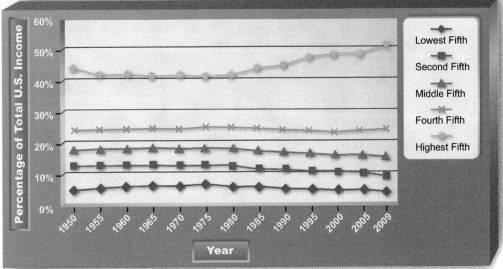

Sources: DeNavas-Walt, 2006, U.S. Census Bureau. U.S. Census Bureau, "Share of Aggregate Income Received by Each Fifth and Top 5 Percent of Households, All Races: 1967 to 2009," www.census.gov/compendia/statab/2011/tables/11s0693.xls.

Inequality: Poverty and Wealth

U.S. Income Change 1970–2000

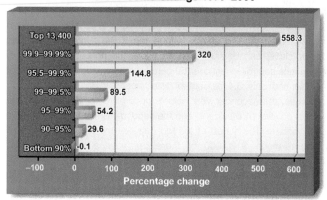

Source: Data from David Cay Johnson, *Perfectly Legal: The Covert Campaign to Rig Our Tax System to Benefit the Super Rich and Cheat Everybody Else* (New York: Penguin Group Inc., 2003).

income, but their share of the "pie" has declined steadily ever since. Meanwhile, the wealthiest fifth of the population has been increasing its share of total U.S. income since 1975.[12]

Is the income gap widening between the wealthy and the poor? The numbers show that it is. Over time, the top fifth of the population has been earning an increasing share of the total U.S. income.[13] The graph above shows income change over the last 30 years. During this

period, the pretax incomes for the bottom 90 percent of Americans actually dropped 0.1 percent.[14] At the same time, incomes grew for those people in the top 10 percent of the population. To put it another way, people in the top 5- to 10-percent income group saw their pay increase almost 30 percent.[15] Those households in the top 95–99% of incomes saw an even greater increase of just over 54 percent.[16] The top 13,400 households in the country experienced the biggest gain. Over 30 years, this group's income increased over 558 percent.[17] That means that if a person had a household income of $5 million in 1970, then his or her income would have increased to $27.9 million by 2000.

The famous sociologist Max Weber suggests that when we stratify people in society, we should do so based on their wealth, power, and prestige. In other words, your rank in society won't change a great deal just because your income rises or falls temporarily. Lasting rank in society is determined by accumulated wealth and property, level of prestige, and amount of power to do what one wants.[18]

WEALTH

Wealth includes income and assets. It can consist of stocks, bonds, real estate, cash, and a host of other items. As you review the pie chart you might at first believe that it represents a relatively equal distribution. However, taking a closer look, you'll see that each piece does not represent the same number of people. Astonishingly, the top 1 percent of wealth holders in the United States has more total wealth than the entire bottom 90 percent of the population.[19]

For the majority of Americans, **owning their own car and home is a big step toward the achievement of the American dream.**

In part this is due to unequal inheritance issues. Only 1.6 percent of Americans receive $100,000 or more as an inheritance. The bottom 91.9 percent of Americans receive nothing.[20] Wealth, once accumulated, tends to stay in the same place. Let's say I have 100 students and start out with 100 Tootsie Rolls. I give 34 pieces of candy to one person and 37 pieces to the next nine people (averaging about four pieces per person). To the remaining 90 people, I give 29 pieces to divide. Because the one person cannot eat all 34 Tootsie Rolls, she is likely to take them home and give them to her family members. Wealth tends to accumulate.

POWER

Income and wealth often bring with them power or access to power. Power is discussed in a variety of ways. First, we can address it as a coercive element in society that manipulates people to do things that they might not otherwise do. According to this line of thinking, **power** is the ability to get people to do what you want without having to make them do so. Sometimes, however, others may not do what you want unless you coerce them. When a professor makes a course so difficult that the only way a student can receive a passing grade is to help her with her research, she is using coercion. On the other hand, **force** is a type of power that occurs when you make someone do something against his or her will. Dictators often use force or the threat of force to make people follow orders.

Persuasive power means that you use direct or indirect methods to get what you want. It is much easier to get people to follow along if they believe it is in their best interests. Oprah Winfrey is considered to be one of the most powerful women in the media today because of her ability to persuade her audience. Books selected for her Book Club often skyrocket to The New York Times' best sellers list.

It is very difficult to convince someone that his or her long-standing ideas about an issue are not necessarily true. For example, most of my students believe that the social class structure in the United States is entirely fair, making chapters such as this one difficult to swallow. That's

POWER is the ability to carry out your will and impose it on others.

FORCE is a type of power that occurs when you make someone do something against his or her will.

PERSUASIVE POWER refers to using direct or indirect methods to get what you want.

PRESTIGE is the level of esteem associated with one's status and social standing.

because if you believe that everyone has an equal chance to succeed, then you are persuaded to keep the system unchanged.[21]

PRESTIGE

Prestige refers to the level of esteem associated with our status and social standing. As I'm sure you've noticed, different jobs have different levels of prestige. Occupations are generally ranked on a scale from 0 to 100, with 0 as the lowest. Doctors and lawyers, as you might suspect, are on the high end of the scale with ratings of 86 and 75, whereas janitors rank a 22. Generally speaking, the less a job pays, the less prestige it carries. Not only do low-wage workers have to struggle financially, they must struggle to earn respect in society as well.

A prestigious job has benefits other than the obvious monetary ones. For example, you might be inclined to take career advice from a successful airline pilot, but it's doubtful that the advice of a minimum-wage service station attendant would merit your respect. Naturally, you don't expect someone who pumps gas for a living to be able to give you great advice on how to build a successful career. Occupational prestige varies according to the job and reflects which work a society respects the most.

Few parents look at their children and dream of them becoming burger flippers rather than engineers, because an engineer attains more occupational prestige in our society. A combination of wealth, power, and prestige form the stratification and class systems used to characterize the population of the United States.

Occupational Prestige Rankings			
Occupation	Prestige Rating	Occupation	Prestige Rating
Physician	86	Housewife	51
Lawyer	75	Manager of a supermarket	48
College professor	74	Secretary	46
Airline pilot	73	Insurance agent	46
Engineer	71	Bank teller	43
Medical technician	68	Househusband	36
Clergy	67	Assembly line worker	35
Registered nurse	66	Housekeeper	34
Accountant	65	Cook in a restaurant	34
Elementary school teacher	64	Sales person in a store	31
Police	61	Garbage collector	28
Journalist	60	Bartender	25
Farm owner	53	Janitor	22
Firefighter	53	Service station attendant	21
Social worker	52	Grocery bagger	18
Electrician	51	Street-corner drug dealer	13

Source: Data from Keiko Nakao and Judith Treas, "Updating Occupational Prestige and Socioeconomic Scales: How the New Measures Measure Up." *Sociological Methodology*, 1994. 24: 1–72.

How Does Inequality Affect the Lives of People?

CLASS IN AMERICA

Ask yourself this: When it comes to social class, where do you stand? When asked to identify themselves in the social class scheme, most people claim to be part of the middle class.[22] But are these claims accurate?

Sociologists have varying opinions on how many classes exist and what the distinctions between each class are. For example, Karl Marx suggested that there are two: the proletariat and the bourgeois. Others, like Max Weber, suggest that there are more. But regardless of how many classes one believes there to be, the lower you are on the social class ladder, the more social problems you're likely to experience. For the purposes of this chapter, we'll take a look at five different social classes that exist in the United States: upper class, upper middle class, middle class, working class, and lower class.

Upper or Elite Class

The **upper** or **elite class** is very small in number and holds significant wealth. Approximately 3 million of the 300 million people in the country are considered upper class. Who are these people? Many are considered "old money"; their class standing comes from wealth, power, and prestige.[23] Others are entertainers or professional athletes who have generally earned, not inherited, their wealth. In his studies on the upper class, sociologist G. William Domhoff found that prerequisites for membership in this class may include attendance at an exclusive prep school, belonging to exclusive social clubs, and being born into a wealthy or powerful family.[24]

Upper Middle Class

The **upper middle class** consists of high-income members of society who are well educated but do not belong to the elite membership of the super wealthy. They tend to occupy professional positions with high prestige and hold places of authority in the workplace.[25] Their income usually exceeds $100,000 a year—enough for them to live comfortably—and they own property or other outside investments. Owning a small business, having a professional career, or holding a high-status job often guides a person into the upper middle class.[26] This group makes up about 15 percent of the U.S. population.

Social Class in the United States

Upper/ Elite Class

Middle Class

Working Class

Urban Underclass

Middle Class

As mentioned above, most Americans claim to belong to the middle class. If you're not rich and you're not poor, you should fall somewhere in the middle, right? Sociologists, however, have a more complex definition.

In general, **middle-class** people have moderate incomes. They vary from low-paid white-collar workers (e.g., teachers, policemen) to well-paid blue-collar workers (e.g., restaurant managers, factory foremen). Middle-class workers may be skilled laborers (e.g., plumbers), but they are generally not manual laborers. Members of the middle class have at least a high school diploma, and many have trade school or college experience. The middle class makes up approximately 34 percent of the U.S. population, and incomes of members in this group range from $40,000 to $80,000 per year.[27]

Working Class

The **working class** makes up about 30 percent of the population and comprises people who have completed high school and lower levels of education.[28] Most of its members hold jobs that require manual labor or clerical skills such as construction workers and bank tellers. Unlike those in higher classes, working-class citizens earn an hourly wage instead of a salary. Unfortunately, there are very limited opportunities for job improvement because they work by the hour and lack a formal education.

Lower Class

Those in the **lower class** are the ones who truly feel the effects of poverty. In the United States, close to 37 million people are in this category.[29] Members often live paycheck to paycheck, if they are employed at all. More than two-thirds of African Americans and 60 percent of Hispanics in the nation live near or below the poverty line.[30] Almost half of the children in the United States live in or near poverty, along with 10 percent of senior citizens.[31]

The Urban Underclass

The homeless and the chronically unemployed are classified as the **urban underclass**. Truly impoverished, they often live in substandard housing in neighborhoods with poor schools, high crime, and heavy drug use.[32] Some are lucky enough to receive financial assistance from the government. Members of this class rarely have health care coverage and often lack a high school education. The jobs they find are usually minimum-wage positions that propel them no higher than the low end of the working class. Despite all these disadvantages, sociologist William J. Wilson notes that both their lack of vision and lack of role models are what make it difficult for many to imagine any other way of life.[33] Yes, they are disadvantaged, experiencing broken homes, poor schools, and substandard housing, but what makes them truly disadvantaged is that they know of almost nothing else. This perpetuates the situation, as the young have very few positive role models that can show them how to escape poverty. This leads them to live their entire lives mired in many social problems without viable solutions.

THE EFFECTS OF SOCIAL CLASS

Neighborhoods

Recent studies show that people in the United States are increasingly segregating themselves by income. All one needs to do is to take a drive past the gated communities in the suburbs to know that spatial segregation between the rich and poor is increasing in the United States. It appears that the segregation of affluence is responsible for creating this pattern. As those with money move away from the poor, society becomes increasingly separated based on social class.[34]

So, how does growing up in a wealthy neighborhood affect a child? Studies have shown that children from these areas do better in school, have a lower risk of teen pregnancies, and have higher standardized test scores. In contrast, children who grew up in disadvantaged communities have lower birth weights, poorer health, and lower levels of education.[35]

Health

When you're sick, do you go to the doctor? Studies find that poor women with children, who frequently have insufficient diets, suffer from higher rates of mental depression and worse physical health than their wealthier counterparts.[36] Poverty influences access to food, and food influences both physical and mental health. A great body of research supports the notion that poor people generally have poor health.[37] This may be associated with a lack of medical care as well as other environmental factors. A poor child living in a home with broken windows may suffer from more colds than a child living in a middle-class neighborhood, for example.

Health and socioeconomic status (SES) have been found to be linked; those with a greater SES tend to enjoy better health, whereas those with a lower SES tend to have poorer health. Furthermore, poor health has been shown to have direct and significant effects on other issues as well. The outlook for educational attainment of sick children is not as promising as for healthy ones. Sick children grow into adults who have less education and earn less than their healthy counterparts. An individual's health influences his social stratification across a lifetime.[38]

UPPER or **ELITE CLASS** is a social class that is very small in number and holds significant wealth.

UPPER MIDDLE CLASS is a social class that consists of high-income members of society who are well educated but do not belong to the elite membership of the super wealthy.

MIDDLE CLASS is a social class that consists of those who have moderate incomes.

WORKING CLASS is a social class generally made up of people with a high school diploma and a lower level of education.

LOWER CLASS is a social class living in poverty.

URBAN UNDERCLASS is a social class living in disadvantaged neighborhoods that are characterized by four components: poverty, family disruption, male unemployment, and lack of individuals in high-status occupations.

Family

There are a variety of factors that differentiate families, but a particularly important one is social class. Are there predictable patterns of income directly related to the composition of families?

The U.S. Census Bureau has found correlations between family form and poverty rates. For example, female-headed households have poverty rates that are nearly three times higher than the national rate for all families.[39] Female poverty rates are also higher than the rates for households headed by single men.[40] Thus, family composition appears to be a main factor that affects whether or not children live in poverty. Since the 1970s, the poverty rate for children under 18 years old has been higher than the poverty rate for any other age bracket.[41] In fact, in 2007, children represented almost 36 percent of all the people in poverty, even though only 25 percent of the total population were children.[42] In recent years, the federal government has attempted to aggressively address this issue by attempting to curb non-marital pregnancy rates and stressing the importance of children's growing up in two-parent households.[43] However, is the difference in family composition appropriately linked to an increase in the rates of women giving birth outside of marriage?

In a 2006 article, Molly A. Martin discusses the history of family structure and its impact on social inequality.[44] She finds that two-parent households have the highest income levels, and female-headed households

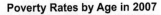

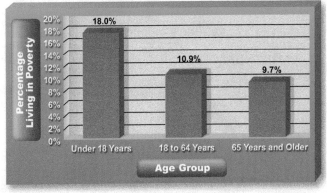

Poverty Rates by Age in 2007

Source: Data from Carmen DeNavas-Walt, Bernadette D. Proctor, and Jessica C. Smith, U.S. Census Bureau, Current Population Reports, P60-235, Income, Poverty, and Health Insurance Coverage in the United States: 2007, U.S. Government Printing Office, Washington, DC, 2008.

have the lowest. But, she asks, what are the reasons for female-headed households and how are these households perceived? Three possible reasons a woman might be raising children without a husband are divorce, death of spouse, or a conscious decision not to marry. The most common reason that children live in single-parent households is divorce. Children raised in homes in which their mother and father never married suffer not only from higher rates of poverty, but they also experience greater levels of social stigmatization. Families headed by widows have the highest social standing among mother-only families, whereas those headed by divorced women are somewhere in the middle. Martin notes that non-marital fertility is on the rise in the United States and remains an important contributing factor to the likelihood of children growing up poor.[45]

Education

It's true that, in the United States, a free 12-year education is available to every child regardless of family or class. However, not all educational opportunities are the same. In a two-year study of public schools, Jonathan Kozol found that the schools he visited in urban communities frequently lacked basic educational supplies. In some cases, chemistry labs didn't have beakers or test tubes and students were forced to share textbooks.[46] Meanwhile, suburban schools often had a surplus of supplies and staff.

What accounts for such dramatic differences? Kozol found that the answer lay in the very structure of the system. Because local taxes fund schools, places with higher property taxes receive more educational funding. Children living in poor urban areas need more help but actually get less. Therefore, he concluded that educational equality does not exist in United States.[47] Because poor neighborhoods lack access to high-quality education, most residents are denied opportunities to overcome poverty.

Social Mobility

Those of us who are lucky enough to win big at Mega Millions or invest in the right stock at the right time might soar quickly to upper-class standing. In a poor economy, however, we might as easily be laid off and subsequently plunge into poverty. These are examples of **social mobility**, a term that describes the ability to change social classes. If you've ever played the board game *Chutes and Ladders*, you know that players can climb ladders to the top or slide down chutes to the bottom, depending on the number they roll. Social mobility works in much the same way. According to sociologists, different patterns of social mobility occur.

Horizontal mobility refers to moving within the same status category. For example, a paralegal who leaves one law firm for a position at another law firm across town experiences horizontal mobility. In this example, the

> V
> V Is life just a game of Chutes and Ladders? **As long as social mobility is possible, our lives**
> V **can always take a turn for the better—or for the worse.**

What Is Social Mobility?

CHUTES and LADDERS Social mobility can be a result of making a wise investment or getting laid off. How do you think this possibility for change affects the lower class? The upper class?

paralegal is earning the same amount of money and performing the same tasks, she is simply employed at a different firm in a different location. **Vertical mobility** involves moving from one social status to another. For example, if the same paralegal completed law school and passed the bar exam to become a lawyer, this exemplifies vertical mobility because, with her passing the bar exam, she has entered a higher social status.

Intragenerational mobility occurs when an individual changes social standing, especially in the workforce. An employee who works his way up from the mail room to senior executive is experiencing intragenerational mobility.

Intergenerational mobility refers to the change that family members make from one social class to the next through generations. Many of your relatives probably immigrated to the United States as members of the lower class and never dreamed of ever being able to achieve the level of education that you have achieved. If you hope to someday live a better life than your parents did, you too are hoping for upward intergenerational mobility.

Structural mobility occurs when social changes cause many people to change social status simultaneously. Whether you're a member of the upper or lower class, there's always a chance that something could happen that would drastically change your status. Think of the recent economic slump. Large numbers of workers have been laid off, and the job market is more competitive than in previous years, causing large groups to shift in social class. Research suggests that the downward structural mobility of low-skilled workers whose jobs have been sent overseas contributes significantly to the wage inequality of the United States. In short, when workers lose factory jobs, they often replace those jobs with ones offering lower pay and fewer benefits. This downgrade has influence on the inequality of this country.[48]

The concept of **exchange mobility** suggests that within the United States, each social class contains a relatively fixed number of people. As some families move into a higher class, others must move down. The data we saw earlier on the changes in income over time support the idea that social stratification levels change very little. However, they don't tell us whether the people who make up each layer have stayed there or exchanged places in the meantime.

What Do Societies Do About This?

HISTORY OF POVERTY

Throughout human history, there have always been people who are poor. The roots of the popular U.S. viewpoint of poverty have their origins in European, particularly British, ideals. The system of welfare and care for the needy arose from the religious concepts of charity and compassion for the less fortunate.

The Elizabethan "Poor Law" of 1601 was the first real law dealing with "welfare and poverty" in Britain.[49] What was the reason behind this? It was simply that churches could no longer adequately handle the job. The Elizabethan Poor Law attempted to accomplish four things: separate the church from the delivery of social services, eliminate begging and crime in the streets, bring social assistance under government control, and set standards to determine those eligible to receive help and the amount of help they should receive.[50] Since that time, a great many changes in policies toward the poor have occurred both in Britain and the United States. However, both countries share an ideology for welfare and a "Protestant work ethic" of hard work, thrift, and individualism.[51]

SOCIAL MOBILITY is the ability to change social classes.

HORIZONTAL MOBILITY refers to moving within the same status category.

VERTICAL MOBILITY refers to moving from one social status to another.

INTRAGENERATIONAL MOBILITY occurs when an individual changes social standing, especially in the workforce.

INTERGENERATIONAL MOBILITY is the change that family members make from one social class to the next through generations.

STRUCTURAL MOBILITY is when social changes affect large numbers of people.

EXCHANGE MOBILITY is a concept suggesting that, within the United States, each social class contains a relatively fixed number of people.

TRANSITIONAL POVERTY refers to a temporary state of poverty that occurs when someone goes without a job for a short period of time.

From the time of the colonies through the Civil War, welfare in the United States was largely left up to the local areas. However, because of large numbers of injured soldiers and increases in immigration, the need to help the poor became greater than many localities could handle. Two welfare ideas arose. The first was the settlement house movement. Neighborhood centers already provided educational, social, and cultural activities, but the settlement houses provided social services and financial assistance. Settlement houses were based on three key concepts: Social change could occur, social class distinctions could be narrowed through information and education, and change could only come when social workers immersed themselves in the neighborhoods they served.[52]

The second movement was the Charity Organization Society. They held that a foundation of "moral beliefs" was essential to combat poverty and that individuals were personally responsible for their plight and could overcome it.[53]

Perhaps the key historical event in the United States in a discussion of poverty is the Great Depression of 1929. The country experienced massive unemployment, with millions seeking assistance from volunteer organizations and completely overwhelming the system. President Franklin D. Roosevelt's New Deal was the answer to the devastated United States. This was a revolutionary, wide-reaching plan to save the economy. The main focus was on aiding struggling farmers, reforming questionable financial and business practices, and promoting the recovery of the economy. Later, the Social Security Act of 1935 further alleviated poverty in the ranks of the elderly, widowed, unemployed, and disabled.[54]

The Great Society and War on Poverty of the 1960s and 1970s attempted to address poverty with the formation of new social programs, which included the Peace Corps, Job Corps, Head Start, and Volunteers in Service to America (VISTA). Additional enhanced and expanded programs included Medicare, Medicaid, the Older Americans Act, and the Food Stamp Act.[55]

HOW DOES THE UNITED STATES DEFINE POVERTY?

"Are you poor?" I often ask my students. Most immediately say yes and then they pull out their iPhones to text their friends during class. But what does it mean to be poor? Sociologists often divide poverty into five separate categories. **Transitional poverty** is a temporary state that occurs

MARGINAL POVERTY refers to a state of poverty that occurs when a person lacks stable employment.

RESIDUAL POVERTY refers to chronic and multigenerational poverty.

ABSOLUTE POVERTY refers to poverty so severe that one lacks resources to survive.

RELATIVE POVERTY is a state of poverty that occurs when we compare ourselves to those around us.

GINI INDEX is scale that measures incoming inequality.

DECILE RATIO measures the distance between income groups in the top 10 percent and the bottom 10 percent by averaging the income of the highest group and dividing it by the average income of the lowest group.

U.S. Department of Health and Human Services Poverty Guidelines, 2011 (for the 48 Contiguous States and District of Columbia)	
Number of Persons in Family	Poverty Guideline
1	$10,890
2	14,710
3	18,530
4	22,350
5	26,170
6	29,990
7	33,810
8	37,630

For families with more than eight persons, add $3,820 for each additional person.

Source: *Federal Register*, Vol. 76, No. 13, January 20, 2011, pp. 3637–3638, http://aspe.hhs.gov/poverty/11fedreg.shtml

when someone goes without a job for a short period of time. **Marginal poverty** occurs when a person lacks stable employment. A handyman bouncing between jobs is experiencing marginal poverty. The next, more serious level, is **residual poverty**. This type is chronic and multigenerational. A family living in residual poverty will pass the poverty on to their children, who will pass it to their children, and on and on down the line. People who experience **absolute poverty** are so poor that they don't have the resources necessary to survive. Farmers starving to death in the Orissa region of India are living in absolute poverty. **Relative poverty** is a state that occurs when we compare our financial standing and material possessions to those around us. You might experience relative poverty if your friend pulls out the latest smartphone, and you're still using a flip phone. You feel poor because you're comparing yourself to others who have more than you, when, in fact, neither of you is really poor. On the flip side, if you live in a poor neighborhood but drive a fancy car, your neighbors are experiencing relative poverty.

The U.S. government has different standards for defining poverty. Using a benchmark known as the poverty line, the government can determine what services are needed by whom. If you fall below the poverty line, you're eligible to receive health care, food, and career aid from the government. If your income is above the poverty line, however, you receive little or no government assistance.[56]

The poverty line dates from 1963–1964, when Mollie Orshansky, an analyst at the Social Security Administration, developed the official U.S. poverty thresholds. The thresholds, now updated for inflation, were originally calculated by multiplying three times the cost of an economy food plan. These calculations were made based on the assumption that people spend about one-third of their income on food.[57] But what are the actual dollar amounts? In the United States, how low does your yearly income have to be for you to be living below the poverty line? The table above provides this information.

Can you predict any problems associated with this system? For one, using a national standard for poverty can be misleading. Living in a beautiful 2,500-square-foot house in a suburb in Texas can easily cost less than living in a cramped Manhattan apartment. Because the poverty line is identical in 48 states, cost-of-living issues aren't accounted for.[58]

Gender issues also come into play, since women are more likely to be poor than men. Even in this day and age, a woman still earns three-quarters of what a man who hold the same job makes.[59] As a result, poverty in the United States is mostly concentrated in female-run households.[60]

▶▶▶ GO GL⊕BAL

Measuring Inequality: The Gini Index and Decile Ratio

The Gini index and the decile ratio are two measures that quantify income inequality . The **Gini index** uses a scale from zero to one, where zero represents perfect equality, in which every person receives an equal share of total income, and one represents perfect inequality, in which only one person controls 100 percent of the income. The higher the Gini index, the higher the level of inequality. Internationally, Sweden boasts the lowest income inequality, with a Gini coefficient of 0.23, while Namibia has the highest, at 0.70. In 2009, the United States had a Gini index of 0.468, meaning that the gulf between the rich and poor was greater than in Canada, the United Kingdom, Denmark, Norway, Sweden, Finland, Germany, France, Egypt, and Tunisia. That same year, the poverty level was higher than it had been in 15 years, yet the 400 richest Americans saw an 8 percent gain in their combined net worth.[61] The **decile ratio** measures the distance between income groups in the top 10 percent and the bottom 10 percent by averaging the income of the highest group and dividing it by the average income of the lowest group. This measure also ranks the United States higher than other wealthy, industrialized, and free countries in terms of inequality.[62]

think social problems: HOW DO SOCIOLOGISTS VIEW INEQUALITY?

> **MERITOCRACY ARGUMENT** states that those who get ahead in society do so according to their own merit.
>
> **BLAMING THE VICTIM** refers to the act of accusing those who suffer from a social problem for that problem.

Functionalism

According to functionalists Kingsley Davis and Wilbert Moore, every system tends toward equilibrium, and so the inequality of the United States is inevitable—even essential—for society to function smoothly.[63] We need janitors and garbage collectors as well as surgeons and astronauts. But why do janitors make so much less than doctors?

Society has various positions that need to be filled; the more important the position is, the rarer the skill or the longer the training period required for it. Generally, these jobs have greater rewards in order to entice people to take them. Thus, the occupations that are greatly rewarded in our society are the ones that require the most skills. This idea suggests that the United States is a meritocracy, a country in which people can rise to the top if they have special skills and/or abilities. The **meritocracy argument** states that those who get ahead in society do so based on their own merit.

Conflict Theory

Conflict theorists generally follow the ideas of Karl Marx, noting that stratification occurs because the proletariat (workers) are exploited by the bourgeoisie (owners). How does the meritocracy argument hold up against this line of thinking? Sociologist Melvin Tumin argued against Davis and Moore, offering a different point of view. Few things affect a person as much as his or her social class. Being born into a wealthy family opens doors to high-quality education and college degrees (the necessary training) that establish a person for a life of affluence. I know a family with three generations of medical doctors. Do they have the "doctor gene," or are their children socialized to think about going to medical school? Tumin also questions the logic that important jobs must necessarily offer high pay to get people to do them. Not so. Consider why kindergarten teachers, soldiers, and firefighters are paid so little. Is there some other type of reward, perhaps social respect, that these people might receive? Why does it have to be money? Furthermore, don't we need soldiers more than we need professional baseball players? Yet who reaps the monetary rewards from society? Something doesn't quite fit the meritocracy argument here. Tumin suggests that we reward certain occupations because we're forced to. We want to watch pro baseball, so teams

fight for the best hitters and pitchers. We need heart surgeons, but they are so rare that they can demand high salaries. Those who receive proper training are also rare. Many people cannot afford college. Does that mean they can't be doctors? Probably not.

Symbolic Interactionism

Interactionists often look at the meaning behind social problems. Does social class really matter? Look around a college campus. Can you distinguish working-class students from upper middle-class students by their clothing or cell phones? Some of my students who come from homes with higher SESes aren't forced to make the tough financial decisions that students from working-class families have to make. It is not uncommon for a student to ask me, "Will I really need the book?" Usually, this student comes from a working-class family and frequently struggles with success in college.

William Ryan suggests that when people look at inequality, they tend to view those at the bottom as creators or co-creators of their problem. He refers to this as **blaming the victim**. In short, it involves blaming those who suffer from a social problem for that problem. So, if you consider the issue of poverty, it is often easy to make assumptions about why people suffer from it. Perhaps they dropped out of school at a young age. Perhaps they waste money on lottery tickets. Maybe they have a drug or alcohol problem. Part of the process of blaming the victim involves saying any of these issues are the cause of poverty. Students who support such a claim often say, "If they'd just stop drinking, they'd be able to keep a job," as if getting over an addiction is as easy as turning off a light switch. Furthermore, we know that the *cause* of any social problem is far more complex than any simple statement, but that doesn't stop our habit of

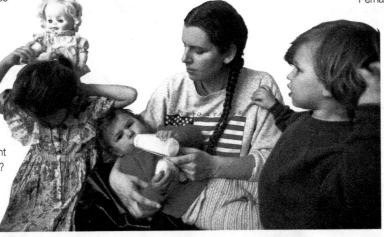

∧ ∧ ∧ Contrary to stereotypes, **families on welfare are not living easy on government money.**

blame. Ryan believes that such a process ignores the structural problems of the society, such as lack of good jobs, low pay, and preexisting inequalities.[64] Sociologist William J. Wilson (2009) suggests that this mentality of blaming the victim prevents us from actually seeing the social structural problems that lead to inequality. Certainly, many who are poor have made poor choices, yet it's not fair to say all poor people have done so.[65]

In her book *So You Think I Drive a Cadillac?*, author Karen Seccombe investigates the social stigma associated with female welfare recipients and suggests that some of them even blame themselves. Of the women she interviews, many use denial as a way of coping with the negative feelings associated with being on welfare.

WRAP YOUR MIND AROUND THE THEORY

Author J. K. Rowling was a single mother on welfare before the success of the *Harry Potter* series. **What factors might have contributed to her rise in society?**

FUNCTIONALISM

Functionalism is based on the idea that stratification is a natural and necessary process in society. As the old saying goes, "The cream rises to the top." Thus, some suggest that your starting position on the economic ladder is not important—those who get ahead in society do so because of the decisions they make and the skills they possess. According to functionalists, the social class you start in has no lasting effect on the rest of your life.

CONFLICT THEORY

Conflict theory focuses on the struggle between those who have wealth and power and those who don't. To theorists such as Tumin, those born without the proverbial silver spoon will likely never obtain it. The rich do the best they can to stay rich, and their luxuries are passed on to the next generation. Wealthier families can provide their children with music lessons, private tutoring, and workplace connections, all of which contribute to a child's eventual success.

WHY DO SOCIETIES HAVE DIFFERENT SOCIAL CLASSES?

SYMBOLIC INTERACTIONISM

The better off a person is, the less he or she tends to perceive the effects of social class. To those in need, however, there is great shame in being poor. Society often frowns upon government aid, and those who qualify for Section Eight housing or welfare are looked down upon even by their peers.[66] Unfortunately, children raised in poor households set lower expectations for themselves than middle- or upper-class children do. Instead of "reaching for the stars," poor children grow up to find themselves trapped in a lifestyle similar to that of their parents.

Both George H. W. Bush and George W. Bush served as presidents of the United States. **How might the younger George Bush's upbringing have steered him toward this career choice?**

Begging for food or money **is a social stigma** in our society. **In what sort of environment do you think this man was raised?**

discover solutions to social problems:
WHAT SOCIAL POLICIES ADDRESS ECONOMIC INEQUALITY?

The Welfare System

As mentioned earlier, there is a harsh social stigma associated with those who receive welfare. As one of my students once put it, "I have to work, and they get to drive around in Hummers and live off the government!" Many people equate welfare with sitting at home living on the taxpayers' dime. Others insist that women at the poverty level have more children to increase benefits. However, few people take the time to understand the recent welfare reform and its results on the lower-class community.

Until 1996, the U.S. welfare system was run as an entitlement program. To demonstrate this, picture a burglar breaking into your house in the middle of the night. When you call the police, you expect them to come and help you no matter who you are, where you live, or how many times you've called the police before. In 1996, however, President Bill Clinton signed the Personal Responsibility and Work Opportunity Reconciliation Act. This act created the Temporary Assistance to Needy Families (TANF) program, which changed the welfare system drastically.

Let's say a burglar breaks into your house again and you call the police. However, this time you are told that you've already used up your two police requests and from now on, you're on your own. This is how the present welfare system works. Through the TANF program, a person is only allowed to receive government assistance for a total of five years total and only up to two years at a time. Among other ramifications, this means that that person's children will not receive aid throughout their childhood.

This restriction prevents freeloaders from living off of the system for years, right? Recent data show that two-thirds of those who were on Aid to Families with Dependent Children (the program in effect before TANF) were never on the program longer than two years. Less than 15 percent were continuous users of the system.[67] It seems that before TANF was put into

Poverty Rates Before and After Government Benefits

Country	Before	After
Sweden	26.7%	5.3%
Denmark	23.6%	5.3%
Austria	23.1%	6.6%
Norway	24.0%	6.8%
France	30.7%	7.1%
Finland	17.6%	7.1%
Netherlands	24.7%	7.7%
United Kingdom	26.3%	8.3%
Switzerland	18.0%	8.7%
Belgium	32.7%	8.8%
New Zealand	26.6%	10.8%
Germany	33.6%	11.0%
Italy	33.8%	11.4%
Canada	23.1%	12.0%
Australia	28.6%	12.4%
Greece	32.5%	12.6%
Spain	17.6%	14.1%
Ireland	30.9%	14.8%
Japan	26.9%	14.9%
United States	26.3%	17.1%
Average excluding U.S.	26.4%	9.8%

Source: Data from Organisation for Economic Co-operation and Development. http://www.stateofworkingamerica.org/charts/view/117.]

MAKE CONNECTIONS

Does Your Neighbor's Income Affect You?

Have you ever been the richest kid on the block? What about the poorest? Either way, you would have noticed that you had either relative advantage or disadvantage. The sociological question is how these issues might affect the happiness of a person who lives in such a setting. In general, those who live in a neighborhood surrounded by people who are wealthier than them tend to be happier. This does not mean that the poorest kid on the block does not feel some level of relative deprivation. Rather, it appears that this negative feeling is superseded by the benefits of being around those who have "more," raising feelings of prestige and improving happiness levels. So, buy the best house you can afford in a neighborhood where people will earn more than you, and you are likely to experience higher levels of happiness.[70]

>>> **Kramer from the hit show *Seinfeld* never held down a real job, and yet was able to enjoy a life of eccentric luxury.** Characters on TV shows often live financially impossible lives.

place, most were already living by its rules. Now, however, there is no support for the less than 15 percent of the population who are truly desperate.

One of the driving forces behind TANF was the emphasis on job training for the poor. It makes sense that higher education and increased skills translate into better paying jobs. However, because TANF assistance only lasts for two years at a time, long-term training options, such as obtaining a college degree, are impossible. Data show that the transition from welfare to work usually results in jobs that don't pay a living wage.[68] Spending the summer sweeping up popcorn or serving food for only $7.25 per hour may seem exasperating, but imagine doing it for the rest of your life. About 79 percent of minimum-wage workers are older than 25 years of age.[69]

There are actually two separate philosophies that guide the U.S. welfare system; we'll call them residual and institutional. What we have been discussing up until now is the former. **Residual welfare** is a system of relief intended for people with jobs whose earnings are not enough to support them. As we have seen, this aid is temporary, only used in emergencies and handed out as infrequently as possible. TANF is of this sort.

Alternatively, **institutional welfare** is part of the first line of defense against poverty. Assistance is offered on a preventive basis, and no time limit is imposed. Unlike residual welfare, no social stigma is attached. Because the money comes from the government and all citizens receive some form of governmental aid, it's seen as no more embarrassing than a tax deduction. Public schools, for example, qualify for institutional welfare. When I ask my students, "Who's on welfare?" only a few of them raise their hands. I then point out that because they attend a state college, their tuition is subsidized by taxpayers, and, in fact, all of them receive a form of institutional welfare. After hearing this, they become aware of the immediacy and relevance of welfare to their lives.

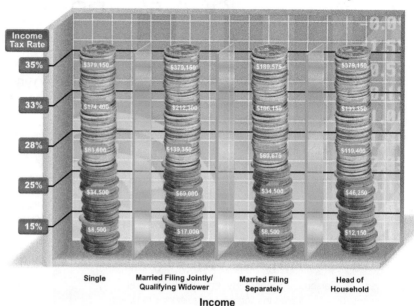

Income Tax Rates: What Percentage do the Poor Pay? What Percentage do the Rich Pay?

Source: Data from "2011 Tax Rate Schedules." http://www.irs.gov/publications/p505/ch02.html#en_US_2011_publink1000234349. Accessed November 21, 2011.

From Classroom to Community } Rags to Riches

As mentioned early in this chapter, purchasing a lottery ticket can often provide hope that the ticket could lift one out of poverty. Instead, it drags many people deeper into debt. As a part of her sorority's community service requirement, Eva volunteered at a human services office downtown where she witnessed this behavior with her own eyes.

"Once a week, this girl about my age would come in with two young boys to collect her check. One day she came to my window, and I commented on her adorable little brothers. She looked at me oddly and told me they were her sons.

"From then on, I got to know Alexia a little better. Over time, she told me about her life: How her mother had died when she was younger, how her boyfriend had left when she was pregnant with their second son, and how her father worked the graveyard shift as a security guard to support the family. My parents had divorced when I was 13, but that felt like nothing compared to Alexia's story.

"On my way home one night, I stopped at the 7-Eleven for a soda. I was standing in line when I noticed Alexia at the front with some friends. She had a stack of lotto tickets in her hands. I was in shock. There must have been over $100 there. I knew from her checks that she couldn't afford to throw away a single dime.

"Alexia turned and saw me. She seemed surprised, but greeted me cheerfully. I asked her how she could afford the tickets.

"Alexia rolled her eyes at me. 'Girl, you can't win it if you're not in it! My boys might have a millionaire mommy.'

"She left, and I walked home alone, that silly slogan from the state lotto commercials still ringing in my head. *You can't win it if you're not in it!* I realized she must have been buying tickets whenever she got the money to do so. It seemed like such a waste.

"Eventually, I was able to place myself in Alexia's shoes. I imagined living every day in poverty, seeing movie stars on TV and wishing I could live like them. With a lottery ticket, there was a small chance to escape into the good life. It gave people like Alexia hope, and blended the lines between the rich and the poor if only for a few moments of hopeful suspense.

"I saw Alexia a couple more times, and then she was gone. I asked around, and someone said she was living with her ex after her father kicked her out. Someone else said he'd seen her on the street. I never did find out what became of her, but every time I see a figure hunched over on the sidewalk, shaking a metal can, I can't help but think sadly, *You can't win it if you're not in it!*"

Taxation

Despite how it sometimes feels, having to pay taxes is not a punishment. Taxes pay for roads, parks, schools, firefighters, and even military protection. They're essential for successfully functioning in society.

The United States makes use of two separate forms of taxation: **progressive taxation** and **regressive taxation**. Generally, the country operates on a progressive tax system. People who earn more pay higher taxes. Even though your boss makes more than you, her income tax is higher than yours.

Regressive taxation technically charges everyone the same percentage of money, however this actually means that the poor pay a higher percentage than the rich do. If you go shopping with your wealthy friend, both of you will pay a 7 percent sales tax on the jeans you buy. Regressive taxes may seem fairer because everyone is charged equally; however, consider the example below:

	Aiden	Lilly	Nathan
Monthly income	$1,000	$5,000	$10,000
Price per gallon of gasoline	$4	$4	$4
Gallons used in a month	40	40	40
7% sales tax paid in dollars	$11.20	$11.20	$11.20
Percent of monthly income	1.12%	0.224%	0.112%

RESIDUAL WELFARE is a temporary system of relief when a person's job or family has failed to be enough to support them.

INSTITUTIONAL WELFARE is a preventive "first line of defense" against poverty. There is no time limit, and no social stigma is associated with receiving this aid.

PROGRESSIVE TAXATION is a system in which people who earn more pay higher taxes.

REGRESSIVE TAXATION is a system that taxes everyone the same percentage of money, but results in the poor paying a higher percentage than the rich.

Aiden ends up paying 10 times more of his monthly income in taxes than Nathan does. Although all three individuals are paying the same amount of monthly tax, its effect is much greater on Aiden. Generally, sales taxes on necessities are regressive. In theory, the United States has a progressive tax structure, but does it really? New research from economists Piketty and Saez calls this into question. Looking at federal tax rates by income and including both individual and corporate taxes, they find that the "progressive" nature of the U.S. tax system has dramatically declined. This is due to a drop in corporate taxes, gift and estate taxes, and taxes on income and capital gains—in short, all the things that Warren Buffett thinks should be raised. Thus, the notion of progressive taxation has been on a steady decline over the last 30 years, resulting in less revenue for the federal government from these sources. Could this decline be a part of our nation's high levels of inequality?[71]

Pro & Con

Progressive Taxes

Progressive taxes tax the wealthy at a higher rate than the poor. Is this a system the United States should continue?

Pro

- Progressive taxes are "fairer," allowing the less fortunate to pay less.
- This arrangement evens out the playing field, closing the gap between the rich and the poor.
- The system promotes political stability, since most of the nation's money isn't concentrated in the hands of a wealthy few.[72]
- Even with the current system of progressive taxes in place, the rich still pay nearly half what middle-class Americans do.[73] Stricter progressive taxes may need to be instituted.

Con

- More complex tax laws lead to more bureaucracy.
- The majority (middle to lower class) might continue to vote for higher taxes for the minority (higher classes). This is called "soaking the rich."
- Even though congress passes these higher tax rates, it also approves exclusions and deductions that give tax shelters to the rich, rendering the higher rates ineffective.[74]
- Economically, progressive taxes are inefficient, since they discourage the upper classes to work and invest, thus reducing the productivity of society.[75]
- Some studies argue that these taxes don't aid in redistribution of money, since the gap between the rich and the poor remains as wide as ever.

<<< **Warren Buffett may be one of the richest men in the world, but he's also the number one advocate of progressive taxes.** In 2007, Buffett made news when he traveled to Washington to convince Congress not to repeal a number of taxes on the rich, including a 55 percent estate tax. **"I see nothing wrong with those who have been blessed by this society to give a larger portion of their income to the society than somebody that's working very, very hard to make ends meet,"** Buffett said.[76]

WHAT IS INEQUALITY AND HOW DOES IT AFFECT PEOPLE?

the difference in income, wealth, power, and prestige that leads to social stratification in society

HOW DO SOCIOLOGISTS VIEW INEQUALITY?

functionalists: inequality is necessary for society to function smoothly

conflict theorists: social inequality begins at birth because of the struggle for limited resources; we reward certain professions (such as doctors) because we have no choice

symbolic interactionists: there is a social stigma associated with being poor, and children growing up in poor households set lower expectations for themselves than children from affluent families; the wealthier a person is, the less that person perceives social inequality

WHAT SOCIAL POLICIES ADDRESS ECONOMIC INEQUALITY?

welfare programs such as the Temporary Assistance to Needy Families; residual welfare temporarily aids citizens while institutional welfare acts as a first line of defense against poverty

get the topic: WHAT IS INEQUALITY, AND HOW DOES IT AFFECT PEOPLE?

Defining Economic Inequality
How Does Inequality Affect the Lives of People?

What Do Societies Do about This?
Functionalism
Conflict Theory

Symbolic Interactionism
The Welfare System
Taxation

Theory

FUNCTIONALISM

- different positions need to be filled in society, from busboys to marine biologists
- social inequality is necessary for a civilization to function properly
- the meritocracy argument claims that certain people get ahead in society because of their personal skills and drive

CONFLICT THEORY

- there are limited resources in the world that we all must compete for
- social inequality begins at birth, and mobility is limited

- we reward professions that are vital to our society (such as surgeons) because we're forced to do so

SYMBOLIC INTERACTIONISM

- the wealthier a person is, the less he or she perceives social class inequalities
- the poor are stigmatized in our society
- in general, poor children set lower expectations for themselves than higher-class children do

Key Terms

social stratification is the ranking of people and the rewards they receive based on objective criteria, often including wealth, power, and/or prestige.

income is the money received for work or through investments.

wealth is all of an individual's material possessions, including income.

quintiles are the five equal segments into which sociologists and economists divide the population, each group accounting for 20 percent (one-fifth) of the population.

median is the midpoint of a group of numbers ranked from lowest to highest.

power is the ability to carry out your will and impose it on others.

force is a type of power that occurs when you make someone do something against his or her will.

persuasive power refers to using direct or indirect methods to get what you want.

prestige is the level of esteem associated with one's status and social standing.

upper or **elite class** is a social class that is very small in number and holds significant wealth.

upper middle class is a social class that consists of high-income members of society who are well educated but do not belong to the elite membership of the super wealthy.

middle class is a social class that consists of those who have moderate incomes.

working class is a social class generally made up of people with a high school diploma and a lower level of education.

(continued)

lower class is a social class living in poverty.

urban underclass is a social class living in disadvantaged neighborhoods that are characterized by four components: poverty, family disruption, male unemployment, and lack of individuals in high-status occupations.

social mobility is the ability to change social classes.

horizontal mobility refers to moving within the same status category.

vertical mobility refers to moving from one social status to another.

intragenerational mobility occurs when an individual changes social standing, especially in the workforce.

intergenerational mobility is the change that family members make from one social class to the next through generations.

structural mobility is when social changes affect large numbers of people.

exchange mobility is a concept suggesting that, within the United States, each social class contains a relatively fixed number of people.

transitional poverty refers to a temporary state of poverty that occurs when someone goes without a job for a short period of time.

marginal poverty refers to a state of poverty that occurs when a person lacks stable employment.

residual poverty refers to chronic and multigenerational poverty.

absolute poverty refers to poverty so severe that one lacks resources to survive.

relative poverty is a state of poverty that occurs when we compare ourselves to those around us.

Gini index is scale that measures incoming inequality.

decile ratio measures the distance between income groups in the top 10 percent and the bottom 10 percent by averaging the income of

the highest group and dividing it by the average income of the lowest group.

meritocracy argument states that those who get ahead in society do so according to their own merit.

blaming the victim refers to the act of accusing those who suffer from a social problem for that problem.

residual welfare is a temporary system of relief when a person's job or family has failed to be enough to support them.

institutional welfare is a preventive "first line of defense" against poverty. There is no time limit, and no social stigma is associated with receiving this aid.

progressive taxation is a system in which people who earn more pay higher taxes.

regressive taxation is a system that taxes everyone the same percentage of money, but results in the poor paying a higher percentage than the rich.

Sample Test Questions
These multiple-choice questions are similar to those found in the test bank that accompanies this text.

1. A lawyer moving to another law firm downtown is an example of
   a. exchange mobility.
   b. transitional mobility.
   c. horizontal mobility.
   d. stratified mobility.

2. Joe works hard in college and graduates at the top of his class. However, due to the bad economy, he can only find work as a gas station attendant. How would a functionalist account for this?
   a. Because he was previously successful, Joe set low goals for the future.
   b. Joe does not have the skills or drive necessary to find a higher-paying job.
   c. Being a student is not a vital position in our society, and Joe is now experiencing the effects of wasted time.
   d. This situation is to be expected due to the limited resources of a poor economy.

3. A migrant worker would most likely experience
   a. marginal poverty.
   c. residual poverty.
   b. absolute poverty.
   d. relative poverty.

4. Which is an example of progressive taxation?
   a. The wealthy paying estate taxes
   b. A sales tax on imported products
   c. Your poor friend being taxed the same percentage of money as you
   d. A tax increase to spur the economy

5. The lottery can best be described as
   a. an easy opportunity for vertical mobility.
   b. a practice that promotes hopelessness in the lower class.
   c. a tax on the poor.
   d. a source of income for the rich.

ESSAY

1. How would both a functionalist and a conflict theorist explain occupational prestige?
2. Do you think a person living off capital gains would support progressive taxation or regressive taxation?
3. Do you believe that the income gap is increasing? Take into account the concept of exchange mobility and the graph of U.S. income change that appears in this chapter.
4. How might a person in marginal poverty view TANF?
5. Knowing what you do now, would you still consider yourself "middle class?" Why or why not?

WHERE TO START YOUR RESEARCH PAPER

For more information on the U.S. poverty line, go to
http://aspe.hhs.gov/poverty/09poverty.shtml

For information about social policies in place to alleviate poverty, go to
http://www.whitehouse.gov/issues/poverty/

For more information about the U.S. welfare system, go to
http://www.welfareinfo.org/

To view how the progressive rate has varied over time, go to
http://www.treasury.gov/education/fact-sheets/taxes/ustax.shtml

ANSWERS: 1. c; 2. b; 3. a; 4. a; 5. c

Remember to check www.thethinkspot.com **for additional information, downloadable flashcards, and other helpful resources.**

End Notes

1. Gus Lubin and Antonina Jedrzejczak, "The 10 Cheapskate Billionaires Who Live Like Paupers," *BusinessInsider*, April 5, 2010, http://www.businessinsider.com/frugal-billionaires-2010-4?op=1.

2. Warren E. Buffett, "Stop Coddling the Super-Rich," *The New York Times,* August 14, 2011, http://www.nytimes.com/2011/08/15/opinion/stop-coddling-the-super-rich.html?_r=1&pagewanted=print.

3. "State Governments and Lotteries," *Consumers' Research Magazine,* 1999. 82(8): 12–14.

4. National Gambling Impact Study Commission, "Lotteries," Accessed July 7, 2009, http://govinfo.library.unt.edu/ngisc/research/ lotteries.html.

5. William C. McConkey and William E. Warren, "Psychographic and Demographic Profiles of State Lottery Ticket Purchasers," *The Journal of Consumer Affairs,* 1987. 21(2): 314–327.

6. Charles T. Clotfelter and Phillip Cook, "On the Economics of State Lotteries," *The Journal of Economic Perspectives*, 1990. 4(4): 105–119; "State Governments and Lotteries," *Consumers' Research Magazine,* 1999. 82(8): 12–14.

7. Philip Carl Salzman, "Is Inequality Universal?" *Current Anthropology,* 1999. 40: 31–61.

8. Sergio Diaz-Briquets and Jorge Perez-Lopez, *Corruption in Cuba: Castro and beyond.* Austin: University of Texas Press, 2006.

9. U.S. Census Bureau, "Share of Aggregate Income Received by Each Fifth and Top 5 Percent of Households, All Races: 1967 to 2009," http://www.census.gov/compendia/statab/2011/tables/11s0693.xls.

10. Ibid.

11. Ibid.

12. Carmen DeNavas-Walt, *Current Population Survey, Annual Social and Economic Supplements.* Washington, DC: Government Printing Office, 2006.

13. David Cay Johnson, *Perfectly Legal: The Covert Campaign to Rig Our Tax System to Benefit the Super Rich and Cheat Everybody Else.* New York: Penguin Group Inc., 2003.

14. Ibid.

15. Ibid.

16. Ibid.

17. Ibid.

18. Max Weber, *Readings in Social Theory: The Classical Tradition to Post-Modernism.* New York: McGraw-Hill, 2004.

19. Lawrence Mishel, Jared Bernstein, and Sylvia Allegretto, *State of Working America 2006/2007.* Ithaca, NY: Cornell University Press, 2007.

20. G. William Domhoff, *Who Rules America? Power and Politics.* New York: McGraw-Hill, 2002.

21. Mark Haugaard, "Reflections on Seven Ways of Creating Power," *European Journal of Social Theory,* 2003. 6(1): 87–113.

22. Elia Kacapyr, "Are You Middle Class? Definitions and Trends of the U.S. Middleclass Households," *American Demographics,* 1996. 18: 30–36.

23. Austin Scaggs, "Paris Hilton," *Rolling Stone,* 2004. 964: 92–94.

24. G. William Domhoff, *Who Rules America? Power and Politics.* New York: McGraw-Hill, 2002; G. William Domhoff, *The Higher Circles.* New York: Random House, 1970.

25. Harold R. Kerbo, *Social Stratification and Inequality: Class Conflict in Historical, Comparative and Global Perspective, 6th Edition.* New York: McGraw-Hill, 2006.

26. Dennis Gilbert, *The American Class Structure in an Age of Growing Inequality.* Belmont, CA: Wadsworth, 2003.

27. Ibid.

28. Ibid.

29. Ibid.

30. Carmen DeNavas-Walt, Bernadette D. Proctor, and Cheryle Hill Lee, "Income, Poverty and Heath Insurance Coverage in the United States: 2005," *Current Population Reports,* 2007. http://www.census.gov/prod/2004pubs/p60–226.pdf.

31. Ibid.

32. Ibid.

33. Ibid.

34. Sean F. Reardon and Kendra Bischoff, "Income Inequality and Income Segregation," *American Journal of Sociology,* 2011. 116(4): 1092–1153.

35. Jeanne Brooks-Gunn, Greg Duncan, Pamela Klebanove, and Naomi Sealand, "Do Neighborhoods Influence Child and Adolescent Development?" *American Journal of Sociology,* 1993. 99: 353–395; Catherine L. Garner and Stephen W. Raudenbush, "Neighborhood Effects on Educational Attainment: A Multilevel Analysis," *Sociology of Education,* 1991. 64: 251–262; Gary Solon, Marianne Page, and Greg J. Duncan, "Correlations Between Neighboring Children and Their Subsequent Educational Attainment," *Review of Economics and Statistics,* 2000. 82: 383–393.

36. Jeanne Brooks-Gunn, Greg Duncan, Pamela Klebanove, and Naomi Sealand, "Do Neighborhoods Influence Child and Adolescent Development?" *American Journal of Sociology,* 1993. 99: 353–395.

37. Jonathan Kozol, *Savage Inequalities: Children in America's Schools.* New York: Crown Publishers Inc., 1991.

38. Vincent Roscigno, Donald Tomaskovic-Devey, and Martha Crowley, "Education and the Inequalities of Place," *Social Forces,* 2006. 84: 2121–2145.

39. Carmen DeNavas-Walt, Bernadette D. Proctor, and Jessica C. Smith, *Current Population Reports, P60-235, Income, Poverty, and Health Insurance Coverage in the United States: 2007.* Washington, DC: U.S. Government Printing Office, 2008.

40. Ibid.

41. Ibid.

42. Ibid.

43. White House, "Working Toward Independence," Accessed March 11, 2007, http://www.whitehouse.gov/news/releases/2002/02/welfare-reform-announcement-book.pdf.

44. Molly A. Martin, "Family Structure and Income Inequality in Families with Children, 1976 to 2000," *Demography,* 2006. 43(3): 421–445.

45. Ibid.

46. Jonathan Kozol, *Savage Inequalities: Children in America's Schools.* New York: Crown Publishers Inc., 1991.

47. Ibid.

48. Ted Mouw and Arne L. Kalleberg," Do Changes in Job Mobility Explain the Growth of Wage Inequality Among Men in the United States," *Social Forces*, 2010. 88(5): 2053-2078.

49. Frank J. McVeigh and Loreen Wolfer, *Brief History of Social Problems: A Critical Thinking Approach*. Lanham, MD: University Press of America, 2004.

50. Ibid.

51. Ibid.

52. Ibid.

53. Ibid.

54. Ibid.

55. Ibid.

56. U.S. Department of Health and Human Services, "Frequently Asked Questions Related to the Poverty Guidelines and Poverty," Accessed July 15, 2008, http://aspe.hhs.gov/poverty/faq.shtml.

57. U.S. Department of Health and Human Services, "The Development and History of the U.S. Poverty Thresholds—A Brief Overview," Accessed July 15, 2009, http://aspe.hhs.gov/poverty/papers/hptgssiv.htm.

58. Ibid.

59. Carmen DeNavas-Walt, Bernadette D. Proctor, and Cheryle Hill Lee, "Income, Poverty and Heath Insurance Coverage in the United States: 2005," *Current Population Reports*, 2007. http://www.census.gov/prod/ 2004pubs/p60-226.pdf.

60. United States Department of Health and Human Services, "Special Populations of American Homeless," Accessed July 15, 2008, http://aspe.hhs.gov/progsys/homeless/symposium/2-Spclpop.htm.

61. "Superrich Americans Driving Income Inequality," National Public Radio, September 23, 2010, http://www.npr.org/templates/story/story.php?storyId=130052776.

62. Andrea Brandolini and Timothy Smeeding. "Inequality: International Evidence," The New Palgrave Dictionary of Economics, March 2007, http://www.irp.wisc.edu/aboutirp/people/affiliates/Smeeding/12-Palgrave_0407.pdf.

63. Kingsley Davis and Wilbert E. Moore, "Some Principles of Stratification," *American Sociological Review,* 1944. 10: 242-249.

64. William Ryan, *Blaming the Victim, Revised Edition*. New York: Vintage Books, 1976.

65. William Julius Wilson, *More Than Just Race: Being Black and Poor in the Inner City.* New York: W.W. Norton and Company Inc., 2009.

66. Kathryn Edin and Laura Lein, "Stratification Processes: Women, Work, and Wages: Work, Welfare, and Single Mothers' Economic Survival Strategies," *American Sociological Review,* 1997. 62: 253-266.

67. "Dethroning the Welfare Queen: The Rhetoric of Reform," *Harvard Law Review*, 1994. 107: 2013-2030.

68. Kathryn Edin and Laura Lein, "Stratification Processes: Women, Work, and Wages: Work, Welfare, and Single Mothers' Economic Survival Strategies," *American Sociological Review*, 1997. 62: 253-266.

69. U.S. Department of Labor, Bureau of Labor Statistics, "Characteristics of Minimum Wage Workers: 2008," Accessed July 9, 2009, http://www.bls.gov/cps/minwage2008.htm.

70. Glen Firebaugh and Matthew B. Schroeder, "Does Your Neighbor's Income Affect Your Happiness?" *American Journal of Sociology*, 2009. 115(3): 805-831.

71. Thomas Piketty and Emmanuel Saez, "How Progressive is the U.S. Federal Tax System? A Historical and International Perspective," *Journal of Economic Perspectives*, 2007. 21(1): 3-24.

72. Marjorie E. Kornhauser, "The Rhetoric of the Anti-Progressive Income Tax Movement: A Typical Male Reaction," *Michigan Law Review*, 1987. 86(3): 465-523.

73. "Warren Buffett: The Rich Need to Pay More Taxes," *ABCNews.com*, November 15, 2007, http://abcnews.go.com/GMA/story?id53869458&page51.

74. Marjorie E. Kornhauser, "The Rhetoric of the Anti-Progressive Income Tax Movement: A Typical Male Reaction," *Michigan Law Review*, 1987. 86(3): 465-523.

75. Ibid.

76. "Warren Buffett: The Rich Need to Pay More Taxes," *ABCNews.com*, November 15, 2007, http://abcnews.go.com/GMA/story?id53869458 &page51.

Credits

Credits are listed in order of appearance.

PHOTO CREDITS

Global Inequality

GLOBALIZATION AND INEQUALITY

G20 FRANCE 2011
NOUVEAU MONDE, NOUVELLES IDÉES

GLOBALIZATION
AND INEQUALITY

If you

have been paying attention to the news recently, you have probably heard stories about the European debt crisis. On the heels of global recession, public debt in Greece has reached levels so high that many people have said it will be necessary for the Greek government to default on at least part of its debt. Because Greece is part of the eurozone, a group of European Union countries that all use the euro as their currency, Greek's debt directly affects the financial stability of all other eurozone countries. Other eurozone countries, led by Germany and France, have attempted to solve the crisis through bailouts, but the crisis continues and appears to be spreading to other countries such as Ireland, Spain, Portugal, and Italy.

President Barack Obama recently held a news conference to discuss the U.S. economy, and he named the European debt crisis as a key factor in the slow recovery of the U.S. economy following the global recession. This is because the economies of countries throughout the world have become more intertwined than ever before through globalization. As Treasury Secretary Timothy Geithner said, "Our direct financial exposure to those governments and their financial institutions is quite small, but Europe is so large and so closely integrated with the United States and world economies that a severe crisis in Europe could cause significant damage by undermining confidence and weakening demand."[1]

During the news conference, President Obama said that he discusses the issue regularly with Chancellor Angela Merkel of Germany and President Nicolas Sarkozy of France, and he wants to see a concrete plan of action from the Group of 20, finance ministers from 20 of the world's largest economies, when it meets next month. He also acknowledged, however, that it is difficult to get anything done in the European Union, because it requires the agreement of 27 different governments. This is one of the many new challenges the world faces as globalization continues to spread. As the economies of different countries become more intertwined, their governments must make more decisions together. It remains to be seen if these governments will rise to the challenge.

---When I look at the clothes in my closet, what do I see? There are shirts made in Pakistan, shoes made in China, jeans from Mexico, and so forth.

In fact, my world is interconnected to all parts of the world through the products I own. Look in your closet; you'll see that most of your clothes come from different countries as well.

This is because of globalization, which we'll discuss in detail in this chapter. In the 1960s, Marshall McLuhan declared the world a "global village" because of the impact of immediate communications.[2] Technology helps us interact with the world, and it helps the world interact with us. For example, let's say a typhoon hits the coast of China, an event that you watch on TV. But do you notice when the price of shoes rises? That occurrence may be a direct result of the typhoon and its effect on Chinese manufacturing. Today, this international trend continues not just because of rapid communication but also because of globalization.

The world is more interconnected than we might think. Go to the grocery store and look around: The strawberries are from Mexico, the bananas are from Ecuador, and both types of fruit are presented to us on metal racks that are made with Brazilian steel. Although this interconnection can help nations such the United States acquire more goods at lower prices, how does it affect poorer countries? What social problems might occur when developing nations sell off their resources or their labor to build manufacturing plants that employ low-paid workers to produce these goods? How does society respond to the social problems that are linked to globalization? We'll explore these questions and more throughout this chapter.

get the topic: WHAT IS GLOBALIZATION AND HOW DOES IT AFFECT THE WORLD?

GLOBALIZATION is a complex process by which the world and the international economy are becoming more and more intertwined.

GLOCALIZATION occurs when countries seek to combine the local and the global into a unique structural blend to maintain their native customs while fitting into the global environment.

BRAIN DRAIN occurs when the best talent leaves poor countries and thereby provides an even greater advantage to wealthy countries.

Globalization

Today, nations are becoming much more closely linked through business, travel, immigration, health issues, and the production of goods.[3] **Globalization** is a complex process by which the world and its international economy are growing more and more intertwined. As a result, the consequences of one nation's actions become shared by all. This can, in theory, bring about a convergence in the world as people from different areas become increasingly alike and have more and more shared experiences. On the other hand, globalization can also create a backlash against external forces, increasing the strength of the local community.[4] For example, across the globe, the English language is expanding, mostly as a language of commerce. This is in large part because of the colonial history of Great Britain, but more recently because of the economic power of the United States. Those who wish to engage in international business generally learn the English language, which allows the world to converge even more. At the same time, some nations are placing great emphasis on saving their native languages, in fear that these dialects will be eliminated by this trend. **Glocalization** occurs when countries seek to combine the local and the global into a unique structural blend to maintain their native customs while fitting into the global environment.[5]

What exactly drives globalization is a debated issue. Is it the force of capitalism, causing some nations to seek cheaper labor so that prices can remain low? Is it a desire to spread political principles throughout the world? Is it a product of greed and consumption, causing countries to need more and more "stuff," even if these products are not available locally? The truth is that all of these notions are interrelated in the motivation toward globalization; no one cause can explain this trend.[6]

PROBLEMS ASSOCIATED WITH GLOBALIZATION

Sometimes, the lean toward globalization can have negative effects. Different countries have different natural resources to offer, and they may sell these resources to become part of the global game. Furthermore, many poor nations have rapidly growing populations, which results in large numbers of young people seeking work. Having an abundant supply of workers allows employers to pay less and less for the labor. There has been a great deal of controversy over exploitation and "sweatshop" labor as big manufacturers outsource work to poorly managed factories in developing countries.[7]

Additionally, increasing globalization has also encouraged trade between nations, although existing trade agreements do not always promote free trade. Instead of leveling the playing field between nations, these agreements sometimes have the opposite effect—they benefit wealthy nations and put poorer nations at a greater disadvantage. For example, the United States and European nations provide subsidies to agribusinesses, making it cheaper to produce crops. These foods are then exported to developing countries, where local farmers are unable to compete with the lower prices of these goods. As a result, local farmers stop producing certain foods, and when prices rise for imported goods—due to fuel costs or other reasons—the local poor are unable to afford basics such as rice and soy.[8]

Another problem that has arisen from globalization is **brain drain**. This occurs when individuals with the greatest talents leave poor countries, thereby providing an even greater advantage to wealthy countries.[9] This occurs throughout the world as developing nations send their best and brightest to the developed world where work, education, and other opportunities abound. These men and women are able to enjoy better standards of living and higher salaries than they would otherwise. But how does this affect the countries that they left?[10]

One concern with brain drain is that developing nations who send their best and brightest generally receive nothing in return; while they lose those with the most ability and talent, the receiving nations reap the benefits of having even more talented and intelligent people in their society. This is particularly true for small nations, which have much higher likelihoods of losing their most educated individuals.[11] In this way, brain drain only helps widen the gap between wealthy and less fortunate nations.

Many of the best and brightest from foreign nations have relocated to wealthier nations. What are the worldwide effects of brain drain?

GLOBALIZATION AND CULTURE

One of the questions surrounding globalization is whether it unites the world culturally. It's not uncommon to see citizens in other countries eating Big Macs or wearing Dallas Cowboy shirts and Nike tennis shoes. Certainly, globalization influences the spread of material culture throughout the world. Some suggest that because of this expansion of common influences, our differences will eventually become nonexistent; in the future, all cultures may meld into one large homogenous society.[12]

GLOBALIZATION AND MIGRATION

Globalization influences migration patterns in ways that do not only involve brain drain. Recently there has been a rapid increase in international migration. The influx of people—both legal and illegal—is associated with various social problems. For example, foreign workers represent increased competition for jobs. Mexican President Felipe Calderon has warned the United States that renegotiating NAFTA will cause many more Mexicans to cross the U.S. border desperately seeking jobs. With unemployment on the rise, a number of American workers view this as a significant problem. As a result of this and other issues, many developed nations are now seeking policies to slow the rate of immigration. In the United States, for example, the government has built

fences along the Mexican border in an effort to minimize undocumented entry. Migration can also create a backlash against the people who enter a new country, resulting in issues of violence, victimization, and abuse.[13]

Globalization has resulted in roughly 3 percent of the world's population living outside their nation of birth. As I write this, two of my family members are living in other countries, while at least two others are considering taking jobs in New Zealand and India. This increase in interaction and travel means that diseases can also spread more easily. West Nile virus—an illness that infects mosquitoes and birds—came to the United States from Africa, most likely transported here by travelers or in containers with agricultural products.[14] Recent fears over the spread of avian flu (H5N1) and swine flu (H1N1) are influenced by the migration of people around the world. Clearly, interconnectedness is not always a positive thing for our health.

Are these issues social problems? It probably depends on which side of the globe you're sitting. When capitalist nations use developing countries as a source of cheap labor, it can have negative effects on the poor citizens of those nations while at the same time benefiting consumers in the wealthy nations. In a sense, the price of cheap clothing in the United States is borne on the backs of the underpaid workers in Bangladesh and elsewhere.[15]

But some see it a different way. The opposing point of view suggests that globalization is a major opportunity for poorer nations to improve their economic status. Another interesting question raised in the debate is whether cultures around the world are becoming more similar as a result of working together more closely. Some suggest that the world's cultures are adopting more Western values. On the flip side, others feel that globalization is causing local groups to work harder to maintain their own customs, religions, and languages.[16]

How Did the World Become Stratified?

Exactly how human societies arose is beyond the scope of this chapter. However, globalization is related to how the world is divided between the rich and the poor. At the earliest point in human history, all humans were on equal footing, and yet we know that some societies advanced technologically, whereas others did not.

There are a lot of factors that contribute to how quickly a society develops. In his book *Guns, Germs, and Steel,* author Jared Diamond explains why the Western world advanced so quickly and other regions of the world did not. Climate, geography, and available natural resources all played a role, as did the ability to use trade and interaction for the citizens' own advantages. Gunpowder, for example, was developed in China but the use of it for weapons was perfected by Europeans, who learned the power of this material through the process of trade—a precursor to globalization today. An increase in trade results in an increase in knowledge, which allows civilizations to flourish through an improved quality of life.[17]

Over many centuries, Europeans became powerful by using the information they gained from other parts of the world, as well as those they developed themselves to increase their relative wealth. Intercontinental struggles led to the development of alliances, technologies, increased trade for goods, and the spread of knowledge into Europe. These trends continue today through globalization.[18]

Global Stratification

Poverty exists in all parts of the world, but the biggest gaps in social inequality are not within nations but between them. **Global stratification** is the categorization of countries based on objective criteria such as wealth, power, and prestige, which highlight social patterns and inequality throughout the world. For instance, although the United States still struggles with social problems related to poverty, the standard of living is extremely high in a global context.

INCOME

Income is difficult to use to measure the standard of living of an entire population, as it is not evenly distributed, and not all countries are the same size. However, sociologists often use a country's **per capita income** as a marker. This is calculated by dividing the country's total gross income by the number of people in that country. The majority of top income-producing countries are in Europe, and most of the bottom income-producing countries are in Africa. The wealthiest U.S. citizens have a larger share of the national income than wealthy citizens in other nations. Beneficial taxation policies allow affluent U.S. citizens to keep more of their income by paying less in taxes than their counterparts in other developed nations.[19]

UNDERDEVELOPED NATIONS AND STRATIFICATION

A country is considered an underdeveloped nation if it is relatively poor and has not yet been industrialized. The United Nations provides some assistance to underdeveloped countries based on three criteria: (1) The country must have a low gross national income; (2) the population must meet health and education criteria; and (3) population size and proximity to other developed nations must be taken into consideration.

Some countries are considered developing or in the process of becoming industrialized. Issues such as poverty and hunger still affect these countries, though not as greatly as in underdeveloped countries.

The sub-Saharan region of Africa is the most disadvantaged area in the world. Infant mortality, childhood death, hunger, and poverty rates are worse there than anywhere else. Poor sanitation also leads to high rates of illness and death.[20] Those living in impoverished areas have control over their lives but are certainly limited by the low standards of living. It is difficult to get ahead when food and resources in your country are scarce. Does globalization aid these people? The consensus is no. Generally, development in these areas is rare. Add to this the reality that many of these countries have unstable political environments, and you can see that globalization may take a long time to help these nations climb out of poverty.[21]

Two major dividing factors between modern developed and underdeveloped nations are communication and literacy. You probably don't stop to think when you use these throughout your day—communication through e-mail, text messaging, and more is common in the United States. Access to these forms of technology is low in underdeveloped countries, however, which provides a distinct disadvantage in communication. Literacy is more or less taken for granted in the United States but not in all parts of the world. When people lack the ability to read, they are forced to take unskilled, labor-intensive jobs to support their families. For example, the United Nations estimates that literacy rates for adults in the developed world stand at about 95 percent, whereas those same rates are only about 62 percent in sub-Saharan Africa.[22]

Modern-Day Slavery?

One serious problem related to globalization and the extension of capitalism throughout the world involves increasing levels of slavery around the globe. In his book Disposable People: New Slavery in the Global Economy, sociologist Kevin Bales estimates that 27 million people are currently enslaved around the world. In some parts of the world, human trafficking includes individuals (often women) sold into prostitution by family members.[23] This modern form of slavery does not quite fall into the same category as slavery in the past. Slavery in the past was legal, and owners viewed slaves as long-term investments. Today, however, slaves are disposable; once they

>>> **Camel racing** is a popular sport in many Middle Eastern countries. Because of their light weight, **children are traditionally used as jockeys,** and over the years, this has led to a profitable child trafficking industry. It's estimated that, because of this sport alone, **over 40,000 children are currently living as slaves** in the Middle East and South Asia.

Asian Human Rights Commission, "Child Jockeys: 40,000 children on slave labour as 'child camel jockeys' in Middle East and Arab countries," Accessed November 13, 2009, http://acr.hrschool.org/mainfile.php/0205/390; UNICEF, "Child camel jockeys return home," Accessed November 13, 2009, http://www.unicef.org/infobycountry/pakistan_27517.html.

Gross National Income Per Capita, 2009

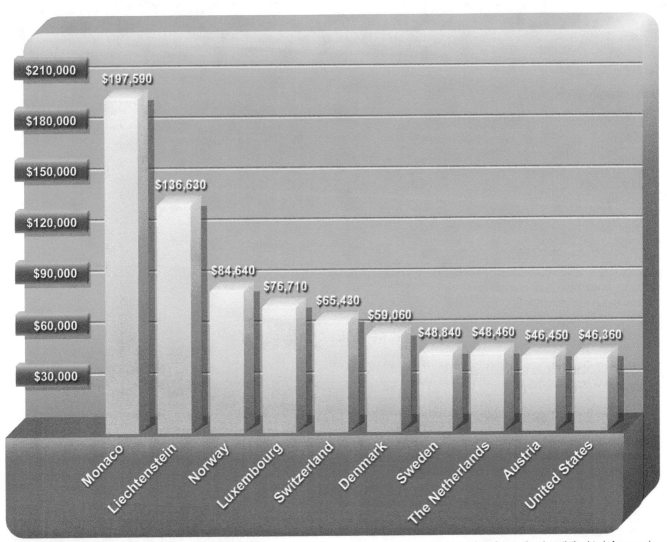

$210,000	$197,590 (Monaco)
$180,000	$136,630 (Liechtenstein)
$150,000	
$120,000	
$90,000	$84,640 (Norway)
	$76,710 (Luxembourg)
	$65,430 (Switzerland)
$60,000	$59,060 (Denmark)
	$48,840 (Sweden) $48,460 (The Netherlands) $46,450 (Austria) $46,360 (United States)
$30,000	

Source: Data from the U.S. Census Bureau, "2012 Statistical Abstract," http://www.census.gov/compendia/statab/cats/international_statistics.html. Accessed October 12, 2011.

Average Wealth by Region, 2000				
Region (Number of Countries)	Share of World Population (%)	Wealth Per Capita (PPP$)	Share of World Wealth (%)	Share of World GDP (%)
North America (5)	5.2	138,417	27.1	23.6
Latin America and Caribbean (46)	8.6	19,781	6.4	8.6
Europe (48)	12.0	62,024	28.1	25.7
Africa (56)	13.4	5,225	2.6	3.9
China	20.6	11,267	8.8	10.3
India	16.8	6,513	4.1	5.9
Rich Asia-Pacific (17)	4.0	102,846	15.6	12.1
Other Asia-Pacific (55)	19.5	9,684	7.2	10.0

Source: Data from James B. Davies, Susanna Sandström, Anthony Shorrocks, and Edward N. Wolff, "Estimating the Level and Distribution of Global Household Wealth," http://www.wider.unu.edu/publications/working-papers/research-papers/2007/en_GB/rp2007-77/. Accessed October 12, 2011.

Globalization and Inequality

Average Poverty by Region, 2011

Region	Percent Living on Less Than $1.25 a day	Percent of Children under Age 5 Who Are Underweight	Percent with Improved Water	Percent with Improved Sanitation
Northern Africa	2.6	6	87	89
Sub-Saharan Africa	50.9	22	47	31
Latin America and the Caribbean	8.2	4	80	80
East Asia	15.9	6	82	56
South Asia	38.6	43	83	57
Southeast Asia	18.9	18	81	79
Western Asia	5.8	7	78	94
Central Asia	19.2	5	80	96
Least Developed Countries	53.4	23	76	53

Source: Created by author. Data from the United Nations, "The Millennium Development Goals Report," http://mdgs.un.org/unsd/mdg/Resources/Static/Data/2011%20Stat%20Annex.pdf. Accessed October 12, 2011.

▶▶▶ GO GL◉BAL

Poor Countries and the World's Economy

Throughout late 2008 and 2009, the state of the world's economy was a hot topic. The United States faced the worst economic downturn since the Great Depression, and other countries suffered in the wake of that loss. The recession had the greatest impact on developing countries. The growth forecast for developing nations was 7.7 percent in 2007 but fell to 1.2 percent in 2009.[29] Leaders of these countries were, in many ways, powerless to do anything about the world's economic problems. Because their nations were already relying on aid from the wealthier countries of the world, they were unable to offer a financial contribution to the solution. However, leaders of developing countries were quick to point out the necessity of their role in economic reform. "Reforms are needed to enhance productivity and capacity to cope with risks," said Bangladeshi Foreign Minister Dipu Moni on behalf of the world's poorest nations.[30]

After drafting a plan, the United Nations held a three-day summit to discuss possible reforms that would turn the economy back around. During their talks, the UN attempted to find solutions that would aid developing countries, where a continued economic crisis could mean an additional 200,000 infants dying each year from malnutrition or disease.[31] Nobel Laureate in Economics Joseph Stiglitz suggested that the plan set out in the draft was inadequate. The plan called for the World Bank, as well as lenders across the globe, to be flexible with developing countries, an idea that Stiglitz said limited the power of change to the richest nations. The 20 key economic powers represented in the UN account for 80 percent of the global economy; however, Stiglitz insisted that all 192 members of the UN should be included in the decision-making process.[32]

Stiglitz further called for a change in how wealthier countries provide aid to developing countries. Grants, rather than loans, should be used for aid, Stiglitz argued, in order for countries to avoid a debt crisis. Chinese Foreign Minister Yang Jiechi presented the plan to keep exchange rates stable. He said that taking this action would further aid developing countries, allowing them to "make more effective use of external funds for their development."[33]

>>> As **Joseph Stiglitz notes,** although globalization has proceeded at a staggering rate, **we have yet to create a global financial institution.**[34] What issues might arise from an attempt to form a universal economy?

Poverty Rates of Developed Countries

Country	Percent of Total Population in Poverty	Percent of Children in Poverty	Percent of Children in Poverty after Taxes and Welfare Transfers	Percent of Elderly in Poverty
United States	17.0	26.6	21.9	24.7
Ireland	16.5	24.9	15.7	35.8
United Kingdom	12.4	25.4	15.4	20.5
Canada	11.4	22.8	14.9	5.9
Denmark	9.2	11.8	2.4	6.6
Germany	8.3	18.2	10.2	10.1
France	8.0	27.7	7.5	9.8
Belgium	8.0	16.7	7.7	16.4
Austria	7.7	17.7	10.2	13.7
Switzerland	7.6	7.8	6.8	18.4

Source: Data from Lawrence Mishel, Jared Bernstein, and Sylvia Allegretto, *State of Working America 2004/2005* (Ithaca, New York: Cornell University Press, 2005).

> ∧∧∧ Although the United States ranks high in per capita income, a large percentage of its citizens are living in poverty. Why do you think this is the case?

are used up, they are released.[24] Although they may be given their freedom, the physical and mental condition in which most slaves are released is poor. In Thailand, female prostitutes are often HIV positive, mentally ill, or both. When given their freedom, they are essentially left to die on the streets.[25]

Even though slavery is illegal everywhere, it is common for companies to use slave laborers in their factories around the world. **Contract slavery** is a form of slavery in which a person signs a work contract, receiving food and shelter from an employer, but is threatened when he or she tries to leave.

Although you may think that these workers' difficulties do not affect you directly, you're wrong. Even if you avoid buying certain clothing or shoe brands, you may still unknowingly buy products that are indirectly related to slave labor. According to Bales, most of the products available on the market today were either produced under or are somehow related to slave labor.[26] Globalization, the pursuit of cheap labor, rapid population growth, weak local governments, and consumer desires for cheap goods all contribute to the fact that we now have more slaves on the planet than at any other time in history. Bales asks the question, "Are we willing to live in a world with slaves?"[27] For most of us, the knee-jerk reaction to this question is "no!" even though our spending habits indicate otherwise. But how do we abolish this new form of slavery? Our system of living seems to encourage it.

One reason slavery is so difficult to eradicate is because of an idea Ritzer calls grobalization. **Grobalization** refers to the idea that capitalist countries use their corporate interests to expand their power throughout the world. These groups seek to constantly increase their influence, until expanded influence becomes an end in and of itself. Grobalization increases profits for companies as well as control. Of course, this influence often comes at the expense of the environment and the freedom of the people who live in the nations that are exploited.[28]

DEVELOPED NATIONS AND STRATIFICATION

We have discussed underdeveloped nations, but what exactly qualifies a nation as "developed"? Some characteristics of developed nations are a

CONTRACT SLAVERY is a form of slavery in which a person signs a work contract, receiving food and shelter from an employer but is threatened when he or she tries to leave.

GROBALIZATION refers to the idea that capitalist countries use their corporate interests to expand their power and influence throughout the world.

well-educated population, regular elections, abundant industry, and free enterprise. The United States, Germany, Japan, and Great Britain are all examples of developed countries. Living in a developed nation is certainly a privilege compared to living in an underdeveloped nation, but it's not a guarantee that one will be privileged. As you can see in the chart above, a large percentage of citizens in developed countries still live in poverty.

The United States is a good example—it may have a high per-capita income, but the huge gap between the rich and the poor leaves many in poverty. In fact, the United States has the highest percentage of people living in poverty of any developed nation, with 17 percent of the total population below the poverty line, even after taking into account government-sponsored programs such as welfare. Of the 21 wealthiest nations in the world, the distance between the top 10 percent of incomes and the bottom 10 percent of incomes is the greatest in the United States. In the 1990s, the incomes of the top 10 percent were 5.64 times higher than incomes in the bottom 10 percent. This means that if the bottom 10 percent made an average of $20,000 a year, the top 10 percent made 5.64 times more, or $112,800! This is a sizable gap, to say the least. In contrast, Sweden has the lowest ratio, with the top 10 percent earning 2.59 times more than the bottom 10 percent. In Sweden, if the average income for the bottom were $20,000, the average income for the top would be $51,800.[35]

QUALITY OF LIFE

What characteristics make a country a desirable place to live? One way to measure quality of life in a country is to measure health and longevity.

<<< According to Kai Müller, **Norway ranks top in quality of life,** whereas the United States doesn't even make it into the top 20.[40]

A country with a low infant mortality rate and a long life expectancy seems as though it would have a high quality of life. Andorra, a small nation in Europe, has the highest life expectancy in the world at 83.5 years, while Swaziland in southern Africa has the shortest at 31.9 years.[36] Singapore has the lowest infant mortality rate at 2.3 deaths per 1,000 babies born, whereas the impoverished nation of Angola has 80 times that rate, with 184.4 deaths per 1,000 births.[37] So, does this mean that Andorra and Singapore are the best places to live? Not necessarily. There are many other factors to consider in quality of life.

Income is an important measure. Other measures include access to telephones, televisions, and newspapers. Sociologists and economists also take measures such as debt ratio and gross national product into consideration. Kai Müller created a ranking system based on all of these criteria.[38] Using this system, Müller determined that Norway is the best country in the world in which to live and the Democratic Republic of Congo is the worst.

With the exceptions of Japan, New Zealand, Australia, and Canada, all of the top 20 ranked countries are located in Western Europe. The bottom 20 countries are all in Africa. You may be surprised to learn that the United States is not considered one of the 20 best countries in which to live.

Of course, this a subjective study, and results can vary greatly depending on how you weigh different factors. Daniel Slottje conducted a different study using older data but similar variables. Slottje found the United States to be the 13th best country to live in and Switzerland to be the first.[39] Regardless of the criteria used, it's clear that every country does not boast the same quality of life, and some countries are better places to live in than others.

think social problems: WHAT ARE THE THEORIES ABOUT GLOBALIZATION?

NEOCOLONIALISM is a process by which powerful nations use loans and economic power to maintain control over poor nations.

Conflict Theory

WALLERSTEIN'S WORLD SYSTEMS THEORY

When I was in college, we learned that the world was divided into three parts: the first, second, and third worlds. The first world was made up of the United States and our allies, the second was made up of the Soviet Union and their allies, and the third contained everyone else. Sociologists do not use this system today for a number of reasons. First, this system is based on political and economic ideologies, and is largely ethnocentric, placing the Western world first. Second, the Soviet bloc has largely dissolved. Third, putting 60 percent of the world into one category fails to provide an accurate description of the differences among these nations.

Immanuel Wallerstein's world systems theory, however, provides an alternative to the old theory. He suggests that the world is divided by connections to economic power. The core is made up of nations that are constantly trying to expand their markets, decrease costs, and increase profits. These nations are at the core because their economies largely influence the actions of the rest of the world.[41]

Because these core nations are constantly seeking expansion, they find ways to enter periphery countries. As we discussed, colonization was the popular method in the past but is no longer practiced in the same way. Today, core nations use multinational corporations and loans to tap into the periphery nations. Periphery nations, in turn, seek to benefit by generating wealth through these arrangements. Nigeria and Iraq are examples of desirable periphery nations, as they have abundant natural resources such as natural gas and oil.

If a periphery nation can generate enough wealth to stabilize its economy, select members of that society will begin to develop industries of their own. When a country reaches this level, it is considered semi-periphery—a developing nation that uses its raw materials to create goods that can be sold to core nations to generate more wealth. Continued industrial advancement will improve the economy, giving the nation a chance to move closer to the core. Brazil and South Korea are current examples of semi-periphery nations.

External nations are located outside this sphere. These are underdeveloped nations that have little interaction with the rest of the system. A lack of natural resources often makes it difficult for these countries to attract investors or interest from the core nations. Examples of external nations are Burundi, Chad, and many of the countries of sub-Saharan Africa. External nations have little to no economic impact on other nations.

NEOCOLONIALISM

The United States is no stranger to conquest and colonization. As you know, the United States developed from a series of colonies settled by Europeans. Sociologist Michael Harrington asserts that a new kind of colonialism exists in the modern world. He calls it **neocolonialism**, a process by which powerful nations use loans and economic power to maintain control over poor nations.[42] Poor nations become dependent on wealthier nations for food, weapons, and development through the

World Systems Theory

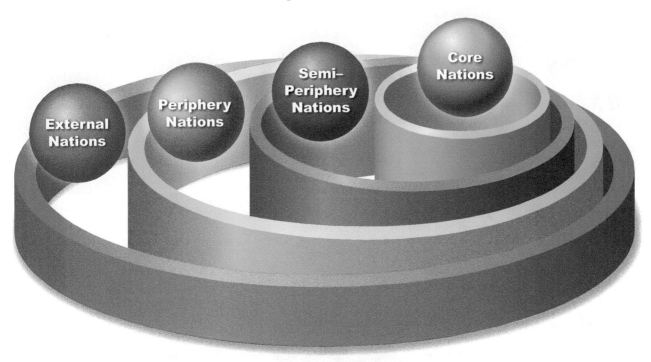

Source: Adapted from data from Wallerstein's The Modern World Systems, 1974.

According to Wallerstein, **the world is divided into countries with different levels of economic power.**

use of loans. This debt is often too great for the poor nations to repay, so they have to agree to alliances, sale of natural resources, and trade agreements that mostly benefit the wealthier nations.

The idea of neocolonialism extends to wealthy nations that use multinational corporations to control poorer nations. These corporations provide jobs and income to the poorer nations, and benefit greatly by gaining tax-free status in that nation, or by other concessions that are not in the best interest of the poorer country. The conditions in manufacturing plants in poor countries are often disastrous. It's unlikely that executives of these companies want to be involved in slave labor, but they are under pressure to maximize profits.

Through the use of outsourcing, multinational corporations allow wealthy countries to control weaker ones through corporate investment. The jobs provided are often the only opportunities that these workers have, and poor countries are easily enticed to perform hard labor to make money.

For Thomas Friedman, such interconnection means that the world is growing increasingly "flat." Through the interconnection between nations caused by low-cost communications, the world is becoming a place where those with means can win at the expense of those without them. In such a system, the weak will end up falling farther and farther behind. For example, throughout the world, outsourced jobs in the service sector require certain skills: speaking English, understanding accounting, programming computers, and so forth. In such a setting, American businesses are likely to further outsource jobs to areas of the world where English is spoken and workers require lower pay for the same skill set. This is all made possible as the world flattens

through use of rapid and cheap intercommunication technologies such as the Internet.[43]

Symbolic Interactionism

At the conclusion of World War II, European nations decided to work together to prevent future wars. Meetings of diplomats led to treaties that ultimately led to the creation of the European Union. The European Union has grown from simple trade relations between six countries to a collection of more than 20 nations.[44]

The countries of the European Union have a weak central government to handle trade disputes among nations, a common currency (the euro), and an increasingly common language (English). There is no military force exclusive to the European Union, but the North Atlantic Treaty Organization (NATO) has troops that come from a variety of European Union nations and the United States.

If the European Union banded together to form a single nation, it would be the wealthiest, most powerful country in the world. T. R. Reid notes that Europeans are in fact seeing themselves less as members of specific nations and more as members of the European Union. What might such a definition mean for globalization? There have already been considerable results. Many of the world's largest banks and most successful businesses have risen to prominence in the European Union. The E.U. makes more scientific discoveries than any other country. Additionally, E.U. countries have the highest standards of living in the world, and, as you can see in the chart on page 249, Europeans work fewer hours while receiving more paid vacation time than United States workers.[45]

WRAP YOUR MIND AROUND THE THEORY

Many wealthy countries have corporate interests in underdeveloped nations. **Globalization creates jobs in poorer countries, but at what cost?**

FUNCTIONALISM

Functionalists believe that stratification is mostly a result of geographic conditions. Historically, certain areas thrived while others did not as a result of these differences. Today, globalization benefits not only the countries that have risen to prominence but also the poorer nations around the world. Globalization brings needed wealth and technology, which helps less developed nations advance.

CONFLICT THEORY

Conflict theorists feel that the imbalance of power between the rich and the poor creates stratification. This is true on a national as well as domestic scale; in the United States, the gap between wealthy people and poor people is significant. Internationally, this gap exists between rich and poor nations. Recall Wallerstein's world systems theory, in which core nations use periphery nations to get what they need or want. This creates competition and conflict between these nations. As the world "flattens" due to cheap technologies, Friedman suggests that only those with the necessary skills will survive, while others will be left behind. Certainly, each country is trying to get ahead, with its own best interests in mind. The external nations are perceived to have nothing to offer the rest of the world and are left to fall by the wayside.

HOW DOES GLOBALIZATION INFLUENCE THE LIVES OF PEOPLE?

SYMBOLIC INTERACTIONISM

Symbolic interactionists look at how language and symbolic events affect society. T. R. Reid suggests that, since the formation of the European Union, Europeans increasingly identify themselves as citizens of a continent, rather than the individual country of which they were born. If the EU were to form a United States of Europe, it would be the world's greatest superpower. What impact might this have on the long-term influence of Europe over the rest of the world?

Conflict theorists believe that stratification is caused by the imbalance of power between the rich and the poor. **What chance do poor nations have to get ahead?**

The European Union has changed the way Europeans view their nationalities. **How would the world be different if they decided to unite further?**

Average Weekly Working Hours

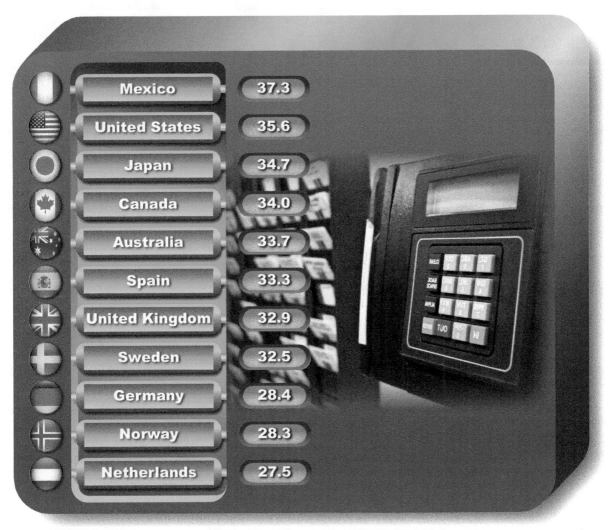

Country	Hours
Mexico	37.3
United States	35.6
Japan	34.7
Canada	34.0
Australia	33.7
Spain	33.3
United Kingdom	32.9
Sweden	32.5
Germany	28.4
Norway	28.3
Netherlands	27.5

Source: Data from the Organisation for Economic Co-operation and Development (OECD), 2010.

> People in the United States work more hours per week than residents of most other developed countries. **Does this affect quality of life?**

discover solutions to social problems:
HOW DOES SOCIETY DEAL WITH GLOBALIZATION?

Foreign Aid

I have had students up in arms about the issue of foreign aid. The most common argument is "Why should I pay huge amounts of tax dollars to other nations when there are people in my own country who are in need?" This is a valid question, as the United States certainly has its fair share of poverty. But does this mean that we should adopt a strictly isolationist policy and let the rest of the world fend for themselves? The U.S. government does not think so.

The government's stance on foreign aid is as follows: "Helping the world's poor is a strategic priority and a moral imperative. Economic development, responsible governance, and individual liberty are intimately connected. The United States must promote development programs that achieve measurable results—rewarding reforms, encouraging transparency, and improving people's lives."[46] This policy sounds good on paper, but does it help or hinder the world in practice?

The stated purpose of foreign aid by the United States is that it aids the strategic interests and safety of the nation while also promoting development and freedom in the underdeveloped parts of the world. This strategy should benefit all countries involved, both those giving aid and those receiving it. Many of the world's wealthiest countries have agreed to donate 0.7 percent of their gross national product to foreign aid. However, only the top five wealthiest countries have met this goal.

Total Dollar Amount and Percent of GNI Given to Foreign Aid, 2009

Country	Amount (In Millions of U.S. Dollars)	Percent of GNI	Country	Amount (In Millions of U.S. Dollars)	Percent of GNI
Sweden	4,548	1.12	Germany	12,079	0.35
Norway	4,086	1.06	Austria	1,142	0.30
Luxembourg	415	1.04	Canada	4,000	0.30
Denmark	2,810	0.88	Australia	2,762	0.29
Netherlands	6,426	0.82	New Zealand	309	0.28
Belgium	1,006	0.54	Portugal	513	0.23
Finland	2,610	0.55	United States	23,831	0.21
Ireland	1,290	0.54	Greece	607	0.19
United Kingdom	11,491	0.52	Japan	9,469	0.18
France	12,600	0.47	Italy	3,297	0.16
Spain	6,584	0.46	Total of EU countries	67,418	0.44
Switzerland	2,310	0.45	TOTAL	120,000	0.31

GNI = gross national income, the total amount produced by that nation (GDP) plus incomes received from other countries

Source: Created by the author. Data from the Organisation for Economic Co-operation and Development, "Statistical Annex of the 2009 Development Co-operation Report," http://www.oecd.org/document/9/0,3343,en_2649_34447_1893129_1_1_1_1,00.html. Accessed October 12, 2011.

The table above is sorted by percentage of gross national income given to foreign aid. While the United States ranks first in number of total dollars provided, it falls at 19th on the list, donating only 0.21 percent of its gross national income to countries in need. This translates into less than one-third of what has been promised. You may wonder, perhaps, how private donations compare to official ones. Among these same nations, the United States still provides the most dollars in private foreign aid, but ranks 10th in its percentage of GNI (0.49 percent). The United Kingdom ranks first in private donations, contributing 2.6 percent of its GNI. So, is the United States really the most generous country? If you consider the matter in terms of total dollars, then the answer is yes. If you're talking about a percentage of income, the answer is no. Which do you think is more important?[47]

MAKE CONNECTIONS

Inequality Comparisons

Data on inequality shows interesting things. The table below shows you the Gini index for the selected countries. The Gini index is a measure of inequality where a 0 would represent perfect equality and 1 would indicate complete inequality. The higher the number, the more inequality. You'll quickly notice that no country has total equality, but the United States has a greater rate of inequality than any similar country.

These data show only a few selected countries; however, a review of international statistics shows some interesting comparisons. According to the United Nations, the most unequal place on Earth is Angola, with a Gini index of 58.6. In fact, the countries in the world with an index over 0.5 are all located in either Africa or South America. By these numbers the United States is the 41st most unequal country on the planet, making our inequality worse than countries like Vietnam (48), India (54), and Canada (71).[48] How might such inequality affect opportunities for social mobility in these nations?

Country	Gini index	Country	Gini index
United States	0.47	Germany	0.28
United Kingdom	0.36	Sweden	0.25
Australia	0.35	Japan	0.25
France	0.33	Denmark	0.25

Pro & Con

Globalization

Across the globe you will find people with differing opinions on globalization. When political, cultural, and economic boundaries blend together, some countries benefit more than others. Globalization can encourage familiarity with cultural norms outside your own personal beliefs. It also allows companies to do business in multiple countries. However, although developed countries often see the benefits of a global economic market, developing countries are less likely to see any profit from the elimination of boundaries. What are the arguments for and against the continuation of this international trend?

Pro

- Globalization is a possible solution to the world's economic crisis.
- Globalization allows for the expansion of business; having a global market allows goods and services to move across borders.
- Globalization creates global standards of living and human rights, and decreases discrimination against minorities by encouraging familiarity with people of different races, ethnicities, and cultures.
- By developing worldwide regulations and standards for working conditions, globalization can end the use of sweatshops and child labor and promote the development of environmentally friendly technologies.

Con

- Globalization creates many of the world's economic hardships.
- Globalization allows industrialized countries to gain control over the economic development of developing countries.
- Globalization spreads disease and increases migration, which, in certain situations, leads to conflict.
- When multinational companies outsource labor and build manufacturing plants in other countries, resources (and therefore profits) are being taken from these poorer countries.

From Classroom to Community } Medical Aid in Botswana

Tamara is a nursing student who spent three months of her summer vacation working as a medical assistant in Botswana. Her job was to aid the doctors in educating the poorer communities on health practices as well as administering medications.

"It was sometime after winter break that I learned Dr. Koeller was making the trip to Africa with his church. I thought I knew what to expect when I signed up, but I was surprised by what I saw when we finally arrived in the first village. Having lived in a large city for most of my life, I was used to seeing the poor and homeless, but this was so much worse. More than half of the town was HIV positive, and some suffered from malaria or typhoid. Since they were far from the city, the people relied on local doctors who traveled between towns, and those who were ill were malnourished due to the parasitic tapeworms that spawned in the river water. I walked two miles with the other missionaries just so we could bring back clean water to wash our hands before seeing patients.

"Dr. Koeller had gotten his hospital to donate vaccines for the children. I was surprised that some children were 12 years old and had never been vaccinated for diseases I'd been inoculated for as a baby. I learned that measles was common in the area, as was hepatitis A.

"The people I met in these villages taught me a lot about what life is really like in many places outside of the United States. In one of the towns, Dr. Koeller introduced me to a 5-year-old boy who he knew from previous trips. Kufuo had been born with HIV and with a lack of health care, wasn't expected to live to his seventh birthday. Dr. Koeller told me it was a miracle he'd made it so far. My heart broke as I saw him playing with the other children, and I couldn't help but think that if we'd been here only a few years earlier, we might have been able to prevent this while he was still in the womb. In a developed country, this would have been a standard practice.

"By the end of the summer I'd made up my mind—I plan on going back to Botswana, and perhaps other countries in need of aid, as soon as I get my nursing degree."

WHAT IS GLOBALIZATION AND HOW DOES IT AFFECT THE WORLD?

globalization is the process by which the world and the international econo-my become more closely intertwined; this results in an increase of shared culture and experiences, as well as glocalization, brain drain, and grobalization

WHAT THEORIES EXIST ABOUT GLOBALIZATION?

conflict theory: the imbalance of power between the rich and the poor cre-ates stratification; this is true on a national scale, as exhibited by the gap between the rich and poor in the United States; on an international scale, this gap is between rich and poor nations; wealthy countries use neocolonialism to benefit from poorer countries that have desirable natural resources and cheap labor

symbolic interactionism: the creation of the European Union is an example of how language and symbolic events influence society; members of the European Union identify themselves as Europeans, rather than as members of various smaller nations; the European Union shows how unity and cooper-ation can drastically benefit a region and its people

functionalism: stratification is a result of geographic conditions; today, global-ization bring wealth to less developed nations, benefitting both rich and poor areas of the world

HOW DOES SOCIETY DEAL WITH GLOBALIZATION?

foreign aid is offered by countries around the world to poorer nations in order to assist in economic development

get the topic: WHAT IS GLOBALIZATION AND HOW DOES IT AFFECT THE WORLD?

Globalization
How Did the World Become
  Stratified?

Global Stratification
Conflict Theory

Symbolic Interactionism
Foreign Aid

Theory

CONFLICT THEORY

- the imbalance of power between the elite and the poor creates strati-fication
- richer countries exploit poorer countries to preserve and augment their own wealth

FUNCTIONALISM

- stratification is mostly a result of geographic differences
- globalization does not solely benefit the countries that have risen to prominence; it also brings needed wealth and technology to poorer nations, which helps them advance

SYMBOLIC INTERACTIONISM

- Europeans are beginning to view themselves less as members of their individual home countries and more as members of the European Union

Key Terms

globalization is a complex process by which the world and the international economy are becoming more and more intertwined.

glocalization occurs when countries seek to combine the local and the global into a unique structural blend to maintain their native customs while fitting into the global environment.

brain drain occurs when the best talent leaves poor countries and thereby provides an even greater advantage to wealthy countries.

global stratification is the categorization of countries based on objective criteria, such as wealth, power, and prestige, which highlight social patterns and inequality throughout the world.

per capita income is calculated by dividing a country's total gross income by the number of people in that country.

contract slavery is a form of slavery in which a person signs a work contract, receiving food and shelter from an employer but is threatened when he or she tries to leave.

grobalization refers to the idea that capitalist countries use their corporate interests to expand their power and influence throughout the world.

neocolonialism is a process by which powerful nations use loans and economic power to maintain control over poor nations.

Sample Test Questions

These multiple-choice questions are similar to those found in the test bank that accompanies this text.

1. Which of the following is a result of globalization?
   a. Countries in the world interact less with one another economically.
   b. Multinational corporations have factories in many poor nations.
   c. Countries with abundant natural resources dominate the world politically.
   d. Worldwide literacy rates have declined.

2. Brain drain
   a. is detrimental to core countries.
   b. demonstrates an unhealthy Western influence in the world.
   c. is a result of migration.
   d. leads to glocalization.

3. Which of the following is not part of the criteria for global stratification?
   a. The amount of wealth possessed by a country
   b. The level of prestige a country carries
   c. The amount of power and influence a country has over others
   d. The type of government a country possesses

4. Which of the following is a characteristic of a developed nation?
   a. A well-educated population
   b. A democratic government
   c. A lack of profitable industry
   d. Government-sponsored health care and education

5. Immanuel Wallerstein's world systems theory divides the world into
   a. first-, second-, and third-world countries.
   b. countries that are the most feared by others.
   c. core, semiperiphery, periphery, and external nations.
   d. primary and secondary spheres of influence.

ESSAY

1. How does globalization affect your life? Think about the prices of the things you buy, such as clothing and electronics. Without globalization, what do you think would happen to the prices of these goods?

2. How would your life be different if you lived in an underdeveloped nation? Do you think that you would feel the same as you do now, or would it significantly decrease your level of satisfaction with life?

3. What factors do you believe affect the quality of life in a country? Are these "ranked" lists biased towards a Western point of view, or do they objectively take all factors into consideration?

4. How do you think the world will change over the course of the next 50 years as a result of globalization? Do you believe that the United States will continue to be the most powerful economic influence, or will this position belong to a United States of Europe or another superpower?

5. Do you think that it's possible for nations that are currently underdeveloped to become influential? Does the current system of neocolonialism allow for such a possibility?

WHERE TO START YOUR RESEARCH PAPER

For U.S. Census facts and information, go to http://www.census.gov

To learn more about neocolonialism, visit http://www.postcolonialweb.org/poldiscourse/neocolonialism1.html

For more information about the North Atlantic Treaty Organization (NATO), see http://www.nato.int

For more information on the European Union, go to http://europa.eu

To learn more about U.S. foreign aid policy, check out http://www.usaid.gov/

ANSWERS: 1. b; 2. c; 3. d; 4. a; 5. c

Remember to check www.thethinkspot.com for additional information, downloadable flashcards, and other helpful resources.

1. Hans Nichols and Mike Dorning, "Obama Says Europe Crisis 'Severe Strain' on World Economy," *Bloomberg Businessweek*, October 6, 2011, http://www.businessweek.com/news/2011-10-06/obama-says-europe-crisis-severe-strain-on-world-economy.html.

2. Marshall McLuhan, *The Gutenberg Galaxy: The Making of Typographic Man.* Toronto: University of Toronto Press, 1962.

3. A. Aboubakr Badawi, "The Social Dimension of Globalization and Health," *Perspectives on Global Development and Technology*, 2004. 3(1-2): 73-90.

4. George Ritzer, *The Globalization of Nothing.* Thousand Oaks, CA: Pine Forge Press, 2004; Jeffrey G. Williamson, "Globalization, Convergence, and History: Papers Presented at the Fifty-Fifth Annual Meeting of the Economic History Association," *The Journal of Economic History*, 1996. 56(2): 277-306; Hugo Radice, "Globalization and National Capitalisms: Theorizing Convergence and Differentiation," *Review of International Political Economy*, 2000. 7(4): 719-742.

5. Chauncy D. Harris, "English as International Language in Geography: Development and Limitations," *Geographical Review*, 2001. 91(4): 675-689; George Ritzer, *The Globalization of Nothing.* Thousand Oaks, CA: Pine Forge Press, 2004.

6. George Ritzer, *The Globalization of Nothing.* Thousand Oaks, CA: Pine Forge Press, 2004.

7. George Ross, "Labor versus Globalization," *Annals of the American Academy of Political and Social Science*, 2000. 570: 78-91.

8. Frank Bajak, "After APEC, Free Trade Orthodoxy Questioned," *The Associated Press*, November 25, 2008, http://abcnews.go.com/Business/wireStory?id5 6330029.

9. Jonathan Crush, "The Global Raiders: Nationalism, Globalization and the South African Brain Drain," *Journal of International Affairs*, 2002. 56 (1): 147-173.

10. Donald Lien and Yan Wang, "Brain Drain or Brain Gain: A Revisit," *Journal of Population Economics*, 2005. 18(1): 153-163.

11. Jean-Christophe Dumont and Georges Lemaître, "Beyond the Headlines: New Evidence on the Brain Drain," *Revue économique*, 2005. 56(6): 1275-1299.

12. Manfred B. Steger, "Global Culture: Sameness or Difference?" in *Globalization: The Transformation of Social Worlds,* eds. D. Stanley Eitzen and Maxine Baca Zinn. Belmont, CA: Wadsworth, 2009.

13. Susan F. Martin, "Heavy Traffic: International Migration in an Era of Globalization," in *Globalization: The Transformation of Social Worlds,* ed. D. Stanley Eitzen and Maxine Baca Zinn. Belmont, CA: Wadsworth, 2009.

14. D. Stanley Eitzen, "Dimensions of Globalization," in *Globalization: The Transformation of Social Worlds,* ed. D. Stanley Eitzen and Maxine Baca Zinn. Belmont, CA: Wadsworth, 2009.

15. Harold Kerbo, *World Poverty: Global Inequality and the Modern World System.* New York: McGraw-Hill, 2006.

16. Jonathan Crush, "The Global Raiders: Nationalism, Globalization and the South African Brain Drain," *Journal of International Affairs*, 2002. 56 (1): 147-173.

17. Jared Diamond, *Guns, Germs, and Steel: The Fates of Human Societies.* New York: W.W. Norton & Company, 1997.

18. Ibid.

19. Urban Institute and Brookings Institution, Tax Policy Center, "OECD Taxes as Share of GDP 1999-2005," Accessed September 2, 2009, http://www.taxpolicycenter.org/taxfacts/displayafact.cfm?Docid5307&Topic2id595.

20. United Nations, "The Millennium Development Goals Report: Statistical Annex 2006," Accessed August 27, 2009, http://unstats.un.org/unsd/mdg/Default.aspx.

21. Harold Kerbo, *World Poverty: Global Inequality and the Modern World System.* New York: McGraw-Hill, 2006.

22. UNESCO Institution for Statistics, "Towards the Next Generation of Literacy Statistics," http://www.uis.unesco.org/ev_en.php?ID57804_201&ID25DO_TOPIC.

23. Nicholas D. Kristof and Sheryl WuDunn, *Half the Sky: Turning Oppression into Opportunity for Women Worldwide.* New York: Knopf, 2009.

24. Kevin Bales, *Disposable People: New Slavery in the Global Economy.* Berkeley, CA: University of California Press, 1999.

25. Ibid.

26. Ibid.

27. Ibid.

28. George Ritzer, *The Globalization of Nothing.* Thousand Oaks, CA: Pine Forge Press, 2004.

29. Michael Astor, "Poor Countries Want Greater Role in World Economy," *The Associated Press*, June 25, 2009, http://abcnews.go.com/Business/wireStory?id57923886.

30. Ibid.

31. Ibid.

32. Ibid.

33. Ibid.

34. Ibid.

35. Timothy M. Smeeding and Lee Rainwater, "Comparing Living Standards Across Nations: Real Incomes at the Top, the Bottom, and the Middle," *Social Policy Research Centre*, 2002. 120: 1-39, http://www.sprc.unsw.edu.au/dp/DP120.pdf.

36. Global Policy Forum, "The World Economic and Social Development," http://www.globalpolicy.org/nations/kaiswork.htm.

37. Ibid.

38. Daniel J. Slottje, "Measuring the Quality of Life Across Countries," *Review of Economics and Statistics*, 1991. 73(4): 684-693.

39. Michael Harrington, *The Vast Majority: The Journey to the World's Poor.* New York: Simon and Schuster, 1977.

40. Immanuel Wallerstein, *The Modern World System: Capitalist Agriculture and the Origins of the European World-Economy in the Sixteenth Century.* New York: Academic Press, 1974; Immanuel Wallerstein, *The Capitalist World-Economy.* New York: Cambridge University Press, 1979.

41. Thomas L. Friedman, *The World Is Flat: A Brief History of the Twenty-first Century.* New York: Farrar, Straus & Giroux, 2005.

42. T.R. Reid, *The United States of Europe: The New Superpower and the End of American Supremacy.* New York: Penguin, 2004.

43. Ibid; Jeremy Rifkin, *The European Dream.* New York: Jeremy P. Tarcher/Penguin, 2005.

44. USAID, "New Frontiers in U.S. Foreign Aid," Accessed September 3, 2009, http://www.usaid.gov/policy/.

45. Organisation for Economic Co-operation and Development, "Statistical Annex of the 2009 Development Cooperation Report," Accessed September 3, 2009, http://www.oecd.org/document/9/0,3343,en_2649_34447_1893129_1_1_1_1,00.html.

46. Ibid.

47. Ibid.

48. Jill Littrell, Fred Brooks, Jan Ivery, and Mary L. Ohmer, "Why You Should Care About the Threatened Middle Class," *Journal of Sociology & Social Welfare*, 2010, 37(2): 87-113.

Credits

Credits are listed in order of appearance.

PHOTO CREDITS

The Global Divide: Globalization and International Inequality

AP Wide World Photos

- What are the economic differences between the industrialized and the less-developed countries?

- What is it like to live in a poor country?

- How do sociologists explain the huge gap between the rich and the poor countries?

- What can be done to make life better for all the world's people?

From Chapter 17 of *Social Problems*, 10/e. James William Coleman. Harold R. Kerbo. Copyright © 2010 by Pearson Education. All rights reserved.

Aposi Lakwemwe is a boy of 16 living in Kampala, the capital city of Uganda, one of the world's poorest countries. About 75 percent of people in Uganda live on less than what $2 per day would buy in the United States. When Aposi caught the attention of reporters in 2002 he was homeless, living under a plastic sheet in one of Kampala's huge slums. The boy owned nothing but the old T-shirt and tattered jeans he wore and the plastic sheet. Thousands of other children are homeless and living alone in the streets of Kampala, "begging and robbing their way from one day to the next."[1] Aposi told reporters, "Most of us are thieves but not all of us. You have to be careful around us. The problem is that not enough people give to us. What are we supposed to do?" Most of these children have lost their parents to the AIDS epidemic in Uganda. Children such as Aposi exist in the streets of almost all the major cities in sub-Saharan Africa, but many are even worse off. At least things are improving in Uganda where not too many years ago a ruthless dictator destroyed the economy, stole much of the government's money, and killed hundreds of thousands of people. The World Bank has recently listed Uganda as a "success story" because of its prudent use of foreign aid to improve social and economic conditions, if only slightly.[2]

The images of global poverty are becoming more familiar every day: homeless children like Aposi, desperate young mothers begging for food, crowds of refugees fenced off in a pen like cattle. Bit by bit, media coverage is helping the people of the rich countries to realize how fortunate they are. The media, though, cover only the most dramatic and desperate problems, so many people have a distorted concept of what life in the rest of the world is really like. The angry protests against the World Trade Organization and other powerful international organizations have led more Americans to become aware of the process of globalization and its possible dangers, but only a few know much about the causes of global poverty or what to do about them. The question of why the countries of the world are so sharply divided into an affluent minority and a poor majority is one of the most controversial issues in all social science. This chapter will examine the most common explanations for this global divide and the kinds of solutions they each imply. First, before we attempt to explain this problem, we must describe it.

Globalization and Global Inequality

Each of the more than 200 nations on this planet has its own unique economic, political, and social institutions. At the same time, all these countries are growing increasingly interdependent. Some are fabulously wealthy, while others are mired in seemingly hopeless poverty. A few exercise awesome global power, while others are hardly noticed on the world stage. It wasn't always this way. Only a few centuries ago, people had little contact with anyone outside of their local territory, and the standard of living was more or less the same in most parts of the world.[3] Now the ever-growing process of **globalization** has changed all that.[4] Today, goods, services, information, and people move around the world at an unprecedented speed. People everywhere on the planet are becoming more dependent on the world economy for their livelihood, every nation is enmeshed in a complex web of political and military relations, and a global culture is beginning to emerge, especially among the more affluent members of the world community.

Globalization ▪ The growth of a worldwide economic, political, and cultural system.

One of the best ways to make sense of the bewildering complexity of the modern world is to think of the nations of the world as making up a kind of international class system, similar in many ways to the classes found within individual countries. A century ago, the industrialized world, which makes up the "upper class," included only the United States and a few western European nations. Today it encompasses countries as far away as Japan and Australia. The countries in the "lower class," collectively known as the **less-developed countries** (**LDCs**) or the **third world,** are concentrated in the southern two-thirds of the planet in Latin America, Africa, and much of Asia. Although they have some manufacturing industries, they are more likely to depend on agriculture and the sale of raw materials to get by.

Less-developed countries (LDCs), third world ▪ Two terms for the poor nations of the world.

Between these two extremes is a smaller group of nations, including Malaysia and Mexico, that have characteristics of both kinds of societies. They are more industrialized and have higher standards of living than the poorest nations, but they are still a long way from the affluence enjoyed by the established industrialized powers. More often than not, these "middle-class" nations are counted as part of the third world, but several more narrow terms are also used, including "moderately developed" or "newly industrialized nations." In addition, there are the numerous independent nations that emerged from the collapse of the communist empire in Eastern Europe and the Soviet Union. Many of these nations have a well-educated population and a lot of heavy industry, but their standard of living is far below that of the developed capitalist countries in the global upper class and even below many of the newly industrialized nations of East Asia. Therefore, it is important to remember that the world is a complex place and that there is a broad spectrum of nations on both sides of the global divide.

Just as individuals occasionally move up or down in the class system of their nation, so the status of the nations changes. Some of the countries in the world's "middle class" seem likely to become full-scale industrial powers; others do not. Several nations have been knocked out of the elite club of industrial powers by wars or internal chaos but later rejoined it. Still other countries appear to be permanently stuck at the bottom of the heap.[5]

Wealth and Poverty

Many people look at the differences between the industrialized nations and the third world as simply a matter of money. When seen in these terms, the gap is certainly enormous. Statistics show that billions of people live in poverty around the world. Approximately 1.3 billion people are now living on less than $1 per day, and another 2.8 billion people live on less than $2 per day. Because these figures are calculated in *purchasing power parity* (PPP) estimates for each country, this $1 per day figure does not mean what $1 would buy in another country (for example, Uganda) but rather what $1 would buy in the United States, perhaps a cheap sandwich.[6] Thus, about 1.3 billion of the world's people can afford only one sandwich per day. United Nations' figures show that the top 20 percent of the world's population now receive 150 times the average income of the bottom 20 percent. Just 30 years before, the income gap was less than half that much.[7] In 2006, the average industrialized nation produced about $27,790 in goods and services for each of its citizens, while the less-developed countries produced only $4,950 per citizen—a difference of more than 5 to 1.[8] (See Figure 1.)

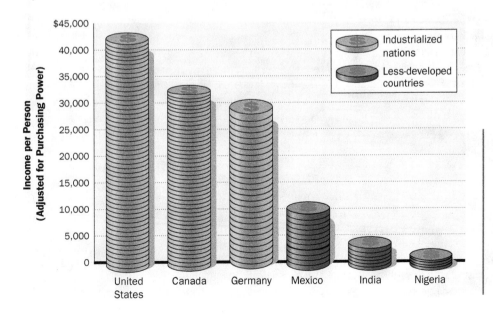

Figure 1

The Privileged and the Deprived

There is a huge gap between the income of the average person in industrialized nations and in less-developed nations.

Source: World Bank, *World Development Report, 2007* (New York: Oxford University Press, 2007), p. 288.

279

For the first time, in 2006 the United Nations sponsored research estimating the level of wealth (the assets held by a person or family including such things as land, a home, car, stocks, or bonds). In a rather shocking finding, the report estimated that the richest 2 percent of people in the world own half of the world's wealth. The poorest 50 percent of people in the world own less than 1 percent of the wealth. Ninety percent of the world's wealth is, moreover, held by people in North America, Europe, and Japan. This means that the majority of the world's population has little or no wealth accumulated to fall back on in hard times. In other words, a simple crop failure can lead to starvation.[9]

Sub-Saharan Africa ■ Africa south of the Sahara Desert.

There are also major differences among the less-developed countries. The per capita income in the world's poorest region, **sub-Saharan Africa,** is less than one-fourth as large as it is in Latin America or in most parts of Asia.[10] As we will see, however, the differences go far beyond money. Another way to compare different nations is to look at how much wealth they have accumulated. Some of this wealth is kept in dollars or yen, but more important are the physical assets of a nation—its roads and bridges, its power plants, its sewers and canals, its supply of housing, and its factories. The simplest way to make this comparison is just to look around. The industrialized nations are crisscrossed with telephone and electric lines and with highways full of cars and trucks. Their buildings are modern and equipped with running water and indoor plumbing. Almost everyone has shoes to wear, and during the cold months most people have warm clothing.

In the less-developed countries, such comforts are far less common, and only a privileged few enjoy the affluent lifestyle taken for granted by so many North Americans. The less-developed countries have paved roads connecting their major cities, but the roads are likely to be much smaller than those in the industrialized nations and in a poor state of repair. Access to smaller towns is often only by footpaths or dirt roads that become hard going when it rains. Most rural areas are further isolated by a lack of telephones and the electricity necessary to run radio transmitters. Even on major highways, the traveler will see far fewer private cars, and the trucks and buses are often dilapidated, noisy, and polluting. These motor vehicles must often share the road with a host of oxcarts, horses, bicycles, and pedestrians.

The standard of living is far lower in the third world than in the industrialized nations, and transportation and communication are much slower.

Doranne Jacobson International Images

Sanitation in the less-developed countries is often primitive, with open fields or shallow outhouses serving as the only toilets. In the cities and crowded villages, human waste may flow down the sides of streets in open sewers. Underground plumbing is now more common, but untreated sewage is often dumped directly into rivers and lakes, which can create serious health problems. In what the World Bank defines as "low-income" countries, for example, only about 40 percent of the population has the toilet facilities people in rich countries take for granted.[11] The quality of housing varies enormously. The wealthy live in sumptuous mansions with servants and all the latest conveniences, while in most big cities hundreds of thousands of people live on the streets with no permanent shelter; huge shantytowns of squatters have grown up on whatever vacant land is available. Because these squatters have neither the legal rights to the land they occupy nor the money to build homes, their structures are primitive affairs, often lacking electricity and plumbing and providing little protection against the elements. In rural areas, most villagers at least have the legal right to live where they do, but construction techniques are still primitive—buildings often have walls of mud bricks and thatched or corrugated iron roofs, and the basic amenities are lacking.

Of course, the poor countries are not all alike. Some are much poorer than others, and those have less hope of moving their people out of poverty.[12] One of the most fundamental problems in the poor nations is the absence of economic opportunities for their young people. Rapid population growth and a weak educational system mean there is almost always a large surplus of unskilled labor. In the past, these young people would have just gone to work on the family farm, but because so many more children now reach adulthood, there is often not enough land to support them all. To make matters worse, birthrates are the highest in the poorest countries and among the poorest people within each country. Young people from throughout the third world are, therefore, migrating to the cities in search of work, but only the lucky find permanent jobs. Most become part of what is sometimes called the **urban subsistence economy**. They work a few temporary jobs, trade their labor for the help of other poor people, receive an occasional handout from the government or a relief agency, and in some cases turn to begging or even crime to make ends meet. (See this chapter's Personal Perspectives box for an account of what it was like growing up as a Guatemalan peasant.)

Urban subsistence economy ■ The way of life of the city dwellers in poor countries who make just enough to get by.

Health and Nutrition

There is nothing more fundamental to the quality of life than good health, and the health statistics show the same global divide as the economic statistics. A baby born in a less-developed country is at least five times more likely to die in its first year of life than a baby born in a wealthy nation (see Figure 2).[13] Overall, demographers say that the people of the industrialized world can expect to live 11 years longer than their counterparts in the poor nations.[14]

Many of the causes of these staggering differences can be traced to the poverty of the third world—more specifically, poor sanitation, lack of clean drinking water, and not enough food to eat.[15] The United Nations' Food and Agriculture Organization estimates that more than 800 million people in the world are chronically undernourished, with another 2 billion people experiencing deficiencies in some crucial nutrients.[16] UNICEF reports that malnutrition is a factor in about 55 percent of the 12 million preventable deaths that occur annually among children younger than 5 years old.[17]

These problems are caused by more than just the lack of food. Lack of refrigeration and poor sanitation mean that a lot of food goes to waste, and the food itself is often a cause of illness. Moreover, more than 30 percent of the agricultural products from countries with the worst malnutrition are exported to rich countries.[18] On the average, almost one in three people in the poor nations does not have access to safe drinking water, and it is one in two in sub-Saharan Africa.[19] Waterborne diseases such as typhoid and cholera, almost unknown in the wealthy nations, sweep through the less-developed countries in epidemic after epidemic, taking millions of lives every year. Another of the most lethal diseases, malaria, is transmitted by insects and not water. The World Health

Personal Perspectives

Growing Up as a Guatemalan Peasant

Rigoberta Menchu is a Quiche Indian who grew up in a poverty-stricken Guatemalan village. Her father and brother were murdered by the Guatemalan military, and her struggle for justice in her country won her the 1992 Nobel Peace Prize. The following is an account of some of her memories of growing up.

I worked from when I was very small, but I didn't earn anything. I was really helping my mother because she always had to carry a baby, my little brother, on her back as she picked coffee. It made me very sad to see my mother's face covered in sweat as she tried to finish her workload, and I wanted to help her. But my work wasn't paid, it just contributed to my mother's work. I either picked coffee with her or looked after my little brother, so she could work faster. My brother was two at the time. Indian women prefer to breastfeed their babies rather than give them food because, when the child eats and the mother eats, that's duplicating the food needed. So my brother was still feeding at the breast and my mother had to spend time feeding him and everything.

I was five when she was doing this work and I looked after my little brother. I wasn't earning yet. I used to watch my mother, who often had the food ready at three o'clock in the morning for the workers who started work early, and at eleven she had the food for the midday meal ready. At seven in the evening she had to run around again making food for her group. In between times, she worked picking coffee to supplement what she earned. Watching her made me feel useless and weak because I couldn't do anything to help her except look after my brother. That's when my consciousness was born. It's true. My mother didn't like the idea of me working, of earning my own money, but I did. I wanted to work, more than anything to help her, both economically and physically. The thing was that my mother was very brave and stood up to everything well, but there were times when one of my brothers or sisters was ill—if it wasn't one of them it was another and everything she earned went on medicine for them. This made me very sad as well. It was at that time, I remember, that when we went back to the Altiplano after five months in the finca [a large farm] I was ill and it looked as if I'd die. I was six and my mother was distressed because I nearly died. The change of climate was too abrupt for me. After that, though, I made a big effort not to get ill again and, although my head ached a lot, I didn't say so.*

*Rigoberta Menchu, *I Rigoberta Menchu: An Indian Woman in Guatemala* (New York: Verso, 1984), p. 33.

Organization recently warned the world about the rapid increase in this global killer.[20] As with so many other problems in the third world, poverty is a major contributor to the malaria problem because the poor nations often cannot afford the expensive mosquito eradication programs that are the best way to deal with the disease. Although AIDS–HIV is not yet the number-one killer among the world's diseases, the future looks ominous.

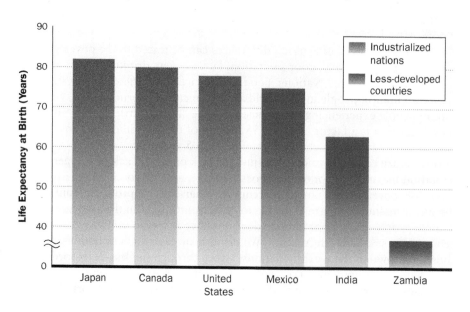

Figure 2

Life Expectancy

People in the rich countries live longer than people in the poor ones.

Source: Population Reference Bureau, *World Population Data Sheet, 2006* (Washington, DC: Population Reference Bureau, 2006).

Bob Daemmrich/Stock Boston

Robert Caputo/Stock Boston

Good health care can be hard to come by in the less-developed countries, and educational facilities, where they are available, are often primitive affairs. The photo on the top is from an American-sponsored medical clinic in rural Honduras, and the other photo shows students in Sudan.

The problem is particularly severe in Africa—more than a quarter of the population in such countries as Botswana and Zimbabwe are believed to be infected, and numerous other countries have double-digit infection rates. The people in such poor countries simply cannot afford the expensive new drugs that can often hold the infection at bay. Barring some new and inexpensive medical breakthroughs, almost all of those currently infected can be expected to die from the disease.[21]

When people in the poor countries do get sick, they are often unable to find a doctor to help. There is only one doctor for every 5,833 people who live in the less-developed countries, but in the industrialized nations there is one doctor for every 341 people.[22]

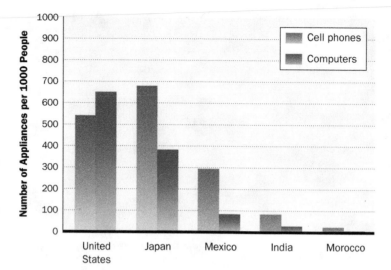

Figure 3

Communications

Communication is much faster and easier in the rich countries than in the poor ones.

Source: U.S. Bureau of the Census, *Statistical Abstract of the United States, 2006* (Washington, DC: U.S. Government Printing Office, 2006), p. 891.

Even those who are lucky enough to find a doctor who will see them are likely to have their treatment hampered by shortages of everything but the least expensive medicines and equipment. The lack of medical care is particularly acute in the rural areas of most poor countries, where traditional healers often provide the only medical help available.

Education

Another major economic advantage of the industrialized nations is their high level of education. In most industrialized nations, less than 1 percent of the population is completely illiterate. But in the less-developed countries one in three people cannot read and write, and the majority of people are illiterate in the 45 countries the United Nations ranks at the bottom of its Human Development Index.[23] Again, however, we must recognize the important regional differences among developing nations. In such Asian nations as Thailand and the Philippines, the illiteracy rate is only about 5 percent, whereas it is more than 50 percent in Mozambique, Chad, and Haiti.[24] Workers in the industrialized countries are also far more likely to have specialized skills—for example, in word processing or automobile mechanics. The labor force in industrialized nations contains large numbers of physicians, engineers, scientists, and other highly trained specialists. Moreover, many of the skilled professionals the poor nations do produce migrate to the industrialized countries, where wages are far higher. As computer skills are becoming ever more important in the global economy, a "digital divide" is emerging around the world—even greater than the digital divide among the rich and poor within the developed nations (see Figure 3).

The system of universal education in the rich nations also serves as a kind of social cement to help hold their people together. Children of widely different backgrounds acquire similar values and attitudes as they learn the history of their nation and read its literature. Mass communication contributes to the sense of national unity because people who read the same newspapers and watch the same television programs tend to develop a similar perspective on the world. In contrast, the perspective of most people in the poor countries is much more local. They often know little of the history or politics of their country. Many can't read the newspaper, and televisions, much less computers, are few and far between. To complicate matters, ethnic and linguistic differences are often far more pronounced in less-developed countries. Thus, these nations must deal with traditional ethnic animosities and suspicions without the benefit of the strong mass institutions that help hold the wealthy nations together.

Women and Children

Women suffer from prejudice and discrimination in every nation, but the problem is far more severe in the less-developed countries. Traditional agricultural societies usually have a high degree of gender inequality. Although all poor nations have undergone some degree of economic development, the traditional attitude that sees women as second-class citizens remains strong. Female infanticide, inadequate care for childbearing women, and the preference often given to male children when resources become scarce mean that there are considerably more males than females in the poorer nations of the world. (In industrialized nations, women normally live longer than men and thus out-number them.) In the industrialized countries, there are no overall gender differences in the literacy rate, but in the less-developed countries women are twice as likely to be unable to read and write as men. According to United Nations figures, 44 percent of the administrators and managers are women in the industrialized nations, but only 12 percent are women in the less-developed nations.[25]

The industrialized nations have made great progress toward the goal of giving women and men equal treatment under the law. In many parts of the world, however, equal treatment is not even recognized as a social goal, and women are commonly given second-class legal status similar to that of a dependent child. Property often passes from fathers to sons, and daughters do not receive an equal share of the inheritance. Husbands are commonly given the legal right to control the household property, and women find it difficult or impossible to get credit or establish financial independence. Women are expected to follow the orders of their husbands, and the legal authorities seldom intervene to prevent a husband from beating a wife who disobeys him. In most Islamic nations, men are allowed up to four wives, but a wife is permitted only a single husband. In many places around the world, it is also far easier for a husband to win a divorce than for a wife.

Children in the less-developed countries also face a host of special problems. As in all societies, they are the most vulnerable to famines and plagues, and young children have a far higher death rate than any other age group. The mortality rate among infants is almost nine times higher in the less-developed countries than in the industrialized ones.[26]

In agricultural societies, children were traditionally seen as a source of farm labor. When people in poor countries move to urban areas, they often send their children off to find jobs. There is a world of difference, however, between having children work on the family farm under the supervision of their parents and having children work for strangers in a factory or shop. The World Bank estimates that about 19 percent of the 10- to 14-year-olds in the low-income nations are in the labor force outside the home. In some places, this rate is much higher—for example, in sub-Saharan Africa it is around 30 percent.[27]

Such problems as poverty, warfare, and just too many mouths to feed have combined to force a growing number of children out of their homes to fend for themselves in the streets of the big cities. The United Nations Children's Fund (UNICEF) estimates that there are about 30 million such "street children" in the less-developed countries,[28] but others have placed that figure much higher.[29] Life is hard for these children. They usually live in desperate poverty, begging, stealing, selling sex, or doing whatever work they can find. To make matters worse, they are often viewed with suspicion and hostility by the adult population. In Brazil, where such attitudes seem to be at their most extreme, thousands of these children have been murdered by police and vigilante organizations.

Social Structure

Underlying the disparities in the quality of life are fundamental differences in the social structures of rich and poor societies. The class system, political institutions, and economic structures are all markedly different in the less-developed countries. For example, farming is only one of dozens of industries in the wealthy nations, but it is still the most common way people make their living in many parts of the world. Many of these nations depend heavily on the exploitation of natural resources such as petroleum, timber, copper, and uranium—if they are lucky enough to have them. A third major source of employment is low-wage jobs in industries that require large amounts of relatively unskilled labor. Sometimes the factories are owned by local businesspeople or governments, but more often they are branches of huge multinational corporations run from headquarters in one of the industrialized nations. As already mentioned, rapid population growth and weak overall economies mean that there is a huge group of workers without steady jobs.

Another important difference between the rich and poor nations is their class systems. Both types of societies have a relatively small upper class that commands a disproportionate share of wealth and power. The industrialized nations also have a large middle class that has the skills necessary to keep the technological economy going. In less-developed countries, the middle class is much smaller and weaker, and the gap between the rich and the poor is far larger. For example, the bottom 20 percent of people in Germany and Japan receive from 8 percent to 10 percent of total income in the country, while the top 20 percent of the people receive about 35 percent. Although income inequality is higher in the United States than in other industrialized nations, the gap is still wider in the third world.[30] For example, in Brazil, Guatemala, Honduras, Colombia, Paraguay, South Africa, and Zimbabwe, the bottom 20 percent of people get about 2 percent of national income while the top 20 percent get more than 60 percent.[31] As in the wealthy countries, the disparities in wealth tend to be even greater than the disparities in income. In Mexico, for example, just 37 families control half the wealth, while millions live in severe poverty.[32]

The nations on the two sides of the global divide also have significant differences in their political institutions. The most obvious is that the rich industrialized nations have stable democratic governments, while less-developed countries are much more likely to have some type of dictator or a small group of bureaucratic rulers who are not elected by the public. (Of course, many of these nations hold elections, but the results are rigged against the government's opponents.) Although there has been a trend toward more democracy in the less-developed countries, such governments are usually fragile affairs. Elected leaders often face a constant threat of a military coup or a disruptive outbreak of social violence if they make the wrong move.

Whether dictatorships or democracies, governments in the less-developed countries tend to be weaker and more unstable than their counterparts in the wealthy nations. Sharp ethnic and class differences and the lack of strong unifying institutions produce a high level of conflict in many poor nations. Popular discontent often leads to a succession of new governments that seem unable to get at the roots of the nation's problems or to an entrenched dictatorship that ignores public opinion.[33] Significant parts of some countries are not actually controlled by their central government at all, but by bands of organized rebels such as in the Tamil Tigers in Sri Lanka or the drug warlords in Burma. Even relatively stable governments are hopelessly outmatched by the military and economic power of the industrialized nations. No matter how independence-minded third world leaders may be, they often find that their destiny is determined by decisions made in Washington, Tokyo, or Berlin.

QUICK REVIEW

- What is the "global class system"?
- Describe the differences between life in the industrialized countries and life in the third world in terms of economic conditions, education, and health.
- What are the special problems faced by women and children in the third world?
- What are the differences in social structure between the rich and poor countries?

Explaining the Global Divide

The huge gap between the world's rich and poor is a relatively recent development in human history. As recently as 200 years ago, the World Bank estimates that some 90 percent or more of the world's populations lived in similar economic conditions.[34] The transition to an agricultural economy greatly increased social inequality, but the beginnings of today's global divide can be found in the **Industrial Revolution** and the capitalist economic system that made it possible. This new kind of society was based not on farm-

Industrial Revolution ▪ The change from an agricultural to an industrial society.

ing but on trade, commerce, and manufacturing, and as it took shape in Western Europe, it stimulated one technological advance after another at an ever-quickening pace. The European countries used their technological superiority for political gains as well. They built up a huge network of colonies (foreign territories under their political control) throughout the world. Even areas that managed to stay outside these colonial empires were often dominated by the economic and military power of the European nations. From the beginning of the colonial period (around the end of the fifteenth century), the standard of living of the European elites grew at an unprecedented rate as wealth and resources poured in from their overseas empires. Most of the rest of the world, however, remained mired in poverty. Although European **colonialism** lasted well into the twentieth century, its days are now over. Nonetheless, the economic inequality between the rich and poor nations is still growing larger year by year.[35]

Today's global inequalities clearly stem from the fact that some nations have undergone a full process of industrialization while others have not. The key question is, Why? In the early days of their colonial expansion, most Europeans simply assumed that their technological advantage was the result of their biological and religious superiority. Although such **ethnocentrism** is certainly still around, few social scientists take that attitude seriously. The effort to explain these differences scientifically has been a long and difficult process. Many of our greatest sociologists and historians have struggled with this crucial question, and even today, opinions remain sharply divided along political lines. In this chapter, we will examine two broad theories—modernization theory and world system theory—that both seek to explain this global divide. The aim of this section is to present each approach in a clear and coherent form, but it is important to keep in mind that there are many disagreements among those who support the same theory and that many social scientists freely combine insights from both approaches or hold to other theories altogether.

Modernization Theory

This theory, which borrows heavily from the classic sociological work of Max Weber (1864–1920), was developed in the 1950s and 1960s by a group of functionalists who saw industrialization as part of a process of social evolution they called **modernization**.[36] According to this perspective, modernization is the result of the buildup of numerous improvements in the structure and function of social institutions. The most obvious are the countless technological innovations that have been made throughout the course of human history, but modernization also involves what economists call **capital accumulation**—that is, the buildup of wealth. The important thing is not so much amassing money, which is only a symbol of wealth, but also increasing real assets (such as roads, buildings, and power plants) and improving the education and skill of the workforce. There are also important changes in the organization of society as its institutions become more specialized and more efficient. For example, in most agricultural societies, the extended family serves as the school, the employer, the welfare agency, and the punisher of deviant behavior, all rolled into one. As part of the process of modernization, a great deal of the responsibility for these functions is transferred to more specialized social institutions such as the schools and the criminal-justice system.

Although modernization takes place as a result of the buildup of one improvement on another, this process does not necessarily occur at a steady pace. In fact, economist Walter W. Rostow has shown that industrialization in the Western nations took place in distinct stages, and he argues that all the less-developed countries will eventually follow this same road.[37] According to Rostow, all nations begin at the traditional stage, in which people cling to their old ways and are reluctant to accept sweeping changes. As a nation enters the "takeoff stage," there is a slow but steady accumulation of wealth, assets, and skills until the nation reaches a kind of critical mass. Once it reaches this third stage, which Rostow terms the "drive for technological maturity," society undergoes a rapid process of industrialization and social change. A more stable balance returns in the fourth and final stage when the society emerges as a mature industrial power. This

Colonialism ■ A system in which one nation extends its political and economic control over other nations or peoples and treats them as dependent colonies.

Ethnocentrism ■ The tendency to view the norms and values of one's own culture as absolute and to use them as a standard against which to measure other cultures.

Modernization ■ The process by which a nation moves from a traditional agricultural society to an industrialized state.

Capital accumulation ■ The buildup of wealth in a nation including not only money but also the skills of its labor force and its infrastructure.

Lessons from Other Places

Poverty in Cambodia

During 2006 and 2007 I have been conducting comparative research on conditions of poverty and poverty programs in Thailand, Cambodia, and Vietnam. Funded by the Abe Foundation in Japan, I have spent most of my research time interviewing government officials, Nongovernmental organization officials (from the United Nations, for example), and people in very poor villages in these countries. Before I began the research I knew the World Bank figures which indicated things are getting better for the poor of Thailand and Vietnam, while there has been almost no improvement in the rural areas of Cambodia. Poverty rates in Thailand have been cut from more than 50 percent 30 years ago to around 15 percent today. In Vietnam, poverty has been cut from more than 50 percent to around 25 percent just since 1990. In contrast, although there has been some poverty reduction in the Cambodian capital of Phnom Penh, there has been little improvement in the Cambodian countryside. One of my main tasks is to figure out why these three countries are so different, and what lessons there are for the other poor nations of the world. What I have found in short is that corruption, lack of educated governmental officials on the local level, and simple incompetence are key problems in Cambodia. As one well-educated and dedicated government official in Phnom Penh told me, "We have a lot of good planning and poverty reduction programs designed, but then nothing happens."

During my visits to villages in Thailand, I saw a much higher standard of living. And in Vietnam I saw impressive rural development projects in progress. In Cambodia, I had read that rural people are living much like they did 1,000 years ago. After spending four months in and out of these peasant villages, I found that to be an accurate statement. Very few villages in Cambodia have electricity or running water, and the main mode of transportation seems to be ox carts. There is almost no health care provided by the government (in a big contrast to Thailand and Vietnam), which means that when peasant families need to hospitalize their children, they must sell what little land or property they might have to pay for this hospital care or watch their children die.

The tragedy of it all for Cambodia is that it would take so little to improve the lives of poor village people. I found that a small investment by the Cambodian government or an aid agency to provide some irrigation for their rice fields could more than double their crops, giving these village people enough rice to eat and sell to get cash for other things. Currently, only 15 percent of the fields have any irrigation in Cambodia, compared to more than 40 percent in Vietnam and much more than that in Thailand. Just $60 per year for a few bags of fertilizer could also substantially increase their rice production, again providing them with enough to eat and sell. Despite the millions of dollars a year international donors give to Cambodia, very little development money gets out to the villagers who need it so desperately.

Harold Kerbo

Source: World Bank, *Cambodian Poverty Assessment, 2006* (New York: Oxford University Press, 2006).

process of transition is a tumultuous one, and Rostow held that the instability it causes may leave the developing nation vulnerable to communism or some other totalitarian system.

Why are some nations so much further ahead in the process of modernization than others? Max Weber pointed out several unique conditions in Western Europe that helped make the Industrial Revolution possible. Weber argued that the spread of Puritan religions, which placed an enormous value on hard work and frugality, stimulated the accumulation of wealth necessary for industrialization. He also felt that the political disunity of Europe and the independence of its cities and towns prevented its feudal rulers from repressing the development of capitalism as they did, for example, in China.[38] Contemporary modernization theorists tend to put the blame on the "traditionalism" of less-developed countries, which has made them resist the kind of changes necessary to create a modern industrial society. Rostow, for example, argues that less-developed countries tend to have a religious, rather than a scientific, cultural orientation, which makes it more difficult to develop and utilize modern technology. According to this view, people in less-developed countries often cling to their traditional ways of doing things and resist the innovations that inevitably go with the process of modernization. Rostow and other modernization theorists also cite the centralization of wealth and power in the hands of a small elite, the numerous restrictions on competitive markets, and the low overall level of education as other important barriers to modernization.[39]

Topham/The Image Works

This photograph is from the US lead invasion of Iraq. World system theorists argue that the rich nations are able to dominate most third world countries through economic means, but when that fails, they resort to military power.

World System Theory

The perspective known as *world system theory* is one of the fastest-growing theoretical schools in contemporary sociology. Whereas modernization theory has its source in the functionalist perspective, world system theory is a conflict theory that can trace its roots back to Karl Marx. The immediate origins of this theory are often credited to Andre Gunder Frank's studies of Latin America,[40] but it was Immanuel Wallerstein who actually created world system theory.[41] Much of the inspiration for this approach came from a critique of modernization theory and what the world system theorists saw as its ethnocentrism and its hidden bias in favor of the status quo. Some world system theorists nonetheless accept many of the points made by modernization theory, and many have also been heavily influenced by the works of Max Weber. Virtually all world system theorists agree, however, that modernization theory leaves out the most fundamental cause of third world poverty—exploitation by the rich industrialized powers.

The most fundamental insight of this new perspective is that industrialization does not take place in isolated individual nations, as modernization theory assumes, but within a complex web of international economic and political relationships known as the **world system.** In its beginnings, the modern world system was a rather small affair limited to a part of northern Europe, but it eventually grew into the global financial and political network that now dominates the planet. At the center of the world system are the rich and powerful industrialized nations known as the **core.** These core nations are surrounded by a much larger number of poor nations called the **periphery.** The core nations exploit the periphery for its natural resources and cheap labor while using their military and economic power to prevent peripheral nations from growing strong enough to challenge the interests of the core. Between these two extremes is the **semiperiphery.** Countries in this category are more industrialized than the peripheral nations but are far behind the core. Although they are still subject to the economic and political domination of the core, the semiperipheral nations are themselves able to exploit their poorer neighbors.

World system theorists disagree about how to classify the remaining communist nations. The most common view is that communism represented an effort by exploited nations to pull out of the world system and industrialize on their own without foreign interference. The collapse of European communism is seen as evidence of how powerful the capitalist world system is and how difficult it is for any nation to challenge it. World system theorists argue that the former communist countries, such as Russia and the

World system ■ The network of economic and political relationships that links the world together.

Core ■ The wealthy industrialized nations that dominate the world system.

Periphery ■ The poor nations of the world, which are subject to the economic and political domination of the core nations.

Semiperiphery ■ The partially industrialized nations that have characteristics of both the core and the periphery.

289

eastern European nations, are now back in the capitalist world system and once again in a subordinate role. Even countries such as China and Vietnam, which still claim to be communist, have realized they must play the capitalist game if they are to survive in today's global economy.

Hegemonic power ■ The strongest of the industrialized powers that assumes leadership of the world system.

The historical record shows that the core is often led by a single **hegemonic power,** a dominant nation that is far stronger economically, militarily, and politically than the other core states. The first hegemonic power was Holland, followed by Great Britain and then the United States. However, the military and economic costs of protecting the world system impose a heavy burden on the hegemonic power, and many world system theorists argue that the United States is already slipping from its position of dominance, as Holland and Great Britain did before it.

According to world system theory, the fundamental cause of poverty in the peripheral nations is not that they are too traditional but that the core nations have forced them into a position of economic and political dependence. Whereas modernization theory sees poor nations as simply places where economic development has yet to take place, world system theorists point out that the peripheral nations have, in fact, undergone enormous social and economic changes. However, those changes have not been dictated by their own needs but by those of the core nations. Many poor countries have great natural resources, but it is the needs of the core nations that determine which minerals are to be produced and the price that such things as timber and petroleum will bring. Many poor nations have lush plantations, but their agricultural bounty is consumed by the people of the rich nations. Many poor nations have beautiful beaches and resorts, but they are full of wealthy tourists from the industrialized countries. Underlying all these inequities is the fact that many of the most productive assets in the poor nations are owned and operated by multinational corporations from the core nations.

Critics of world system theory complain that it is too ideological and that its supporters see only the bad side of capitalism. Such critics point out that both life expectancy and the standard of living in the third world are actually much higher now than they were in the past. They argue that far from exploiting the less-developed countries, the industrialized countries are actually helping them. The critics claim that if industrial capitalism had never developed in Western Europe, the third world would still be suffering from the extreme poverty and class exploitation typical of most agricultural societies. Defenders of world system theory respond that the standard of living as calculated by the economists is not a good measure of actual conditions in the third world. World system theorists argue that even though monetary income may have gone up, the quality of life has declined as the traditional lifestyles of third world peoples have been destroyed and that conditions certainly would have been much better in the periphery without foreign interference.[42] (See the Debate "Are the Rich Nations Exploiting the Poor Ones?")

Evaluation

It may seem frustrating to students that the enormous amount of time and effort social scientists have spent analyzing global inequality hasn't produced more agreement about its causes. Behind the academic and political rivalry between these two theoretical camps, however, are considerable areas of actual agreement. The naive version of world system theory would blame all the world's problems on the capitalist core nations, whereas naive modernization theorists see the "traditionalism" of the third world as the cause of all its difficulties. More sophisticated members of both camps recognize that no single factor can explain the complexities of the modern world. Traditional values, the lack of capital, low educational levels, weak government, and the other factors cited by the modernization theorists have certainly played a major role in creating today's global divide, but so has the exploitation of the poor nations by the rich ones. To understand our current problems, we must look at both the internal conditions within individual nations that impede development and the world system of economic and political relationships in which those nations are embedded.

Debate

Are the Rich Nations Exploiting the Poor Ones?

YES All you have to do is look around any third world country. The evidence of victimization is everywhere. The children are sickly and malnourished while their parents are often tired and hopeless. Those who live in mud huts and crowded tenements are actually the lucky ones, for whole families often sleep in the streets. Most third world cities are jammed with legions of unemployed young men and women who have little real chance of ever finding a steady job. Yet this poverty and deprivation occur in the shadow of the incredible abundance of the industrialized nations. The per capita income in the world today is far higher than it has ever been before, but most of that wealth stays in the hands of a privileged few.

Exactly how do the rich nations take advantage of the poor countries? First, third world people are exploited for their labor. The third world is now dotted with factories producing consumer goods for the rich nations. The wages paid by the multinational corporations that own most of these factories are pitifully low—sometimes less than $1 a day. Not only are the hours long and the pay low, but also the factories are hot, polluted, and dangerous. Hundreds of thousands of workers die every year because of working conditions that would never be tolerated in the wealthy nations. Second, third world nations are exploited for their natural resources. Their forests are stripped, their petroleum reserves pumped out, and their mineral deposits depleted in order to satisfy the core nations' voracious appetite for raw materials. Although the peripheral countries receive some money for these commodities, the economic monopoly of the industrialized nations enables them to keep the price of raw materials far below their real value. Third, the poor nations are forced to follow political and economic policies dictated by the rich ones. Through the careful use of bribes, covert operations, and outright military force, the core keeps the poor nations from mounting an effective challenge to the world order that exploits them. In addition, a new form of exploitation is developing as the southern part of the planet becomes the dumping ground for toxic wastes and unsafe products manufactured in the core.

The next time someone tells you how much good our corporations and our governments are doing in the third world, stop and think for a moment. Picture Europeans and North Americans dying from the clogged arteries that come from overeating while millions of people starve to death in the third world. Or picture a third world dictator slaughtering his people with the guns, tanks, and aircraft supplied by his supporters in the core nations. The truth will soon become obvious.

NO It's human nature to try to find someone to blame for our problems. When we compare the poverty of the third world with the affluence of the industrialized nations, it is natural to blame one on the other. When we place these problems in historical perspective, however, it is apparent that the industrialized nations have actually helped to improve the standard of living in the third world. The most useful comparison is not between the rich and poor nations of today's world but between the third world today and the way most countries in Africa, Asia, and Latin America were before they were influenced by the industrialized powers. When seen in these terms, there is simply no question that the people of the third world are far better off as the result of their contacts with the industrialized nations. Their average income and standard of living are much higher than they used to be. Even though most people in the third world do not have all the latest technological innovations, they still have electric lights, radios, bicycles, and other inventions created in the industrialized nations. Health conditions have vastly improved, infant mortality has plummeted, and the average life expectancy in the third world is probably double what it was five centuries ago. Although there are a lot of complaints about "political meddling" in the third world, the industrialized nations have actually been a vital force encouraging democracy and fighting communism and other totalitarian systems. Five hundred years ago, there wasn't a single democracy in the entire world; today, democracy is flowering even in many of the poorest nations.

The charges that the industrialized nations are exploiting the third world are just ideological rhetoric intended for political purposes. When revolutionary leaders come to power and cut their nations off from "foreign influence," the people's standard of living goes down, not up. It is easy to complain about the low wages of the workers in the third world, but the economic fact is that these workers are less educated and less productive than workers in the industrialized nations. If their wages were raised too much, third world factories would no longer be competitive with those in the industrialized nations. Besides, the third world workers employed by foreign multinationals are actually the lucky ones because they earn far more than they could in almost any of the other jobs available to them. Of course, none of this means that the multinationals or the governments of the industrialized nations never take advantage of the people in the poor nations; the real world is not that simple. It is clear, however, that the industrialized nations have done far more to help than to hurt the third world.

QUICK REVIEW

- What impact did the Industrial Revolution have on global inequality?
- Compare and contrast the ways the modernization theory and world system theory explain the inequality among nations.
- What are the strengths and weaknesses of the modernization and world system theories?

Solving the Problems of Global Inequality

As we have seen, the less-developed countries are faced with daunting and complex problems. Many social scientists and political leaders have a pet proposal they see as a solution to our global crisis, but just as there is no one cause of the global divide, there is no single solution. This section will examine some of the most common suggestions, but there are still strong disagreements about the wisdom and the possible effectiveness of all these proposals. We will begin by exploring some ideas about what the industrialized world can do to help the less-developed countries, and then we will look at what those nations can do themselves.

The Industrialized Nations

Although there are a number of ways the industrialized nations could help the less-developed countries, there is a real question about whether they will make a serious effort to do so. Of course, virtually all the governments of the core nations say they want to assist the poor countries, but those fine words are seldom translated into effective programs. Many influential people in the industrialized nations simply don't care what happens in the far-off countries of the third world, while others may fear that the industrialization of those countries would mean more economic and political competition for their own nations. Thus, the first step is to educate the people of the industrialized countries about the acute problems of the less-developed countries and the international dangers posed by their poverty and political instability.

DROPPING TRADE BARRIERS Most wealthy nations use a complex system of import taxes, quotas, and other restrictions to protect their own industries and limit the flow of goods from the low-wage countries. There are hundreds of examples: Duties on clothes imported into the United States are relatively high unless they are made using American textiles. In the European Union, the duties on agricultural products are usually less than in the United States, but there are still many restrictions to protect European producers.[43] For example, African countries can export cocoa beans to European manufacturers such as Nestlé, but if the African countries process the beans themselves and attempt to sell chocolate in Europe (a more profitable venture), the duties are high.

Despite much political rhetoric, the reality is that most nations want other countries to have open markets so they can sell goods freely while they continue to protect their own industries from foreign competition. This is why the United States and the European countries fight with each other about who has the most subsidies to its farmers and other industries: What they are doing is trying to maneuver for advantage to protect their own industries while making other countries open their markets. Poor nations want the same things but lack the power to get them as effectively.[44]

One estimate is that the 49 least-developed nations in the world lose about $2.5 billion a year because of tariffs and quotas placed on their products by rich nations. In the case of Bangladesh, the international aid agency Oxfam estimates the United States gets back $7 from import barriers for every $1 given in aid. Oxfam also estimates that rich countries subsidize their own agribusinesses at a level of about $1 billion per day, which floods the world market with cheap food, while the International Monetary Fund (IMF) pushes these least-developed countries to keep their markets open to these agricultural products. Another estimate suggests that although the rich nations give about $56 billion in aid to the poor countries, they subsidize their own industries to the tune of $300 billion, thus making them more competitive against industries in the third world. In the European Union, the average cow is subsidized at about $2 per day—a sum greater than the average income of almost half of the world's people.[45] The least-developed nations simply have no means to support their own farmers or businesses with such subsidies. When forced to open their markets to subsidized products from rich nations, they cannot compete and are forced out of business.

When leaders of the less-developed countries discuss the problems of economic development with their counterparts in the core nations, one of their most frequent requests is that those trade barriers and subsidies be dropped and their goods be allowed to compete freely on the open market. The North American Free Trade Agreement (NAFTA), for example, gave Mexico far greater access to the North American market, and since then many other similar pacts have been signed around the world. However, many open and hidden subsidies are still allowed to continue. So such treaties may actually harm the poor nations unless they are structured in a way that recognizes the fact that the economic needs of the poor nations are much more urgent and pressing than those in rich nations.

FORGIVING DEBT One of the most serious problems facing the less-developed countries is what has come to be known as the *debt crisis*. The roots of this problem can be traced to the oil crisis of the early 1970s. When sharp increases in the price of petroleum sent hundreds of billions of dollars in new income to the Middle Eastern oil producers, Western banks were flooded with huge new deposits. At the same time, however, the oil crisis also created a severe recession in the world economy, so there were few attractive investment opportunities in the industrialized nations. The bankers' response was to make massive new loans to various less-developed countries. Unfortunately, most of this money simply went to pay for higher oil bills or was wasted through corruption and inefficiency.

Today, many of the less-developed countries are saddled with debts so large that they cannot even pay the interest, much less the principal, and as a result they are falling further and further behind (see Figure 4). In 1990, the external debt of all the less-developed countries was about $1,350 billion; by 2004 it was more than $4,260 billion.[46] Third world nations now pay far more in interest on their debt than they receive in foreign aid. In other words, more money is flowing from the poor countries into the rich countries than from the rich to the poor—money the poor countries desperately need to overcome their poverty. Most poor nations have turned to development agencies such as the IMF as their only possible sources of capital to meet their debt payments. In exchange for their money, international development agencies typically demand that national governments take harsh austerity measures to balance their budgets and reduce imports. The effects of these government cutbacks fall hardest on the poor: Whatever meager government assistance they receive is reduced or eliminated while new economic policies drive their countries into recession.

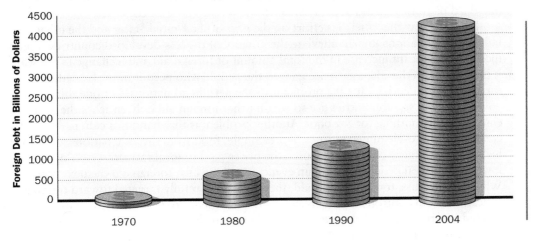

Figure 4
Debt

There has been a staggering increase in the debt poor nations owe to foreign lenders.

Source: World Bank, *World Development Report, 2007* (New York: Oxford University Press, 2007), p. 296; World Bank, United Nations Human Development Programme, *Human Development Report, 1994* (New York: Oxford University Press, 1994), p. 63.

The most effective foreign aid is often targeted to the specific needs of the recipient. This photo shows a project to plant new trees and bushes in Niger.

Markus Matzel/Peter Arnold, Inc.

There is, however, some new hope for these poor nations. At the summer 2000 meetings of the G-7 nations (the seven richest countries in the world), there was an agreement to provide debt relief to some of the very poorest nations, although various limitations and restrictions still applied.[47] What is needed, then, is to give debt relief to all the poor nations that need it, not to only a lucky few.

FOREIGN AID Many Americans think that their government spends huge sums in foreign aid to help the developing nations. Actually, the United States spends only one-tenth of 1 percent of its national income on foreign economic assistance. Although the U.S. economy is twice as large as Japan's, the Japanese actually give twice as much foreign aid. In fact, when viewed in terms of the percentage of their total economy that nations give in foreign aid, the United States is far down on the list. Norway gives about nine times more, Canada almost four times more. Considered another way, while people in Denmark give $348 per person in foreign aid each year, Americans give just $34 per person, the lowest amount of any industrial nation.[48] Moreover, most U.S. aid is not targeted to help the world's poorest people. The politically sensitive Middle East gets more American money than Latin America, Africa, and East Asia put together, although it has only a tiny fraction of their population. Unfortunately, the United States is not alone in this politicized approach to foreign aid. Otherwise, it would be hard to explain why only one-third of all foreign aid actually went to the world's poorest countries.[49]

It seems clear that a serious effort on the part of the United States and the other industrialized nations to help alleviate the poverty of the less-developed countries should include a significant increase in the total amount of foreign aid and a change in the way it is allocated so that the assistance goes to the people who need it most. Nonetheless, foreign aid is no cure-all for the problems of the peripheral nations. For one thing, the governments of some countries are so corrupt that foreign aid only enriches the local elites and does nothing for the poor. Another problem is that handouts can inadvertently create a vicious cycle of dependency. For example, food from the core nations given to help feed the hungry often drives down the prices paid to local farmers, resulting in lower agricultural production and an even greater need for foreign aid the next year. Wherever possible, foreign aid should, therefore, be carefully targeted toward training, education, birth control, and other specific development projects. Even the World Bank now admits that many of the big foreign aid projects, like building big dams, have done more harm than good. Rather, smaller aid projects—for example, helping individual farmers buy water pumps to irrigate their crops—will do more to reduce poverty in the long run. One of the most popular of these projects is the so-called micro-loan program, which loans small amounts of money to peasants who can benefit from the investment.[50]

FOREIGN WORKERS A 2006 World Bank study estimated that in workers in foreign countries sent $166 billion dollars a year back home. The vast majority of this money goes to poor countries. China and India receive the highest amount of these "remittances," slightly more than $21 billion each. Mexico receives more than $18 billion in remittances, mostly from the United States. Worldwide, the World Bank estimates that world poverty was reduced by about 20 percent because of the money foreign worker send back home.

The two central recommendations from this World Bank report are that the rich nations accept more of these workers from poor countries, and that the rich countries make it cheaper for this money to be transferred to poor family members back home. Although proposals to allow in more foreign workers are highly controversial in the industrialized nations, they make obvious sense given their declining birthrates and aging populations.

BEING GOOD NEIGHBORS Traditionally, most nations haven't been very concerned with anything outside their borders that didn't have a direct impact on them. If neighbors were weak, they were looked on as possible prey; if strong, they were viewed as possible aggressors; otherwise, they were usually ignored. Modern technology and the growth of the world system have made all the world's nations neighbors, but most nations still see the world in terms of narrow self-interest. Even after the end of European colonialism, the rich industrialized nations continued to advance their own interests by meddling in the internal affairs of the poor countries. Since World War II, the United States has fought four full-scale wars in the third world (in Korea, in Vietnam, and two in Iraq); invaded the Dominican Republic, Grenada, Panama, and Afghanistan; organized and funded independent armies in such places as Nicaragua and Cambodia; made assassination attempts against third world leaders; supported and even arranged numerous coups and revolutions, such as the one that brought the Shah of Iran to power and the one that killed Salvador Allende, the leftist president of Chile; and given huge amounts of secret financial assistance to help some political causes and hurt others.[51]

Defenders of these actions claim they actually benefited the countries involved, but the foreign policy of the United States is, after all, designed to advance U.S. interests and those of its upper class, not those of the less-developed countries.[52] Most countries would still like to see the United States and the other industrialized nations take action to help out during acute international crises. But it is critical that such actions be supported by international law and a consensus of the international community, not based simply on naked self-interest. The United States and the other core powers will undoubtedly continue to be politically involved in the third world in one way or another, and it is essential that they act like good neighbors and not the local bullies.

The Less-Developed Countries

Economic development is obviously a much more vital issue in the poor nations than in the industrialized ones, but that does not mean that peripheral nations do not have their own powerful vested interests that oppose significant change. Elite groups that reap the benefits of the current system obviously have little desire for reform. Nonetheless, a growing number of third world leaders realize that it is not a question of whether their societies will change but *how* they will change.

Those governments committed to major reforms face many perplexing issues. Some third world leaders feel that the best path is simply to copy the nations that are already industrialized. Others, however, despite being attracted by the wealth and power of Japan and the Western nations, are also deeply disturbed by the threat industrialization poses to their traditional moral standards and way of life. In the Middle East, for example, many leaders advocate some kind of distinctive "Islamic" approach to development, but it is not clear exactly what that might be or what chances such an approach would have for success. A related question concerns the role of the core powers. Should the leaders of the less-developed countries encourage foreign investment and accept the risk of domination it brings, or should they try to go it alone without much outside money? No matter which course they take, funds are likely to be in short supply, and third world governments will have to make difficult choices among competing options.

POPULATION CONTROL By itself, population control will not solve the problems of the less-developed countries, but neither can those problems be solved without it. Despite some recent improvements, the current rate of population growth in Asia is 1.6 percent a year; and in Latin America, it is 1.5 percent. This means that there must be at least that much economic growth every year just to keep the standard of living from falling. The situation is far worse in sub-Saharan Africa, where the population growth rate is 2.4 percent, and in the Middle East, where it is about 2.0 percent.[53] It is not just an issue of making the economy grow faster than the population, however. There are concrete environmental limits on how many people can comfortably live in a given area. Even if the average income grows, the quality of life declines as overcrowding and pollution make conditions more and more difficult. An increasing number of governments are coming to see excessive population growth as a serious national problem and are starting to take measures to control it.[54] It remains to be seen how effective these programs will be.

ECONOMIC DEVELOPMENT Practically all third world leaders say they are committed to **economic development**, but that phrase has different meanings to different people. One of the biggest issues concerns priorities and goals. Those who want to emulate the industrialized nations tend to focus on large-scale development projects in urban areas. Typically, local governments use loans, foreign investments, or their own funds to build modern factories like those in the core nations. Critics charge that expensive factories with laborsaving equipment make little sense in nations that are short on money but have vast resources of unused labor. They advocate simpler, "low-tech" industries that utilize inexpensive technology and local labor to turn out low-cost products. Others claim that the whole emphasis on industrialization is misguided and that the number-one priority of the governments in the poor nations should be rural development. They argue that because the majority of the people live in rural areas, an effort to increase farm production and prevent runaway urban growth will create the greatest benefits for the most people.

Most leaders in the poor nations nonetheless want to see their countries grow powerful enough to compete on equal terms with the core nations, and that means industrialization. How is that to be achieved? One key ingredient is capital—that is, the money to build the schools, roads, and factories necessary to an industrial economy. Unless a country is blessed with unusually rich natural resources, there are only two ways to get capital: raise it locally or rely on foreign investment. The latter is often a far more attractive alternative to the leaders of the less-developed countries because foreign investors can provide huge sums of money immediately and without the sacrifices and political tensions necessary to raise significant amounts of local capital.

However, a great deal of research indicates that although investment by foreign multinational corporations provides a short-term boost to a local economy, in the long run, self-reliance is the most effective approach.[55] Investments by multinational corporations represent a quick infusion of cash, but once the factories are built, the flow of capital is reversed as the firms take their profits back home. Moreover, the more multinational investment a country allows, the greater the percentage of its economy that will be under foreign control. Time and again, the vast financial resources of the multinationals have enabled them to corrupt local officials and win economic concessions that benefit the corporations to the detriment of the host economy.[56] These generalizations do not mean that multinational investment cannot be beneficial in some circumstances. For example, nations so poor and disorganized that they have few sources of local capital may have no choice but to rely on foreign investors. At the other extreme, the most well-organized of the less-developed countries may be able to accept significant amounts of multinational investment and still maintain strict enough controls to ensure that it provides real benefits to their own economies. Several Asian nations with strong central governments have been able to overcome the negative effects of outside investments from multinational corporations. But even for them, it has proven

Economic development ■ Economic growth in the poor nations.

Signs of Hope

The Quality of Life Improves

It is extremely difficult to measure something as intangible as the "quality of life" in the different countries of the world. The United Nations attempts to do this with what it calls the Human Development Index. This index is based on the combination of the scores for three variables that most people would agree reflect the quality of life in a particular country (at least to some degree). Those three factors are the standard of living, which is measured by the average income per person adjusted to take account of the local cost of living; education, as measured by adult literacy and the average years of schooling; and longevity, measured by life expectancy at birth. When you look at the way the Human Development Index has changed over the years, you get an optimistic picture. In 1960, almost three-fourths of the world's people lived in countries classified as having a low level of human development; today, only about one-third of all people do. The proportion of people living in countries with a high level of human development increased by about one-third, from 16 percent to 23 percent of the world's population, and the percentage living in countries with a medium level of human development more than tripled, from 11 percent to 45 percent. Norway is now rated as having the world's highest level of human development, the United States is seventh, and Sierra Leone is the lowest.*

*United Nations Human Development Programme, *Human Development Report, 2003* (New York: Oxford University Press, 2003), pp. 237–240.

difficult to balance the needs of the country with the demands of the multinational corporations.

POLITICAL REFORM All the nations that have undergone a successful process of industrialization, such as the United States, Germany, and Japan, have had strong, unified governments.[57] The process of industrialization is a grueling one that creates enormous social pressures that cannot be effectively managed in a weak, divided country. In a sharp break with its previous position, even the World Bank in its *World Development Report, 2000* finally recognized the fact that good government is an essential first step to economic improvement, and the poor countries need better governments before "opening economic markets." Since 2000, the World Bank has sponsored many reports that highlight "good governance" as a key to economic development, although it and similar agencies have not been able to give much guidance on how to achieve that goal.[58]

Of course, it is easy to tell the people of less-developed countries that they need to pull together and support a unified government, but how are they to do so? Some nations, such as Japan, had a long tradition of powerful government and obedience to authority, which gave them a significant advantage from the beginning of their drive for industrialization. As we have seen, however, governments in the peripheral nations are likely to be weak and deeply divided along class and ethnic lines. In some cases, democratic reforms can be extremely helpful because they bring a much wider spectrum of people into the process of government and help create more popular support for the regime. Social movements based on religious or economic ideologies have sometimes served to bring a new sense of organization and purpose to floundering governments as well. At other times, violent revolutionary change is required before an unstable government can be replaced by a strong one. Revolution was necessary in Europe, the United States, Russia, and even Japan before those nations could launch effective drives for industrialization. Even the current trend toward fragmentation of large countries into smaller nations with more ethnic homogeneity may be beneficial if the end result is the creation of more unified nations with stronger governments. It is clear, however, that no single factor—including a unified and well-run government—can guarantee economic success.

The emperors of classical China used the authority of their government to prevent the merchant class from becoming prosperous enough to threaten the power of the feudal landlords, and they thereby also prevented the growth of a modern economy. The situation was similar in Japan, where the process of industrialization could not begin until after the shogun (military dictator) was overthrown in 1868. More recently, the powerful communist state in the old Soviet Union was extremely effective in carrying out a crash program of industrialization, but the militarism and rigid bureaucratic mentality of that regime eventually choked off its own economic growth.

In contrast to the vexing problems in Russia after the collapse of the old Soviet Union and the economic stagnation in many developing nations in Africa and Latin America, the poor nations of East Asia have undergone some remarkable growth. A key difference in Asia has been the presence of more efficient governments that can promote economic development while still protecting the interests of the nation's people. What scholars sometimes call a "hard state" can, if it keeps the interests of the whole nation in mind, not only make the tough decisions that are necessary for economic growth but also carry them out even though they may cause a create a great deal of pain and public resistance in the short run.[59]

QUICK REVIEW

- What can we in the industrialized nations do to help the poor nations of the world?
- What are the poor nations' best options for improving themselves?

Sociological Perspectives on the Global Divide

Most sociologists are convinced that in order to deal with social problems effectively, we must first understand their causes and then formulate our response based on that understanding. As we have seen, functionalism (by shaping modernization theory) and conflict theory (through its influence on world system theory) have played a major role in explaining the deep divisions in today's world; each approach implies a different program of action. Feminists and interactionists have also given their attention to these problems and have made their own important contributions to our understanding of global inequality.

The Functionalist Perspective

Wherever functionalists look at the less-developed countries, they see the problems of social disorganization. Under pressure from rapid economic change, the extended family is breaking down and its traditional power is slowly ebbing away. There is a growing cultural lag as people cling to traditional attitudes that were useful in the past but have now become a serious drawback. For example, most people in the less-developed countries still place a high importance on having a large family, even though rapid population growth in most poor countries makes that an extremely dysfunctional attitude. Traditional religious beliefs are being challenged by secular ideas from the West and a rising tide of materialism. The educational institutions that foster the scientific worldview are often so weak that they do not even reach large segments of the population. As we have noted, governments are ineffective and deeply divided. Perhaps most serious of all, economic institutions have not made a smooth transition from an agricultural to an industrial system and often flounder somewhere between the two. A flood of immigrant villagers pours into cities that lack enough jobs, sanitation, and housing to support them. Thus, functionalists see the less-developed countries as being in a difficult state of transition from one kind of social and cultural system to another.

Because functionalists generally assume that the less-developed countries will ultimately end up as Western-style industrial nations, they feel that the best way to help is to speed up the process of transition so these societies can regain their balance as quickly as possible. Functionalists, therefore, recommend a much stronger emphasis on education in less-developed countries in order to teach people the skills necessary in an industrial economy. They advocate a strong program of family planning to help change dysfunctional attitudes favoring large families. Urban development programs must be launched to create enough housing for the expanding urban population. Because functionalists are not especially concerned about the issue of economic exploitation, they often advocate more foreign investment by multinational corporations as a good way to spread modern attitudes and economic structures. Finally, the governments of the less-developed countries need to be made more democratic so that they can gain the support of their population for the difficult reforms that must be made.

The Conflict Perspective

Where the functionalists see disorganization, the conflict theorists see the results of international exploitation. In the past, the exploitation was obvious. When the Europeans first colonized a new area, they would loot whatever gold and jewels they could find and then take over direct political control of the native peoples. Today the exploitation is more subtle, but conflict theorists are convinced that it is just as real. The peripheral nations now have their own governments, but conflict theorists feel that the armies and the secret agents of the industrial powers are always waiting to punish any third world leader who gets out of line. The people of the peripheral nations are no longer forced to work as slaves in the mines and plantations, but they work for wages so low that they are barely better off than slaves. Foreigners no longer simply steal the wealth of the peripheral countries—they buy up their precious natural resources at a fraction of their real value.

To the conflict theorists, the answer to the problems of the third world is a simple one: end the economic exploitation that has victimized so much of the Earth's population. Exactly how that is to be done is a more difficult matter. Despite the failure of the communist government of the Soviet Union, many conflict theorists are still strong supporters of third world revolutionary movements that seek to overthrow their local governments. They urge the revolutionaries to create new regimes that are free from foreign dominance and represent the interests of all their people and not just a small elite. Conflict theorists also encourage third world nations to band together in the struggle against the industrialized nations. They point to the success the Organization of Petroleum Exporting Countries (OPEC) had in increasing the price of oil, and they call for the creation of similar cartels for other raw materials. Many conflict theorists feel that the key to liberating the third world lies in the core nations. They argue that because the multinational corporations are exploiting workers in the industrialized nations in much the same way they exploit the workers in the third world, the two groups must join together to demand the creation of a more just world order that will benefit them all.

The Feminist Perspective

From the feminist perspective, the poor women of the third world are the most exploited of all the exploited. Not only are their countries exploited by foreigners, but also the poor people within a country are exploited by the rich, and the poor women are exploited by their husbands and their other male family members. As we have seen in this chapter, the women of the third world are denied the most basic human rights to control their own lives and are often treated as little more than domestic servants by their family members.

Aside from its obvious injustice, this system also wastes the talents and leadership abilities of the third world's women. Feminists therefore advocate the kind of female-oriented development projects that have proved not only to improve the status of women but also to be one of the most effective techniques to stimulate economic development. One of the best examples is the Grameen Bank, whose founder won the Nobel Peace Prize in 2006. The bank started in Bangladesh but now has more than 1,000 branches around the world. The Grameen Bank specializes in making small loans to poor women in order to help them do such things as set up businesses or improve their farms. The bank prefers female clients because they have found that money loaned to women was more likely to be used to benefit the whole family and that women were more likely to repay their loans than men. The results of these modest loans have often proved to be revolutionary, not only improving the local economy but also helping liberate women from the domination of their husbands.[60]

The Interactionist Perspective

Interactionists' primary contribution to the study of global inequality has been through their efforts to understand the psychological consequences of modernization. Agricultural societies are characterized by mass poverty and a huge gap between the elite and the common people. Nonetheless, these tradition-bound societies provide their members with a sense of security and belonging seldom found in the industrialized world. Most people are born, live, and die in the same close-knit villages. The important transitions in life are all marked by religious rituals, and everyone holds similar definitions of the world and of each other. Because poverty is the rule, not the exception, it holds no shame. The difficulty of social mobility and the absence of a profit-oriented economy minimize competition and the tensions it causes.

Sooner or later, the process of modernization shatters this traditional perspective, and people must grope for a new way to define the world. Many leave their familiar villages and move into urban environments, where few of the old rules seem to apply. Even if they can maintain strong family ties in this new world, the old sense of belonging is gone. The pressures of overpopulation and a changing economy create an intensely competitive environment in which those who fail may literally starve to death. Even those who remain in the villages are likely to find their lives changing in disturbing ways. Increasing levels of education and exposure to the media slowly undermine the old perspectives and spread the new commercial orientation. At the same time, economic dislocation and environmental deterioration make it harder and harder to make a living off the land.

Solutions to these problems must come from the kinds of proposals advanced by the macro theories, but interactionists make two additional recommendations. First, they urge the governments of the less-developed countries to focus their efforts on improving the rural economy so that people can stay in their villages and avoid the wrenching psychological changes that accompany urban migration. Second, they advise the leaders of these nations to learn from the mistakes of the West and do their best to maintain strong family and community institutions.

QUICK REVIEW

■ Compare and contrast the functionalist and conflict approaches to global inequality.

■ What solutions do feminists offer for the problems of global inequality?

■ What has been the psychological impact of modernization?

Summary

The people from different parts of the world used to have little contact with each other, but the process of globalization is creating a worldwide economic, political, and social system that is becoming increasingly important in our daily lives. The nations of the world make up a kind of international class system with the rich industrialized nations at the top and a much larger group of what are often called *less-developed countries* below them. The most obvious difference between these two groups of nations is their wealth—both in terms of money and accumulated assets such as buildings, roads, and factories. Because of runaway population growth and rapid urbanization, most cities in the less-developed countries have a large number of homeless people and huge shantytowns. Inadequate nutrition and contagious disease make the life expectancy far below that in the industrialized nations. Women are commonly denied the most basic rights men enjoy, and children face serious health and economic problems. Literacy rates are low, and because there is only a small middle class, the gap between the rich and the poor is usually a large one. The less-developed countries are also more likely to have deep ethnic divisions and ineffective governments.

The enormous difference between the wealthy nations and the poor nations developed in the modern era as some countries underwent a rapid process of industrialization while others did not. Modernization theorists see industrialization as a universal process that has simply taken place more quickly in some parts of the world than in others. The less-developed countries have made slower progress because they have clung to traditional attitudes and values that impede industrialization. World system theory, on the other hand, sees industrialization as a global process, not a national one. All nations are seen to be part of a single world system dominated by the industrialized nations (the core), which exploit the poor nations (the periphery).

The rich countries can help the less-developed ones by opening up their markets, forgiving the debts owed by the poor nations, increasing foreign aid, allowing in more foreign workers, and ending their political interference in the internal affairs of the poor nations. The less-developed countries themselves are faced with many difficult choices. Do they emphasize industrialization or rural development? Do they encourage investment by multinational corporations or depend on their own resources? How are their limited development funds best spent? There are no simple answers to these questions, but it does seem clear that most of the less-developed countries need better population-control programs, a greater effort at economic development, and stronger governments.

Functionalists see today's global divide as the product of social disorganization in the less-developed countries, and they recommend programs to speed up the transition to full industrialization in order to bring more stability to these societies. Conflict theorists see most of today's global problems as the direct result of European colonialism and the exploitative economic system that developed from it. They recommend an international effort by poor and working-class people around the world to create a more just international order. Feminists call for more female-oriented development programs both to improve the status of women and to promote general economic improvements. Interactionists point out that the destruction of the traditional worldview and way of life in agricultural societies has also meant a great deal more insecurity and anxiety for the average person. They urge the leaders of the less-developed countries to work to keep their family and community institutions strong.

QUESTIONS FOR CRITICAL THINKING

When most Americans think about improving conditions in the third world, they think of making those countries more like us, but is that really a good idea? What problems has our process of industrialization created for us? Is there some way the developing countries can avoid repeating our mistakes? Would it even be possible for the whole world to consume as many resources and produce as much pollution as we do?

KEY TERMS

capital accumulation
colonialism
core
economic development
ethnocentrism
hegemonic power

globalization
industrial revolution
less-developed countries
  (LDCs), third world
modernization
periphery

semiperiphery
sub-Saharan Africa
urban subsistence economy
world system

INTERNET EXERCISE

The gap between the rich and the poor of this world has increased substantially in recent decades. The new trend toward globalization of economies has threatened to make this inequality even worse in coming years. International agencies such as the United Nations and the World Bank have been exploring the extent of world poverty and its causes for many decades. To begin your exploration of these Websites, go to the *Companion Website* at www.pearsonhighered.com/coleman. Enter Chapter 17 and choose the Web destination module from the navigation bar.

Go to the International Fund for Agricultural Development's Website at www.ifad.org and click on Documents and Publications. Then click on Publications, and click on "Rural Poverty Report 2001," which describes the extent and problems of rural poverty in the world. Click on Introduction and Overview to download. Why does this agency believe we should give greater attention to rural poverty in the world rather than only urban poverty? How has rural poverty changed around the world since 1970?

NOTES

1. *International Herald Tribune, New York Times*, March 26, 2002.

2. World Bank, *Aid and Reform in Africa* (New York: Oxford University Press, 2002).

3. World Bank, *World Development Report, 2000–2001* (New York: Oxford University Press, 2001).

4. See Christopher Chase-Dunn, Yukio Kawano, and Benjamin D. Brewer, "Trade Globalization Since 1795: Waves of Integration in the World-System," *American Sociological Review* 65 (2000): 77–95; David Held, Anthony McGrew, David Golblatt and Jonathan Perraton, *Global Transformations: Politics, Economics, and Culture* (Palo Alto, CA: Stanford University Press, 1999).

5. See Harold R. Kerbo, *Social Stratification and Inequality*, 6th ed. (New York: McGraw-Hill, 2003), Chapter 14.

6. See Harold R. Kerbo, *World Poverty at the 21st Century: The Modern World System and the Roots of Global Inequality* (New York: McGraw-Hill, 2006), Chapter 1.

7. United Nations, *A Better World for All* (New York: Author, 2000); United Nations Development Programme, *Overcoming Human Poverty* (New York: Author, 2000).

8. Population Reference Bureau, *World Population Data Sheet, 2006* (Washington, DC: Author, 2006).

9. James B. Davies, Susanna Sandstrom, Anthony Shorrocks, and Edward N. Wolff, *The World Distribution of Household Wealth*, www.un.org, 2006.

10. World Bank, *World Development Report, 2007* (New York: Oxford University Press, 2007), p. 288.

11. World Bank, *World Development Report, 2004* (New York: Oxford University Press, 2004), p. 259.

12. Kerbo, *World Poverty at the 21st Century*.

13. United Nations, *Human Development Report, 2003* (New York: Oxford University Press, 2003), p. 265.

14. Ibid.

15. World Bank, *World Development Report, 2004*, pp. 159–171.

16. United Nations Food and Agricultural Organization, *The State of Food Security in the World, 2003* (Rome: United Nations, 2004), p. 6.

17. United Nations, *A Better World for All*; United Nations Development Program, *Overcoming Human Poverty, 2004*.

18. United Nations Food and Agricultural Organization, *The State of Food Security in the World, 2003*, p. 16.

19. United Nations, *Human Development Report, 2003*, p. 257.

20. World Health Organization, *The World Health Report, 2003; Shaping the Future* (Geneva, Switzerland: World Health Organization, 2003).

21. Ibid.

22. World Bank, *World Development Report, 2004*, pp. 259–260.

23. Ibid., p. 273.

24. Ibid., pp. 274–275.

25. United Nations Development Programme, *Overcoming Human Poverty*, pp. 149–151, 172–173.

26. Population Reference Bureau, *World Population Data Sheet, 2006*.

27. UNICEF, *The State of the World's Children*, www.unicef.org., 2006.

28. Ibid.

29. Germaine W. Shames, "The World's Throw-Away Children," in Jackson, ed., *Global Issues 94/95*, pp. 229–232.

30. World Bank, *World Development Report*, pp. 288–289.

31. ibid.

32. Mark Fineman, "Anxious Mexicans Await Day of the Vote," *Los Angeles Times*, August 21, 1994, pp. A1, A10.

33. Kerbo, *World Poverty in the 21st Century*, Chapter 2.

34. World Bank, *World Development Report, 2002* (Oxford University Press, 2002), p. 8.

35. See World Bank, *World Development Report, 2000–2001* for some comparative statistics; and see L. S. Stavrianos, *Global Rift: The Third World Comes of Age* (New York: Morrow, 1981) for a comprehensive history of the development of the Third World.

36. See, for example, Talcott Parsons, *Societies: Evolutionary and Comparative Perspectives* (Upper Saddle River, NJ: Prentice-Hall, 1966), and Wilbert Moore, *Social Change*, 2nd ed. (Upper Saddle River, NJ: Prentice-Hall, 1974).

37. Walter W. Rostow, *The Stages of Economic Growth* (New York: Cambridge University Press, 1960).

38. For a contemporary discussion of these issues from a Weberian perspective, see Daniel Chirot, "The Rise of the West," *American Sociological Review* 50 (1985): 181–195.

39. See Walter W. Rostow, *The World Economy: History and Prospect* (Austin: University of Texas Press, 1980).

40. Andre Gunder Frank, *Capitalism and Underdevelopment in Latin America* (New York: Monthly Review Press, 1967).

41. See, for example, Immanuel Wallerstein's three-volume historical work, *The Modern World System* (New York: Academic Press, 1974, 1980, 1988).

42. For an excellent summary of world system theory and an analysis of its strengths and weaknesses, see Thomas Richard Shannon, *An Introduction to the World-System Perspective*, 2nd ed. (Boulder, CO: Westview, 1996).

43. *International Herald Tribune*, April 27, 2004.

44. For example, see *International Herald Tribune*, February 21, 2004.

45. *International Herald Tribune*, April 27, 2004, September 24, 2003, May 4, 2001.

46. World Bank, *World Development Report, 2007*, p. 296.

47. See *International Herald Tribune*, September 18, 2000; World Bank, *Heavily Indebted Countries Progress Report* (2001).

48. United Nations, *Human Development Report, 2002* (New York: Oxford University Press, 2002), pp. 202, 216.

49. World Bank, *World Development Report, 2000–2001*, p. 196. United Nations, *Human Development Report, 2003*, p. 253.

50. See *International Herald Tribune*, September 27, 2000.

51. See James William Coleman, *The Criminal Elite: Understanding White Collar Crime* (New York: St. Martin's Press, 1998), pp. 61–66.

52. On the control of foreign policy by elite groups, see G. William Domhoff, *The Power Elite and the State* (New York: Aldine de Gruyter, 1990).

53. Population Reference Bureau, *World Population Data Sheet, 2006*.

54. See ibid. for a description of each nation's official view of its current rate of population growth.

55. See Volker Bornschier and Christopher Chase-Dunn, *Transnational Corporations and Underdevelopment* (New York: Praeger, 1985).

56. For a summary of this research see Kerbo, *World Poverty in the 21st Century*, Chapter 4.

57. See Daniel Chirot, *Social Change in the Modern Era* (San Diego: Harcourt Brace Jovanovich, 1986).

58. World Bank, *World Development Report, 2000–2001*; see Kerbo, *World Poverty in the 21st Century*, Chapter 2.

59. Chalmers Johnson, *MITI and the Japanese Miracle* (Stanford: Stanford University Press, 1982); Harold Kerbo and John McKinstry, *Who Rules Japan? The Inner Circles of Economic and Political Power* (Westport, CT: Greenwood/Praeger, 1995); Ezra Vogel, *The Four Little Dragons: The Spread of Industrialization in East Asia* (Cambridge, MA: Harvard University Press, 1991); Ezra Vogel, *One Step Ahead in China: Guangdong Under Reform* (Cambridge, MA: Harvard University Press, 1989).

60. World Bank, *World Development Report, 2000–2001*; Muhammad Yunus, "Helping the Poor to Help Themselves," *Los Angeles Times*, February 17, 1997, p. B5; Robin Wright, "Women as Engines Out of Poverty," *Los Angeles Times*, May 27, 1997, pp. A1, A6.

Problems in Politics and the Global Economy

THINKING SOCIOLOGICALLY

- Do the rich actually get richer while the poor get poorer? What part does the political economy play in the distribution of wealth in the United States?

- How is uneven economic development related to problems in the global economy?

- "Politics is a rich man's game." Based on this chapter, do you agree or disagree with this statement?

From Chapter 13 of *Social Problems in a Diverse Society*, Sixth Edition. Diana Kendall. Copyright © 2013 by Pearson Education, Inc. Published by Pearson Social Science & Art. All rights reserved.

((••—[Listen to the Chapter Audio on mysoclab.com

Mrs. Parry is a woman battered by events that were outside her control. I met her in the centre of Ashington, a 27,000-strong community about seventeen miles north of Newcastle. It was the world's biggest mining village until the local pit closed in 1986, just a year after the defeat of the Miners' Strike. Thousands were thrown out of work; the community has never recovered.

When I asked Mrs. Parry what impact the pit's closure had on the community, she interrupted me before I had even finished the question. "We died!" she responded with a combination of grief and conviction. "Once all the mines closed, all the community had gone. It's just been a big depression ever since, just struggling to survive, that's all." Both her father and her then-husband were miners. They split up the year he lost his job. "We owed not just our livelihoods, but our lives to the pits as well. My dad retired, and then he died. My marriage broke up."

—Owen Jones (2011), author of Chavs: The Demonization of the Working Class, *describes the long-term effects that closing all the mines in Ashington (England) had on*

the community and on Mrs. Parry's family. This is one of many examples of how numerous villages in Great Britain were devastated by the collapse of mining and other local industries, as well as the lack of a governmental response to such economic conditions.

Even if we had depressing issues before [in Detroit, Michigan], the decline [in population] makes it so much harder to deal with. Yes, the city feels empty physically, empty of people, empty of ambition, drive. It feels empty.

—Samantha Howell, a Detroit resident, explains to journalist Katharine Q. Seelye (2011) how it feels to live in Detroit, which saw the largest percentage loss (25 percent) of any American city with more than 100,000 residents (other than New Orleans) between 2000 and 2010. Deindustrialization and loss of automobile manufacturing plants devastated this urban area and caused many residents to flee to the suburbs and elsewhere.

Whether in Great Britain or the United States, stories such as these are being told by ordinary citizens and journalists who want to describe the effects that changes in the economy have had on people, communities, and the larger society. Coupled with these stories is the question of what, if anything, should governments do about job loss, unemployment, and rising inequality. In most high-income nations, many people see their economic fate as being intricately linked not only to local, national, and global economic conditions but also to decisions made by political leaders that affect their livelihood and overall economic situation. In this chapter we examine politics and the economy together because they are deeply interrelated.

Politics **is the social institution through which power is acquired and exercised by certain individuals and groups.** Although political decisions typically are made on a nation-by-nation basis, many of these decisions affect the lives and economic status of people in other nations as well. The *economy* **is the social institution that ensures that a society will be maintained through its production, distribution, and consumption of goods and services.** Because of the extent to which politics and the economy are related in high-income, industrialized nations such as the United States, some sociologists believe that it is more accurate to refer to the "political economy" as one entity—a combined social institution where the players, rules, and games often overlap. The *political economy* **refers to the interdependent workings and interests**

DID YOU KNOW

- Many people who make money from the underground economy have legitimate jobs and are thought of as "law-abiding" citizens.

- Some individual transnational corporations have more financial clout than entire nations.

- If we divided all of the personal debt in the United States among all citizens, each person would owe at least $52,000.

of political and economic systems. To gain a better understanding of how the political economy works, it is important to take a closer look at various types of economic systems, the global economy, and the role of governments and corporations in shaping economic conditions around the world.

MODERN ECONOMIC SYSTEMS AND THE UNDERGROUND ECONOMY

There are three major modern economic systems: capitalism, socialism, and mixed economies. Of course, there is no such thing as "pure" capitalism or "pure" socialism, but each is characterized by several key tenets that distinguish it as an approach to producing and distributing goods and services in a society. In addition to these three "legitimate" economies, the underground ("illegal") economy is also growing around the world.

Capitalism

Capitalism **is an economic system characterized by private ownership of the means of production, from which personal profits can be derived through market competition and without government intervention.** There are four distinctive features of "ideal" capitalism: private ownership of the means of production, pursuit of personal profit, competition, and lack of government intervention.

Read the Document

Asceticism and the Spirit of Capitalism on mysoclab.com

First, capitalism is based on the right of individuals to own various kinds of property, including those that produce income (e.g., factories and businesses). In a capitalist economy, individuals and corporations not only own income-producing property, but they also have the right to "buy" people's labor.

Second, capitalism is based on the belief that people should be able to maximize their individual gain through personal profit, which is supposed to benefit everyone, not just the capitalists. The idea that "rising tides lift all boats" is central to the pursuit of personal profit being a major tenet of capitalism: the belief is that, if some businesses have high profits, these profits will benefit not only the capitalists who own those businesses, but also their workers and the general public, which will benefit from increased public expenditures for things that everyone uses, such as roads and schools.

Third, capitalism is based on competition, which is supposed to prevent any one business from making excessive profits. For example, when companies are competing for customers, they must offer innovative goods and services at competitive prices. The need to do this, it is argued, prevents excessive profits. One twenty-first century economic problem is the extent to which competition has been reduced or eliminated in many economic sectors by the business practices of major corporations.

Finally, capitalism is based on a lack of government intervention in the marketplace. According to this *laissez-faire* (meaning "leave alone") policy, also called *free enterprise*, competition in a free marketplace should be the force that regulates prices and establishes workers' wages, rather than the government doing so.

Socialism

As compared to capitalism, *socialism* **is characterized by public ownership of the means of production, the pursuit of collective goals, and centralized decision making.** Under socialism, there are governmental limits on the right of individuals and corporations to own productive property. In a truly socialist economy, the means of production are owned and controlled by a collectivity or by the state, not by private individuals or corporations. Unlike capitalist economies, in which the primary motivation for economic activity is personal profit, the primary motivation in a socialist economy is supposed to be the collective good of all citizens. Although socialist economies typically have less economic inequality than the United States, there has been a move in many nations toward *privatization*, a process in which resources are converted from state ownership to private ownership, and the government maintains an active role in developing, recognizing, and protecting private property rights. Privatization continues today in formerly socialist countries such as the Republic of Turkey, where the nations iron and steel industry has been privatized so that it could compete with similar businesses in the rest of the world. Through privatization of the steel maker, political leaders hoped to realize a profit that would help pay down the country's budget deficit and attract foreign investors (Presidency of the Republic of Turkey, 2010). As socialist countries continue to develop a capitalist model of economic production and distribution, it is important to reflect on how

Karl Marx viewed socialism as an answer to the problems produced by capitalism.

Highly critical of the growing economic inequality that emerged as capitalism flourished in the 1800s, the early economist and social thinker Karl Marx argued that socialism could serve as an intermediate stage on the way to an ideal communist society in which the means of production and all goods would be owned by everyone. Under communism, Marx said, people would contribute according to their abilities and receive according to their needs. Moreover, government would no longer be necessary, since government existed only to serve the interests of the capitalist class. However, in actual practice, problems of economic and political instability, low standards of living, and other internal issues plagued the former Soviet Union as well as Cuba, the Republic of China, and other nations that have tried to establish socialist and communist economic systems.

Mixed Economies

No economy is purely capitalist or purely socialist; most are mixtures of both. A **mixed economy combines elements of both capitalism (a market economy) and socialism (a command economy)**. In one type of mixed economy, *state capitalism*, the government is involved in the dealings of privately owned companies, including having a strong role in setting the rules, policies, and objectives of the businesses. Countries such as Japan and Singapore in Asia and Saudi Arabia in the Middle East are examples of state capitalism; however, the outcomes are quite different. In Asia, greater government involvement may have resulted in greater good for more individuals, but in Saudi Arabia, it appears to have only made a few people extremely wealthy.

Some western European nations, including Sweden, Britain, and France, have an economic and political system known as *democratic socialism*, in which private ownership of some of the means of production is combined with governmental distribution of some essential goods and services and free elections. In these nations, the government is heavily involved in providing services such as medical care, child care, and transportation for all residents. For this reason, some analysts refer to these economies as *welfare capitalism* to highlight the fact that privately owned companies coexist with extensive governmental programs that provide certain essential services to everyone without cost or at a greatly reduced cost.

The Underground (Informal) Economy

As compared to the legitimate economy in which taxes are paid on income and people have licenses or credentials that allow them to perform the work they do, the *underground economy* is made up of money-making activities that people do not report to the government and for jobs they may not have the licenses or credentials to perform (such as the "gypsy" cabs in New York City that do not have proper medallions, or permits, to operate as taxis for hire). Sometimes referred to as the "informal" or "shadow economy," one segment of the underground economy is made up of workers who are paid "off the books," which means that they are paid in cash, their earnings are not reported, and no taxes are paid. Lawful jobs, such as nannies, construction workers, and landscape/yard workers in the United States, are often part of the shadow economy because workers and bosses make under-the-table deals so that both can gain through the transaction: Employers pay less for workers' services, and workers have more money to take home than if they paid taxes on their earnings.

The underground economy also involves trade in lawful goods that are sold "off the books" so that no taxes are paid and unlawful goods, such as the worldwide sale of "designer alternative fashion" products that are counterfeit ("knockoff") merchandise. Demand for such products is strong at all times but frequently improves in difficult economic times because many people retain a desire for luxury goods, particularly those that are widely discussed and publicized by the media even when individuals have fewer resources to allocate to luxury purchases (Box 1).

According to one way of thinking, operating a business in the underground economy reveals capitalism at its best because it shows how the "free market" might work if there were no government intervention. However, from another perspective, selling goods or services in the underground economy borders on—or moves into—criminal behavior. For some individuals, the underground economy offers the only means for purchasing certain goods or for overcoming unemployment, particularly in low-income and poverty areas where people may feel alienated from the wider world and believe that using shady means is the only way to survive (Venkatesh, 2006). The underground economy operates on a global basis. Labor and products easily flow across national borders despite the efforts of law enforcement officials to curb such practices.

Box 1

The Media and the Underground Economy

While some people love their [knockoff] Chanel bags (I spot those fakes all over campus!), others would rather rock Target than fake designer anything. . . . Personally, I'm not 100% against knockoffs—they make design affordable for everyone. . . . On the other hand, I'd never carry a faux Chanel bag—it would be sacrilegious! I don't think I could live with myself if I pretend a fake Chanel was real. Every time I wore it (which would be almost every day), I'd know I was lying to myself and the world. I'd rather save up and earn the real thing or not have one at all.

—*One woman expresses the ambivalence some women feel about buying "knockoff" or illegal "designer alternative" handbags, but this does not keep millions of people around the world from purchasing such merchandise (Zephyr, 2009).*

We are pretty use[d] to seeing stories about fake Apple products that stream out of China but it seems that some bootleggers have decided to raise the bar and have opened up "Apple Stores" in some Chinese cities. According to one American couple who came across one in the city of Kunming, several hundred miles from the nearest official Apple Store. . . . [It takes] careful observation to spot the fake stores [because they] are faithful reproductions of the Apple Store theme. The really amazing things is that the employees in these stores believe that they are actually working for Apple, blue t-shirts and all.

—*Steve Hodson (2011) posted this sighting (with photos) of a fake "Apple Store" that sells fake "Apple" products in China on The Inquisitr website.*

From ads to "celebrity sightings" of media stars wearing designer handbags to using their Apple iPads, iPhones, and iPods, everyday people are bombarded with images of the rich and famous carrying or wearing the latest name-brand products. Media framing of stories about luxury merchandise (legally or illegally produced) typically uses a "price-tag framing" approach. *Price-tag framing* occurs when the cost and "exclusivity" of a luxury item is a key feature in a media story or blog. This type of framing focuses on *how much*? and encourages potential consumers to focus on the cost of a luxury item and on the high-profile status of people who own similar goods (Kendall, 2011). A second type of framing also comes into play in heightening consumers' desire for Apple products or other communications technology: *Show-off framing* is the use of a name-brand product to make a person feel important, in-the-know, and on the cutting edge of technology. For example, to have an iPhone 3 when iPhone 4 came out was to be unimportant, out-of-the-loop with

other people, and not on the cutting edge. Real and fake products are used to fill this need in people and the image of the company—real or fake—is used to lure customers.

Consumers' desires for trendy and luxury products are fulfilled in the underground economy because manufacturers make look-alike products that are sometimes offered for lower prices. These products typically are made by low-wage workers who use less expensive materials and shoddy workmanship. Then unscrupulous—or unsuspecting, in the case of the Apple store in China—salespersons hawk the goods on the streets, in fake stores, or the Internet. In the underground economy, knockoff products are sold at global tourist attractions such as the Eiffel Tower in Paris and streets bordering the Venice canals to "Counterfeit Triangle" along Canal Street in New York City and Internet websites.

Why do people purchase fake merchandise? How do the media become involved in this charade? Although full equality does not exist in any society, consumers around the world tend to view themselves as having an "equal right" to purchase items that will make them equal to others regardless of their position in the economic hierarchy. If luxury merchandise that they want comes from the underground economy, so be it, at least from their perspective. The media become involved through endless ads and journalistic descriptions about the intangible aspects of clothing, handbags, cell phones, and other smart technologies that suggest that consumption of certain products defines who we are and elevates us in the eyes of other people, and apparently this approach works despite the origins of the merchandise.

Questions for Consideration

1. What effect does the underground economy have on the legitimate economy in high-income nations such as the United States? What about low-income nations?

2. How does media framing influence consumer desires even in difficult economic times?

3. To what extent do political leaders encourage (or discourage) the growth of an underground economy in their country?

Independent Research

If you are interested in doing further research on this topic, find websites that offer fashion knockoffs or other high-demand merchandise for sale. Analyze these ads or blurbs to see what claims are being made and how these claims compare with "legitimate" advertising and media stories about the same products. Discuss ways in which the underground economy makes it possible for individuals to purchase products they otherwise might not have. Identify problems the underground economy causes for the legitimate economy in a nation.

PROBLEMS IN THE GLOBAL ECONOMY

The global financial crisis that began in 2007–2008—and has not been fully resolved—demonstrates how closely connected problems in the U.S economy are with those of other nations. When U.S. financial institutions were in crisis, the economic well-being of many other nations was also in question because it was widely assumed that high-income nations with advanced economic development would continue to set the pace of global economies.

▣ Watch on mysoclab.com
Globalization on mysoclab.com

Not all nations are at the same stage of economic development, however, and this creates a widely stratified global economy in which some countries are very wealthy, some are much less wealthy, and still others are very poor. We refer to these as high-income, middle-income, and low-income nations. How these nations are classified is related to their level of economic development and the amount of national and personal income in the country. This development can be traced back to the economic organization of societies in the past.

Inequality Based on Uneven Economic Development

Depending on the major type of economic production, a society can be classified as having a preindustrial, industrial, or postindustrial economy. In preindustrial economies, most workers engage in *primary-sector production*—**the extraction of raw materials and natural resources from the environment**. In this type of economy, materials and resources are used without much processing. Today, extracting gold and silver from mines in Indonesia is an example of primary-sector production.

By comparison with preindustrial economies, most workers in industrial economies are engaged in *secondary-sector production*—**the processing of raw materials (from the primary sector) into finished products**. Work in industrial economies is much more specialized, repetitive, and bureaucratically organized than in preindustrial economies. Assembly-line work, now done on a global basis, is an example. Here is Ben Hamper's (1991:88–89) description of his first day working on the rivet line at a truck and bus manufacturing plant here in the United States:

The Rivet Line was the starting point for all that went on during the three-day snake trail needed to assemble a truck. The complex birth procedure began right here. It started with a couple of long black rails. As the rails were hoisted onto crawling pedestals, the workers began riveting them together and affixing them with various attachments. There weren't any screws or bolts to be seen. Just rivets. Thousands upon thousands of dull gray rivets. They resembled mushrooms. . . . I looked around at [other workers] who would soon be my neighbors. I'd seen happier faces on burn victims.

Although Hamper's discussion about assembly-line work is more than two decades old, the basic description of how factories work remains largely unchanged with the exception of additional technology and robotics in some industrial settings. In other countries where secondary-sector production is moving from the United States, even greater abuses of workers are often found. In China, for example, workers in grim factories have high rates of suicide and job turnover because they cannot stand the working conditions. After a number of suicides at Foxconn Technology in Shenzhen, China, journalist David Barboza (2010) wrote about factory life as follows:

[Ma Xiangqian, who committed suicide, hated his job which included] . . . an 11-hour overnight shift, seven nights a week, forging plastic and metal into electronic parts amid fumes and dust. Or at least that was Mr. Ma's job until, after a run-in with his supervisor, he was demoted to cleaning toilets. Mr. Ma's pay stub shows that he worked 286 hours in the month before he died, including 112 hours of overtime, about three times the legal limit. For all of that, even with extra pay for overtime, he earned the equivalent of $1 an hour.

Although computers and other technology have changed the nature of the production process in some settings, the kinds of factory work described previously are often repetitive, heavily supervised, and full of rules for workers to follow, whether these assembly plants are located in the United States, China, or other nations in today's global economy.

Unlike preindustrial and industrial economies, postindustrial economies are characterized by *tertiary-sector production*, which means that **workers provide services rather than goods as their primary source of livelihood**. Tertiary-sector production includes work in such areas as food service, transportation, communication, education, real estate, advertising, sports,

Industrial and postindustrial economies often blend in the twenty-first century workplace. Shown here is a clean room (a factory-type setting) at a computer hard-drive manufacturing plant where products are made for use in the communication and information technology sectors.

and entertainment. Inequality typically increases in postindustrial economies where people in high-tech, high-wage jobs often thrive financially and have business connections throughout the world while, at the same time, workers in low-tech, low-wage jobs in the service sector (such as fast-food servers or hotel cleaning personnel) may have a hard time paying their basic bills and may feel very isolated from the economic mainstream of their own society. Today, manufacturing and production accounts for slightly more than 10 percent of U.S. economic output, and the service sector is the most rapidly growing component. For this reason, some sociologists refer to the United States as an advanced industrial society, which is characterized by greater dependence on an international division of labor (R. Hodson and Sullivan, 2008). In the United States, corporations rely on workers throughout the

world to produce goods and services for paying customers in this country and elsewhere.

At one end of the international division of labor is low-wage labor. For example, along the U.S.–Mexican border, some U.S. corporations run *maquiladora* plants—factories in Mexico where components manufactured in the United States are assembled into finished goods and shipped back to the United States for sale. In countries such as Mexico, where the economy has been less robust, it was possible to find workers who are willing to work for lower wages and fewer benefits than the typical worker in a high-income nation. Recently, employment opportunities have expanded in Mexico, and average family income has increased more than 45 percent since 2000. At the other end of the international division of labor are workers in countries such as Ireland and India, where U.S. corporations are able to find well-educated workers who view jobs in fields such as insurance claims processing, reading of certain types of medical tests, and filling out tax returns for U.S. workers to be a source of economic stability and upward mobility. As a result, what may be viewed as a problem in the global economy for some in the United States, namely the shifting of jobs from this country to other nations, may be viewed as a solution in those countries where young workers see their employment opportunities expanding and no longer feel a need to move elsewhere to work. Transnational corporations headquartered in high-income nations have had a major influence on economies and governments worldwide.

Transnational Corporations and the Lack of Accountability

Today, the most important corporate structure is the *transnational corporation*—**a large-scale business organization that is headquartered in one country but operates in many countries, which has the legal power (separate from individual owners or shareholders) to enter into contracts, buy and sell property, and engage in other business activity.** Some transnational corporations constitute a type of international monopoly capitalism that transcends the boundaries and legal controls of any one nation. The largest transnationals are headquartered in the United States, Japan, Korea, other industrializing Asian nations, and Germany. Currently, transnational corporations account for more than half of total world production. The shareholders in transnational corporations live throughout the world. Although corporate executives often own a great number of shares, most shareholders have little control over where plants

The Malling of Dubai: Transnational Corporations in the Midst of Affluence and Poverty

The Dubai Mall is the world's largest shopping mall based on total area and fifth largest by gross leasable area. Located in Dubai, United Arab Emirates, it is part of the 20-billion-dollar Burj Khalifa complex, and includes 1,200 shops. . . . The Dubai Mall has 10–15 distinct 'malls-within-a-mall.' . . . It also has a 250-room luxury hotel, 22 cinema screens plus 120 restaurants and cafes.

In addition to the features described in this listing for the Dubai Mall, the center includes an indoor theme park with 150 amusement games, an aquarium, a discovery center, and an Olympic-sized ice rink that can host up to 2,000 guests.

With transnational corporations and shops such as Galeries Lafayette (France), Bloomingdale's (the United States), and others from around the world backing this massive enterprise, how might the Mall of Dubai possibly be viewed as a problem for anyone? According to some social analysts who closely examined the issue of wealth and poverty in Dubai, the building of the world's tallest building (Burj Khalifa) and the malling of Dubai have a hidden, "dark side" that is unknown to outsiders.

What tourists and other outsiders do not see are the shantytown conditions where workers live when they are not building the gleaming new towers and luxury hotels and residences in Dubai. Labor violations in Dubai have attracted the attention of human rights organizations. Many workers live eight to a room and send most of the money they make home to their family in another country.

Labor camps are often gated and guarded, and some of the workers live in dirty conditions, such as the smell of raw sewage, and ride on roads that are full of garbage.

In the aftermath of the worldwide economic crisis in 2007–2008, some of the migrant workers were let go. Some have returned to their countries of origin; others have remained in the low-paid workforce in Dubai where service workers in general have low wages and few opportunities for advancement. Some of the migrant workers came to Dubai in hopes of a better life for themselves and their families back home, but they have found instead problems of poverty and not being able to afford a flight home.

Descriptions of the lifestyles of the rich and affluent in Dubai and other major world cities stand in stark contrast to the poverty and lack of opportunity of many of the people who help make such opulence possible for those at the top of the hierarchy. What unique problems do nations face if their economy is largely based on tourism and trade?

Questions for Consideration

1. Do you believe that global consumerism is a problem? If so, are corporations responsible for the problem?
2. What is the relationship between consumerism and the demand for cheap labor?
3. How does the glamour of Dubai and some cities in the United States, such as Las Vegas, hide the poverty that exists in high-profile, luxury-oriented areas?

are located, how much employees are paid, or how the environment is protected.

Because transnational corporations are big and powerful, they play a significant role in the economies and governments of many countries. At the same time, by their very nature, they lack accountability to any government or any regulatory agency. Because of this lack of accountability, some major corporations offshore their profits in countries such as the Cayman Islands to avoid paying taxes. Transnational corporations do not depend on any one country for labor, capital, or technology, and they can locate their operations in countries where political and business leaders accept their practices and few other employment opportunities exist. Although many workers in low-income nations earn less than a living wage from

transnational corporations, the products they make are often sold for hundreds of times the cost of raw materials and labor. Designer clothing and athletic shoes are two examples of this kind of exploitation.

Still another concern is that transnational corporations foster global consumerism that inevitably changes local cultures and encourages a "shop till you drop" mentality through extensive advertising and strategic placement of their business operations around the world. McDonald's golden arches and Coca-Cola signs can be seen from Times Square in New York to Red Square in Moscow, and the malls in Dubai might be mistaken for those located anywhere except that they are much larger and they had the darker side of a poverty and an immigrant work force in that nation (see Box 2).

Traditional and ultramodern are often found in close proximity in the global economy.

PROBLEMS IN THE U.S. ECONOMY

Although an economic boom occurred late in the twentieth century, corporate wealth became increasingly concentrated. Economic concentration refers to the extent to which a few individuals or corporations control the vast majority of all economic resources in a country. Concentration of wealth is a social problem when it works to society's detriment, particularly when people are unable to use the democratic process to control the actions of the corporations.

Concentration of Wealth

The concentration of wealth in the United States can be traced through several stages. In the earliest stage (1850–1890), most investment capital was individually owned. Before the Civil War, about 200 families controlled all major trade and financial organizations. By the 1890s, even fewer—including such notables as Andrew Carnegie, Cornelius Vanderbilt, and John D. Rockefeller—controlled most of the investment capital in this country (Feagin et al., 2006).

Explore the Concept

Social Explorer Activity: The Nation's Wealthiest [report] on mysoclab.com

In early monopoly capitalism (1890–1940), ownership and control of capital shifted from individuals to corporations. As monopoly capitalism grew, a few corporations gained control over major U.S. industries, including the oil, sugar, and grain industries. A *monopoly* **exists when a single firm controls an industry and accounts for all sales in a specific market**. In early monopoly capitalism, some stockholders derived massive profits from such companies as American Tobacco Company, F. W. Woolworth, and Sears, which held near-monopolies on specific goods and services (Hodson and Sullivan, 2008).

In advanced monopoly capitalism (between 1940 and the present), ownership and control of major industrial and business sectors became increasingly concentrated. After World War II, there was a dramatic increase in *oligopoly*—**a situation in which a small number of companies or suppliers control an entire industry or service**. Today, a few large corporations use their economic resources—through campaign contributions, PACs, and lobbying—to influence the outcome of government decisions that affect their operations. Smaller corporations have only limited power and resources to bring about political change or keep the largest corporations from dominating the economy.

Today, mergers often occur across industries. In this way, corporations gain near-monopoly control over all aspects of the production and distribution of a product because they acquire both the companies that supply the raw materials and the companies that are the outlets for the product. For example, an oil company might hold leases on the land where the oil is pumped out of the ground, own the refineries that convert the oil into gasoline, and own the individual gasoline stations that sell the product to the public. Corporations that have control both within and across industries and are formed by a series of mergers and acquisitions across industries are referred to as conglomerates—combinations of businesses in different commercial areas, all of which are owned by one holding company. Media ownership is a case in point.

Concentration of wealth and excessive consumer spending have reached new highs among an elite few in the United States and other high income nations.

Further complicating corporate structures are *interlocking corporate directorates*—members of the board of directors of one corporation who also sit on the board of one or more other corporations. Although the Clayton Antitrust Act of 1914 made it illegal for a person to sit on the boards of directors of two corporations that are in direct competition with each other at the same time, a person may serve simultaneously on the board of a financial institution (a bank, for example) and the board of a commercial corporation (a computer manufacturing company or a furniture store chain, for example) that borrows money from the bank. Directors of competing corporations also may serve together on the board of a third corporation that is not in direct competition with the other two. The problem with such interlocking directorates is that they diminish competition by producing interdependence. People serving on multiple boards are in a position to forge cooperative arrangements that benefit their corporations but not necessarily the general public. When several corporations are controlled by the same financial interests, they are more likely to cooperate with one another than to compete. The directors of some of these corporations are highly paid for their services: Annual compensation for board members of some top corporations is well over a million dollars per person with stock and stock options. Many directors serve on the boards of several companies, receiving lucrative salaries and benefits from each of them.

Corporate Welfare

Corporate welfare occurs when the government helps industries and private corporations in their economic pursuits. Corporate welfare refers to financial aid, such as a subsidy or tax break, that the government provides to corporations or other businesses. Some analysts prefer the more neutral term, corporate subsidies, for this practice, because they argue that "corporate welfare" implies that the aid is wasteful or unjust. Corporate welfare is not new in the United States. Between 1850 and 1900, corporations received government assistance in the form of public subsidies and protection from competition. To encourage westward expansion, the federal government gave large tracts of land to privately owned railroads. Antitrust laws that were originally intended to break up monopolies were used against labor unions that supported workers' interests. Tariffs, patents, and trademarks all serve to protect corporations from competition. Today, government intervention includes billions of dollars in subsidies to farmers through crop subsidy programs, tax credits for

corporations, and large subsidies or loan guarantees to auto makers, aircraft companies, railroads, and others. In 2009, the federal government spent $11 trillion in an effort to stable the financial and housing markets in the United States. Overall, most financial institutions and other corporations have gained much more than they have lost as a result of government involvement in the economy. Obviously, they do not refer to these programs as corporate welfare or corporate handouts, but rather by names that make the programs sound more deserving. The words used can be very important in the political process (see Box 3).

The National Debt and Consumer Debt

The national debt—the U.S. total public debt—is a major concern in the twenty-first century. The national debt is the amount of money owed by the federal government to creditors who hold U.S. debt instruments. In other words, the national debt consists of the total amount of money the federal government has borrowed over the years from U.S. citizens and foreign lenders to finance overspending. As of July 2011, the total U.S. federal debt was approximately $14.5 trillion, or about $46,544 per U.S. resident. This figure does not include other promises that the government will disburse future funds for Social Security, Medicare, and Medicaid.

Throughout U.S. history, this nation has had public debt, and for many years, this debt has continued to grow. However, after decades of the federal government spending more money each year than it was making, in the late 1990s, a period of economic expansion occurred and slower growth in some spending areas made it possible for the government to produce a surplus of more than $100 billion a year (between 1999 and 2001). But, as the nation entered the twenty-first century, a combination of tax cuts and increased spending as a result of terrorism and war (among other factors) resulted in a growing budget deficit—which is excess of spending over income over a particular period of time. When a budget deficit is accumulated by the federal government, this deficit must be financed by the issuance of Treasury bonds. The federal deficit increased from $318 billion in 2005 to approximately $1.4 trillion in 2010.

National debt and the budget deficit are only two of the major problems we face; another is the amount of consumer debt in this country. Like the federal government, many individuals and families in this country are deeply in debt. Consumer debt has grown significantly since the 1980s, and in 2008, it had reached more than $2.52 trillion. In July 2011, consumer debt was $2.44 trillion for the

Critical Thinking and You

Box 3

Are You a Conservative or a Liberal? The Language of the Political Economy

The American Heritage Dictionary of the English Language (2011) defines *conservatism* and *liberalism* as follows:

Conservatism

1. The inclination, especially in politics, to maintain the existing or traditional order
2. A political philosophy or attitude emphasizing respect for traditional institutions (such as family, education, and religion), distrust of too much government involvement in business and everyday life, and opposition to sudden change in the established order

A conservative is one who favors traditional views and values. A conservative is a supporter of political conservatism.

Liberalism

1. The state or quality of being liberal
2. A political theory founded on the natural goodness of humans and the autonomy of the individual and favoring civil and political liberties, government by law with the consent of the governed, and protection from arbitrary authority

A liberal is one who is open to new ideas for progress, favors proposals for reform, and is tolerant of the ideas and behavior of others.

This sounds simple enough, doesn't it? However, politicians, scholars, and everyday people constantly argue about the meaning of these words as they seek to determine where individuals fit on the political spectrum, a continuum that represents the wide range of political attitudes. Linguistics scholar George Lakoff (2002) raises a number of interesting points that might assist us in our critical thinking about our views on the political economy. According to Lakoff, conservatives and liberals not only choose different topics on which to focus their attention, but they also use different words to discuss these topics:

> Here are some words and phrases used over and over in conservative discourse: character, virtue, discipline, tough it out, get tough, tough love, strong, self-reliance, individual responsibility, backbone, standards, authority, heritage, competition, earn, hard work, enterprise, property rights, rewards, freedom,

intrusion, interference, meddling, punishment, human nature, traditional, common sense, dependency, self-indulgent, elite, quotas, breakdown, corrupt, decay, rot, degenerate, deviant, lifestyle.

Lakoff asks us to think about the following questions: What unifies this collection of words? Why do conservatives choose the words they do? What do these words mean to conservatives? Now, let's look at Lakoff's list of words that are favorites among liberals:

> Liberals talk about: social forces, social responsibility, free expression, human rights, equal rights, concern, care, help, health, safety, nutrition, basic human dignity, oppression, diversity, deprivation, alienation, big corporations, corporate welfare, ecology, ecosystem, biodiversity, pollution, and so on.

Obviously, we cannot easily sort everyone into either the conservative or liberal school of thought based on their choice of words. In fact, people move around somewhat on the political spectrum: Individuals may have more liberal attitudes on some social issues and more conservative attitudes on others.

Where does this discussion leave you? Do you most often use the language of liberalism or of conservatism? Are you a middle-of-the-road type of person when it comes to political issues? What words do you most often use in discussing political and economic issues? Think about your attitudes on the following topics and state what, if anything, you believe the government should do about the following: abortion; death penalty; government funds for victims of floods, earthquakes, fires, and other natural disasters; health care as a commodity; health care as a right; increasing/decreasing budgets for the military, prisons, and homeland security; increasing/decreasing spending for regulatory agencies that control businesses and seek to protect the environment; and welfare for individuals who are chronically poor and homeless. These are only a few of the social concerns that face our nation today. Listen to local, state, and national political leaders: What language do they use? Do their actions reveal attitudes that are conservative, liberal, or somewhere in between as they confront social problems and seek to reduce or eliminate them? Where would you place the Tea Party movement in this regard?

first nine months of the year and some analysts suggested that consumer spending was decreasing because of major concerns about the U.S. economy and the high unemployment rate (Bater, 2011). Even more worrisome to analysts

was the fact that the ratio of consumer debt to income has increased. Two factors contribute to high rates of consumer debt. The first is the instability of economic life in modern society; unemployment and underemployment are commonplace. The second factor is the availability of credit and the extent to which credit card companies and other lenders extend credit beyond people's ability to repay. Recent increases in consumer debt have largely been attributed to heavier use of revolving credit, primarily credit cards, in which consumers, at best, paid only their minimum balance rather than the total amount owed on a card in a given month. Some people run up credit card charges that are greatly out of proportion to their income; others cannot pay off the charges they initially believed they could afford when their income is interrupted or drops. Having a high level of consumer debt is a personal problem for individuals, but it is also a public issue, particularly when credit card issuers give fifth, sixth, or seventh credit cards to people who are already so far in debt that they cannot pay the interest, much less the principal, on their cards.

In recent years, many homeowners who have been having trouble juggling their credit card debts have turned to home equity loans as a means of reducing their bills. Home equity loans consist of borrowing money from a mortgage company and pledging the equity in your home (the difference between what you previously owed and the value of the residence) as collateral for the new debt. For a number of years, large numbers of U.S. homeowners refinanced their residential mortgages only to see the housing boom in their region of the country become a national housing bust, or to have other unexpected events occur (such as loss of a job or a medical emergency), which resulted in foreclosure on their home. Federal National Mortgage Association (FNMA or "Fannie Mae") and Federal Home Loan Mortgage Corporation (FHLMC or "Freddie Mac") are stockholder-owned corporations that were originally set up as government entities in the 1930s and 1970s, respectively. As buyers of home mortgages, they have been a critical part of the nation's housing finance system for decades, owning or guaranteeing more than half of all home mortgages outstanding. However, in 2008, Fannie Mae and Freddie Mac were placed under federal control as the U.S. government took over these massive corporations because they recorded combined losses of about $14 billion and had a history of accounting scandals, questionable management practices, and maintaining inadequate capital reserves. The bailout and recapitalization of Fannie Mae and Freddie Mac was only the beginning of what became a major financial crisis: The U.S. housing market continued to experience a meltdown with homeowners seeing the value of their residences decline sharply in some areas of the country. In addition, the financial market lost confidence in government-sponsored mortgage entities, and numerous mortgage companies and banks were either bought out by other financial institutions or were bailed out by the federal government. This institutional crisis then spread around the globe and to individuals in this country who were heavily in debt. Many of these persons have filed for bankruptcy and lost their homes to foreclosure. When this major economic crisis will end is unknown at this time, even though the decline has leveled off in some areas of the country and housing values have risen somewhat. A full recovery appears to be a long way off at this time.

Unemployment

There are three major types of unemployment—cyclical, seasonal, and structural. *Cyclical unemployment* occurs as a result of lower rates of production during recessions in the business cycle; a recession is a decline in an economy's total production that lasts at least six months. Although massive layoffs initially occur, some of the workers will eventually be rehired, largely depending on the length and severity of the recession. *Seasonal unemployment* results from shifts in the demand for workers based on conditions such as the weather (in agriculture, the construction industry, and tourism) or the season (holidays and summer vacations). Both of these types of unemployment tend to be relatively temporary.

By contrast, structural unemployment may be permanent. *Structural unemployment* arises because the skills demanded by employers do not match the skills of the unemployed or because the unemployed do not live where the jobs are located. This type of unemployment often occurs when a number of plants in the same industry are closed or when new technology makes certain jobs obsolete. Structural unemployment often results from capital flight—the investment of capital in foreign facilities, as previously discussed. Today, many workers fear losing their jobs, exhausting their unemployment benefits (if any), and still not being able to find another job.

The **unemployment rate** **is the percentage of unemployed persons in the labor force actively seeking jobs.** The second decade of the twenty-first century has seen a significant increase in unemployment. By contrast, the U.S. unemployment rate in 2000 was 4.0 percent. By 2011 the overall rate hovered around 9 percent with some people no longer actively seeking work and thus not being counted as "unemployed." In 2011, the unemployment rate for adult men was 8.7 percent, as compared to 8.0 percent for adult women. However, the breakdown for unemployment across racial-ethnic and age categories tells a more complete story: Teenagers of all racial-ethnic categories had a 23.9 percent unemployment rate. African Americans of all ages had a 15.3 percent unemployment rate; Hispanics (Latinos/as) had an 11.6 percent rate, as compared to a rate for whites (non-Hispanics) of 8.0 percent and for Asian Americans of 6.8 percent (U.S. Bureau of Labor Statistics, 2011a). However, individuals who become discouraged in their attempt to find work and no longer actively seek employment are not counted as unemployed. According to a Bureau of Labor Statistics (2011a) report, 1 million "discouraged workers" are not currently looking for work because they believe that no jobs are available for them. Another 8.3 million people report that they are employed part time because they cannot find full-time employment. Both in the United States and other nations of the world, the linkage between the economy, levels of employment, and how people view government and politics are closely linked together.

PROBLEMS IN POLITICAL PARTICIPATION AROUND THE WORLD

Social scientists distinguish between politics and government: *Politics*, as previously defined, is the social institution through which power is acquired and exercised by some people and groups. The essential component of politics is *power*—the ability of people to achieve their goals despite opposition from others. People who hold positions of power achieve their goals because they have control over other people; those who lack power carry out the wishes of others. Powerful people get others to acquiesce to their demands by using persuasion, authority, or force.

In contemporary societies, the primary political system is *government*—**a formal organization that has legal and political authority to regulate relationships among people in a society and between the society and others outside its borders**. The government (sometimes called the state) includes all levels of bureaucratized political activity such as executive, central, and local administrations; the legislature; the courts; and the armed forces and police.

Political participation varies widely because political freedom is uneven worldwide. Although people in the United States might take elections as a given and decide not to participate even when they have the freedom to do so, people in many other nations do not have the opportunity to participate in free and fair elections. As a result, issues pertaining to political participation remain a concern both in the United States and around the world.

PROBLEMS IN U.S. POLITICS

The United States is a *democracy,* **a political system in which the people hold the ruling power either directly or through elected representatives**. In a *direct participatory democracy,* citizens meet regularly to debate and decide issues of the day. Ancient Athens was a direct democracy, as was colonial New England with its town meetings. Even today, many New England towns use the town meeting. However, even in its beginnings as a nation, the United States was not a direct democracy. The framers of the Constitution believed that decisions should be made by representatives of the people. To ensure that no single group could control the government, they established a *separation of powers* among the legislative, executive, and judicial branches of government and a *system of checks and balances,* giving each branch some degree of involvement in the activities of the others.

In countries that have some form of *representative democracy,* such as the United States, citizens elect representatives who are responsible for conveying the concerns and interests of those they represent. If these representatives are not responsive to the wishes of the people, voters can unseat them through elections. This is not to say that representative democracy is equally accessible to all people in a nation. The framers of the U.S. Constitution, for example, gave the right to vote only to white males who owned property. Eventually, nonlandowners were given the vote, then African American men, and finally, in 1920, women. Today, democratic participation is at least theoretically available to all U.S. citizens age eighteen and over.

Political Parties, Elections, and Public Discontent

A *political party* is an organization whose purpose is to gain and hold legitimate control of government. Persons who make up a specific political party typically have similar attitudes, interests, and socioeconomic status. In the democratic process, political parties are supposed to develop and articulate policy positions, educate voters about issues and simplify the choices for them, and recruit and support candidates for public office. To accomplish these goals, political parties create a *platform*, a formal statement of the party's political positions on various social and economic issues. Since the Civil War, the Democratic and Republican Parties have dominated the U.S. political system. Although one party may control the presidency for several terms, at some point the voters elect the other party's nominee, and control shifts. Although both parties have been successful in getting their candidates elected, these parties are dominated by active elites who hold views further from the center of the political spectrum than the views of a majority of party members. As a result, voters in primary elections (in which the nominees of political parties for most offices other than president and vice president are chosen) may select nominees whose views are closer to the center of the political spectrum and further away from the party's own platform. Overall, party loyalties appear to be declining among voters, who may vote in one party's primary but then cast their ballot in general elections without total loyalty to that party, or cast a "split-ticket" ballot (voting for one party's candidate in one race and another party's candidate in the next one).

Although most individuals identify themselves as Republicans or Democrats, a growing number of people have expressed discontent with the existing U.S. political parties. In 2009 a movement emerged to support more constitutionally limited government and to oppose various stimulus and bailout programs that require the use of federal monies. These protesters have referred to themselves as the "Tea Party" movement, based on the 1773 Boston Tea Party, a protest by American colonists against "taxation without representation" by the British government because the colonists were not represented in the British Parliament but were required to pay taxes to that government. According to a *New York Times*/CBS News poll, Tea Party supporters are "wealthier and more well-educated than the general public, and are no more or less afraid of falling into a lower socioeconomic class" (Zernike and Thee-Brenan, 2010:A1). A demographic analysis reveals that the typical Tea Party supporter is white, male, married, and over forty-five years of age. Most are registered Republicans, but they disagree with party leadership about various issues. Although some movement members have been accused of being racist and homophobic, others have applauded the movement for opening up new arenas for political debate when few other options have existed in the U.S. two-party system. Clearly, Tea Party activists are pessimistic about the direction that the United States is going and want to do something about it (Zernike and Thee-Brenan, 2010).

What will become of the Tea Party movement? Will it take a place alongside other, more established political parties, or will it disappear? At the time of this writing, the Tea Party movement does not have a formal organizational structure, and the majority of the group's participants surveyed in the recent *New York Times*/CBS poll stated that they did not want a third party and would still vote Republican. Regardless of how formally organized the group becomes, it appears that participants will remain vocal on a number of issues, including protection of the Constitution, demand for a balanced budget and tax reform, an end to "runaway spending," and other measures that emphasize fiscal restraint and limited government and deemphasize putting government money into social issues (Zernike and Thee Brenan, 2010). Those who participate in the Tea Party movement are engaged in a form of political activism; however, many people in the United States respond in a different manner to current political parties and social issues: They simply do not participate and, as a result, contribute to high levels of voter apathy in many elections. Unfortunately, today voter apathy and influence-buying through campaign contributions threaten to undermine the principles on which our government is based.

Voter Apathy and the Gender Gap

Since democracy in the United States is defined as a government "of the people, by the people, and for the people," we would assume that citizens would participate in their government at any or all of four levels: (1) voting, (2) attending and taking part in political meetings, (3) actively participating in political campaigns, and (4) running for and/or holding political office. At most, about 10 percent of the voting-age population in this country participates at a level higher than simply voting, and over the past forty years, less than half of the voting-age population has voted in nonpresidential elections. Even in presidential elections, voter turnout often is relatively low. In the 2008 presidential election, about 62 percent of the 208.3 million eligible voters cast ballots, compared with 60.6 percent in the 2004 presidential election. The number of ballots cast in 2008 was the highest in history because about 6.5 million more people were registered to vote in 2008. The larger turnout in 2008 was partly a result of significant increases in voting by younger people, Latinos/as, and African American voters. Women's votes were also a significant factor in the election of Barack Obama because women strongly preferred Obama (56 percent) to John McCain (43 percent), whereas men split their votes almost evenly between Obama (49 percent) and McCain (48 percent). State-by-state differences in voting preferences are also highly visible in what political analysts refer to as the "red states" and the "blue states."

Why is it that so many eligible voters in this country stay away from the polls? During any election, millions of voting-age persons do not go to the polls due to illness, disability, lack of transportation, nonregistration, or absenteeism. However, these explanations do not account for why many other people do not vote. According to some conservative analysts, people may not vote because they are satisfied with the status quo or because they are apathetic and uninformed—they lack an understanding of both public issues and the basic processes of government.

By contrast, liberals argue that people stay away from the polls because they feel alienated from politics at all levels of government—federal, state, and local—due to political corruption and influence peddling by special interests and large corporations. Participation in politics is influenced by gender, age, race-ethnicity, and, especially, socioeconomic status (SES). One explanation for the higher rates of political participation at higher SES levels is that advanced levels of education may give people a better understanding of government processes, a belief that they have more at stake in the political process, and greater economic resources to contribute to the process. Some studies suggest that during their college years, many people develop assumptions about political participation that continue throughout their lives.

In the 2010 midterm election, when candidates ran for governor in some states and the U.S. Senate and House of Representatives, approximately 40 percent of eligible voters participated in the election. More people vote in presidential election years than in midterm elections, but the overall percentage of voters is not dramatically higher. In the 2000 and 2004 presidential elections, for example, slightly over 50 percent of the voting-age population (age eighteen and older) voted. The 2004 election was one in which the winning candidate (George W. Bush) received only slightly more than one-half of all votes cast.

When elections can be that close, what causes voter apathy? According to studies by the Pew Research Center for the People and the Press, many people do not vote because they see no reason for change, others are turned off by excessive polling by media and other groups (people see no point to voting if the outcomes are predictable), and still others either disagree with negative advertising by candidates and parties or believe that the issues raised by the candidates are not important or will have no effect on their personal economic situation.

Along with voter apathy, the emergence and persistence of the *gender gap*—**the difference between a candidate's number of votes from women and men**—is a dominant feature of U.S. politics today. Political analysts first noticed a gender gap in the early 1980s, but the gap grew wider and more apparent in subsequent elections. In 1980, the gender gap was about eight points (men were 8 percent more likely than women to support Ronald Reagan for president). In 2004, the gap increased to eleven points (women were 11 percent more likely than men to vote for John Kerry than for George W. Bush). In 2008, a sizable gender gap was evident in the presidential election results. Women strongly preferred Obama (56 percent) to McCain (43 percent) while men split their votes about evenly, with Obama receiving 49 percent of the votes to 48 percent for McCain. The gender gap for 2008 was 7 percentage points, which was virtually identical to the seven-point gap in 2004.

Gender gaps in voting were even more evident in the 2010 races for governor and the U.S. Senate than in previous elections. In races where a gender gap was evident, women were much more likely than men to a support Democratic candidate, and less likely to support the Republican contender. According to the Center for American Women and Politics (2010), "Gender gaps of 4 to 19 percentage points were evident in 17 or 18 gubernatorial races where exit polls were conducted. Similarly, among the 26 U.S. Senate races with exit polls, gender gaps of 4 to 17 points were evident in 15." In the past, gender gaps might have been evident in about two-thirds of statewide races, but in 2010, gender gaps existed in virtually all of the political races.

Why is there a gender gap? Most analysts agree that the gap is rooted in how women and men view economic and social issues, such as welfare reform, abortion, child care, and education, and what they believe the nation's priorities should be. Voter apathy and an increase in the gender gap have received substantial attention in recent years but nothing like the scrutiny given to allegations of political influence-buying by large campaign contributors.

Politics and Money in Political Campaigns

Presidential and congressional candidates and their supporters raise and spend millions of dollars every two years on the elections for national political positions.

Where does all the money go? The cost of running for political office has skyrocketed. The costs of advertising and media time, staff, direct-mail operations, telephone banks, computers, consultants, travel expenses, office rentals, and many other campaign expenses have increased dramatically over the past two decades. Unless a candidate has private resources, contributions can determine the success or failure of his or her bid for election or reelection.

In the past certain kinds of campaign contributions were specifically prohibited by law: Corporate contributions to presidential and congressional candidates have been illegal since 1907, and contributions from labor unions were outlawed in 1943. In 1974, Congress passed a law limiting an individual's total contribution to federal candidates to $25,000 a year and no more than $1,000 per candidate. In 2002, these limits were raised to $2,000 per candidate and no more than $95,000 in any two-year period. However, these individual limits have been sidestepped by bundling, which occurs when a donor collects contributions from family members, business associates, and others and then "bundles" them together and sends them to a candidate. For example, during the 2000 presidential election, supporters of Republican candidate George W. Bush included a group of volunteer fundraisers referred to as the "pioneers," each of whom pledged to raise at least $100,000 which would be bundled as hard money contributions and given to Bush's campaign for use in getting him elected (Nyhart, 2001).

Federal law also limits individual contributions to a political action committee to a maximum of $5,000. **Political action committees (PACs) are special-interest groups that fund campaigns to help elect (or defeat) candidates based on their positions on specific issues.** PACs were originally organized by unions to get around the laws that prohibited union gifts. Today, there are thousands of PACs representing businesses, labor unions, and various single-issue groups (such as gays and lesbians and environmental groups).

Finally, federal law limits contributions made to political parties for campaigning to $28,500, but until 2002, there was no limit on contributions made for the purpose of party-building, such as distributing "vote Democratic" or "vote Republican" bumper stickers or organizing get-out-the-vote drives. However, both the Democratic and Republican parties used these contributions to pay for administrative expenses and overhead, thus freeing up other party money to support candidates. This *soft-money loophole*—contributing to a political party instead of to a specific candidate—became a

TABLE 1 Top Ten Corporate Campaign Contributors, 2010	
AT&T	$45.6 million
Goldman Sachs	$36.7 million
Citigroup	$27.5 million
United Parcel Service	$24.9 million
Altria (formerly Philip Morris)	$24.3 million
Microsoft	$21.0 million
J. P. Morgan	$20.3 million
Time Warner	$20.0 million
Morgan Stanley	$19.8 million
Lockheed Martin	$19.3 million

Source: Based on data from The 10 Biggest Corporate Campaign Contributors in U.S. Politics at http://www.dailyfinance.com/2010/10/13/the-10-biggest-corporate-campaign-contributors-in-u-s-politics/

major issue, and the same law that increased contribution limits in 2002 allegedly closed this loophole.

But the most controversial recent change occurred in 2010 when the U.S. Supreme Court ruled that corporations can spend unlimited money on behalf of political candidates. Now, corporations can legally pay for extensive political advertising on behalf of candidates and causes, and they will not be required to disclose these contributions (Palmer, 2010). By donating anonymously to nonprofit civic leagues and trade associations, corporations and labor unions can in essence donate to candidates' campaigns (see Table 1).

What agency monitors campaign contributions and how effective has this agency been? The Federal Election Commission—the enforcement agency that monitors campaign contributions—is considered "one of the most toothless agencies in Washington" (Cohn, 1997). Violations, when discovered, are typically not punished until some time after an election is over. As a result, a very small percentage of the U.S. population is contributing extraordinarily large amounts to get their candidates elected. Is this sort of influence-buying a recent phenomenon? According to journalist Kevin Phillips (1995), influence-buying has been going on for some time in this country, and most political candidates and elected officials do not refuse such contributions.

Although the general public realizes that special-interest groups and lobbyists often have undue influence on political decisions and the outcome of elections, most people believe that they are powerless to do anything about it. When respondents in a 1990s Gallup Poll survey were asked "Would you say the government is pretty much run by a few big interests looking out for themselves or that it is run for the benefit of all the people?" 76 percent said that they believed big interests ran the country, only 18 percent believed the government operates for the benefit of all, and 6 percent had no opinion (Golay and Rollyson, 1996). Do you think that their answer would be different today? How might the percentages have changed in the meantime?

Government by Special-Interest Groups

What happens when special-interest groups have a major influence on how the government is run? Some special-interest groups exert their influence on single issues such as the environment, gun ownership, abortion, or legislation that affects a particular occupation (e.g., the American Medical Association) or business (e.g., the National Restaurant Association).

Other special-interest groups represent specific occupations and industries and make contributions to candidates who will protect their interests and profits. Lawyers and law firms were among the top contributors in the 2008 presidential election with the American Association for Justice and a number of nationwide law firms contributing in the range of $100,000 to $300,000 to both presidential candidates. Other industries that engage in heavy lobbying efforts are health professionals, securities and investment firms, real estate groups, and public sector unions that want to be heard in regard to such matters as health care and pension plans. Another highly effective lobby is AARP (American Association of Retired Persons), which spent $21 million lobbying, particularly for candidates who were seen as friendly toward the issues that affect older persons, such as Social Security and Medicare.

Government by Bureaucracy

Special-interest groups wield tremendous political power, but so does the federal bureaucracy. The federal bureaucracy, or *permanent government*, **refers to the top-tier civil service bureaucrats who have a strong power base and play a major role in developing and implementing government policies and procedures.**

The federal government played a relatively limited role in everyday life in the nineteenth century, but its role grew during the Great Depression in the 1930s. When faced with high rates of unemployment and persistent poverty, people demanded that the government do something. Under a series of "New Deal" initiatives, security markets were regulated, federal jobs and relief programs were instituted, and labor-management relations were regulated. In the ensuing decades, as voters continued to demand that the government "do something" about the problems facing society, government has continued to grow. In fact, since 1960, the federal government has grown faster than any other segment of the U.S. economy. Today, slightly more than 2.1 million people are employed by the federal bureaucracy, in which much of the actual functioning of the government takes place.

Sociologists point out that bureaucratic power in any sphere tends to take on a life of its own over time, and this is evident in the U.S. government. Despite efforts by presidents, White House staffs, and various presidential cabinets, neither Republican nor Democratic administrations have been able to establish control over the federal bureaucracy (Dye, Zeigler, and Schubert, 2012). In fact, many federal bureaucrats have seen a number of presidents come and go. The vast majority of top-echelon positions have been held by white men for many years. Rising to the top of the bureaucracy can take as long as twenty years, and few white women and people of color have reached these positions.

The government bureaucracy is able to perpetuate itself and expand because many of its employees possess highly specialized knowledge and skills and cannot easily be replaced. As the issues facing the United States have grown in number and complexity, offices and agencies have been established to create rules, policies, and procedures for dealing with such things as nuclear power, environmental protection, and drug safety. These government bureaucracies announce about twenty rules or regulations for every one law passed by Congress (Dye, Zeiger, and Schubert, 2012). Today, public policy is increasingly made by agencies rather than elected officials. The agencies receive little direction from Congress or the president, and although their actions are subject to challenge in the courts, most agencies are highly autonomous.

The federal budget is the central ingredient in the bureaucracy. Preparing the annual federal budget is a major undertaking for the president and the Office of Management and Budget, one of the most important agencies in Washington. Getting the budget approved by Congress is an even more monumental task. However, as Dye, Zeigler, and Schubert, (2012) point out, even with the highly publicized wrangling over the budget by the president and Congress, the final congressional appropriations usually are within 2 to 3 percent of the budget that the president originally proposed. In the difficult economic and political climate of 2011, however, there is no guarantee that these percentages will hold as budget negotiations move forward.

As powerful as the federal bureaucracy has become, it is not immune to special-interest groups. Special-interest groups can help an agency get more operating money. Although the president has budgetary authority over the bureaucracy, any agency that believes that it did not get its fair share can raise a public outcry by contacting friendly interest groups and congressional subcommittees. This outcry can force the president to restore funding to the agency or prod Congress into appropriating money that was not requested by the president, who might go along with the appropriation to avoid a confrontation. Special-interest groups also influence the bureaucracy through the military-industrial complex.

The Military-Industrial Complex

The term *military-industrial complex* **refers to the interdependence of the military establishment and private military contractors**. The complex is actually a three-way arrangement involving one or more private interest groups (usually corporations that manufacture weapons or other military-related goods), members of Congress who serve on congressional committees or subcommittees that appropriate money for military programs, and a bureaucratic agency (such as the Defense Department). Often, a revolving door of money, influence, and jobs is involved: Military contractors who receive contracts from the Defense Department also serve on advisory committees that recommend what weapons should be ordered. Many people move from job to job, serving in the military, then in the Defense Department, then in military industries (Feagin et al., 2006).

In the 1970s, sociologist C. Wright Mills (1976) stated that the relationship between the military and private industry was problematic and could result in a "permanent war economy" or "military economy" in this country. But economist John Kenneth Galbraith (1985) argued that government expenditures for weapons and jet fighters stimulate the private sector of the economy, creating jobs and encouraging spending. In other words, military spending by Congress is not an economic burden but a source of economic development. It also enriches those corporations that build jet fighters and other warplanes, such as Boeing and Lockheed Martin. According to one executive who spent much of his career

Corporations in the military-industrial complex produce weapons systems such as the F-22 Raptors shown here. What are the benefits of spending billions of dollars on advanced military equipment such as this? What are the economic and noneconomic costs?

involved in building jet fighters for the U.S. military, getting a $1 trillion Pentagon contract for a new generation of jet fighters was of utmost importance to his company: "It's the Super Bowl. It's winner takes all. It's the huge plum. It's the airplane program of the century. If you don't win this program, you're a has-been in tactical aircraft" (quoted in Shenon, 1996:A1).

The 2011 fiscal year budget provides $553 billion for the base budget of the Department of Defense, an increase of $22 billion above the 2010 appropriation. Many believe that the United States will always have an active military-industrial complex because of our emphasis on *militarism*—a societal focus on military ideals and an aggressive preparedness for war. The belief in militarism is maintained and reinforced by values such as patriotism, courage, reverence, loyalty, obedience, and faith in authority, as sociologist Cynthia H. Enloe (1987:542–543) explains:

> Military expenditures, militaristic values, and military authority now influence the flow of foreign trade and determine which countries will or will not receive agricultural assistance. They shape the design and marketing of children's toys and games and of adult fashions and entertainment. Military definitions of progress and security dominate the economic fate of entire geographic regions. The military's ways of doing business open or shut access to information and technology for entire social groups. Finally, military mythologies of valor and safety influence the sense of self-esteem and well-being of millions of people.

SOCIOLOGICAL PERSPECTIVES ON THE POLITICAL ECONOMY

Politics and the economy are so intertwined in the United States that many social scientists speak of the two as a single entity: the political economy. At issue for most social scientists is whether political and economic power are concentrated in the hands of the few or distributed among the many in this country. Functionalists adopt a pluralistic model of power, whereas conflict theorists adopt an elitist model.

The Functionalist Perspective

Pluralism is rooted in the functionalist perspective, which assumes that people generally agree on the most important societal concerns—freedom and security—and that government fulfills important functions in these two regards that no other institution can fulfill. According to the early functionalists, government serves to socialize people to be good citizens, to regulate the economy so that it operates effectively, and to provide necessary services for citizens (Durkheim, 1933/1893). Contemporary functionalists identify four similar functions: A government maintains law and order, plans society and coordinates other institutions, meets social needs, and handles international relations, including warfare.

But what happens when people do not agree on specific issues or concerns? Functionalists say that divergent viewpoints lead to political pluralism; that is, when competing interests or viewpoints arise, government arbitrates. Thus, according to the *pluralist model*, **power is widely dispersed throughout many competing interest groups in our political system** (Dahl, 1961). In the pluralist model, (1) political leaders make decisions on behalf of the people through a process of bargaining, accommodation, and compromise; (2) leadership groups (such as business, labor, law, and consumer organizations) serve as watchdogs to protect ordinary people from the abuses of any one group; (3) ordinary people influence public policy through voting and participating in special-interest groups; (4) power is widely dispersed in society (the same groups aren't equally influential in all arenas); and (5) public policy reflects a balance among competing interest groups, not the majority-group's view (Dye, Zeigler, and Schubert, 2012).

How might a social analyst who uses a functionalist framework address problems in politics and the economy? Such an analyst might begin by saying that since dysfunctions are inevitable in any social institution, it is important to sort out and remedy the specific elements of the system that are creating the problems. It should not be necessary to restructure or replace the entire system. Consider, for example, government regulations: Some regulations are good, and some are bad. The trick, functionalists say, is to keep the good ones and get rid of the bad. Too often, the U.S. government moves between two extremes: overregulation of business and society or seeking to end most, if not all, regulation. As social analysts Donald L. Barlett and James B. Steele (1996:214) suggest, "We must preserve the rules that assure the quality of American life: the food you eat, the medicines you take, the air you breathe and the water you drink. They have evolved over a century." Barlett and Steele also state, however, that demanding that U.S.-owned companies comply with regulations that are not required of their competitors in foreign countries creates an uneven playing field. Hence, a tariff should be imposed on imported products equal to the amount of money that U.S. businesses must spend to comply with government regulations (Barlett and Steele, 1996). This perspective is based on the belief that a certain amount of government intervention in the economy is appropriate but that too much—or the wrong kind—is detrimental. Since the time when Barlett and Steele made these comments, the national and international playing field in regard to business and regulation has become much more, not less, complicated and has many more players involved.

The Conflict Perspective

Most conflict theorists believe that democracy is an ideal, not a reality, in our society today because the government primarily benefits the wealthy and the politically powerful, especially business elites. In fact, according to conflict theorists, economic and political elites use the powers of the government to impose their will on the masses. According to the *elite model*, **power in political systems is concentrated in the hands of a small group, whereas the masses are relatively powerless**. In the elite model, (1) elites possess the greatest wealth, education, status, and other resources and make the most important decisions in society; (2) elites generally agree on the basic values and goals for the society; (3) power is highly concentrated at the top of a pyramid-shaped social hierarchy, and those at the top set public policy for everyone; (4) public policy reflects the values and preferences of the elite, not of ordinary people; and (5) elites use the media to shape the political attitudes of ordinary people (Dye, Zeigler, and Schubert, 2012).

According to sociologist C. Wright Mills (1959a), the United States is ruled by a *power elite,* **which at the**

323

top is composed of business leaders, the executive branch of the federal government, and the military (especially the "top brass" at the Pentagon). The corporate rich—the highest-paid CEOs of major corporations—are the most powerful because they have the unique ability to parlay their vast economic resources into political power. The next most powerful level is occupied by Congress, special-interest groups, and local opinion leaders. The lowest (and widest) level of the pyramid is occupied by ordinary people, the unorganized masses who are relatively powerless and vulnerable to economic and political exploitation.

Individuals in the power elite have similar class backgrounds and interests and interact on a regular basis. Through a revolving door of influence, they tend to shift back and forth between and among business, government, and military sectors. It is not unusual for people who have served in the president's cabinet to become directors of major corporations that do business with the government, for powerful businesspeople to serve in the cabinet, or for former military leaders to become important businesspeople. Through such political and economic alliances, people in the power elite can influence many important decisions, including how federal tax money will be spent and to whom lucrative subsidies and government contracts are awarded.

In his lengthy analysis of the political economy over many decades, sociologist G. William Domhoff (1978) has identified a ruling class, which is made up of the corporate rich, a relatively fixed group of privileged people who wield power over political processes and serve capitalist interests. The corporate rich influence the political process in three ways: (1) by financing campaigns of candidates who favor their causes; (2) by using PACs and loophole contributions to obtain favors, tax breaks, and favorable regulatory rulings; and (3) by gaining appointment to governmental advisory committees, presidential commissions, and other governmental positions. For example, some members of the ruling class influence international politics through their involvement in banking, business services, and law firms that have a strong interest in overseas sales, investments, or raw materials extraction (Domhoff, 1990).

Some analysts who take a conflict perspective say that the only way to overcome problems in politics and the economy is to change the entire system. Our present system exploits poor whites, people of color, women of all colors, people with disabilities, and others who consider themselves disenfranchised from the political and economic mainstream of society. Other conflict theorists think that we can solve many

problems by curbing the abuses of capitalism and the market economy and thereby reducing the power of political and economic elites. Political scientist Benjamin R. Barber (1996:242) believes that we cannot rely on the capitalist (market) economy to look after common interests:

> It is the job of civil society and democratic government and not of the market to look after common interests and make sure that those who profit from the common planet pay its common proprietors their fair share. When governments abdicate in favor of markets, they are declaring nolo contendere [no contest] in an arena in which they are supposed to be primary challengers, bartering away the rights of their people along the way. . . . Markets simply are not designed to do the things democratic polities do. They enjoin private rather than public modes of discourse, allowing us as consumers to speak via our currencies of consumption to producers of material goods, but ignoring us as citizens speaking to one another about such things as the social consequences of our private market choices. . . . They advance individualistic rather than social goals. . . . Having created the conditions that make markets possible, democracy must also do all the things that markets undo or cannot do. It must educate citizens so that they can use their markets wisely and contain market abuses well.

ARE THERE SOLUTIONS TO PROBLEMS IN POLITICS AND THE ECONOMY?

A number of key factors will establish the future course of politics, both in the United States and in other nations. The level of economic growth will have a significant effect on the amount of money that high-income nations will be able to invest in domestic programs (such as education, the environment, health care, and elder care) and in alleviating international problems (such as growing economic inequality within and among nations, the spread of HIV/AIDS and other diseases, and political upheavals and wars). However, political decisions also will be crucial in determining where money is spent and how much is allocated for war, international programs, and domestic programs.

In the United States, the future of our well-being is, at least to some extent, in the hands of our political leaders, whom—at least in most instances—we have elected.

Our future is also in the hands of powerful economic leaders, such as corporate decision makers whom we did not elect. Some political leaders and corporate officers appear to seek the common good; however, others have proven themselves to be unworthy of our trust, as revealed in numerous media headlines and articles. The media provide us with most of the information we have about the current political and economic issues that confront us today and in the future.

SUMMARY

✓•─[Study and Review on mysoclab.com

◼ What kind of economic system does the United States have?

The United States has a capitalist economy. Ideally, capitalism is characterized by private ownership of the means of production, pursuit of personal profit, competition, and lack of government intervention.

◼ How are societies classified by their predominant type of work?

Societies are classified as preindustrial, industrial, or postindustrial. Preindustrial societies engage in primary-sector production—the extraction of raw materials and natural resources from the environment. Industrial societies engage in secondary-sector production—the processing of raw materials (from the primary sector). Postindustrial societies engage in tertiary-sector production—providing services rather than goods.

◼ What are transnational corporations, and why do they pose social problems?

Transnational corporations are large-scale business organizations that are headquartered in one country but operate in many countries. Transnationals lack accountability to any government or regulatory agency. They are not dependent on any one country for labor, capital, or technology. They can play important roles in the economies and governments of countries that need them as employers and accept their practices.

◼ Why is the national debt a serious problem? How is consumer debt a public issue?

When we increase the national debt, we are borrowing from future generations, which will leave them with higher taxes, fewer benefits, and a lower rate of economic growth. Consumer debt becomes a public issue when people cannot repay their credit card loans.

◼ What is corporate welfare?

Corporate welfare occurs when the government helps industries and private corporations in their economic pursuits. Many subsidies that were originally put in place to help stabilize the economy continue unnecessarily because of labor union and PAC lobbying and campaign contributions.

◼ Why is voter apathy a problem? What is the gender gap?

Voter apathy undermines the basis on which representative democracy is built; if large numbers of people don't vote, the interests of only a few are represented. The gender gap is the difference between a candidate's number of votes from women and men. More than ever today, women and men seem to view economic and social issues differently.

◼ Why have campaign contributions been an issue in recent elections?

Campaign contributions are regulated, but individuals, unions, and corporations have circumvented the law through the soft-money loophole—contributing to a political party instead of to a specific candidate—and through political action committees. Political action committees (PACs) are special-interest groups that fund campaigns to help elect (or defeat) candidates on the basis of their positions on specific issues. Because running for office is expensive, contributions can make the difference between a candidate's success or defeat. A recent Supreme Court decision has made it possible for corporations to make unlimited contributions in political elections. It remains to be seen what effect this will have on funding of elections and the overall political process.

◼ What is the military-industrial complex?

The military-industrial complex refers to the interdependence of the military establishment and private military contractors. The military-industrial complex can be a revolving door of money, influence, and jobs.

◼ What are the sociological perspectives on the political economy?

The functionalists use a pluralist model, believing that power is widely dispersed through many competing interest groups in our political system. Functionalists therefore believe that problems can be solved by identifying dysfunctional elements and correcting them. Conflict theorists use an elite model, believing that power in political systems is concentrated in the hands of a small group, whereas the masses are relatively powerless. Sociologist C. Wright Mills used the term *power elite* for this small group of top business leaders, the executive branch of the federal government, and the "top brass" of the military.

KEY TERMS

capitalism
democracy
economy
elite model
gender gap
government
military-industrial complex
mixed economy

monopoly
oligopoly
permanent government
pluralist model
political action committees (PACs)
political economy
political party
politics

power elite
primary-sector production
secondary-sector production
socialism
tertiary-sector production
transnational corporation
unemployment rate

QUESTIONS FOR CRITICAL THINKING

1. Imagine that you are given unlimited funds and resources to reverse the trend in voter apathy. What would you do at the local level? What would you do at the state and national levels to bring about change?

2. How would you respond to the Gallup Poll survey question, "Would you say the government is pretty much run by a few big interests looking out for themselves or that it is run for the benefit of all the people?" Explain your answer.

3. What do you think should be done to reduce unemployment in the United States? Should employers be given a financial incentive or tax credit for creating additional jobs? Should a compulsory retirement age be reestablished for older workers? Should the government start new public works projects similar to those used in the Great Depression to reduce unemployment? What solutions would you suggest?

Succeed with MySocLab®   www.mysoclab.com

The new MySocLab delivers proven results in helping students succeed, provides engaging experiences that personalize learning, and comes from a trusted partner with educational expertise and a deep commitment to helping students and instructors achieve their goals.

Here are a few activities you will find for this chapter:

Watch on mysoclab.com

Core Concepts video clips feature sociologists in action, exploring important concepts in the study of Social Problems. Watch:
• Globalization

Explore on mysoclab.com

Social Explorer is an interactive application that allows you to explore Census data through interactive maps. Explore:
• Social Explorer Activity: The Nation's Wealthiest [report]

Read on mysoclab.com

MySocLibrary includes primary source readings from classic and contemporary sociologists. Read:
• Asceticism and the Spirit of Capitalism

Glossary

capitalism   an economic system characterized by private ownership of the means of production, from which personal profits can be derived through market competition and without government intervention.

democracy   a political system in which the people hold the ruling power either directly or through elected representatives.

economy   the social institution that ensures that a society will be maintained through its production, distribution, and consumption of goods and services.

elite model   a view of society in which power in political systems is concentrated in the hands of a small group, whereas the masses are relatively powerless.

gender gap   the difference between a candidate's number of votes from women and men.

government   a formal organization that has legal and political authority to regulate relationships among people in a society and between the society and others outside its borders.

military-industrial complex   the interdependence of the military establishment and private military contractors.

mixed economy   an economic system that combines elements of both capitalism (a market economy) and socialism (a command economy).

monopoly   a situation that exists when a single firm controls an industry and accounts for all sales in a specific market.

oligopoly   a situation in which a small number of companies or suppliers control an entire industry or service.

permanent government   the top-tier civil service bureaucrats who have a strong power base and play a major role in developing and implementing government policies and procedures.

pluralistic model   the view that power is widely dispersed throughout many competing interest groups in our political system.

political action committees (PACs)   special-interest groups that fund campaigns to help elect (or defeat) candidates based on their positions on specific issues.

political economy   the interdependent workings and interests of political and economic systems.

political party   an organization whose purpose is to gain and hold legitimate control of government.

politics   the social institution through which power is acquired and exercised by some people and groups.

power elite   rulers of the United States, which at the top is composed of business leaders, the executive branch of the federal government, and the military (especially the "top brass" at the Pentagon).

primary-sector production   the extraction of raw materials and natural resources from the environment.

secondary-sector production   the processing of raw materials (from the primary sector) into finished products.

socialism   an economic system characterized by public ownership of the means of production, the pursuit of collective goals, and centralized decision making.

tertiary-sector production   providing services rather than goods as the primary source of livelihood.

transnational corporation   a large-scale business organization that is headquartered in one country but operates in many countries, which has the legal power (separate from individual owners or shareholders) to enter into contracts, buy and sell property, and engage in other business activity.

unemployment rate   the percentage of unemployed persons in the labor force actively seeking jobs.

References

NOTE: References in blue are new to the Sixth Edition.

American Heritage Dictionary. 2000. *American Heritage Dictionary of the English Language.* Boston: Houghton Mifflin.

Barber, Benjamin R. 1996. *Jihad vs. McWorld: How Globalism and Tribalism Are Reshaping the World.* New York: Ballantine Books.

Barboza, David. 2010. "After Suicides, Scrutiny of China's Grim Factories." *New York Times* (June 6). Retrieved July 19, 2011. Online: http://www.nytimes.com/2010/06/07/business/global/07suicide.html

Bater, Jeff. 2011. "Budget-Deficit Figures Narrow From a Year Ago." *Wall Street Journal* (July 13). Retrieved July 18, 2011. Online: http://online.wsj.com/article/SB10001424052702304911104576444202308329060.html#printMode

Center for American Women and Politics. 2010. "Gender Gap Widespread in 2010 Elections: Women Less Likely Than Men to Support Republican Candidates." Rutgers University (November 4). Retrieved July 18, 2011. Online: http://www.cawp.rutgers.edu/press_room/news/documents/PressRelease_11-04-10-GG.pdf

Cohn, Jonathan. 1997. "Reform School." *Mother Jones* (May–June):62.

Dahl, Robert A. 1961. *Who Governs?* New Haven, CT: Yale University Press.

Domhoff, G. William. 1978. *The Powers That Be: Processes of Ruling Class Domination in America.* New York: Random House.

Domhoff, G. William. 1990. *The Power Elite and the State: How Policy Is Made in America.* New York: Aldine De Gruyter.

Durkheim, Emile. 1933. *Division of Labor in Society.* Trans. George Simpson. New York: Free Press (orig. published in 1893).

Dye, Thomas R., Harmon Zeigler, and Louis Schubert. 2012. *The Irony of Democracy: An Uncommon Introduction to American Politics* (15th ed.). Belmont, CA: Cengage.

Enloe, Cynthia H. 1987. "Feminists Thinking about War, Militarism, and Peace." In Beth Hess and Myra Marx Ferree (Eds.), *Analyzing Gender: A Handbook of Social Science Research.* Newbury Park, CA: Sage, pp. 526–547.

Feagin, Joe R., David Baker, and Clairece Booher Feagin. 2006. *Social Problems: A Critical Power-Conflict Perspective* (6th ed.). Upper Saddle River, NJ: Prentice Hall.

Galbraith, John Kenneth. 1985. *The New Industrial State* (4th ed.). Boston: Houghton Mifflin.

Golay, Michael, and Carl Rollyson. 1996. *Where America Stands: 1996.* New York: John Wiley.

Hamper, Ben. 1991. *Rivethead: Tales from the Assembly Line.* New York: Warner Books.

Hodson, Randy, and Teresa A. Sullivan. 2008. *The Social Organization of Work.* Belmont: Wadsworth.

Hodson, Steven. 2011. "Fake Apple Store Employees Believe They Work for Apple." The Inquisitr (July 20). Retrieved July 20, 2011. Online: http://www.inquisitr.com/127725/fake-apple-store-employees-believe-they-work-for-apple/

Jones, Owen. 2011. *Chavs: The Demonization of the Working Class.* London: Verso. Excerpt from Chapter 7: Broken Britain. Reprinted at nytimes.com (July 12). Retrieved July 19, 2011. Online: http://www.nytimes.com/2011/07/13/books/excerpt-chavs-by-owen-jones.html?scp=4&sq=long%20term%20unemployment?&st=cse

Kendall, Diana. 2011. *Framing Class: Media Representations of Wealth and Poverty in America* (2nd ed.). Lanham, MD: Rowman & Littlefield.

Lakoff, George. 2002. *Moral Politics: How Liberals and Conservatives Think.* Chicago: University of Chicago Press.

Mills, C. Wright. 1959a. *The Power Elite.* Fair Lawn, NJ: Oxford University Press.

Mills, C. Wright. 1976. *The Causes of World War Three.* Westport, CT: Greenwood Press.

Nyhart. Nick. 2001. "Raising Hard-Money Limits: An Incumbent Protection Plan." Retrieved December 14, 2002. Online: http://www.rollcall.com/pages/columns/observers/01/guest0329.html

Palmer, Griff. 2010. "Decision Could Allow Anonymous Political Contributions by Businesses." *New York Times* (February 27). Retrieved July 18, 2011. Online: http://www.nytimes.com/2010/02/28/us/28donate.html?scp=31&sq=Citizens+United&st=nyt

Phillips, Kevin. 1995. *Arrogant Capital: Washington, Wall Street, and the Frustration of American Politics.* Boston: Little, Brown.

Presidency of the Republic of Turkey. 2010. "Business World Should Always Be Consolidated" (February 11). Retrieved July 18, 2011. Online: http://www.tccb.gov.tr/news/397/77861/busineb-world-should-always-be-consolidated.html

Seelye, Katharine Q. 2011. "Detroit Census Confirms a Desertion Like No Other." *New York Times* (March 22). Retrieved July 19, 2011. http://www.nytimes.com/2011/03/23/us/23detroit.html

Shenon, Philip. 1996. "Jet Makers Preparing Bids for a Rich Pentagon Prize." *New York Times* (March 12): A1, C4.

U.S. Bureau of Labor Statistics. 2010. "Women in the Labor Force: A Databook." U.S. Bureau of Labor Statistics (December). Retrieved June 10, 2011. Online: http://www.bls.gov/cps/wlf-data-book-2010.pdf

U.S. Bureau of Labor Statistics. 2011a. "Employment Status of the Civilian Population by Race, Sex, and Age." Retrieved June 5, 2011. Online: http://www.bls.gov/news.release/empsit.t02.htm

Venkatesh, Sudhir. 2006. *Off the Books: The Underground Economy of the Urban Poor.* Cambridge, MA: Harvard University Press.

Watson, Bruce. 2010. "The 10 Biggest Corporate Campaign Contributors in U.S. Politics." Dailyfinance.com (October 13). Retrieved July 19, 2011. Online: http://www.dailyfinance.com/2010/10/13/the-10-biggest-corporate-campaign-contributors-in-u-s-politics/

Zephyr (A pseudonym). 2008. "Would You Wear … Designer Knockoffs?" College Fashion—College Girl Blog and Fashion Blog with Fashion Tips for the College Fashionista. Retrieved February 4, 2012. Online: http://www.collegefashion.net/would-you-wear/would-you-wear-designer-knockoffs/

Zernike, Kate, and Megan Thee-Brenan. 2010. "Poll Finds Tea Party Backers Wealthier and More Educated." *New York Times* (April 14). Retrieved July 21, 2011. Online: http://www.nytimes.com/2010/04/15/us/politics/15poll.html

Photo Credits

Credits are listed in order of appearance.

Maurizio Brambatti/EPA/Newscom; Adrian Bradshaw/EPA/Newscom; ©Lain Masterton/Alamy; Richard B. Levine/Newscom; ©AP Photo/U.S. Air Force, Airman 1st Class Courtesy Witt.

Text Credits

Credits are listed in order of appearance.

Excerpt from Owen Jones, *Chavs: The Demonization of the Working Class.* Copyright © 2011 Owen Jones. Reprinted by permission of Verso Books; From Seelye, Katharine Q. "Detroit Census Confirms a Desertion Like No Other." *The New York Times*, March 22, 2011 © 2011 The New York Times. All rights reserved. Used by permission and protected by the Copyright Laws of the United States. The printing, copying, redistribution, or retransmission of this Content without express written permission is prohibited. www.nytimes.com; Excerpt from "Would You Wear . . . Designer Knockoff's?" by Zephyr. *CollegeFashion.net*. http://www.collegefashion.net/would-you-wear/would-you-wear-designer-knockoffs/. Reprinted by permission of the author; From Steven Hodson, "Fake Apple Store Employees Believe They Work for Apple." *The Inquisitr*, July 20, 2011. Reprinted by permission; Hamper, Ben. 1991. *Rivethead: Tales from the Assembly Line.* Grand Central Publishing. Reprinted by permission; From Barboza, David. "After Suicides, Scrutiny of China's Grim Factories." *The New York Times*, June 6, 2010 © 2010 The New York Times. All rights reserved. Used by permission and protected by the Copyright Laws of the United States. The printing, copying, redistribution, or retransmission of this Content without express written permission is prohibited. www.nytimes.com; Copyright © 2011 by Houghton Mifflin Harcourt Publishing Company. Reproduced by permission from *The American Heritage Dictionary of the English Language, Fifth Edition*; From Zernike, Kate, and Megan Thee-Brennan. "Poll Finds Tea Party Backers Wealthier and More Educated." *The New York Times*, April 14, 2010 © 2010 The New York Times. All rights reserved. Used by permission and protected by the Copyright Laws of the United States. The printing, copying, redistribution, or retransmission of this Content without express written permission is prohibited. www.nytimes.com; Based on data from Watson, Bruce. 2010. "The 10 Biggest Corporate Campaign Contributors in U.S. Politics." *DailyFinance.com*, October 13, 2010. http://www.dailyfinance.com/2010/10/13/the-10-biggest-corporate-campaign-contributors-in-u-s-politics/; From Shenon, Philip. "Jet Makers Preparing Bids for a Rich Pentagon Prize." *The New York Times*, March 12, 1996 © 1996 The New York Times. All rights reserved. Used by permission and protected by the Copyright Laws of the United States. The printing, copying, redistribution, or retransmission of this Content without express written permission is prohibited. www.nytimes.com; Excerpt from *Jihad vs. McWorld: How Globalism and Tribalism Are Reshaping the World*, by Benjamin Barber. Reprinted by permission of Ballantine Books, a division of Random House, Inc.

Part Four: The Problems of Changing World

Population Problems

Population

Richard Lord Photographer

- What has been the cause of runaway population growth?

- How does population growth affect our way of life?

- What kinds of problems does migration create?

- What kinds of population problems do the rich developed countries have?

- Can food production keep up with population growth?

- How can population growth be controlled?

From Chapter 15 of *Social Problems*, 10/e. James William Coleman. Harold R. Kerbo. Copyright © 2010 by Pearson Education. All rights reserved.

Amanda Blanco is a slim, dark-eyed woman in her early 40s. She lives behind her husband's tiny store in El Naranjo, Guatemala. On the clapboard wall of her home hang several pictures of the youngest of her nine children, Edwin, who died from diarrhea when he was just 4 months old. When asked whether she will have any more children, she simply says, "If God wishes." It's been almost three years since Edwin was born, and after a moment she asks: "I would be pregnant again by this time, right, if I were going to be pregnant at all?" Having so many children, she says, "may have hurt my health, and I think that is why I am always tired." When asked about which birth-control methods are available in her town, she only giggles and says, "My husband won't allow it. He thinks it will make me go with other men."[1]

The attitudes expressed by Amanda Blanco are typical of many poor people around the world, and they are still shared by some people in the middle and upper classes as well. The number of men, women, and children on this planet is now more than 6 billion—twice as many as there were only a few decades ago. If the rate of population growth only 15 years ago had continued, the world's population would have doubled in only 50 years. This would mean 12 billion people by 2050.[2] Fortunately, however, the world's **population explosion** has been slowing down, and most experts expect that birthrates will continue to decline. Instead of 12 billion people by 2050, the predictions are that there are more likely to be about 9 billion people.[3] Although that is certainly an improvement, most of those *3 billion* new mouths to feed will be in the poor countries—countries that often have trouble feeding the people they have now.

Many scientists wonder how long the Earth can support such growth. To understand the problems caused by this population explosion, it is helpful to look at the history of world population in units of 1 billion people. It took all of human history until 1800 for the world's population to reach 1 billion, but the next unit of 1 billion was added in only 130 years (1800–1930), the unit after that in 30 years (1930–1960). The next billion people were added in 15 years (1960–1975) and the next in only 12 years (1975–1987).[4] (See Figure 1.) If this trend had continued, the world would soon have been adding 1 billion people every year and eventually every month. Obviously, the world could not sustain such enormous population growth indefinitely. Fortunately, the pace of population growth has slowed in recent years, and the last billion people took 13 years to add (1987–2000). Experts now expect the world's population to stabilize sometime in the next 100 years. However, estimates vary widely as to when that will be and at what size. The crucial task facing the human race is to ensure that the population explosion is curbed by a rational program of population control and not by massive famines or devastating wars.

The long-range forecasts are, of course, educated guesswork, but the population crisis is not a thing of the future. It is here now. Next year, the world must house, clothe,

Population explosion ■ The rapid increase in the human population of the world.

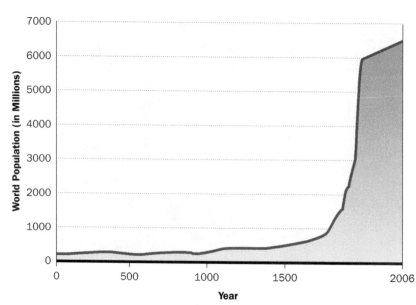

Figure 1

World Population

In the last three centuries, the world's population has been growing faster than at any other time in human history. There are now more than 6 billion people on this planet.

Source: Population Reference Bureau, *World Population Data Sheet, 2006* (Washington, DC: Population Reference Bureau, 2006).

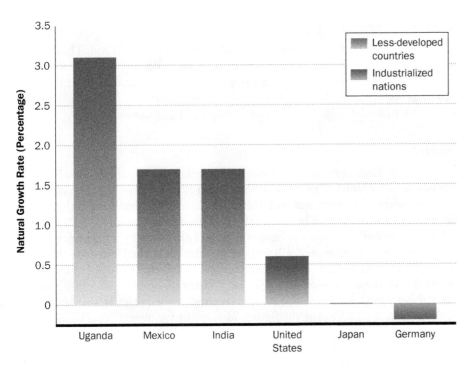

Figure 2

Growth in the Rich and Poor Nations

The population of the poor countries is growing much faster than the population of the rich ones.

Source: Population Reference Bureau, *World Population Data Sheet, 2006* (Washington, DC: Population Reference Bureau, 2006).

and feed about 79 million more people.[5] To make matters worse, most of them will be born in the underdeveloped nations of Africa, Latin America, and Asia—countries that are often too poor to provide for the populations they already have (see Figure 2). Although these nations may seem alike to Western eyes, there are important differences in their population problems. The most immediate crisis is in the overcrowded nations of Southern Asia (including Bangladesh, India, and Pakistan), which already contain one-fourth of the world's people, and in some of the rapidly growing states of sub-Saharan Africa (Africa south of the Sahara Desert).

The natural growth rates (excluding migration) of the industrialized nations of Western Europe (0.1 percent), North America (0.5 percent), and Japan (no growth) are much lower. Most other areas of the third world are somewhere in between. Eastern Asia is doing well (0.5 percent) because of China's successful population-control program, while the growth rate is higher in Latin America (1.5 percent) and Africa (2.3 percent).[6] These continent-wide generalizations cover up many important differences among nations. The Philippines, for example, has a growth rate of 2.1 percent a year, which is much higher than the average in Asia as a whole. At that rate, its population of more than 85 million will double in about 30 years. In 60 years, if its growth rate does not go down, the Philippines will have a larger population than the United States today but with less than one-thirtieth the land area.[7]

There is, moreover, a different kind of "population time bomb" ticking in the wealthy countries with declining birthrates. One might think that such a decline is a positive trend given the rapid population growth in other parts of the world, but the situation is much more complicated. As the birthrates have dropped, the population of elderly people has exploded while there are fewer and fewer people of working age. Adding this up, the questions becomes, who is going to keep the economy running? Who is going to take care of all the elderly people? Major adjustments will be necessary if the rich countries are to avoid a new kind of population crisis. We will begin our review with the more pressing problems associated with the population explosion in the poor countries, and then turn our attention to the rich countries with the aging populations.

QUICK REVIEW

■ What is the population explosion?

■ How do population growth rates differ among the different regions of the world?

What Caused the Population Explosion?

If population growth is to be brought under control, it must be understood. That understanding comes largely from the scientific discipline known as **demography,** which studies the causes and effects of changes in human population. Demographers must be mathematicians as well because they study such things as the rates of births and deaths, the flow of migration, and the age and sex distribution of a population.

Growth Rates

A nation's rate of population growth is obviously affected by the number of people who move into or out of the country. The world's population is not affected by **migration,** however: It is determined by **birthrates** and **death rates** alone. The birthrate is the number of babies born in a year divided by the total population. The death rate is the number of people who die. For convenience, the figures refer to 1,000 members of the population rather than to the total. For example, in 2003, the population of the United States was estimated to be 291 million. In that year there were 4,091,000 births and 2,443,000 deaths. Dividing by the size of the total population, we get a birthrate of 14.1 per 1,000 and a death rate of 8.4 per 1,000. The **growth rate** is determined by subtracting the death rate from the birthrate and then adjusting the figures to account for migration. Thus, for every 1,000 Americans in 2003, there were about six more births than deaths (for a natural growth rate of about 0.6) and 1,221,000 more people immigrated to the United States, bringing the growth rate up to 1.0 percent.[8]

However, these are only crude rates. They are called "crude" by demographers because they do not take the sex and age composition of the population into account. National populations usually consist roughly of half men and half women (although there are some important exceptions, as we will see), but age composition varies from time to time. Therefore, the age composition of a population must be examined to determine whether its growth rate is unusually high or low. The percentage of the population below age 15 is much higher in poor countries (32 percent) than in industrialized ones (17 percent). Because the girls in this age group are normally too young to have children, the crude birthrate actually underestimates the differences in fertility between women in the rich and poor countries. To measure this more accurately, demographers calculate the **total fertility rate,** which is an estimate of the number of children a woman is likely to have in her lifetime. The average woman in an industrialized country is now projected to have about 1.6 children, whereas a woman in a poor country can be expected to have 2.9 children.[9] The **replacement rate**—the number of children each woman must have to keep the population from growing or shrinking—is between 2.1 and 2.5, depending on the death rate. Therefore, if the total fertility rate does not change, the population in the industrialized countries can be expected to decline slowly while the population of the poor countries continues its rapid growth. Migration from the poor countries is likely to keep the population of most industrialized nations from actually shrinking, however.

Many people believe that increasing birthrates are the cause of the population explosion, but overall birthrates have actually declined. The real origins of the population crisis are to be found in the remarkable decline in death rates that began in Western Europe in the second half of

Demography ■ The scientific discipline that studies human population.

Migration ■ The movement of people from one geographic area to another.

Birthrate ■ The number of babies born in a year divided by the total population.

Death rate ■ The number of people who die in a year divided by the total population.

Growth rate ■ The birthrate minus the death rate.

Total fertility rate ■ The average number of children a woman is likely to have in her lifetime.

Replacement rate ■ The average number of children each woman must have to keep the population from growing or shrinking.

> On the average, women in industrialized nations have only about half as many children as those in third world nations, but infant mortality is much lower in industrialized countries.

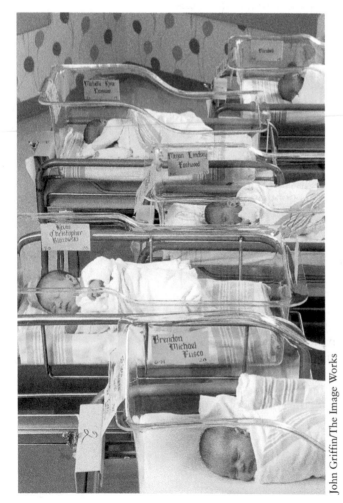

John Griffin/The Image Works

the eighteenth century and later spread around the world. Throughout most of human history, average life expectancy seldom exceeded 30 years, but today it is about 67 years worldwide, and the result is an exploding population.[10] In the early years of the population explosion, the European nations led the world in population growth. However, birthrates began decreasing in most of the industrialized nations in the latter part of the nineteenth century, reducing their rates of population growth. In the poor agricultural nations, birthrates did not begin to decrease until much more recently, and they have not gone down nearly as rapidly as death rates in those countries. As a result, the patterns of world population growth have been reversed, and the poor nations are now growing much faster than the rich ones. In 2006, the growth rate in the less-developed countries (excluding migration) was more than 15 times higher than in the industrialized nations.[11]

The Demographic Transition

Explaining these trends in world population has been one of the central tasks of modern demography. The most popular explanation is known as the theory of **demographic transition**, which attempts to put these changes in a long-term historical perspective. According to this theory, there are three distinct stages of population growth. In the first stage, which is characteristic of all traditional societies, both birthrates and death rates are high and population growth is moderate. In the second stage, the process of industrialization begins, and technological improvements bring a sharp decline in death rates. However, birthrates decline more slowly, and there is a population explosion. Finally, in the last stage, birthrates drop far enough to balance death rates, and population stabilizes.

Demographic transition ■ The changes in the birthrates and death rates that occur during the process of industrialization.

Why does industrialization bring down death rates? For one thing, industrial technology increases the food supply, thereby reducing the number of deaths from starvation. Industrialization also prolongs life by giving people safer water and better diets, clothing, housing, and sanitation. Insecticides prevent epidemics spread by insects and thus increase life spans even more. Improvements in medical technology also contribute to declining death rates. Vaccinations have brought numerous contagious diseases under control, and the discovery of antibiotics produced a cure for such killers as syphilis and pneumonia.

Although it takes longer, the economic changes created by industrialization eventually bring down birthrates as well. Children in agricultural societies make an important contribution to farm labor and usually support their parents when they grow old. In contrast, children in industrial societies are economic liabilities rather than assets. They make little economic contribution to the family, and they consume considerably more resources than their counterparts in agricultural societies. Thus, the economic rewards no longer go to those with big families, but to those with small families. Changes in traditional gender roles are another factor in the lowering of birthrates. In industrial societies, women have a far wider range of economic opportunities, and bearing and rearing children is no longer seen as their main social responsibility.

More efficient methods of birth control, such as the contraceptive drugs and the intrauterine device (IUD), and improvements in abortion and sterilization techniques have also helped bring down birthrates. Although modern technology has made it easier for couples to have the number of children they want and no more, we should not overestimate its impact. As Charles F. Westoff has pointed out, many European countries had low birthrates during the Great Depression of the 1930s, before the invention of the pill and the IUD, and before the legalization of abortion.[12] Thus, it appears that social change was a more important factor in bringing down birthrates than the mere availability of contraceptive technology.

The theory of demographic transition has clear implications for the future of world population. According to the theory, the less-developed countries with rapidly growing populations are in the second phase of the demographic transition; once these countries become industrialized, their birthrates will come down and their population problems will be over. Critics point out, however, that this theory was based on population changes that occurred during the industrialization of the Western countries; however, the situation in the less-developed countries is quite different than the theory implies. There is little doubt that industrialization was the direct cause of the decrease in the birthrates and death rates in the Western nations (and in Japan as well). The decline of death rates in the less-developed countries has not been caused by industrialization but by the spread of foreign technology and know-how. Because the population explosion in the third world started before the process of industrialization, it may take much longer for industrialization to progress far enough to bring the birthrates and death rates back into balance naturally (if indeed that ever happens).[13]

QUICK REVIEW

■ How do demographers calculate a nation's growth rate?

■ Explain the theory of the demographic transition and what its critics say about it.

The Impact of Population Growth

As we have seen, environmental limitations will make it impossible for the human population to keep growing at its current pace forever. The question is not whether the growth rate will decrease but, rather, how it will decrease. There are only two possibilities: Either birthrates will drop or death rates will rise.

One of the first people to recognize the dangers of unrestricted population growth was an English minister, Thomas Malthus. His famous *Essay on the Principle of Population* raised a storm of controversy when it was published in 1798.[14] Malthus argued that the human population naturally increases much more rapidly than its food supply. Food supplies increase arithmetically (1, 2, 3, 4, 5, etc.), but uncontrolled populations increase geometrically (1, 2, 4, 8, 16, etc.). This doubling effect occurs because two parents can produce four children; each of the four children can marry and produce four more children; and so on. Eventually, Malthus said, a population that keeps doubling in this way is doomed to outrun its food supply. He believed that only death-dealing disasters—famine, pestilence, and war—kept the human population within its environmental limits. This gloomy theory was not popular in Malthus's time, when most Europeans believed in the inevitability of progress and saw a bright future for the human race. Although Malthus clearly underestimated the world's capacity to produce food for its people, many demographers fear that he will be proved right in the long run. Today's farming techniques require much more energy than before, and as the world's supply of fossil fuel is used up, food production may fall short of the need.

But for many people in the third world, the lack of enough food is not a problem for the distant future but a constant daily threat. Of course, famines were a common event long before the population explosion. Although modern technology has enabled the industrialized nations to banish this ancient scourge, millions still starve in the overpopulated third world nations every year.

Since the end of World War II, the world's food supplies have grown faster than its population. Between 1950 and 1985, new technology helped world food production increase faster than it ever had before. Despite record population growth, the amount of food

Rapid population growth contributes to hunger and overcrowding in the third world.

Richard Lord Photographer

334

produced per person increased by almost 30 percent.[15] The increases have slowed down since then,[16] but some significant improvements in the diet of the world's people has clearly been made since 1950. Although per capita food consumption went up in the less-developed countries as a whole, most of the increase occurred in the industrialized nations that were already well fed, and there are significant regional differences within the third world as well. Since 1980, the Asian nations have made great improvements and Latin America has made more modest gains, but per capita food production has actually dropped in sub-Saharan Africa.[17]

Even though most people are able to get enough food to survive, some 800 million people, about 15 percent of the world's population, suffers from chronic hunger or malnutrition.[18] A poor diet during the childhood years delays physical maturity, produces dwarfism, impairs brain development, and reduces intelligence, even if the children affected later receive an adequate diet. The undernourished adult is apathetic, listless, and unable to work as long or as hard as the well-fed adult. Diseases caused directly by dietary deficiency, such as beriberi, rickets, and marasmus, are common in poor nations. Malnutrition also lowers resistance to disease, so the undernourished are likely to have a number of other health problems. The danger of epidemics is always high in overpopulated and underfed areas.[19] Moreover, research shows that the damage of malnutrition is passed on from one generation to the next. Babies born to malnourished mothers are weaker and in poorer health than the babies of well-fed mothers.[20]

The lack of adequate nutrition is, unfortunately, only one of a host of problems explosive population growth creates for less-developed countries. One of the most difficult is the pressure it places on traditional village lifestyles. The tiny plots of family land typical of the third world can support only a limited number of people. Many young men and women are forced to migrate to the cities, adding to the flood of unskilled and uneducated immigrants that is creating a crushing burden on the urban centers of the less-developed countries. A substantial percentage of people in the major cities of the poor nations already live in slums or in shantytowns built by squatters on land they do not own. These homes often lack running water, sewers, and electricity, and the rapid urbanization projected for the next decade can only make matters worse.

Poverty is another problem intensified by the population explosion. Because the population of the poor nations is growing so much faster than the population of the rich ones, the percentage of the world's people who live in poverty is increasing every year. Moreover, rapid population growth in the less-developed countries makes it far more difficult to improve the living conditions of the average person. More people inevitably mean more congestion, more crowding, and more damage to the environment. At the current rate of population growth, the economies of most poor nations must grow almost 2 percent a year just to keep their standard of living from falling.

Societies with rapid growth rates also have a disproportionate number of children in their population. In many less-developed countries, there are so many children that working-age adults make up a bare majority of the total population. For example, western Africa is growing much faster than North America, and as a result only 53 percent of all Africans are in their most productive years (15 to 65), compared with 68 percent of all North Americans.[21] Because a smaller percentage of working-age adults actually have jobs in Africa, each African worker must support almost twice as many people as each North American worker. These problems, moreover, are just the beginning: As today's children grow up, they must find jobs, and huge numbers of people in less-developed countries are already unemployed or underemployed.

The Graying of the Industrialized Nations

Demographers, environmentalists, and sociologists have been worried about the population explosion for decades. Sharp decreases in the birthrate and an aging population, however, are spreading a new fear among the advanced industrialized nations. In a rich country with a low death rate, the number of children the average woman needs to have in her lifetime (the total fertility rate) to keep the population stable is about 2.1. If the

Table 1

LOW FERTILITY RATES AND THE FUTURE POPULATION DECLINES IN ADVANCED
INDUSTRIAL NATIONS

Country	Total Fertility Rate, 2006	Population Size 2006 (millions)	Population Size 2050 (millions)
United States	2.0	299	420
Canada	1.5	33	42
Japan	1.3	128	100
United Kingdom	1.8	60	69
France	1.9	61	64
Germany	1.3	82	75
Italy	1.3	59	56
Russia	1.3	142	110

Source: Population Reference Bureau, *World Population Data Sheet, 2006* (Washington, DC: Population Reference Bureau, 2006).

The population of the industrialized nations is rapidly aging, and many economists are concerned about how society will shoulder the burden of their care.

Jim West

total fertility rate falls below that level without extensive immigration, there will be a population decline. Table 1 shows the current total fertility rate for most advanced industrial nations, their current population size, and population size projections for 2050.

The United States is the only one of these industrial nations with a total fertility rate high enough to maintain a stable population, and because the United States also has high rates of immigration, it is expected to see substantial population growth in the next 50 years. A few other advanced industrial nations with a history of immigration will also see an increase in population despite a total fertility rate below 2.0. Many other industrialized nations, however, are expected to see substantial declines in their populations.[22]

The problem for the industrial nations with low fertility rates is not just that their population may decline sometime in the future. There are also serious problems they must face almost immediately. The most important has to do with the "graying" of the population. As the birthrate drops, there are fewer children as a percentage of the total population. In addition, all over the industrial world, people are living longer as death rates are declining among the older population. Simply adding these changes up, we find more and more older people in the society and fewer and fewer young people. The problem then is how to take care of those older people with fewer working-age adults. People in their 20s to 60s are the most productive segment of the population; they make the cars, build the roads, run the hospitals. They also pay taxes that help take care of the elderly population that is no longer in the labor force. Thus, if the elderly are to be taken care of, if the work of running the economy is to be done, then the relatively smaller percentage of the working-adult population must save more for their own future, pay more taxes (for Social Security and hospital care), and perhaps work longer hours in order for the country's standard of living not to decline drastically.

Governments in Japan and Europe have been trying to deal with the problem, but with little success thus far. One approach would be to somehow increase the total fertility rate. Japan has had a government campaign in operation for several years to encourage women to have more children by appealing to their sense of national duty. However, it hasn't worked. Japan and several countries in Europe are also trying material incentives for families to have more children.[23] Most incentives involve paying a family a small monthly allowance when they have children, providing free medical care, or education subsidies. So far, these incentives also have not worked, probably because the total amount of the subsidies is still far less than the costs of raising a child. Another obvious response to this problem, of course, is to allow more immigration. Canada and Great Britain have allowed sufficient immigration in recent years to overcome their reduction

Lessons from Other Places

Human Trafficking, Modern Slavery

While spending some time at a Thai university close to the Malaysian border a few years ago, I happened upon a tragic story unfolding in the local newspapers. At first, it seemed simply a sad but routine occurrence: A young girl had committed suicide while being held in a jail. But the local press soon found that there was far more to the story. The girl, who had hanged herself, had been arrested for the third time by local police. The two previous times, the police turned her back over to the local brothel where she was being held in slavery to work as a prostitute. As is often the case, this young girl was lured in from one of the desperately poor countries near Thailand with the promise of a good job that would allow her to send money back to her hungry relatives. After the story broke, the brothel was raided and closed, but a private agency working to stop "sex tourism" reported later that it was only closed about three weeks. Southeast Asian countries, however, are making some progress in reducing sex slavery and trafficking in women and children. Many non-governmental organizations have induced rich nations to prosecute their own citizens coming back from Southeast Asia after committing sex crimes. Cambodia, one of the countries with an extremely high rate of child prostitution, is taking strong actions. In 2007, there were signs all over the country saying "Make Sex Tourists Ex-Tourists." Taxi drivers and motorcycle taxi drivers have been organized and instructed by the government to report tourists who seem to be picking up children for sex, and neighborhood organizations have started secretly following tourists to see if they are picking up small children and then reporting them to the police.

Because of the recent media attention, most people in the West think that the trafficking in women and children is only an Asian problem. Although many of the women and children in the international sex trade are from poor Asian countries, there are almost as many coming from other poor countries, especially the former communist countries and territories of the old Soviet Union. The International Labor Organization estimates that human trafficking produced $36 billion in profits in 2005 alone. Most of this profit was from sex trafficking, and most was made by people in rich countries. When the Central Intelligence Agency, better known in Cold War days as just the CIA, was asked by the U.S. government to look into the issue, it found much the same problem here. Its detailed analysis published in the spring of 2000 reported that as many as *50,000 women and children* a year from Asia, Latin America, and Eastern Europe were brought to the United States under false pretenses, and many were held as sex slaves while others were forced to work in sweatshops making cheap clothing for Americans. State and federal government agencies, however, prosecuted only 250 cases between 1998 and 2000!

Harold Kerbo

Sources: International Labor Organization, Global Alliance Against Forced Labor, 2005 (www.ilo.org/declaration); U.S. Central Intelligence Agency, *Growing Global Migration and Its Implications for the United States, 2001* (Washington DC: U.S. Government Printing Office).

in the fertility rate. As we will see next, however, this option has proven difficult for other advanced industrial nations such as Japan to accept.

QUICK REVIEW

- Why did the future look so gloomy to Thomas Malthus?
- Compare and contrast the effects of population change on the poor and the rich countries.

Migration

Next to its exploding size, the most significant development in world population is the waves of migration that have affected every country on Earth in one way or another. We have already discussed one of the most important of these human tides: the steady flow of people from overpopulated rural villages to the urban slums of the third world. Although such migrants often face enormous hardships, their problems pale in comparison to those of people caught up in the forced migrations that follow such disasters as floods, famines, and wars that so often strike the less-developed countries. Such crises can send millions of refugees running for safety. Sometimes they are able to escape to a neighboring country, but more often they are turned back at the borders and must find a new place to live in their own nation. Most of these desperate people end up in refugee camps that are crowded, dirty, and dangerous. All the basic necessities—food, water, sanitation, shelter—are likely to be in short supply, and deaths from malnutrition, epidemic disease, and violence are common.

Many of the world's growing number of refugees end up in camps such as the one shown here.

AP Wide World Photos

A Political Refugee

There is a constant flow of world population from the less-developed countries to the wealthier and more politically stable nations. This story comes from a woman who fled from political persecution in Afghanistan.

I left Afghanistan in 1979, after the Russian invasion. My main reason for leaving was not because of the economic opportunities in the United States, but that Afghanistan had become unsafe for me. I was from a wealthy family and my boss warned me that the communists had my name on a list and I would be arrested. I wasn't able to take any of my things . . . nothing. I just had to go to the airport and get on the first plane I could.

I became an American citizen in 1989, and that was one of the saddest days of my life. I felt as if I had betrayed my country and my past. I did feel like I was losing part of my identity. My passport meant something to me, part of my personal life, and when I was asked to give it up, it was giving a part of my life away.

My children don't mention it, but they do suffer to live in a family where a mother has a very thick accent. For example, I used to make them sandwiches, so-called Afghan sandwiches, and when the other kids would smell the hamburger and spices I used, they would say, "Yuk." My children said, "Mama, we want peanut butter, just to be like everybody else." They feel threatened, they do feel powerless, and they do want to be accepted by the dominant culture. During the Gulf War my son was so upset because someone called him a "camel jockey."

Sometimes I think America gives the illusion that it is everybody's land and is a land of immigrants. There seems to be much more negativism toward immigrants in the '90s than there was before. When I lived in Europe they made it very clear you were not wanted, whereas in America the kind of discrimination you confront is very covert—they say there is no discrimination, but in fact there is discrimination.

Leaving the Third World

A second tide of human population runs from the third world to the industrialized nations. Although the United States has traditionally been thought of as a land of immigrants, Western Europe actually accepted more new people in recent years, and the percentage of foreign-born residents in many European nations is rapidly approaching or even exceeding that of the United States. In 2002, 11.8 percent of the U.S. population was foreign born, as were 20 percent of residents of Switzerland, 8.9 percent of the Germans, 4.6 percent of the British, and 2.4 percent of the Italians. The largest percentage was in Australia, where almost a quarter (23.2 percent) of the population was born someplace else.[24] Although not all these migrants were from the poor nations, the majority were. Given the desperate poverty and rapidly growing population in so many countries, most experts expect the current tide of immigration to grow even stronger in the years ahead. (For an account of the problems faced by one refugee, see the Personal Perspectives box, "A Political Refugee.")

The millions of immigrants who come to the industrialized nations every year face a host of daunting problems, starting with all the psychological ramifications of leaving friends, family, and native country. Some try the legal route—filling out applications and going through lengthy waiting periods in hopes that they will ultimately be given permission to come. Most people, though, have little chance of success unless they have a lot of money, special skills, or close relatives in an industrialized nation. For most people who want to immigrate, the only realistic option is to come illegally. Sometimes they hire what Latin Americans call a "coyote"—a professional who smuggles them into a country like the United States for a big fee. Other immigrants buy forged papers, stow away on boats, climb fences, swim rivers, or do anything else they can think of to get across a border on their own. However it is done, an illegal border crossing is a dangerous affair. Many illegal immigrants drown, are smothered, or die in extreme desert heat before they ever reach their new homes, and even if they arrive safely, they are often the targets of both government officials and a host of unscrupulous criminals.

If third world migrants have relatives or close friends in their new country, their immediate adjustment is likely to be easier. Most immigrants, however, face a myriad of problems. They have to find a job, learn a new language, and adjust to a whole new culture. Although their new country may be far richer than their old one, they are likely to find that it is also a dangerous and extremely competitive place. If they came illegally, the new migrants must live with the constant danger of being caught and deported, and they are likely to find that, without official documents, all but the most marginal jobs are closed to them. To make matters worse, both legal and illegal immigrants are often the targets of racism, cultural prejudice, and bitter resentment from members of the native population who feel threatened by the new arrivals.

Although tearing up their roots and moving to a foreign land is usually traumatic for the immigrants themselves, this migration has two beneficial effects for the less-developed countries they leave. First, the flow of immigrants (who tend to be young males) acts as a pressure valve to help reduce their huge problems of overpopulation and unemployment. Second, these immigrants send billions of dollars a year to their relatives back home. On the one hand, for many countries—Turkey, India, and Morocco, for example—those remittances total more than all the foreign aid they receive. On the other hand, however, many poor nations are experiencing a "brain drain" because of this migration—that is, they are losing many of their best-trained and most highly skilled people because they cannot compete with the wages paid in the industrialized nations.

The Impact on the Industrialized Nations

The impact of immigration from the third world on the industrialized nations is an emotional and hotly debated issue. In the past, immigrants provided a valuable pool of cheap labor for the industrialized nations, but automation has made unskilled jobs more scarce, and public opinion in the industrialized nations has turned against immigration. Nonetheless, the new immigrants are an economic asset overall. Some bring desperately needed talents and special skills, and, as a whole, immigrants tend to be more ambitious and harder-working than most other people. They do the jobs nobody else wants to do for less money than anyone else would be willing to accept. Another benefit is demographic. Because the native population of all the industrialized nations is rapidly aging, and most immigrants are young people in their prime earning years, they are likely to be an essential link in the support network for the growing number of retirees.

Despite their need for such immigration, however, many industrial nations without the benefit of the U.S. tradition of immigration are experiencing severe difficulties. As we saw in the previous section, nations such as Japan and France are aging rapidly and must face the prospect of significant declines in population in the future. These countries, however, tend to view citizenship as a matter of race and ethnic background and find it hard to accept immigrants with a different cultural tradition. These countries seem headed for serious economic problems if their views of immigration and immigrants do not change.

The benefits derived from immigrant labor are not evenly distributed throughout society—some segments tend to gain while others lose. The biggest winners are, of course, businesspeople and corporate stockholders, who benefit from the productivity and low cost of immigrant labor. The elderly and infirm are also winners because they gain the services of healthy young immigrant workers. The biggest losers are the low-skilled native workers who must compete with the new immigrants for jobs. Not only do immigrants take some jobs away from native-born citizens, but also they may hold down the overall wages paid for low-skilled work. Among the other losers are the big cities where most of the immigrants end up living. In the United States, for example, new immigrants tend to gravitate to Los Angeles, New York City, Miami, and Chicago, and those cities and their surrounding communities shoulder a disproportionate share of the costs of the social needs of immigrant populations such as health care, education, and police services.

QUICK REVIEW

- What are the different patterns of migration we see in today's world?
- What problems do immigrants from the poor countries face?
- Describe the different impact immigration to industrial countries has on the rich and the poor countries.

Solving Population Problems

Some observers argue that there is no population crisis at all and that dire warnings about the future are just the cries of a few alarmists. However, most demographers, politicians, and informed citizens have come to agree that the world indeed faces a grave population problem. There now seems little doubt that we need both to work to feed the hungry people already on the planet and to take stronger action to reduce population growth.

Feeding the Hungry

Many people believe that the use of better technology for agricultural production is the best way to feed the hungry people of the world. The greatest single advance in recent times was the **green revolution**—the creation of new strains of wheat and rice that yielded much more food per acre. This development has been one of the main reasons that world food production has kept ahead of population growth in the last half century. However, the green revolution was no cure-all for world hunger. The new strains of wheat and rice require more fertilizer, insecticides, and irrigation if they are to produce higher yields, and many poor farmers simply cannot afford such things. Moreover, all three depend on petroleum, which can also be extremely costly. Research shows that increasing inputs of water, fertilizer, and pesticides produce diminishing returns: In the first few years, the new crops produce dramatically improved yields, but as time goes on, productivity levels off. Finally, the green revolution has encouraged the trend toward larger farms, and that has often had devastating effects on peasants who have been forced off their traditional lands.[25]

Green revolution ■ The increase in agricultural production created by the use of new strains of wheat and rice.

Despite the limitations of the green revolution, some experts believe that another new technique—biological engineering—provides the best hope of keeping food production up with population growth. These new techniques allow scientists to directly manipulate the genetic structure of plants and animals so they can create new organisms that better satisfy human needs. Many crops that are currently in use, for example, have been genetically altered to make them more resistant to insects, and the proponents of this technology feel that many far more useful new organisms will soon be on the market. Critics of this technology take a strikingly different view, however. They fear that releasing a host of new synthetic organisms into the environment could have disastrous and unpredictable results, perhaps disrupting existing ecosystems and actually causing a drop instead of an increase in world food production.[26] Agribusiness in the United States rapidly embraced the use of such **genetically modified organisms (GMOs)** without much public debate or involvement. In Europe, however, a strong popular movement in opposition to GMO products has sprung up and many consumers refuse to buy them.

Genetically modified organisms (GMOs) ■ Plants or animals that scientists have genetically altered.

The American way of improving agricultural production also relies heavily on mechanization, but this approach is often not appropriate for poor countries with severe population problems. Few of the world's farmers can afford even the least expensive tractors. When the price of such machines is subsidized by the government or some other agency, they still cannot be operated economically on the small plots of land owned by most peasant farmers. It is sometimes suggested that small farms be consolidated so they can be worked with such laborsaving equipment, but even if a program of this sort were politically feasible, it would create a staggering unemployment problem. Moreover, it is hard to imagine anything that makes less sense for third world countries with runaway population growth and high unemployment than spending their precious reserves on laborsaving machinery. Furthermore, a greater dependence on sophisticated mechanized equipment will only exhaust the planet's supply of petroleum that much faster and make the poor nations that much more dependent on the rich ones.

The late English economist E. F. Schumacher advocated an ingenious compromise. He proposed that poor nations use **intermediate technology**: machines that are less sophisticated than the gas-guzzling marvels of the industrialized nations but more effective than the traditional reliance on human and animal power.[27] What the world needs, Schumacher said, is simple machines that can be manufactured in poor nations at low cost and are suitable for small-scale farming. Schumacher himself helped design a small gasoline-powered plowing machine that is more efficient than a horse or an ox but much less costly than a tractor.

Intermediate technology ■ Technology that is less complicated and less expensive than that typically used in the industrialized nations but more efficient than animal power and other traditional technologies.

Another way to get farmers to grow more food is to reorganize the agricultural economy. One program that has proved effective is **land reform**: taking land away from rich landlords and redistributing it among the peasants who actually do the work. Land reform programs in Mexico and Taiwan have shown that people work harder and produce more when they own their own land and receive the benefits of their own labor. A different version of this approach has also proved effective in the communist and formerly communist nations. The old communist-style collective farms provide few incentives for individual farmers to increase production, and agricultural production usually increases significantly when farmers are allowed to sell their own crops and keep the profits.

Land reform ■ The redistribution of land from wealthy landlords to peasant farmers.

A serious problem in some poor nations, especially in Africa, is that their governments intentionally hold down the price of agricultural products to keep the cost of food for urban workers low. Although that is a worthwhile objective, the result is that farmers often lose money on their crops and production decreases. A better approach is to encourage farm prices to rise and subsidize the food budgets of the urban poor by taxing the local elites.

Some people propose feeding the world's hungry by merely cultivating more land, but almost all the good land is already in use. The remainder would require large amounts of oil and other energy to produce even low yields. Some arid soil could be put into production with new irrigation projects, and perhaps new hydroelectric power would come as a bonus. However, such projects are extremely expensive, and unless carefully thought out, they often do more harm than good. The proposal that tropical jungles be cleared for farming is even less realistic. Jungle land is not farmland. Brazil's attempts to farm the Amazon valley have shown that rain forest land has few plant nutrients and that tropical rains quickly wash away artificial fertilizers.[28]

As open land runs out, humanity has turned to the sea. Fish and other seafoods now make up almost one-fourth of all the animal protein consumed by humans.[29] Like agricultural production, the world's catch of fish increased rapidly after World War II. It more than quadrupled between 1950 and 1989. Since then, however, the world's total catch has leveled off, while the human population has kept on growing. The World Resources Institute estimates that 60 percent of the world's important fish stocks are in urgent need of management to rehabilitate them or prevent them from being overfished. A 2006 report funded by the National Science Foundation concluded that the populations of one-third of the species that are commonly fished including Atlantic cod, Pacific salmon, and bluefin tuna have already collapsed.[30] The lakes and oceans can support only a limited number of fish, and some species are already near extinction. Nevertheless, experts believe that the total catch of fish could be expanded by concentrating on smaller and less-appetizing species of fish and through more careful management and control of the fishing industry. Many countries now raise fish specifically for human consumption, and "fish farming" is bound to increase as the human population grows. Future efforts to get more food from the sea will, however, have to focus on plants as well as animals. Various forms of edible algae and seaweed are already being harvested

Debate

Should We Try to Stop the New Wave of Third World Immigration?

YES The flood of new immigrants is out of control and must be stopped as soon as possible. Factory owners and investors reap huge profits from cheap immigrant labor while the poor suffer—because immigrants are willing to work for wages far below the minimum standards accepted in our society. They take jobs away from our own workers and drive down the pay for all unskilled work. Because several immigrant families are often willing to share the same cramped apartment, they outbid our own poor people for the limited supply of affordable rental housing. This human flood places a heavy burden on taxpayers, who must finance new schools, hospitals, prisons, and other facilities to meet the needs of all these new residents. It also creates serious new health problems by bringing contagious third world diseases into this country.

Although some people claim that the current wave of immigration is no different from those of the past, such statements are clearly false. The most obvious difference is that so many of today's immigrants come into this country illegally, thus showing disrespect for the laws and standards of the country they claim to admire. By allowing so many illegals to stay here, we reward their criminal behavior and in effect punish their law-abiding countrymen who stay at home. Another important difference is not in the immigrants but in the economic realities of present-day America. When previous waves of immigration reached these shores, there was a vast untamed continent to be explored and developed. Now the frontier is gone, and with it has gone our ability to assimilate large numbers of new immigrants. Effective action to stem this new tide of immigration is needed before the problem gets any worse.

NO The plain fact is that we need immigrant labor, and we need it badly. Birthrates throughout the industrialized world have plummeted, and a steady supply of young new immigrants is essential if we are to care for our aging population. Some people claim that immigrants hurt our economy by taking away jobs from local citizens and placing an extra burden on our state and local governments. The exact opposite is true. Immigrants have always taken the dirty, dangerous, and low-paying jobs that nobody else wants. Without the steady supply of low-cost labor that immigrants provide, many domestic industries would be driven into bankruptcy by foreign competition. Moreover, immigrants pay the same taxes as anyone else, and many of them actually receive fewer services for their money because they are afraid of being deported if they step forward to claim their due.

The greatness of this nation was founded on the determination, sacrifice, and skill of the millions of immigrants who came to these shores over the years. Everyone now recognizes the great contribution immigrants have made to our nation, but the same objections raised about immigrants a hundred years ago are still being voiced today. The real reason for these complaints also remains the same: fear and prejudice. The Italians, Jews, Poles, and Irish helped strengthen, not weaken, this country, and so will the Latin Americans and Asians. The fact that the color of their skin is a little different does not mean their contribution will be any less.

Even if these new immigrants made no economic contribution at all (which is clearly not true), it would still be morally unconscionable to shut the door to the world's poor and oppressed. How can we, the daughters, sons, and grandchildren of immigrants, tell those courageous people that they may not gamble their future on a new land?

---

in Asia, but if marine plants are to make a major contribution to the human food supply, they too will have to be farmed. Several experimental sea farms are now in operation, but it will be some time before this technology is economically feasible for large-scale use.

Finally, a different way to get more food for the hungry is to waste less. It has been estimated that people in the wealthy nations throw away one pound of food for every three that are eaten.[31] Poor nations also waste a great deal of food but for different reasons: Insects and rodents eat food held in storage, and slow and inefficient methods of distribution allow more food to rot before it can be eaten. Another way to increase food supplies without increasing food production is to get more people to eat a vegetarian diet. A cow must be fed 8 kilograms to 10 kilograms of grain to produce 1 kilogram of meat, and it is far more efficient, and often more healthful, for humans simply to eat the grain and other vegetable products themselves.[32]

Controlling Population Growth

Gaining control over the world's explosive population growth is one of the most urgent tasks before the human race today. If we fail, we will surely have to face our ancient enemies—famine, pestilence, and war—on a new and unprecedented scale. Currently, the industrialized nations are much closer than their less-developed neighbors to achieving population control. The population of the industrialized nations is growing at less than 0.1 percent a year, which is only about one-fifteenth the rate for poor nations. The following discussion therefore focuses on the less-developed countries, although the proposals and programs designed for the poor nations can be modified to fit the industrialized nations if the need arises.

Some political leaders see a large population as a national asset, and they have used government programs to encourage growth. As far back as the thirteenth century, a number of European nations established tax benefits for parents. Hitler's Germany enacted a variety of measures aimed at increasing its population, as have several communist countries. Romania's communist dictator Nicolae Ceauşescu created a program designed to increase his country's population by one-third. He forbade abortion and birth control and created so-called baby police to give monthly tests to female workers to guard against any illegal termination of pregnancy. In late 1990, shortly after Ceauşescu's overthrow, there were 200,000 abandoned children in state care in Romania's orphanages.[33] Fortunately, such efforts are the exception, not the rule. The harsh realities of unchecked population growth have forced most poor nations to adopt population-control programs.

SOCIAL CHANGE Many political leaders who are interested in controlling population focus their efforts on industrialization, believing that attitudes toward the family and reproduction will change as the economy develops. As we have already shown, industrialization does bring about a demographic transition—a change in birthrates and death rates that ultimately results in slower overall growth. Many leaders insist that the population problem will take care of itself if we wait for this "natural" process to occur in the agricultural nations. Unfortunately, such expectations are ill founded. The fact that industrialization has occurred in a few poor countries hardly means that it will occur in all of them. Moreover, even if all the poor nations of the world were somehow to industrialize, the demographic transition could not possibly occur quickly enough to limit the world's population to a manageable size.

Industrialization is not, however, the only economic influence on population control. The key variable may be the maintenance of a minimum standard of living for the poor. As Jon Bennett put it: "High birth rates are primarily related to economic uncertainty. In nearly every country where malnutrition has been reduced and child death rates have decreased, birthrates have also dropped dramatically."[34]

There is a growing consensus of world opinion that one of the most effective ways to help stabilize population growth is to focus on the needs of women. The World Bank, for example, has concluded that improving the status of women was the key to both economic development and population control.[35] In less-developed countries, women often live extremely restricted lives under the domination and control of their husbands and other relatives. They have few roads to status or social rewards other than bearing and rearing large families. One of the best ways to reduce this pressure is, as John R. Weeks put it, to change "the sex roles taught to boys and girls, giving equal treatment to the sexes in the educational and occupational spheres. If a woman's adulthood and femininity are expressed in other ways besides childbearing, then the pressures lessen to bear children as a means of forcing social recognition."[36] The power of women's labor can also provide a big boost to industrialization, thus making an indirect contribution to lower birthrates as well. Equal opportunities and equal status for women are revolutionary ideas in many third world countries, but the success of that revolution would go a long way toward solving the problems of poverty and overpopulation.

BIRTH CONTROL Most population-control programs try to encourage people to use birth control and limit the size of their families voluntarily. The assumption is that the birthrate will drop if couples have only the number of children they desire. To help achieve that goal, information and birth-control devices are usually given to the poor without charge. Such programs are called **family planning,** but the real objective is to cut the birthrate. Some countries support their family planning programs with publicity stressing the desirability of small families and the dangers of overpopulation. In India, for example, the symbol of population control—a red triangle with the smiling faces of two parents and two children—can be seen in every village.

Family planning ▪ A program that seeks to control population by helping families to have only the number of children they desire.

Such programs help reduce the number of unwanted children, but by themselves they are unlikely to achieve the kind of reduction in birthrates that the world needs to stabilize its population at a manageable size. For one thing, many family planning programs in the less-developed countries have been poorly organized and underfunded. There is a more basic problem, however. Publicity campaigns and speeches simply cannot change deeply rooted attitudes favoring large families. The most successful family planning programs therefore have been in countries such as South Korea, Thailand, and Taiwan, which have also been undergoing rapid industrialization.

The traditional attitude in most cultures is that having more children means a stronger family. In the past, big families have been essential to the prosperity of the peasants and often to their very survival. The belief in the value of having many children is often reinforced by religious and political doctrines as well. Of all the world's major religions, Roman Catholicism is the most strongly opposed to birth control. In 1968, Pope Paul VI reaffirmed church doctrine by ruling that all forms of artificial contraception block the normal "transmission of life" in marriages and thereby violate the "creative intention of God." According to Catholic doctrine, only two methods of birth control are permitted: total abstinence from sexual relations or periodic abstinence during a woman's most fertile period (that is, the rhythm method). However, both methods have proved unreliable because they demand a higher level of self-control than most people appear to possess.

The weaknesses in family planning programs have led some nations to provide additional incentives for parents to limit the size of their families: bonuses for couples with few children and penalties for those with many children. Some countries have even proposed mandatory restrictions that require all families to limit the number of children they have.

David Austen/Stock Boston

Voluntary family planning programs are common all over the world, but such programs have little chance of success unless traditional attitudes about the value of a large family are changed.

Of all the large third world nations, the People's Republic of China has made the greatest progress in reducing its birthrate). China's powerful central government has put intense pressure on its people to abstain from premarital sex, to delay marriage and childbearing, and to use birth control and abortion. China also has a strong incentive program designed to encourage each family to have no more than one child. Couples who agree to this limit are given a "single-child certificate," which entitles them to such benefits as priority in housing, better wages, a special pension, and preference in school admissions. Couples who have too many children are often fined and required to pay for all the maternity, medical, and educational costs their children may incur. As a result of this program, China's birthrate has shown a significant decline. China's current growth rate is only 0.6 percent a year—an extremely low figure for a poor agricultural nation.[37] It is clear that China is now firmly committed to an all-out effort to stabilize the size of its population. Not only is that good news for the future of China, it is good news for the entire world, for one of every five people now lives in China.

These gains have not been made without considerable social cost, however. The government pressure for population control in China's highly centralized society has been so intense that the one-child limitation has become virtually mandatory for some Chinese. Peasants have traditionally put a high value on having sons, who live with the extended family throughout their lives. Daughters, on the other hand, are expected to move in with their husbands' families and thus are considered more of a burden than an asset. The Chinese have always taken better care of male than female children, and the new population limitation measures seem to have encouraged more female infanticide and selective abortion as well. The result has been a growing gender imbalance in the population. In some regions of China, there are 135 men to every 100 women. Because there is normally a rough biological balance in the number of boys and girls who are born, we can estimate there are about 80 million missing girls throughout the world, mostly in China and India. China will soon have 40 million men without women to marry.[38] Although this tendency poses some obvious problems for unmarried Chinese men, some experts believe that the growing scarcity of women will help improve their status in Chinese society. There is little doubt that this imbalance in the sex ratio will also help to further slow the growth of the Chinese population because demographers have found that it is the number of women that determines the overall birthrate, not the number of men. (This is because one man can father a much larger number of children than a woman can bear.)

QUICK REVIEW

- Describe and critically evaluate the proposals to feed the world's hungry.
- Critically evaluate the different approaches to controlling population growth.

Sociological Perspectives on Population

Only a few centuries ago, the main population problem was not how to reduce population growth but how to encourage it. Plagues and disasters sometimes brought sharp declines in population, and at times people must have thought the very survival of humanity to be in doubt. As we have seen, improvements in technology and changes in social organization sent death rates plummeting and created a new problem: overpopulation. Most people were slow to recognize this fundamental change and continued in their old ways. Social scientists, including sociologists, were the first to recognize these new realities and to urge government leaders to take action. Although there is now a specialized discipline devoted to the study of population, a great many demographers are trained as sociologists as well, and the major sociological perspectives provide important insights into the population problem.

The Functionalist Perspective

Functionalists argue that population growth can perform several important functions: Because greater size often means greater strength, a large population offers more security during natural disasters and a stronger defense against foreign aggressors. Many economists believe that economic growth is essential to the prosperity of an industrial society and that an increasing population promotes economic growth by providing labor and creating new markets for consumer goods.

Population growth may also be dysfunctional, however. Although all the services an expanding population requires—such as the construction of more houses, the cultivation of more land, and the manufacture of more clothing—may stimulate the economy, these activities may also produce serious environmental damage and a shortage of natural resources. Moreover, young adults face intense competition for jobs, and unemployment fosters alienation and even despair. Overcrowding contributes to urban decay, the spread of disease, and a general decline in the standard of living.

When the world's population was low and there was no shortage of natural resources, the functions of population growth far outweighed its dysfunctions. Now the same social forces that promoted population growth in the past, when it was desirable, produce hunger, poverty, and social instability. For this reason, functionalists say, the population problem will be solved only when dysfunctional attitudes, values, and institutions that promote excessive birthrates are changed. Given time, the social system will reach a new balance. The critical question is whether this balance will come about as a result of famine, wars, or other disasters or because of well-organized programs to change traditional attitudes toward childbearing.

The Conflict Perspective

The conflict perspective sees the population crisis in the third world as a direct result of European colonialism and the growth of a world economy that is divided between rich industrialized nations and poor agricultural ones. In the nineteenth century, when technological advances were producing a sharp decline in death rates in Western Europe, the process of industrialization was creating economic incentives that were eventually to bring the birthrate down as well. Conflict theorists note that these same technological developments also began lowering the death rate in the third world, but the European nations prevented their colonies from industrializing. As a result, the economic system continued to reward those with large families, and the population of the third world exploded. Daniel Chirot cites the role of the British in India as a classic example of this process:

> Along with maintaining a colonial class structure, the British also prevented the imposition of protective tariffs which would have helped Indian industry compete against the more advanced British industries. . . . By the time India had escaped from British colonial rule, . . . the country's overpopulation problem was quite severe, and world technology still more advanced and capital intensive than in the early 1900s [thus making it still harder for India to industrialize.][39]

Conflict theory also provides important insights into the forces that oppose population control. Official opposition to contraception and abortion is viewed as a reflection of a conflict between the interests of the masses and those of leaders and ruling elites. Overpopulation is harmful to most people, but an expanding population is an economic and political asset to the ruling class. A large national population means greater international power. Population growth among a society's lower classes also helps the elite by keeping wages down and providing a large pool of labor. Unionization and strikes are less likely when jobs are scarce, and there are many unemployed workers waiting to replace those who protest poor working conditions. In the long run, religious groups that prevent their followers from practicing birth control are likely to have more members than those that allow contraception.

Perhaps the most significant contribution of the conflict perspective is its analysis of the causes of malnutrition and hunger. Conflict theorists point out that the current "food shortage" is really a problem of distribution, not production. The world currently produces more than enough food to provide an adequate diet for all people. Starvation and malnutrition result from the unequal distribution of the food that is produced. The rich industrialized countries have less than one-fourth of the world's people, but they consume more than half of its food.[40] Every year, millions of people starve to death in the poor countries, while in the wealthy nations many others die from heart conditions caused by overeating. Moreover, the same system of unequal distribution is found within nations. The ruling elites of even the poorest countries eat well while poor people in rich countries such as the United States and Canada are often malnourished.

The obvious solution to this problem is to redistribute the world's food so that everyone is adequately fed, but there are enormous political and economic barriers to such a project. Most of the surplus food is in the wealthy industrialized nations, and most of the hungry are too poor to pay for it. Even in the unlikely event that the wealthy nations could be persuaded to give away a substantial proportion of their surplus food, redistribution might drive many marginal third world farmers out of business and create even more poverty and deprivation. On a national level, however, the outlook for an effective program of redistribution is brighter. Such countries as Sweden and Norway already guarantee a good diet to their poor by means of welfare programs, and some third world governments ration food supplies during hard times to ensure that most people get enough to eat.

The Feminist Perspective

Traditionally, most demographers have seen economic and technological causes at the root of the population explosion: Technological advances linked to the process of industrialization brought down death rates faster than cultural changes brought down birthrates. In recent years, however, feminists have proved that social restrictions placed on women also play a critical role in the population problem. The cultures with the highest birthrates are also those that deny women equal access to education and jobs. When women are restricted to their family roles as mothers and as subordinates of their husbands, their whole social status and personal security derive from their ability to bear and raise children.

The feminist response to the population crisis therefore is obvious: Give the women of the developing nations more rights and more freedoms. Following the urgings of the feminists, development workers have found that the most successful family planning programs are indeed those that focus on women—not just to provide birth-control technology but also to provide the education, economic assistance, and emotional support necessary to help women create a more powerful and independent role for themselves. It is not surprising that such programs have often proved highly controversial in traditional patriarchal cultures. The obstacles have not, however, proved insurmountable because husbands also benefit from the extra income their wives are able to earn and from the overall advantages of family planning.

The Interactionist Perspective

Interactionists see the problem of overpopulation as the result of the way traditional cultures define the world, including their attitudes and beliefs about childrearing and family life. Peasant farmers in traditional societies have a fatalistic attitude toward life. The idea of planning a family, let alone a world population, is alien to them. Fertility continues to be seen as a sign of virility and competence. The "real man" is one who has fathered many sons, and the "real woman" is one who has borne and reared them. Even in the industrialized nations, childless couples are sometimes pitied, and the inability to bear children may be reason enough for a husband to divorce his wife.

From the interactionist perspective, it is obvious that such learned attitudes and beliefs must change before birth-control measures can be effective. Such attitudinal changes do not occur in a vacuum; rather, they interact with shifting economic, social, and political conditions. Mere propaganda and personal appeals are not enough; they must be accompanied by concrete economic and social improvements. For example, a sound social security plan can do much to convince people that a large family is not necessary for support in their old age. Similarly, like the feminists, many interactionists argue that women who are provided with alternatives to the roles of wife and mother will soon learn that caring for a large family is not the only important activity in life, and their birthrates will drop.

QUICK REVIEW

- What are the functions and dysfunctions of population growth?
- What role does exploitation play in the population problem?
- How do feminists say we should respond to the population problem?
- How do interactionists explain the causes of the population explosion?

Summary

Even though it has slowed somewhat in recent years, the world's population continues to grow at a rapid rate. Demographers agree that the reason for the population explosion is the dramatic reduction in death rates. According to the theory of demographic transition, this process is caused by industrialization, which raises the average life span by increasing food production and improving public health conditions. In the early stages of industrialization, birthrates remain high and there is a population explosion. Eventually, economic changes make children more of a financial liability than an asset, and birthrates come down. Thus, this theory implies that industrialization will soon lower the birthrates in the less-developed countries, where population growth is now the highest. Critics, however, point out that this theory was based on Western societies and does not describe conditions in the less-developed countries very accurately.

Thomas Malthus was among the first to point out the dangers of unrestricted population growth. He argued that the human population naturally multiplies much faster than its food supply. So far, Malthus has been wrong because food supplies have kept up with or exceeded population growth, but many demographers feel that there is a limit to the number of people the world can support and that Malthus will eventually be proved right.

The runaway population growth has caused problems throughout the third world. Poor agricultural nations with high growth rates are exhausting their land and other natural resources. Millions of people starve to death every year, and many of the world's people are underfed. Increasing numbers of people in the less-developed countries are migrating to cities, where unemployment is high and social integration is low. There are also a growing number of refugees seeking to avoid the social and environmental disasters so common in the third world, and a growing tide of migration flows from the poor to the rich countries. Some rich nations, on the other hand, are facing the opposite problem of a declining population with a higher and higher percentage of elderly people.

There are two general ways to deal with runaway population growth: increasing the amount of food and lowering birthrates. Proposals for expanding the world's food supply include enhancing the productivity of agriculture, increasing the sea's food production, and wasting less of the food that we do produce. In order to lower birthrates, the governments of many countries have established family planning programs. Such programs encourage the use of birth control, on the assumption that the birthrate will decline if couples have only the number of children that they desire. Some nations have also introduced incentive programs that give rewards to families with few children and penalize those with many. Another approach is to provide more economic and social opportunities for women so that they will have a real alternative to the role of mother and child rearer.

Sociologists of all theoretical persuasions agree that the population explosion has become a real global crisis. Functionalists note that as death rates have dropped, attitudes encouraging fertility have become dysfunctional. Conflict theorists point out that the food shortage is caused by a distribution system that gives too much food to the wealthy and too little to the poor. Feminists see elimination of restrictions placed on the lives of women as the key to solving the population problem. Interactionists have shown that high birthrates are created by the attitudes and beliefs found in traditional cultures.

QUESTIONS FOR CRITICAL THINKING

Many scientists feel that the population explosion is the most serious problem facing the human race today, but others feel that those who sound such warnings are just alarmists and that we will have no trouble feeding and housing our growing population. After reading this chapter, which side do you think is right? Current projections are that the world's population will increase by more than a third by 2050 from 6.5 billion people to more than 9 billion. How different would a world with 9 billion people be from the one we know today?

KEY TERMS

birthrate	genetically modified	land reform
death rate	organisms (GMOs)	migration
demographic transition	green revolution	population explosion
demography	growth rate	replacement rate
family planning	intermediate technology	total fertility rate

INTERNET EXERCISE

Because of the concern over the "population explosion" around the world, many governmental, international, and nongovernmental agencies have been created to track and deal with the problems of rapid population growth. To begin your exploration of these Websites, go to the *Companion Website* at www.pearsonhighered.com/coleman. Enter Chapter 15 and choose the Web destination module from the navigation bar.

The World Resources Institute (WRI) is an environmental think tank. Their Website posts research and ideas to find practical ways to protect the Earth and the environment around the world. Find an article, "World Population Growth—Past, Present and Future," at http://earthtrends.wri.org/updates/node/61/. Describe what are considered to be trends in world population growth. Is there a difference in population growth between developing and developed nations?

NOTES

1. Mary Jo McConahay, "Seven Children . . . Four Alive," *Sierra*, November–December 1993, pp. 62–73.

2. Population Reference Bureau, *World Population Data Sheet, 2000* (Washington, DC: Author, 2000).

3. Population Reference Bureau, *World Population Data Sheet, 2006* (Washington, DC: Author, 2006).

4. Population Reference Bureau, *World Population Data Sheet, 1994* (Washington, DC: Author, 1994) John Balzar, "Doomsayers of Overpopulation Sound a New Jeremiad," *Los Angeles Times*, June 7, 1994, p. A5.

5. Calculated from Population Reference Bureau, *World Population Data Sheet, 2006* (Washington, DC: Author, 2006).

6. Population Reference Bureau, *World Population Data Sheet, 2006.*

7. Ibid.

8. U.S. Bureau of the Census, *Statistical Abstract of the United States, 2006*, pp. 8, 9, 68.

9. Population Reference Bureau, *World Population Data Sheet, 2006*.

10. Ibid.; John R. Weeks, *Population: An Introduction to Concepts and Issues*, 3rd ed. (Belmont, CA: Wadsworth, 1986), p. 55.

11. Population Reference Bureau, *World Population Data Sheet, 2003*.

12. Charles F. Westoff, "Populations of the Developed Countries," *Scientific American* 231 (1974): 114.

13. For an analysis of the theory of demographic transition, see Weeks, *Population*, pp. 39–48.

14. Thomas Robert Malthus, *Essay on the Principle of Population* (New York: Oxford University Press, 1993).

15. Calculated from John Bennett, *The Hunger Machine: The Politics of Food* (Cambridge, MA: Polity Press, 1987), p. 32; U.S. Bureau of the Census, *Statistical Abstract of the United States, 1993* (Washington, DC: U.S. Government Printing Office, 1993), p. 867; also see Paul Kennedy, *Preparing for the Twenty-first Century* (New York: Vintage, 1993), pp. 65–70.

16. U.S. Bureau of the Census, *Statistical Abstract of the United States, 1999* (Washington, DC: U.S. Government Printing Office, 1999), p. 857.

17. United Nations Development Programme, *Human Development Report, 1997* (New York: Oxford University Press, 1997), p. 179.

18. United Nations Food and Agricultural Organization, *The State of Food Security in the World, 2003* (Rome: Author, 2004), p. 6.

19. See G. Tyler Miller, *Living in the Environment*, 5th ed. (Belmont, CA: Wadsworth, 1988), pp. 242–245.

20. See Robert N. Ross, "The Hidden Malice of Malnutrition," in Robert M. Jackson, ed., *Global Issues 88/89* (Guilford, CT: Dushkin, 1989), pp. 98–101.

21. Population Reference Bureau, *World Population Data Sheet, 2006*.

22. See Harold Kerbo and Hermann Strasser, *Modern Germany* (New York: McGraw-Hill, 2000), Chapter 8.

23. Harold Kerbo and John McKinstry, *Modern Japan* (New York: McGraw-Hill, 1998), Chapters 7 and 12.

24. U.S. Bureau of the Census, *Statistical Abstract of the United States, 2006*, p. 867.

25. United Nations Development Programme, *Human Development Report, 1997*, p. 70; Miller, *Living in the Environment*, pp. 247–249; Bennett, *The Hunger Machine*, pp. 23–27.

26. See Kennedy, *Preparing for the Twenty-first Century*, pp. 65–81.

27. E. F. Schumacher, *Small Is Beautiful: Economics as If People Mattered* (New York: HarperCollins, 1974), pp. 171–190.

28. Weeks, *Population*, pp. 381–383.

29. Miller, *Living in the Environment*, pp. 253–254.

30. World Resources Institute (www.wri.org); Marla Cone, "Fisheries Set to Collapse, Study Warns," *Los Angeles Times*, November 3, 2006, pp. A1, A11.

31. Weeks, *Population*, pp. 385–386.

32. Bennett, *The Hunger Machine*, p. 37.

33. Carol Williams, "The Unwanted Children: Casualties Left by a Tyrant," *Los Angeles Times*, December 10, 1990, pp. A1, A16–A17.

34. Bennett, *The Hunger Machine*, p. 22.

35. World Bank, *Engendering Development* (New York: Oxford University Press, 2001); World Bank, *World Development Report, 2000* (New York: Oxford University Press, 2000).

36. Ibid., p. 423.

37. Population Reference Bureau, *World Population Data Sheet, 2006*.

38. BBC News, April 5, 2004 (www.bbcnews.org); Nicholas Kristof and Sheryl WuDunn, *Thunder From the East: Portrait of a Rising Asia* (New York: Knopf, 2000), p. 276.

39. Daniel Chirot, *Social Change in the Modern Era* (San Diego: Harcourt Brace Jovanovich, 1986), p. 177.

40. Bennett, *The Hunger Machine*, p. 34.

352

POPULATION PROBLEMS

TRACK 19
TRACK 18

POPULATION PROBLEMS

The world's

population will hit 7 billion early in 2012 and top 9 billion in 2050, with the vast majority of the increase coming in the developing countries of Asia and Africa, according to a UN estimate released Wednesday.

Hania Zlotnik, director of the UN Population Division, said that "there have been no big changes" from the previous estimate in 2006.

"We are still projecting that by 2050, the population of the world will be around 9.1 billion," she said at a news conference. "The projections are based on the assumption that fertility, that is now around 2.56 children per woman, is going to decline to about 2.02 children per woman in the world."

Zlotnik said if fertility remained about where it is now, then world population would reach 10.5 billion by 2050. If fertility fell even more than expected, to about 1.5, then the population would only increase to 8 billion by midcentury, she said.

Population growth will remain concentrated in the most populous countries through 2050. Nine nations are expected to account for half the projected increase: India, Pakistan, Nigeria, Ethiopia, the United States, Congo, Tanzania, China, and Bangladesh, the report said.

In sharp contrast, the populations of 45 countries or regions are expected to decline at least 10 percent over the same period, including Japan, Italy, and many other countries that were once part of the Soviet Union, the UN said.

According to the study, the largest number of migrants will head to the United States—an estimated 1.1 million every year between 2010 and 2050.

The immigrants and the U.S. birth rate will help boost the U.S. population from an estimated 314.7 million in mid-2009 to 403.9 million in 2050, according to Gerhard Heilig, chief of the UN's Population Estimates and Projections Section.[1]

---Even in a developed nation like the United States, the population continues to increase.

In my town, new housing is constantly being built to accommodate the growing number of people. Of course, in a country such as ours, a growing population generally means more economic growth and very few real problems related to providing residents with adequate shelter, water, and sanitation. This is not always true in other parts of the world.

What will it be like to live in a world with 9 billion people, as projected in the opening article?

How will developing nations in Asia and Africa handle the predicted population surges, and how will this change our lives in the developed world as well? These are just a few of the questions that researchers explore when considering the impact of population growth on a world with limited resources and a fragile environment.

get the topic: IS POPULATION GROWTH A PROBLEM?

DEMOGRAPHY is the study of the size and composition of a population.

POPULATION VARIABLES are the changeable characteristics of a given population.

FERTILITY is the number of births that occur in a population.

CRUDE BIRTH RATE is the number of births for every 1,000 people each year.

AGE-SPECIFIC BIRTH RATE is the number of births for every 1,000 women in a specific age group.

TOTAL FERTILITY RATE (TFR) is the average number of births expected from any woman in a population.

ZERO POPULATION GROWTH is a TFR of two, meaning that each woman has two children to replace the mother and father.

LIFE EXPECTANCY is the average number of years of life for a person of any given age.

LIFE SPAN is the maximum length of time that it is possible for a human being to live.

The world's population is constantly changing, as you can see from the graph on the next page. Note that the growth of the population is rather slow for a long period of time and then rapidly increases around the time of the industrial revolution. As nations develop, life expectancies increase, largely due to advances is public health and access to other goods we take for granted, such as clean water and sewage disposal. Notice that it took more than 11,000 years for the world's population to grow to 1 billion; however, it more than doubled again 100 years later, and again from 1940 to 1982. It's projected that the number of people will double again by 2042, bringing the world's total population to over 9 billion people.[3] Demographers refer to this span as doubling time, which we will discuss in more detail later on in the chapter.[4]

Tools for Studying Population

FERTILITY

Fertility refers to the number of births that occur in a population. It's often calculated as **crude birth rate**, which is the number of births each year per 1,000 people. There are several factors that can determine fertility rate, including health, wealth, and education, as well as access to birth control and the number of women of child-bearing age. **Age-specific birth rate** measures the number of births per every 1,000 women in a specific age group. The **total fertility rate (TFR)** is the average number of births expected from a woman in a population. **Zero population growth** refers to a TFR of two, meaning that each woman, on average, is expected to have two children to replace the mother and father. Each of these calculations allows demographers to make predictions about a population and can help the society plan ahead for the future. For example, if a community notices that crude birth rate is declining, they may decide to put off building a new elementary school.

LIFE EXPECTANCY

How long will you live? No one knows for sure, of course, but demographers can calculate how long you might expect to live. **Life expectancy** is the average number of years of life for a person of any given age. This figure should not be confused with **life span**, which is the maximum length of time it is possible for a human being to live. So, while a human being may be capable of living well over 100 years, he or she may only live for a portion of that time based on other factors. Over the last century, the life expectancy for many people around the world has increased

Population by the Numbers

In graduate school, one of my favorite classes was demography. It taught one simple truth: All societies are influenced by their populations. **Demography** is the study of the size and composition of a population, and as a wise old professor once told me, "It's all in the numbers." If a population of a country is large, the nation can face many problems, such as how to provide its people with the necessary resources. Of course, the country also faces many possible opportunities, because more people allows for more economic growth, more innovation, and greater possibilities for development.

What different characteristics might the population of Sweden have from the population of Afghanistan? To study a population, demographers use **population variables**, changeable characteristics of a given population such as size, racial composition, birth rates, and death rates.

As you may already know, the world's population is unevenly distributed. The number of people in the two most populated countries, China and India, is larger than the next 23 countries combined. The United States is the third greatest populated nation, but is home to just 4.6 percent of the world's people.[2]

dramatically, thanks, in large part, to improvements in our standard of living, such as access to clean water and better housing, and expanded availability of health care.[5] Between the 1860s and the 1990s, the human life span increased from 108 years to 116 years.[6]

At the time of birth, all people around the world can expect to live an average of 65 years. This number changes based on other factors that can affect the life expectancy rates in a given area. For example, nations such as France, Italy, and Spain have some of the longest life expectancies at 81, 80.2, and 80.5 years, respectively. On the other hand, countries such as Zimbabwe and Ethiopia have some of the shortest life expectancies, falling in the low 40s. There are 48 other countries with higher life expectancies than the United States, where the life expectancy is 78.1 years. However, when compared to the 10 largest nations on Earth, the United States is second only to Japan. The low life expectancy rate in some African countries is due to a number of factors, including lack of clean water, sewage problems, malaria, and the widespread presence of HIV/AIDS—the leading cause of death in countries such as Angola (in which individuals are only expected to live 38.2 years).[7]

MORTALITY RATES

The **mortality rate** is the number of deaths that occur in a population. Sociologists can examine mortality rates to calculate what is called the **crude death rate**, the number of deaths per 1,000 people each year. Such a number helps in comparisons of nations. A population going through a period of war, disease, or famine would experience an increased mortality rate. One statistic that researchers pay close attention to is the **infant mortality rate**, which is the number of children per 1,000 who are born alive but die before reaching the age of one year.

One of the reasons life expectancies are so low in some countries is because of their high infant mortality rates, which are also affected by

> **MORTALITY RATE** is the number of deaths that occur in a population.
> **CRUDE DEATH RATE** is the number of deaths per 1,000 people each year.
> **INFANT MORTALITY RATE** is the number of children per 1,000 who are born alive but who die before reaching the age of one year.
> **POPULATION PYRAMIDS** are tools that visually represent data about a specific population in relation to age and sex.

environment and access to health care. For example, the infant mortality rate in Angola is 180, while it is only 2.75 in Sweden. This means that 18 percent of children born in Angola die within the first year of life while only 0.275 percent of babies born in Sweden are likely to die before their first birthday. The United States' rate of 6.26 is rather high for a developed nation and falls just behind Cuba in world rankings. More than 40 countries have lower rates of infant mortality. Why might this be the case? Access to prenatal care tends to lower infant mortality rates. Countries such as Angola have weak health care systems with limited access to services. Meanwhile, nations such as Sweden offer universal coverage. The U.S. system does not assure everyone access to medical care, which may be part of the reason for our relatively high rate of infant death.[8]

POPULATION PYRAMIDS

A **population pyramid** visually represents data about a specific population in relation to age and sex. Population pyramids track changes in a population over time, and this information can help researchers assess the potential needs of a society. The population pyramids on the upcoming page demonstrate how the populations of Mexico and the United States are likely to change from 1989 to 2029. Notice that the countries do not have the

World Population Growth

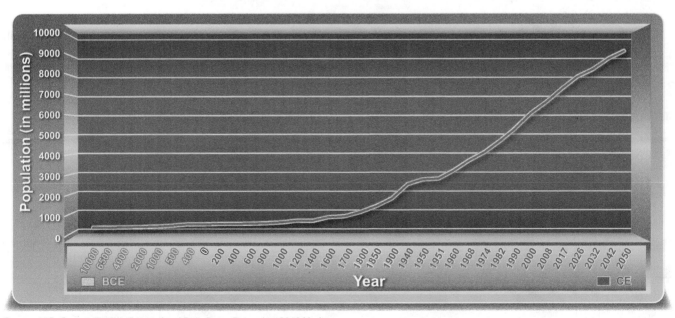

Source: U.S. Census Bureau, International Data Base, December 2010 Update.

∧
∧ The doubling time of the world's population has decreased rapidly. **How long do you predict it will be until the population doubles to 18 billion people?**

MIGRATION is the movement of people from one area to another area.

IMMIGRATION is the movement of people into a nation-state.

EMIGRATION is the movement of people out of a nation-state.

RATE OF NATURAL INCREASE (RNI) is a calculation that demographers use to determine the growth or decline of a population.

BIRTH DEARTH refers to declining birth rates.

DOUBLING TIME is the length of time in which it takes a population to double in size.

same shape. As people begin to live longer and birth rates stabilize, a "squaring" of the pyramids occur, and they begin to take on a more rectangular shape. In the United States, this squaring is already happening. In Mexico, the effect is less pronounced. Can you think of possible social problems that might result as the pyramid of the U.S. squares? Will there

be enough young people to care for and financially support the growing number of elderly citizens? Might older workers need to continue working later in their lives to maintain a reasonable standard of living? What would happen to the pyramid if migration to the United States halted? These are just some of the issues that demographers raise when discussing population predictions.

MIGRATION

Demographers know that people have always migrated. Today, as in the past, population increases and global interaction contribute to **migration**, or the movement of people from one area to another. Migration is usually discussed in terms of immigration and emigration. **Immigration** is the movement of people into a nation-state. **Emigration** is the movement of people out of a nation-state. The vast majority of U.S. citizens are either descendants of immigrants or are immigrants themselves.

Issues like infant mortality and life expectancy can play a role in peoples' decisions to emigrate from their country of birth. People from poorer areas of the world often move to more prosperous areas in hopes of improving their lives. For example, my German ancestors came to America due to lack of work in Germany, just as today some Mexican citizens immigrate to the United States for the same reason.[9]

When large numbers of a group migrate to an area, locals may react with discrimination and violence. For example, in the United States, anti-immigrant sentiment is on the rise. Hate groups are cropping up around the country with their focus on recent immigrants. Such groups often scapegoat the new immigrants as the "cause" of their suffering to justify their bigotry and violence.[10]

RATE OF NATURAL INCREASE

The **rate of natural increase (RNI)** is a calculation that demographers use to determine the growth or decline of a population. Populations with a positive RNI are growing, while populations with a negative RNI are in decline. Infant mortality and life

World Population Tops 7 Billion People

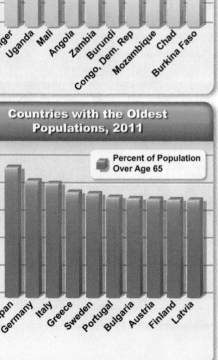

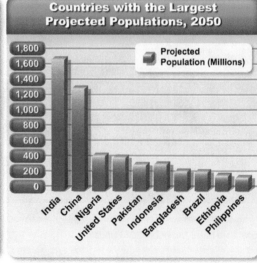

Source: Data from Population Reference Bureau, *The World at 7 Billion*, http://www.prb.org/pdf11/2011population-data-sheet_eng.pdf, Accessed October 13, 2011.

Population Pyramids

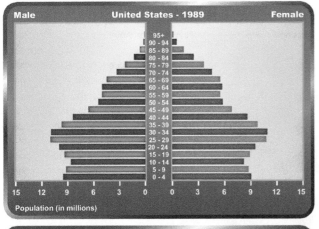

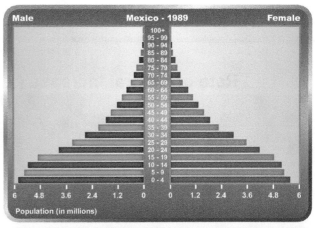

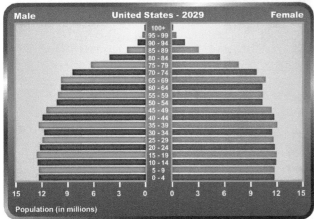

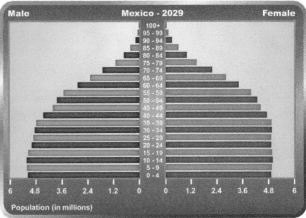

Source: U.S. Census Bureau, Population Division, 2007, www.census.gov/ipc/www/idb/index.php

World Population

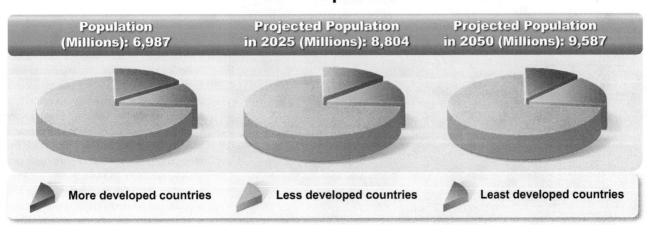

| Population (Millions): 6,987 | Projected Population in 2025 (Millions): 8,804 | Projected Population in 2050 (Millions): 9,587 |

More developed countries   Less developed countries   Least developed countries

Source: Data from Population Reference Bureau, *The World at 7 Billion*, http:// www.prb.org/pdf11/2011population-data-sheet_eng.pdf, Accessed October 13, 2011.

expectancy are only two factors that can contribute to a negative RNI. In some cases, citizens in a population are opting not to have children, or are having fewer children than before, leading to **birth dearth**, or declining birth rates. For example, in the early 1990s, the total fertility rate in Japan dropped to 1.46, below the replacement level of two children per woman.[11] The shrinking population of future workers will have a hard time supporting a growing elderly population. Government policies hope to boost birth rates and temper this demographic imbalance.[12]

DOUBLING TIME

As you will recall, **doubling time** is the length of time in which it takes a population to double in size. The doubling time of a population can have a significant and lasting impact on its future. A shorter doubling time means that there will be less time to sufficiently increase available resources. If, for example, a country's doubling time is 50 years, then that country must be able to double its resources in that 50-year period in order to sustain itself. Otherwise, the growing population will put a strain on resources.

A simple way to calculate doubling time is by using the rule of 70. The **rule of 70** estimates doubling time by dividing 70 by the annual RNI for a population, resulting in an approximate number of years in which that population will double. Looking at the table, you can see that the doubling time for the population of South America is 46.6 years (70/1.5), while the doubling time for the population of Oceania is 70 years (70/1). Because the RNI can vary from year to year, it is important to be aware that most populations do not grow exactly as predicted, and in the past, doubling time estimates have rarely been completely accurate.[13] Even so, demographers can use doubling time calculations to show possible population growth trends and to compare populations. Looking back at the table, notice that in many regions of the world the populations are projected to double within your lifetime. What impact will this have on your life? What social issues will this create for both the young and the old?

Rate of Natural Increase (%)

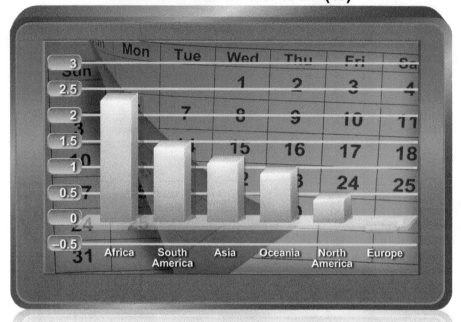

Doubling Time (years)

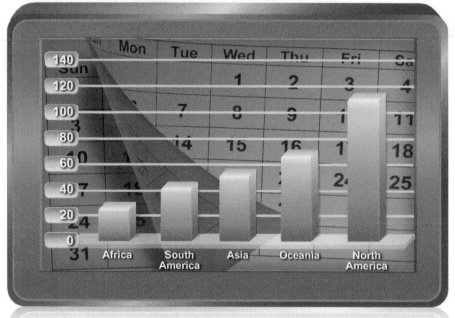

Source: Data from *World Population Data Sheet*, Population Reference Bureau, 2007, http://www.prb.org/pdf07/07WPDS_Eng.pdf

∧
∧ The population of Africa will double long before that
∧ of any other continent. What causes such **discrepancies in rates of natural increase?**

POPULATION PROJECTIONS

Fertility rates, life expectancies, mortality rates, population pyramids, migration rates, and rates of natural increase are all taken into consideration when making population projections. Of course, such projections may not be able to predict factors such as war, disease, or changes in birth rates, so they can be incorrect. However, this does not mean that population projections have no value at all. Scientific estimates are important tools that allow businesses and policy makers to plan for the future. In my hometown, for example, projections suggest that in the next 20 years our population will grow by around 14 percent. Recently, the city council began to discuss how to plan for clean water and sewage for this larger population. Even if the projection is not exactly accurate, and the population grows by 13 percent, the services will still be available. Having advance insight into the potential needs of a population and the challenges that they face helps societies prepare for or even prevent such problems. Population projections can determine potential resource requirements, such as schools, homes, and jobs for growing populations, as well as adequate health care facilities for populations with longer life expectancies.

Economic Issues of Population Growth and Decline

The growth rate of a population can have an impact on its economy. Often, countries with the weakest economies experience the

China and the One-Child Policy

In the future, do you plan on having a large family? You can do this in the United States, but that's not an option for everyone around the world. Can you imagine being rewarded for having one child, but being penalized for having more? That's the way China's "one-child" policy works. Unlike the United States, where couples are given incentives to have children by way of tax breaks, the Chinese approach offers couples incentives to have only one child. After having their first child, Chinese citizens can be penalized if they have any more.

In 1979, the Chinese government implemented the one-child policy in an effort to address a social problem—that of a rapidly growing population. The government hoped to prevent future problems by eliminating the strain on resources and ensuring that opportunities were available for all of its citizens. If the size of the Chinese population was not kept in check and people were permitted to have families of any size, the government foresaw the potential for starvation, uneven distribution of jobs and resources, and conflict resulting from these factors. Aside from limitations placed on the number of children that couples can have, the Chinese government also promotes the use of birth control and encourages its citizens to marry later in life, thereby reducing the amount of time that couples will have to reproduce.[14]

There are rewards for following the rules. In China, after having their first child, couples vow not to have any more children. If they keep that vow, they may receive higher pay, better health options, and more educational possibilities for their child, and the expecting mother receives an extended maternity leave. On the other hand, if they violate their pledge, they can be penalized by having their earnings taxed. There are exceptions to the one-child rule. The rule is most strictly enforced on people who live in highly populated, urbanized areas. People who live in less densely populated rural areas, however, are permitted to have two children without being penalized.[15]

China's one-child policy is not without its critics, who have accused the country of state-mandated sterilizations and abortions.[16] In Chinese society, males retain more power than females and are held in higher regard by parents for their ability to move upward in society in ways that females cannot. A side effect of the one-child rule is that when families are forced to have only one child, they often opt for male children. Women have been known to abort or abandon children once it is known that the child is female or disabled.[17] This abundance of males in the population can lead to future difficulties with the nation's fertility rate, causing an imbalance in the availability of single women and single men. Having so many males in the Chinese population is also seen by some as increasing the likelihood of internal strife, war, and civic unrest as masses of young, single men are shown to exhibit more aggression and may be inclined to pursue military careers.[18]

<<< The **Chinese** government instated the **"one-child" policy** as a means of **population control.**

greatest population growth. Countries in this situation are in a double bind because they can't support the existing population and will have even greater difficulty in trying to support a larger population.

The news isn't all bad, though. Economist Julian Simon found that population growth can improve a country's economy over a span of more than 100 years. When compared to countries with stable population growth, the economies of countries with growing populations saw greater improvement. His explanation was that people living in growing populations need to find jobs to survive, and those jobs slowly help improve the economy over time.[19] In developed countries, population growth leads to greater specialization of labor, increased

RULE OF 70 estimates doubling time by dividing 70 by the annual rate of natural increase for a population.

MALTHUSIAN THEOREM states that populations grow at a geometric rate, while food grows at an arithmetic rate.

development of knowledge, and the promotion of innovation, resulting in the generation of income and improved quality of life for many. The same is not true of developing countries, where growing populations lead to reductions in income and put a greater strain on public resources.[20]

think social problems: HOW DO WE MEASURE POPULATION?

Malthusian Theory

Thomas Malthus was an English clergyman known for making one of the earliest population projections. In 1798, he published *An Essay on the Principle of Population* that introduced his observations on population. Now known as the **Malthusian theorem**, he stated that populations grow at a geometric rate (2, 4, 8, 16 . . .), while food grows at an arith-

metic rate (1, 2, 3, 4 . . .). Even with advanced technology that increases food production, there will come a time when the population cannot be sustained by the food supply. At that point, food shortages are likely to lead to famine, war, and the spread of disease. However, any famine, war, or disease that occurs before that point in history is a positive check on population, because it pushes back the day when the number of people will outgrow the amount of food. Keep in mind that during Malthus's

> **DEMOGRAPHIC TRANSITION THEORY** states that people control their fertility as societies change from being agrarian to industrial.

time, measures such as birth control were not widely available. Today, Malthus's thoughts on population remain highly influential, and many of the environmental arguments are built on the idea that the world has finite resources and populations will eventually overwhelm those resources. If Malthus could see the world today, would he argue that we are close? Some suggest that current famines are due less to shortages of food and more to corrupt governments and poor distribution systems. What do you think?

Demographic Transition Theory

Demographic transition theorists, for example, disagree with Malthus' conclusions. **Demographic transition theory** states that people control their fertility as societies change from being agrarian to industrial, and that this occurs in four basic stages. These findings are based on historical data on population growth trends in Northern Europe, leading critics to point out that this model may not apply to non-European countries.[21]

In the first stage, a society is not industrialized and experiences high birth and death rates. The life expectancy of the population is low, and infant mortality is high. It's beneficial for citizens to have many children because it increases the odds that some will grow into adulthood and be able to assist with labor. The population grows slowly during this stage due to similar rates of birth and death.

In the second stage, a society enters the initial phase of industrialization. New technologies decrease the need for physical labor, and people relocate to urban areas seeking jobs in factories. Along with industrialization comes an increased food supply, improved health care, and a higher standard of living. Birth rates remain high, while infant mortality declines.[22] Life expectancy also increases, leading to a decline in the death rate; because of this, populations see the greatest rates of growth during this period.

In the third stage, as a society establishes its industrialized status, birth rates decline. Death rates also decline and stabilize due to longer life expectancies. Improvements in economic and social conditions affect personal reproductive choices, and people begin to opt for smaller families. Note that the population is still growing at this stage, just at a slower rate.[23]

In the fourth stage, a society becomes postindustrial and experiences either a stable or declining population size. At this point, both birth and death rates are relatively low.

Malthus Curve

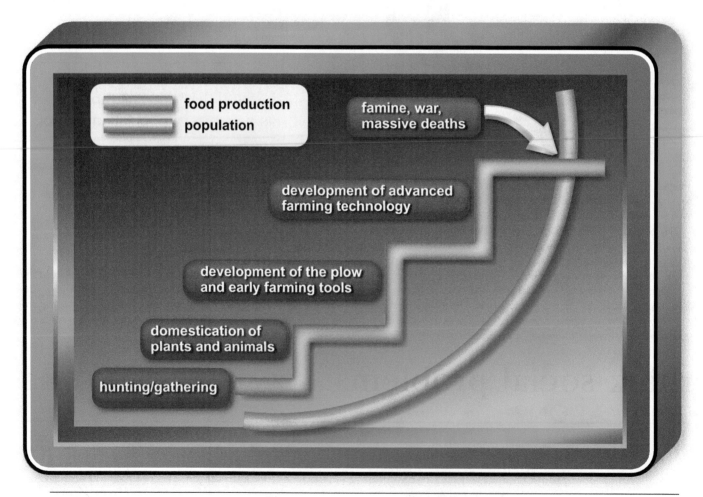

∧
∧ Thomas Malthus argued that food is produced at an arithmetic rate, while populations
∧ grow at a geometric rate. **How close do you think we are from expending all of our resources?**

Demographic Transition Model

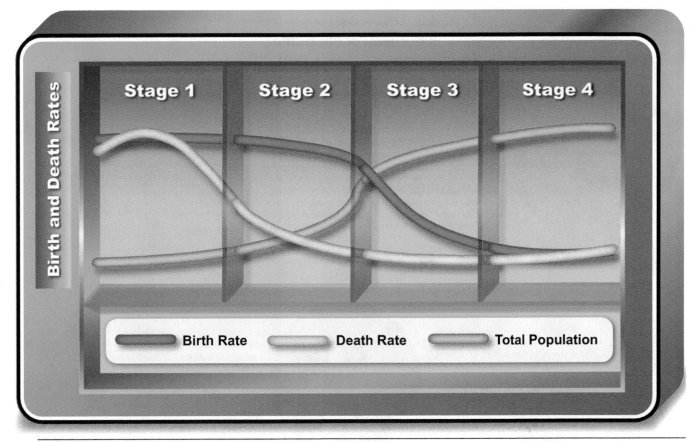

Stage 1 Stage 2 Stage 3 Stage 4

Birth and Death Rates

Birth Rate   Death Rate   Total Population

^^^ According to the demographic transition model, population growth is constantly in flux as a society transitions to an industrialized status. **Where is the United States in this model?**

discover solutions to social problems:
HOW DO DEMOGRAPHERS THINK ABOUT THE ISSUE OF POPULATION?

Population Control

Populations grow as a result of both birth rates and death rates. Because managing the death rate is not an acceptable solution, population control programs must focus on the birth rate. As mentioned before, countries like China focus their policies on how many children a couple can have; conversely, the United States does not have a population control policy and rewards large families with more tax breaks. In a way, small American families subsidize large American families. In other countries around the world, the opposite is true.

Although birth control options such as contraceptives and abortion are available in the United States, these decisions are left to individuals and are provided by private sources. In other parts of the world, this is not the case. For example, Mexico provides publicly funded abortions that are free to all citizens.[24] Likewise, in Colombia, contraception is available to adolescents in an effort to prevent unwanted pregnancies.[25]

From a global perspective, the world's population is still growing, but the rate at which the population is growing has declined.[26] In most parts of the world now, population control efforts tend to focus on educating women on their reproductive rights and making contraceptives widely available.[27]

>>> While the rate of population growth has declined, **the world's population** is still growing and **is projected to reach 9 billion by 2042.**[28]

WRAP YOUR MIND AROUND THE THEORY

Overuse of resources can lead to disaster. **Is our way of life putting a strain on the environment?**

FUNCTIONALISM

Functionalists focus on the relationships between different social structures. What role does a growing population play in society? From a functionalist perspective, having children ensures that a population will be able to carry on. Population growth can lead to economic progress, but it can also lead to problems when a society overtaxes its resources. The ancient inhabitants of Easter Island died off due to deforestation and over-use of resources that stemmed from population growth; we must take precautions to avoid these same issues today.[29]

HOW DOES POPULATION GROWTH AFFECT SOCIETY?

CONFLICT THEORY

A growing population increases competition over resources such as food, water, fuel, and space. Even with the development of new technologies that make necessary resources available to large groups of individuals, a constantly rising number of people will eventually overwhelm our ability to produce and distribute those necessities. Who will "win" this competition? Conflict theorists suggest that the future shortage will divide the population into groups: those with access to resources and those with little or no access to them. Those with access will increase their level of power and influence over society, while those without will have a diminished status. This inequality will lead to conflict not only over resources, but power, influence, and social standing as well. Social problems of this nature have occurred throughout history; a growing population increases the likelihood of similar conflicts occurring in the near future.

SYMBOLIC INTERACTIONISM

Symbolic interactionists examine how society itself affects the growth of the population. By examining the culture of a society, symbolic interactionists hope to gain a better understanding of the causes of population growth. A society's overall feelings about children can have an impact on the size of the population, as can changes in male and female roles. Symbolic interactionists study how attitudes regarding marriage, use of birth control, increased education of women, and other shifts in culture can alter the development of a population. Countries in which people delay marriage until they've reached a certain point in their career or education, for example, might see a decline in the growth rate of their population. An increase in the use of birth control could result in similar trends.

Limited resources can lead to conflict. Can our resources support the entire population?

Some men and women postpone marriage until they've finished school. What effects can this have on population growth?

Rising Population in Niger

Countries throughout the developing world have made efforts to control their populations in order to avoid future problems. Nowhere is this more relevant than in Niger. This country in West Africa is one of the poorest in the world, ranking 176 out of 178 countries in development. Yet it has the fastest population growth and the highest TFR on the planet. Efforts by the government to give away free contraception have had limited effects.

Approximately 15 percent of women in this country use some modern method of fertility control, yet Niger is one of the youngest countries on Earth. Coupled with this population problem is the environmental reality that only 12 percent of its land receives enough rainfall to produce crops. Current food production is insufficient for the needs of this population, and expected population problems are likely to make matters worse.[30] How can a country like this function? What future problems do you see on the horizon for these people? How might government instability, war, and migration be affected by this impending population problem?

Pro & Con

Population Control

To address rapid population growth, some countries have enacted policies and programs to encourage population control. Are these programs ultimately effective or destructive?

Pro

- A controlled population allows for increased opportunities for success. An overpopulated area will have a limited availability of jobs and limited opportunities for education.
- A controlled population benefits women in developing nations who will have increased access to these resources and a greater chance for upward mobility.
- Population control is important for maintaining peace. Conflicts over limited resources are more likely to occur as a result of overpopulation.
- Overpopulation can strain the environment beyond its ability to support itself. If too many of the world's resources are used before they can be replaced, the world's population will suffer as a result.

Con

- Overpopulation is a social problem that will take care of itself, as the entire world continues to go through the demographic transition.
- The state has no inherent right to influence a couple's decision to reproduce or to predetermine the size of their family. Trying to control personal decisions that citizens make violates a person's right to think and decide for himself or herself.
- Such policies encourage abortions and infanticide as well as the abandonment of children. In China, for example, people tend to favor male children, which can increase these social problems.
- Claims of the devastating impact of population growth have been greatly exaggerated, and there is no tangible evidence to support such claims. There is no real way to accurately determine whether societal problems occur as a result of population growth.

Population Problems

From Classroom to Community } Clean Water

Christine was accepted into the Peace Corps after her senior year of college. Armed with a BA in education, she assumed that she'd be assigned to teach undereducated children. Instead, she found herself in the small town of Mafi-Dove, Ghana, as a member of a new clean water initiative.

"At first I was disappointed. Working with water didn't seem nearly as exciting as teaching, or even constructing houses. However, after a few days there, I began to see how much of a problem there really was. Since there weren't enough latrines for everyone in the village, many people went near the river. When it rained, waste would be carried into the river, contaminating it. People in Mafi-Dove routinely suffered from guinea worms and other parasites that were found in the water, and seeing huge boils on the children made me want to cry."

Christine learned that the other Peace Corps members had spent the last year digging shallow wells, but the holes weren't deep enough to reach a clean source of water, or to sustain such a rapidly growing population. "During my second week there, a construction crew was called in by our leader. Using a huge drill, they dug a borehole. It was over a hundred feet deep and, when tested, was found to provide an almost endless supply of sanitary water."

Christine spent the following months overseeing more drilling projects, testing water sources, and educating the residents on sanitary waste practices. "By the time my two years were over, three new boreholes had been dug in the village, and most of the citizens were either getting their water from those pipes or boiling river water before using it. I joined the Peace Corps because I wanted to teach and make a difference—and in a way, I think I did."

IS POPULATION GROWTH A PROBLEM?

yes, if measures are not taken to properly compensate for the strain that will be placed on natural resources, public facilities, and the environment

HOW DO WE MEASURE POPULATION?

through the Malthusian theorem, which states that the population grows at a faster rate than the food supply, and the demographic transition theory, which states that people control their fertility as populations make the transition from agrarian to industrial

HOW DO DEMOGRAPHERS THINK ABOUT THE ISSUE OF POPULATION?

population control programs are the best methods of preventing destructive population growth

get the topic: IS POPULATION GROWTH A PROBLEM?

Population by the Numbers
Tools for Studying Population

Economic Issues of Population Growth and Decline
Malthusian Theory

Demographic Transition Theory
Population Control

Theory

FUNCTIONALISM

- a growing population is necessary for the continuation of society and leads to increased opportunities
- a population that grows too large can lead to a scarcity of resources and inhibit the planet's ability to support a population of any size
- it is important for people to know the sustainable limits of the environment that supports them

CONFLICT THEORY

- even the development of new technologies will not be able to support a constantly growing population forever, and the result will be an inevitable shortage of resources
- a shortage of resources will lead to two groups of people: those with access to resources who will grow in power and influence as a result, and those without, who will lose power and influence in society

- these divisions will lead to conflict over resources, power, and influence in society

SYMBOLIC INTERACTIONISM

- it is important to look at the role society plays in a population, since studying a culture can lead to a better understanding of population growth
- factors such as how a society views children can have an impact on the growth rate of a population
- major shifts in the attitudes and behaviors of a society, like changes in male and female roles, opinions about marriage, the use of birth control, and the education of women can have a lasting impact on how quickly a population grows

Key Terms

demography is the study of the size and composition of a population.

population variables are the changeable characteristics of a given population.

fertility is the number of births that occur in a population.

crude birth rate is the number of births for every 1,000 people each year.

age-specific birth rate is the number of births for every 1,000 women in a specific age group.

total fertility rate (TFR) is the average number of births expected from any woman in a population.

zero population growth is a TFR of two, meaning that each woman has two children to replace the mother and father.

life expectancy is the average number of years of life for a person of any given age.

life span is the maximum length of time that it is possible for a human being to live.

mortality rate is the number of deaths that occur in a population.

crude death rate is the number of deaths per 1,000 people each year.

infant mortality rate is the number of children per 1,000 who are born alive but who die before reaching the age of one year.

population pyramids are tools that visually represent data about a specific population in relation to age and sex.

migration is the movement of people from one area to another area.

immigration is the movement of people into a nation-state.

emigration is the movement of people out of a nation-state.

rate of natural increase (RNI) is a calculation that demographers use to determine the growth or decline of a population.

birth dearth refers to declining birth rates.

doubling time is the length of time in which it takes a population to double in size.

rule of 70 estimates doubling time by dividing 70 by the annual rate of natural increase for a population.

Malthusian theorem states that populations grow at a geometric rate, while food grows at an arithmetic rate.

demographic transition theory states that people control their fertility as societies change from being agrarian to industrial.

Sample Test Questions

These multiple-choice questions are similar to those found in the test bank that accompanies this text.

1. According to Malthus,

   a. populations grow at arithmetic rates.

   b. doubling time is calculated by the rule of 70.

   c. population control is primarily a method of maintaining peace.

   d. famine, war, and disease can be beneficial to a population.

2. Getting married and having children later in life is likely to

   a. increase the size of the population.

   b. decrease the size of the population.

   c. have no effect on the size of the population.

   d. only be an effective means of population control in first-world countries.

3. The average age to which a member of a population can expect to live is called

   a. life expectancy.

   b. life span.

   c. life term.

   d. life trajectory.

4. Doubling time is

   a. a technique used to determine the original size of a population.

   b. a calculation of the number of people born between two dates in time.

   c. the length of time it takes for a population to increase twofold.

   d. a comparison of the length of time taken by two separate societies to become industrialized.

5. One of the criticisms of China's one-child policy is that it favors women over men and may lead to a predominantly female population in the future.

   a. True

   b. False

ESSAY

1. Do you think that government should have any involvement in controlling population size? Why or why not?

2. Which model best describes global population growth: the Malthus Curve or the Demographic Transition Model (or neither)? Explain your answer.

3. Do you think that it would be a good idea for the United States to implement population control policies?

4. Which resources have you seen diminish as a result of population growth? How has it affected you?

5. With careful planning, can a population continue to grow for an unlimited amount of time? Explain your conclusion using one or more of the sociological theories.

WHERE TO START YOUR RESEARCH PAPER

For information and statistics on the world's population, go to
http://www.census.gov/ipc/www/idb

For information on China's one-child policy, see
http://www.ncbi.nlm.nih.gov/pmc/articles/PMC1116810

To see a presentation about the effects of overpopulation, go to
http://www.nationalgeographic.com/eye/overpopulation/overpopulation.html

To read about possible solutions to overpopulation, go to
http://www.overpopulation.org/solutions.html

To see a map of the world with countries sized by population, visit
http://www.worldmapper.org/countrycartograms

To view a running population clock, check out
http://www.worldometers.info/population/

ANSWERS: 1. d; 2. b; 3. a; 4. c; 5. b

Remember to check www.thethinkspot.com **for additional information, downloadable flashcards, and other helpful resources.**

End Notes

1. Edith M. Lederer, "UN Says World Population to Hit 7 Billion in 2012," *ABCNews.com*, March 11, 2009, http://abcnews.go.com/US/wireStory?id57061338.

2. Central Intelligence Agency, "Population 2007," Accessed April 20, 2007, https://www.cia.gov/cia/publications/factbook/rankorder/2119rank.html.

3. Ibid.

4. Ibid.

5. Eric Neumayer, "HIV/AIDS and Cross-National Convergence in Life Expectancy," *Population and Development Review*, 2004. 30(4): 727–742.

6. John R. Wilmoth and Jean-Marie Robine, "The World Trend in Maximum Life Span," *Population and Development Review*, 2003. 29: 239–257.

7. Central Intelligence Agency, "Life Expectancy at Birth," https://www.cia.gov/library/publications/the-world-factbook/rankorder/2102rank.html.

8. Central Intelligence Agency, "Country Comparison: Infant Mortality Rate," Accessed September 21, 2009, https://www.cia.gov/library/publications/the-world-factbook/rankorder/2091rank.html.

9. Douglas Massey, Rafael Alarecon, Jorege Durand, and Humberto Gonzalez, *Return to Aztlan: The Social Process of International Migration from Western Mexico*. Berkeley, CA: University of California Press, 1987; Alejandro Portes and Ruben G. Rumbaut, *Immigrant American: A Portrait*. Berkeley, CA: University of California Press, 1996.

10. "Blood on the Border," *Intelligence Report*, 2001. 101: http://www.splcenter.org/intel/intelreport/article.jsp?pid5418; "Anti-Immigration Groups," *Intelligence Report*, 2001. 101: http://www.splcenter.org/intel/intelreport/article.jsp?sid5175.

11. Naohiro Ogawa and Robert D. Retherford, "The Resumption of Fertility Decline in Japan: 1973–92," *Population and Development Review*, 1993. 19(4): 703–741.

12. Cynthia G. Wagner, "Promoting Parenthood in Japan," *Futurist*, 2007. 41(3): 9–13; Hayashi Yuka and Sebastian Moffett, "Cautiously, and Aging Japan Warms to Foreign Workers," *Wall Street Journal*, May 25, 2007.

13. John R. Bermingham, "Exponential Population Growth and Doubling Times: Are They Dead or Merely Quiescent?" *Population and Environment*, 2003. 24(4): 313–327.

14. James Lee and Feng Wang, *One Quarter of Humanity: Malthusian Mythology and Chinese Realities, 1700-2000*. Cambridge, MA: Harvard University Press, 1999; Rachel Murphy, "Fertility and Distorted Sex Ratios in a Rural Chinese County: Culture, State, and Policy," *Population and Development Review*, 2003. 29(4): 595–626; Nancy E. Riley, "China's Population: New Trends and Challenges," *Population Bulletin*, 2004. 59(2): 3–36.

15. Rachel Murphy, "Fertility and Distorted Sex Ratios in a Rural Chinese County: Culture, State, and Policy," *Population and Development Review*, 2003. 29(4): 595–626; Nancy E. Riley, "China's Population: New Trends and Challenges," *Population Bulletin*, 2004. 59(2): 3–36.

16. *The International Herald Tribune*, "Report: China's One-Child Policy has Prevented 400 Million Births," November 9, 2006, http://www.iht.com/articles/ap/2006/11/09/asia/AS_GEN_China_One_Child_Policy.php.

17. Ibid.

18. Therese Hesketh and Zhu Wei Xing, "Abnormal Sex Ratios in Human Populations: Causes and Consequences," *Proceedings of the National Academy of Sciences of the United States of America*, 2006. 103(36): 13271–13275, http://www.pubmedcentral.nih.gov/articlerender.fcgi?artid51569153.

19. Julian L. Simon, *Theory of Population and Economic Growth*. New York: Basil Blackwell, 1986; Julian L. Simon, "One Aggregate Empirical Studies Relating to Population Variables to Economic Development," *Population and Development Review*, 1989. 15(2): 323–332.

20. Gary S. Becker, Edward L. Glaeser, and Kevin M. Murphy, "Population and Economic Growth," *The American Economic Review*, 1999. 89(2): 145–149.

21. Kingsley Davis, "The World Demographic Transition," *The Annals of the American Academy of Political and Social Science*, 1945. 237: 1–11; Sarah F. Harbison and Warren C. Robinson, "Policy Implications of the Next World Demographic Transition," *Studies in Family Planning*, 2002. 33(1): 37–48.

22. Dudley Kirk, "Demographic Transition Theory," *Population Studies*, 1996. 50(3): 361–387.

23. Kingsley Davis, "The World Demographic Transition," *The Annals of the American Academy of Political and Social Science*, 1945. 237: 1–11.

24. United Nations Population Fund, "UNFPA Global Population Policy Update," http://www.unfpa.org/parliamentarians/news/newsletters/issue49.htm.

25. Ibid.

26. Carl Haub, "Global Aging and the Demographic Divide," *Public Policy & Aging Report*, 2007. 17(4): http://www.prb.org/Articles/2008/globalaging.aspx.

27. Matthew Conelly, "New Perspectives on the International Campaign to Limit Population Growth," *Comparative Studies in Society and History*, 2003. 45(1): 122–147.

28. Central Intelligence Agency, "Population 2007," Accessed April 20, 2009. https://www.cia.gov/cia/publications/factbook/rankorder/2119rank.html.

29. Jared Diamond, *Collapse: How Societies Choose to Fail or Succeed*. London: Penguin Books Ltd., 2005.

30. Malcolm Potts, Virginia Gidi, Martha Campbell, Sarah Zureick, "Niger: Too Little, Too Late," *International Perspectives on Sexual & Reproductive Health*, 2011. 37(2): 95–101.

Credits

Credits are listed in order of appearance.

PHOTO CREDITS

Chris Stowers/DK Images; Picsfive/Photos.com; Szefei/Shutterstock; Eddie Lawrence/Dorling Kindersley, Ltd.; **(from top):** Timothy Epp/Shutterstock; Andresr/Shutterstock; Getty Images

TEXT, TABLE, AND FIGURE CREDITS

Edith M. Lederer, "UN Says World Population to Hit 7 Billion in 2012," *ABCNews.com*, March 11, 2009, http://abcnews.go.com/US/wireStory?id57061338. © ABC News - Permissions Dept.

Can Social Problems Be Solved?

THINKING SOCIOLOGICALLY

- What shocking lessons did we learn from the 2001 terrorist attacks, the 2005 Hurricane Katrina disaster, and the passive BP oil spill in 2010 about the importance of prevention and/or preparedness in dealing with major emergencies and massive social problems?

- When do macrolevel efforts work better than midrange or microlevel attempts to deal with social problems?

- What do social movements and special-interest groups have in common in their ideologies and efforts to influence politicians and other influential people? How do they differ in their goals and methods?

From Chapter 18 of *Social Problems in a Diverse Society*, Sixth Edition. Diana Kendall. Copyright © 2013 by Pearson Education, Inc. Published by Pearson Social Science & Art. All rights reserved.

Before 9/11 the Federal Emergency Management Agency listed the three most likely catastrophic disasters facing America: a terrorist attack on New York, a major earthquake in San Francisco, and a hurricane strike in New Orleans. "The New Orleans hurricane scenario," The Houston Chronicle wrote in December 2001, "may be the deadliest of all." It described a potential catastrophe

very much like the one [that occurred in August, 2005]. So why were New Orleans and the nation so unprepared?

—Paul Krugman (2005a), a Nobel laureate economist, Princeton University professor, and columnist for the New York Times, criticizing the slow response by the federal government to Hurricane Katrina's devastation

Described by many as one of the worst natural disasters in U.S. history, Hurricane Katrina in 2005 not only left a wide path of death and destruction in its wake but also raised many serious questions about emergency preparedness and how we deal with social problems in this country. Some analysts suggest that local, state, and federal governments were not adequately prepared for unprecedented emergencies such as this devastating hurricane on the Gulf Coast (Shane and Lipton, 2005). Lack of adequate funding, resulting in part from federal income tax cuts and shifting national priorities after the 2001 terrorist attacks coupled with the continuing conflict in Afghanistan and Iraq, had left many emergency programs in a "bare-bones" condition. Funding problems and lack of long-range planning may also contribute to failures in components of the infrastructure at a time when it is most needed. *Infrastructure* **refers to a framework of support systems, such as transportation and utilities, that makes it possible to have specific land uses** (commercial, residential, and recreational, for example) **and a built environment** (buildings, houses, highways, and such) **that facilitate people's daily activities and the nation's economy.** Problems with the infrastructure create major crises, such as when transportation systems malfunction, utilities fail or are inadequate, and *infrastructural capital* (including bridges, dams, and levees) is unable to fulfill its purpose. Infrastructure failure contributed to existing problems in New Orleans when, in the aftermath of Hurricane Katrina, water pumps and several levees on Lake Pontchartrain were breached, spilling millions of gallons of polluted water onto the city's already-flooded streets, forcing residents from their homes, and leaving thousands of people homeless. Many Gulf Coast communities in Louisiana and Mississippi were also hard-hit by this hurricane, and some of these areas once again experienced extensive environmental degradation and social harm from the Deepwater Horizon (BP) oil spill in 2010. Both of these crises, which involved elements of natural and technological disasters, received extensive media coverage, but the nature and extent of news reporting in each was different (see Box 1).

Explore the Concept

Social Explorer Activity: Transportation and Social Status on mysoclab.com

The tragedy in New Orleans also reflects social problems experienced by many people but seldom seriously discussed in this country, including the high rate of poverty (28 percent) among African Americans living in that city, which was more than double the national poverty rate for all U.S. citizens (Whitesides, 2005). Many people across a variety of political spectrums, lifestyles and economic conditions, and racial-ethnic categories were extremely critical of the length of time that it took for political leaders, the military, and other governmental agencies to mobilize and help rescue victims, care for the ill and dying, and bring some order to the city.

Although Hurricane Katrina was a *natural disaster* (which includes floods, hurricanes, tornadoes, and earthquakes), from a sociological perspective it also was a *social disaster*. If Hurricane Katrina's first wave was the storm itself, the second wave of this hurricane was a *manmade disaster* because large numbers of injuries, deaths, and property damage may have resulted not from the devastating effects of the hurricane itself but rather from earlier decisions about priorities, allocation of funds, and the importance of certain kinds of preparedness. In essence, Hurricane Katrina revealed that our nation may have "penny pinched" in the wrong places, ignoring deep divisions of race, class, gender, and age

Covering Hurricane Katrina and the BP Oil Spill: Similar Location but Different Issues

More than 1,800 people lost their lives. There was more than $81 billion in damage. Eighty percent of New Orleans was submerged. Thousands of victims were forced to rooftops, and hundreds of thousand scattered to shelters around the country. . . . The hurricanes of 2005 destroyed or severely damaged approximately 350,000 homes within 90,000 square miles from southeastern Texas to the Florida Keys—an area the size of Great Britain. They were the costliest hurricanes in U.S. history.

—An American Red Cross (2010) report describing the loss of life and destruction that resulted from Hurricane Katrina

Dear Fellow Shareholder:
2010 was a profoundly painful and testing year. In April, a tragic accident on the Deepwater Horizon rig claimed the lives of 11 men and injured others. . . . The accident should never have happened. We are shocked and saddened that it did. The spill that resulted caused widespread pollution. Our response has been unprecedented in scale, and we are determined to live up to our commitments in the Gulf.

—Brief excerpts from a letter written by Carl-Henric Svanberg, chair of BP, explaining to the company's shareholders about the tragic gulf oil spill and vowing that the company would do everything necessary to clean up the disaster and ensure that similar disasters did not occur again (quoted in BP, 2010)

Images of destruction, death, and desperation such as the ones described have become an all-too-common sight on our television screens, computer monitors, smartphones, iPads and other tablets, and daily newspapers. Through photos, audio and video clips, and journalists' accounts we have witnessed numerous acts of terrorism, wars, earthquakes, tsunamis, bombings, and other horrendous occurrences. But all of the coverage has not been identical. It has depended on answers to journalists' questions of who?, what?, when?, where?, how?, and why?

Based on research about coverage of the BP oil spill and cleanup by the Pew Research Centers Project for Excellence in Journalism (www.journalism.org), let's briefly compare media framing of Katrina coverage with that of the BP oil spill. Obviously, both disasters were tragic and had a strong human interest angle: Many people were harmed, either directly or indirectly, by both tragic events. In Katrina, many journalists on the scene at least briefly lost their pro-

fessional detachment when they saw the magnitude of the disaster and the desperate plight of helpless victims. Images of death and despair that media audiences saw from afar were close and personal for reporters, some of whom temporarily left behind their dispassionate, journalistic demeanor and began to tell the story with a tone of advocacy, making demands on political leaders and relief workers to explain why help for the victims was so slow in arriving.

Although the deaths of eleven workers on the BP oil rig were devastating to family, friends, and coworkers, less media attention was paid to individual workers or their families, and most of the focus was on stopping the flow of oil into the Gulf of Mexico and expert opinions about what happened and why it occurred. Reporters and television crews spent extensive amounts of time interviewing experts about how to stop the flow and minimize the problem. According to the Pew study, the oil spill was by far the dominant story in all mainstream media coverage in the 100-day period after the explosion. At first the story lines focused on the explosion and the missing workers. Then the emphasis shifted to the size of the spill and who was responsible for the disaster. Finally, the story line moved to the environmental and economic effects of the spill (Journalism.org, 2011). At that time, paid workers and volunteers cleaning up the gulf water and along the shoreline were interviewed with regularity, and dead or dying birds, fish, and other animals were key props in heartrending stories about the short-term and long-term effects of the oil spill. Fisherman and other people who make money from tourism were extensively interviewed to learn how they planned to get by without the money they usually made from fishing or tourism.

If nature was identified as the antagonist in the Katrina story, the adversary in the oil spill story was BP and its CEO, who was characterized as not having control over the situation and not doing enough about the problem. In media coverage of both the Katrina aftermath and the BP oil spill, the U.S. government came out with mixed to negative media reviews. Katrina coverage focused on the ineptitude of the Bush administration in getting help to various disaster sites, the many problems associated with FEMA and disaster preparedness, and what was perceived to be the apathy of then-President George W. Bush about this tragic occurrence. Similarly, the Obama administration initially received mixed media reviews about its role in the oil spill saga, but this perspective generally diminished, except for a few cable news channels and in the blogosphere.

Box 1 continued

Finally, the Katrina and BP stories will not be exhausted for many years to come because they provide a near-perfect story line for television, social media, and the Internet. Disaster stories start with an initial burst of event-driven coverage and are followed by postmortems, extensive follow-ups, and commentary. Then, a slower trickle of related stories comes out in the years following the tragedy. In 2011, for example, media coverage of Katrina focused on the trial and conviction on civil rights violations and obstruction charges of local police officers who were accused of killing unarmed citizens on a New Orleans bridge in the hours following the flooding of portions of the city. In 2011, media coverage also discussed how some of Katrina's low-income victims reached a legal settlement in a civil rights lawsuit over Louisiana's Road Home program, which had failed to distribute aid to persons trying to rebuild homes after they were destroyed by Hurricane Katrina. Fewer stories have focused on the many unresolved problems in New Orleans, including the lack of low-income housing, problems in rebuilding and improving public schools, and inadequate hospitals and medical services partly as a result of Katrina's devastation. In 2011, coverage of the BP oil spill looked at how the affected areas had been restored to a higher level of cleanliness, particularly the water and beaches. Stories also emphasized that fish caught in the Gulf were now safe to eat, and that life had nearly returned to normal in the area. Of course, some media critics argue that some positive reporting resulted by spin placed on the coverage by public relations firms hired by BP to ensure that its side of the cleanup story was fairly told by the media.

In sum, the media coverage of Hurricane Katrina and the BP oil spill were similar in some significant ways because both crises involved disasters beyond the imagination of most people. However, each disaster had its own unique story, and various media sources took different approaches to framing those stories. What the Pew study concluded about media coverage of the BP oil spill might be changed slightly to reflect a truth

about coverage of both Katrina and BP: "The BP oil spill in the Gulf of Mexico [and Hurricane Katrina and its aftermath] proved to be a complex, technical and long-running saga that taxed the media's resources and attention span." And, perhaps, media coverage of these two tragedies had the same effect on media audiences and bloggers as well.

Questions for Consideration

1. Throughout this text, we have looked at how the media frame stories about social problems. We have also examined media representations of race, class, gender, age, and other ascribed characteristics. Do you think that issues such as race and class may have affected media coverage of stories such as Hurricane Katrina and its aftermath? How about the BP oil spill coverage? Did it make any difference that a massive transnational corporation was seeking to control the spin on stories about this disaster? Why or why not?

2. How do you think various kinds of media will cover disasters in the future? How might social media influence people's perceptions about the causes, effects, and possible solutions to social problems?

Independent Research

Hopefully, other major natural or technological disasters have not occurred since the time this box was written, but if they have, you might wish to gather information from newspapers, electronic media, websites, and social media about the disaster and identify key recurring themes or issues that are presented in various sources. How are the issues in the data you found similar to the ones highlighted in the Katrina and/or BP oil spill media coverage? How do they differ?

If you are unable to find information on newer disasters, how about revisiting the aftermath of Katrina and/or BP oil spill at "x" number of years later (the year in which you are conducting your research) to see which, if any, of the issues discussed in this box have been resolved and which remain as ongoing problems for people and for the environment.

that we usually do not examine or seek to remedy except when faced with massive disaster such as terrorist attacks or natural disasters of great magnitude.

Following in the aftermath of Hurricane Katrina was the *technological disaster* of the Deepwater Horizon (BP) oil spill in 2010, which also extensively damaged the coastline and gulf waters in some of the same areas that Hurricane Katrina had already damaged. The Deepwater Horizon oil spill, also known

as the BP oil spill, was the largest marine oil spill in history with crude oil gushing out of a 5,000-foot pipe that connected the well at the ocean floor to the drilling platform on the surface. Although BP was eventually able to cap the well and stop the flow of oil into the Gulf of Mexico, massive damage had been done to the environment, the economy, and other areas below the water's surface. Unlike the cleanup from Katrina, which was the responsibility of the government and voluntary relief organizations such as the Red Cross, the cleanup of the Deepwater Horizon oil spill was the responsibility of one of the world's largest oil companies. Although both events constituted major social problems in the United States, outlines for their solution were different in that the resolution in the Katrina disaster focused on money, personnel, and other resources from the government. By contrast, resolution in the BP disaster focused primarily on the role of private corporations in reducing the problem with the government playing a secondary, legalistic, oversight role in which certain timetables and demands had to be met in cleaning up the disaster and its fallout, such as the harm caused to water, beaches, the fishing industry, tourism, and a myriad of other things that were damaged or killed by the disaster.

In this chapter we look at the role of the U.S. government, voluntary organizations, and corporations in preventing and/or reducing social problems. However, persistent underlying social problems, such as the growing gap between the rich and the poor and the continuing significance of racial inequality in the United States, also rise to the surface for analysis in times of national crisis. In this chapter, we look at what might be done to reduce or eliminate social problems. Thinking sociologically about the causes and effects of, and possible solutions for, problems such as natural disasters like Hurricane Katrina and technological disasters such as the BP oil spill helps focus our attention on what needs to be done to reduce social problems.

DID YOU KNOW

- Preventive measures are less costly and time-consuming than after-the-fact measures when it comes to dealing with social problems.
- Individual solutions to personal problems are generally ineffective because many problems require collective action to bring about change.
- Sociological insights on social problems are used in various fields to help people understand issues and improve social conditions around the world.

THE PROBLEM WITH TACKLING SOCIAL PROBLEMS

Solving social problems is a far more complex undertaking than simply identifying them and pinpointing their social locations. It is much easier for us to call attention to a problem than it is to carry out a solution.

Designing and implementing programs to solve social problems may take years while the needs of individuals and groups are immediate. According to some analysts, programs to bring about positive social change face "innumerable obstacles, delays, and frustrations," and require that we have "immense dedication and perseverance" (Weinberg, Rubington, and Hammersmith, 1981:6).

Ideal versus Practical Solutions

Perhaps the first obstacle that we face in trying to reduce or solve social problems is in dealing with the difference between *ideal* solutions and *practical* solutions. As the sociologists Martin S. Weinberg, Earl Rubington, and Sue Kiefer Hammersmith (1981:6) state, "There is usually considerable conflict between what the *ideal* solution would be and what a *workable* solution might be." Sometimes the ideal solution to a problem entails prohibitive costs. In regard to natural disasters, for example, there is no ideal solution (given the fact that we cannot stop most natural disasters) but we can do far better than we have in regard to advance warnings about a potential disaster, evacuation of individuals regardless of who they are or their ability to pay, immediate help for those who must remain behind, and better fortification against naturally occurring hazards to protect communities and infrastructure.

Preventive measures such as these are costly and time-consuming, which means that they typically are allocated only a small percentage of the money and resources actually needed or they are entirely swept off the table in political discussions by being labeled as "prohibitive" in cost or "impractical" in view of other seemingly more urgent budget demands. Consequently, rather than employing preventive measures to deal with social problems, we frequently rely on *after-the-fact measures* (such as trying to remedy a problem or reduce its effects after it has occurred) to deal with issues and crises. In the case of Hurricane Katrina, for example, engineers, members of the media, and many others had long asserted that money for storm protection needed to be spent to protect New Orleans from massive flooding. The Louisiana congressional delegation had also asked for money for storm protection in the past but had received only a small portion of the amount they requested.

Although the exact cause of the explosion and fire on Deepwater Horizon rig that caused the massive Gulf of Mexico oil spill may never be fully known, the subsea blowout in deep water was what Bob Dudley, group chief executive of BP, referred to as a "very, very low-probability event, by BP and the entire industry—but it happened" (BP, 2010). Whether adequate resources were put into maintaining a safe drilling operation in the gulf will be a point of debate for years to come; however, the focus of the discussion about this disaster became not what had been spent in the past, but how much money BP was going to spend on resolving the problem and making restitution to those individuals and organizations that had experienced physical and/or monetary damage as a result of this crisis. Latest figures in 2011 estimated that more than $40 billion is the pricetag for cleanup, government fines, lawsuits, legal fees, and damage claims resulting from this oil spill (gulfspilloil.com, 2011).

Spending tens of billions of dollars after a disaster such as the BP oil spill, rather than a few billion in advance to prevent a technological disaster from occurring, or, in the case of Katrina, spending money for flood protection and for improving the infrastructure, are examples of an after-the-fact approach to dealing with social problems. Unfortunately, this approach is often used in problems associated with education, crime, and health care. When leaders do not allocate necessary funds for schools and juvenile prevention programs, they later have to spend much more money on programs that deal with school dropouts, juvenile offenders, and others who are left behind (or left out) in the existing system. Similar situations occur in health care when patients do not receive preventive care that might reduce their risk for certain illnesses or disease (such as cardiovascular accidents, diabetes, and cancer) but instead receive expensive "high-tech" medical treatment after the onset of their medical condition—if they are among the fortunate ones who have money, insurance, or a social welfare program (such as Medicare or Medicaid) that partly covers the cost of their treatment.

Defining the Problem versus Fixing It

Sometimes there is no agreement about what the problem *is* and what efforts should be made to reduce or eliminate it. After all, the people and organizations involved in the problem-*defining* stage of a social problem generally are not the same people and organizations involved in the problem-*solving* stage of a social problem. Social problems are often identified and defined by political or social activists, journalists, social scientists, and religious leaders. In contrast, the problem-solving stage usually involves elected officials and/or people working in agencies and governmental bureaucracies. Moreover, sometimes a proposed solution to a problem may only give rise to a whole new set of problems. For example, the Affordable Health Care law passed in 2010 was intended to expand health insurance coverage for all Americans, which would help reduce the problem of obtaining medical care for uninsured people. However, full implementation of this law means that the current health care system may be further swamped because it is already overburdened, particularly in low-income, central cities and in rural areas where physicians and other health care professionals are in short supply. As you can see, fixing a social problem is no easy matter because it often involves new laws or other kinds of social change, which makes many people uncomfortable because they believe that things could indeed get worse rather than better when individuals and groups start to tinker with the status quo (things as they currently are).

SOCIAL CHANGE AND REDUCING SOCIAL PROBLEMS

It should be clear from the preceding discussion that the concept of social change is an important factor in any attempt to reduce social problems. *Social change is the alternation, modification, or transformation of public policy, culture, or social institutions over time.* Notice that this definition states that social change occurs "over time." Thus, social change has temporal dimensions. Some efforts to deal with social problems are *short-term* strategies, whereas others are *middle-term* remedies, and still others constitute *long-term* efforts to alleviate the root causes of a social problem. In other words, efforts to alleviate individual unemployment or reduce unemployment rates in a community have a different temporal dimension than efforts to change the political economy in such a manner that high levels of employment and greater wage equity are brought about throughout a nation or nations. Clearly, efforts to alleviate individual unemployment are a short-term solution to the problem of unemployment, while efforts to reduce unemployment in a community or to change the political economy are middle-term and long-term solutions. Sometimes discussions of social change sound idealistic or utopian because they are middle-term or long-term strategies that attempt to target the root causes of a social problem. For many social problems, however, a combination of strategies is required to reduce social problems.

MICROLEVEL ATTEMPTS TO SOLVE SOCIAL PROBLEMS

Sociologist C. Wright Mills (1959b) believed that we should apply the sociological imagination to gain a better understanding of social problems. According to Mills, the sociological imagination is the ability to see the relationship between individual experiences and the larger society. For Mills, social problems cannot be solved at the individual level alone: These problems are more than personal troubles or private problems. Consequently, solutions must be found through social institutions such as the economy, politics, and education. However, sometimes social institutions cannot deal with a problem effectively, and political and business leaders are unwilling or unable to allocate the resources that are necessary to reduce a problem. In these situations, we have no choice but to try to deal with a problem in our own way.

Seeking Individual Solutions to Personal Problems

Microlevel solutions to social problems focus on how individuals operate within small groups to try to remedy a problem that affects them, their family, or friends. Usually, when individuals have personal problems, they turn to their *primary groups*—**small, less specialized groups in which members engage in face-to-face, emotion-based interactions over an extended period of time.** Primary groups include one's family, close friends, and other peers with whom one routinely shares the more personal experiences in life.

How can participation in primary groups help us reduce personal problems? According to sociologists, members of our primary groups usually support us even when others do not. For example, some analysts believe that we have many more people who are without a domicile (technically homeless) than current statistics suggest but that, whenever possible, these people live with relatives or friends, many of whom may already live in overcrowded and sometimes substandard housing. Most people who seek individualized solutions to personal troubles believe the situation will be temporary. However, if the problem is widespread or embedded in the larger society, it might stretch out for months or years without resolution. At best, individualized efforts to reduce a problem are short-term measures that some critics refer as the "Band-Aid approach" to a problem because these efforts do not eliminate the causes of the problem.

Some microlevel approaches to reducing social problems focus on how individuals can do something about the problems they face. For example, a person who is unemployed or among the "working poor" because of low wages, seasonal employment, or other factors might be urged to get more education or training and work experience in order to find a "better" job and have the opportunity for upward mobility. Individuals who appear to have eliminated problems in their own lives through such efforts are applauded for their determination, and they are often used (sometimes unwillingly or unknowingly) as examples that others are supposed to follow.

An example of this approach is columnist John Tierney's assessment of Hurricane Katrina and his encouragement to readers to "fight floods like fires, without the feds." According to Tierney, urbanites in cities such as New York have learned to protect themselves from fire losses by purchasing insurance, and the people of New Orleans and along the Gulf Coast should do likewise:

> Here's the bargain I'd offer New Orleans: the feds will spend the billions for your new levees, but then you're on your own. You and others along the coast have to buy flood insurance the same way we all buy fire insurance—from private companies with more at stake than Washington bureaucrats. . . . If Americans had to pay premiums for living in risky areas, they'd think twice about building oceanfront villas. Voters and insurance companies would put pressure on local politicians to take care of the levees, prepare for the worst—and stop waiting for that bumbling white knight from Washington. (Tierney, 2005:A29)

Although Tierney raises an interesting point, his approach does not take into account the fact that many who experienced devastating losses in this disaster were individuals and families with the fewest material possessions and little or no hope of ever affording an oceanfront villa, much less the insurance to protect it from fire and hurricanes.

Limitations of the Microlevel Solutions Approach

Although individuals must certainly be responsible for their own behavior and must make decisions that help solve their own problems, there are serious limitations to the assumption that social problems can be solved one person at a time. When we focus on individualistic solutions to reducing social problems, we are not taking into account the fact that secondary groups and societal institutions play a significant part in creating, maintaining, and exacerbating many social problems. ***Secondary groups* are larger, more**

specialized groups in which members engage in impersonal, goal-oriented relationships for a limited period of time. Without the involvement of these large-scale organizations, which include government agencies and transnational corporations, it is virtually impossible to reduce large-scale social problems. Consider, for example, the problem of air pollution:

If I live in a city with excessive amounts of air pollution, I can decide to stay inside all the time, or, if I can afford it, I could move to a low-density suburb with lots of trees where I will not have to inhale the polluted air, but this is only an individual solution that does not solve the greater problem of air pollution in the United States and around the world. My individualistic approach also does not address the role of others (vehicle manufacturers, gasoline producers, and consumers) in the creation of air pollution. With the excessively high price of gasoline and other fuels due to factors such as wars in the Middle East, damage to oil-producing facilities, and disruptions in oil production due to disasters like the Deepwater Horizon spill, people may seek out more fuel-efficient vehicles as an economic survival strategy. At the bottom line, however, personal choices alone cannot do much to reduce most national and global problems. Given this fact, what typically happens is a political mandate to reduce the level of pollution in the environment or to establish a new standard of fuel efficiency that vehicle manufacturers must follow for cases sold in the United States. Such a measure was announced in 2011 by the Obama administration when major automakers agreed to increase fuel economy in cars and light-duty trucks by 2025 (EPA, 2010). Social problems such as environmental pollution and excessive fuel usage require larger-scale solutions such as this because, if one person decides to reduce fuel usage for a day or a year, the environment continues to be contaminated, and the air quality for future generations comes more and more into question. However, if a larger group of people banded together in a grassroots effort to deal with a social problem, the effects of their efforts might be more widespread.

MIDRANGE ATTEMPTS TO SOLVE SOCIAL PROBLEMS

Midrange solutions to social problems focus on how secondary groups and formal organizations can deal with problems or assist individuals in overcoming problems such as drug addiction or domestic violence. Some groups help people cope with their own problems, and some groups attempt to bring about community change.

Groups That Help People Cope with Their Problems

Most midrange solutions to social problems are based on two assumptions: (1) that some social problems can best be reduced by reaching one person at a time and (2) that prevention and intervention are most effective at the personal and community levels. Groups that attempt to reduce a social problem by helping individuals cope with it or by eliminating it from their own lives are commonplace in our society (see Table 1). Among the best known are Alcoholics Anonymous (AA) and Narcotics Anonymous (NA); however, a wide range of "self-help" organizations exist in most communities. Typically, self-help groups bring together individuals who have experienced the same problem and have the same goal: quitting the behavior that has caused the problem, which can be anything from abuse of alcohol, tobacco, and other drugs to overeating, gambling, or chronic worrying. Volunteers who have had similar problems (and believe that they are on the road to overcoming them) act as role models for newer members. For example, AA and NA are operated by alcoholics and/or other substance abusers who try to provide new members with the support they need to overcome alcohol addiction or drug dependency. According to some analysts, AA is a subculture with distinct rules and values that alcoholics learn through their face-to-face encounters with other AA members. Social interaction is viewed as central for individual success in the programs. Confessing one's behavioral problems to others in an organizational setting is believed to have therapeutic value to those who are seeking help. Like other midrange approaches, organizations such as AA and NA may bring changes in the individual's life; however, they do not systematically address the structural factors (such as unemployment, work-related stress, and aggressive advertising campaigns) that might contribute to substance abuse problems. For example, AA typically does not lobby for more stringent laws pertaining to drunk driving or the sale and consumption of alcoholic beverages. As a result, larger, societal intervention is necessary to reduce the problems that contribute to individual behavior.

Read the Document
Community Building: Steps Toward a Good Society on mysoclab.com

Grassroots Groups That Work for Community-Based Change

Some grassroots organizations focus on bringing about a change that may reduce or eliminate a social problem in a

TABLE 1 A Brief List of the Best-Known Self-Help Groups

Alcoholics Anonymous
www.aa.org/?Media=PlayFlash

Al-Anon and Alateen
www.al-anon.alateen.org/

Alzheimer's Support Group
www.alz.org/index.asp

Breast Cancer Support Group
www.komen.org/

Bulimia, Anorexia Self-Help
www.nationaleatingdisorders.org/

Cocaine Anonymous
www.ca.org/

Co-Dependents Anonymous
www.coda.org/

Diabetes Support Group
www.diabetes.org/

Gamblers Anonymous
www.gamblersanonymous.org/

Narcotics Anonymous
www.na.org/

National Coalition for the Homeless
www.nationalhomeless.org/

Overeaters Anonymous
www.oa.org/

Parents Without Partners
www.parentswithoutpartners.org/

People with a Lesbian, Gay, Bisexual, Transgender,
or Queer Parent
www.colage.org/

Step-Families Association of America
www.stepfamilies.info/

United Fathers of America
www.unitedfathers.org/

specific community or region. ***Grassroots groups* are organizations started by ordinary people who work in concert to change a perceived wrong in their neighborhood, city, state, or nation.** Using this approach, people learn how to empower themselves against local and state government officials, corporate executives, and media figures who determine what constitutes the news in their area:

> By their nature, grassroots groups emerge to challenge individuals, corporations, government agencies, academia, or a combination of these when people discover they share a grievance. In their search for redress, they have encountered unresponsive, negative public agencies, self-serving private businesses, or recalcitrant individuals and groups. The answer for them is to select specific issues and find like-minded others. (Adams, 1991:9)

A central concern of those who attempt to reduce a social problem through grassroots groups is the extent to which other people are apathetic about the problem. Some analysts suggest that even when people are aware of problems, they do not think that they can do anything to change them or do not know how to work with other people to alleviate them:

> The biggest problem facing Americans is not those issues that bombard us daily, from homelessness and failing schools to environmental devastation and the federal deficit. Underlying each is a deeper crisis. Some see that deeper problem in the form of obstacles that block problem solving: the tightening concentration of wealth, the influence of money in politics, discrimination, and bureaucratic rigidity, to name a few. These *are* powerful barriers. But for us the crisis is deeper still. The crisis is that *we as a people don't know how to come together to solve these problems.* We lack the capacities to address the issues or remove the obstacles that stand in the way of public deliberation. Too many Americans feel powerless. (Lappé and Du Bois, 1994:9)

According to social analysts, more community dialogue is needed on social issues, and more people need to become involved in grassroots social movements. A ***social movement* is an organized group that acts collectively to promote or resist change through collective action.** Because social movements when they begin are not institutionalized and are outside the political mainstream, they empower outsiders by offering them an opportunity to have their voices heard. For example, when residents near Love Canal, located in Niagara Falls, New York, came to believe that toxic chemicals were damaging the health of their children, they banded together to bring about change in government regulations concerning the disposal of

379

TABLE 2 Selected Organizations That Seek to Address a Social Problem

Category	Organization	Website Address
Environment	Earth First!	www.earthfirst.org/
	Sierra Club	www.sierraclub.org/
	Slow Food USA	www.slowfoodusa.org/
Driving While Drinking	Mothers Against Drunk Driving	www.madd.org/
Wages and Working Conditions	American Rights at Work	www.americanrightsatwork.org/
	Industrial Workers of the World	www.iww.org/
Neighborhoods/Poverty	National Low Income Housing Coalition	www.nlihc.org/template/index.cfm
	National Urban League	www.nul.org/
Homelessness Violence and War	National Coalition for the Homeless	http://nationalhomeless.org/
	Food Not Bombs	www.foodnotbombs.net/
	International Fellowship of Reconciliation	www.ifor.org/
	The Nonviolence Web	www.nonviolence.org/

toxic wastes. Indeed, Love Canal was the birthplace of the environmental movement against dumping toxic waste. Social movements such as Mothers Against Drunk Driving (MADD), Earth First!, People for the Ethical Treatment of Animals (PETA), and the National Federation of Parents for Drug Free Youth began as community-based grassroots efforts. Over time, many midrange organizations evolve into national organizations; however, their organization and focus often change in the process. Table 2 provides examples of activist organizations that seek to reduce specific social problems in communities.

Grassroots organizations and other local structures are crucial to national social movements because national social movements must recruit members and gain the economic resources necessary for nationwide or global social activism. Numerous sociological studies have shown that the local level constitutes a necessary microfoundation for larger-scale social movement activism (Buechler, 2000). According to social movement scholar Steve M. Buechler (2000:149),

[S]ome forms of activism not only require such microfoundations but also thematize local structures themselves as the sources of grievances, the site of resistance, or the goal of change. By consciously identifying local structures as the appropriate areas of contention, such movements comprise a distinct

subset of the larger family of movements that all rely on microfoundations but do not all thematize local structures in this way.

To understand how grassroots organizations aid national social movements, consider the problem of environmental degradation. Leaders of national environmental organizations often make use of social media,

Midrange attempts to solve social problems typically focus on how secondary groups and formal organizations deal with problems or seek to assist individuals in overcoming problems. An example is this grassroots social movement, whose members are protesting the placement of a low-level radioactive dumping site in their neighborhood.

particularly Facebook and Twitter, to get other people involved in rallies, protests, and e-mail campaigns, particularly when politicians are making decisions that environmentalists believe will have a negative effect on the environment. By working with local and regional activists and seeking to influence local and regional power structures—city councils, statewide planning commissions, and legislatures—national organizations assert the need for their existence and attempt to garner additional supporters and revenue for their efforts nationwide or around the globe. By intertwining local, regional, and national organizational structures, these groups create a powerful voice for social change regarding some issue.

Limitations of the Midlevel Solutions Approach

Although local efforts to reduce problems affecting individuals and collectivities in a specific city or region bring about many improvements, they typically lack the sustained capacity to produce the larger, systemic changes at the national or international levels that are necessary to actually reduce or eliminate the problem. For example, organizations that represent the homeless often challenge the attempts of various cities to remove homeless persons and their personal belongings from city sidewalks or public parks. Although it is important for powerless people to have organizations that advocate for their rights, efforts such as these typically do not address the larger, structural factors that cause, or at least contribute to, the problem of homelessness. Examples include lack of affordable housing, few job opportunities, and dollar-strapped social service agencies that cannot help all of the individuals who need assistance.

Many people who are involved in midrange organizations see themselves primarily as local activists. Some display a bumper sticker saying, "Think globally, act locally" (Shaw, 1999). Many activists believe that in the absence of any sustained national agenda, national problems such as child poverty, low wages, and lack of affordable housing can be reduced by community-based organizations; but some analysts now believe that local activists must demand large-scale political and economic support to bring about necessary changes.

According to Randy Shaw (1999:2–3), the director of the Tenderloin Housing Clinic in San Francisco, California, and the founder of Housing America, a national mobilization campaign to increase federal housing funds,

America's corporate and political elite has succeeded in controlling the national agenda because citizen activists and organizations are not fully participating in the struggles shaping national political life. As the constituencies central to reclaiming America's progressive ideas bypass national fights to pursue local issues, their adversaries have faced surprisingly little opposition in dismantling federal programs achieved by six decades of national grassroots struggle. Citizen activities and organizations have steadfastly maintained their local focus even as national policy making drastically cut the resources flowing to communities. From 1979 to 1997, for example, federal aid to local communities for job training, housing, mass transit, environmental protection, and economic development fell by almost one trillion real dollars.

As this statement suggests, those working in grassroots organizations might be fighting a losing battle because the loss of federal aid can only diminish their future efforts. Accordingly, in the 1990s some grassroots activists changed their motto to "think locally and act globally" (Brecher and Costello, 1998), and began to work at the macrolevel, attempting to educate national leaders and corporate executives about the part that governments and transnational corporations must play if social problems are to be reduced or solved.

MACROLEVEL ATTEMPTS TO SOLVE SOCIAL PROBLEMS

Macrolevel solutions to social problems focus on how large-scale social institutions such as the government and the media can be persuaded to become involved in remedying social problems. Sometimes individuals who view themselves as individually powerless bind together in organizations to make demands on those who make decisions at the national or global level. As one social analyst explains,

Most individuals are largely powerless in the face of economic forces beyond their control. But because millions of other people are affected in the same way, they have a chance to influence their conditions through collective action. To do so, people must grasp that the common interest is also their own personal interest. This happens whenever individuals join a movement, a union, a party, or any organization pursuing a common goal. It happens when people push for a social objective—say universal health care or human rights—which benefits them by benefiting all those similarly situated. It underlies the development of an environmental movement which seeks to preserve the environment on which all depend. (Brecher and Costello, 1998:107)

For example, when groups such as AARP (the American Association of Retired Persons) and the American Medical Association (AMA) support new health care legislation their efforts are more likely to culminate in passage of laws such as the 2010 Affordable Care Act, even though the individual interests of retired persons are more on the protection of Medicare and the individual interests of physicians who are members of the AMA may be on protecting the rights and income of physicians and guarding the viability of the doctor–patient relationship. In fact, most social analysts would place AARP and AMA in the following category—special-interest groups—that work for political change.

Working through Special-Interest Groups for Political Change

At the national level, those seeking macrolevel solutions to social problems may become members of a *special-interest group*—a political coalition composed of individuals or groups sharing a specific interest they wish to protect or advance with the help of the political system. Examples of special-interest groups include Common Cause, the League of Women Voters, and other organizations that advocate for specific issues such as the environment, gun control, educational reform, or thousands of other single- or multiple-issue concerns.

Through special-interest groups, which are sometimes called *pressure groups* or *lobbies*, people can seek to remedy social problems by exerting pressure on political leaders. These groups can be categorized on the basis of these factors:

1. *Issues.* Some groups focus on *single issues*, such as abortion, gun control, or school prayer; others focus on *multiple issues*, such as equal access to education, employment, and health care.
2. *View of the present system of wealth and power.* Some groups make *radical demands* that would involve the end of patriarchy, capitalism, governmental bureaucracy, or other existing power structures; others do not attack the legitimacy of the present system of wealth and power but insist on specific social reforms.
3. *Beliefs about elites.* Some groups want to *influence* elites or incorporate movement leaders into the elite; others want to *replace* existing elites with people whom they believe share their own interests and concerns.

Since the 1980s, an increasing number of more special-interest groups have been single-issue groups that focus on electing and supporting politicians who support their views. There might be more than one single-interest group working to reduce or eliminate a specific social problem. Usually, however, these groups do not agree on the nature and extent of the problem or on proposed solutions to the problem. For this reason, competing single-interest groups aggressively place their demands in front of elected officials and bureaucratic policy makers.

Working through National and International Social Movements to Reduce Problems

Collective behavior and national social movements are significant ways in which people seek to resolve social problems. *Collective behavior* **is voluntary, often spontaneous, activity that is engaged in by a large number of people and typically violates dominant-group norms and values.** Everything ranging from public protests and riots to flash mobs that are brought together on the spur of the moment by text messaging and social media, such as Facebook and Twitter, are examples of collective behavior. Since the civil rights movement in the 1960s, one popular form of public demonstration has been *civil disobedience*—**nonviolent action that seeks to change a policy or law by refusing to comply with it.** People often use civil disobedience in the form of sit-ins, marches, boycotts, and strikes to bring about change. When people refuse to abide by a policy or law and challenge authorities to do something about it, they are demanding social change with some sense of urgency. Recent examples include small-scale protester-on-legislator action where advocates backing specific legislation, such as demands for a universal health care system before the Affordable Care Act was passed. In 2009, advocates briefly occupied the offices of public officials, such as Senator Joe Lieberman, to make their wishes known.

Groups that engage in activities that they hope will achieve specific political goals are sometimes referred to as *protest crowds*. In 2011, protests in other nations, including Greece and Eqypt, made headlines around the world. In the United States, we have had fewer organized protests in recent years than might be expected with high rates of unemployment, a sluggish economy, and political turmoil among members of Congress in the nation's capital. However, at the time of this writing, we have to look back to the 2008 Republican National Convention to find a good example of a situation in which at least 10,000 protesters came forward to publicize an

⊙ ⌐Watch on mysoclab.com
Grievances, Anger, and Hope on mysoclab.com

issue. At that time, more than 10,000 protesters marched in St. Paul, Minnesota, to show their opposition to the Iraqi War and call for the return of American troops to the United States. A second group of about 2,000 people marched on behalf of the homeless and the poor and to call attention to injustices they believed were perpetuated and exacerbated by government policies. Among those in the protest crowds were members of Veterans for Peace, Iraq Veterans Against the War, Military Families Speak Out, the Teamsters, Code Pink, the American Indian Movement, and the Poor People's Economic Human Rights Campaign.

What types of national and international social movements can be used to reduce social problems? National social movements can be divided into five major categories: reform, revolutionary, religious, alternative, and resistance movements. *Reform movements* seek to improve society by changing some specific aspect of the social structure. Environmental groups and disability rights groups are examples of groups that seek to change (reform) some specific aspect of the social structure. Reform movements typically seek to bring about change by working within the existing organizational structures of society, whereas *revolutionary movements* seek to bring about a total change in society. Examples of revolutionary movements include utopian groups and radical terrorist groups that use fear tactics to intimidate and gain—at least briefly—concessions from those with whom they disagree ideologically. Some radical terrorists kill many people in their pursuit of a society that more closely conforms to their own worldview.

Religious movements (also referred to as expressive movements) seek to renovate or renew people through inner change. Because these groups emphasize inner change, religious movements are often linked to local

The Raging Grannies is a group of activists who promote peace, justice, and social and economic equality through song and humor. Do you believe that activism will increase in the future? Why or why not?

and regional organizations that seek to bring about changes in the individual's life. National religious movements often seek to persuade political officials to enact laws that will reduce or eliminate what they perceive to be a social problem. For example, some national religious movements view abortion as a problem and therefore lobby for a ban on abortions. In contrast, *alternative movements* seek limited change in some aspects of people's behavior. An example is MADD—Mothers Against Drunk Driving—an organization that specifically targets drunk driving and those who engage in such harmful behavior. Advocates from MADD often show up at court hearings when a person is being tried for a drunken driving offense to call attention to this pressing social problem and to call for justice to be done in this specific case.

Finally, *resistance movements* seek to prevent change or undo change that has already occurred. In public debates over social policies, most social movements advocating change face resistance from reactive movements, which hold opposing viewpoints and want social policy to reflect their own beliefs and values. An example of a resistance movement is an anti-immigrant organization that seeks to close U.S. borders to outsiders or to place harsher demands on employers who hire illegal immigrant workers.

Can national activism and social movements bring about the changes that are necessary to reduce social problems? Some analysts believe that certain social problems can be reduced through sustained efforts by organizations committed to change. According to social activist Randy Shaw (1999), efforts by Public Interest Research Groups and the Sierra Club, the nation's two largest grassroots environmental groups, were successful in stimulating a new national environmental activism in the 1990s. Wanting to strengthen the Clean Air Act of 1967, these two organizations engaged in affirmative national environmental activism, mobilizing people who had previously been disconnected from national environmental debates (Shaw, 1999). As a result, a strong working relationship developed between grassroots activists at the local level and the leaders of the national movement. In previous decades, national groups had believed that their national leaders knew what was best for the environmental movement and had relied solely on their leadership's relationship with lawmakers to bring about change (Shaw, 1999). However, this belief changed as activists sought to strengthen the Clean Air Act:

The Clean Air Act standards became a battle over framing the issue. If the public saw the new standards as a health issue environmentalists would prevail. Industry would win if, as in the health care debate [of the 1990s], it could define its campaign as trying to stop Big Government from hampering the private sector's ability to improve people's lives. The campaign would revisit the philosophical battleground where corporate America had increasingly prevailed in the past decade. Whether environmentalists' new emphasis on national grassroots mobilizing would change this would soon be seen. (Shaw, 1999:157)

Eventually, supporters declared that the clean air campaign had been a success and vowed that they would continue to demand changes that they believed would benefit the environment and improve the quality of life (Shaw, 1999).

What about global activism? Once again, we turn to the environmental movement for an example. In a 2000 *New York Times* article, Jared Diamond, a physiology professor and a board member of the World Wildlife Fund, observed that some transnational corporations were becoming aware that they have a responsibility for the environment. Diamond (2000) described a new attitude taking hold of corporations such as Chevron and Home Depot, both of which claimed to realize that it is better to have a clean operation than to have costly industrial disasters. Of course, consumers also demanded that corporations become more accountable for their actions: "Behind this trend lies consumers' growing awareness of the risks that environmental problems pose for the health, economies, and political stability of their own world and their children's world" (Diamond, 2000:A31). At that time, it was hoped that growing consumer awareness would lead companies that buy and retail forest products to no longer sell wood products from environmentally sensitive areas of the world and instead give preference to certified wood—that is, lumber that has been derived from forests where guidelines for environmentally sound logging practices have been met (Diamond, 2000). However, this belief has proven to be unduly optimistic, coming as it did, before the terrorist attacks of 2001 and eight years of the Bush administration when corporate power grew and government regulations and enforcement were weakened, if not crippled, in some cases.

Other analysts have argued that what is needed is "globalization-from-below" (Brecher and Costello, 1998). In other words, people cannot rely on corporations to solve environmental problems. Indeed, it is necessary to develop a human agenda that will offset the corporate agenda that has produced many of the problems in the first place. Social activists Jeremy Brecher and Tim Costello (1998) suggest these criteria for any proposed human agenda:

- It should improve the lives of the great majority of the world's people over the long run.
- It should correspond to widely held common interests and should integrate the interests of people around the world.
- It should provide handles for action at a variety of levels.
- It should include elements that can be at least partially implemented independently but that are compatible or mutually reinforcing.
- It should make it easier, not harder, to solve noneconomic problems such as protection of the environment and reduction of war.
- It should grow organically out of social movements and coalitions that have developed in response to the needs of diverse peoples.

On the basis of these guidelines, the only way in which a major global social problem, such as environmental degradation or world poverty, can be reduced is through a drastic redirection of our energies, as Brecher and Costello (1998:184) explain:

> The energies now directed to the race to the bottom need to be redirected to the rebuilding of the global economy on a humanly and environmentally sound basis. Such an approach requires limits to growth—in some spheres, sharp reduction—in the material demands that human society places on the environment. It requires reduced energy and resource use; less toxic production and products; shorter individual worktime; and less production for war. But it requires vast growth in education, health care, human caring, recycling, rebuilding an ecologically sound production and consumption system, and time available for self-development, community life, and democratic participation.

Do you believe that such human cooperation is possible? Will it be possible for a new generation of political leaders to separate *politics* from *policy* and focus on discovering the best courses of action for the country and the world? Where do ideas regarding possible social policies come from? Some of the ideas and policies of tomorrow are being developed today in public policy organizations and think tanks (see Table 3). If, as some analysts believe, these think tanks are increasingly setting the U.S. government's

TABLE 3 Examples of Public Policy Organizations and Think Tanks

Action Institute for the Study of Religion and Liberty	Family Research Council
Adam Smith Institute	Fight Internet Taxes!
The AFL-CIO	Frontiers of Freedom Institute
Alliance for America	Galen Institute
American Civil Liberties Union	Goldwater Institute
American Conservative Union	Heartland Institute
American Enterprise Institute	Heritage Foundation
The American Institute for Full Employment	Hoover Institute
Americans for a Balanced Budget	Hudson Institute
Americans for Democratic Action	Independence Institute
Americans for Hope, Growth and Opportunity	Institute for Civic Values
Americans for Tax Reform	Institute for Economic Analysis, Inc.
Amnesty International	Institute for First Amendment Studies
Atlas Economic Research Foundation	Institute for Global Communications
Brookings Institution	Institute for Justice
Campaign for America's Future	Institute for Policy Innovation
The Carter Center	Leadership Institute
Cascade Policy Institute	League of Conservative Voters
Cato Institute	League of Women Voters
Center of the American Experiment	Ludwig von Mises Institute
Center for Defense Information	Madison Institute
Center for Equal Opportunity	Manhattan Institute
Center for Individual Rights	National Organization for Women
Center for Law and Social Policy	National Rifle Association
Center for Policy Alternatives	OMB Watch
Center to Prevent Handgun Violence	People for the American Way
Center for Public Integrity	Pioneer Institute for Public Policy Research
Center for Responsive Politics	Planned Parenthood
Century Foundation	Progress and Freedom Foundation
Children's Defense Fund	Project for Defense Alternatives
Christian Coalition	Public Citizen
Citizens Against Government Waste	RAND Corporation
Citizens for an Alternative Tax System	Reason Foundation
Citizens for Tax Justice	Tax Reform NOW!
Clare Boothe Luce Policy Institute	Union of Concerned Scientists
Claremont Institute	U.S. Term Limits
Discovery Institute	Worldwatch Institute
Economic Policy Institute	Young America's Foundation
Empower America	

agenda, how much do we know about these groups, their spokespersons, and the causes they advocate?

Perhaps gaining more information about the current state of U.S. and global affairs is the first step toward our individual efforts to be part of the solution rather than part of the problem in the future.

Limitations of the Macrolevel Solutions Approach

As C. Wright Mills stated, social problems by definition cannot be resolved without organizational initiatives that bring about social change. Therefore, macrolevel approaches are necessary for reducing or eliminating many social problems. However, some analysts believe that macrolevel approaches overemphasize structural barriers in society and give people the impression that these barriers are insurmountable walls that preclude social change. Macrolevel approaches might also deemphasize the importance of individual responsibility. Reducing the availability of illegal drugs, for example, does not resolve the problem of the individual drug abuser who still needs a means to eliminate the problem in her or his personal life. Similarly, macrolevel approaches usually do not allow for the possibility of positive communication and the kind of *human cooperation* that transcends national boundaries (Brecher and Costello, 1998). Experience, however, has shown us that positive communication and global cooperation are possible.

According to sociologist Immanuel Wallerstein, a former president of the International Sociological Association:

> We live in an imperfect world, one that will always be imperfect and therefore always harbor injustice. But we are far from helpless before this reality. We can make the world less unjust; we can make it more beautiful; we can increase our cognition of it. We need but to construct it, and in order to construct it we need but to reason with each other and struggle to obtain from each other the special knowledge that each of us has been able to seize. We can labor in the vineyards and bring forth fruit, if only we try. (Wallerstein, 1999:250)

In the two decades since this statement was made, Wallerstein has reaffirmed these beliefs on numerous occasions, namely that social justice is the way to improve life for more people around the world. In any case, a sociological approach to examining social problems provides us with new ideas about how to tackle some of the most pressing issues of our times (see Box 2).

We have seen that different theoretical approaches to analyzing social problems bring us to a variety of conclusions about how we might reduce or eliminate certain problems. Let's take a last look at the major sociological theories we have studied so that we can relate them one more time to social problems, an activity which you will hopefully continue in the future as new challenges arise and older problems continue to need resolution.

FINAL REVIEW OF SOCIAL THEORIES AND SOCIAL PROBLEMS

The underlying theoretical assumptions that we hold regarding social problems often have a profound influence on what we feel may be the best solution for a specific problem. Do we believe society is based on stability or conflict? Is conflict typically good for society or bad for society? According to the functionalist perspective, society is a stable, orderly system that is composed of a number of interrelated parts, each of which performs a function that contributes to the overall stability of the society. From the functionalist perspective, social problems arise when social institutions do not fulfill the functions they are supposed to perform or when dysfunctions (undesirable consequences of an activity or social process that inhibit a society's ability to adapt or adjust) occur. For example, in the aftermath of Hurricane Katrina, all levels of government were severely criticized for the excessive amount of time it took to get military personnel and emergency evacuation crews to disaster sites and to provide food, water, sanitation, and transportation for those who were displaced by the storm. If the vast problems experienced by individuals living in the Gulf Coast states are symptomatic of larger gaps in national emergency preparedness, the U.S. government will continue to be accused of indifference, incompetence, or even worse. According to the functionalist approach, dysfunctions create social disorganization, which in turn causes a breakdown in the traditional values and norms that serve as social control mechanisms. As shown in Table 4, the social disorganization approach traces the causes of social problems to social change that leaves

Critical Thinking and You

Box 2

Applying Sociology to the Ordinary and the Extraordinary in Everyday Life

[In the aftermath of Hurricane Katrina in New Orleans], you're now looking at a situation in which, when people return, they may have to find work. . . . Both close ties [with others] and extended relationships will be very important, and it's likely the people who have both will do best.

—Jeanne Hulbert, a sociologist at Louisiana State University in Baton Rouge, talks about studies on hurricane disasters she and her colleagues conducted that show a clear link between people's mental health and the kinds of social relationships they have (Carey, 2005:A20).

People don't know until something like this comes along how much the shape of their house, the texture of their house, the mood of their neighborhood, are important parts of who they are. People take all of this so much for granted that when they return and the house is gone or not habitable it disorients them, makes them more lonely and more afraid, and they don't know why. This is true of public spaces and streets, too. You have no idea how much they mean to you until they are gone or permanently altered.

—Kai Erikson, a sociologist at Yale University and author of several books about disasters, including Everything in Its Path: Destruction of Community in the Buffalo Creek Flood, *looks at the sociological psychology of how people deal with disasters (Carey, 2005:A20).*

In times of crisis, including natural disasters, terrorist attacks, war, and other cataclysmic events, sociologists are often called on to discuss these events as they affect individuals, groups, and nations. Because sociologists in academic and research settings are continually engaged

in research in their areas of specialization, they are authorities on topics such as the social psychology of survival. As a result of years of theorizing and research, scholars such as Jeanne Hulbert and Kai Erikson (quoted previously) gain and share with others significant insights on social phenomenon such as how people react to disasters.

However, we do not necessarily need to be experts in order to put basic sociological ideas into practice. Sociological insights on social problems can be used in a variety of fields, including criminal justice, community and human services, health care and substance abuse programs, and disaster relief efforts. But, perhaps more importantly to each of us, sociology can be used in our everyday life to help us understand what is going on around us and to evaluate the quality of life in our own community. As a final critical thinking activity in this course, let's take a new look at the city where you live.

Questions for Consideration

1. Media discussions about the disaster in New Orleans often called attention to a "rich section" or "poor section" of the city. Can you identify areas of your city that could be classified as upper, middle, or lower class? If so, what sociological factors did you use to distinguish among the various areas and the people who live in each?

2. Can you identify distinct racial or ethnic patterns with regard to where people live in your city? If a reporter asked you the following question, how would you answer: "Do you think that race or class is the most important factor in determining where people in your community live?" In answering this question, is it possible that race and class are so intertwined as factors relating to privilege or deprivation that giving the reporter an "either/or" answer is virtually impossible?

existing rules inadequate for current conditions. In societies undergoing social change—for example, high rates of immigration, rapid changes in technology, and increasingly complex patterns of social life—social disorganization produces stress at the individual level and inefficiency and confusion at the institutional and societal levels. Thus, the functionalist approach to reducing social problems has as central factors the prevention of

rapid social changes, the maintenance of the status quo, and the restoration of order.

In contrast, the conflict perspective assumes that conflict is natural and inevitable in society. Value conflict approaches focus on conflict between the values held by members of divergent groups. These approaches also highlight the ways in which cultural, economic, and social diversity may contribute to misunderstandings

Table 4 Perceived Problems and Possible Solutions

Perspective	Causes	Possible Solutions
Functionalist:		
Social disorganization	Social change; inadequacy of existing social rules	Developing and implementing social rules that are explicit, workable, and consistent
Conflict:		
Value conflict	Conflict between different groups' values; economic, social, and cultural diversity	Groups confronting opponents and working for lasting changes in policy or legislation
Critical conflict (Marxist)	Relations of domination and subordination are reinforced by the global capitalist economy and political leaders who put other priorities ahead of the good of the people	Changing the nature of society, particularly inequalities that grow more pronounced as the wealthy grow richer and the poor worldwide become increasingly impoverished
Symbolic Interactionist:		
Deviant behavior	Inappropriate socialization within primary groups	Resocializing or rehabilitating people so that they will conform
Labeling	How people label behavior, how they respond to it, and the consequences of their responses	Changing the definition through decriminalization; limiting labeling

Source: Based on Weinberg et al., 1981; Feagin et al., 2006.

and problems. According to Marxist (or critical-conflict) theorists, groups are engaged in a continuous power struggle for control of scarce resources. As a result of the unjust use of political, economic, or social power, certain groups of people are privileged while others are disadvantaged. Thus, for critical-conflict theorists, social problems arise out of major contradictions that are inherent in the ways in which societies are organized. When this approach is used, the root causes of social problems—patriarchy, capitalism, and massive spending on the U.S. military-industrial complex at the expense of human services, for example—must be radically altered or eliminated altogether. Focusing on the political economy, one critical-conflict approach states that the capitalist economy, which is now global, maintains and reinforces domination and subordination in social relations. This approach also examines how political leaders might put their own interests ahead of any

common good that might exist. Clearly, any solutions to social problems by this approach would require radical changes in society and thus are not always viewed positively in societies in which economic prosperity based on individual attributes rather than collective activities is considered a mark of personal and social achievement. Other conflict theorists view the interlocking nature of race, class, and gender as systems of domination and subordination as central concerns to social problems. Therefore, their solutions for reducing or eliminating social problems that are embedded in racial and ethnic relations, class relationships, and gender inequalities also require dramatic changes in society.

At the macrolevel, globalization theories make us aware that many social problems transcend the borders of any one nation and are often international in their causes and consequences. As some social scientists have suggested, any solution to global social problems will require new thinking about how business, politics, and civil society ought to work together and how nation-states worldwide must establish policies and enact legislation that will benefit not only their own constituents but also the global community (Richard, 2002).

If we shift to the microlevel, the symbolic interactionist perspective focuses on how people act toward one another and make sense of their daily lives. From this perspective, society is the sum of the interactions of individuals and groups. Thus, symbolic interactionists often study social problems by analyzing the process whereby a behavior is defined as a social problem and how individuals and groups come to engage in activities that a significant number of people view as major social concerns. Symbolic interactionist theories of deviance note that inadequate socialization or interacting with the "wrong" people may contribute to deviant behavior and crime. Similarly, interactionists who use the labeling framework for their analysis of social problems study how people label behavior, how they respond to people engaged in such behavior, and the consequences of their behavior. Essentially, a symbolic interactionist approach helps us understand why certain actions are significant to people and how people communicate what these actions mean to them. For example, fear of potential terrorism can affect how people think and behave, whether or not they are actually in harm's way and have real cause to modify their daily routines and encounters with others.

A symbolic interactionist approach can also help us understand how some low-income people caught up in a natural disaster such as Hurricane Katrina might engage in illegal behavior that they otherwise might never have considered, such as pilfering and looting, because of the magnitude of the tragedy facing them and the brief opportunity that presents itself to get "free" food, supplies, and perhaps "luxury" items such as expensive television sets or jewelry they otherwise would never have been able to afford. Moreover, only limited plans had been made by officials to successfully evacuate these individuals should the need ever arise, as one journalist stated:

> The victims . . . were largely black and poor, those who toiled in the background of the tourist havens, living in tumbledown neighborhoods that were long known to be vulnerable to disaster if the levees failed. Without so much as a car or bus fare to escape ahead of time, they found

Why were some people referred to as "looters" in the aftermath of Hurricane Katrina while others were described as "appropriating what they needed to survive"? According to symbolic interactionists, social problems may be viewed differently based on who is participating in the activity and what is believed to be the cause of their conduct.

> themselves left behind by a failure to plan for their rescue should the dreaded day ever arrive. (Gonzalez, 2005:A1, A19)

And, indeed, when that day did arrive, the majority of the victims who were hardest hit were those who lived at the margins of society and who were left behind not only when people initially evacuated from the city before the storm hit but also when initial rescue efforts were so slow getting started. From a symbolic interactionist perspective, an ordeal such as resulted from Hurricane Katrina is likely to affect how people think and feel about themselves and others, how they view "reality," and the labels they use to identify themselves and their needs in relation to others. For example, some of the poor and black victims who prior to the disaster were struggling mightily now find themselves with new labels, including "homeless," "destitute," and "refugee."

Each of these sociological perspectives suggests ways in which social problems may be identified and remedies may be sought. In doing so, these theories provide divergent views on social change that might reduce or eliminate social problems. We are left with one final question as we conclude this text and our time together: Won't you join with sociologists and others who seek to face up to one of the greatest challenges of the twenty-first century, which is how to bring peace, justice, and greater social equality to as many of the world's people as possible?

SUMMARY

■ **Why is it difficult to reduce or eliminate social problems?**
According to social scientists, reducing or solving social problems is more complex than simply identifying such problems and pinpointing their social locations because many obstacles, delays, and frustrations confront those who attempt to bring about social changes that might alleviate the problems. Solving a problem can entail prohibitive costs and may only give rise to a whole new set of problems.

■ **What is social change and why is it important in reducing social problems?**
Social change refers to the alternation, modification, or transformation of public policy, culture, or social institutions over time. Social change is important in reducing social problems because a combination of strategies, some previously untried, are usually required to reduce major social problems.

■ **What are microlevel solutions to social problems? What are the limitations of this approach?**
Microlevel solutions to social problems focus on how individuals operate within small groups to try to remedy a problem that affects them, their family, or friends. Most people turn to their primary groups to help them deal with a problem. However, solving social problems one person at a time does not take into account the fact that secondary groups and societal institutions play a significant part in creating, maintaining, and exacerbating many social problems.

■ **What are midrange attempts to deal with social problems? What are the limitations of this approach?**
Midrange attempts to deal with social problems focus on how secondary groups and formal organizations deal with problems or seek to assist individuals in overcoming problems such as addiction to drugs or alcohol. Grassroots groups often work to change a perceived wrong in their neighborhood, city, state, or nation. Although local efforts to reduce problems that affect individuals and collectivities in a specific city or region have brought about many improvements in the social life of individuals and small groups, they usually lack the sustained capacity to produce the larger systemic changes needed at the national or international levels to reduce or eliminate the problems.

■ **What are macrolevel attempts to deal with social problems? What are the limitations of this approach?**
Macrolevel solutions to social problems focus on how large-scale social institutions such as the government and the media can become involved in remedying social problems. Some people work through social movements, others through special-interest groups, and still others through various forms of collective behavior. Although macrolevel approaches are necessary for reducing or eliminating

many social problems, some analysts believe that these approaches overemphasize structural barriers in society and give people the impression that these barriers constitute insurmountable walls that preclude social change. Macrolevel approaches can also deemphasize the importance of individual responsibility.

■ **What are three key factors that can be used to differentiate special-interest groups?**
The three factors by which special-interest groups may be categorized are (1) issues (single issue versus multiple demands), (2) view of the present system of wealth and power (positive versus negative), and (3) beliefs about elites (whether to try to influence elites or seek to replace them).

■ **What is collective behavior? How does civil disobedience occur?**
Collective behavior is voluntary, often spontaneous activity that is engaged in by a large number of people and typically violates dominant-group norms and values. As a form of collective behavior, civil disobedience refers to nonviolent action that seeks to change a policy or law by refusing to comply with it.

■ **What are the key characteristics of the five major categories of national social movements?**
National social movements are divided into five major categories: reform, revolutionary, religious, alternative, and resistance movements. Reform movements seek to improve society by changing some specific aspect of the social structure. Revolutionary movements seek to bring about a total change in society. Religious movements seek to renovate or renew people through "inner change." Alternative movements seek limited change in some aspects of people's behavior and currently include organizations such as Mothers Against Drunk Driving (MADD).

■ **What is a human agenda? What might be the major criteria for such an agenda?**
According to some analysts, we need to develop a human agenda that focuses on the needs of people and offsets the corporate agenda that is currently taking precedence over other issues and concerns. Social activists Jeremy Brecher and Tim Costello suggest that any proposed human agenda should (1) improve the lives of the great majority of the world's people, (2) correspond to widely held common interests, as well as integrate the interests of people worldwide, (3) provide handles for action at a variety of levels, (4) include elements that can be implemented independently, at least in part, but that are compatible or mutually reinforcing, (5) make it easier to solve noneconomic problems such as environmental pollution, and (6) grow out of social movements and coalitions that have developed in response to the needs of diverse peoples.

What is the primary focus of functionalist, conflict, and interactionist approaches to solving social problems?
From the functionalist perspective, social problems arise when social institutions do not fulfill the functions they are supposed to or when dysfunctions occur; therefore, social institutions need to be made more effective, and social change needs to be managed carefully. According to critical-conflict theorists, social problems arise out of the major contradictions inherent in the way societ-ies are organized (particularly factors such as patriarchy and capitalism). Consequently, attempting to solve social problems requires major changes in the political economy. Symbolic interactionists focus on how certain behavior comes to be defined as a social problem and why some individuals and groups engage in that behavior. To reduce problems entails more adequate socialization of people as well as a better understanding of how labeling affects people's behavior.

KEY TERMS

civil disobedience
collective behavior
grassroots groups

infrastructure
primary groups
secondary groups

social change
social movement
special-interest group

QUESTIONS FOR CRITICAL THINKING

1. Do you believe that corporations can be trusted to do the right thing when it comes to reducing or eliminating existing social problems? Is good corporate citizenship a possibility in the global economy today? Why or why not?

2. Suppose that you were given the economic resources and political clout to reduce a major social problem. Which problem would you choose? What steps would you take to alleviate this problem? How would you measure your success or failure in reducing or eliminating the problem?

3. What is most useful about applying a sociological perspective to the study of social problems? What is least useful about a sociological approach? How can you contribute to a better understanding of the causes, effects, and possible solutions to social problems?

Succeed with MySocLab® www.mysoclab.com

The new MySocLab delivers proven results in helping students succeed, provides engaging experiences that personalize learning, and comes from a trusted partner with educational expertise and a deep commitment to helping students and instructors achieve their goals.

Here are a few activities you will find for this chapter:

Watch on **mysoclab.com**
Core Concepts video clips feature sociologists in action, exploring important concepts in the study of Social Problems. Watch:
• Grievances, Anger, and Hope

Explore on **mysoclab.com**
Social Explorer is an interactive application that allows you to explore Census data through interactive maps. Explore:
• Social Explorer Activity: Transportation and Social Status

Read on **mysoclab.com**
MySocLibrary includes primary source readings from classic and contemporary sociologists. Read:
• Community Building: Steps Toward a Good Society

Glossary

civil disobedience   nonviolent action that seeks to change a policy or law by refusing to comply with it.

collective behavior   voluntary, often spontaneous, activity that is engaged in by a large number of people and typically violates dominant-group norms and values.

grassroots groups   organizations started by ordinary people who work in concert to change a perceived wrong in their neighborhood, city, state, or nation.

infrastructure   a framework of support systems, such as transportation and utilities, that makes it possible to have specific land uses and a built environment that facilitate people's daily activities and the nation's economy.

primary groups   small, less specialized groups in which members engage in face-to-face, emotion-based interactions over an extended period of time.

secondary groups   larger, more specialized groups in which members engage in impersonal, goal-oriented relationships for a limited period of time.

social change   the alteration, modification, or transformation of public policy, culture, or social institutions over time.

social movement   an organized group that acts collectively to promote or resist change through collective action.

special-interest group   a political coalition composed of individuals or groups sharing a specific interest they wish to protect or advance with the help of the political system.

References

NOTE: References in blue are new to the Sixth Edition.

Adams, Tom. 1991. *Grass Roots: How Ordinary People Are Changing America.* New York: Citadel Press.

American Red Cross. 2010. "Bringing Help, Bringing Hope: The American Red Cross Responds to Hurricanes Katrina, Rita and Wilma." American Red Cross. Retrieved: August 6, 2011. Online: http://www.redcross.org/www-files/Documents/pdf/corppubs/Katrina5Year.pdf

BP. 2010. "Annual Report." Retrieved August 6, 2011. Online: http://www.bp.com/assets/bp_internet/globalbp/globalbp_uk_english/set_branch/STAGING/common_assets/downloads/pdf/BP_Annual_Report_and_Form_20F.pdf

Brecher, Jeremy, and Tim Costello. 1998. *Global Village or Global Pillage: Economic Reconstruction from the Bottom Up* (2nd ed.). Cambridge, MA: South End Press.

Buechler, Steven M. 2000. *Social Movements in Advanced Capitalism: The Political Economy and Cultural Construction of Social Activism.* New York: Oxford University Press.

Carey, Benedict. 2005. "Storm Will Have a Long-Term Emotional Effect on Some, Experts Say." *New York Times* (September 4):A20.

Diamond, Jared. 2000. "The Greening of Corporate America." *New York Times* (January 8):A31.

Environmental Protection Agency. 2010. "Municipal Solid Waste Generation, Recycling, and Disposal in the United States: Facts and Figures for 2009." Retrieved July 29, 2011. Online: http://www.epa.gov/wastes/nonhaz/municipal/pubs/msw2009-fs.pdf

Feagin, Joe R., David Baker, and Clairece Booher Feagin. 2006. *Social Problems: A Critical Power-Conflict Perspective* (6th ed.). Upper Saddle River, NJ: Prentice Hall.

Gonzalez, David. 2005. "From Margins of Society to Center of the Tragedy." *New York Times* (September 2):A1, A19.

gulfspilloil.com 2011. "BP's Oil Spill Costs Look Manageable (January 9). Retrieved February 4, 2012. Online: http://www.gulfspilloil.com/ap-bps-oil-spill-costs-look-manageable

Journalism.org. 2011. "Eight Things to Know about How the Media Covered the Gulf Disaster." Pew Research Center's Project for Excellence in Journalism (August 25). Retrieved August 6, 2011. Online: http://www.journalism.org/analysis_report/100_days_gushing_oil

Krugman, Paul. 2005a. "A Can't Do Government." *New York Times* (September 2):A23.

Lappé, Frances Moore, and Paul Martin Du Bois. 1994. *The Quickening of America: Rebuilding Our Nation, Remaking Our Lives.* San Francisco: Jossey-Bass.

Richard, J. F. 2002. *High Noon: Twenty Global Problems, Twenty Years to Solve Them.* New York: Basic.

Shane, Scott, and Eric Lipton. 2005. "Storm Overwhelmed Government's Preparation." *New York Times* (September 2):A1, A14.

Shaw, Randy. 1999. *Reclaiming America: Nike, Clean Air, and the New National Activism.* Berkeley: University of California Press.

Tierney, John. 2005. "Fight Floods Like Fires, without the Feds." *New York Times* (September 3):A29.

Wallerstein, Immanuel. 1999. *The End of the World as We Know It: Social Science for the Twenty-First Century.* Minneapolis: University of Minnesota Press.

Weinberg, Martin S., Earl Rubington, and Sue Kiefer Hammersmith. 1981. *The Solution of Social Problems: Five Perspectives* (2nd ed.). New York: Oxford University Press.

Whitesides, John. 2005. "Katrina Devastation Highlights Poverty of U.S. Blacks." Reuters.com (September 2). Retrieved September 3, 2005. Online: http://today.reuters.com

Photo Credits

Text Credits

ndex